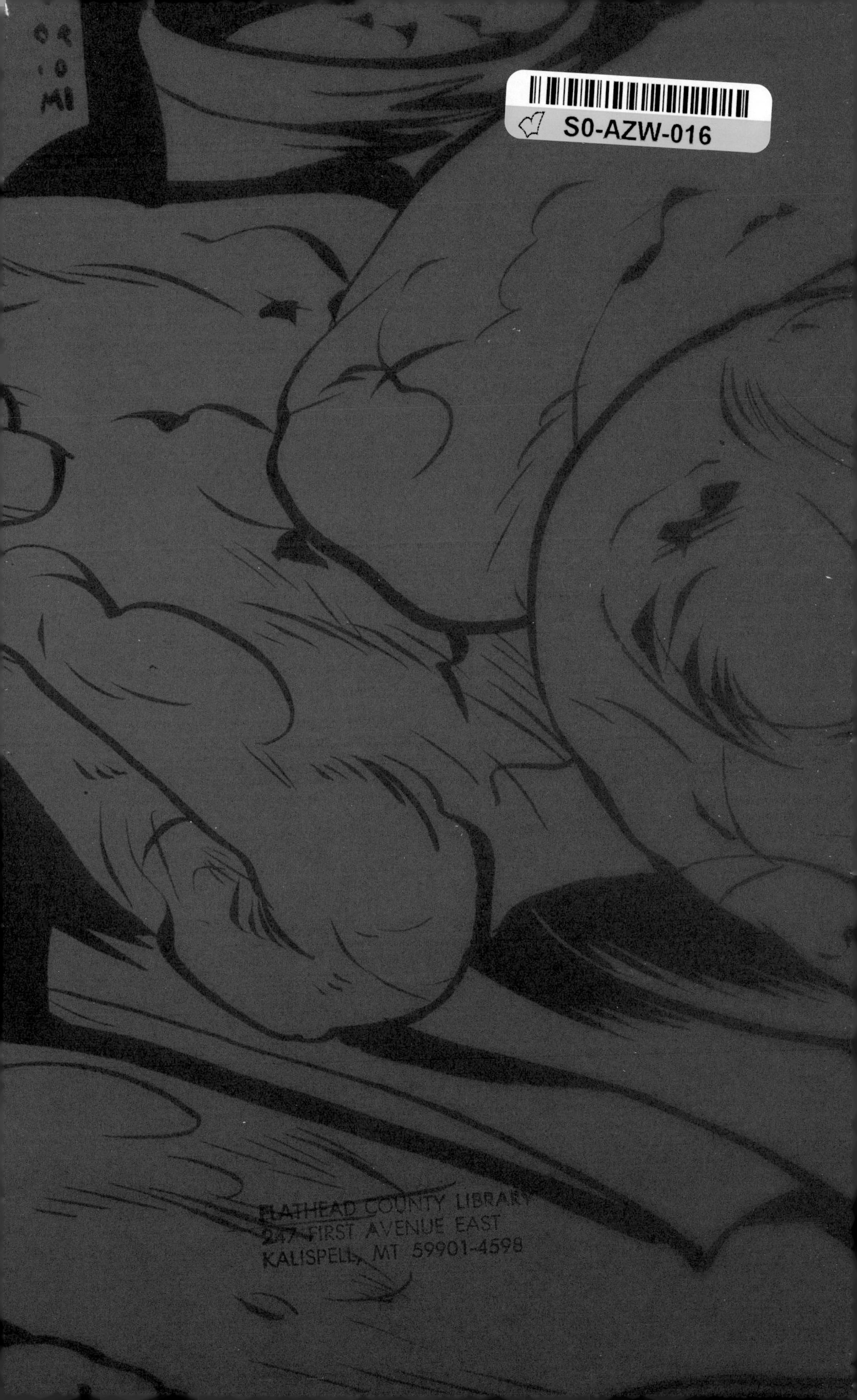

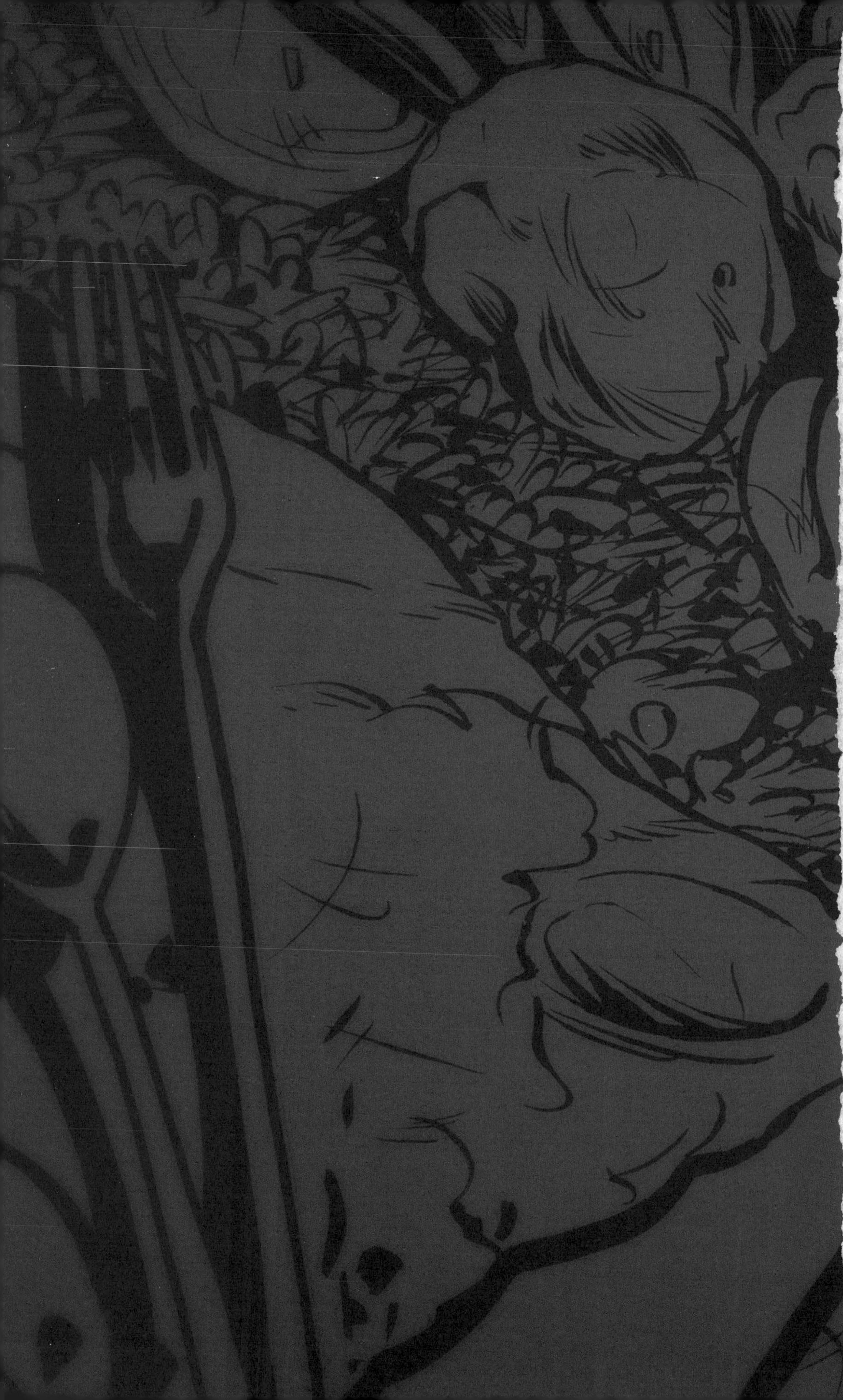

image

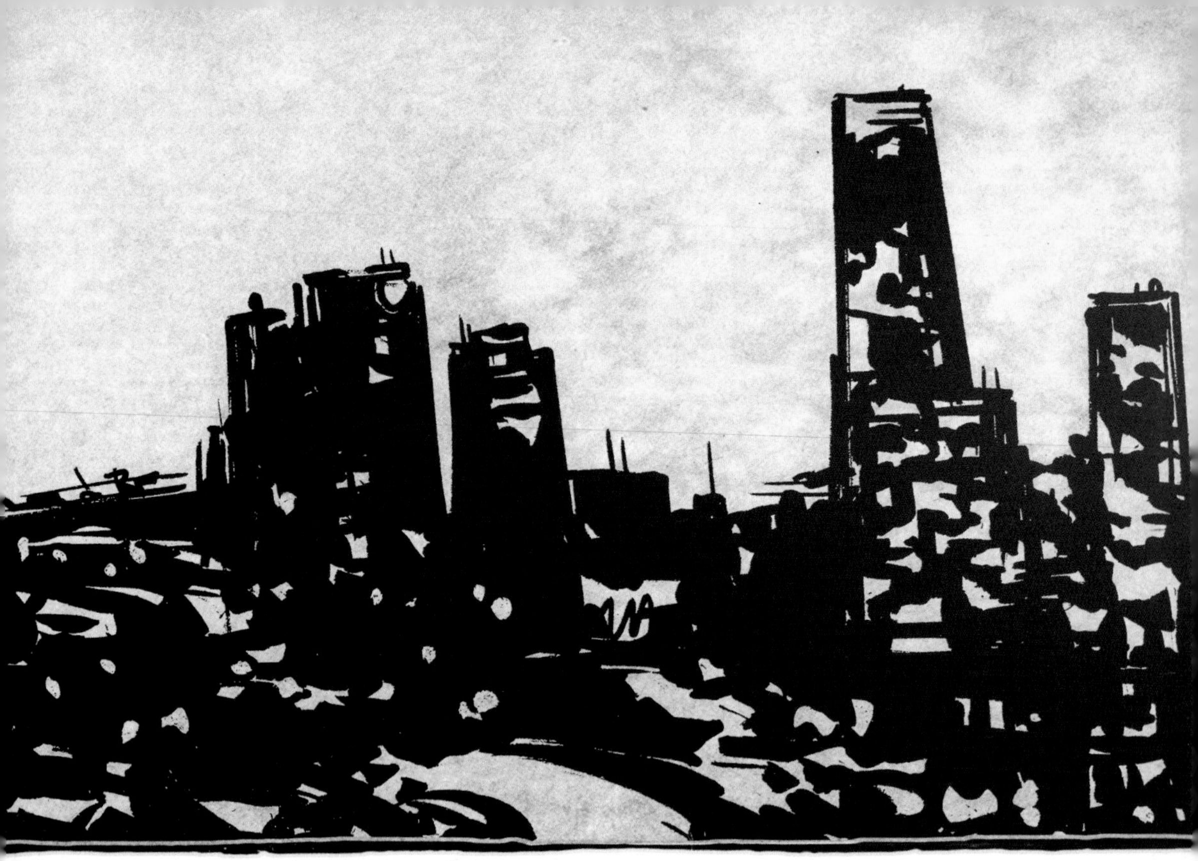

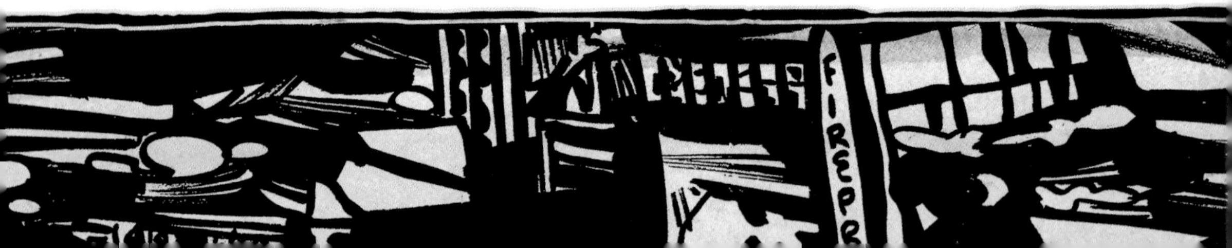
FIREPR

PAUL POPE
THE ONE TRICK RIP-OFF
+ DEEP CUTS

IMAGE COMICS
WWW.IMAGECOMICS.COM

Paul Pope — Story and Art
Jamie Grant and Dominic Regan — Colors
Michael Neno and Jared K. Fletcher — Letters
Jim Pascoe — Design and Production
Casey Gonzalez — Line Producer
Greg Tumbarello — Assistant Editor
Bob Schreck — Editor

For international licensing inquiries, write to: foreignlicensing@imagecomics.com.

First Printing January 2013
Published by Image Comics, Inc.
Office of publication: 2001 Center Street, 6th Floor, Berkeley, CA 94704

ISBN: 978-1-60706-718-4 Regular Edition
ISBN: 978-1-60706-729-0 Signed & Numbered Limited Edition

Printed in CANADA.

Cover illustration by Paul Pope with colors by Dominic Regan.
Logo by Jim Pascoe.

IMAGE COMICS, INC.
Robert Kirkman - chief operating officer
Erik Larsen - chief financial officer
Todd McFarlane - president
Marc Silvestri - chief executive officer
Jim Valentino - vice-president

Eric Stephenson - publisher
Todd Martinez - sales & licensing coordinator
Jennifer de Guzman - pr & marketing director
Branwyn Bigglestone - accounts manager
Emily Miller - accounting assistant
Jamie Parreno - marketing assistant
Jenna Savage - administrative assistant
Sarah deLaine - events coordinator
Kevin Yuen - digital rights coordinator
Jonathan Chan - production manager
Drew Gill - art director
Monica Garcia - production artist
Vincent Kukua - production artist
Jana Cook - production artist
www.imagecomics.com

What you have
learned and done
is safe and fruitful.
Work and learn
in evil days,
in insulted days,
in days of debt
and depression
and calamity.
Fight best in the
shade of the
cloud of arrows.

—RW Emerson, April 1847

I'M AFRAID, TUBBY. I'M SCARED.

TABLE OF CONTENTS

INTRODUCTION by Charles Brownstein **8**

THE ONE TRICK RIP-OFF (1995 – 1996) **13**
(colors by Jamie Grant & Dominic Regan, lettering by Michael Neno)

EXTRAS **120**

DEEP CUTS

COLUMBUS (1993 – 1996)

The Triumph of Hunger **128**
(text by Rimbaud, colors by Dominic Regan)

The Zhuk **134**
(based on a poem by composer Modest Mussorgsky,
colors by Dominic Regan)

The Armadillo **148**
(poem by Francis Richardson, colors by Dominic Regan
lettering by Lorie Witte)

The Island **150**
(poem by Francis Richardson, colors by Dominic Regan
lettering by Lorie Witte)

The Visible Man... **154**
(colors by Dominic Regan)

Portrait of a Girl with
an Unpronounceable Name **160**
(colors by Dominic Regan)

Yes **166**
(colors by Dominic Regan)

Antigone.. **174**
(text excerpt from Sophocles, colors by Dominic Regan,
lettering by Michael Neno)

AREN'T YOU SCARED?

DEEP CUTS (CONTINUED)

COLUMBUS (1993 – 1996)

The Scythe 185
(colors by Dominic Regan)

Super Trouble 186
(graytones by Scott Mou, colors/lettering by Jared K. Fletcher)

TORONTO (1997)

Four Cats 226
(colors by Dominic Regan)

TOKYO (1998)

Night Job 236
(colors/lettering by Jared K. Fletcher)

NEW YORK CITY (1999 – 2001)

The Scarf 270
(colors by Jared K. Fletcher)

Airplanes 284
(colors by Dominic Regan)

BIOS 287

Special thanks to Michael Neno, Lorie Witte,
Scott Mou, Shannon T. Stewart, Dezi Sienty
and Andrew Carl. "Without whom..."

I JUST WANT TO MOVE THE WORLD: PAUL POPE'S GLOBAL 20s

by Charles Brownstein

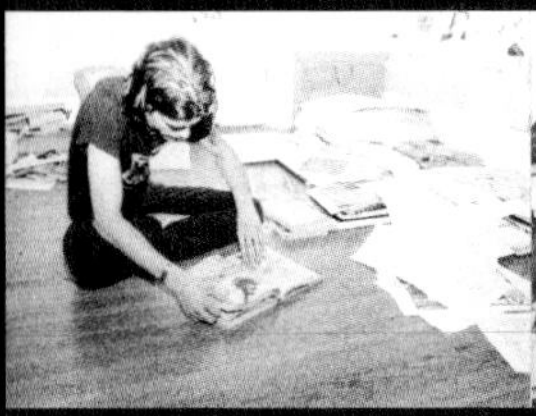

COLUMBUS 1995

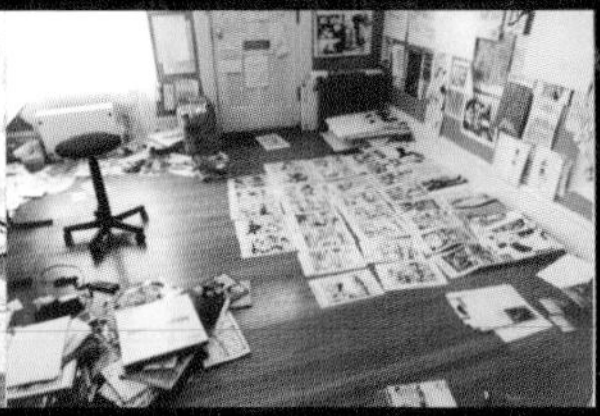

COLUMBUS 1995

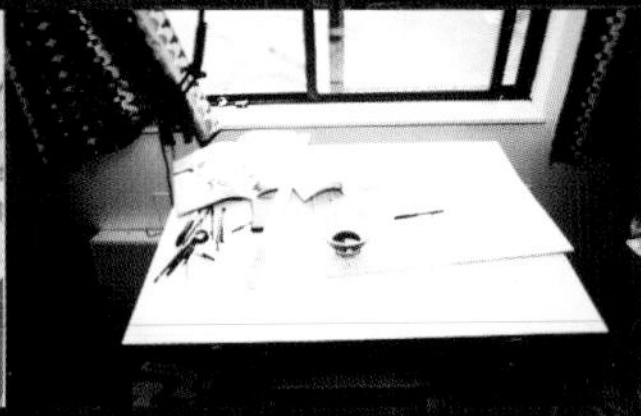

BOWLING GREEN 1995

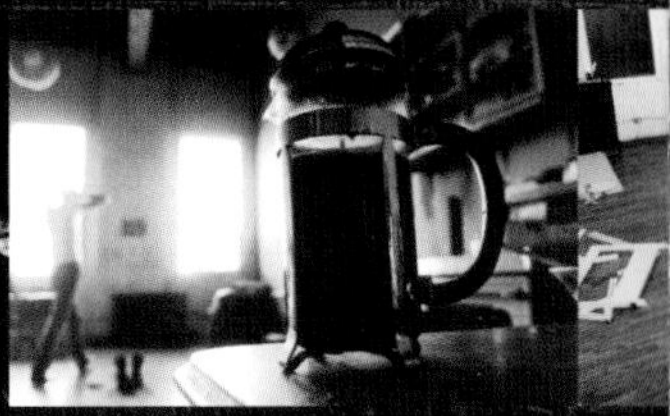

TORONTO 1997

I will lie at your feet / I'll kneel at your door
I'll rock you to sleep / I will roll on the floor
And I will ask for nothing / Nothing in this life
I will ask for nothing / Give me ever-lasting life
I just want to move the world
I just want to move the world
I just want to move the world
I just want to move.

— Nick Cave & The Bad Seeds

In those lines from his lusty hymn to creativity, "There She Goes My Beautiful World," Nick Cave captures the urgency and passion of the artist yearning to make an impact. His description of the fiery, single-minded desire to fully inhabit Art, and to use it to make a difference, could have been describing the young Paul Pope.

An artist who burst into comics like a meteor, Pope had a powerful desire to make his mark by asking the big questions about love, sexuality, beauty, and art. In this volume, you'll view Pope's journey from a Midwestern young man with a powerful need to know the world to a mature artist who fought for and earned his place in it.

Pope popped into comics young, hungry, and nearly fully-formed. In 1992, at the age of 22, he self-published his debut graphic novel ***Sin Titulo***, and followed up early the next year with ***The Ballad of Dr. Richardson***. Those books were both romances, heavily influenced by European comics. They address the emotional borderlands between youth and adulthood, education and experience, navigated by people entering their twenties. Both were strange apparitions in the early '90s American comics field, where the "Death of Superman" and the birth of Image Comics defined the mainstream, and where Dave Sim's multi-layered fantasy influenced epic, ***Cerebus***, and Los Bros. Hernandez's literary, magical realist melodrama, ***Love & Rockets***, epitomized the alternative. Pope's concerns didn't intersect with either camp. "You could choose to be indie/underground or mainstream," Pope recalls. "I wasn't with that. I felt, outside of the obvious options, there wasn't a lot of room for a unique voice."

Those books earned the attention of editor Joe Pruett, who commissioned the artist to create work for the anthology ***Negative Burn***. Pope contributed stories to six issues of that anthology, including

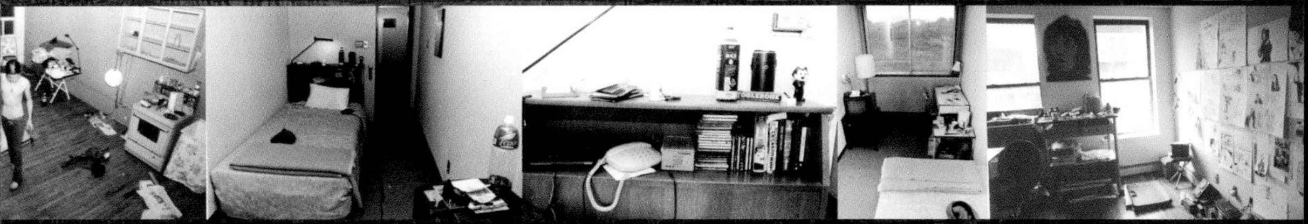

TORONTO 1997 TOKYO 1998 TOKYO 1998 TOKYO 1998 GREENWICH VILLAGE NYC 1999

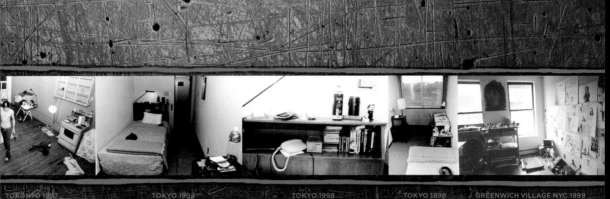

"The Triumph of Hunger," "The Armadillo" & "The Island," which appear in this volume. Pope says, "I was struggling to find and hone a strong and unique artistic voice, but I was also in a state of creative exploration. I wasn't entirely sure what direction I wanted my work to take yet, and used these shorts as a way to experiment in more of what I considered a European mode of story-making for comics." Pope identifies his influences from this period as including Jacques de Loustal and Philippe Paringaux, Jerome Charyn, Yves Chaland, Hugo Pratt, Milo Manara, and François Boucq.

The stories are bold experiments that lean into poetry and employ almost painterly expressions of landscape. Pope says, "If half of our medium is Word, then why not explore the outer territories of Word? A lot of poetry is lost in time but still valuable if used well. I was into trying to bring that back. Also, the sense of space is interesting to me as a metaphor for the clarity of thought, from the possible to the unknown. I have always loved that as a visual metaphor."

While these poetic contributions were hitting the stands, Pope was developing his break-out work, ***THB***, which would drop forcefully into comic book stores late in 1994. ***THB*** arrived as part of the self-publishing movement spearheaded by Dave Sim and protégés Jeff Smith, Colleen Doran, Martin Wagner and James Owen that set the stage for a wide variety of creators, including Pope, to introduce their own periodical comics into the comic book specialty market. Pope's entry was unusual even by the standards of creative diversity that were being set by Sim and his compatriots. ***THB*** was a science fiction series set on Mars that explored the adventures of teenage heiress H.R. Watson. The setting gave Pope a massive canvas for world-building where he could freely mesh influences ranging from comics to pulp fiction to economics in a holistic and adventurous way.

That wasn't the only thing remarkable about ***THB***. It also set itself apart for the sheer volume of work Pope included — the debut issue topped 100 pages, and subsequent ones were at least half that, at a time when the norm for comic books was 22 pages of story in each issue.

THB was also unique for how Pope cultivated his personal image by publishing self-portraits influenced by fashion photography and long, lyrical essays about his interests in art and travel. This facet of

Pope's work was more than mere publicity, it was a component of his overall art practice. In this regard, he was emulating artists like David Bowie and Nick Cave, who used photos and interviews to cultivate a self-image that was designed to reflect the sensibility of their current work. Of this practice he remarks, "It was a way to distinguish myself and my work from the others. I always approached this as a singer/songwriter. Tell the truth and people will listen. Do it well, they will listen. That was what I was thinking. I appreciated that music plays for a wide audience, and so the musician must be tall on the stage so that even the people in the back could see you."

While he was starting ***THB***, Pope got a call from then ***Dark Horse Presents*** editor Bob Schreck, who offered the artist his first paying gig. Schreck recalls discovering Pope's work at the 1993 San Diego Comic-Con. He says, "I read ***The Ballad of Dr. Richardson*** and then immediately called Paul on the way back from the Con." The result was ***The One Trick Rip-Off***. When it hit stores in 1995, the cumulative effect of this stylish new strip alongside the inventive material in ***THB*** made Pope a household name amongst comic book cognoscenti.

Pope says he approached ***Rip-Off*** as an opportunity to "make an early rendezvous into crime fiction's gym." Heavily influenced by noir titans Raymond Chandler and Dashiell Hammett, and affected by the phenomenon of ***Pulp Fiction***, Pope set out to create a morality drama that fully inhabited the crime genre. "I've always been into the great conundrums of literature, and thought I stumbled across one with the rhetorical question, 'Is it wrong to steal from thieves?'" Pope said. "Bob Schreck called me up after reading the proposal and told me he loved it but had one question. It was a simple question, too: Why would Tubby and Vim decide to rip-off the One Tricks to begin with? 'Because they're young, and they've gotten too many ideas from TV, and perhaps they're a little dumb,' I replied."

In ***Rip-Off***, Pope continues to explore his preoccupations with romance and youth, and to express his own longing to get out into the world. While making the book, Pope spent a lot of his time driving and refining the ideas that would find a way into the work. He says, "The world was outside the window, a place you always dreamed of but could never quite touch. I think there is a sense of yearning in that. A feeling like you want to be outside but you're trapped inside. It's a somewhat generous image too, the unknown open space beyond." Tubby and Vim embody Pope's desire to light out into the world, setting up the book's tragic action. He says they "consciously decide to steal from fellow thieves, knowing it is morally wrong, but go ahead with their half-baked scheme anyway. This consciousness of their own wrongdoing in this matter seemed to me to be the only way to tell a story like ***The Rip-Off*** and allow for the protagonists to retain any likeability."

Like Pope's development of an artistic persona, his exploration of morality and doomed romance were influenced by Nick Cave, who was in the midst of examining those same themes in his albums ***Let Love In*** and ***Murder Ballads***. Pope says, "The one clearly intended reference in ***The Rip-Off*** is in the character Jesse James, whom I

GREENWICH VILLAGE NYC 1999

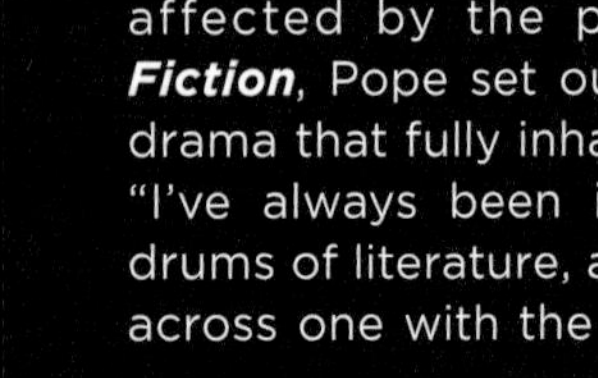

GREENWICH VILLAGE NYC 1999

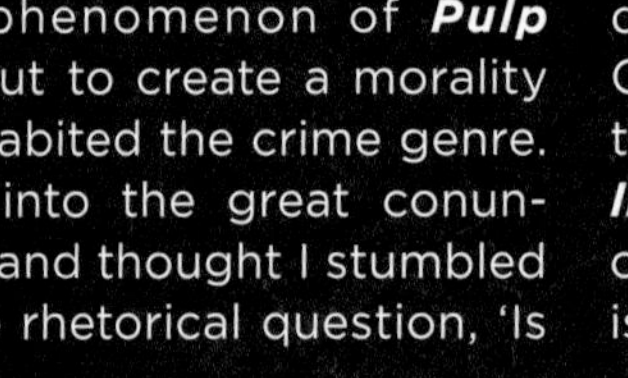

WILLIAMSBURG 2001

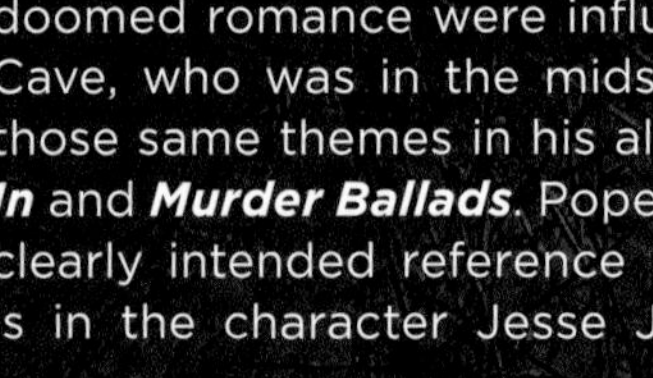

CHINATOWN NYC 2002

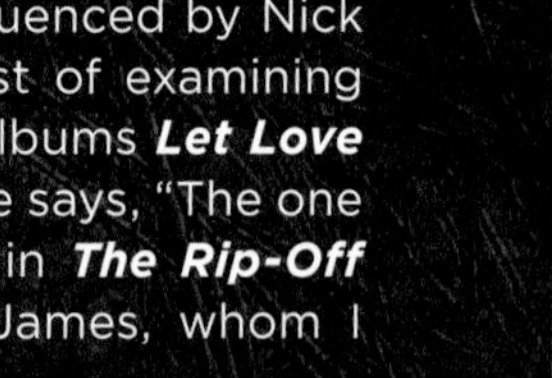

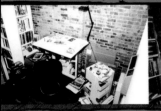

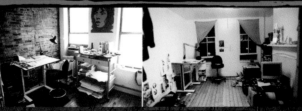

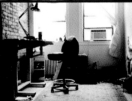

modeled after Nick Cave, or at least that murderous romantic Nick Cave of the time." Pope also explored his passion for restaurants and food, introducing his recurring theme that culinary expression is a kind of worldliness.

After completing ***The One Trick Rip-Off***, Pope began to travel more extensively, moved to Toronto and started a new period of ***THB*** work. The new work defiantly experimented with the presentation of comics, and was released in oversized editions that were extremely unusual in the American marketplace. 1996's ***Buzz Buzz Comics Magazine*** was the first book of this period, a 9.25" x 13" monster that presented comics like a fashion-conscious cosmopolitan magazine. The book included prose articles, photography and new stories by Pope, Moebius and Jay Stephens. "I had no idea it would be such a headache to approach talent, chase deadlines, and edit the materials — not to mention draw my own contributions," he says. "That one issue took nine months to produce, but I get the rare bragging rights to say I published a story by Moebius that debuted in my magazine and didn't appear anywhere else at that point." Pope's seminal mid-'90s romance "Escapo" appeared in ***Giant THB Parade*** later that year. "The Zhuk," a young H.R. Watson story included in this volume, also came out of this period.

At the same time, things were starting to heat up for Pope when Kodansha, the mammoth Japanese publishing house, drafted him to train for the manga marketplace. He explains, "I met with the editors at Comic-Con in 1994, when they were actively looking for American talents, and I was lucky enough to not only meet them, but to meet them with lots of pointed aesthetic questions about the manga format. They asked me to propose some story ideas for them. They loved ***THB***, but only wanted the 'cutie-pie' girl aspect. They didn't get the giant super-meks, surprisingly." This work became "Super Trouble," published for the first time in this book.

"Super Trouble" shows off Pope's other pivotal preoccupation of the 1990s — capturing the mischievous qualities of young girls. "Mainly, I was writing stories about little girls because I have a younger sister, and we were barely out of our teens at that point, so I was writing about what I knew at the time," he explains. "Also, like many cartoonists, I like to draw cute girls. I liked the pro-feminist/pro-humanist idea of showing women and girls who were not merely sexualized objects, but people — something I think I managed to finally achieve in ***100%***. I would say for the time, the young H.R. Watson in ***THB*** is a unique character in American comics — and she has had an influence on cartoonists from the younger generation, the ones after me. She was based more on a meditation about manga and the sort of science fiction I like to read and look at. It reflects the fact that I see women as humans first and women second." Those same attitudes are reflected in the characterization of the lead in "Four Cats" and "Airplanes," herself based on a girlfriend Pope courted.

Ultimately, "Super Trouble" didn't connect with the decision makers at Kodansha, but the work was enough to give Pope his first big ticket to ride — an invitation to go work in Japan. "They asked me to stop 'Super

SOHO NYC 2005

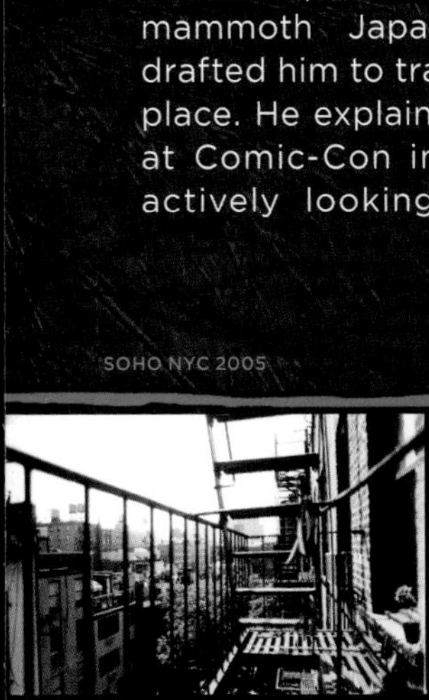

SOHO NYC 2005

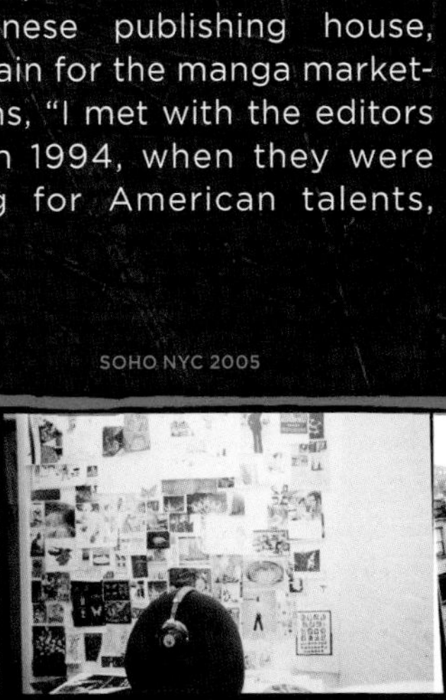

SOHO NYC 2005

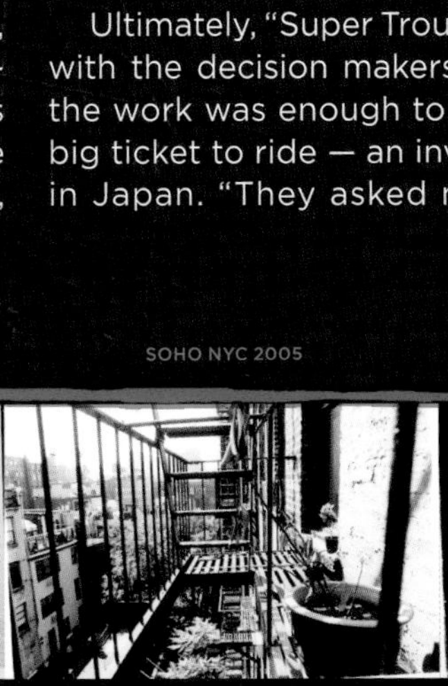

CHARLES DE GAULLE 2006

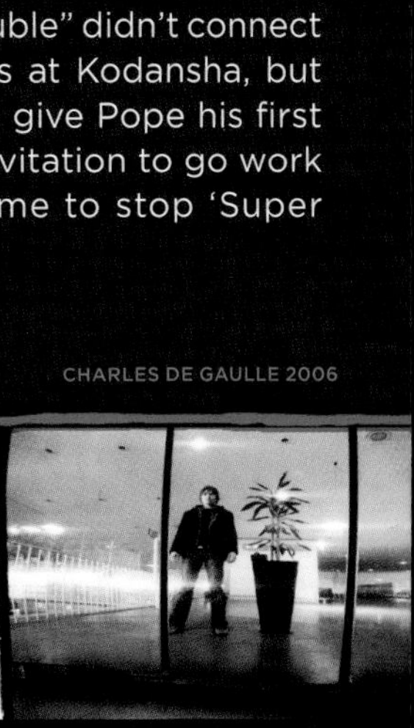

Trouble' and focus on a male-oriented action story after a couple of years. I was invited to live and work in Tokyo by that point. For most of the '90s I thought I'd be making manga for my career and didn't look at much American comics, outside of a few of my self-publishing peers, like Jeff Smith, Rick Veitch, and Steve Bissette."

The manga influence comes out in its most pronounced form here in "Night Job" and "The Scarf." These stories reflect an ethic of storytelling that favors greater exaggeration in both character expressions and actions. "Night Job" builds on the genre lessons learned in *Rip-Off*, while "The Scarf" returns to Pope's motif of the romantic chase seen earlier in "Yes" and *The Ballad of Dr. Richardson*. Within these stories, Pope is surer of his abilities, composing his pages with a swift, kinetic line that allows looser drawing and pacing values to bolt the reader through the narrative.

After a four year courtship, Pope's relationship with Kodansha had cooled off and he moved back to the States, settling at last in New York City in 1999. Once there, Shelly Bond recruited him to do the graphic novels *100%* and *Heavy Liquid* for DC Comics' Vertigo imprint. Pope continued to work for DC Comics and went on to create *Batman: Year 100*, which garnered him two prestigious Eisner Awards in 2007 for Best Writer/Artist and Best Limited Series.

Pope says, "Looking at this work now, I can see that a lot of the themes I was working on and was trying to hammer out eventually came together by the time I was working on *Heavy Liquid* and *100%* for Vertigo. I see those works as the cap on the '90s period. I was super-excited by manga and pretty much dove into the deep end of it while in Japan. I didn't even look at American comics for years, and that had a really positive effect in the long run, I think. By the time I hit NYC, I was in love with a place for the first time. The energy of NYC was informing the work by that point. I wasn't trying to 'escape' a place anymore and I wasn't waiting until I could leave a place — I was there, and I wanted my work to belong there."

Through the process of making the work collected in this book, Pope had come of age by exploring the world, both as a man and as an artist. Along the way he'd assimilated the lessons of Europe, North America and Japan into his lifestyle and art practice. After spending the first decade of his creative life on the move, Paul Pope had finally arrived.

CHARLES BROWNSTEIN *is the Executive Director of the Comic Book Legal Defense Fund (www.cbldf.org), a non-profit organization protecting the First Amendment rights of the comics field. In addition to running the CBLDF, he also writes extensively about comics; his publications include the award-winning books* Eisner/ Miller *and* The Oddly Compelling Art of Denis Kitchen. *His work has also been included in several anthology publications, including* Best American Comics Criticism *and* Comic-Con Annual. *Follow his blog at brownstein.blogspot.com.*

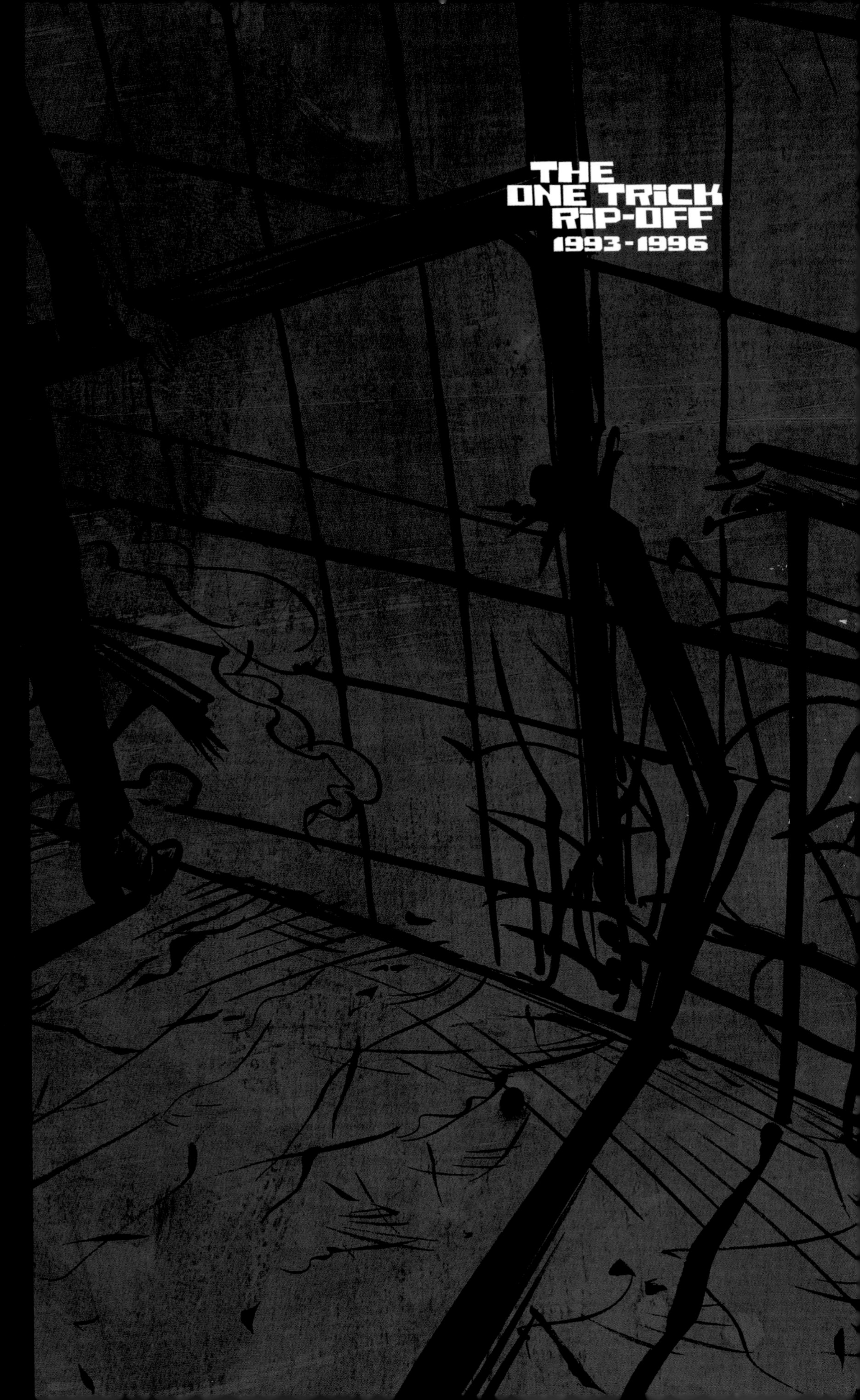
THE
ONE TRICK
RIP-OFF
1993-1996

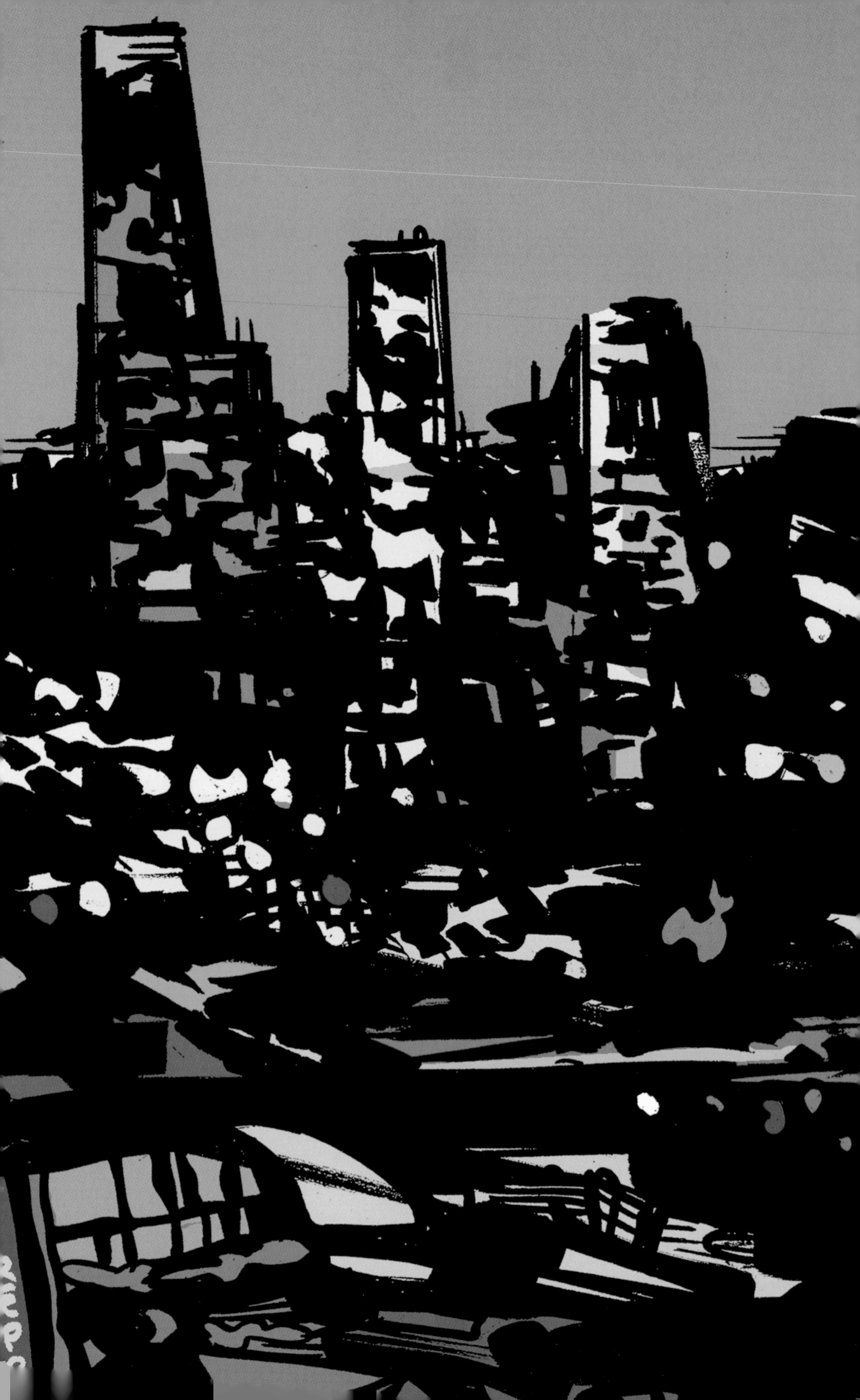

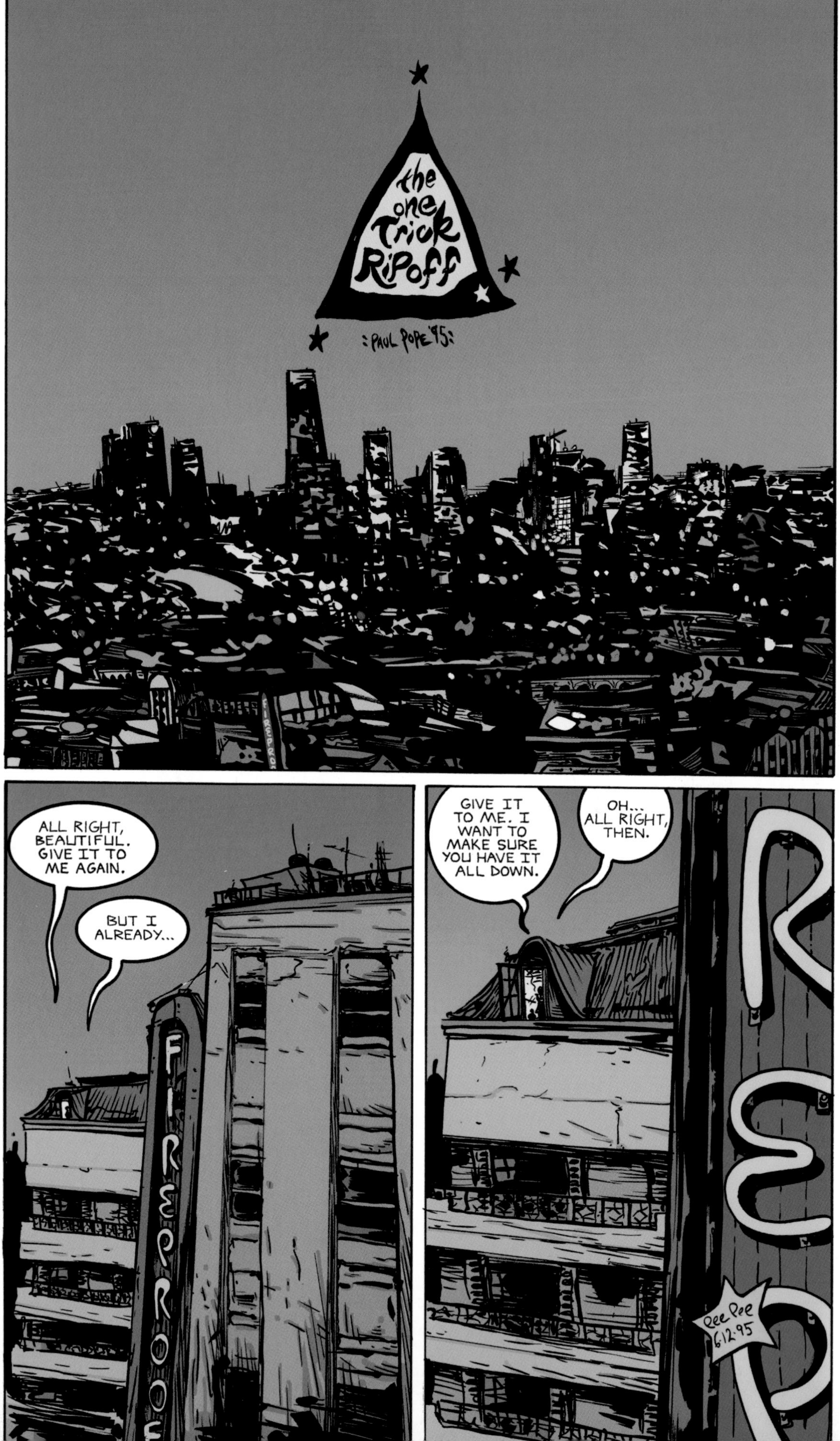
the one Trick Ripoff
PAUL POPE '95
ALL RIGHT, BEAUTIFUL. GIVE IT TO ME AGAIN.
BUT I ALREADY...
GIVE IT TO ME. I WANT TO MAKE SURE YOU HAVE IT ALL DOWN.
OH... ALL RIGHT, THEN.
Pee Pee 6.12.95

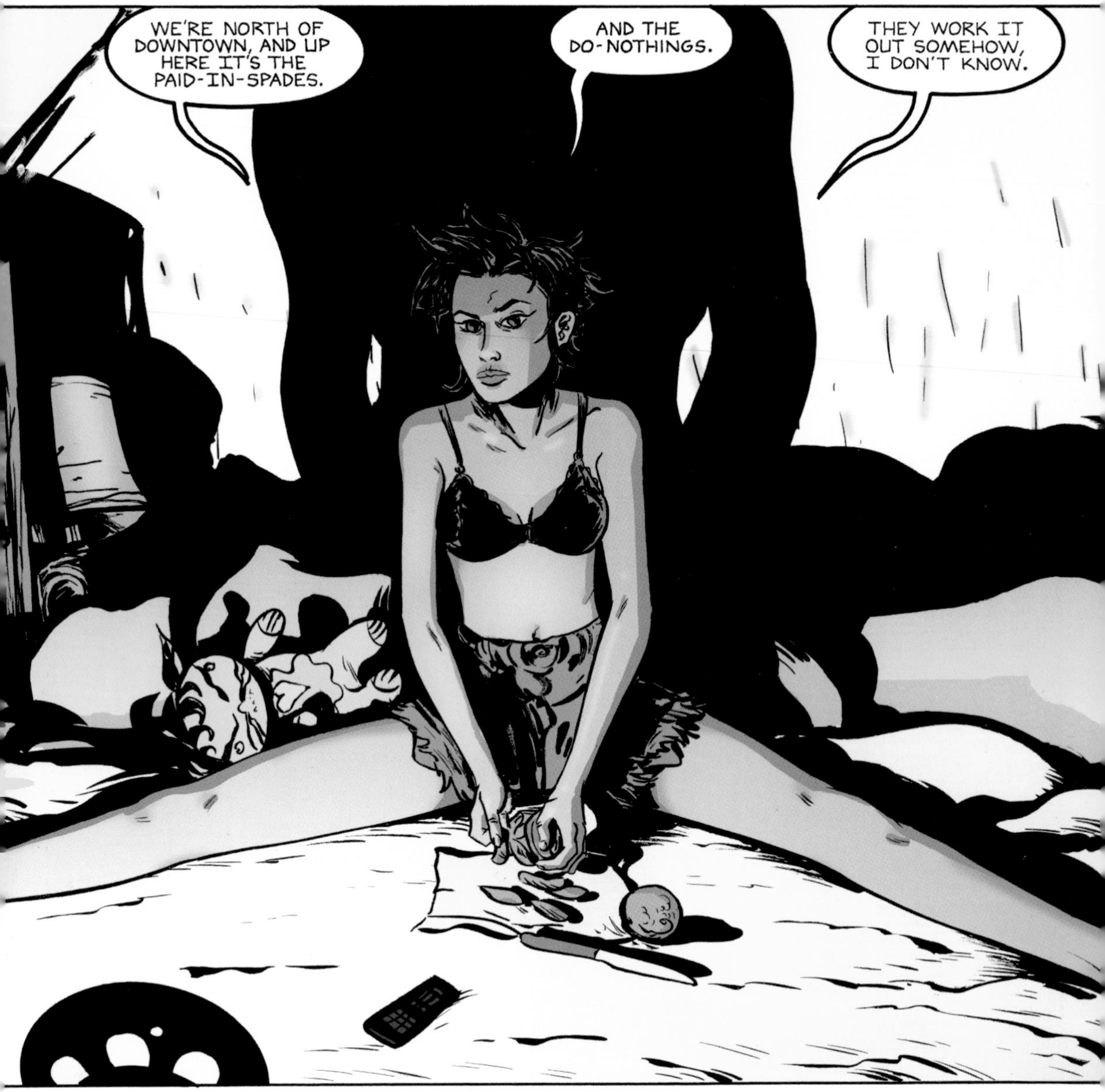
WE'RE NORTH OF DOWNTOWN, AND UP HERE IT'S THE PAID-IN-SPADES.
AND THE DO-NOTHINGS.
THEY WORK IT OUT SOMEHOW, I DON'T KNOW.

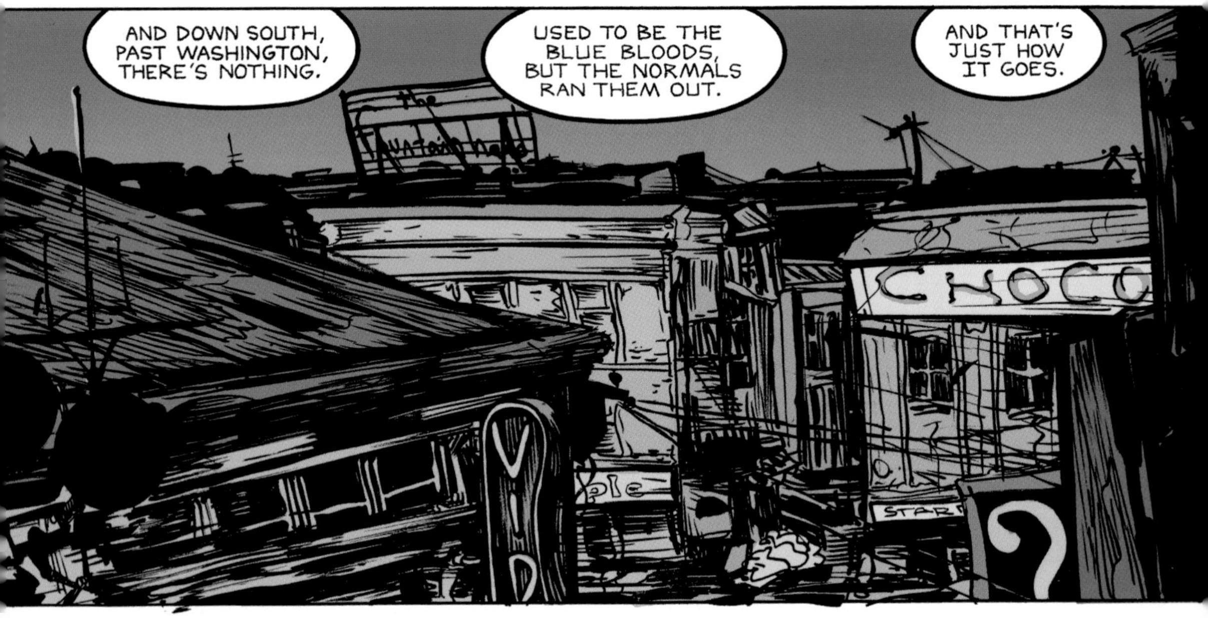
AND DOWN SOUTH, PAST WASHINGTON, THERE'S NOTHING.
USED TO BE THE BLUE BLOODS, BUT THE NORMALS RAN THEM OUT.
AND THAT'S JUST HOW IT GOES.

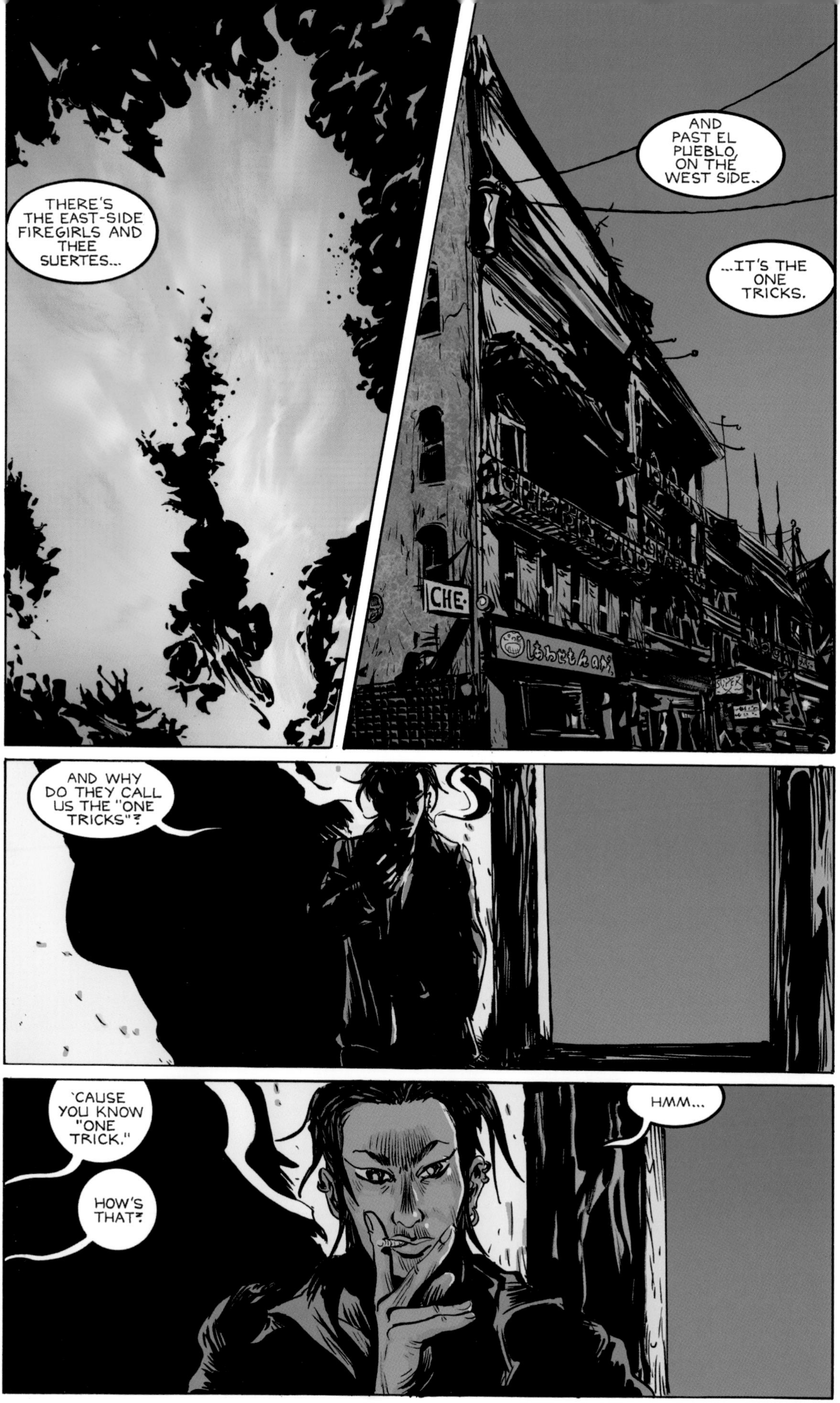
THERE'S THE EAST-SIDE FIREGIRLS AND THEE SUERTES...
AND PAST EL PUEBLO, ON THE WEST SIDE..
...IT'S THE ONE TRICKS.
CHE·
AND WHY DO THEY CALL US THE "ONE TRICKS"?
'CAUSE YOU KNOW "ONE TRICK."
HOW'S THAT?
HMM...

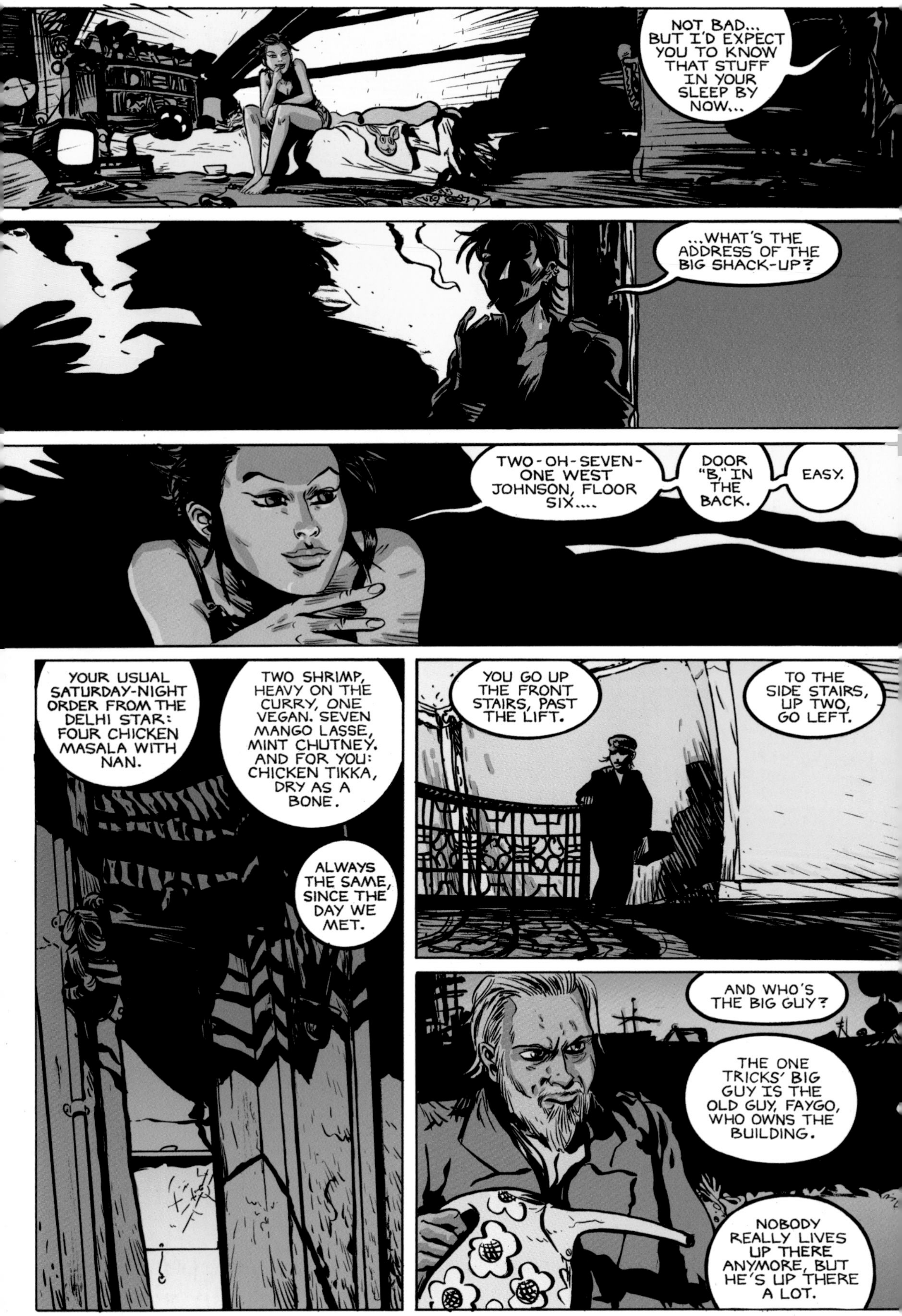
NOT BAD... BUT I'D EXPECT YOU TO KNOW THAT STUFF IN YOUR SLEEP BY NOW...
...WHAT'S THE ADDRESS OF THE BIG SHACK-UP?
TWO-OH-SEVEN-ONE WEST JOHNSON, FLOOR SIX....
DOOR "B," IN THE BACK.
EASY.
YOUR USUAL SATURDAY-NIGHT ORDER FROM THE DELHI STAR: FOUR CHICKEN MASALA WITH NAN.
TWO SHRIMP, HEAVY ON THE CURRY, ONE VEGAN. SEVEN MANGO LASSE, MINT CHUTNEY. AND FOR YOU: CHICKEN TIKKA, DRY AS A BONE.
ALWAYS THE SAME, SINCE THE DAY WE MET.
YOU GO UP THE FRONT STAIRS, PAST THE LIFT.
TO THE SIDE STAIRS, UP TWO, GO LEFT.
AND WHO'S THE BIG GUY?
THE ONE TRICKS' BIG GUY IS THE OLD GUY, FAYGO, WHO OWNS THE BUILDING.
NOBODY REALLY LIVES UP THERE ANYMORE, BUT HE'S UP THERE A LOT.

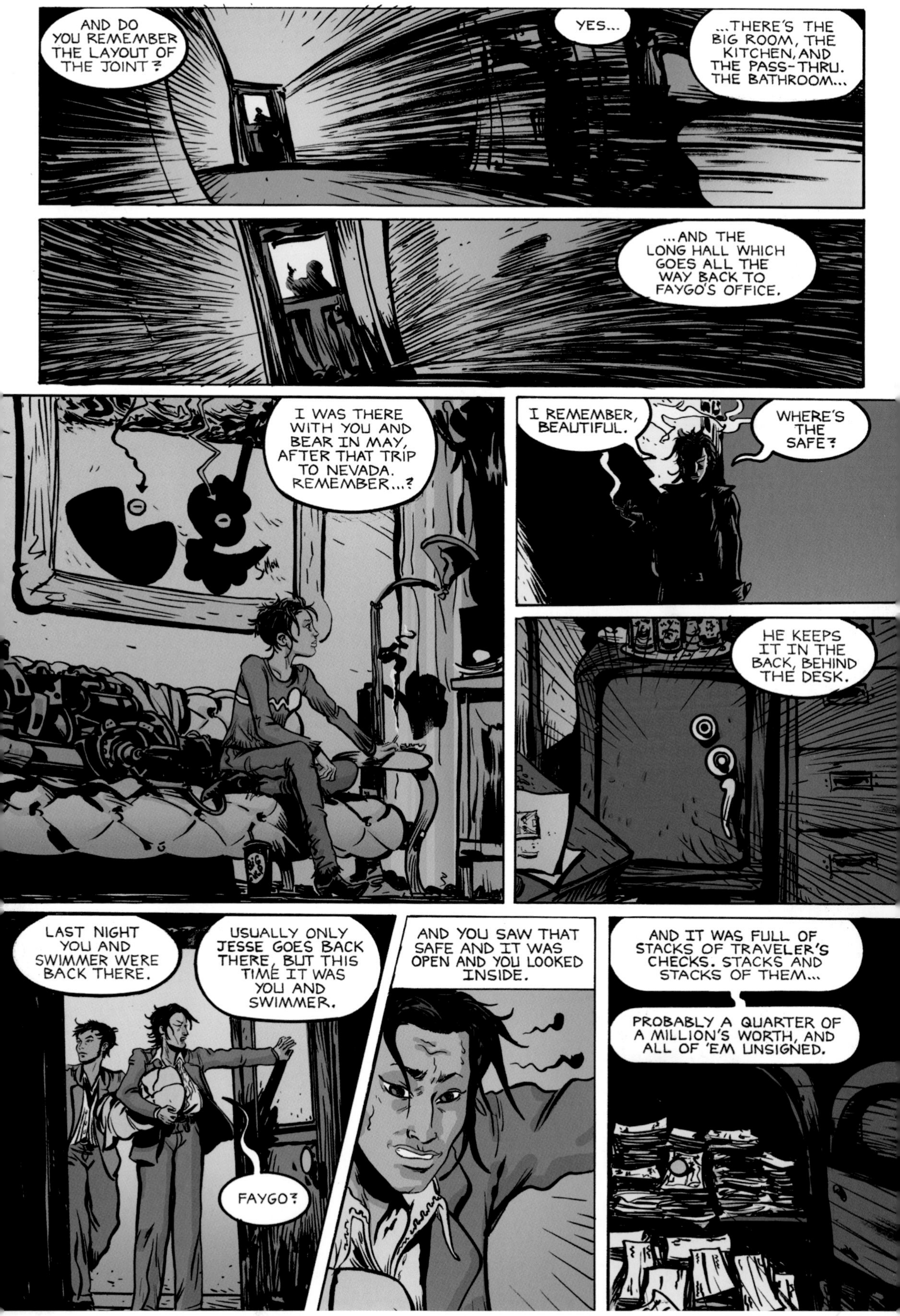
AND DO YOU REMEMBER THE LAYOUT OF THE JOINT?
YES...
...THERE'S THE BIG ROOM, THE KITCHEN, AND THE PASS-THRU. THE BATHROOM...
...AND THE LONG HALL WHICH GOES ALL THE WAY BACK TO FAYGO'S OFFICE.
I WAS THERE WITH YOU AND BEAR IN MAY, AFTER THAT TRIP TO NEVADA. REMEMBER...?
I REMEMBER, BEAUTIFUL.
WHERE'S THE SAFE?
HE KEEPS IT IN THE BACK, BEHIND THE DESK.
LAST NIGHT YOU AND SWIMMER WERE BACK THERE.
USUALLY ONLY JESSE GOES BACK THERE, BUT THIS TIME IT WAS YOU AND SWIMMER.
FAYGO?
AND YOU SAW THAT SAFE AND IT WAS OPEN AND YOU LOOKED INSIDE.
AND IT WAS FULL OF STACKS OF TRAVELER'S CHECKS. STACKS AND STACKS OF THEM...
PROBABLY A QUARTER OF A MILLION'S WORTH, AND ALL OF 'EM UNSIGNED.

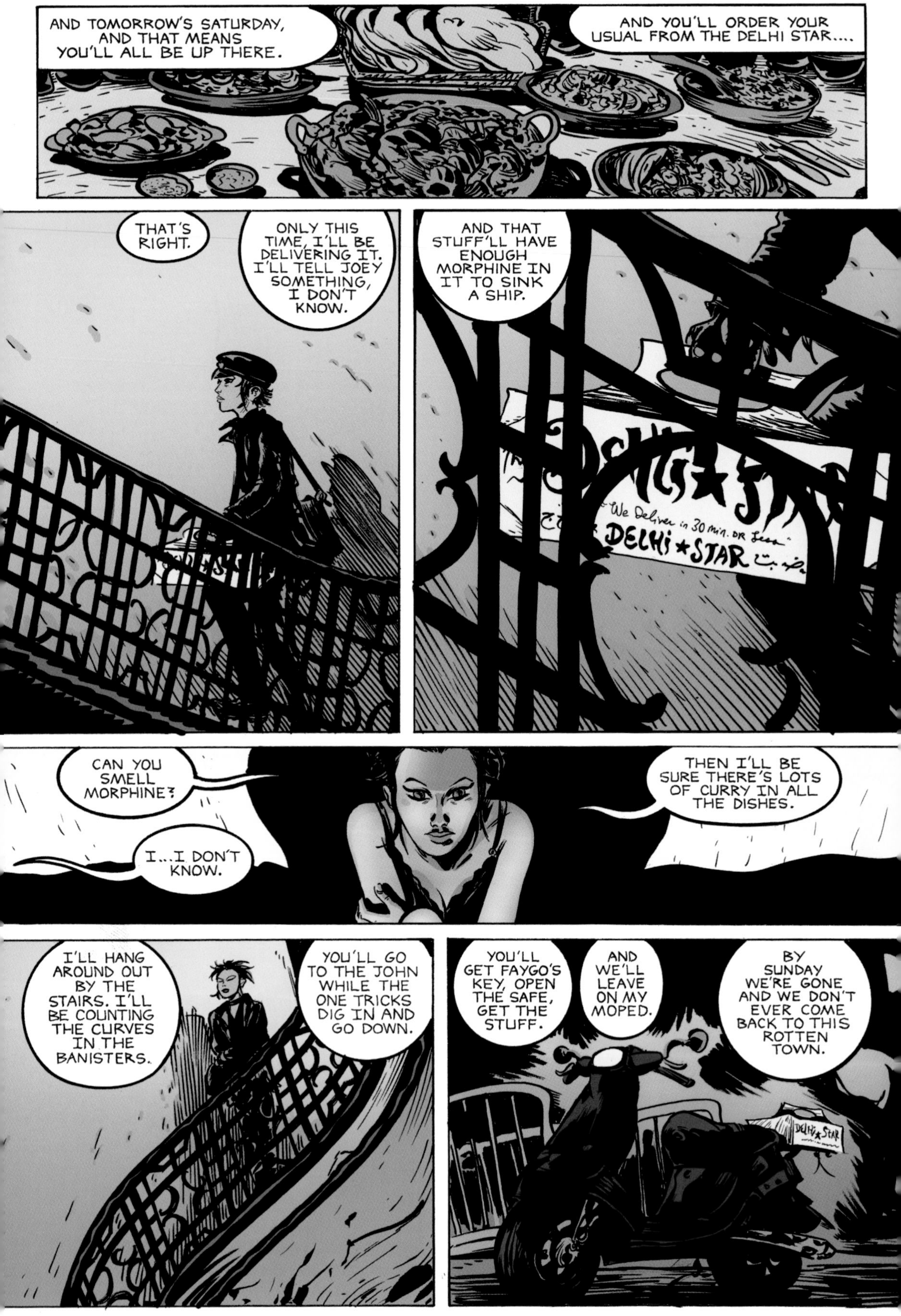
AND TOMORROW'S SATURDAY, AND THAT MEANS YOU'LL ALL BE UP THERE.
AND YOU'LL ORDER YOUR USUAL FROM THE DELHI STAR....
THAT'S RIGHT.
ONLY THIS TIME, I'LL BE DELIVERING IT. I'LL TELL JOEY SOMETHING, I DON'T KNOW.
AND THAT STUFF'LL HAVE ENOUGH MORPHINE IN IT TO SINK A SHIP.
We Deliver in 30 min. or Less
DELHI ★ STAR
CAN YOU SMELL MORPHINE?
I...I DON'T KNOW.
THEN I'LL BE SURE THERE'S LOTS OF CURRY IN ALL THE DISHES.
I'LL HANG AROUND OUT BY THE STAIRS. I'LL BE COUNTING THE CURVES IN THE BANISTERS.
YOU'LL GO TO THE JOHN WHILE THE ONE TRICKS DIG IN AND GO DOWN.
YOU'LL GET FAYGO'S KEY, OPEN THE SAFE, GET THE STUFF.
AND WE'LL LEAVE ON MY MOPED.
BY SUNDAY WE'RE GONE AND WE DON'T EVER COME BACK TO THIS ROTTEN TOWN.
DELHI ★ STAR

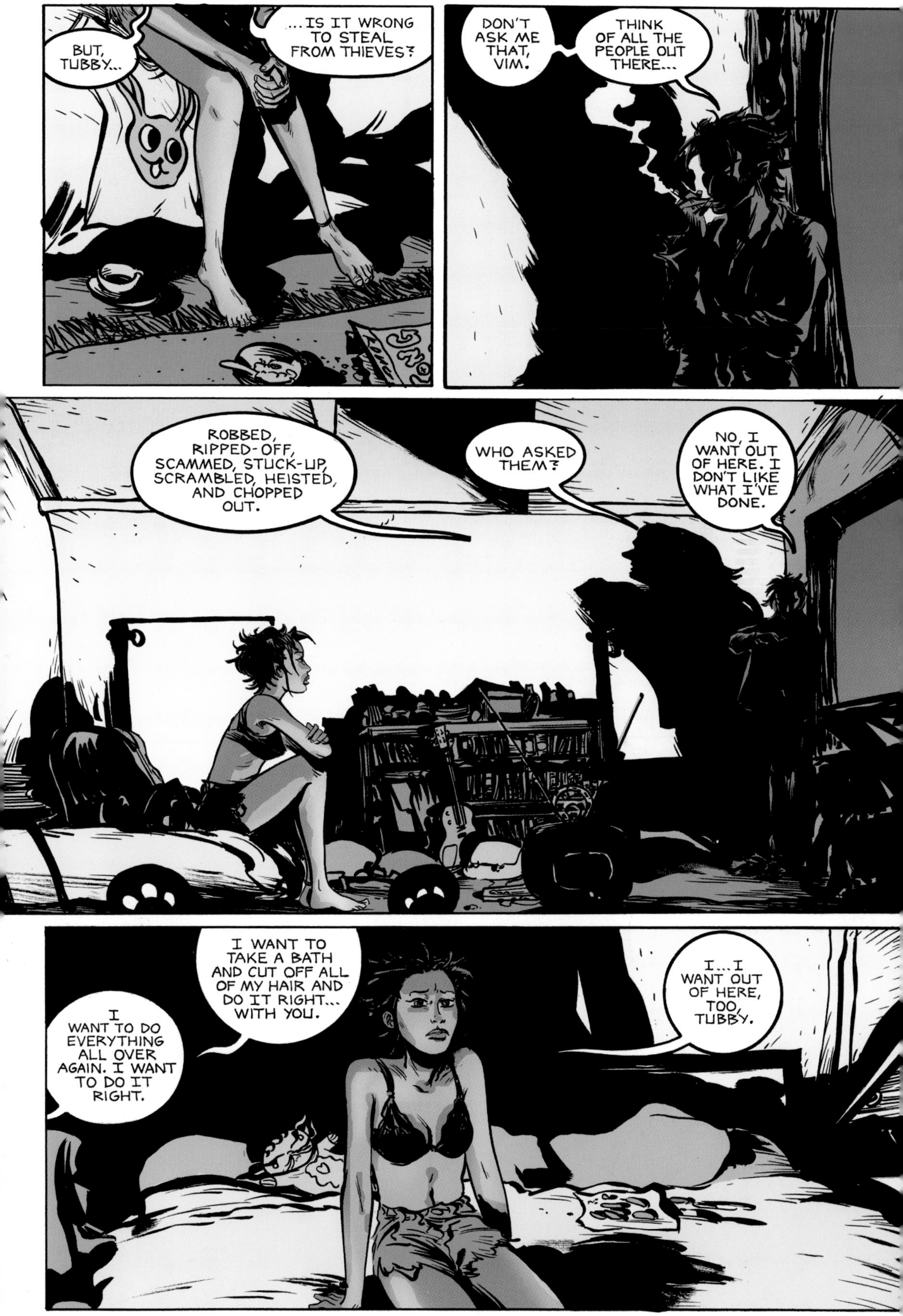
BUT, TUBBY...
...IS IT WRONG TO STEAL FROM THIEVES?
DON'T ASK ME THAT, VIM.
THINK OF ALL THE PEOPLE OUT THERE...
ROBBED, RIPPED-OFF, SCAMMED, STUCK-UP, SCRAMBLED, HEISTED, AND CHOPPED OUT.
WHO ASKED THEM?
NO, I WANT OUT OF HERE. I DON'T LIKE WHAT I'VE DONE.
I WANT TO DO EVERYTHING ALL OVER AGAIN. I WANT TO DO IT RIGHT.
I WANT TO TAKE A BATH AND CUT OFF ALL OF MY HAIR AND DO IT RIGHT... WITH YOU.
I... I WANT OUT OF HERE, TOO, TUBBY.

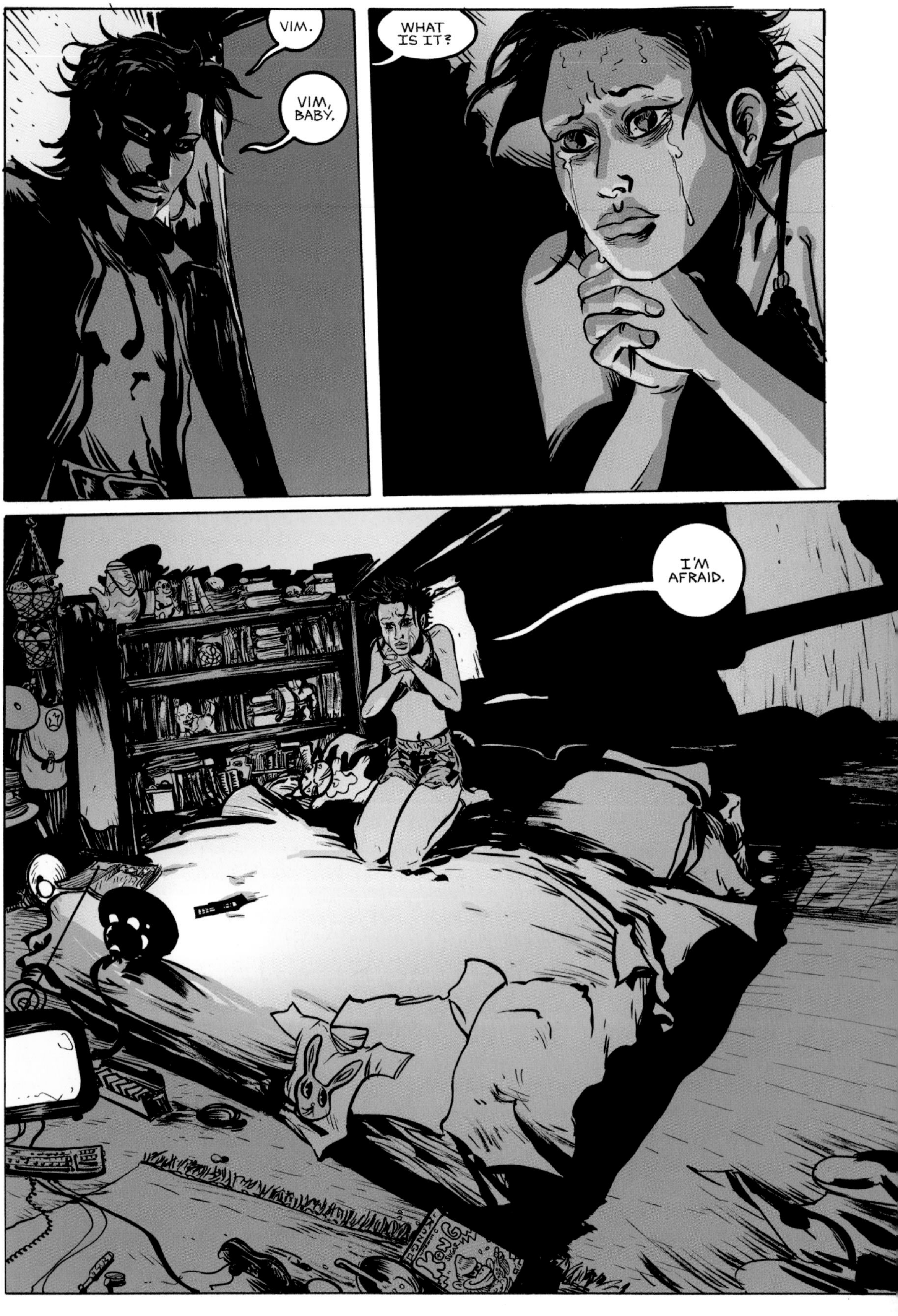
VIM.
VIM, BABY.
WHAT IS IT?
I'M AFRAID.

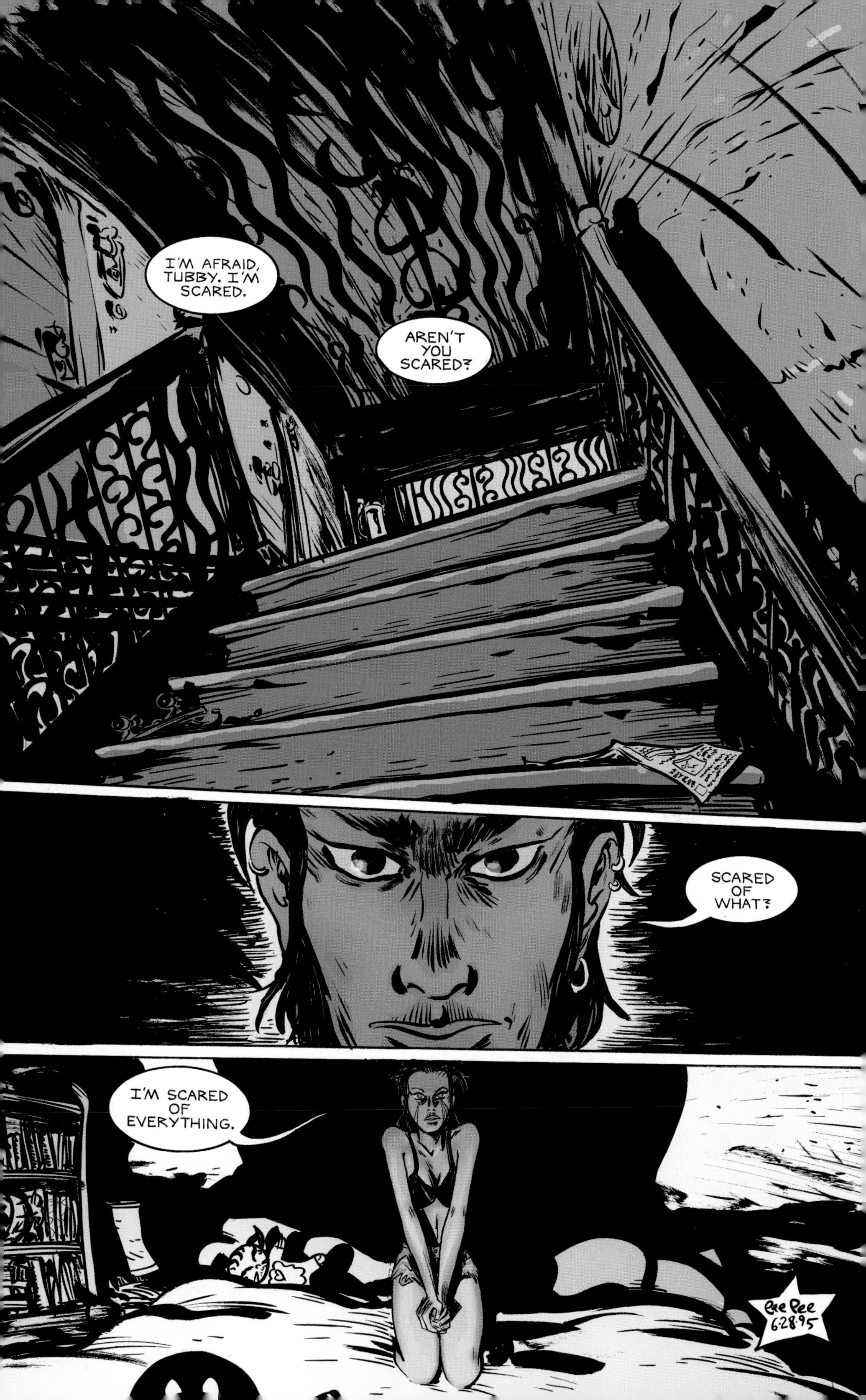
I'M AFRAID, TUBBY. I'M SCARED.
AREN'T YOU SCARED?
SCARED OF WHAT?
I'M SCARED OF EVERYTHING.
Pee Pee 6.28.95

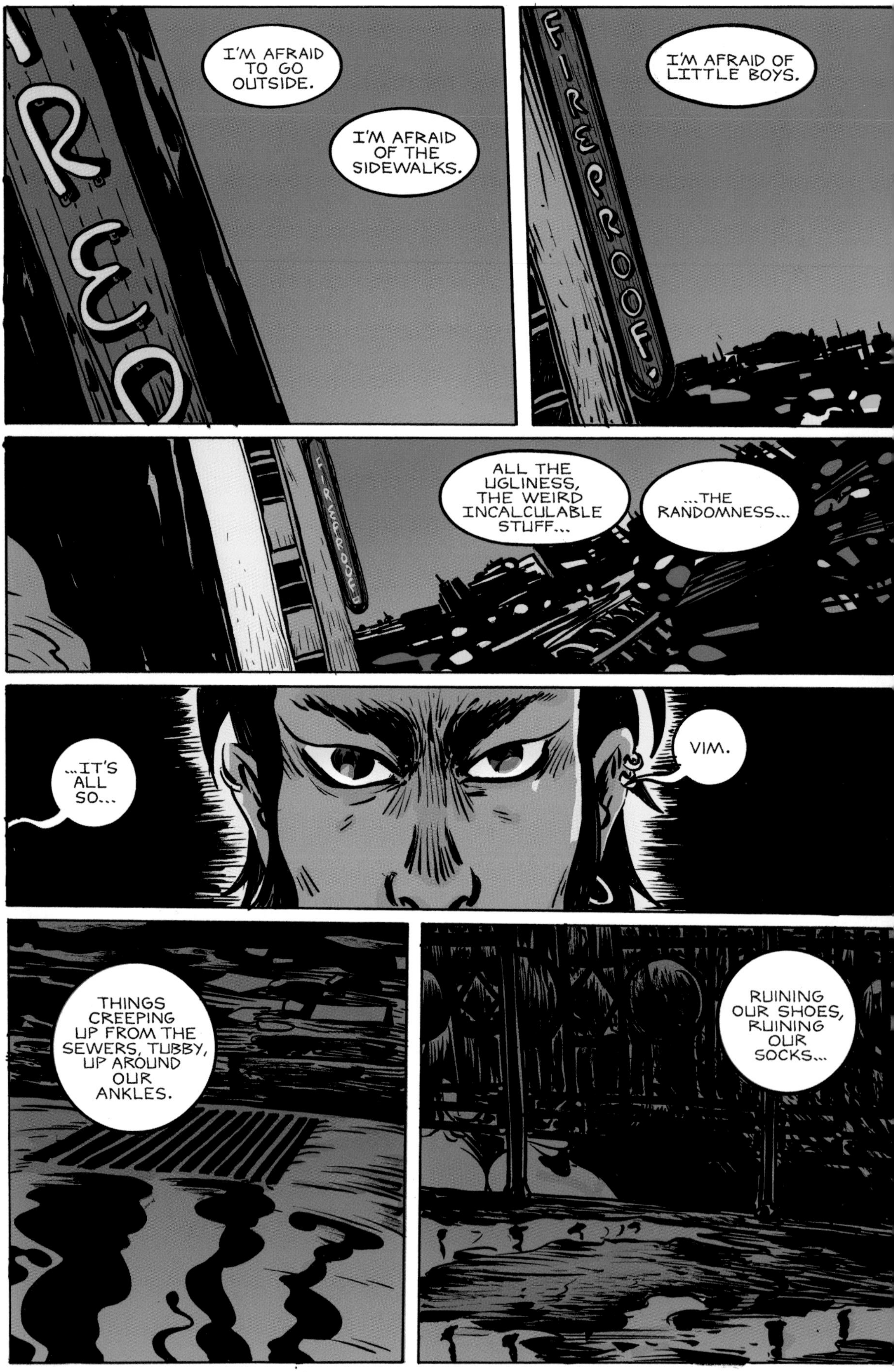
I'M AFRAID TO GO OUTSIDE.
I'M AFRAID OF THE SIDEWALKS.
FIREPROOF
I'M AFRAID OF LITTLE BOYS.
FIREPROOF
ALL THE UGLINESS, THE WEIRD INCALCULABLE STUFF...
...THE RANDOMNESS...
...IT'S ALL SO...
VIM.
THINGS CREEPING UP FROM THE SEWERS, TUBBY, UP AROUND OUR ANKLES.
RUINING OUR SHOES, RUINING OUR SOCKS...

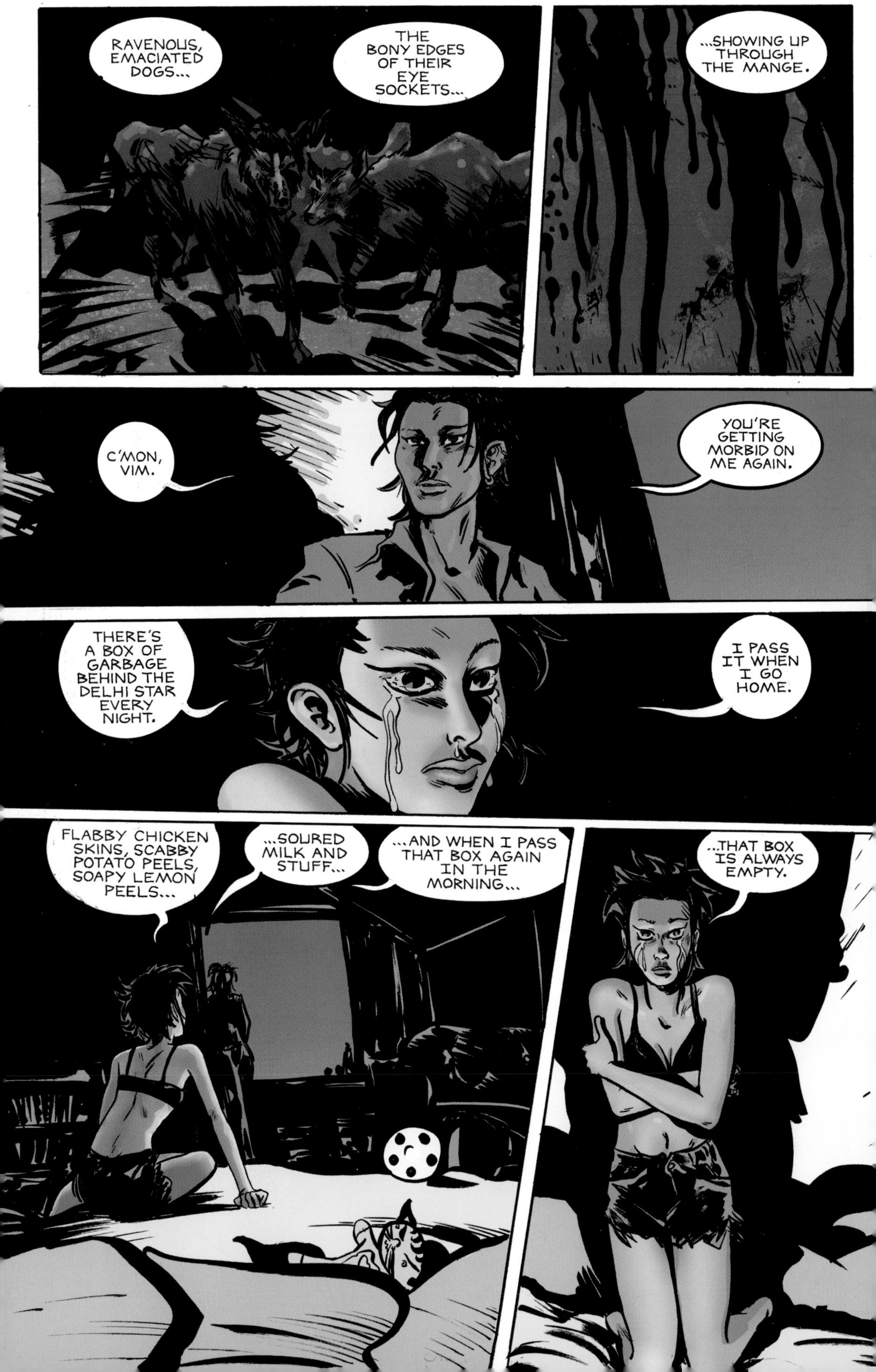
RAVENOUS, EMACIATED DOGS...
THE BONY EDGES OF THEIR EYE SOCKETS...
...SHOWING UP THROUGH THE MANGE.
C'MON, VIM.
YOU'RE GETTING MORBID ON ME AGAIN.
THERE'S A BOX OF GARBAGE BEHIND THE DELHI STAR EVERY NIGHT.
I PASS IT WHEN I GO HOME.
FLABBY CHICKEN SKINS, SCABBY POTATO PEELS, SOAPY LEMON PEELS...
...SOURED MILK AND STUFF...
...AND WHEN I PASS THAT BOX AGAIN IN THE MORNING...
...THAT BOX IS ALWAYS EMPTY.

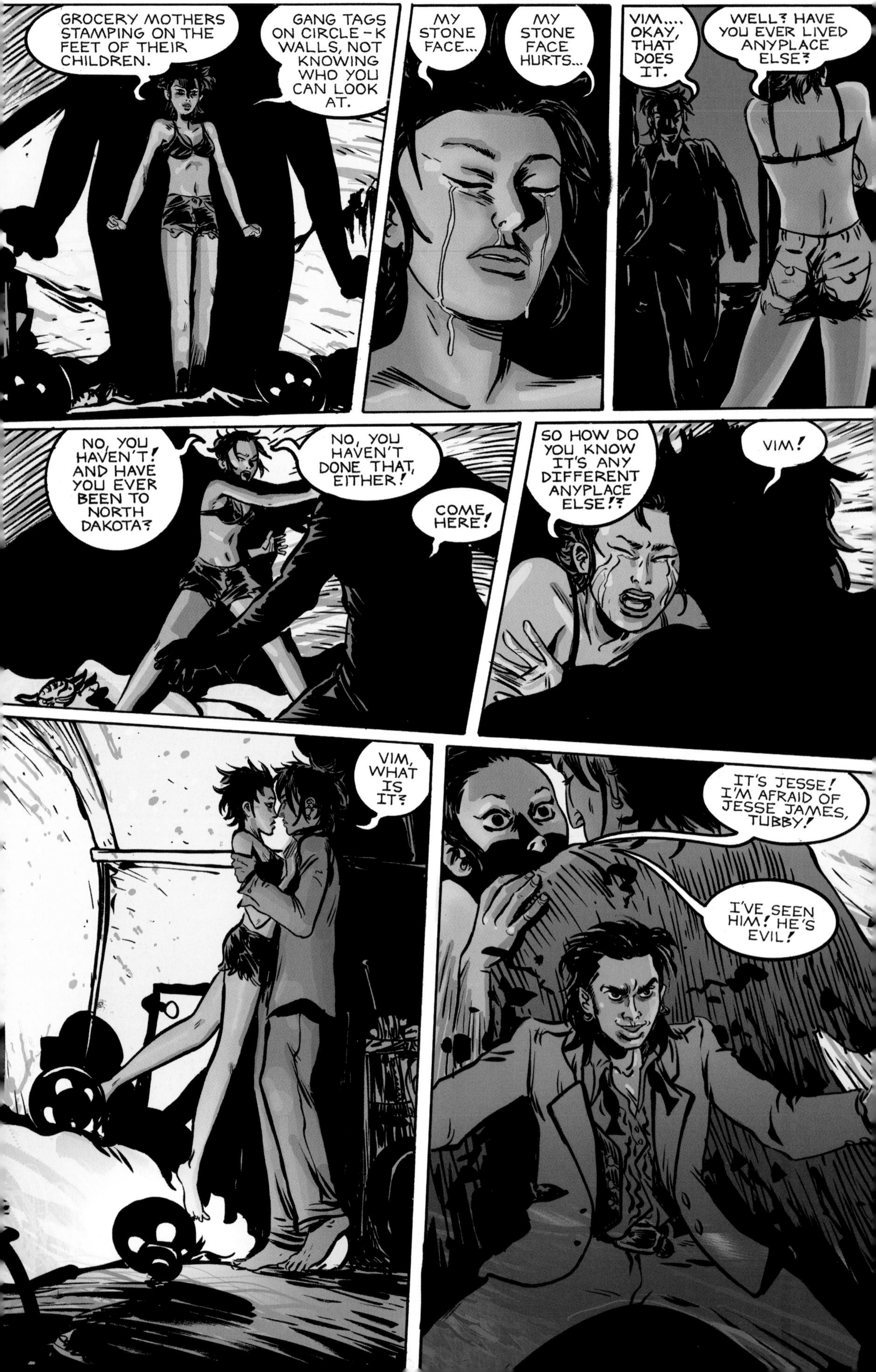
GROCERY MOTHERS STAMPING ON THE FEET OF THEIR CHILDREN.
GANG TAGS ON CIRCLE-K WALLS, NOT KNOWING WHO YOU CAN LOOK AT.
MY STONE FACE...
MY STONE FACE HURTS...
VIM.... OKAY, THAT DOES IT.
WELL? HAVE YOU EVER LIVED ANYPLACE ELSE?
NO, YOU HAVEN'T! AND HAVE YOU EVER BEEN TO NORTH DAKOTA?
NO, YOU HAVEN'T DONE THAT, EITHER!
COME HERE!
SO HOW DO YOU KNOW IT'S ANY DIFFERENT ANYPLACE ELSE!?
VIM!
VIM, WHAT IS IT?
IT'S JESSE! I'M AFRAID OF JESSE JAMES, TUBBY!
I'VE SEEN HIM! HE'S EVIL!

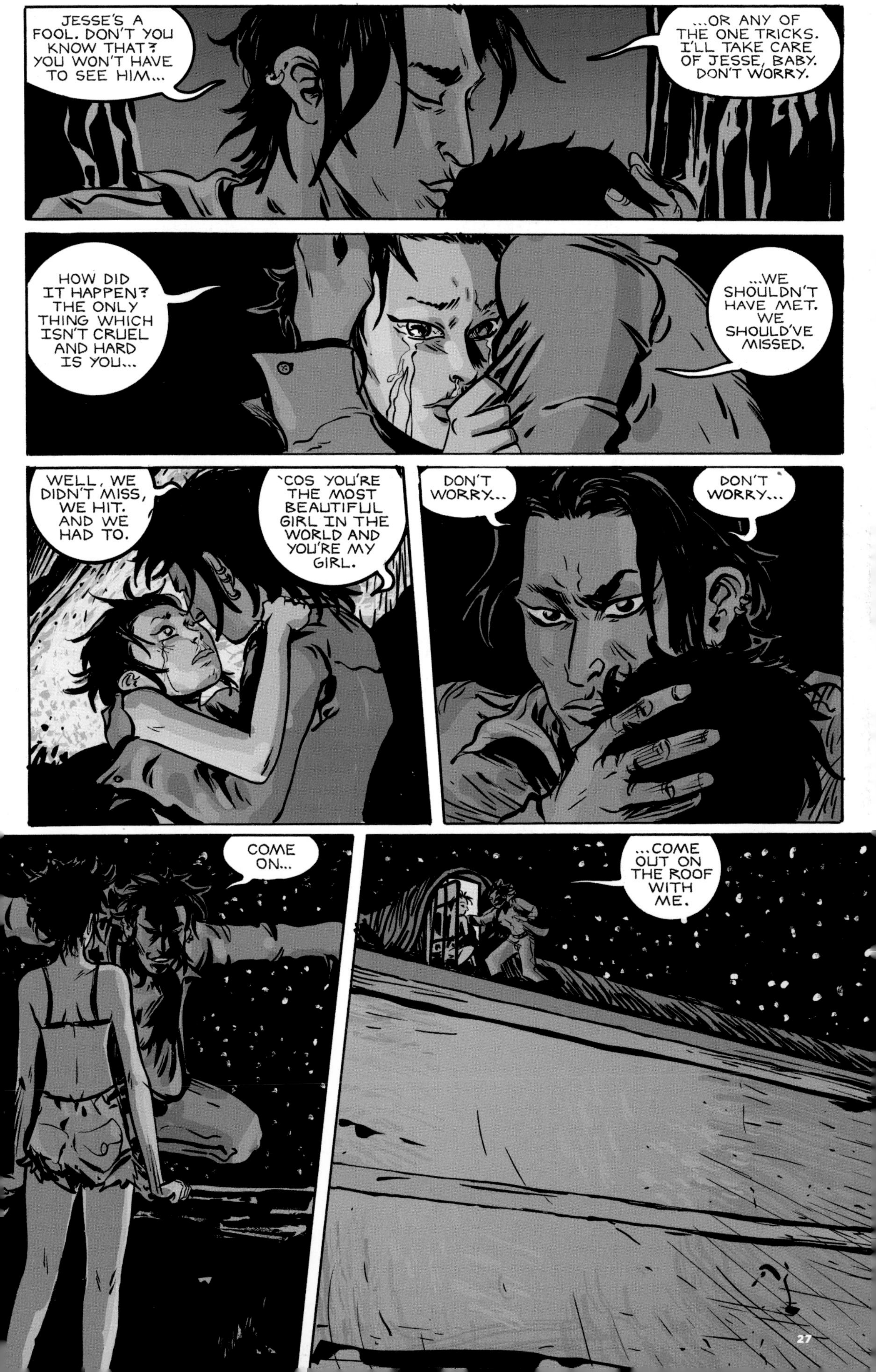
JESSE'S A FOOL. DON'T YOU KNOW THAT? YOU WON'T HAVE TO SEE HIM...
...OR ANY OF THE ONE TRICKS. I'LL TAKE CARE OF JESSE, BABY. DON'T WORRY.
HOW DID IT HAPPEN? THE ONLY THING WHICH ISN'T CRUEL AND HARD IS YOU...
...WE SHOULDN'T HAVE MET. WE SHOULD'VE MISSED.
WELL, WE DIDN'T MISS, WE HIT. AND WE HAD TO.
'COS YOU'RE THE MOST BEAUTIFUL GIRL IN THE WORLD AND YOU'RE MY GIRL.
DON'T WORRY...
DON'T WORRY...
COME ON...
...COME OUT ON THE ROOF WITH ME.

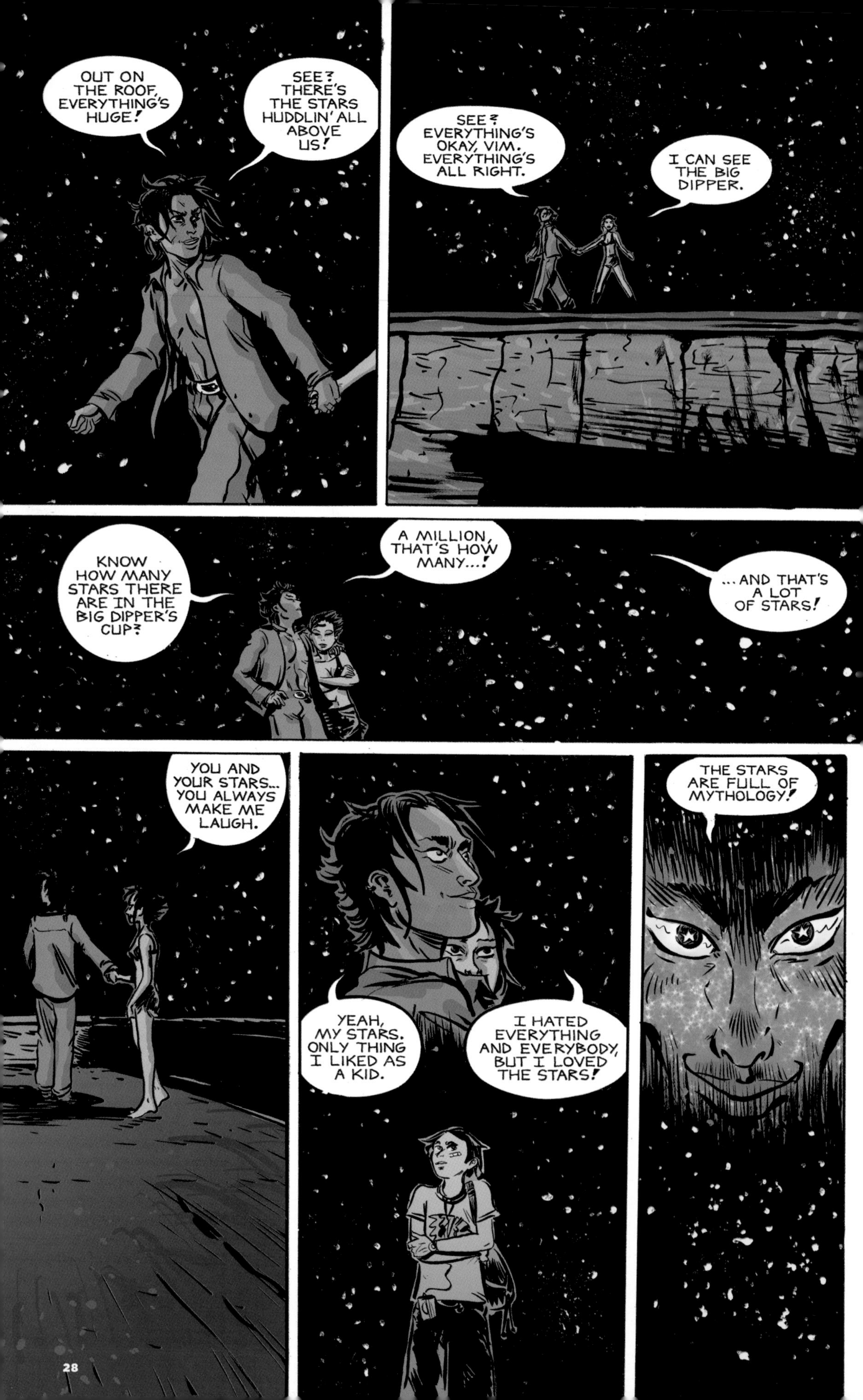

OUT ON THE ROOF, EVERYTHING'S HUGE!
SEE? THERE'S THE STARS HUDDLIN' ALL ABOVE US!
SEE? EVERYTHING'S OKAY, VIM. EVERYTHING'S ALL RIGHT.
I CAN SEE THE BIG DIPPER.
KNOW HOW MANY STARS THERE ARE IN THE BIG DIPPER'S CUP?
A MILLION, THAT'S HOW MANY...!
...AND THAT'S A LOT OF STARS!
YOU AND YOUR STARS... YOU ALWAYS MAKE ME LAUGH.
YEAH, MY STARS. ONLY THING I LIKED AS A KID.
I HATED EVERYTHING AND EVERYBODY, BUT I LOVED THE STARS!
THE STARS ARE FULL OF MYTHOLOGY!

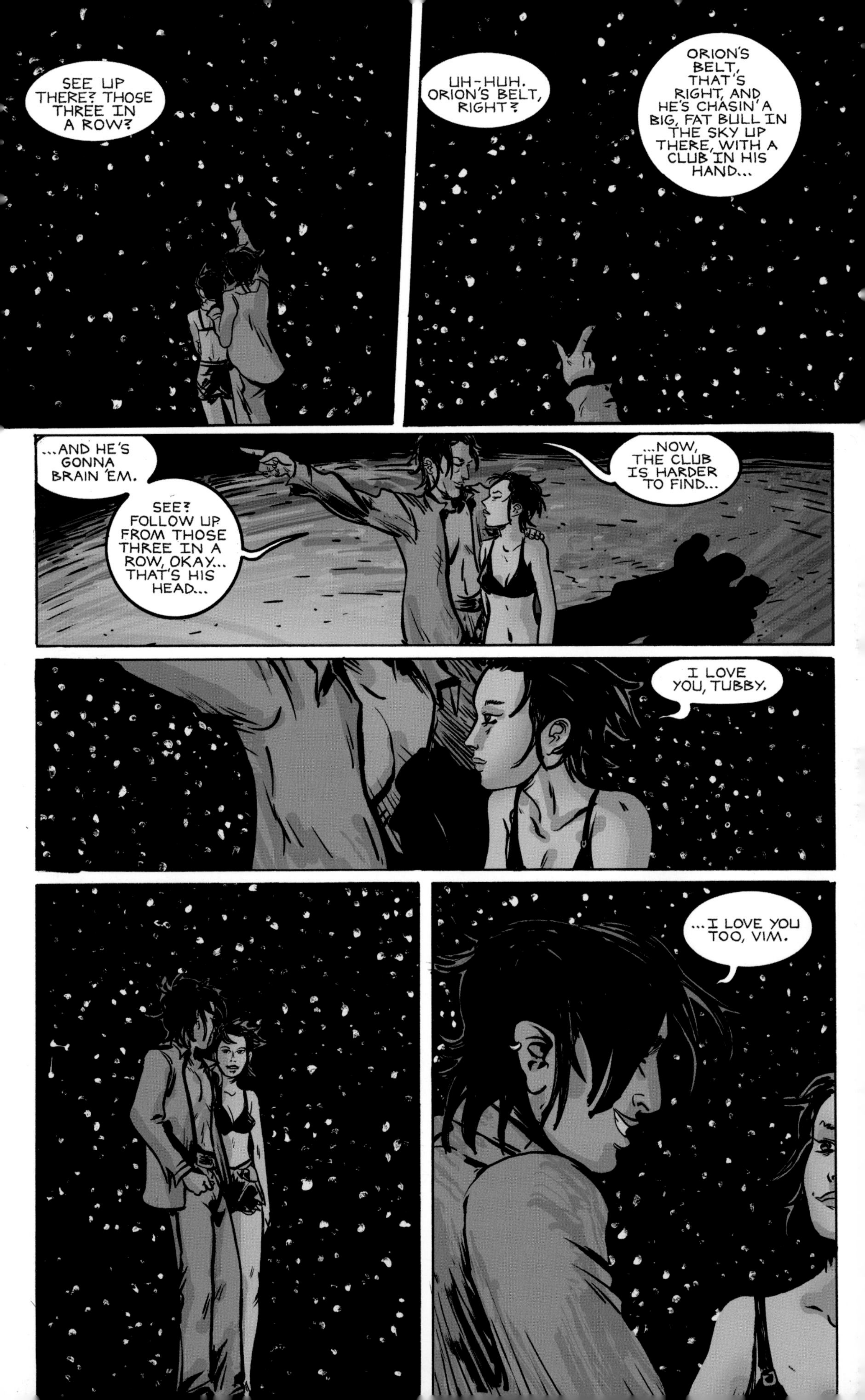
SEE UP THERE? THOSE THREE IN A ROW?
UH-HUH. ORION'S BELT, RIGHT?
ORION'S BELT, THAT'S RIGHT, AND HE'S CHASIN' A BIG, FAT BULL IN THE SKY UP THERE, WITH A CLUB IN HIS HAND...
...AND HE'S GONNA BRAIN 'EM.
SEE? FOLLOW UP FROM THOSE THREE IN A ROW, OKAY... THAT'S HIS HEAD...
...NOW, THE CLUB IS HARDER TO FIND...
I LOVE YOU, TUBBY.
...I LOVE YOU TOO, VIM.

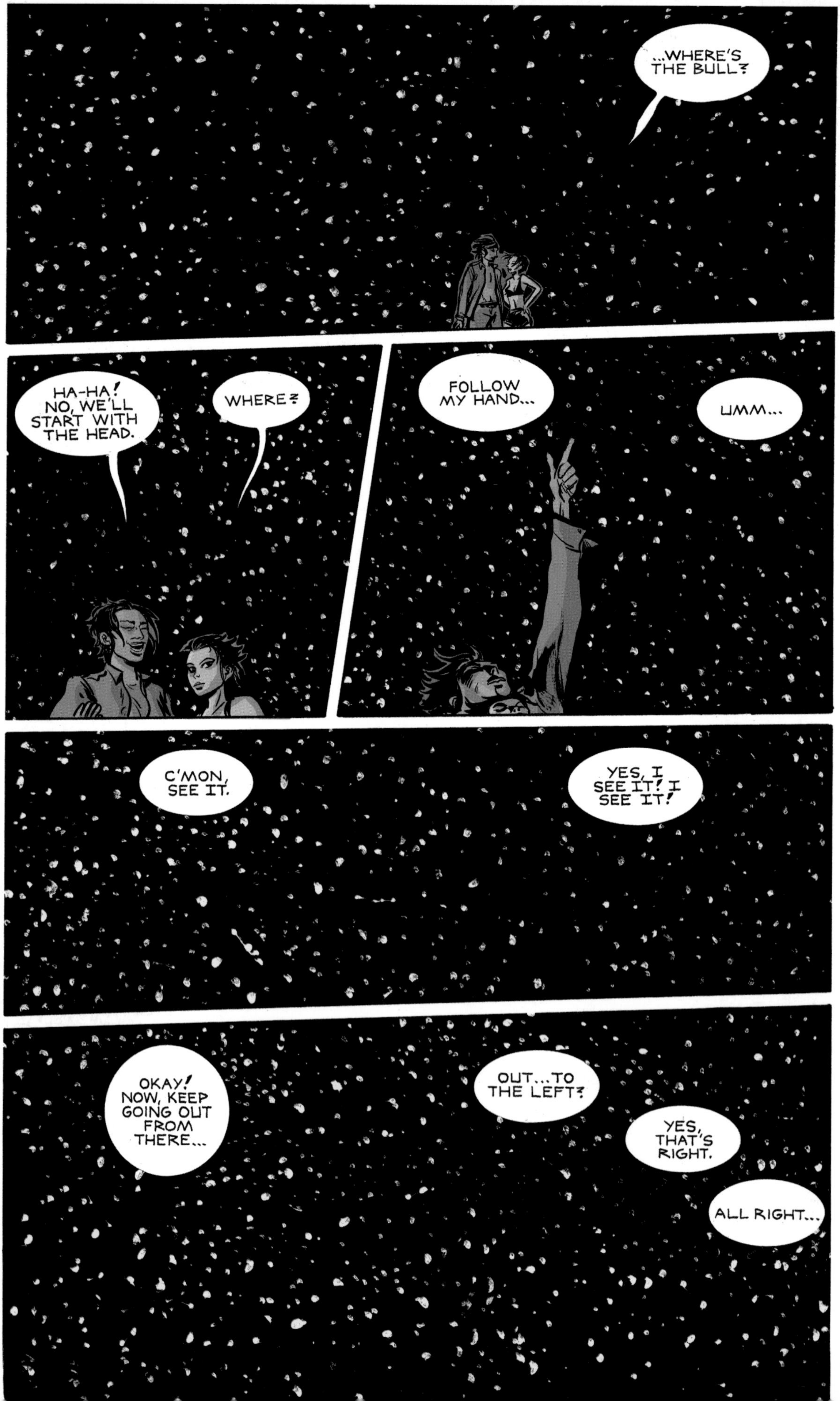
...WHERE'S THE BULL?
HA-HA! NO, WE'LL START WITH THE HEAD.
WHERE?
FOLLOW MY HAND...
UMM...
C'MON, SEE IT.
YES, I SEE IT! I SEE IT!
OKAY! NOW, KEEP GOING OUT FROM THERE...
OUT...TO THE LEFT?
YES, THAT'S RIGHT.
ALL RIGHT...

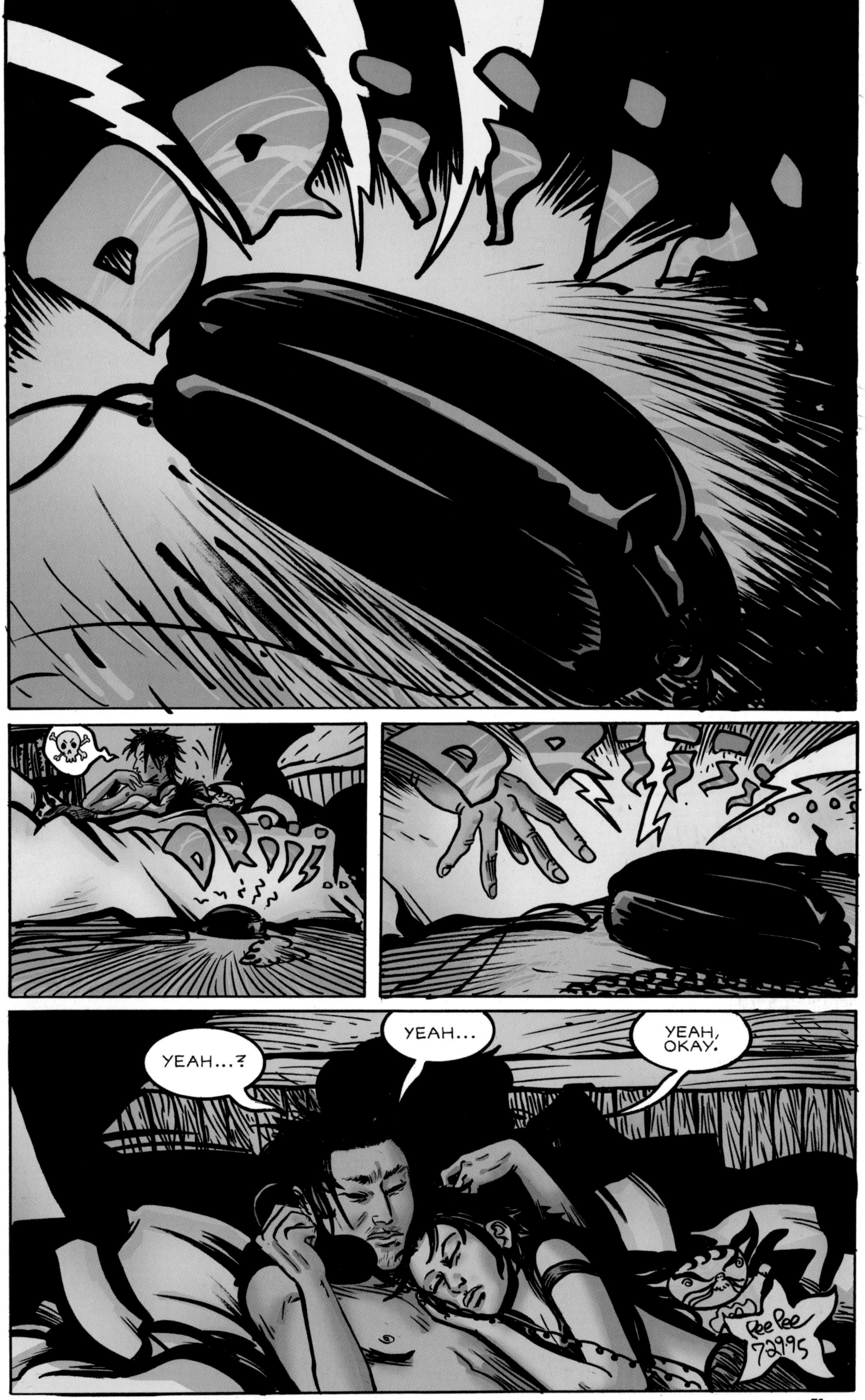
YEAH...?
YEAH...
YEAH, OKAY.
Pee Pee
7.29.95

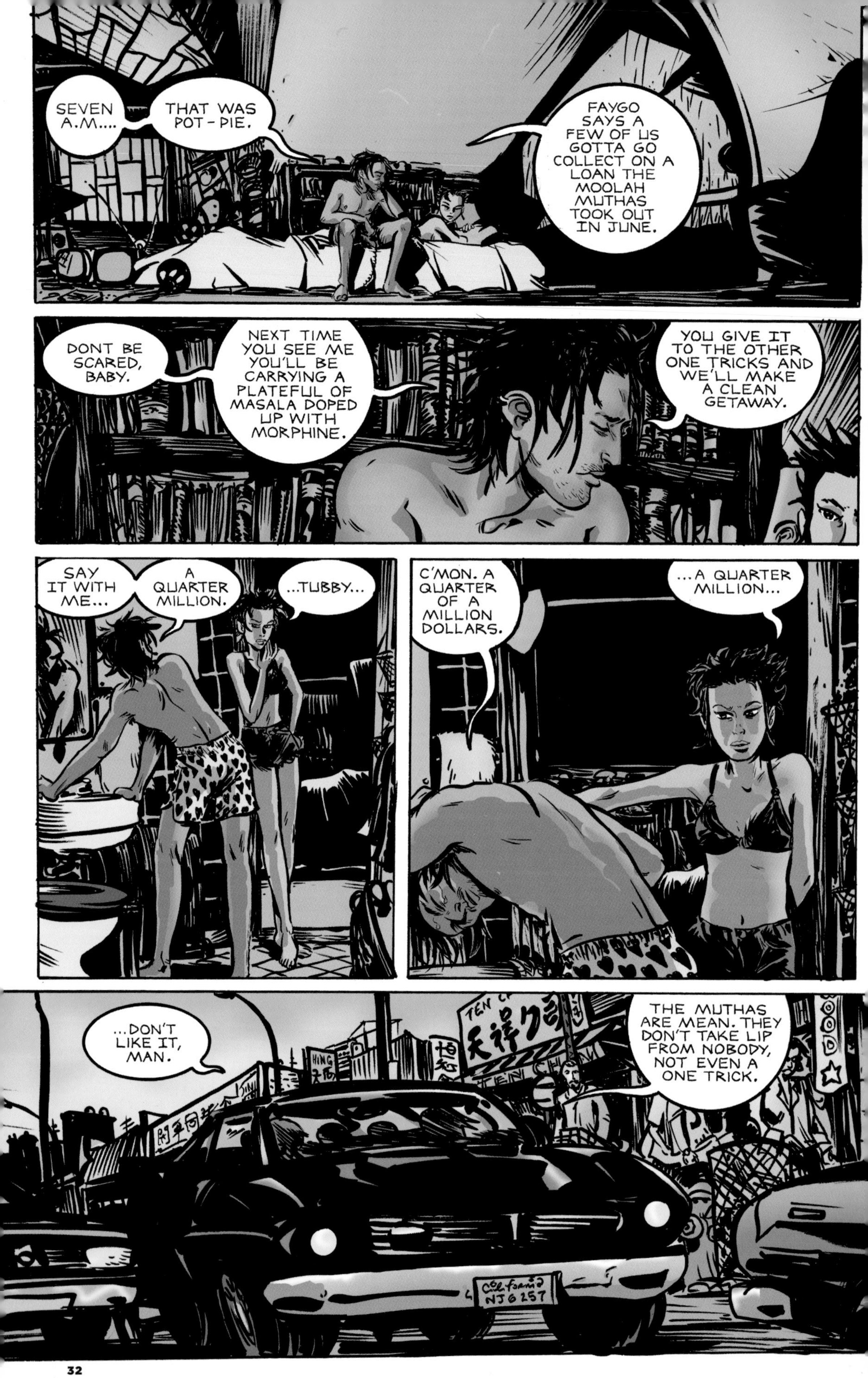
SEVEN A.M....
THAT WAS POT-PIE.
FAYGO SAYS A FEW OF US GOTTA GO COLLECT ON A LOAN THE MOOLAH MUTHAS TOOK OUT IN JUNE.
DONT BE SCARED, BABY.
NEXT TIME YOU SEE ME YOU'LL BE CARRYING A PLATEFUL OF MASALA DOPED UP WITH MORPHINE.
YOU GIVE IT TO THE OTHER ONE TRICKS AND WE'LL MAKE A CLEAN GETAWAY.
SAY IT WITH ME...
A QUARTER MILLION.
...TUBBY...
C'MON. A QUARTER OF A MILLION DOLLARS.
...A QUARTER MILLION...
...DON'T LIKE IT, MAN.
THE MUTHAS ARE MEAN. THEY DON'T TAKE LIP FROM NOBODY, NOT EVEN A ONE TRICK.
NJ6257

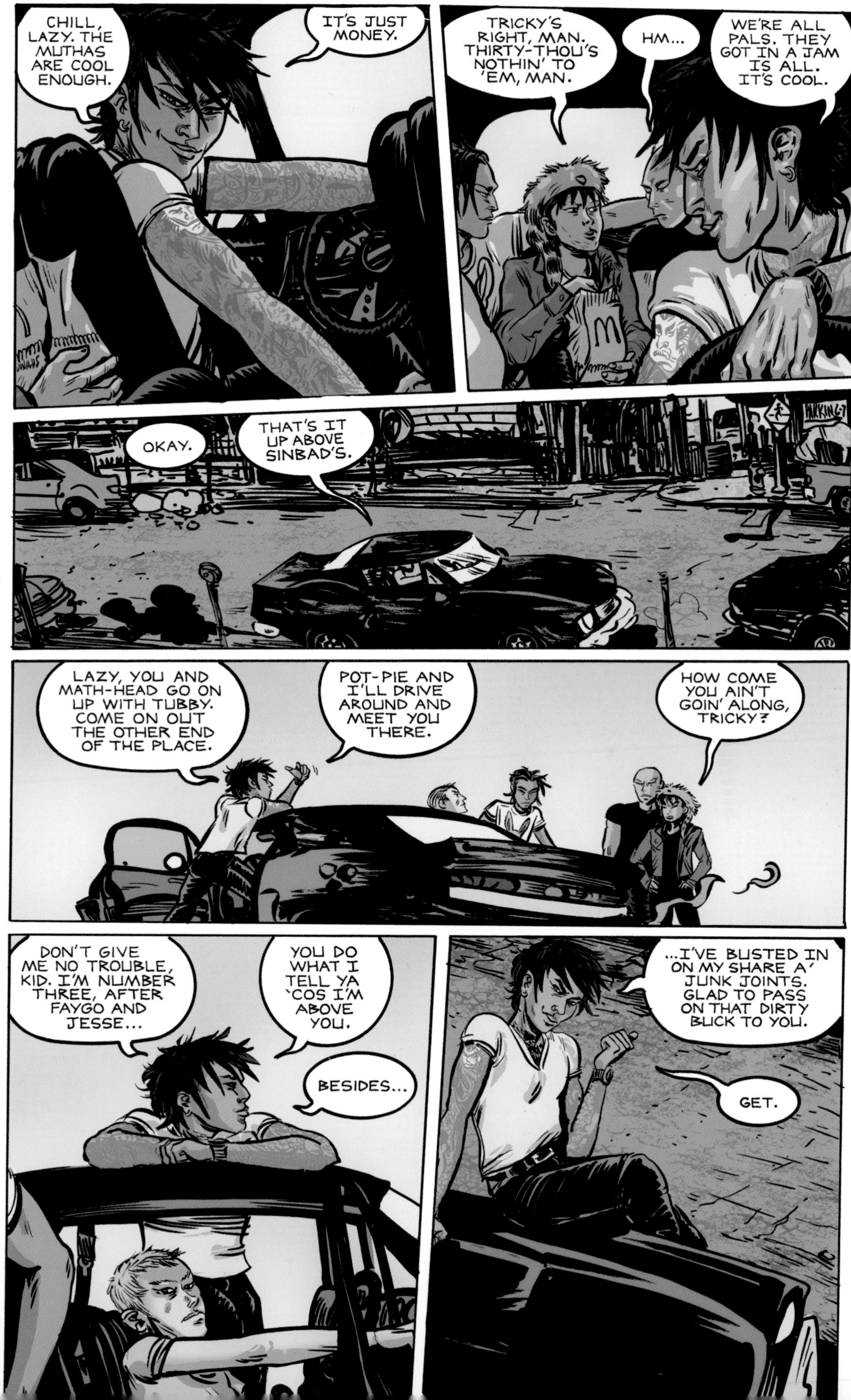
CHILL, LAZY. THE MUTHAS ARE COOL ENOUGH.
IT'S JUST MONEY.
TRICKY'S RIGHT, MAN. THIRTY-THOU'S NOTHIN' TO 'EM, MAN.
HM...
WE'RE ALL PALS. THEY GOT IN A JAM IS ALL. IT'S COOL.
OKAY.
THAT'S IT UP ABOVE SINBAD'S.
LAZY, YOU AND MATH-HEAD GO ON UP WITH TUBBY. COME ON OUT THE OTHER END OF THE PLACE.
POT-PIE AND I'LL DRIVE AROUND AND MEET YOU THERE.
HOW COME YOU AIN'T GOIN' ALONG, TRICKY?
DON'T GIVE ME NO TROUBLE, KID. I'M NUMBER THREE, AFTER FAYGO AND JESSE...
YOU DO WHAT I TELL YA 'COS I'M ABOVE YOU.
BESIDES...
...I'VE BUSTED IN ON MY SHARE A' JUNK JOINTS. GLAD TO PASS ON THAT DIRTY BUCK TO YOU.
GET.

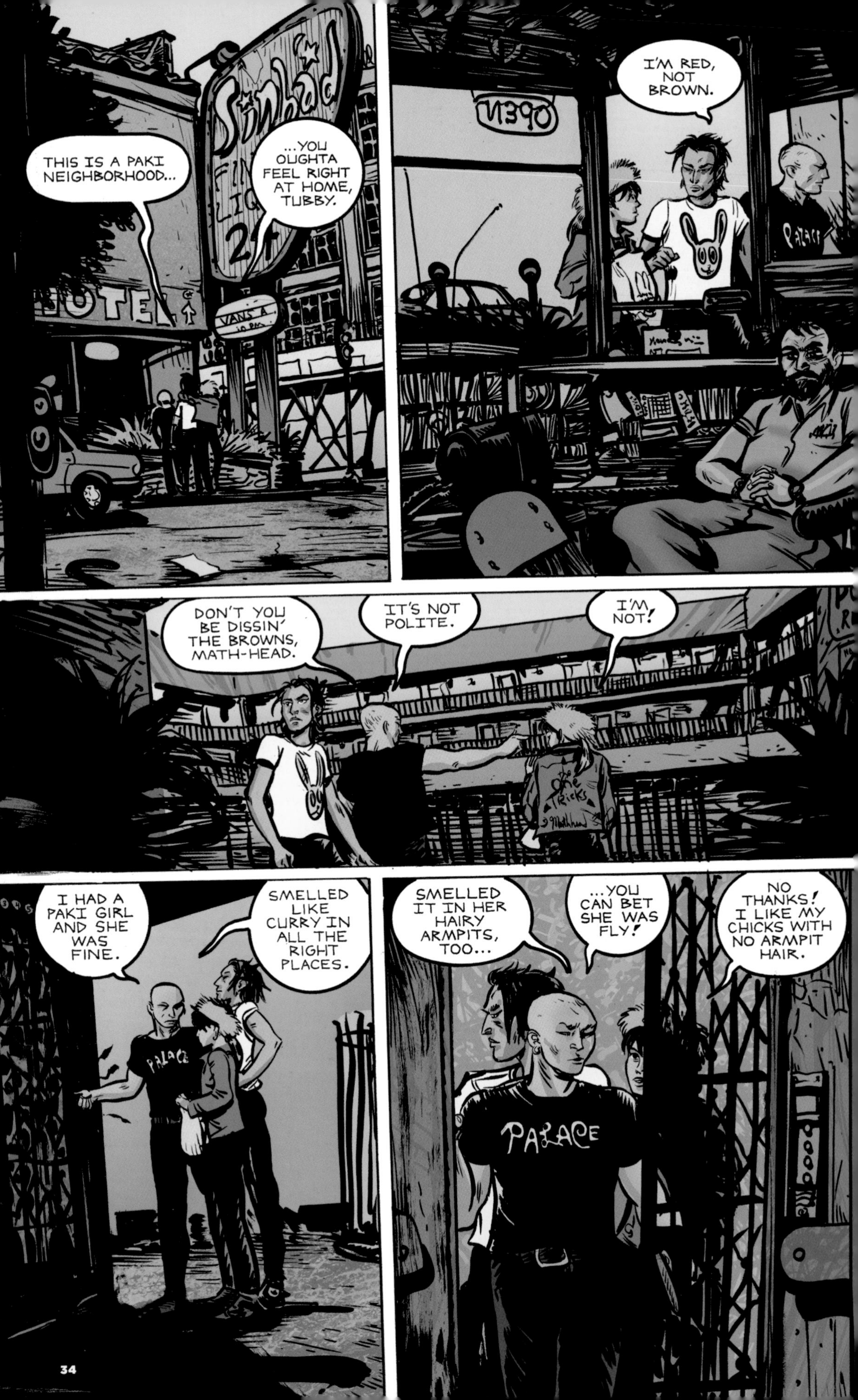
THIS IS A PAKI NEIGHBORHOOD...
...YOU OUGHTA FEEL RIGHT AT HOME, TUBBY.
I'M RED, NOT BROWN.
DON'T YOU BE DISSIN' THE BROWNS, MATH-HEAD.
IT'S NOT POLITE.
I'M NOT!
I HAD A PAKI GIRL AND SHE WAS FINE.
SMELLED LIKE CURRY IN ALL THE RIGHT PLACES.
SMELLED IT IN HER HAIRY ARMPITS, TOO...
...YOU CAN BET SHE WAS FLY!
NO THANKS! I LIKE MY CHICKS WITH NO ARMPIT HAIR.

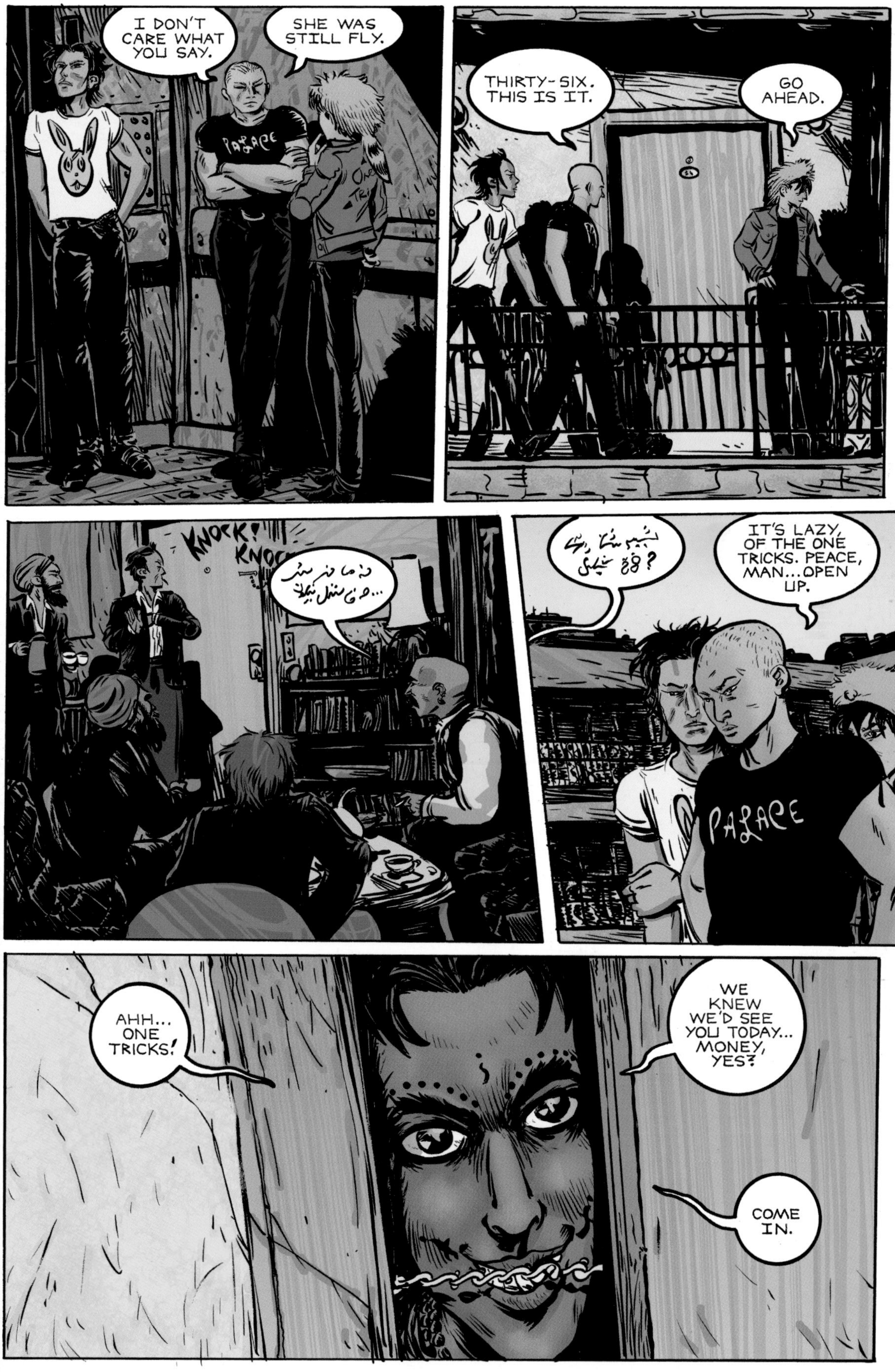
I DON'T CARE WHAT YOU SAY.
SHE WAS STILL FLY.
PALACE
THIRTY-SIX. THIS IS IT.
GO AHEAD.
KNOCK! KNOCK
IT'S LAZY, OF THE ONE TRICKS. PEACE, MAN... OPEN UP.
PALACE
AHH... ONE TRICKS!
WE KNEW WE'D SEE YOU TODAY... MONEY, YES?
COME IN.

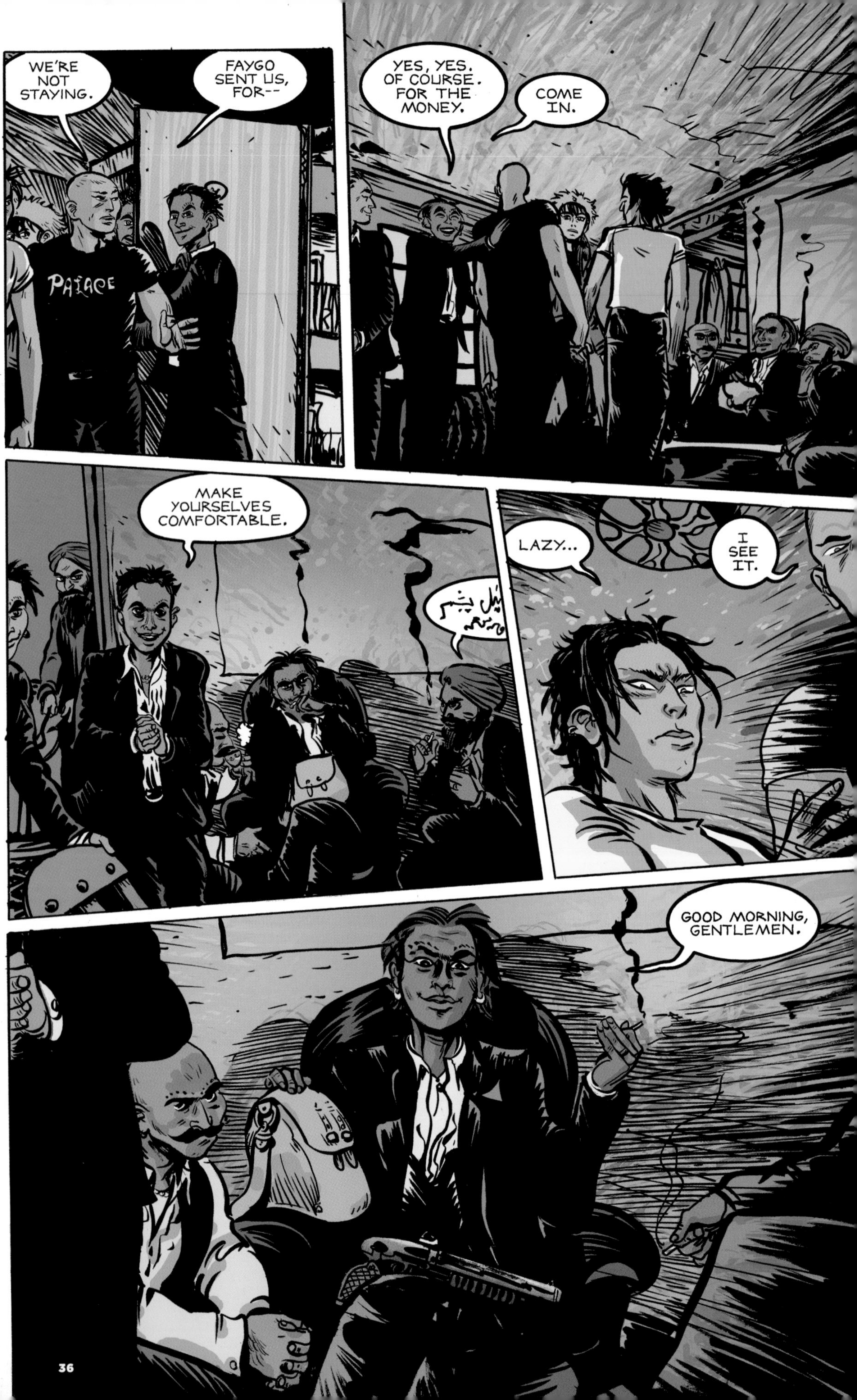
WE'RE NOT STAYING.
FAYGO SENT US, FOR--
YES, YES. OF COURSE. FOR THE MONEY.
COME IN.
MAKE YOURSELVES COMFORTABLE.
LAZY...
I SEE IT.
GOOD MORNING, GENTLEMEN.

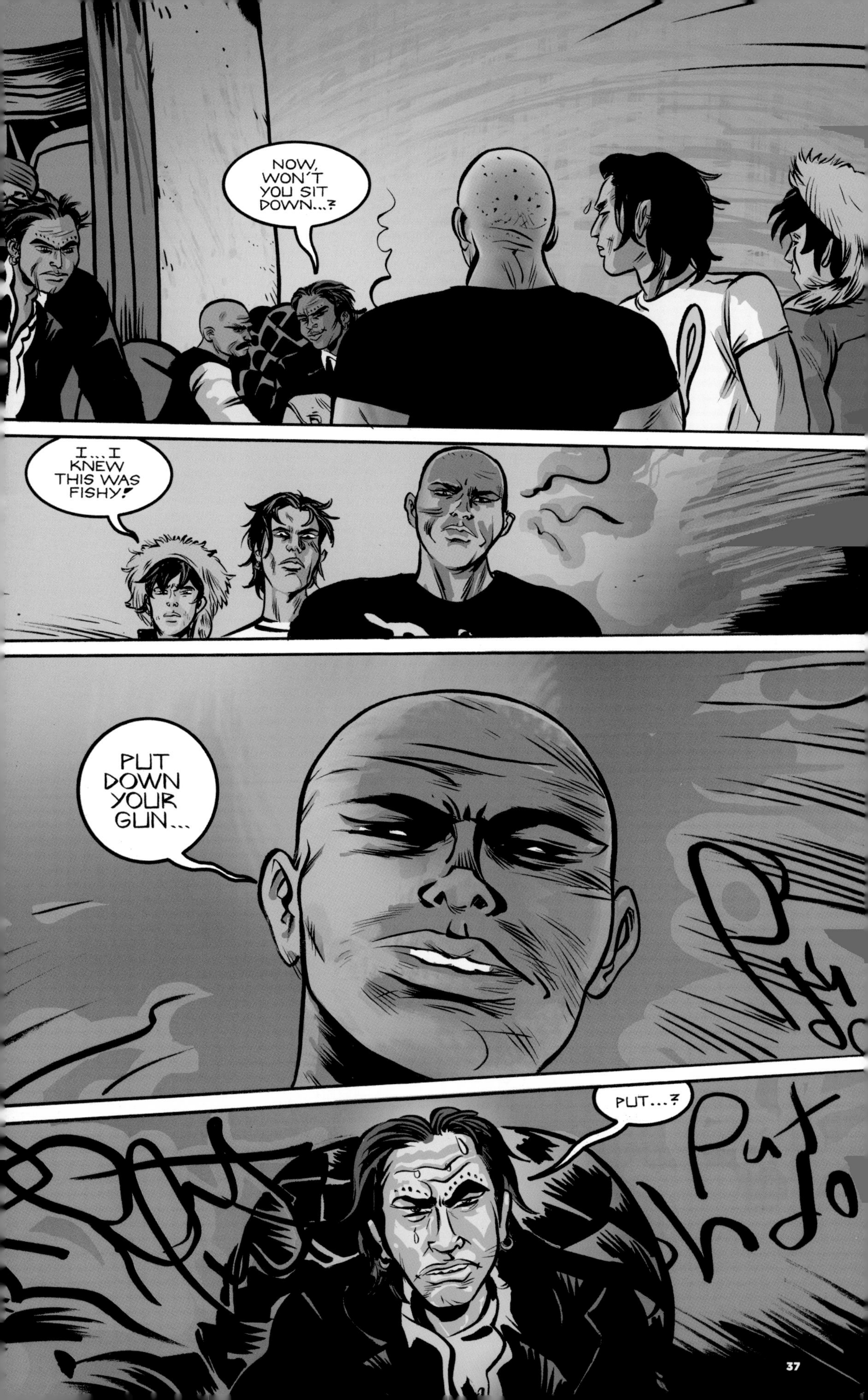
NOW, WON'T YOU SIT DOWN...?
I... I KNEW THIS WAS FISHY!
PUT DOWN YOUR GUN...
PUT...?

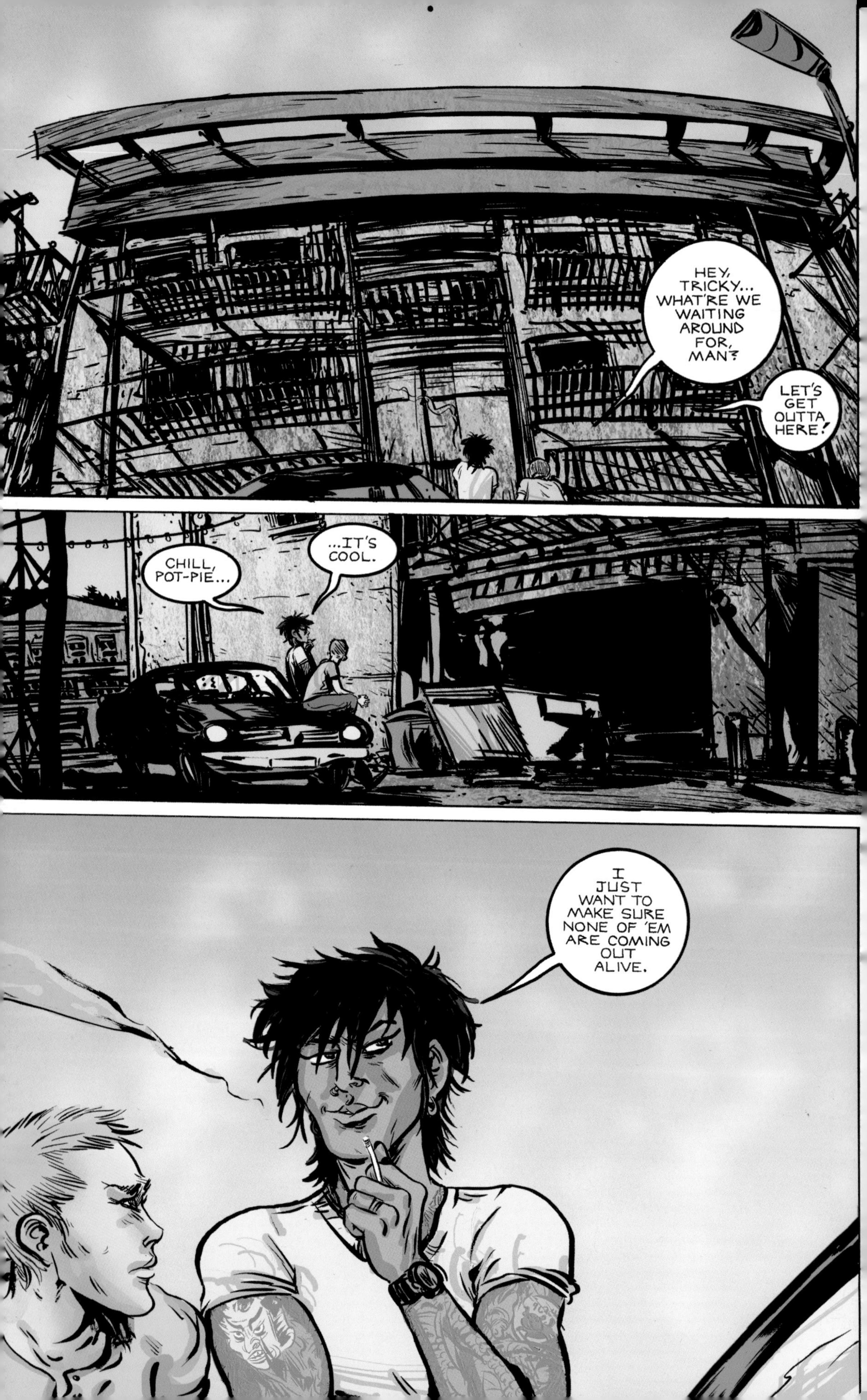
HEY, TRICKY... WHAT'RE WE WAITING AROUND FOR, MAN?
LET'S GET OUTTA HERE!
CHILL, POT-PIE...
...IT'S COOL.
I JUST WANT TO MAKE SURE NONE OF 'EM ARE COMING OUT ALIVE.

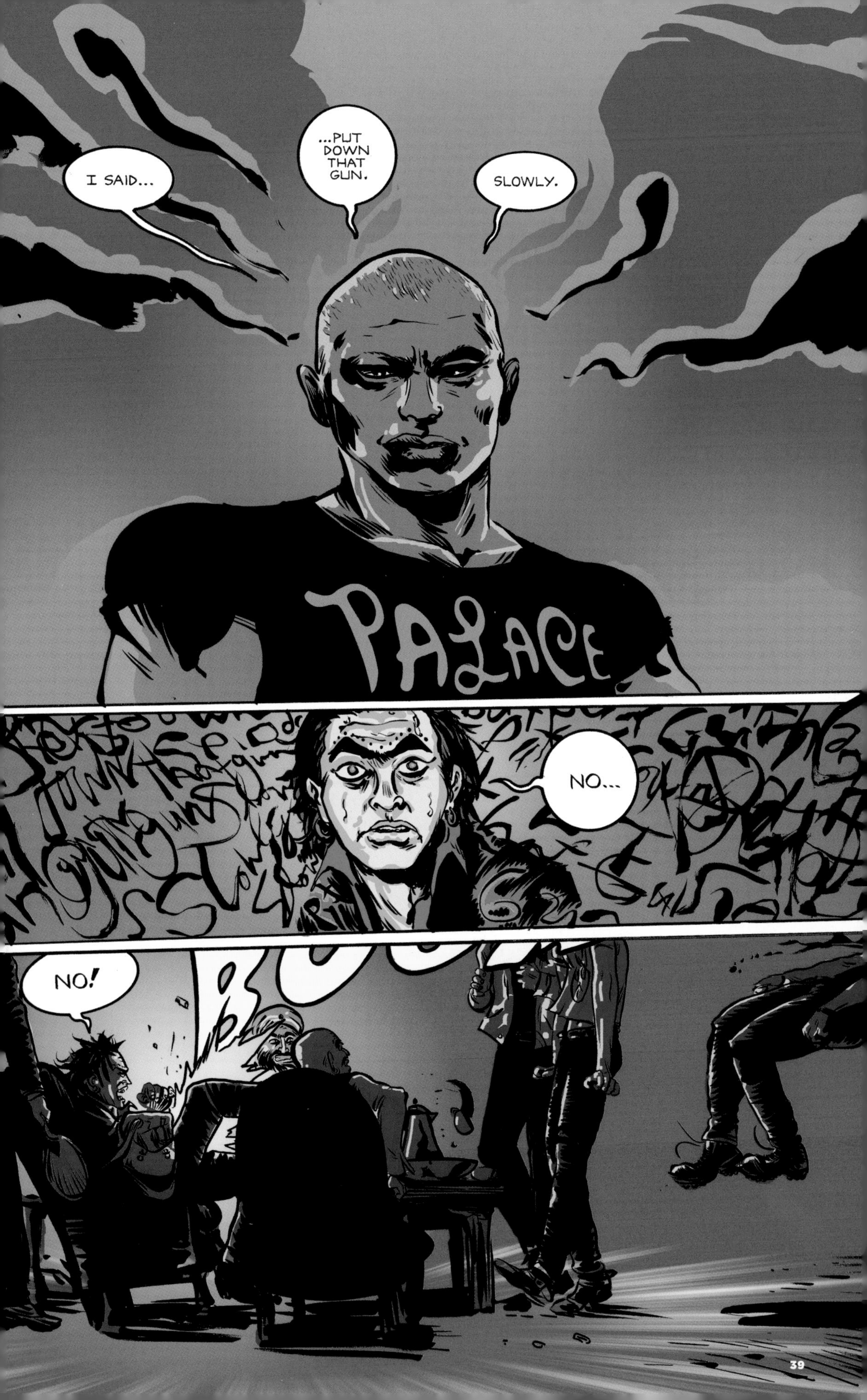
I SAID...
...PUT DOWN THAT GUN.
SLOWLY.
PALACE
NO...
NO!

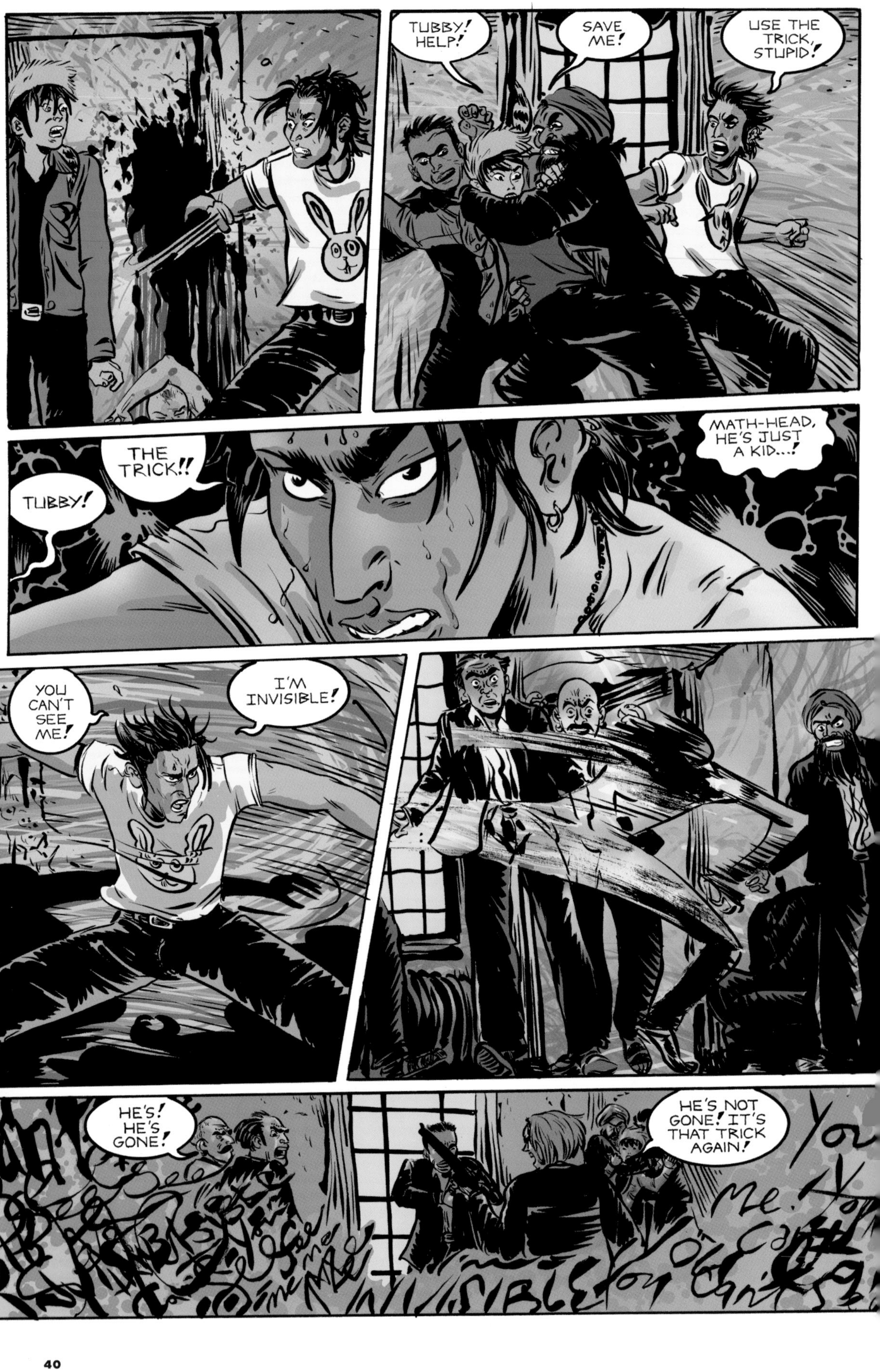
TUBBY! HELP!
SAVE ME!
USE THE TRICK, STUPID!
THE TRICK!!
TUBBY!
MATH-HEAD, HE'S JUST A KID...!
YOU CAN'T SEE ME!
I'M INVISIBLE!
HE'S! HE'S GONE!
HE'S NOT GONE! IT'S THAT TRICK AGAIN!

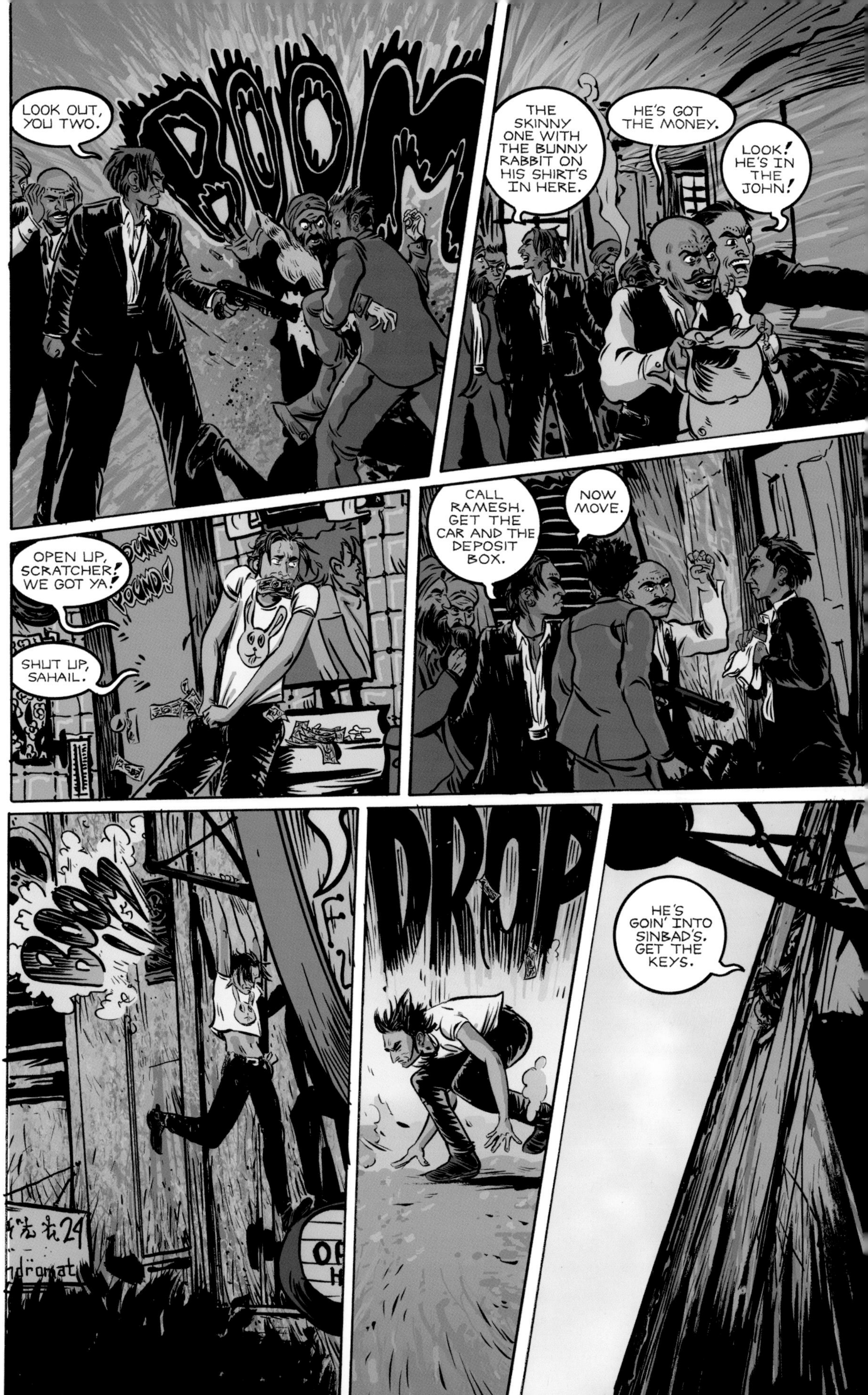
LOOK OUT, YOU TWO.
BOOM
THE SKINNY ONE WITH THE BUNNY RABBIT ON HIS SHIRT'S IN HERE.
HE'S GOT THE MONEY.
LOOK! HE'S IN THE JOHN!
OPEN UP, SCRATCHER! WE GOT YA!
POUND! POUND!
SHUT UP, SAHAIL.
CALL RAMESH. GET THE CAR AND THE DEPOSIT BOX.
NOW MOVE.
BOOM
DROP
HE'S GOIN' INTO SINBAD'S. GET THE KEYS.

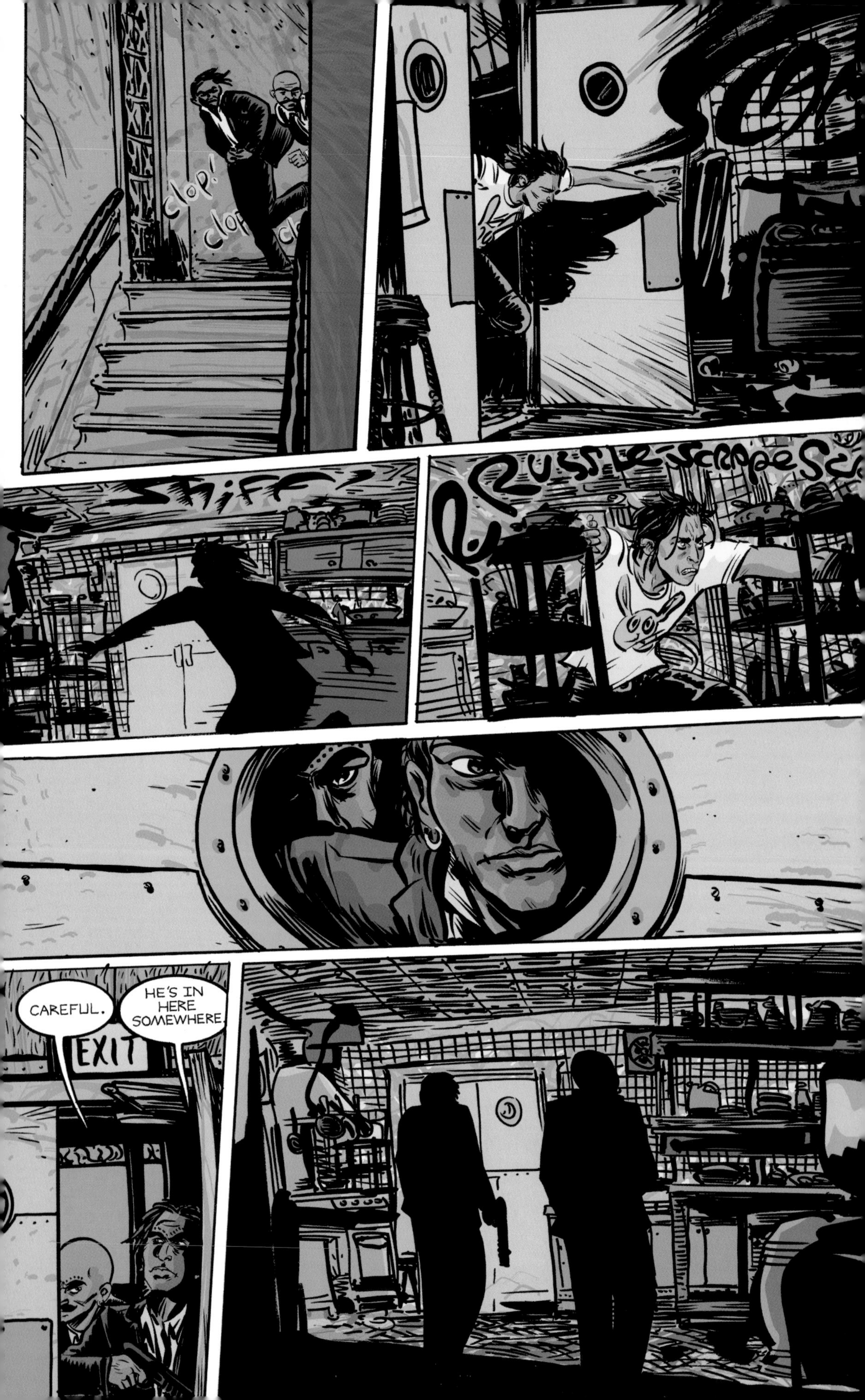
clop!
clop
CAREFUL.
HE'S IN HERE SOMEWHERE.
EXIT

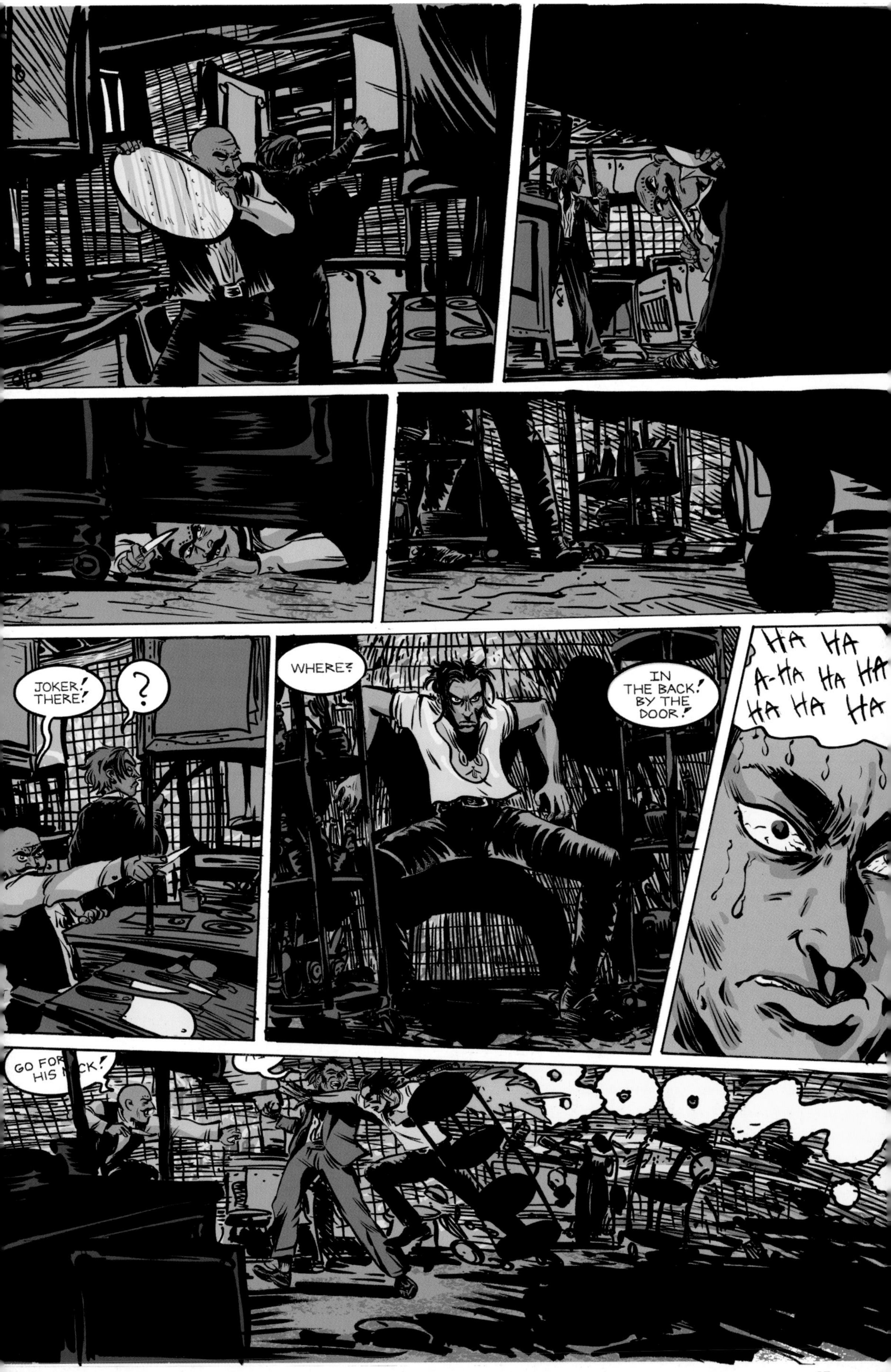
JOKER! THERE!
?
WHERE?
IN THE BACK! BY THE DOOR!
HA HA A-HA HA HA HA HA HA
GO FOR HIS

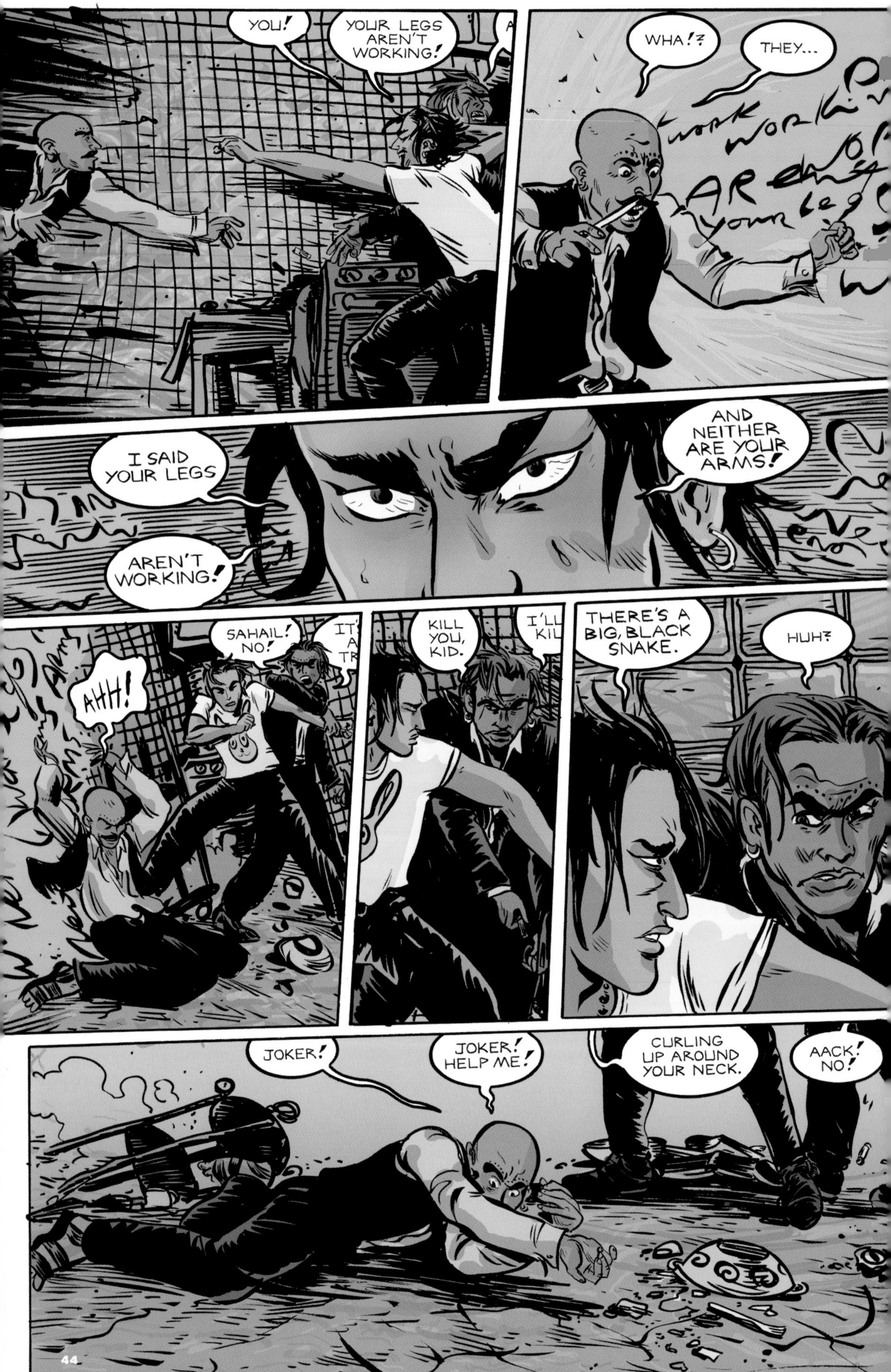
YOU!
YOUR LEGS AREN'T WORKING!
WHA!?
THEY...
I SAID YOUR LEGS
AREN'T WORKING!
AND NEITHER ARE YOUR ARMS!
AHH!
SAHAIL! NO!
KILL YOU, KID.
THERE'S A BIG, BLACK SNAKE.
HUH?
JOKER!
JOKER! HELP ME!
CURLING UP AROUND YOUR NECK.
AACK! NO!

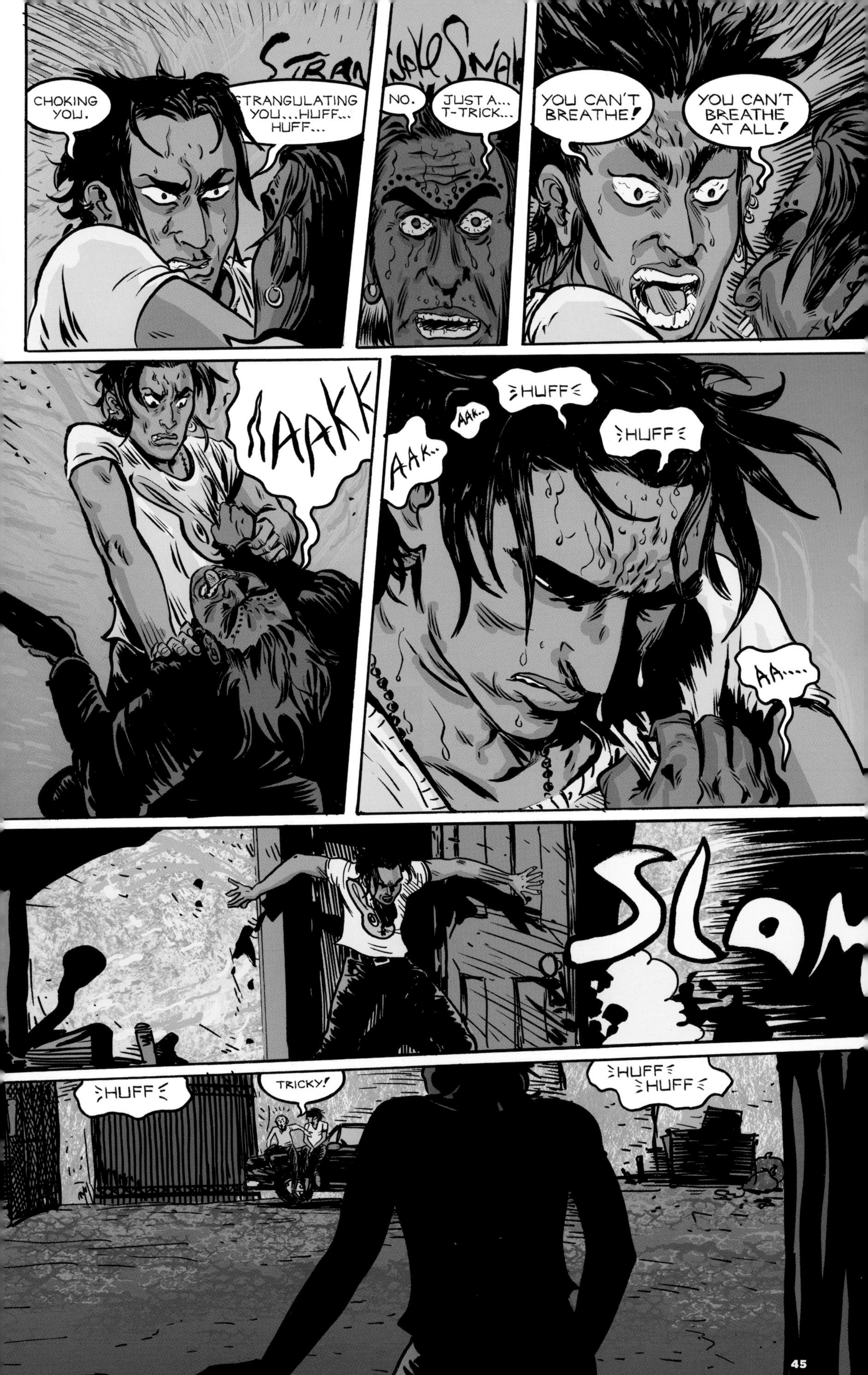
STRAN
CHOKING YOU.
STRANGULATING YOU...HUFF... HUFF...
NO.
JUST A... T-TRICK...
YOU CAN'T BREATHE!
YOU CAN'T BREATHE AT ALL!
AAKK
AAK..
AAK..
HUFF
HUFF
AA....
HUFF
TRICKY!
HUFF HUFF

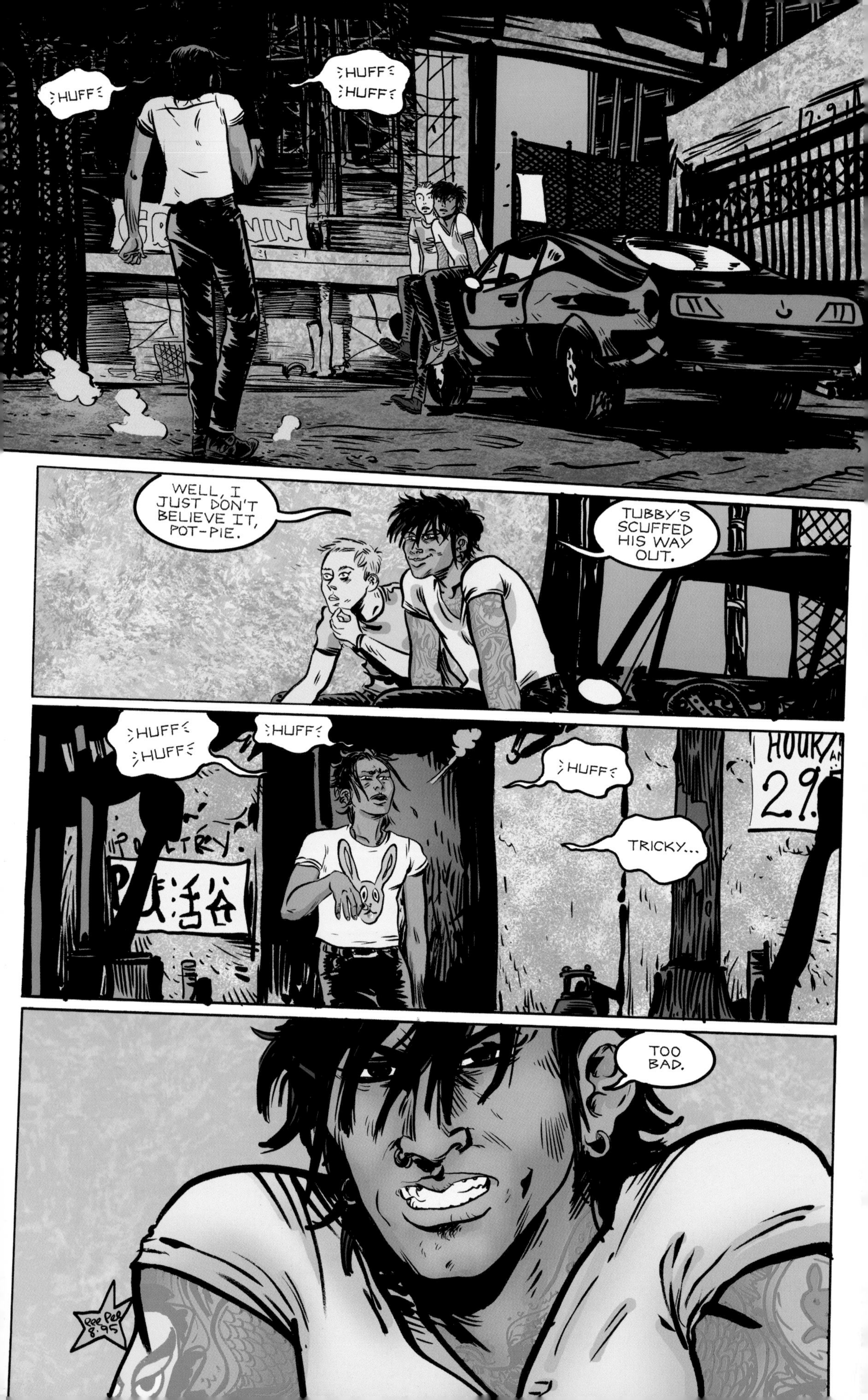
HUFF
HUFF
HUFF
WELL, I JUST DON'T BELIEVE IT, POT-PIE.
TUBBY'S SCUFFED HIS WAY OUT.
HUFF
HUFF
HUFF
HUFF
TRICKY...
TOO BAD.

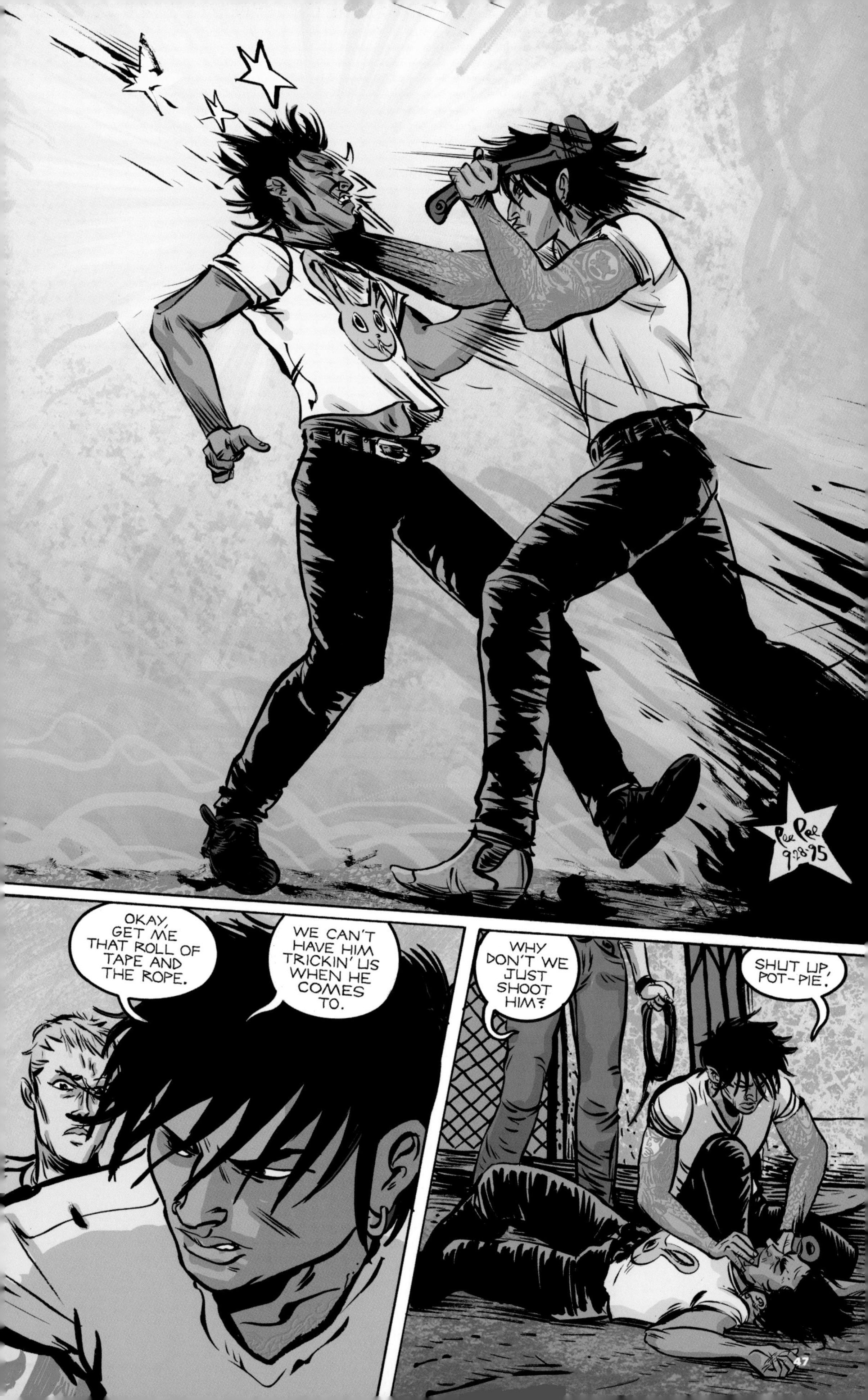
Pee Pee
9.28.95
OKAY, GET ME THAT ROLL OF TAPE AND THE ROPE.
WE CAN'T HAVE HIM TRICKIN' US WHEN HE COMES TO.
WHY DON'T WE JUST SHOOT HIM?
SHUT UP, POT-PIE.

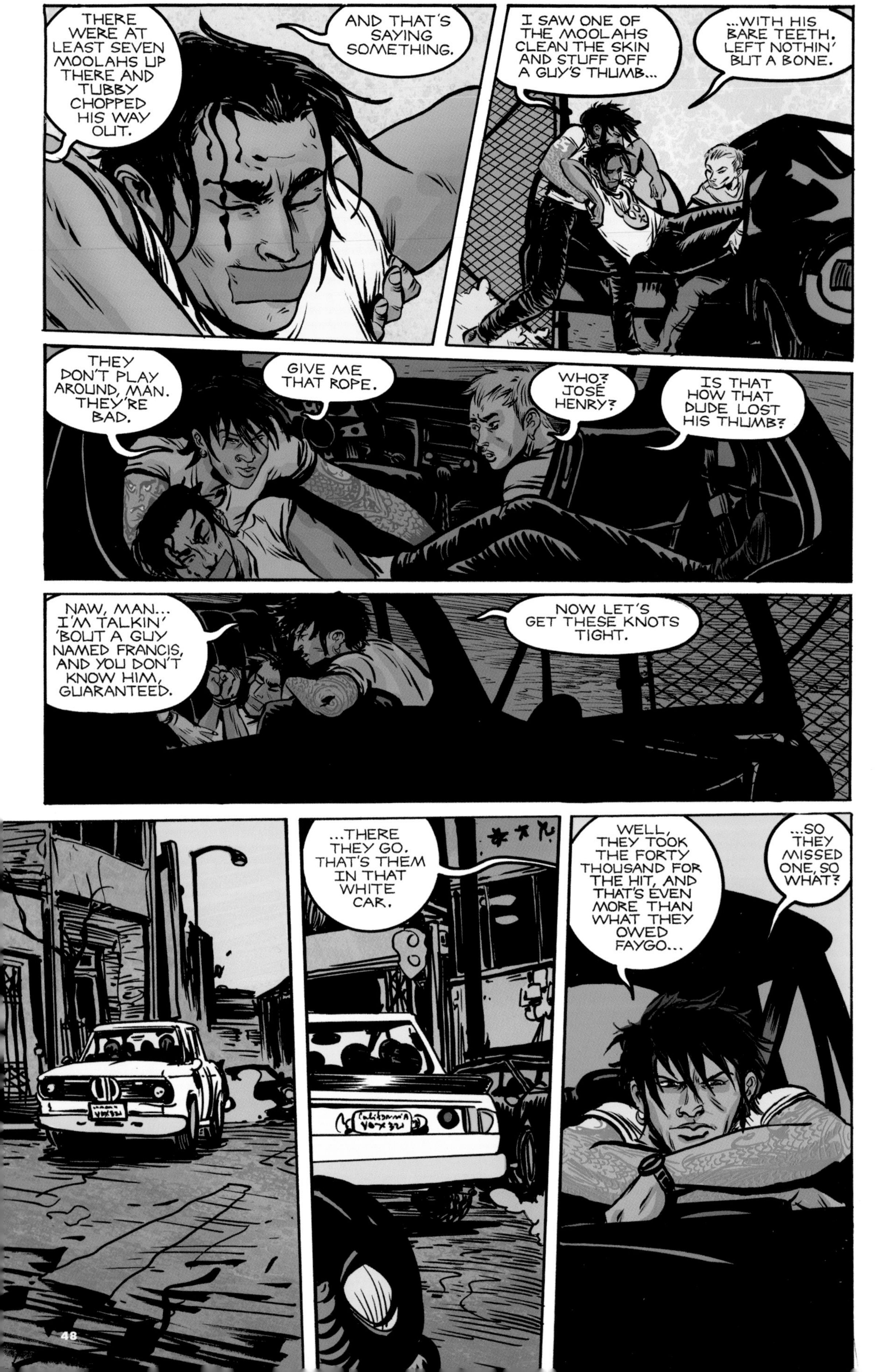
THERE WERE AT LEAST SEVEN MOOLAHS UP THERE AND TUBBY CHOPPED HIS WAY OUT.
AND THAT'S SAYING SOMETHING.
I SAW ONE OF THE MOOLAHS CLEAN THE SKIN AND STUFF OFF A GUY'S THUMB...
...WITH HIS BARE TEETH. LEFT NOTHIN' BUT A BONE.
THEY DON'T PLAY AROUND, MAN. THEY'RE BAD.
GIVE ME THAT ROPE.
WHO? JOSÉ HENRY?
IS THAT HOW THAT DUDE LOST HIS THUMB?
NAW, MAN... I'M TALKIN' 'BOUT A GUY NAMED FRANCIS, AND YOU DON'T KNOW HIM, GUARANTEED.
NOW LET'S GET THESE KNOTS TIGHT.
...THERE THEY GO. THAT'S THEM IN THAT WHITE CAR.
WELL, THEY TOOK THE FORTY THOUSAND FOR THE HIT, AND THAT'S EVEN MORE THAN WHAT THEY OWED FAYGO...
...SO THEY MISSED ONE, SO WHAT?

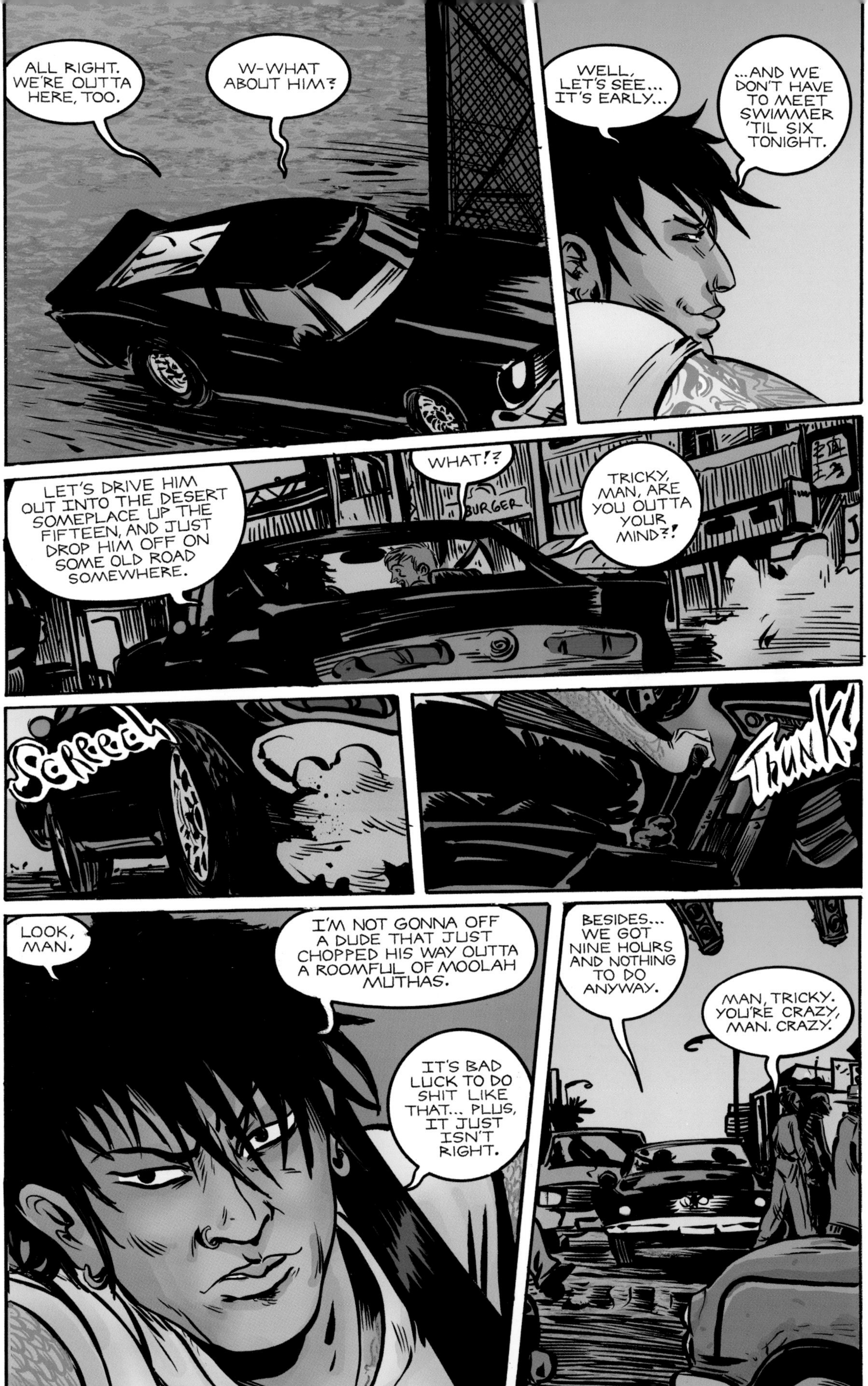
ALL RIGHT. WE'RE OUTTA HERE, TOO.
W-WHAT ABOUT HIM?
WELL, LET'S SEE... IT'S EARLY...
...AND WE DON'T HAVE TO MEET SWIMMER 'TIL SIX TONIGHT.
LET'S DRIVE HIM OUT INTO THE DESERT SOMEPLACE UP THE FIFTEEN, AND JUST DROP HIM OFF ON SOME OLD ROAD SOMEWHERE.
WHAT!?
BURGER
TRICKY, MAN, ARE YOU OUTTA YOUR MIND?!
SCREECH
THUNK!
LOOK, MAN.
I'M NOT GONNA OFF A DUDE THAT JUST CHOPPED HIS WAY OUTTA A ROOMFUL OF MOOLAH MUTHAS.
IT'S BAD LUCK TO DO SHIT LIKE THAT... PLUS, IT JUST ISN'T RIGHT.
BESIDES... WE GOT NINE HOURS AND NOTHING TO DO ANYWAY.
MAN, TRICKY. YOU'RE CRAZY, MAN. CRAZY.

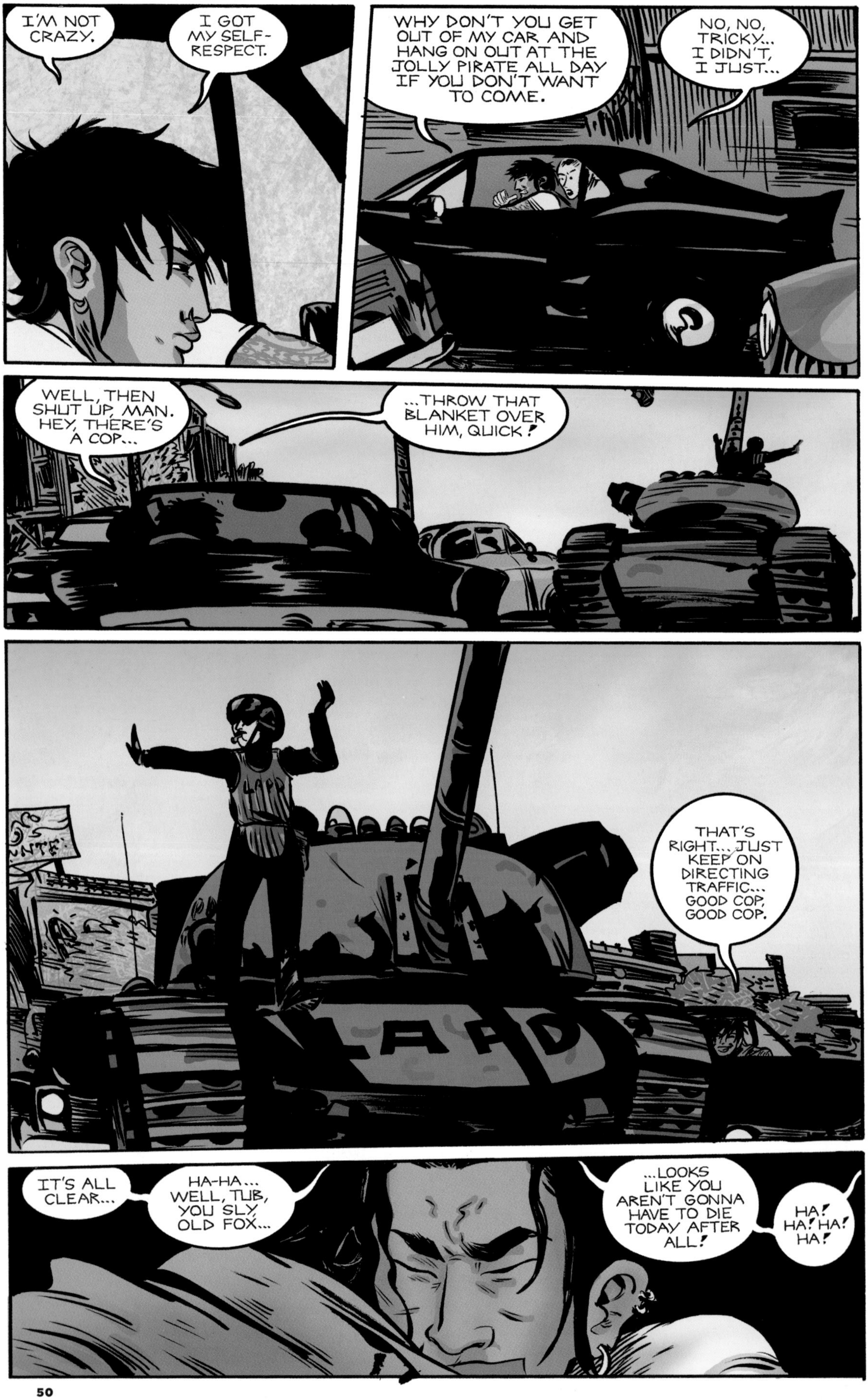
I'M NOT CRAZY.
I GOT MY SELF-RESPECT.
WHY DON'T YOU GET OUT OF MY CAR AND HANG ON OUT AT THE JOLLY PIRATE ALL DAY IF YOU DON'T WANT TO COME.
NO, NO, TRICKY... I DIDN'T, I JUST...
WELL, THEN SHUT UP, MAN. HEY, THERE'S A COP...
...THROW THAT BLANKET OVER HIM, QUICK!
THAT'S RIGHT... JUST KEEP ON DIRECTING TRAFFIC... GOOD COP, GOOD COP.
LAPD
IT'S ALL CLEAR...
HA-HA... WELL, TUB, YOU SLY, OLD FOX...
...LOOKS LIKE YOU AREN'T GONNA HAVE TO DIE TODAY AFTER ALL!
HA! HA! HA! HA!

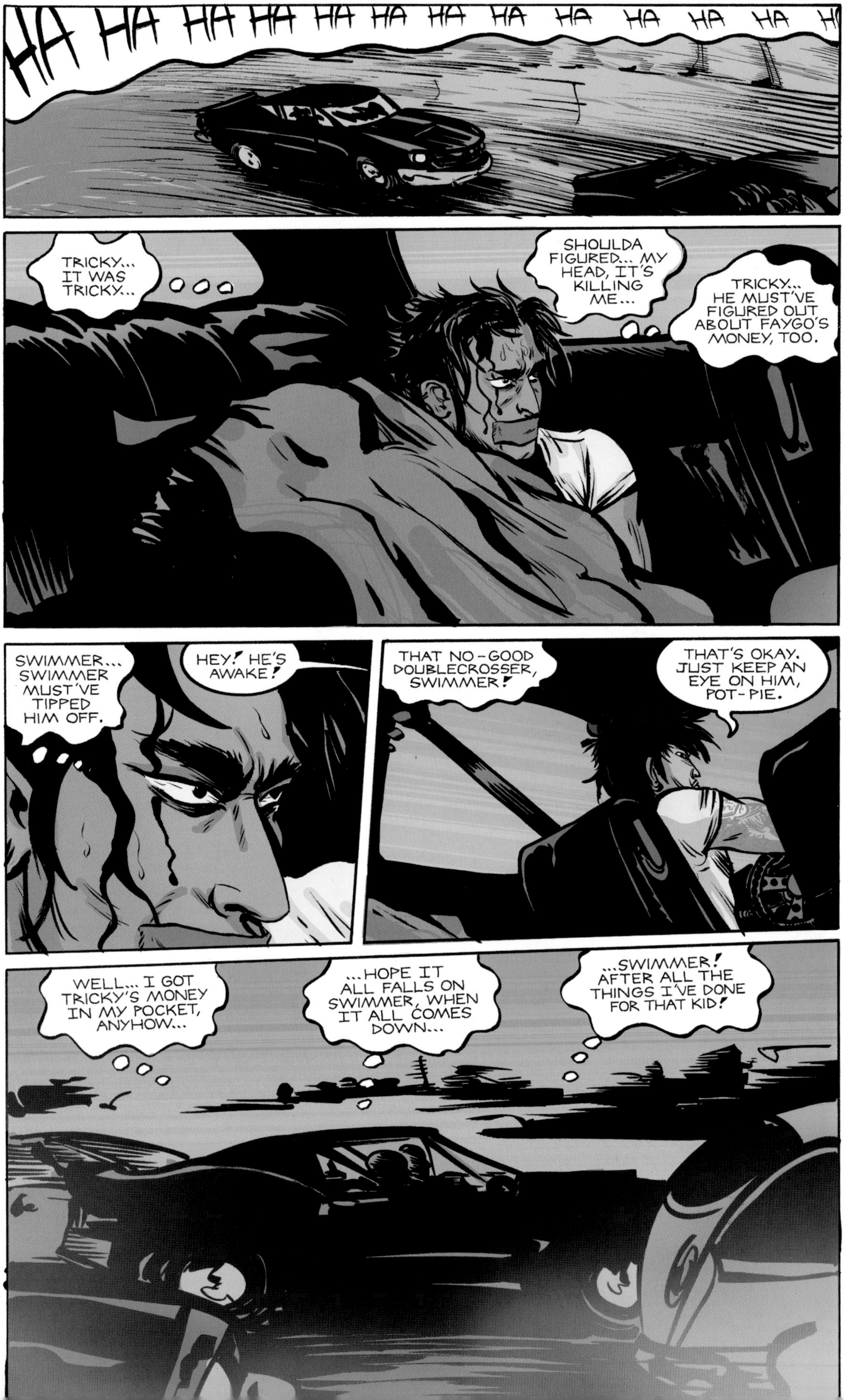
HA HA HA HA HA HA HA HA HA HA HA HA
TRICKY... IT WAS TRICKY...
SHOULDA FIGURED... MY HEAD, IT'S KILLING ME...
TRICKY... HE MUST'VE FIGURED OUT ABOUT FAYGO'S MONEY, TOO.
SWIMMER... SWIMMER MUST'VE TIPPED HIM OFF.
HEY! HE'S AWAKE!
THAT NO-GOOD DOUBLECROSSER, SWIMMER!
THAT'S OKAY. JUST KEEP AN EYE ON HIM, POT-PIE.
WELL... I GOT TRICKY'S MONEY IN MY POCKET, ANYHOW...
...HOPE IT ALL FALLS ON SWIMMER, WHEN IT ALL COMES DOWN...
...SWIMMER! AFTER ALL THE THINGS I'VE DONE FOR THAT KID!

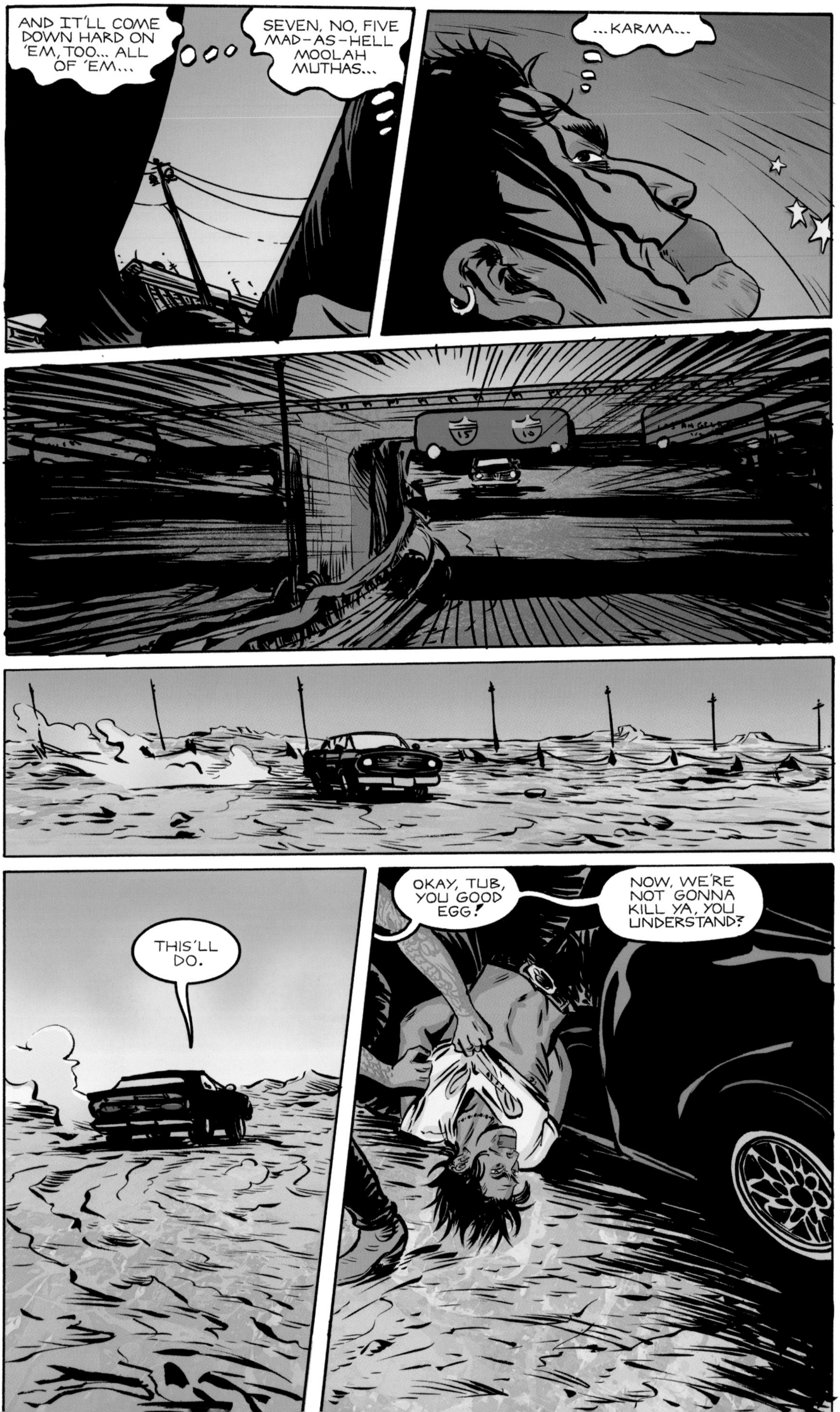
AND IT'LL COME DOWN HARD ON 'EM, TOO... ALL OF 'EM...
SEVEN, NO, FIVE MAD-AS-HELL MOOLAH MUTHAS...
...KARMA...
THIS'LL DO.
OKAY, TUB, YOU GOOD EGG!
NOW, WE'RE NOT GONNA KILL YA, YOU UNDERSTAND?

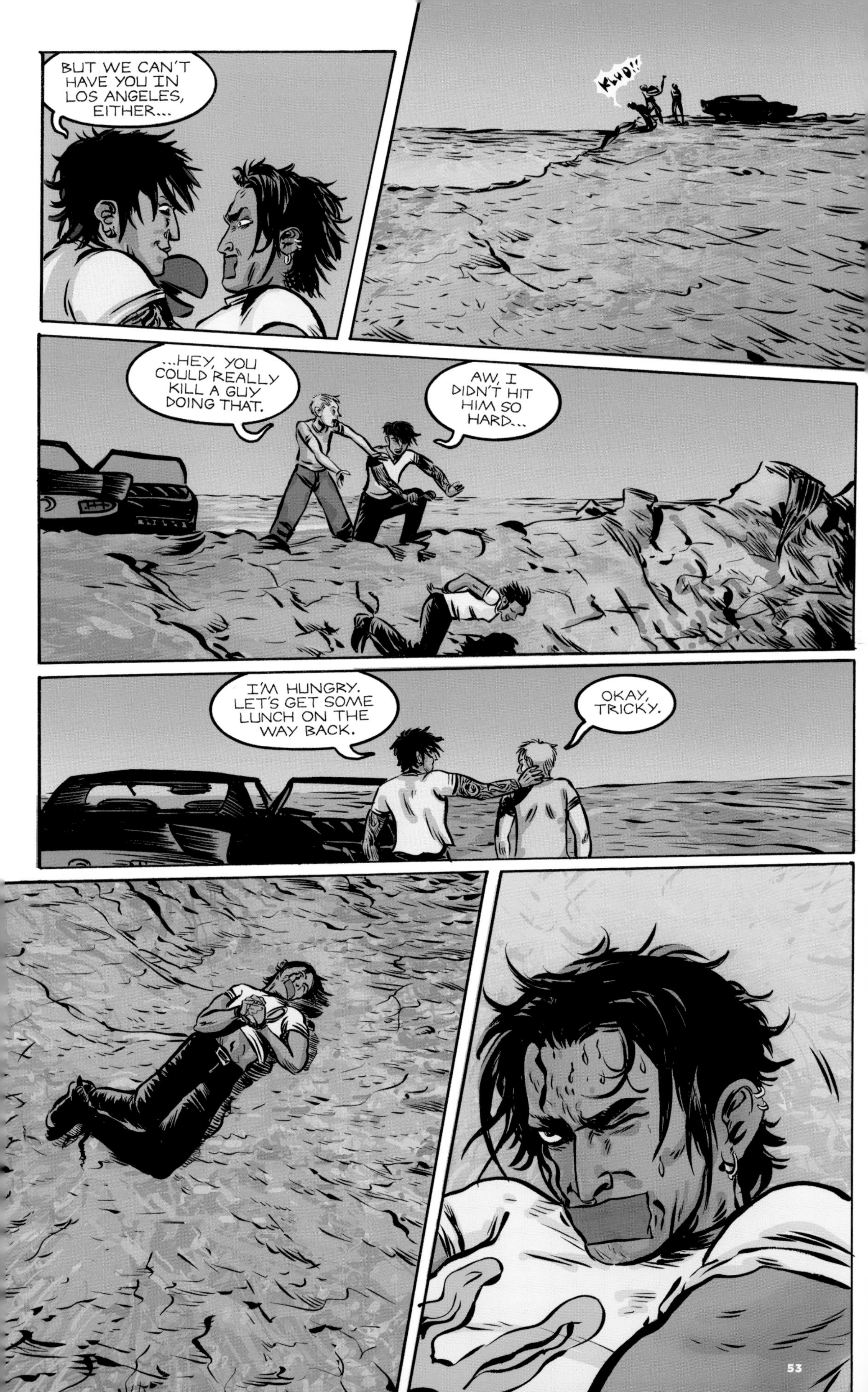
BUT WE CAN'T HAVE YOU IN LOS ANGELES, EITHER...
KLUD!!
...HEY, YOU COULD REALLY KILL A GUY DOING THAT.
AW, I DIDN'T HIT HIM SO HARD...
I'M HUNGRY. LET'S GET SOME LUNCH ON THE WAY BACK.
OKAY, TRICKY.

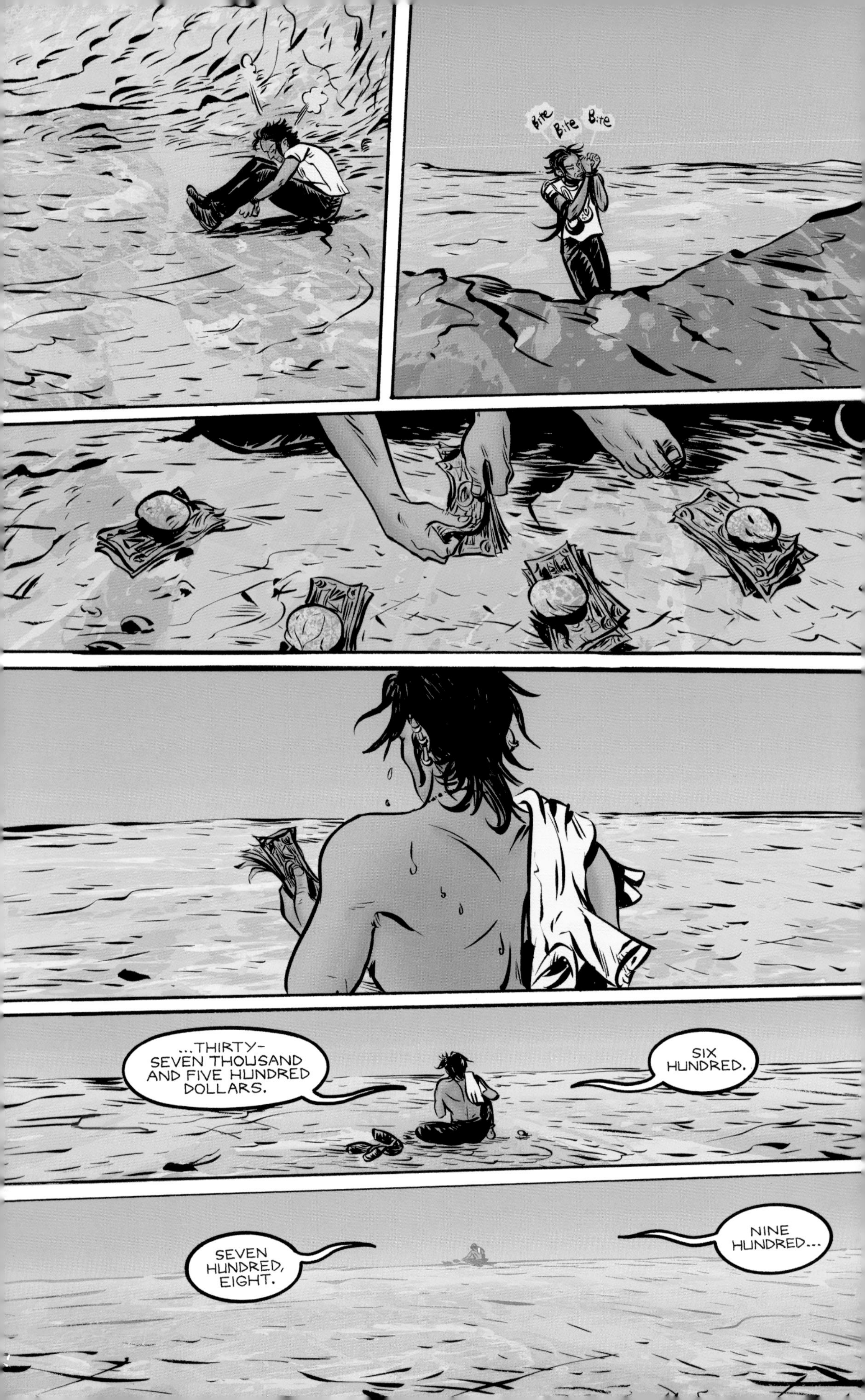
Bite
Bite
Bite
...THIRTY-SEVEN THOUSAND AND FIVE HUNDRED DOLLARS.
SIX HUNDRED.
SEVEN HUNDRED, EIGHT.
NINE HUNDRED...

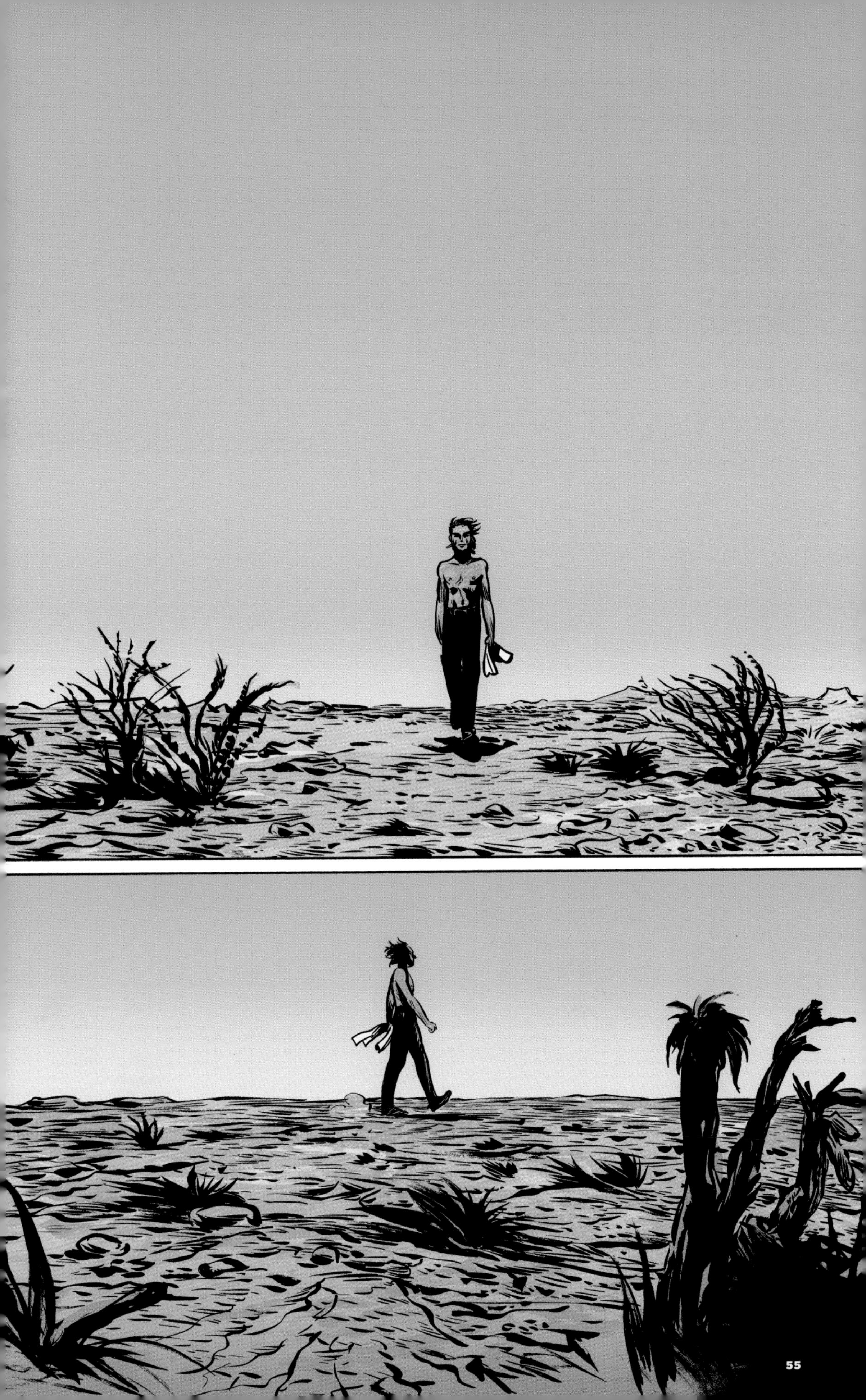

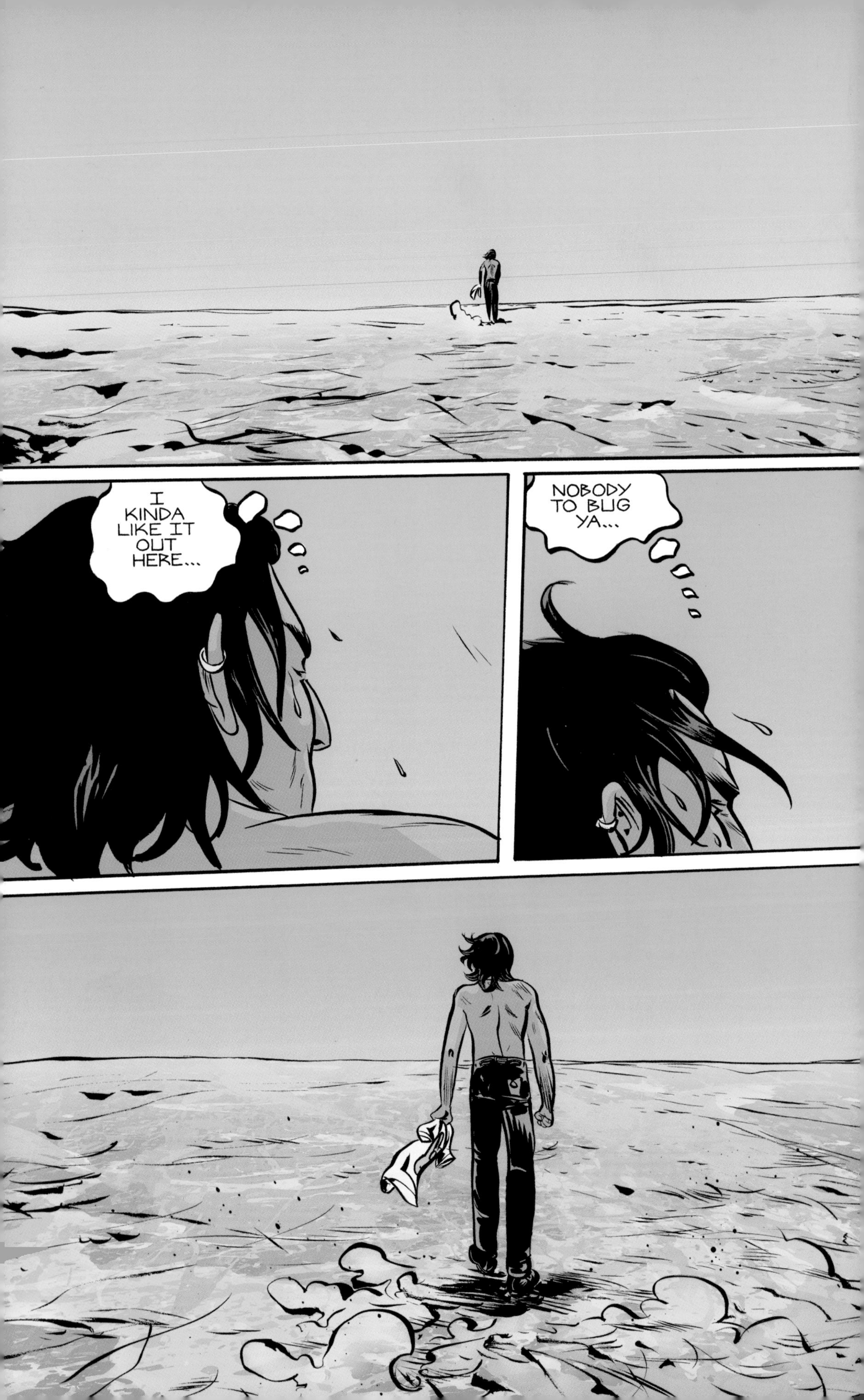
I KINDA LIKE IT OUT HERE...
NOBODY TO BUG YA...

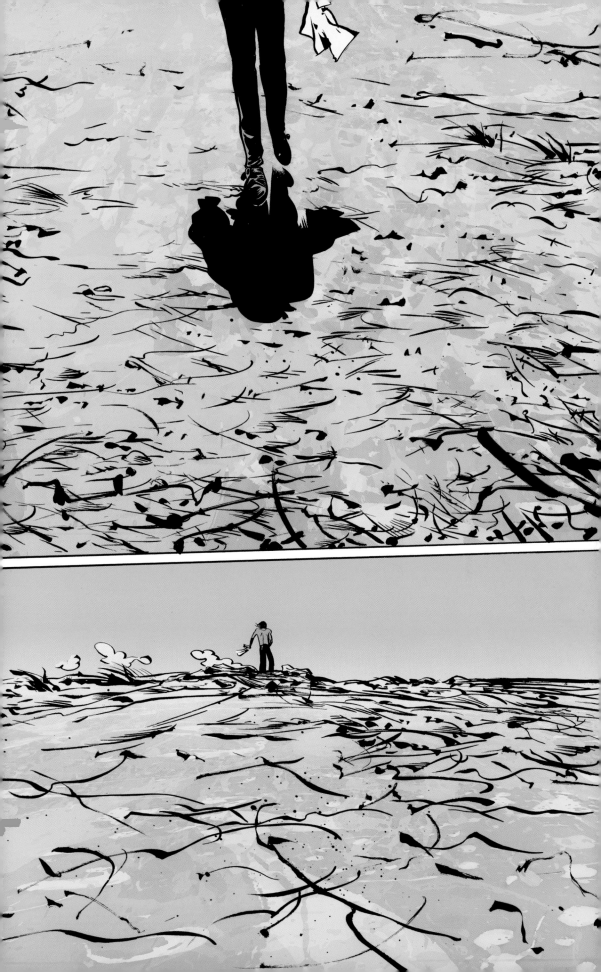

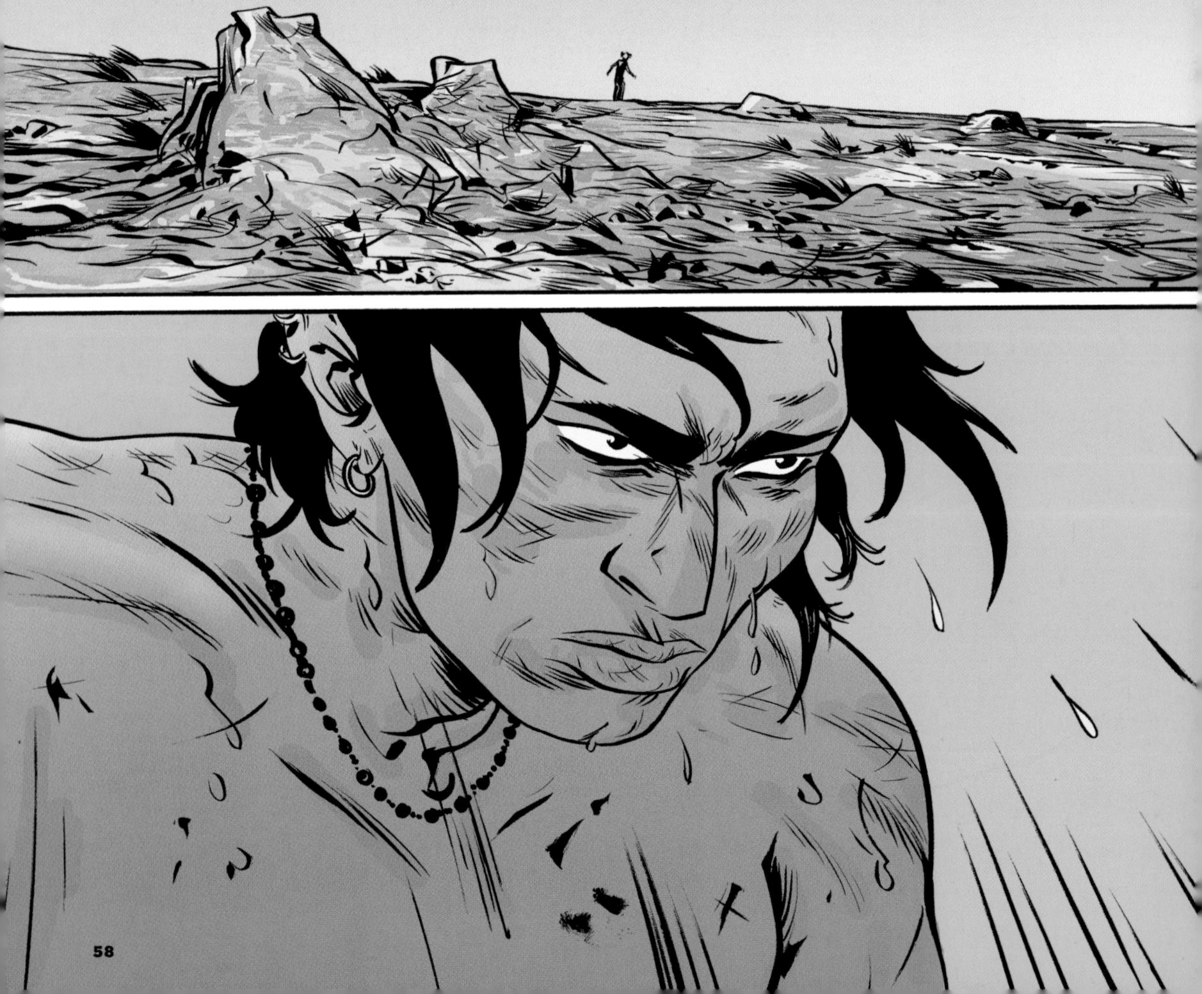

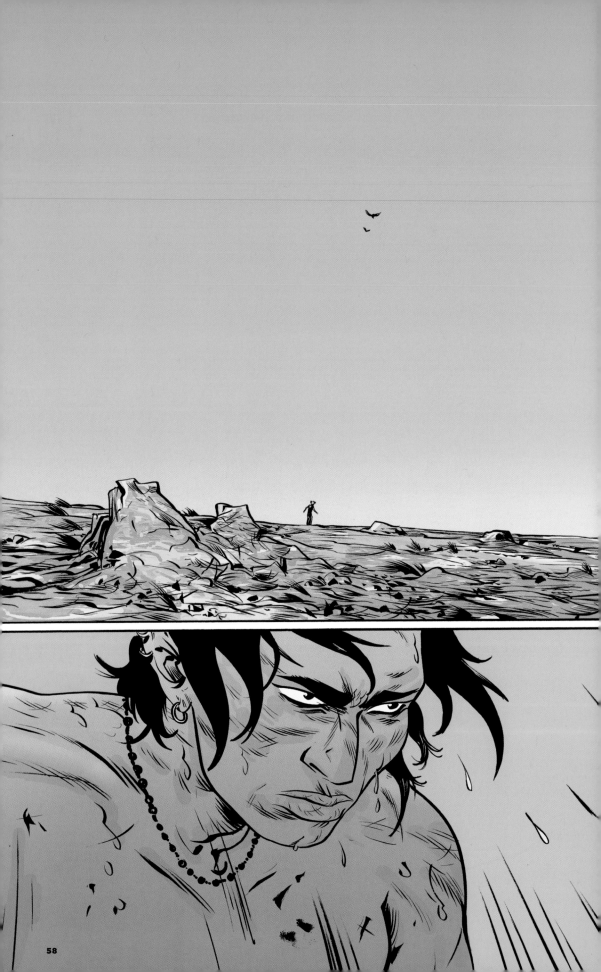

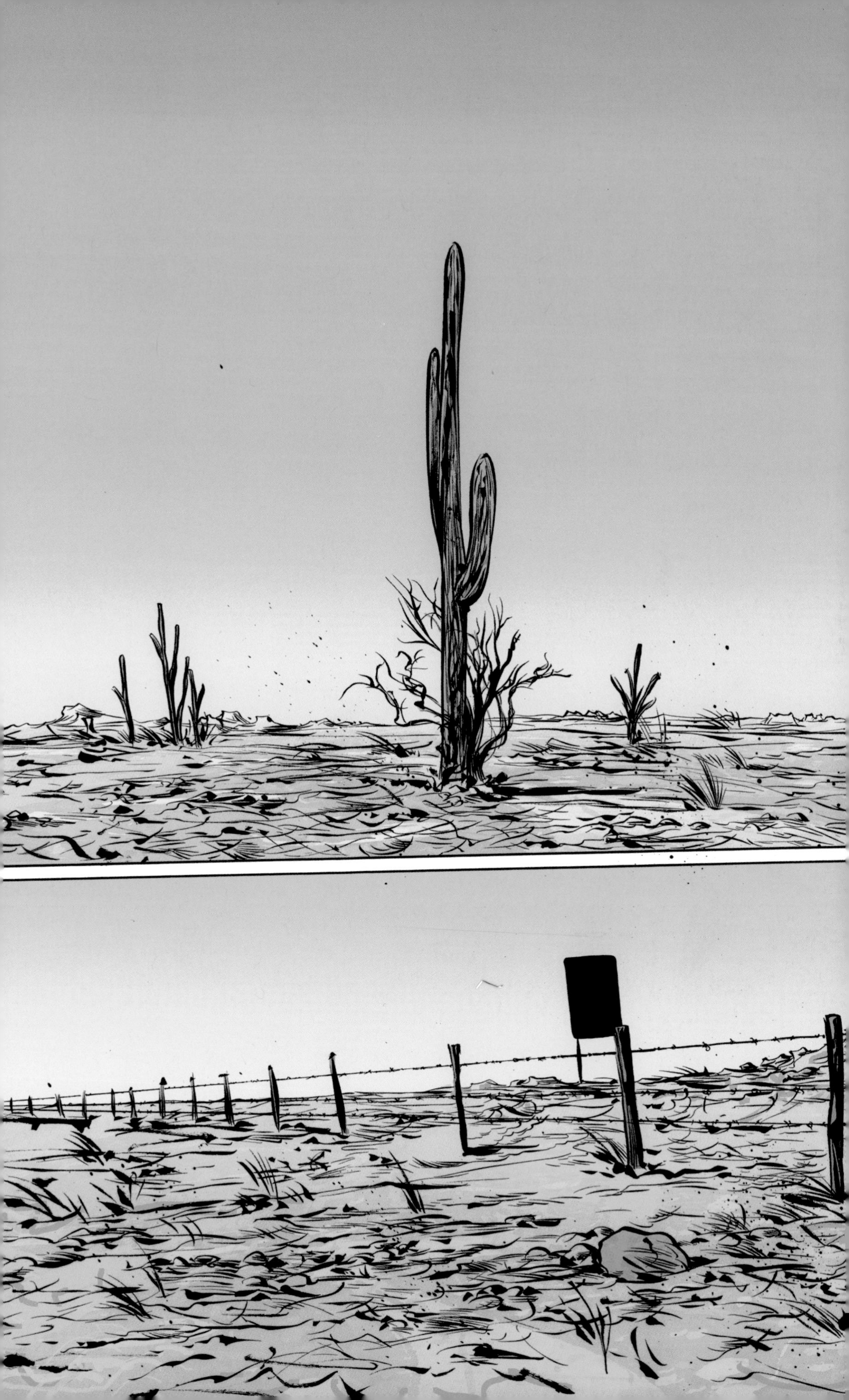

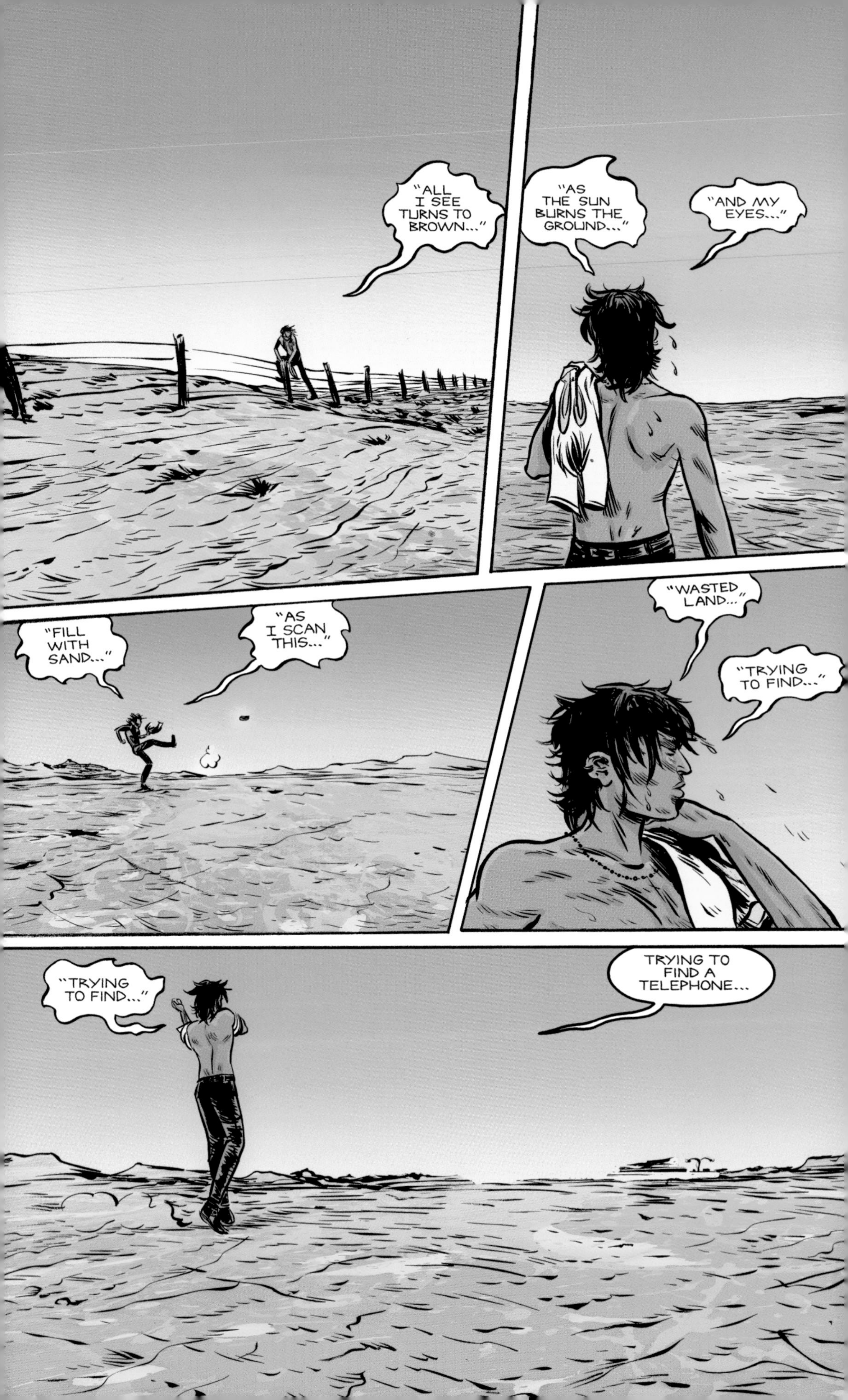
"ALL I SEE TURNS TO BROWN..."
"AS THE SUN BURNS THE GROUND..."
"AND MY EYES..."
"FILL WITH SAND..."
"AS I SCAN THIS..."
"WASTED LAND..."
"TRYING TO FIND..."
"TRYING TO FIND..."
TRYING TO FIND A TELEPHONE...

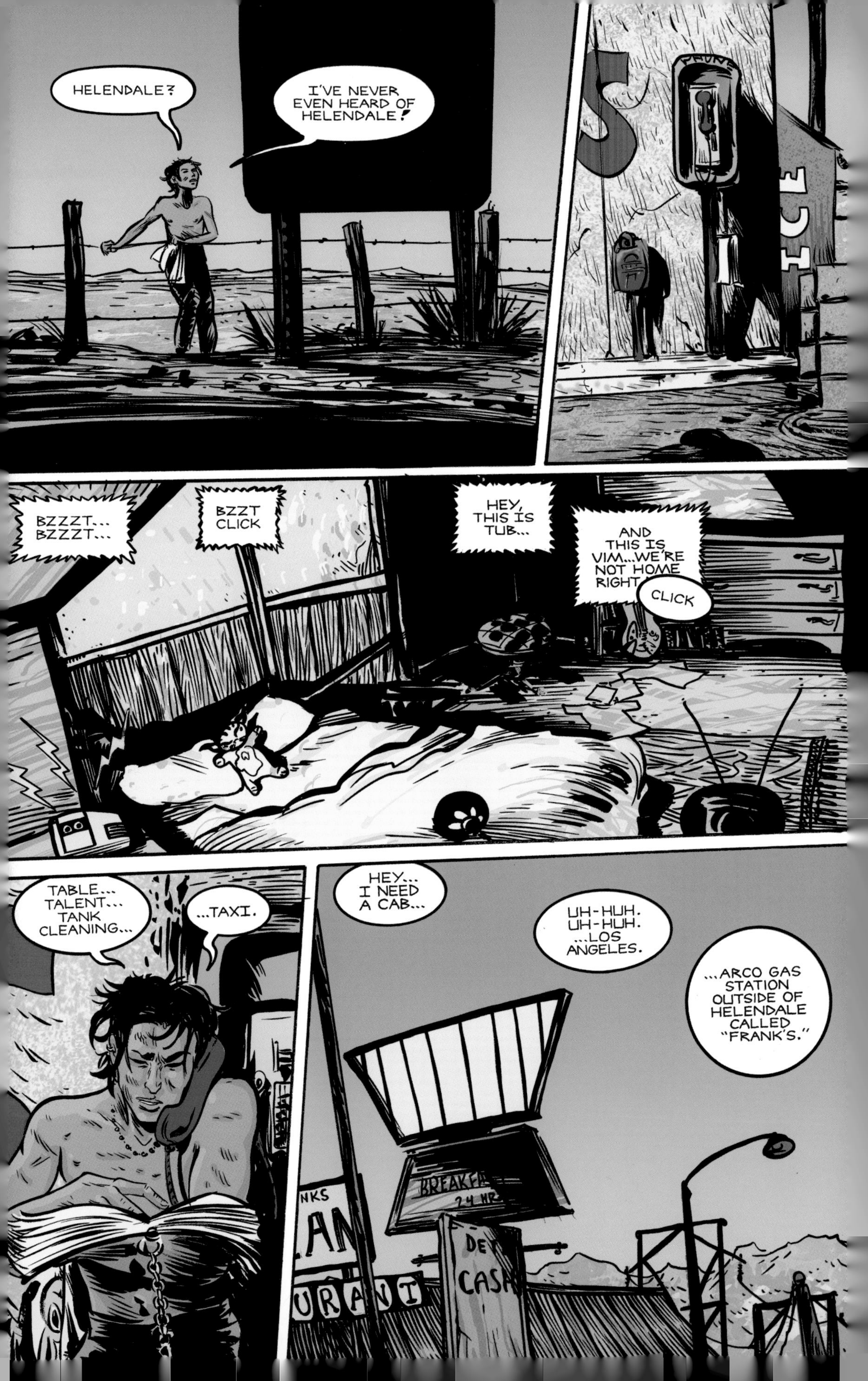
HELENDALE?
I'VE NEVER EVEN HEARD OF HELENDALE!
BZZZT... BZZZT...
BZZT CLICK
HEY, THIS IS TUB...
AND THIS IS VIM...WE'RE NOT HOME RIGHT
CLICK
TABLE... TALENT... TANK CLEANING...
...TAXI.
HEY... I NEED A CAB...
UH-HUH. UH-HUH. ...LOS ANGELES.
...ARCO GAS STATION OUTSIDE OF HELENDALE CALLED "FRANK'S."

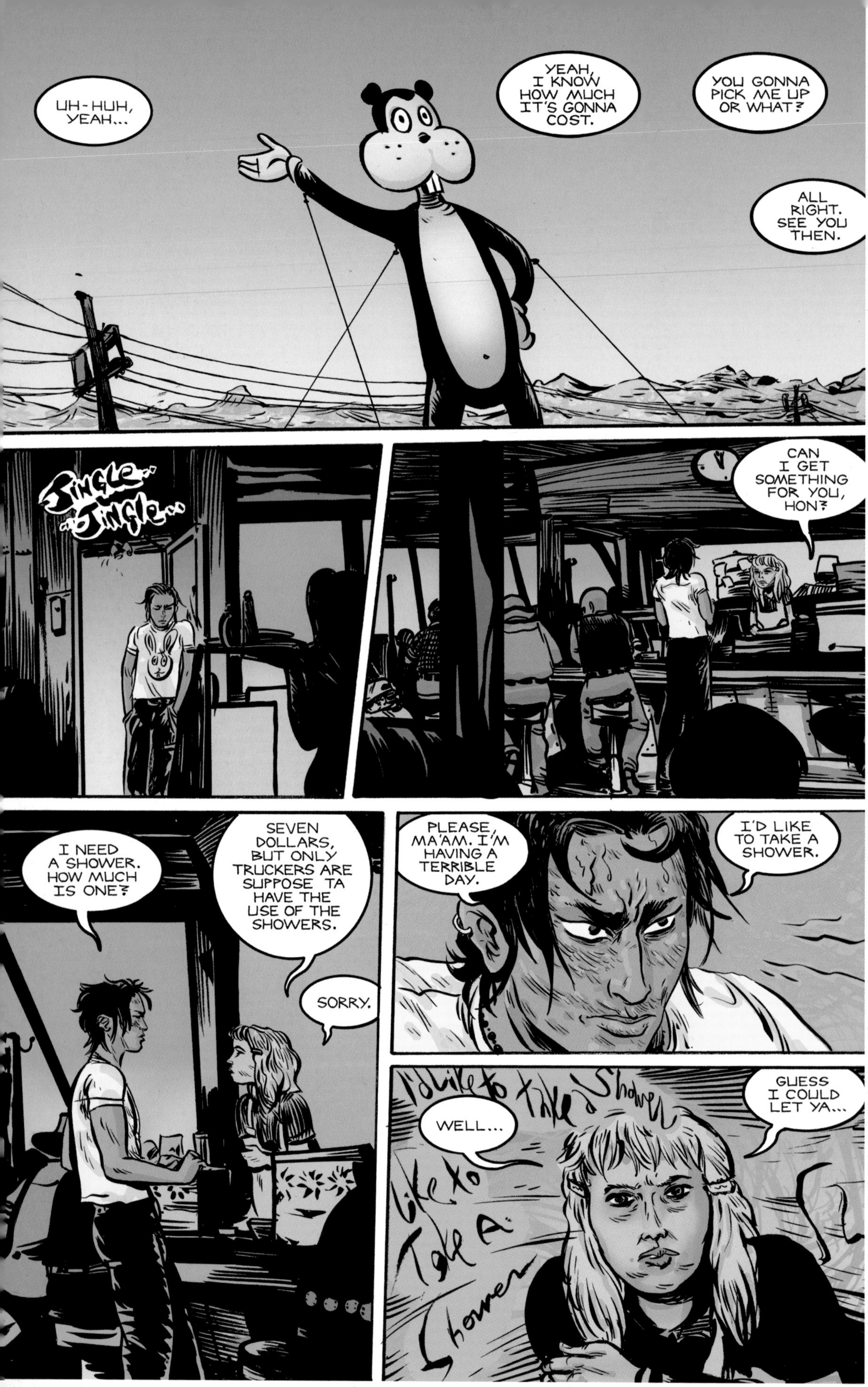
UH-HUH, YEAH...
YEAH, I KNOW HOW MUCH IT'S GONNA COST.
YOU GONNA PICK ME UP OR WHAT?
ALL RIGHT. SEE YOU THEN.
JINGLE JINGLE
CAN I GET SOMETHING FOR YOU, HON?
I NEED A SHOWER. HOW MUCH IS ONE?
SEVEN DOLLARS, BUT ONLY TRUCKERS ARE SUPPOSE TA HAVE THE USE OF THE SHOWERS.
SORRY.
PLEASE, MA'AM. I'M HAVING A TERRIBLE DAY.
I'D LIKE TO TAKE A SHOWER.
WELL...
GUESS I COULD LET YA...

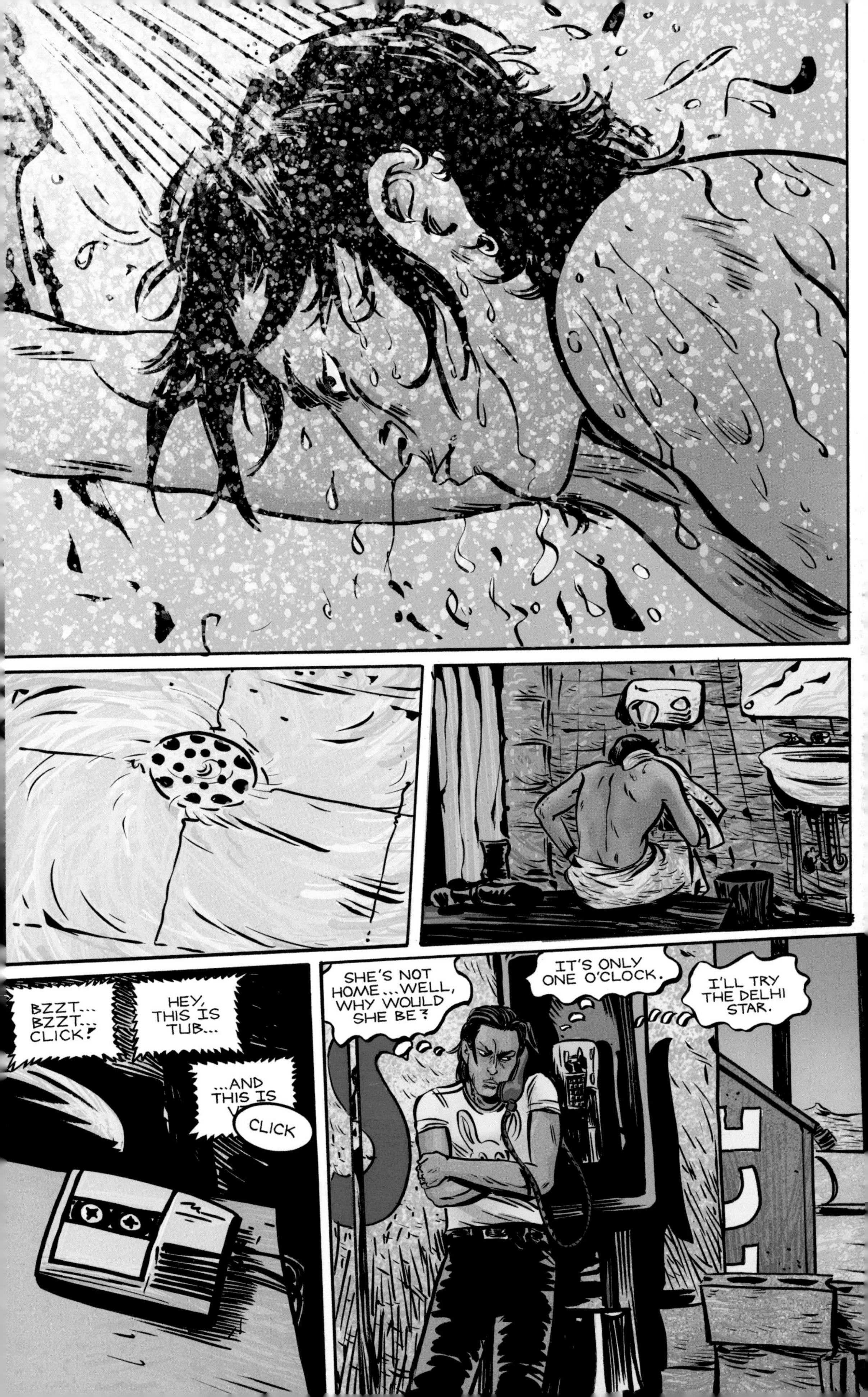
BZZT... BZZT... CLICK!
HEY, THIS IS TUB...
...AND THIS IS
CLICK
SHE'S NOT HOME...WELL, WHY WOULD SHE BE?
IT'S ONLY ONE O'CLOCK.
I'LL TRY THE DELHI STAR.

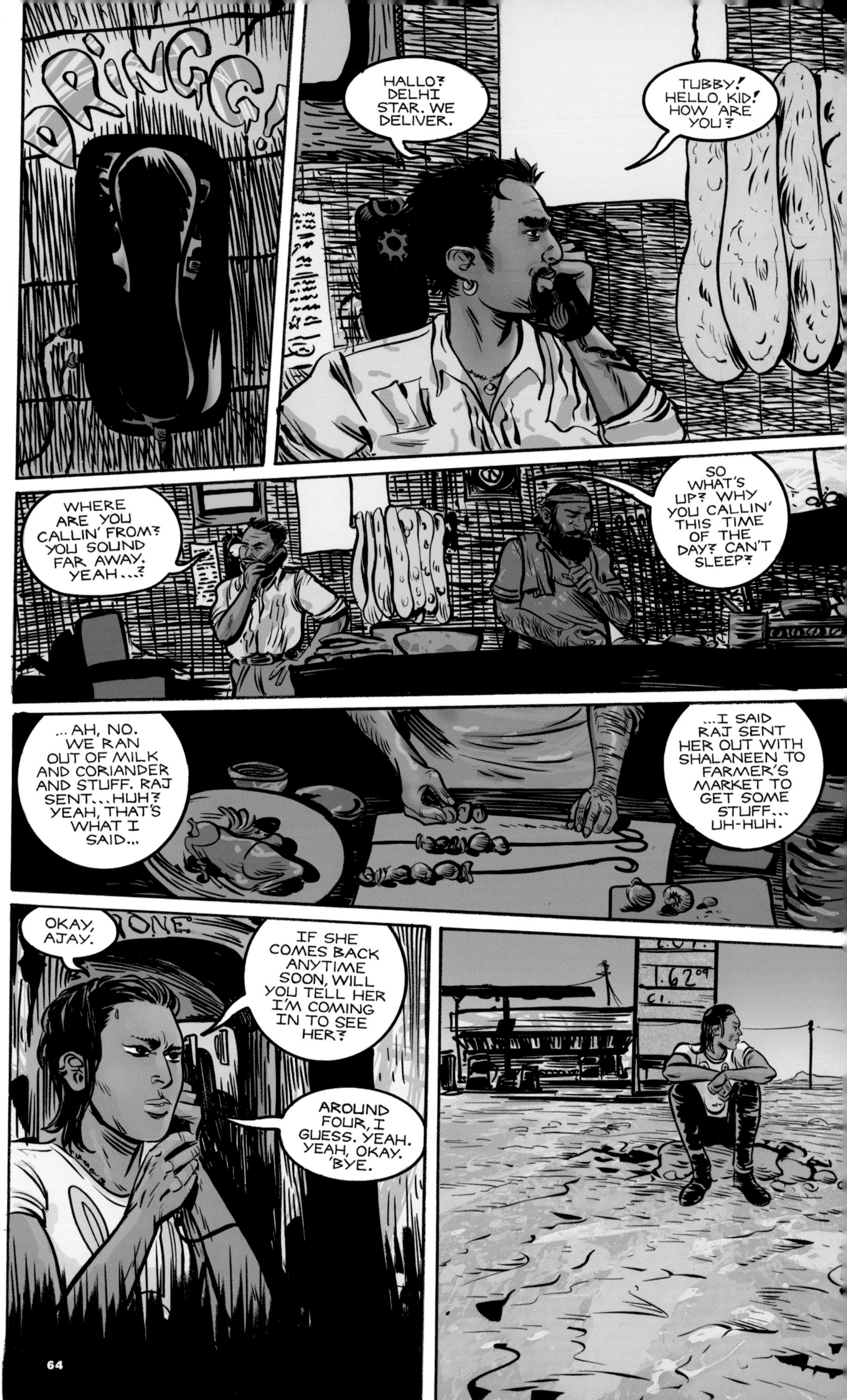
DRINGG!
HALLO? DELHI STAR. WE DELIVER.
TUBBY! HELLO, KID! HOW ARE YOU?
WHERE ARE YOU CALLIN' FROM? YOU SOUND FAR AWAY. YEAH...?
SO WHAT'S UP? WHY YOU CALLIN' THIS TIME OF THE DAY? CAN'T SLEEP?
...AH, NO. WE RAN OUT OF MILK AND CORIANDER AND STUFF. RAJ SENT... HUH? YEAH, THAT'S WHAT I SAID...
...I SAID RAJ SENT HER OUT WITH SHALANEEN TO FARMER'S MARKET TO GET SOME STUFF... UH-HUH.
OKAY, AJAY.
IF SHE COMES BACK ANYTIME SOON, WILL YOU TELL HER I'M COMING IN TO SEE HER?
AROUND FOUR, I GUESS. YEAH. YEAH, OKAY. 'BYE.

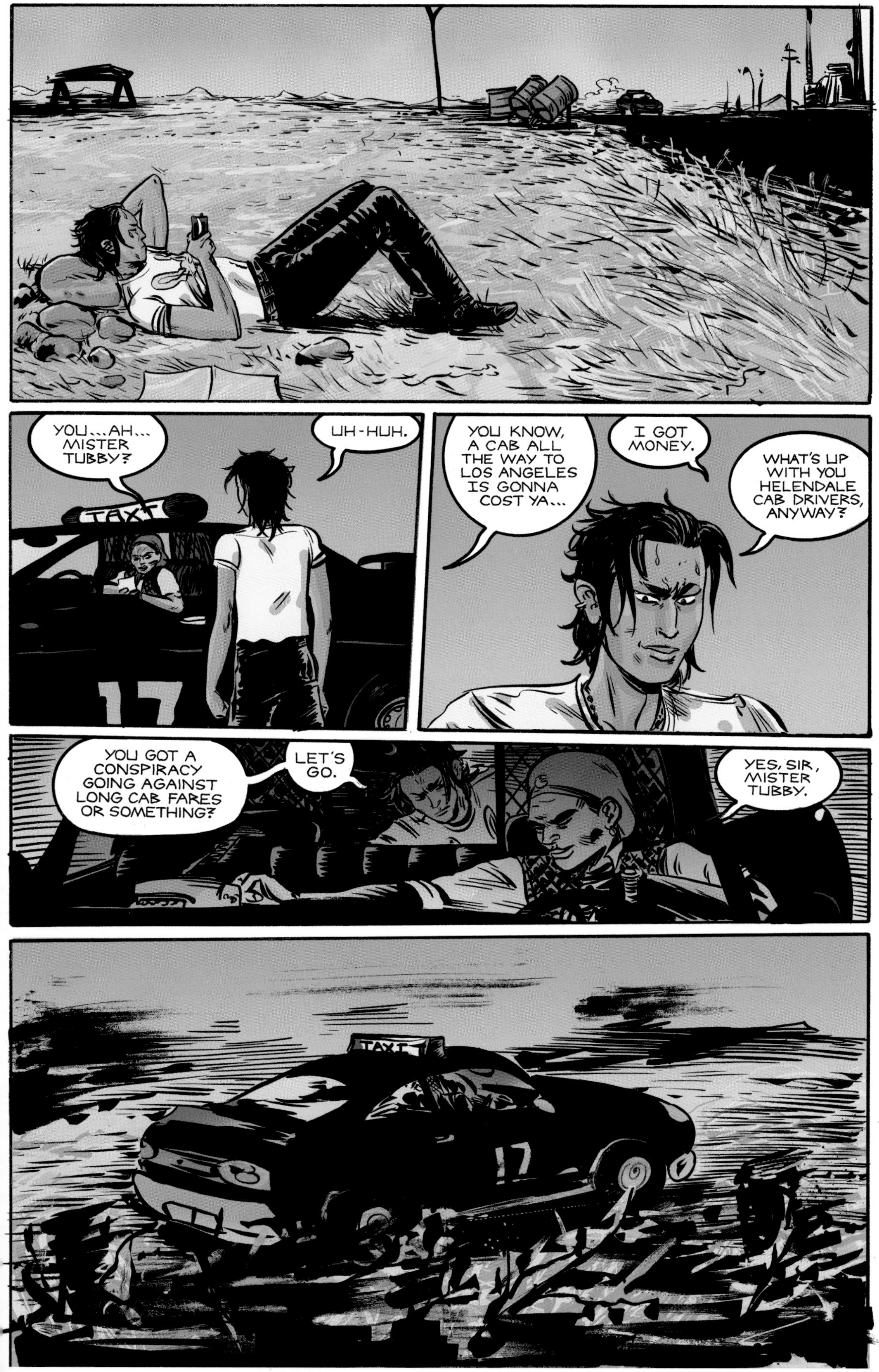
YOU...AH... MISTER TUBBY?
UH-HUH.
YOU KNOW, A CAB ALL THE WAY TO LOS ANGELES IS GONNA COST YA...
I GOT MONEY.
WHAT'S UP WITH YOU HELENDALE CAB DRIVERS, ANYWAY?
YOU GOT A CONSPIRACY GOING AGAINST LONG CAB FARES OR SOMETHING?
LET'S GO.
YES, SIR, MISTER TUBBY.
TAXI
17

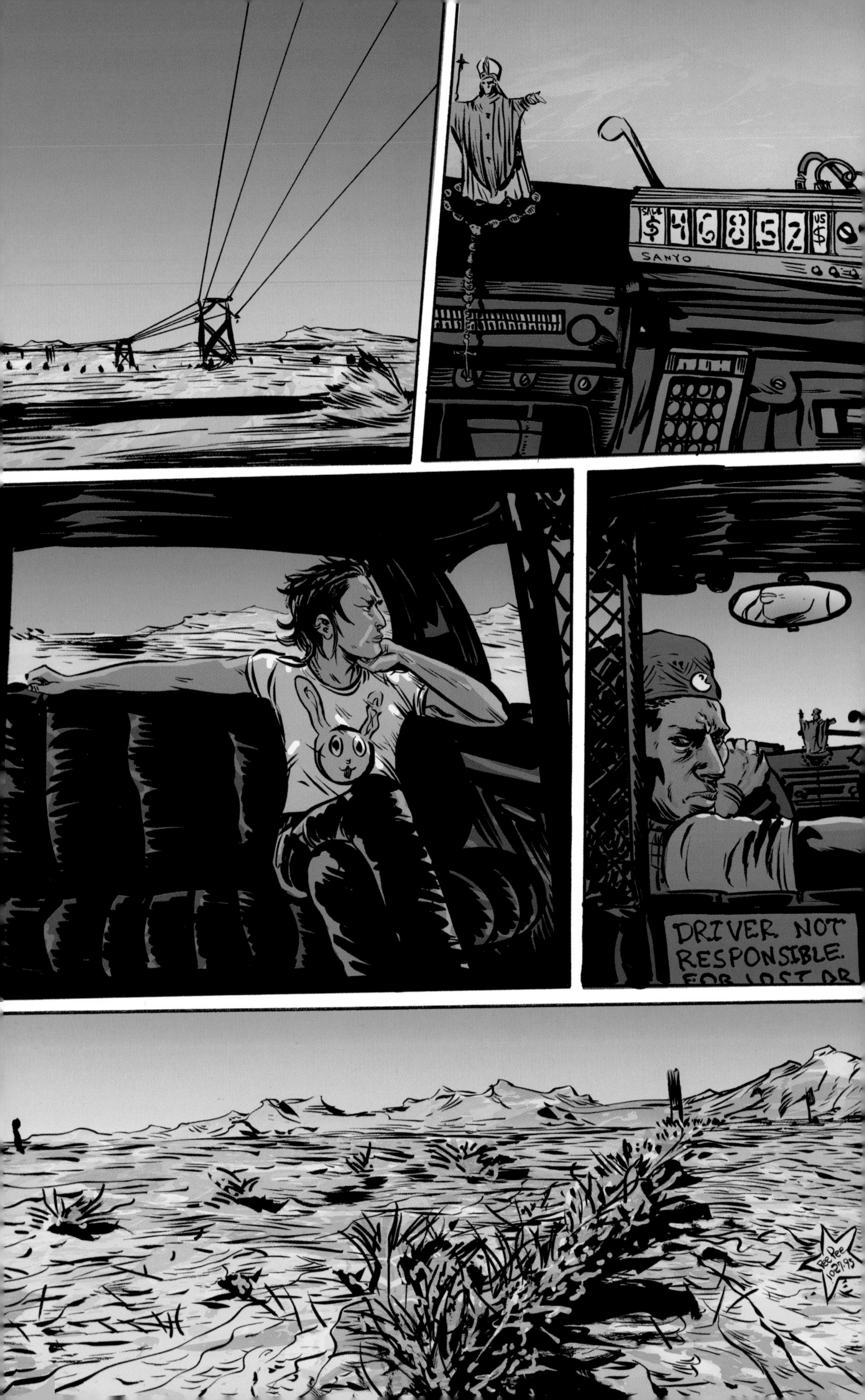
SALE
$468.52
US$
SANYO
DRIVER NOT
RESPONSIBLE.

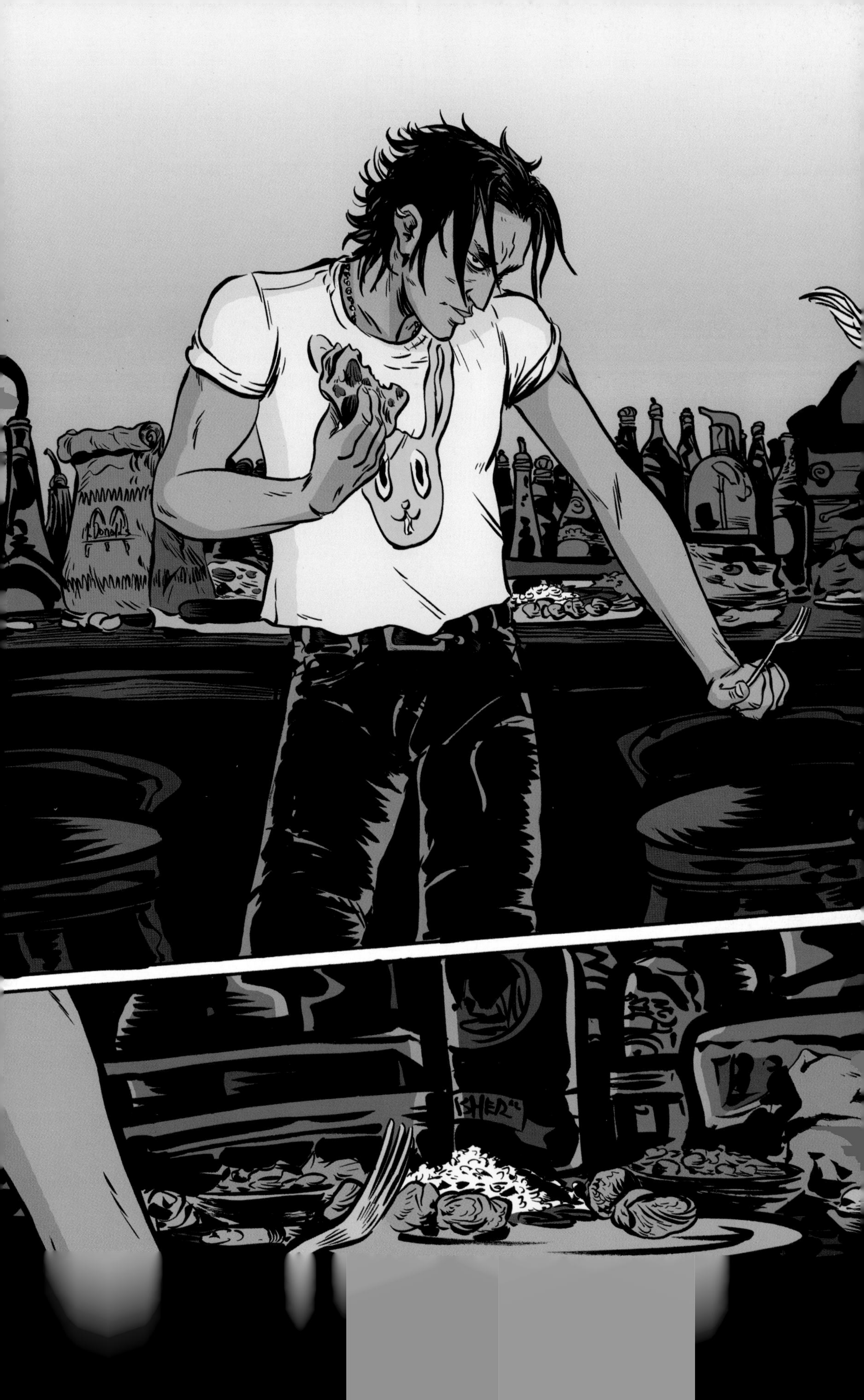

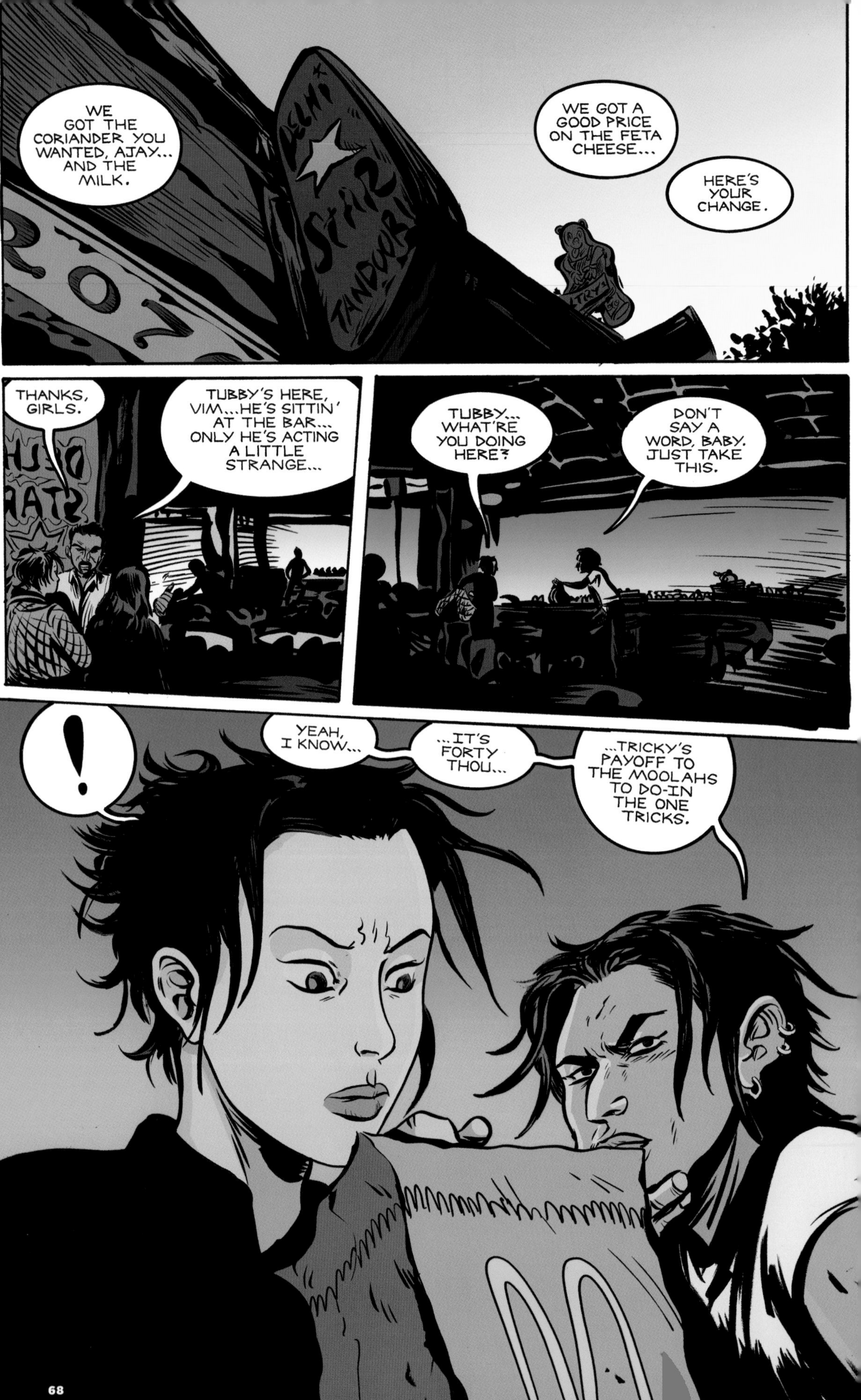
WE GOT THE CORIANDER YOU WANTED, AJAY... AND THE MILK.
DELHI STAR TANDOORI
WE GOT A GOOD PRICE ON THE FETA CHEESE...
HERE'S YOUR CHANGE.
THANKS, GIRLS.
TUBBY'S HERE, VIM... HE'S SITTIN' AT THE BAR... ONLY HE'S ACTING A LITTLE STRANGE...
TUBBY... WHAT'RE YOU DOING HERE?
DON'T SAY A WORD, BABY. JUST TAKE THIS.
!
YEAH, I KNOW...
...IT'S FORTY THOU...
...TRICKY'S PAYOFF TO THE MOOLAHS TO DO-IN THE ONE TRICKS.

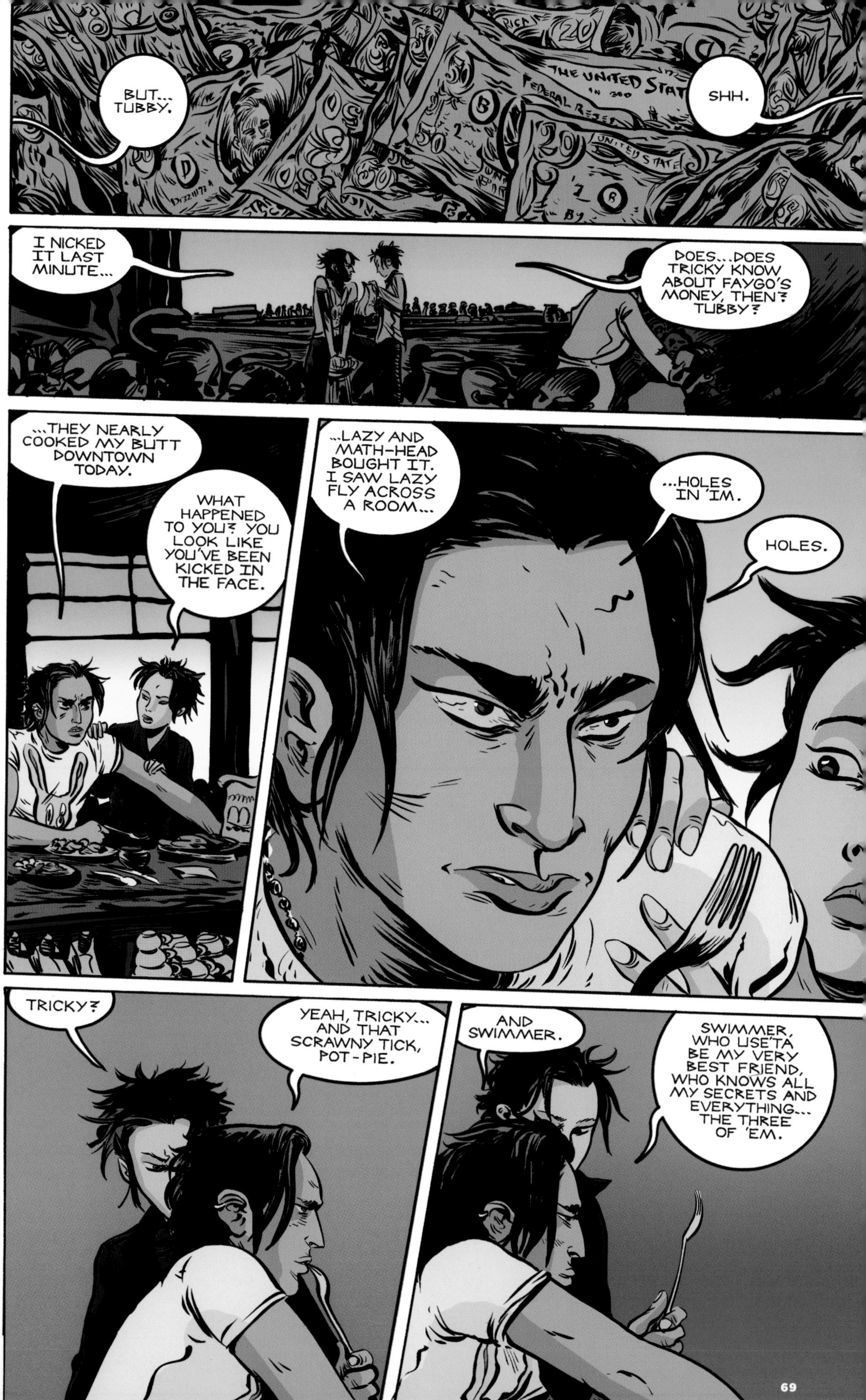
BUT... TUBBY.
SHH.
I NICKED IT LAST MINUTE...
DOES...DOES TRICKY KNOW ABOUT FAYGO'S MONEY, THEN? TUBBY?
...THEY NEARLY COOKED MY BUTT DOWNTOWN TODAY.
WHAT HAPPENED TO YOU? YOU LOOK LIKE YOU'VE BEEN KICKED IN THE FACE.
...LAZY AND MATH-HEAD BOUGHT IT. I SAW LAZY FLY ACROSS A ROOM...
...HOLES IN 'IM.
HOLES.
TRICKY?
YEAH, TRICKY... AND THAT SCRAWNY TICK, POT-PIE.
AND SWIMMER.
SWIMMER, WHO USE'TA BE MY VERY BEST FRIEND, WHO KNOWS ALL MY SECRETS AND EVERYTHING... THE THREE OF 'EM.

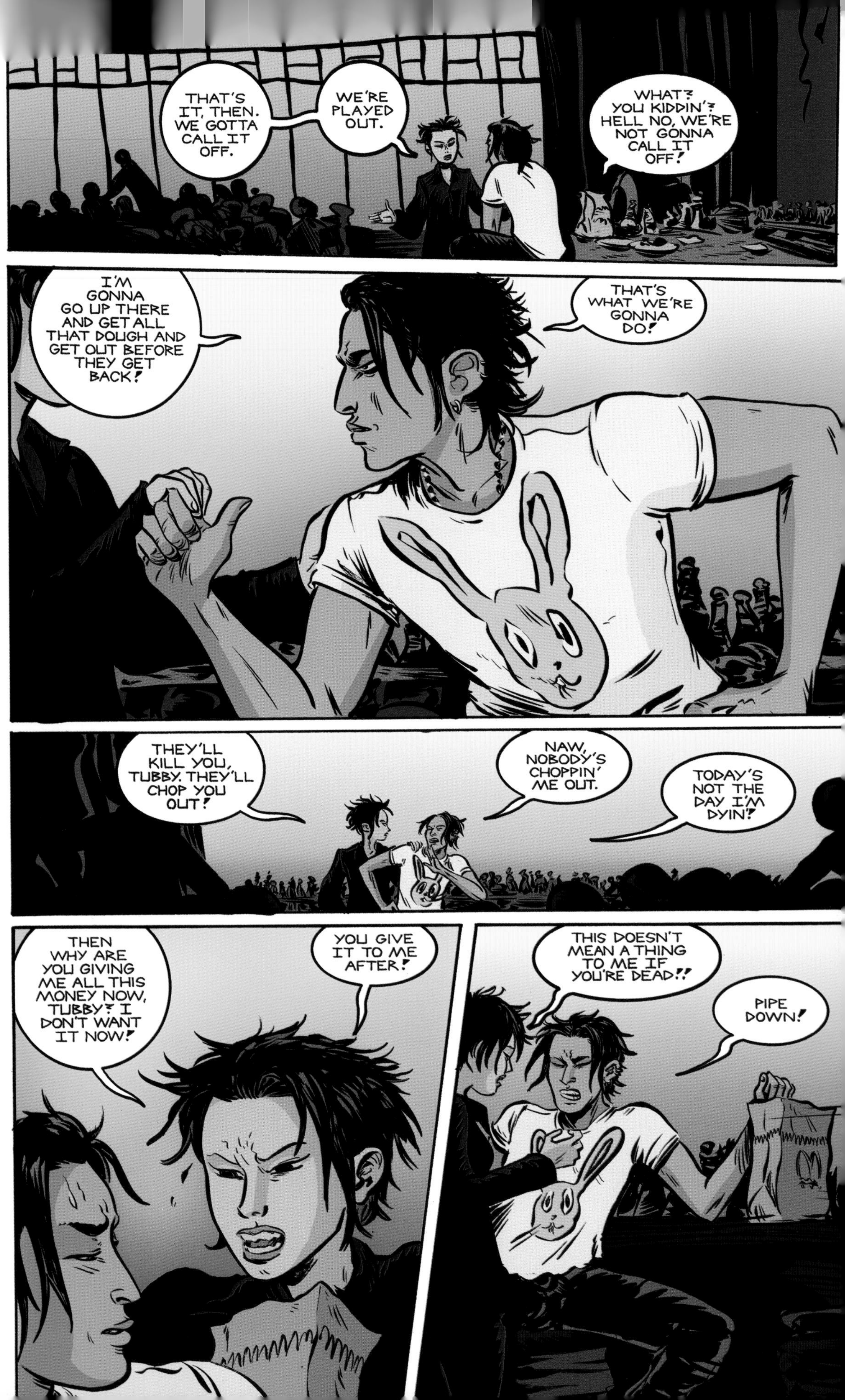
THAT'S IT, THEN. WE GOTTA CALL IT OFF.
WE'RE PLAYED OUT.
WHAT? YOU KIDDIN'? HELL NO, WE'RE NOT GONNA CALL IT OFF!
I'M GONNA GO UP THERE AND GET ALL THAT DOUGH AND GET OUT BEFORE THEY GET BACK!
THAT'S WHAT WE'RE GONNA DO!
THEY'LL KILL YOU, TUBBY. THEY'LL CHOP YOU OUT!
NAW, NOBODY'S CHOPPIN' ME OUT.
TODAY'S NOT THE DAY I'M DYIN'!
THEN WHY ARE YOU GIVING ME ALL THIS MONEY NOW, TUBBY? I DON'T WANT IT NOW!
YOU GIVE IT TO ME AFTER!
THIS DOESN'T MEAN A THING TO ME IF YOU'RE DEAD!!
PIPE DOWN!

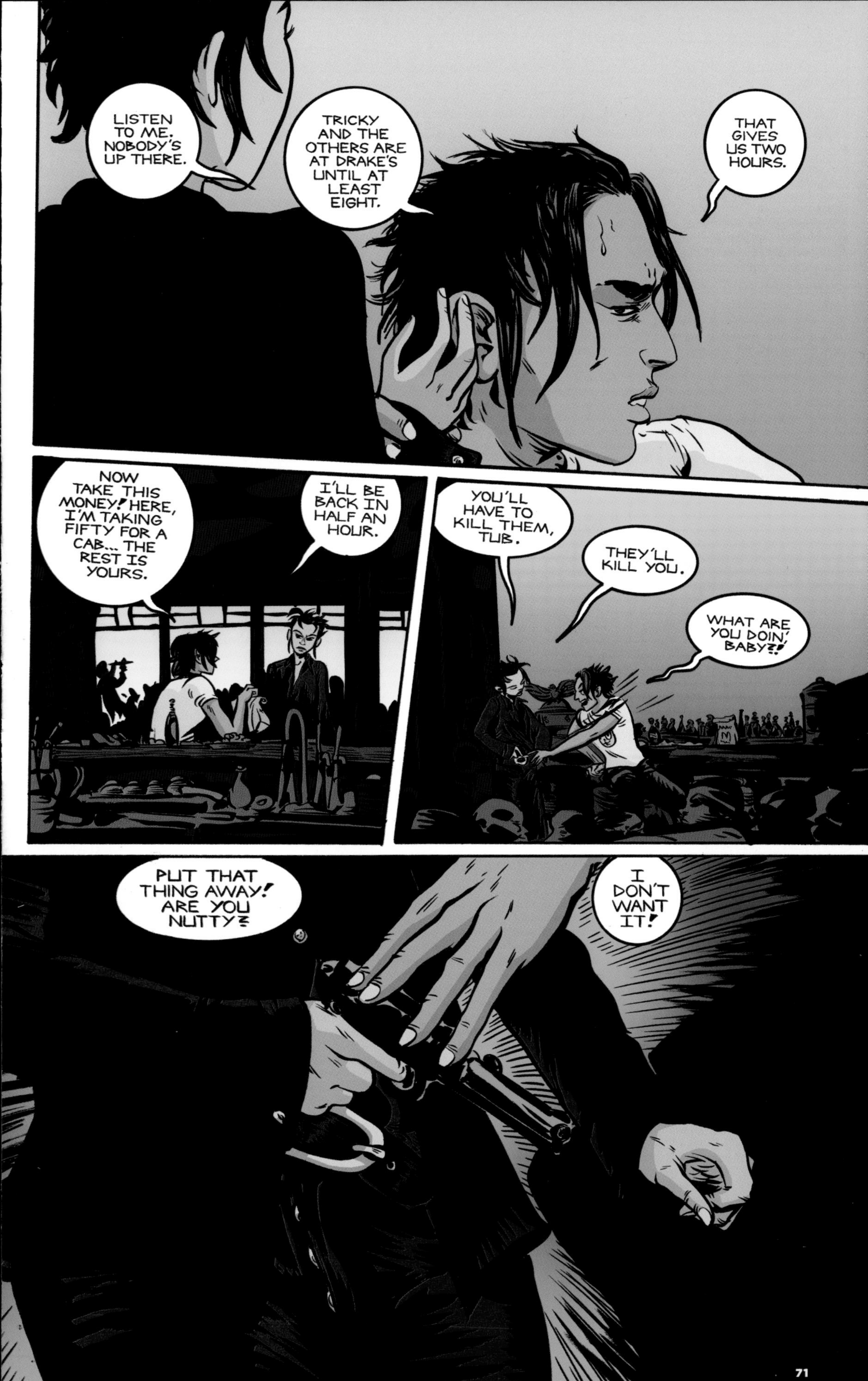
LISTEN TO ME. NOBODY'S UP THERE.
TRICKY AND THE OTHERS ARE AT DRAKE'S UNTIL AT LEAST EIGHT.
THAT GIVES US TWO HOURS.
NOW TAKE THIS MONEY! HERE, I'M TAKING FIFTY FOR A CAB... THE REST IS YOURS.
I'LL BE BACK IN HALF AN HOUR.
YOU'LL HAVE TO KILL THEM, TUB.
THEY'LL KILL YOU.
WHAT ARE YOU DOIN', BABY?!
PUT THAT THING AWAY! ARE YOU NUTTY?
I DON'T WANT IT!

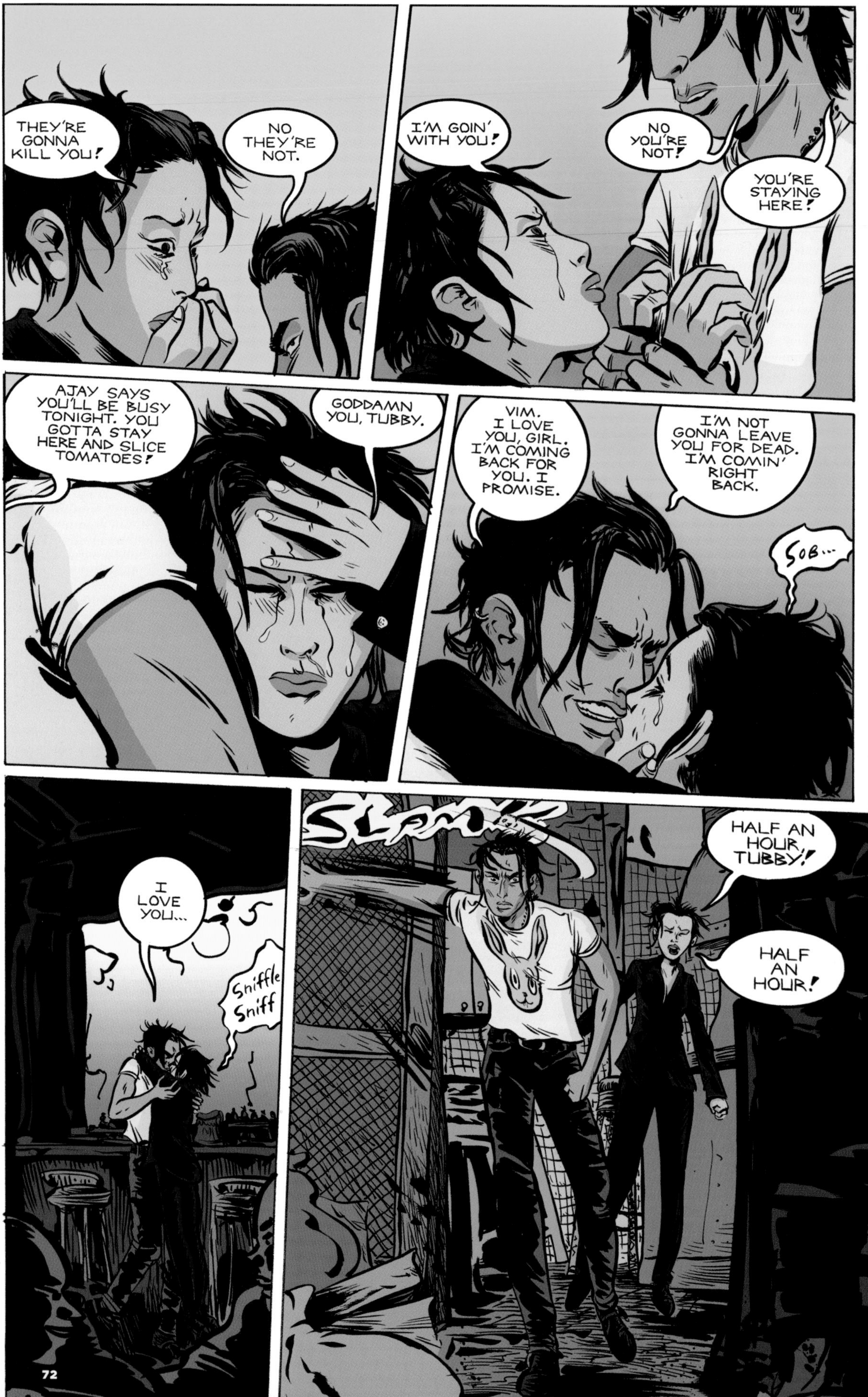
THEY'RE GONNA KILL YOU!
NO THEY'RE NOT.
I'M GOIN' WITH YOU!
NO YOU'RE NOT!
YOU'RE STAYING HERE!
AJAY SAYS YOU'LL BE BUSY TONIGHT. YOU GOTTA STAY HERE AND SLICE TOMATOES!
GODDAMN YOU, TUBBY.
VIM. I LOVE YOU, GIRL. I'M COMING BACK FOR YOU. I PROMISE.
I'M NOT GONNA LEAVE YOU FOR DEAD. I'M COMIN' RIGHT BACK.
SOB...
I LOVE YOU...
SNIFFLE SNIFF
HALF AN HOUR TUBBY!
HALF AN HOUR!

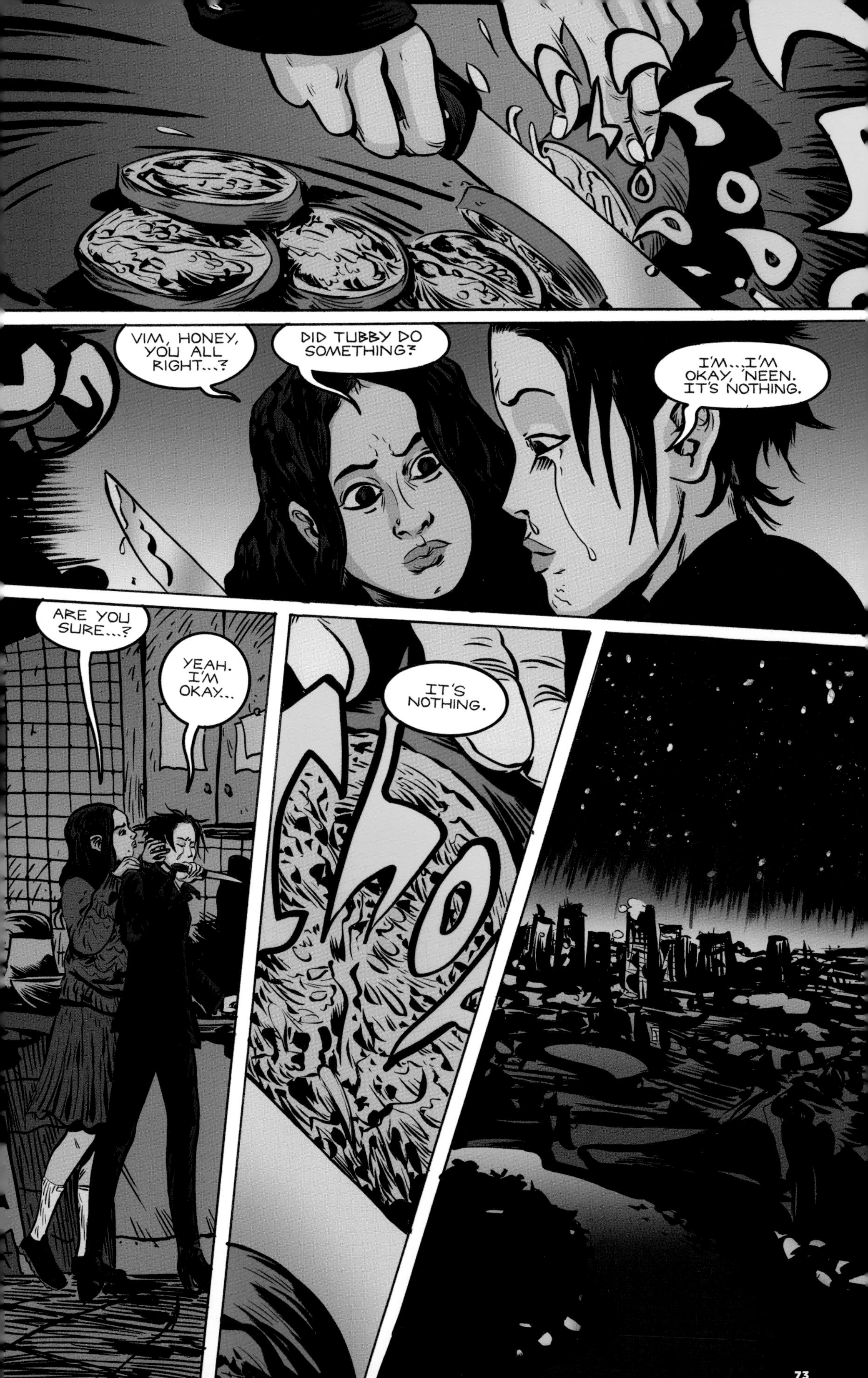
VIM, HONEY, YOU ALL RIGHT...?
DID TUBBY DO SOMETHING?
I'M...I'M OKAY, 'NEEN. IT'S NOTHING.
ARE YOU SURE...?
YEAH. I'M OKAY...
IT'S NOTHING.

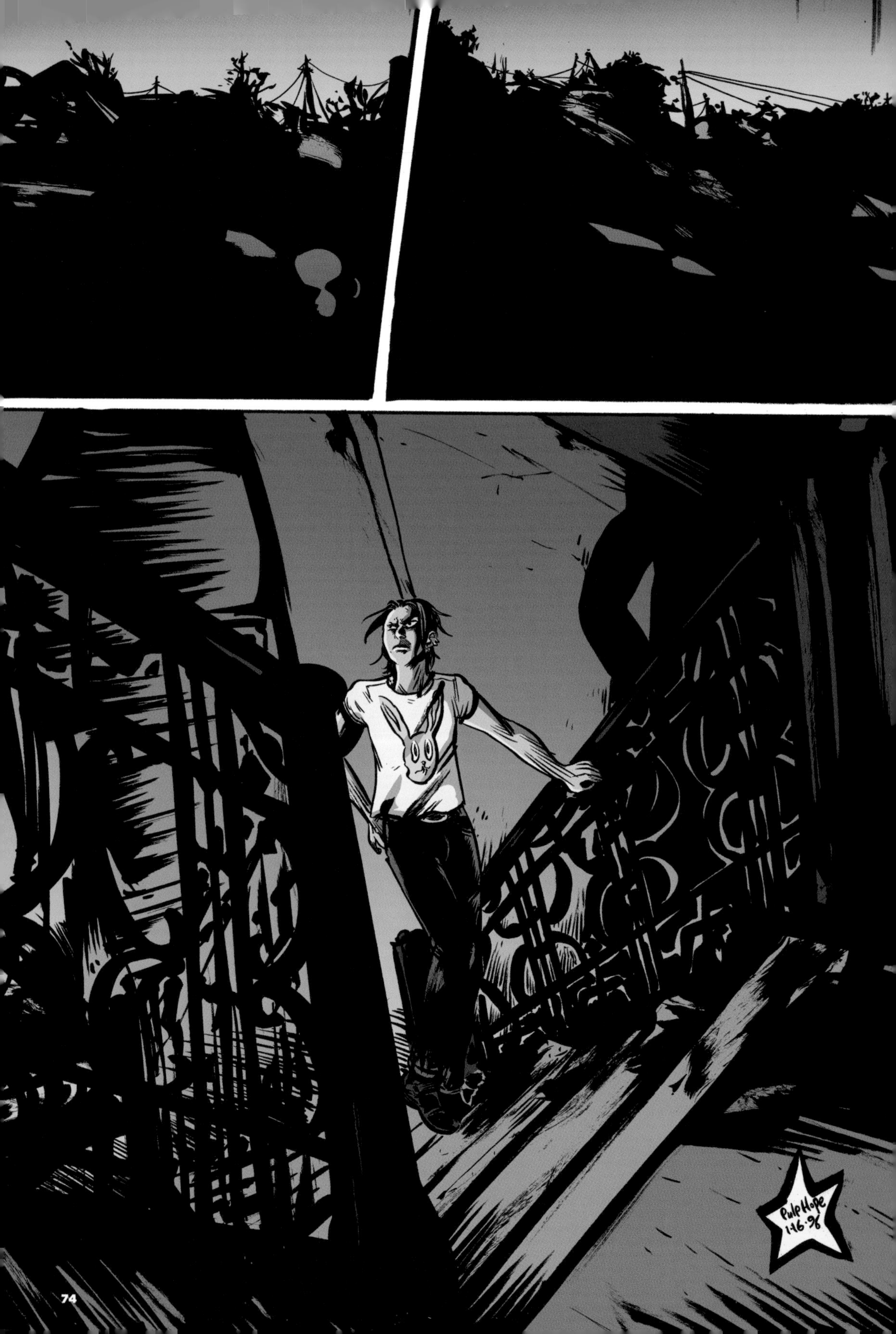
Pulp Hope
1·16·96

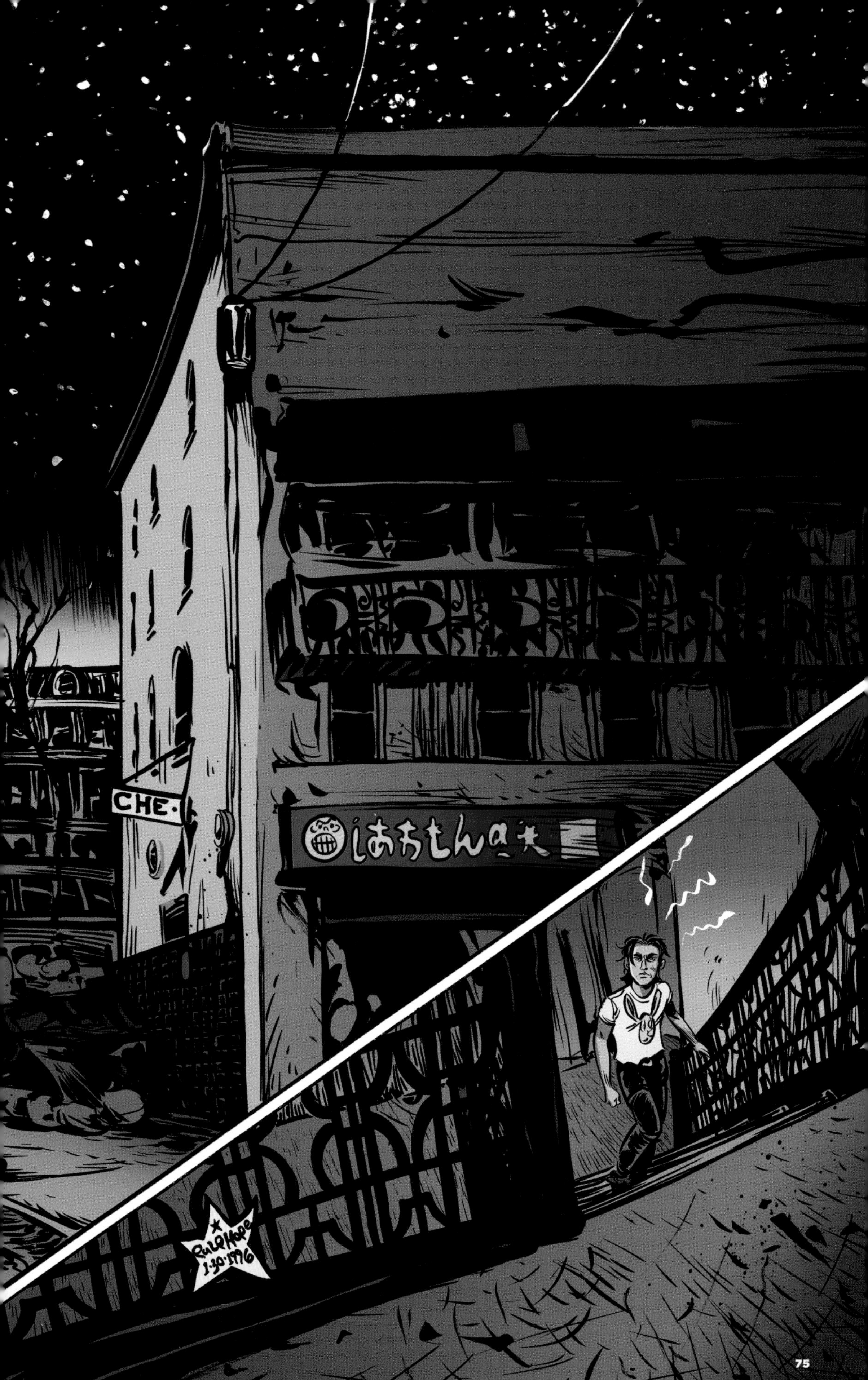
CHE
Paul Hope
1-30-1996

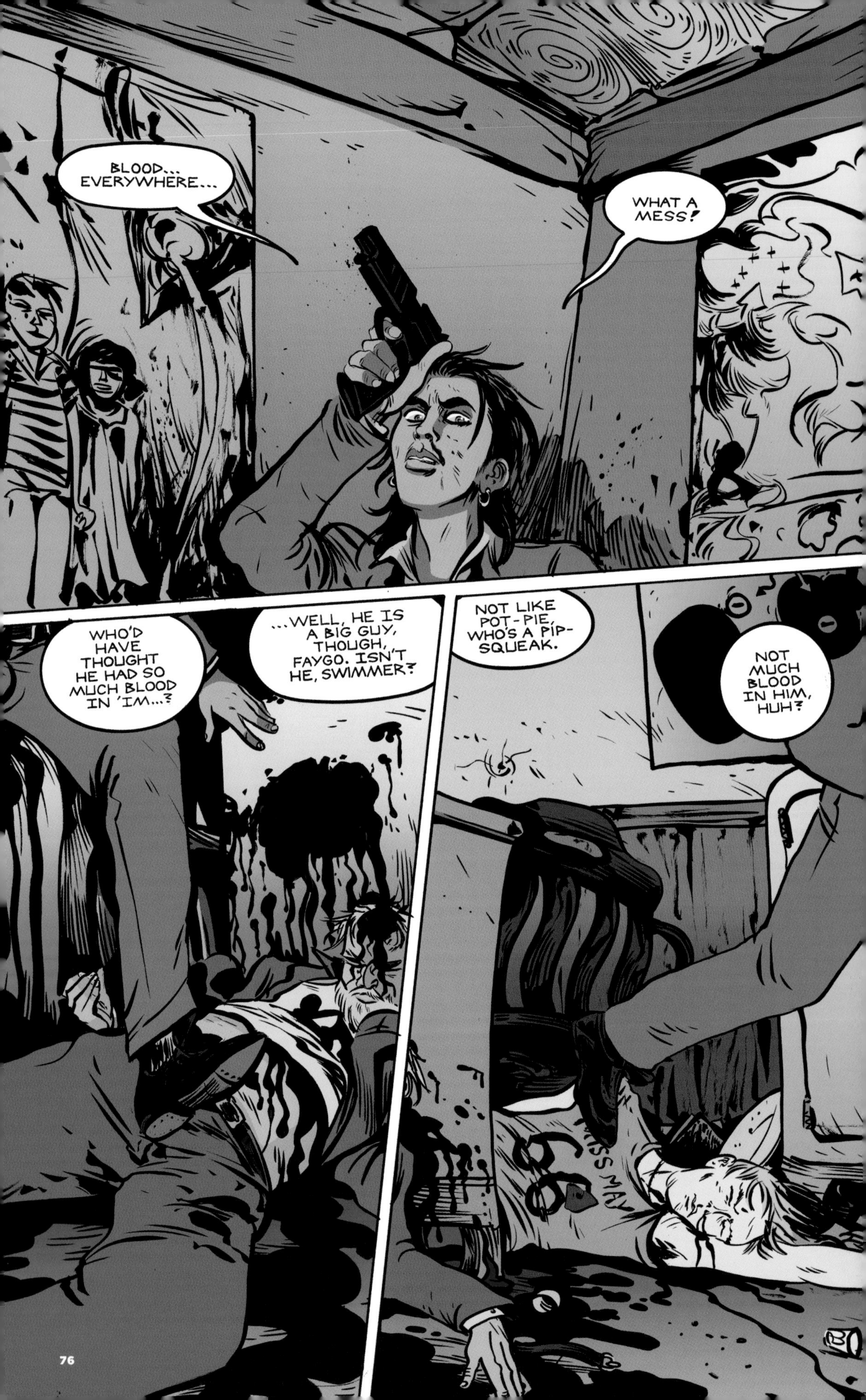
BLOOD... EVERYWHERE...
WHAT A MESS!
WHO'D HAVE THOUGHT HE HAD SO MUCH BLOOD IN 'IM...?
...WELL, HE IS A BIG GUY, THOUGH, FAYGO. ISN'T HE, SWIMMER?
NOT LIKE POT-PIE, WHO'S A PIP-SQUEAK.
NOT MUCH BLOOD IN HIM, HUH?
MISS MAY

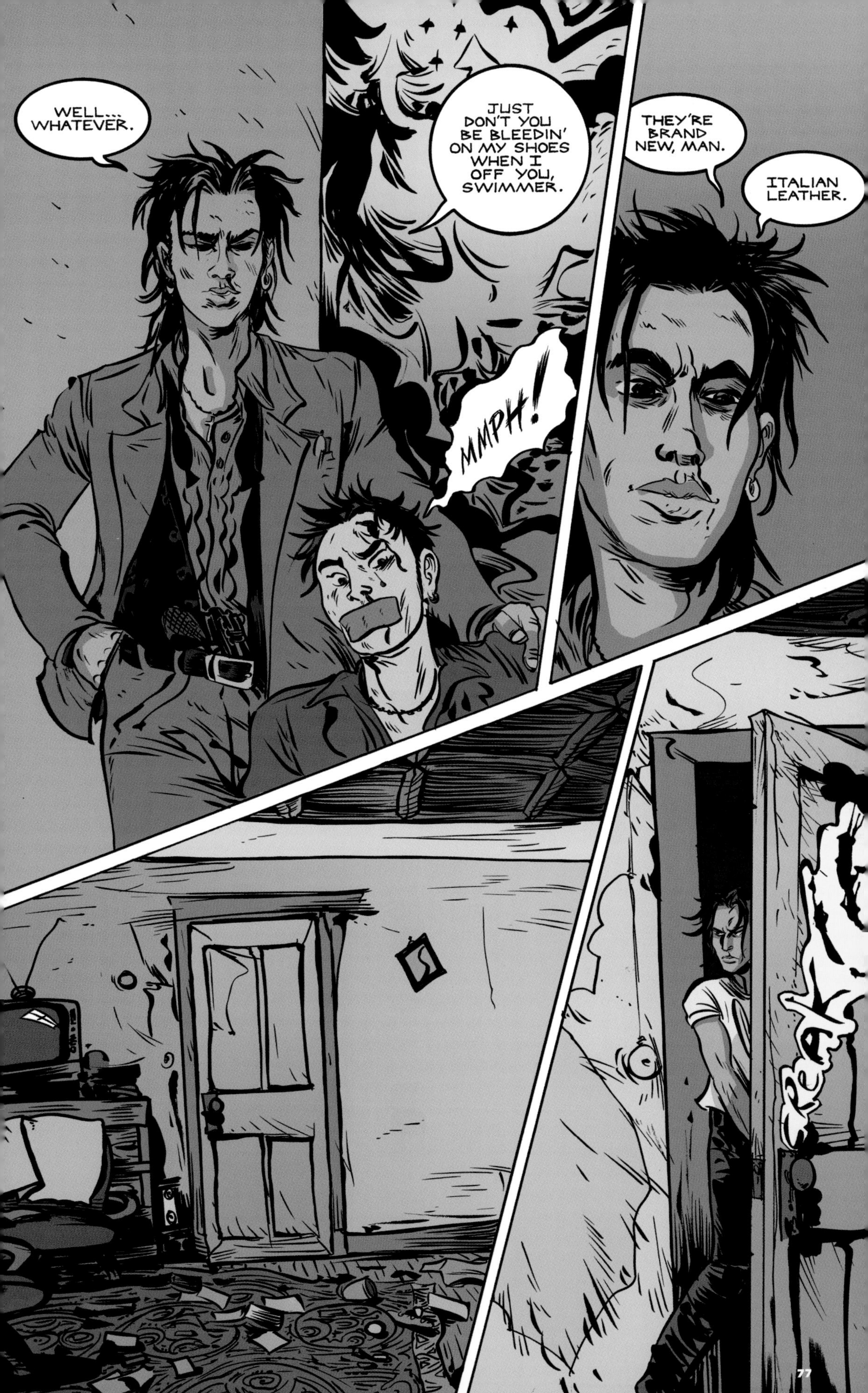
WELL... WHATEVER.
JUST DON'T YOU BE BLEEDIN' ON MY SHOES WHEN I OFF YOU, SWIMMER.
MMPH!
THEY'RE BRAND NEW, MAN.
ITALIAN LEATHER.
CREAK

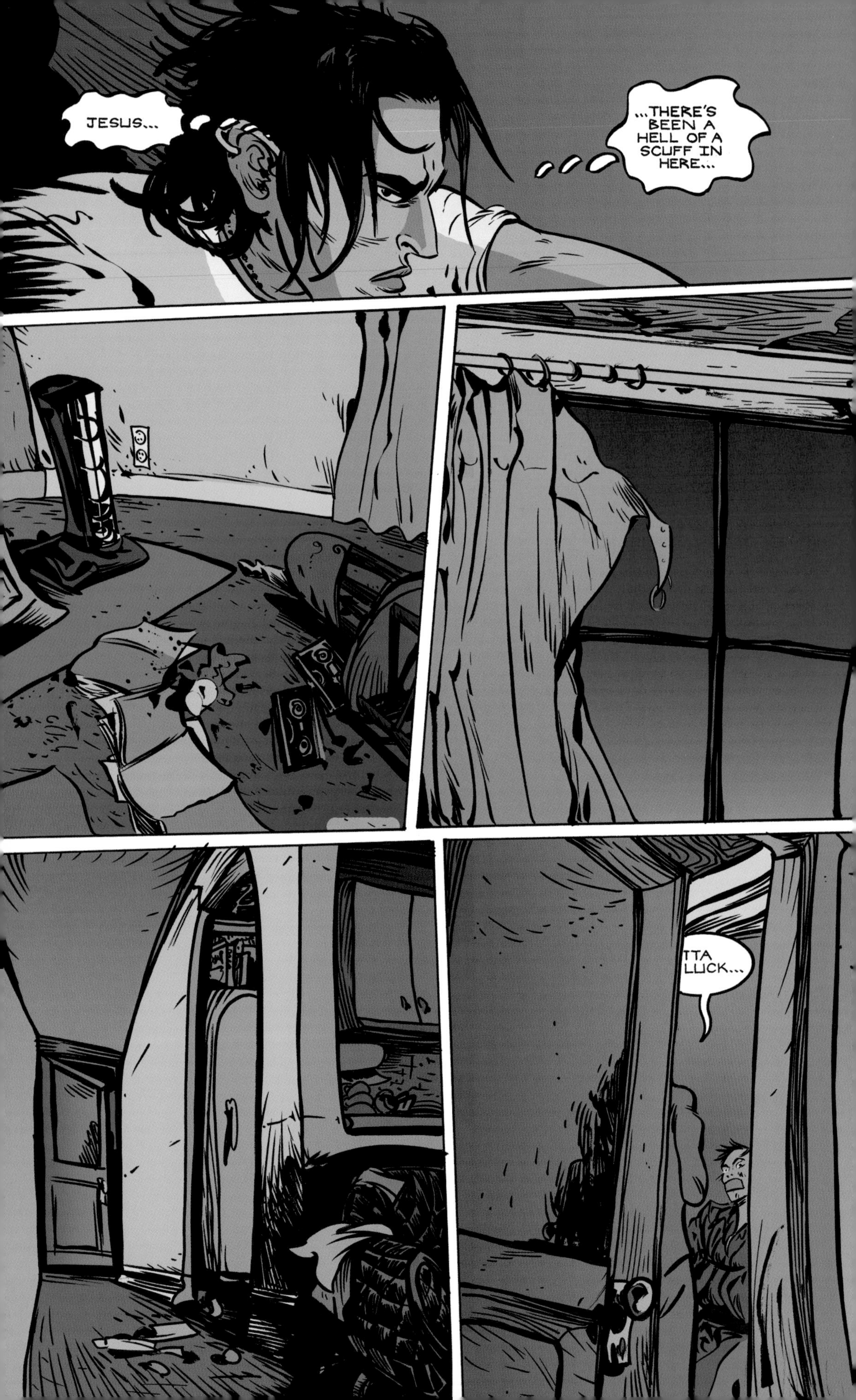
JESUS...
...THERE'S BEEN A HELL OF A SCUFF IN HERE...
TTA LUCK...

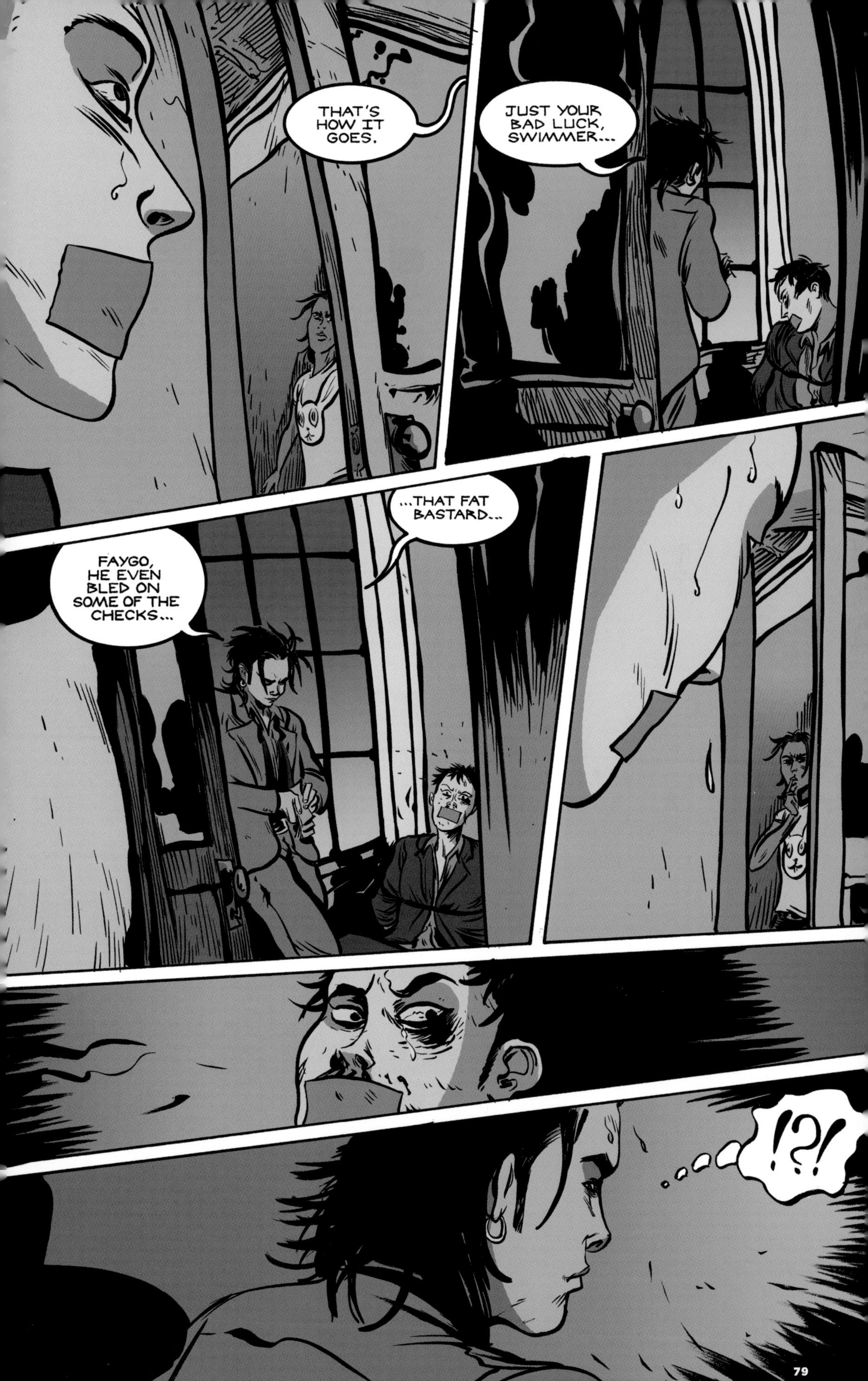
THAT'S HOW IT GOES.
JUST YOUR BAD LUCK, SWIMMER...
FAYGO, HE EVEN BLED ON SOME OF THE CHECKS...
...THAT FAT BASTARD...
!?!

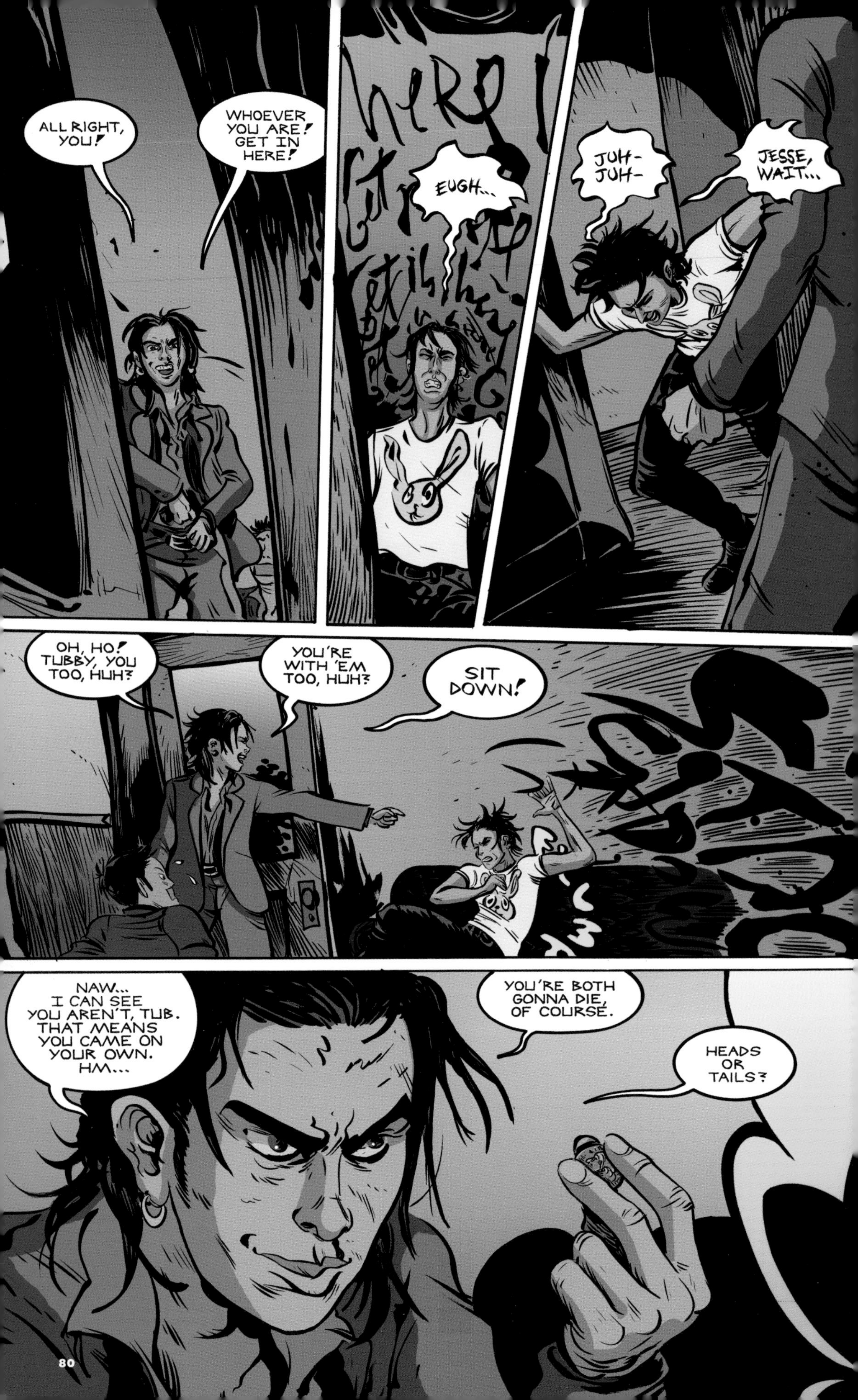
ALL RIGHT, YOU!
WHOEVER YOU ARE! GET IN HERE!
EUGH...
JUH- JUH-
JESSE, WAIT...
OH, HO! TUBBY, YOU TOO, HUH?
YOU'RE WITH 'EM TOO, HUH?
SIT DOWN!
NAW... I CAN SEE YOU AREN'T, TUB. THAT MEANS YOU CAME ON YOUR OWN. HM...
YOU'RE BOTH GONNA DIE, OF COURSE.
HEADS OR TAILS?

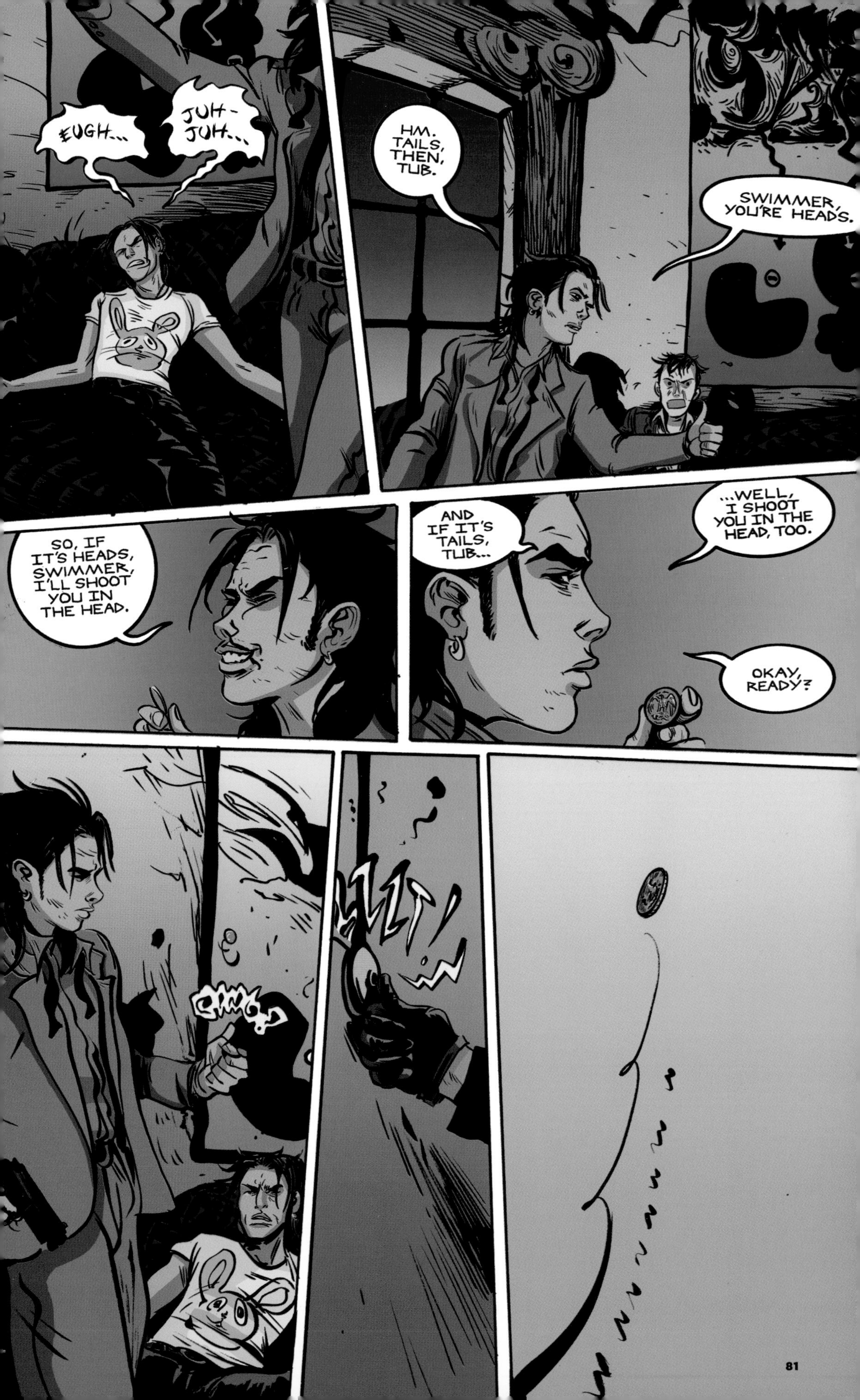
EUGH...
JUH-JUH...
HM. TAILS, THEN, TUB.
SWIMMER, YOU'RE HEADS.
SO, IF IT'S HEADS, SWIMMER, I'LL SHOOT YOU IN THE HEAD.
AND IF IT'S TAILS, TUB...
...WELL, I SHOOT YOU IN THE HEAD, TOO.
OKAY, READY?

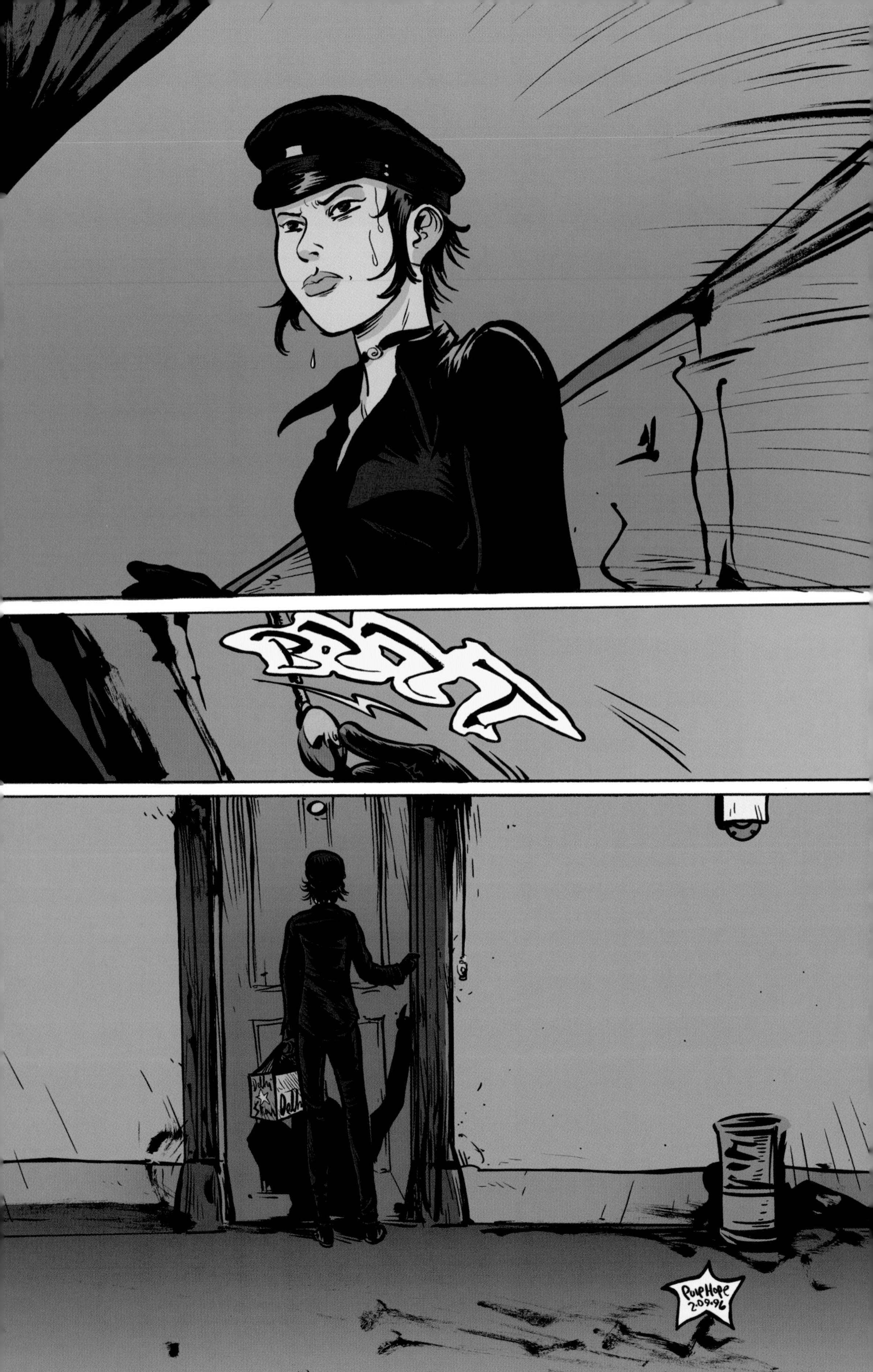
PulpHope
2.09.96

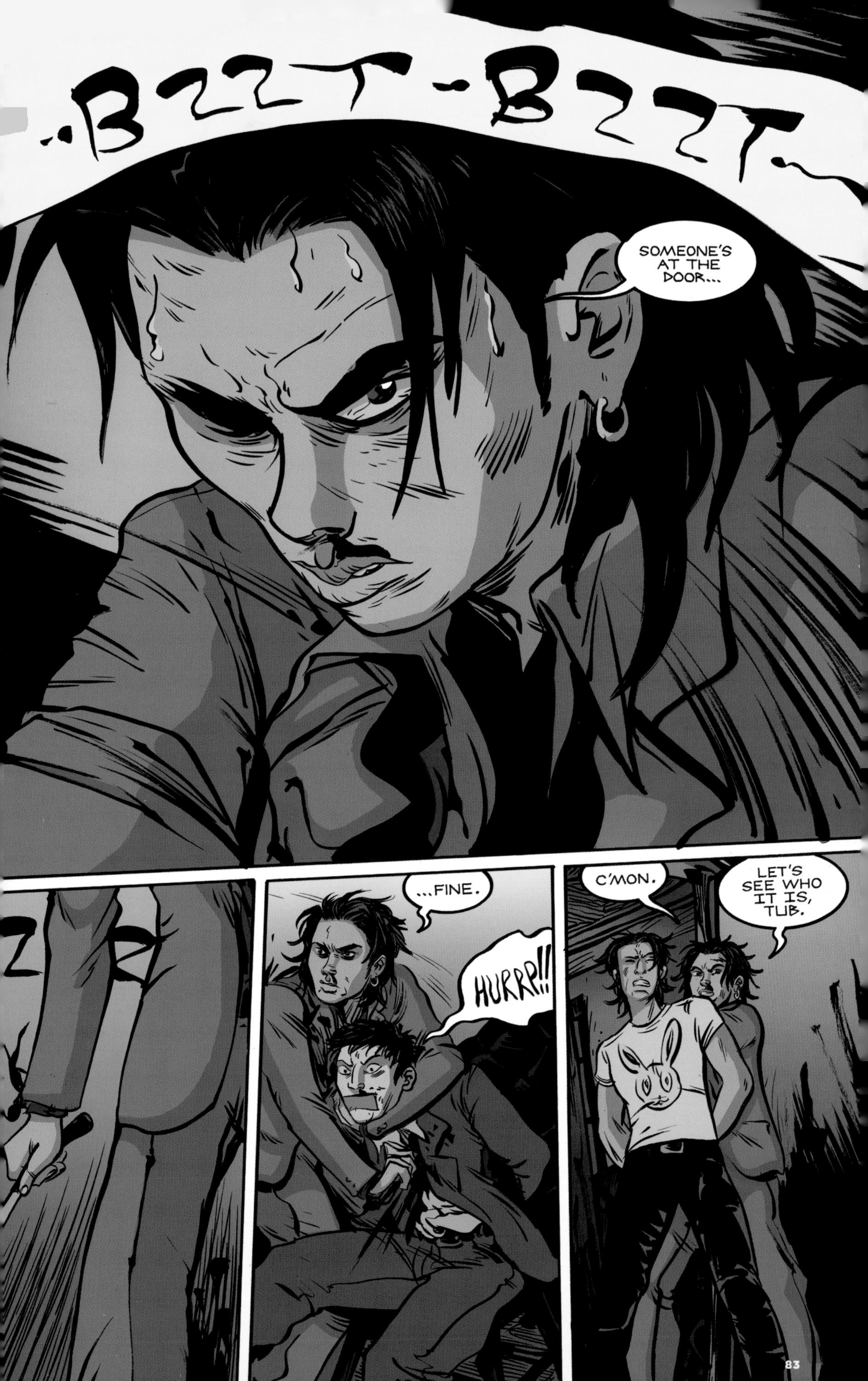
BZZT-BZZT
SOMEONE'S AT THE DOOR...
...FINE.
HURRP!!
C'MON.
LET'S SEE WHO IT IS, TUB.

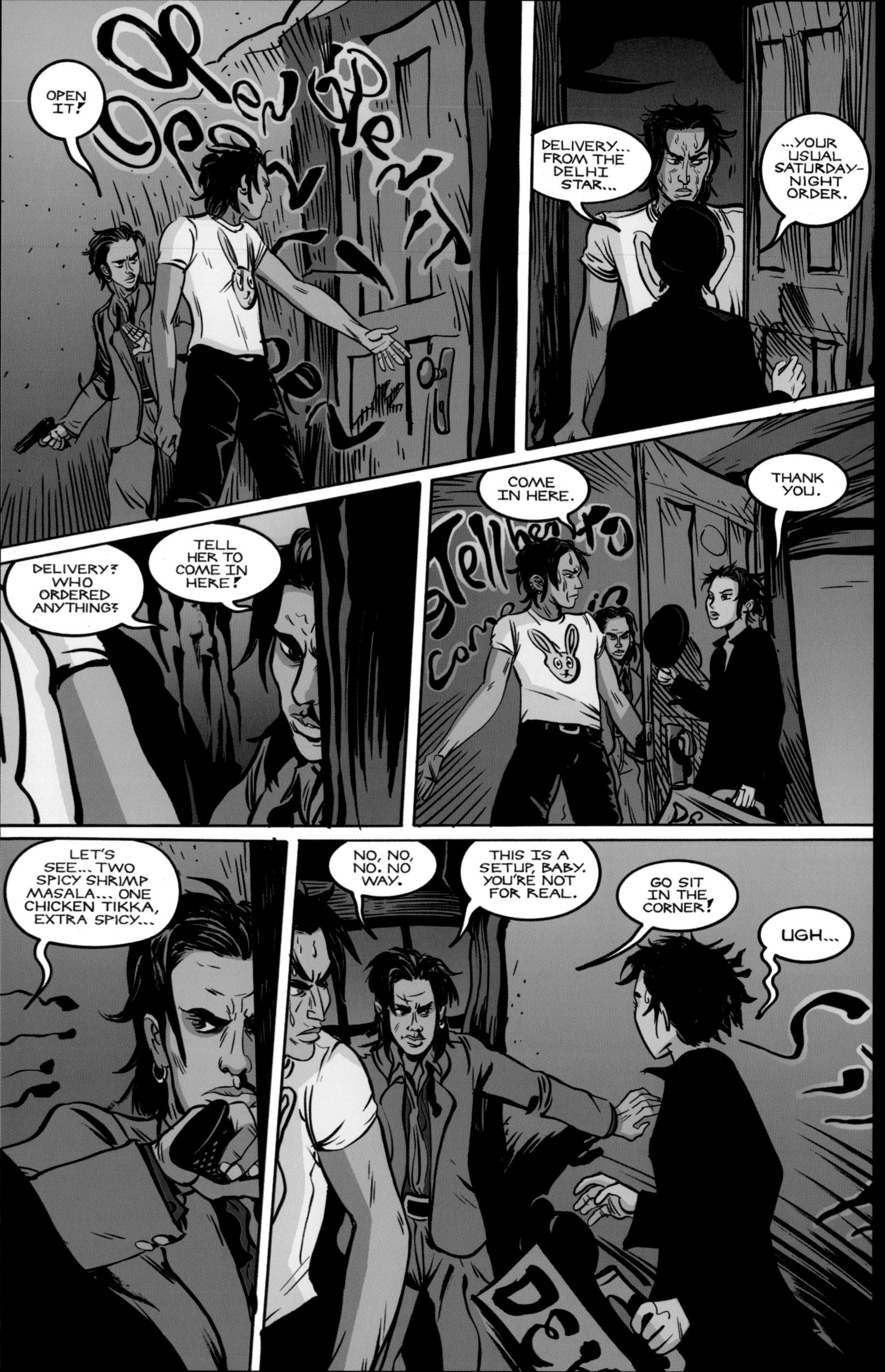
OPEN IT!
DELIVERY... FROM THE DELHI STAR...
...YOUR USUAL SATURDAY-NIGHT ORDER.
DELIVERY? WHO ORDERED ANYTHING?
TELL HER TO COME IN HERE!
COME IN HERE.
THANK YOU.
LET'S SEE... TWO SPICY SHRIMP MASALA... ONE CHICKEN TIKKA, EXTRA SPICY...
NO, NO, NO. NO WAY.
THIS IS A SETUP, BABY. YOU'RE NOT FOR REAL.
GO SIT IN THE CORNER!
UGH...

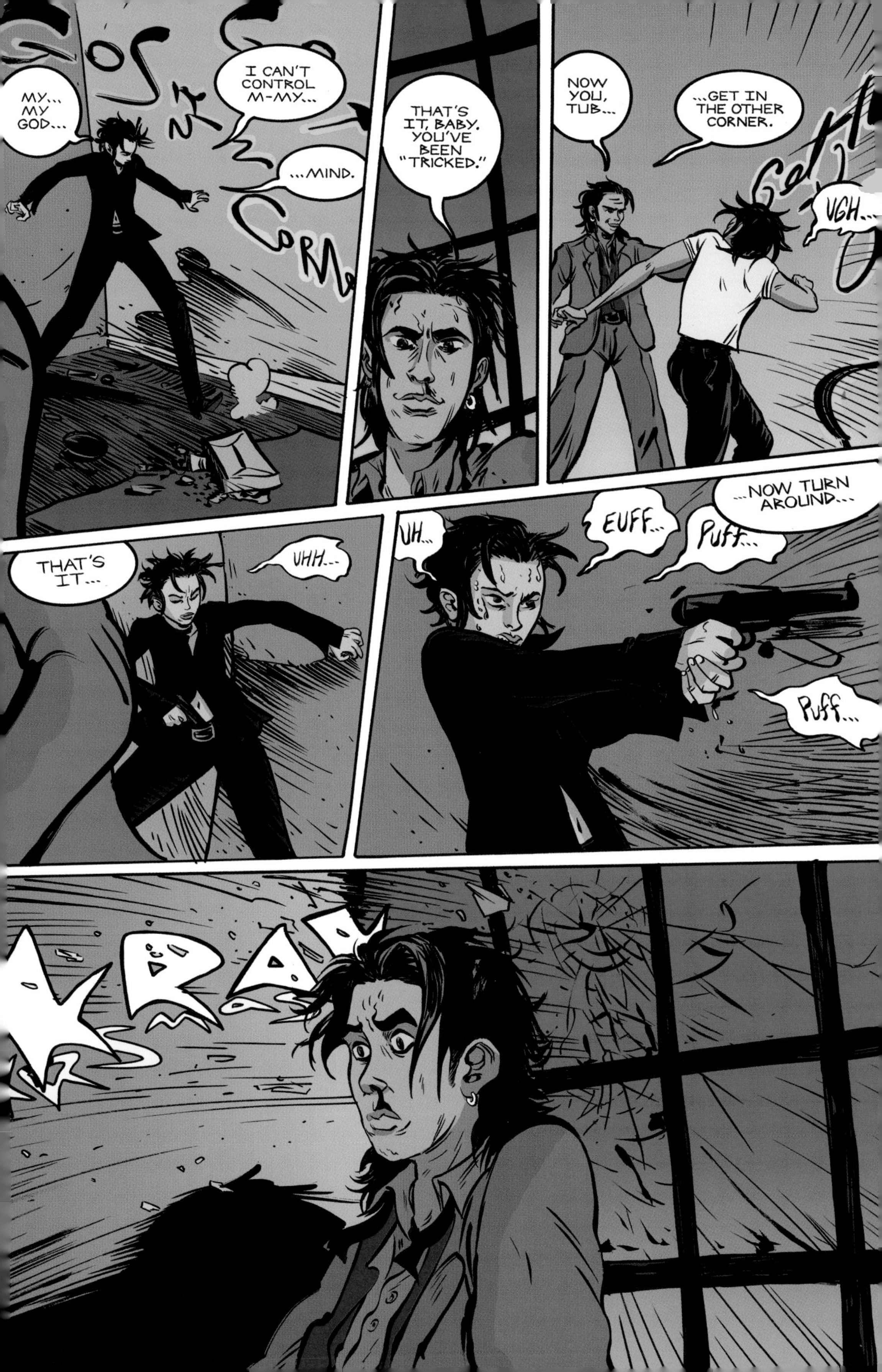
MY... MY GOD...
I CAN'T CONTROL M-MY...
...MIND.
THAT'S IT, BABY. YOU'VE BEEN "TRICKED."
NOW YOU, TUB...
...GET IN THE OTHER CORNER.
UGH...
THAT'S IT...
UHH...
UH...
EUFF...
PUFF...
...NOW TURN AROUND...
PUFF...

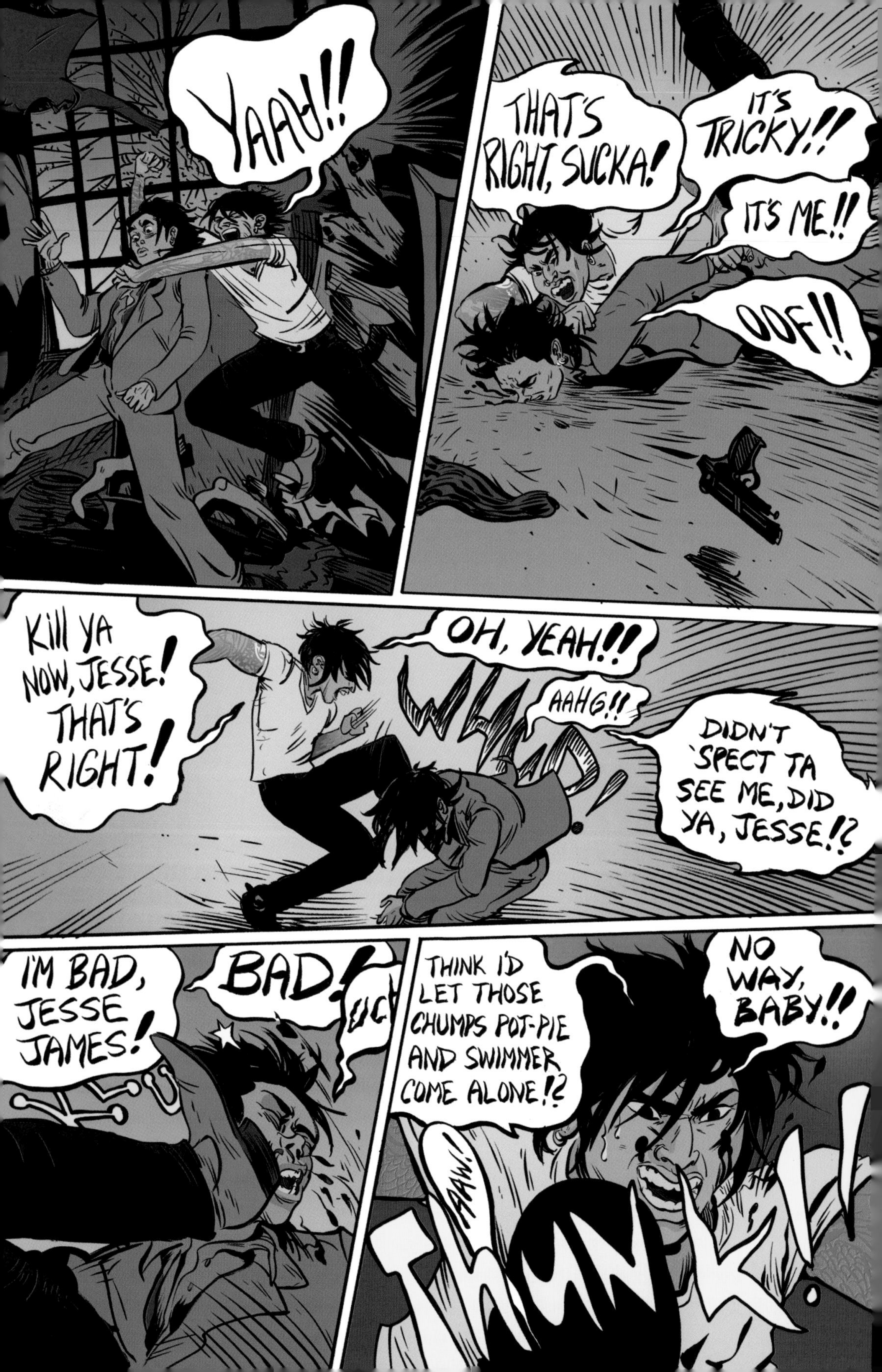
YAAAU!!
THAT'S RIGHT, SUCKA!
IT'S TRICKY!!
IT'S ME!!
OOF!!
Kill YA NOW, JESSE! THAT'S RIGHT!
OH, YEAH!!
WHAMP!
AAHG!!
DIDN'T 'SPECT TA SEE ME, DID YA, JESSE!?
I'M BAD, JESSE JAMES!
BAD!
THINK I'D LET THOSE CHUMPS POT-PIE AND SWIMMER COME ALONE!?
NO WAY, BABY!!
RAW!
THUNK!

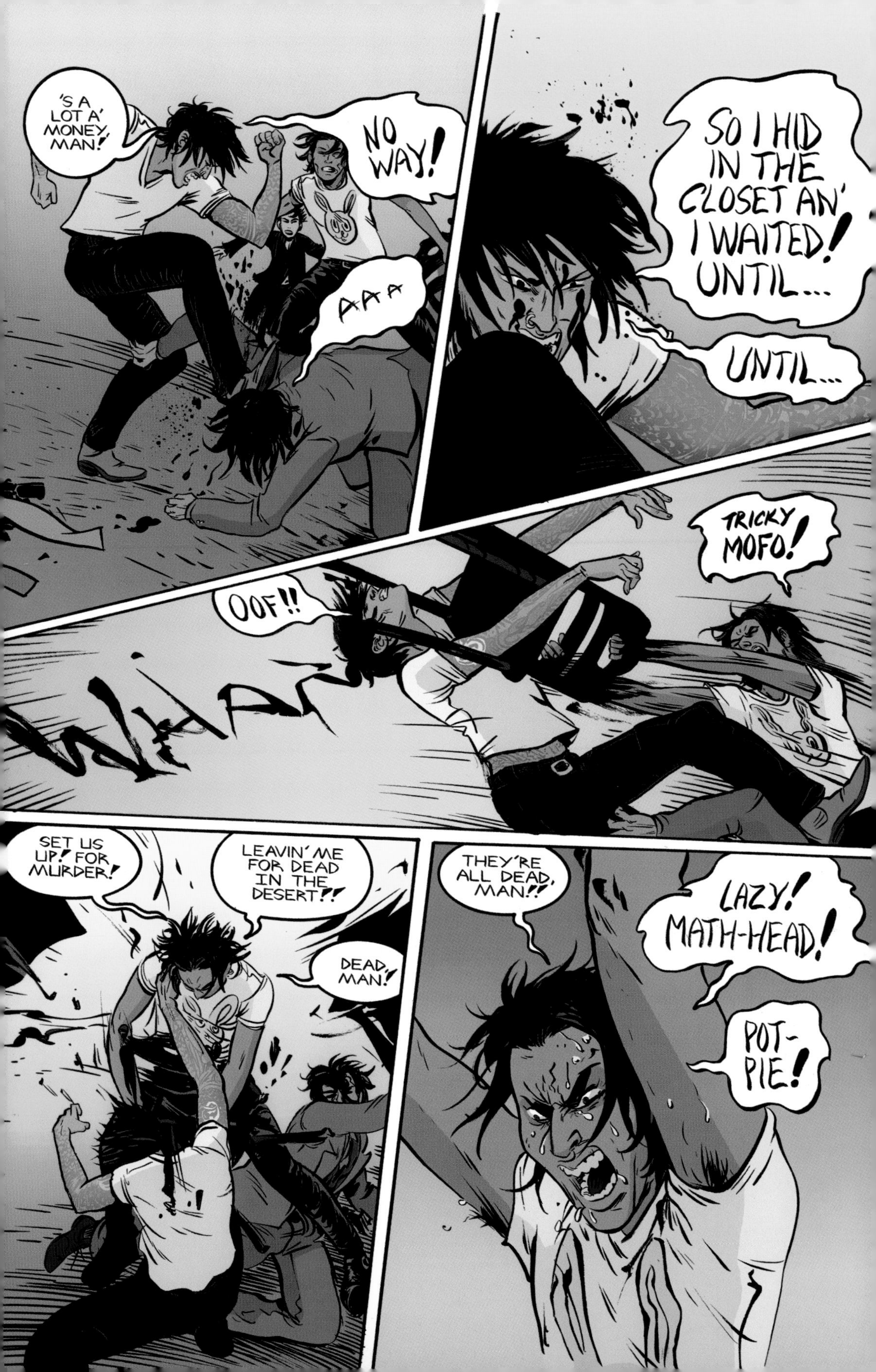
'S A LOT A' MONEY, MAN!
NO WAY!
AAA
SO I HID IN THE CLOSET AN' I WAITED! UNTIL...
UNTIL...
OOF!!
TRICKY MOFO!
WHAP
SET US UP! FOR MURDER!
LEAVIN' ME FOR DEAD IN THE DESERT!!
DEAD, MAN!
THEY'RE ALL DEAD, MAN!!
LAZY! MATH-HEAD!
POT-PIE!

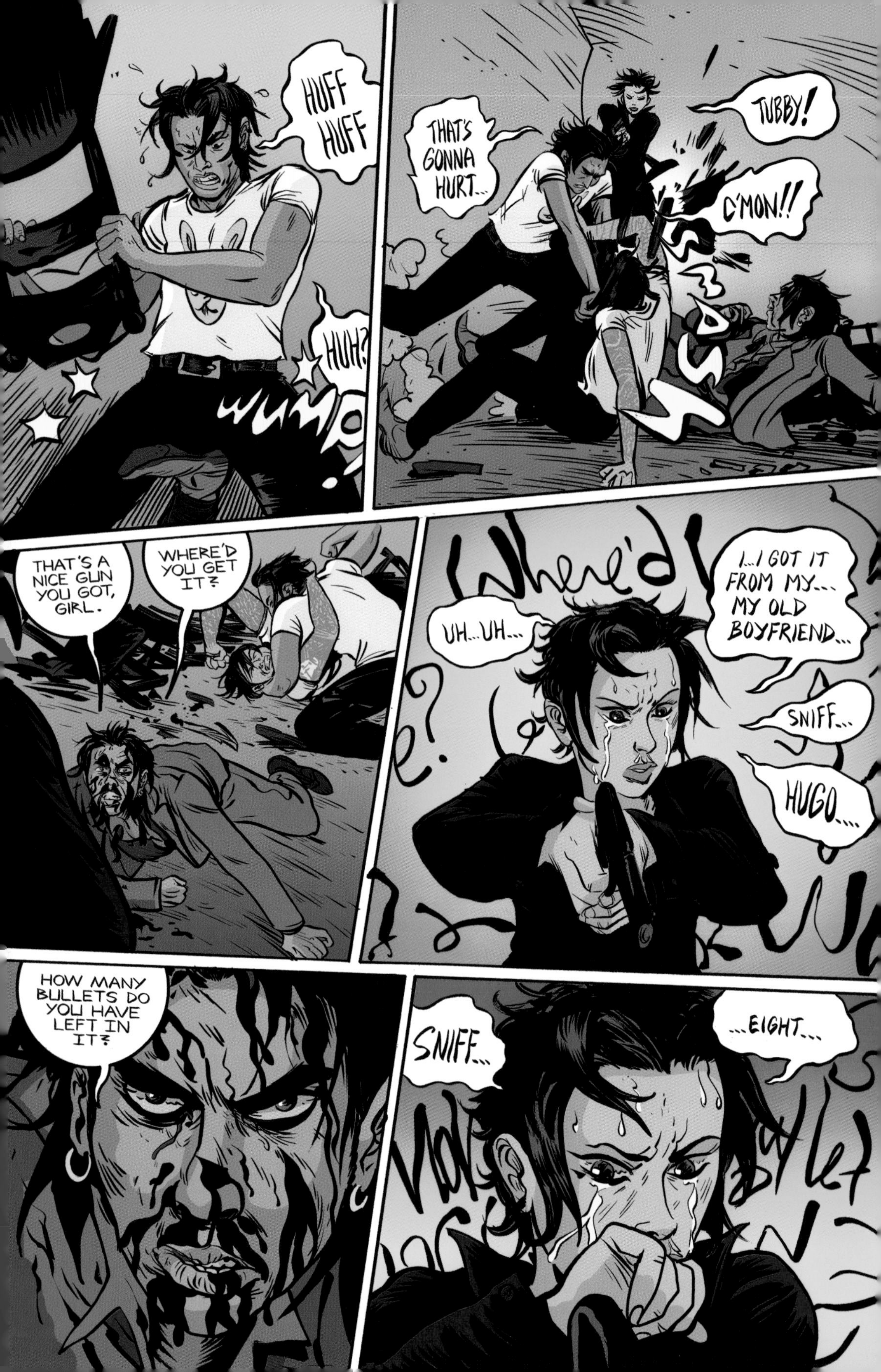
HUFF HUFF
HUH?
WUMP!
THAT'S GONNA HURT...
TUBBY!
C'MON!!
THAT'S A NICE GUN YOU GOT, GIRL.
WHERE'D YOU GET IT?
UH...UH...
I...I GOT IT FROM MY... MY OLD BOYFRIEND...
SNIFF...
HUGO....
HOW MANY BULLETS DO YOU HAVE LEFT IN IT?
SNIFF...
...EIGHT...

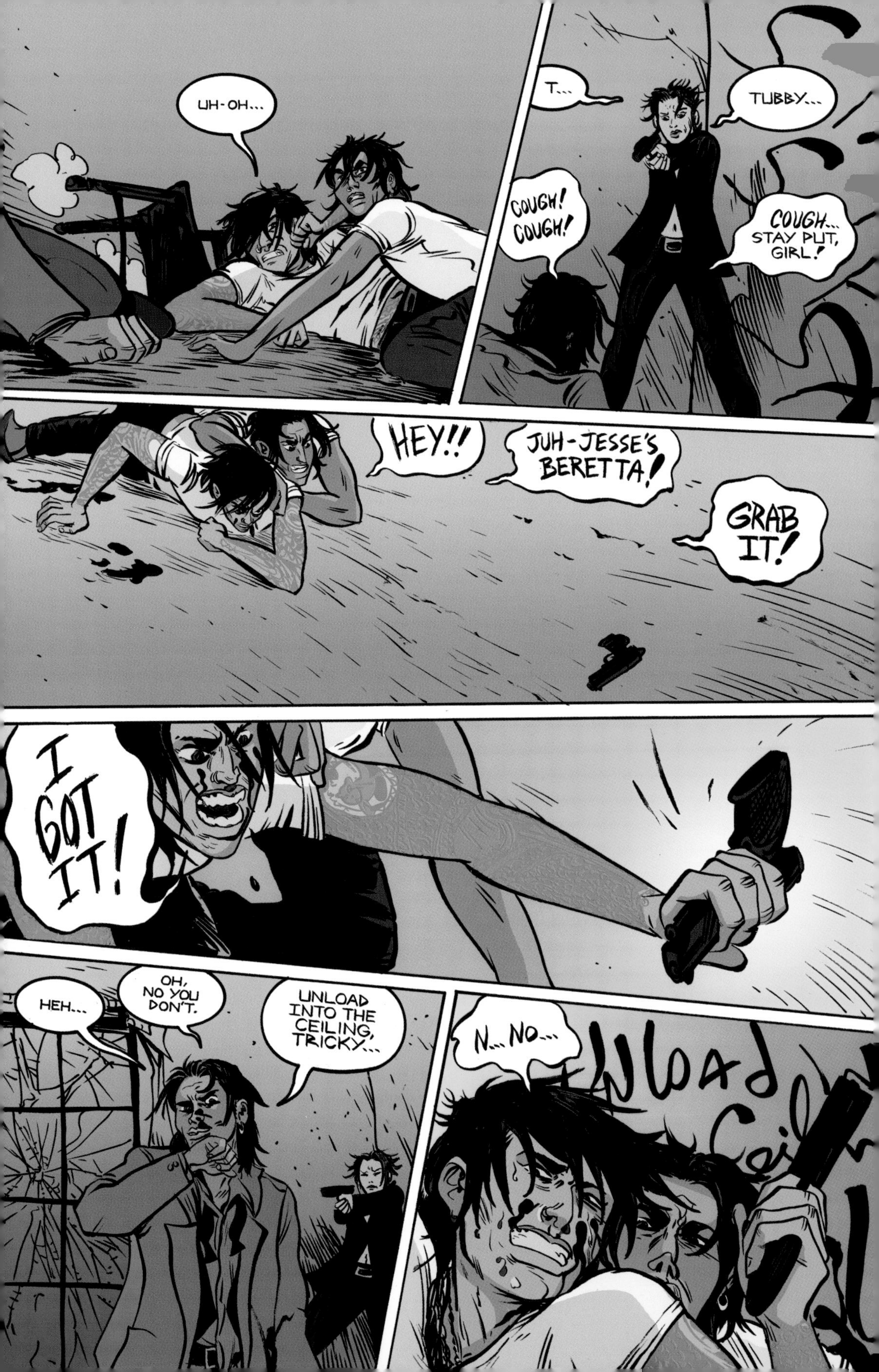
UH-OH...
T...
TUBBY...
COUGH! COUGH!
COUGH... STAY PUT, GIRL!
HEY!!
JUH-JESSE'S BERETTA!
GRAB IT!
I GOT IT!
HEH...
OH, NO YOU DON'T.
UNLOAD INTO THE CEILING, TRICKY...
N... NO...
Unload

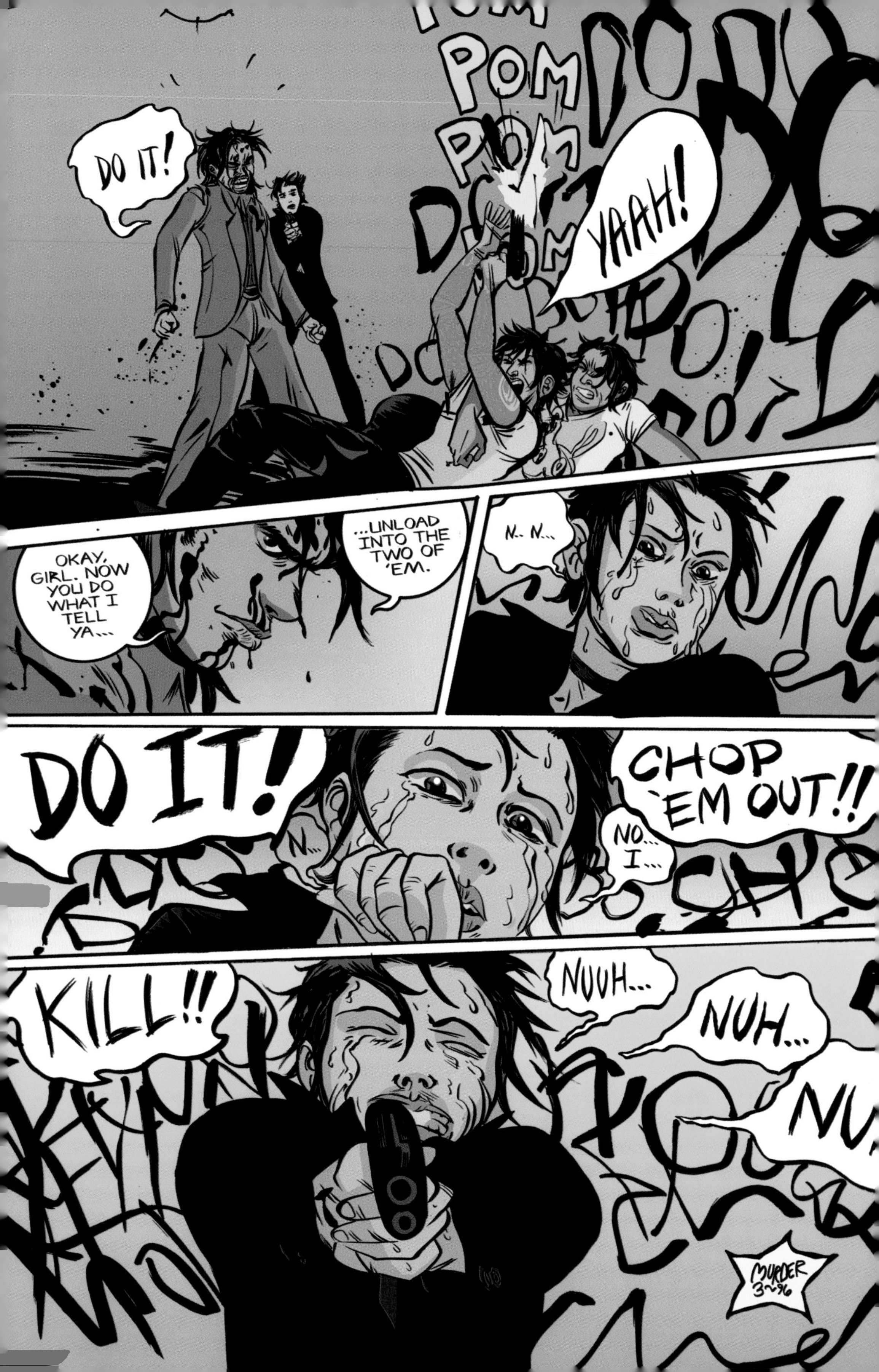
POM
POM
DO IT!
YAAH!
OKAY, GIRL. NOW YOU DO WHAT I TELL YA...
...UNLOAD INTO THE TWO OF 'EM.
N.. N...
DO IT!
N...
CHOP 'EM OUT!!
NO... I...
KILL!!
NUUH...
NUH...
MURDER 3~96

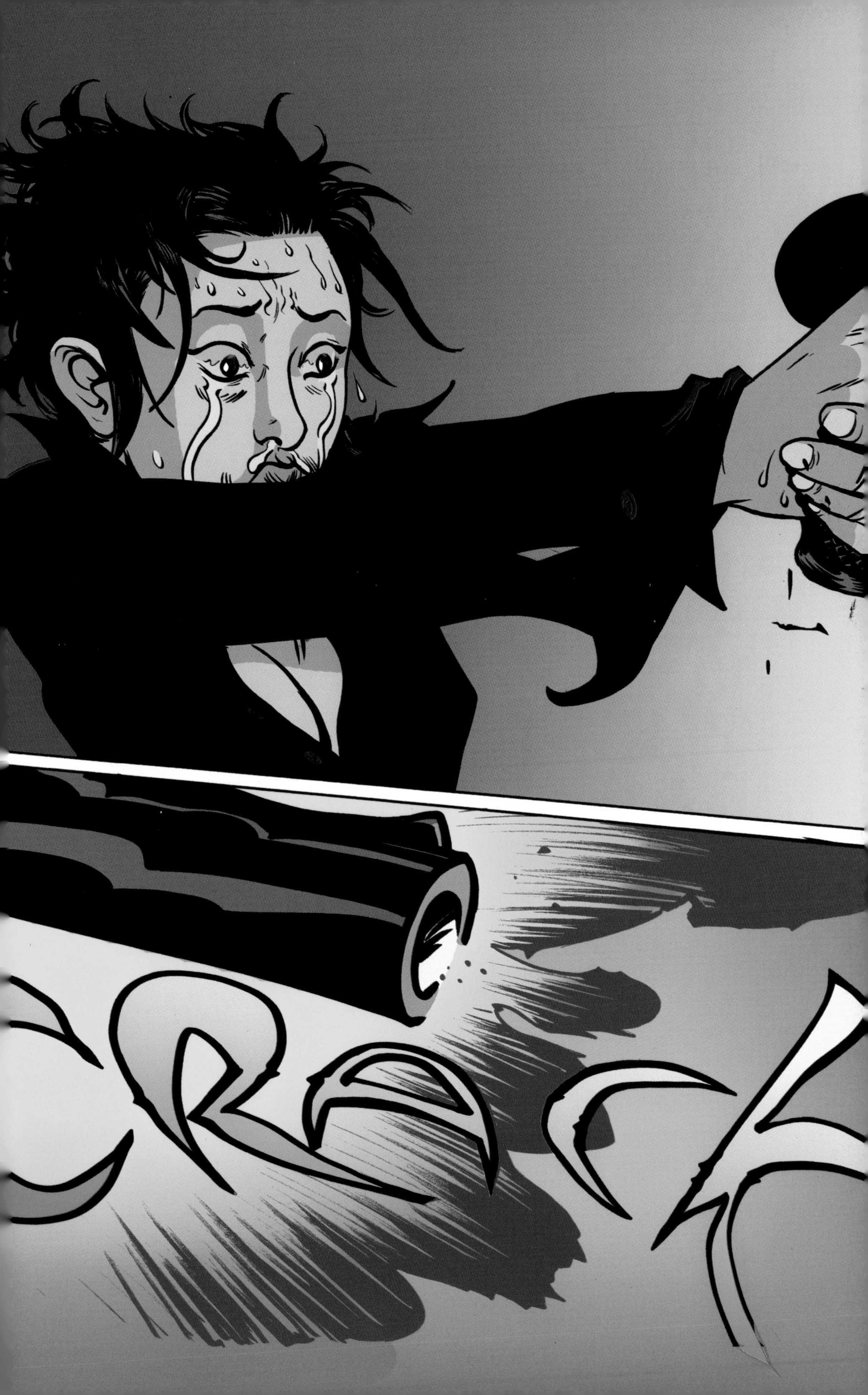
CRACK

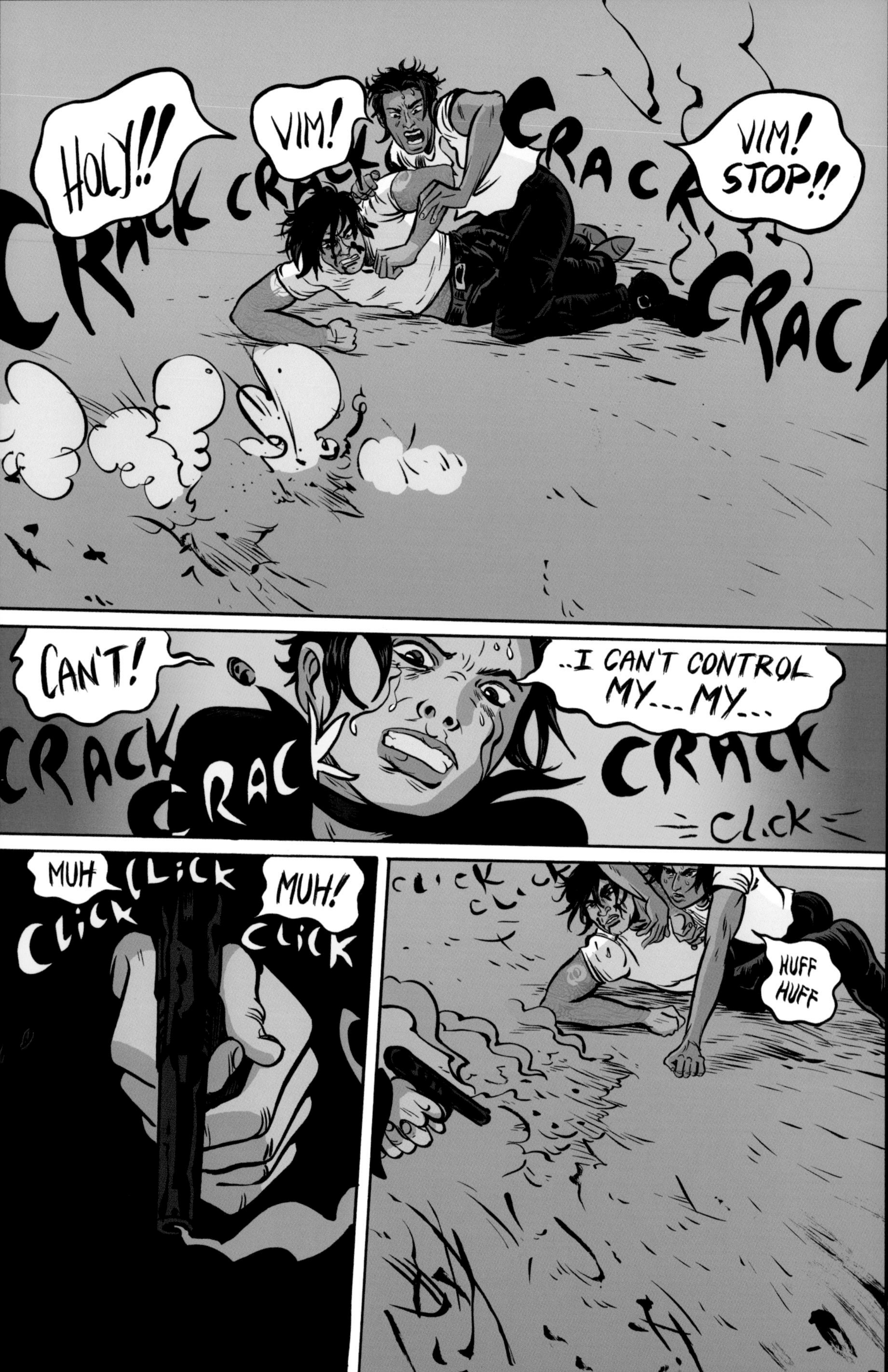
HOLY!!
VIM!
CRACK CRACK
CRACK
VIM! STOP!!
CRACK
CAN'T!
..I CAN'T CONTROL MY... MY...
CRACK CRACK
CRACK
CLICK
MUH
CLICK CLICK
MUH!
CLICK
CLICK CLICK
HUFF HUFF

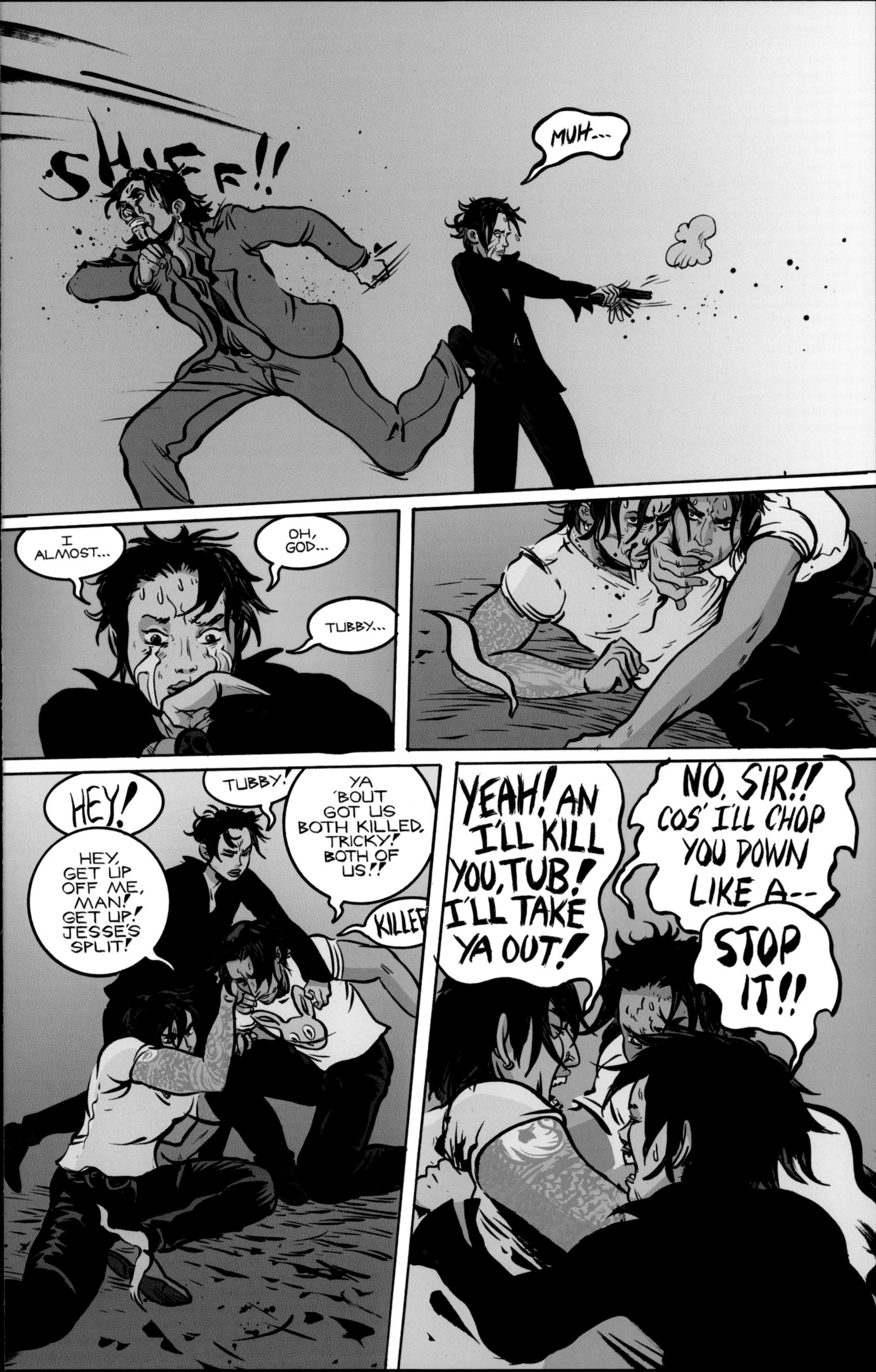
SHIFF!!
MUH...
I ALMOST...
OH, GOD...
TUBBY...
HEY!
TUBBY!
YA 'BOUT GOT US BOTH KILLED, TRICKY! BOTH OF US!!
HEY, GET UP OFF ME, MAN! GET UP! JESSE'S SPLIT!
KILLER
YEAH! AN I'LL KILL YOU, TUB! I'LL TAKE YA OUT!
NO, SIR!! COS' I'LL CHOP YOU DOWN LIKE A--
STOP IT!!

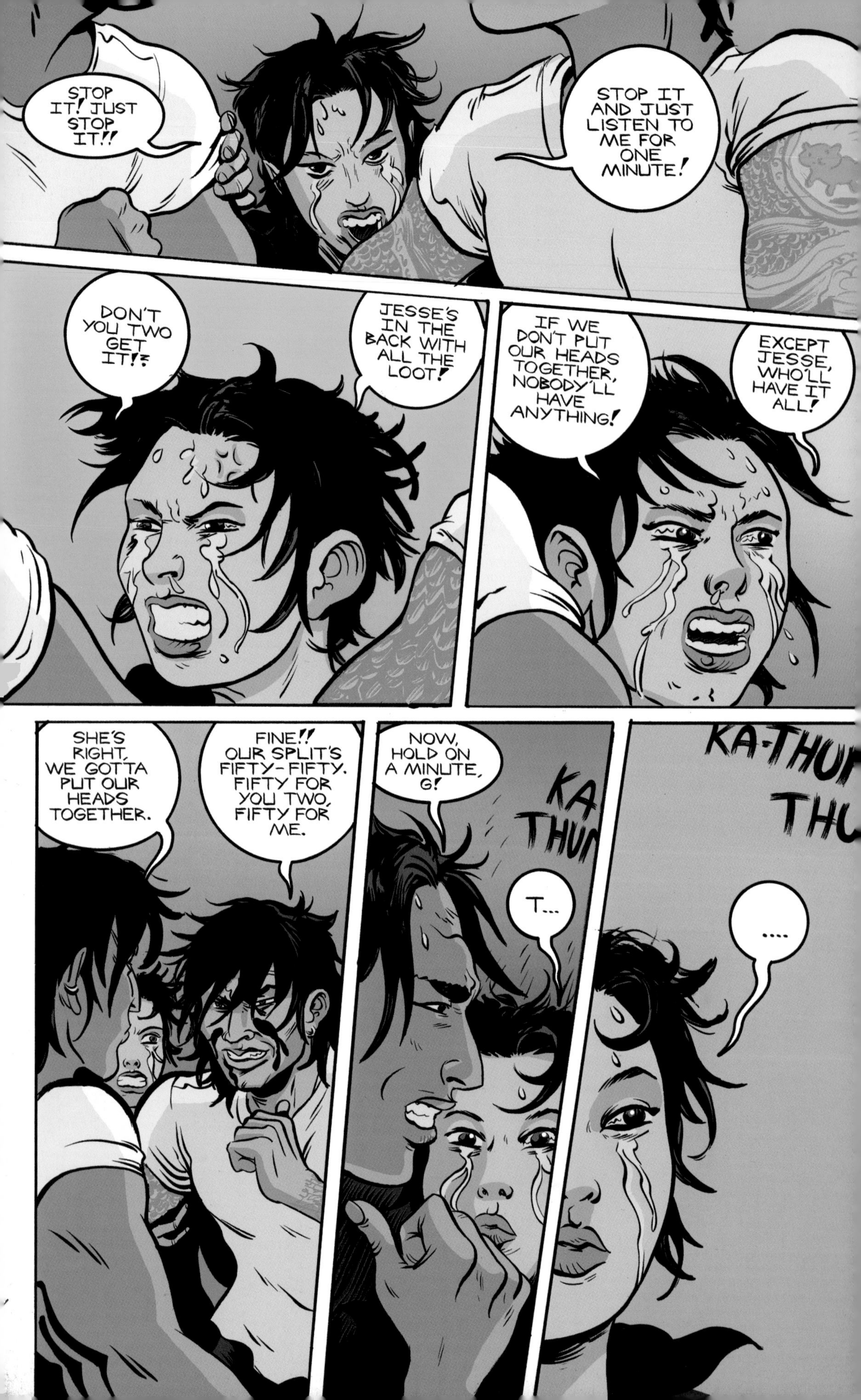
STOP IT! JUST STOP IT!!
STOP IT AND JUST LISTEN TO ME FOR ONE MINUTE!
DON'T YOU TWO GET IT!?
JESSE'S IN THE BACK WITH ALL THE LOOT!
IF WE DON'T PUT OUR HEADS TOGETHER, NOBODY'LL HAVE ANYTHING!
EXCEPT JESSE, WHO'LL HAVE IT ALL!
SHE'S RIGHT. WE GOTTA PUT OUR HEADS TOGETHER.
FINE!! OUR SPLIT'S FIFTY-FIFTY. FIFTY FOR YOU TWO, FIFTY FOR ME.
NOW, HOLD ON A MINUTE, G!
KA THUM
T...
KA-THUM
THU
....

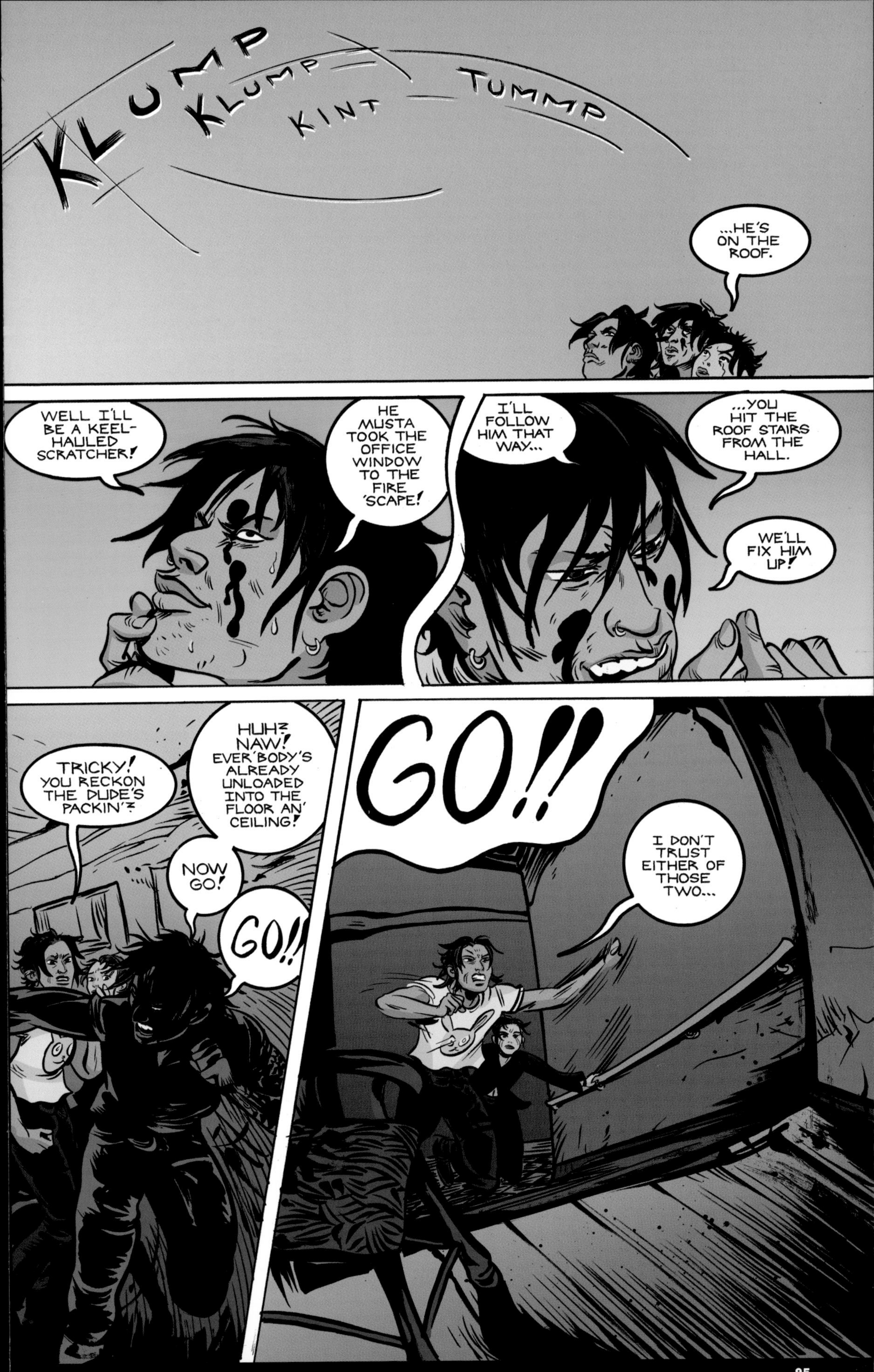
KLUMP KLUMP KINT TUMMP
...HE'S ON THE ROOF.
WELL I'LL BE A KEEL-HAULED SCRATCHER!
HE MUSTA TOOK THE OFFICE WINDOW TO THE FIRE 'SCAPE!
I'LL FOLLOW HIM THAT WAY...
...YOU HIT THE ROOF STAIRS FROM THE HALL.
WE'LL FIX HIM UP!
TRICKY! YOU RECKON THE DUDE'S PACKIN'?
HUH? NAW! EVER'BODY'S ALREADY UNLOADED INTO THE FLOOR AN' CEILING!
NOW GO!
GO!!
GO!!
I DON'T TRUST EITHER OF THOSE TWO...

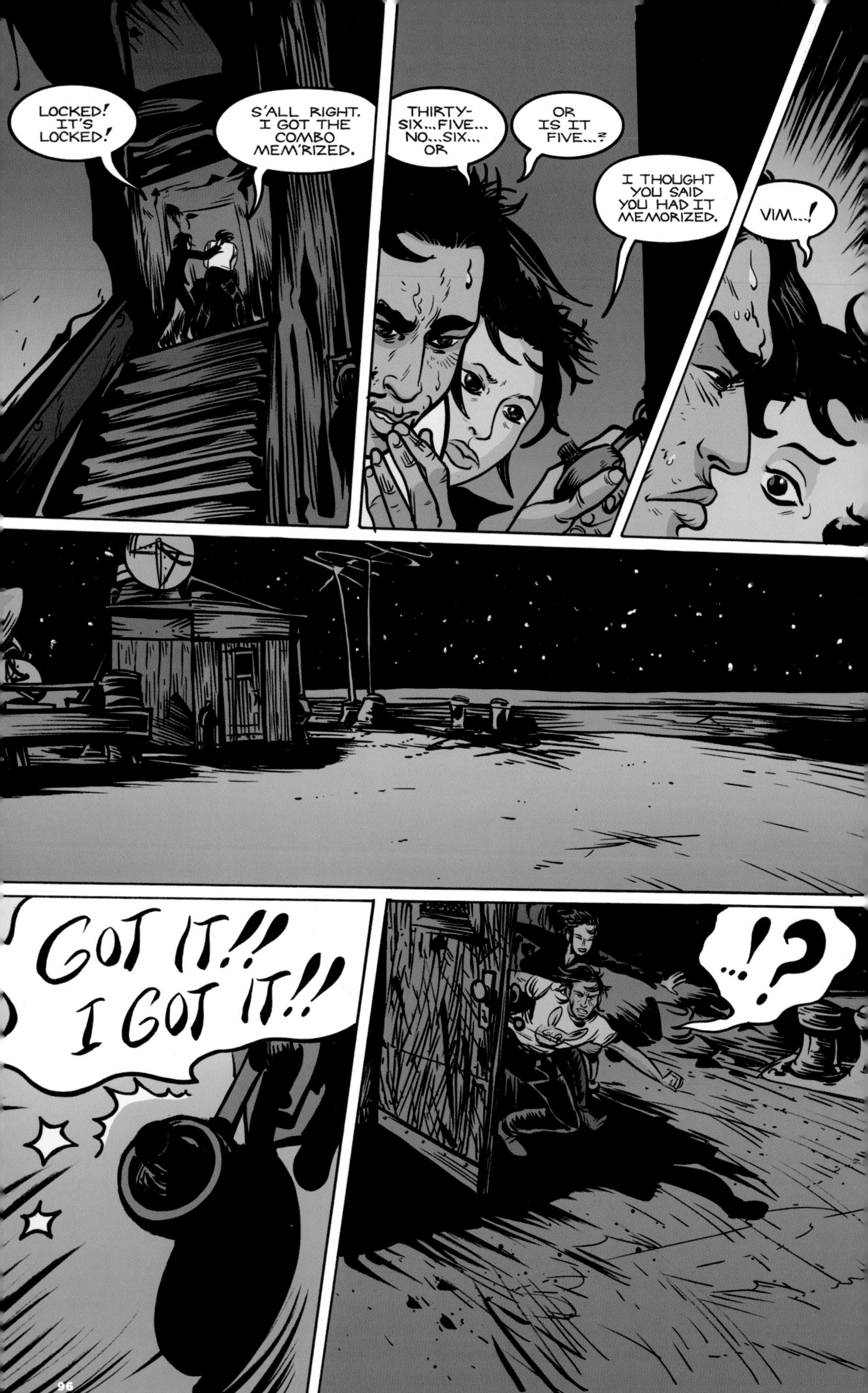
LOCKED! IT'S LOCKED!
S'ALL RIGHT. I GOT THE COMBO MEM'RIZED.
THIRTY-SIX...FIVE... NO...SIX... OR
OR IS IT FIVE...?
I THOUGHT YOU SAID YOU HAD IT MEMORIZED.
VIM...!
GOT IT!! I GOT IT!!
...!?

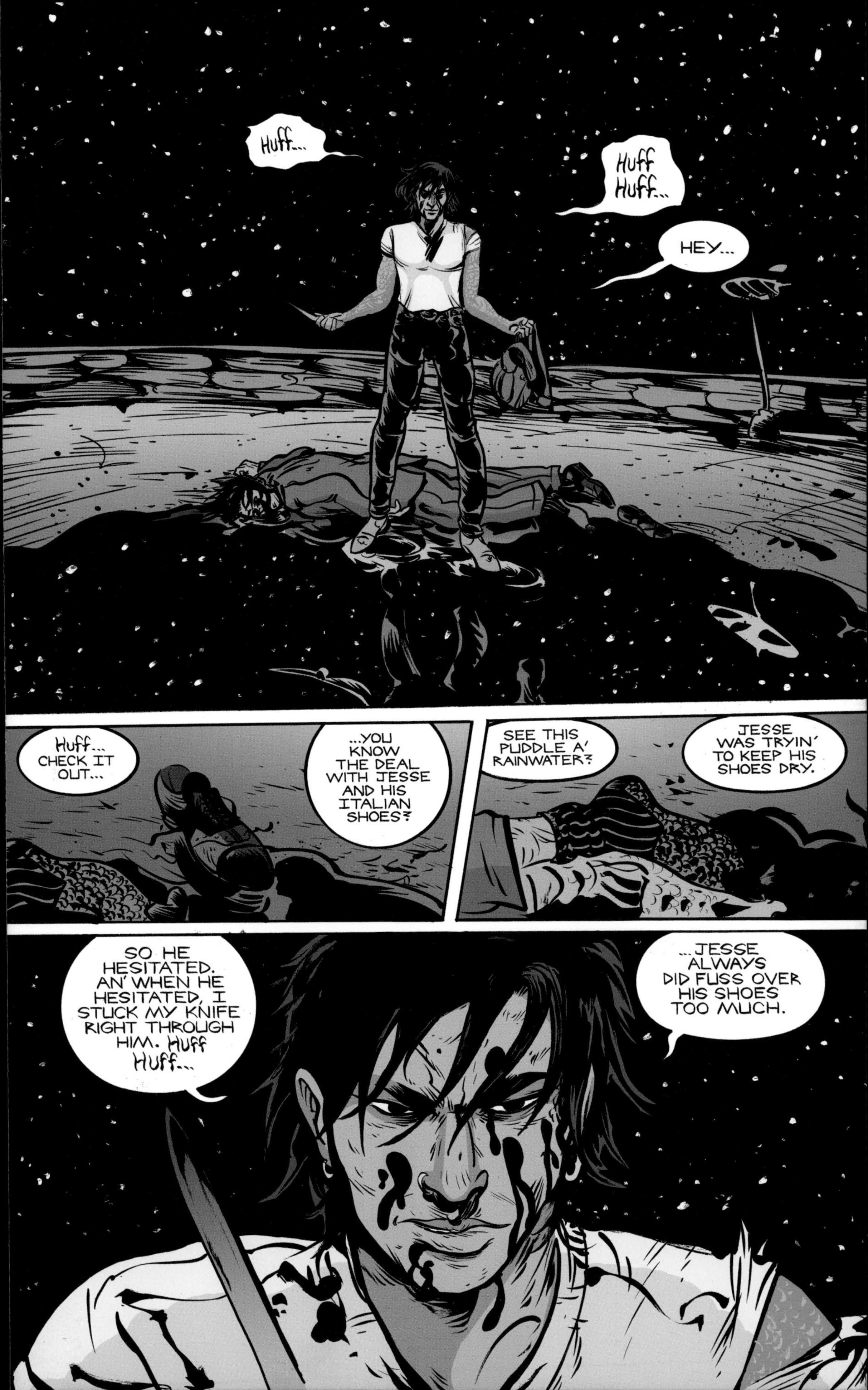
Huff...
Huff Huff...
HEY...
Huff... CHECK IT OUT...
...YOU KNOW THE DEAL WITH JESSE AND HIS ITALIAN SHOES?
SEE THIS PUDDLE A' RAINWATER?
JESSE WAS TRYIN' TO KEEP HIS SHOES DRY.
SO HE HESITATED. AN' WHEN HE HESITATED, I STUCK MY KNIFE RIGHT THROUGH HIM. Huff Huff...
...JESSE ALWAYS DID FUSS OVER HIS SHOES TOO MUCH.

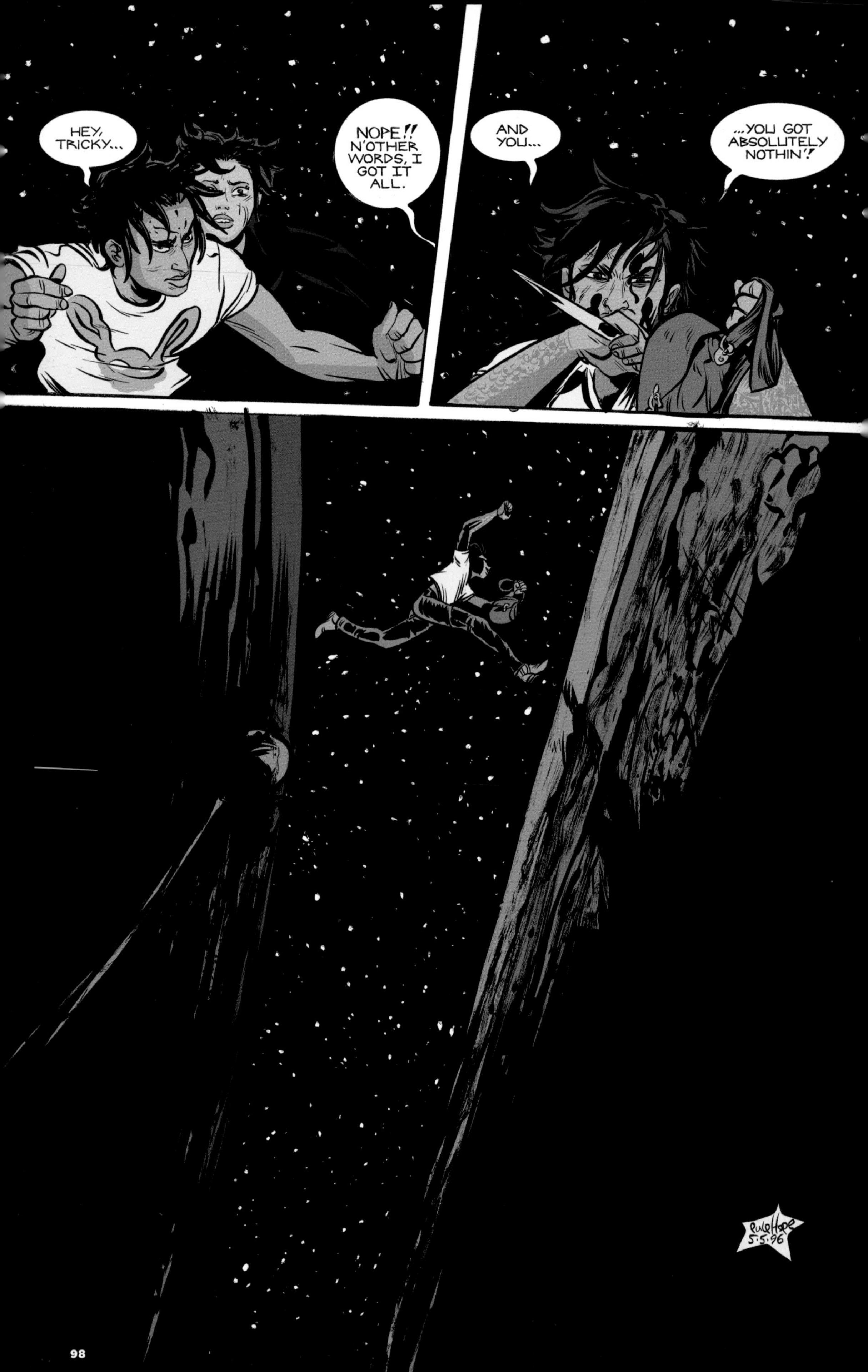
HEY, TRICKY...
NOPE!! N'OTHER WORDS, I GOT IT ALL.
AND YOU...
...YOU GOT ABSOLUTELY NOTHIN'!

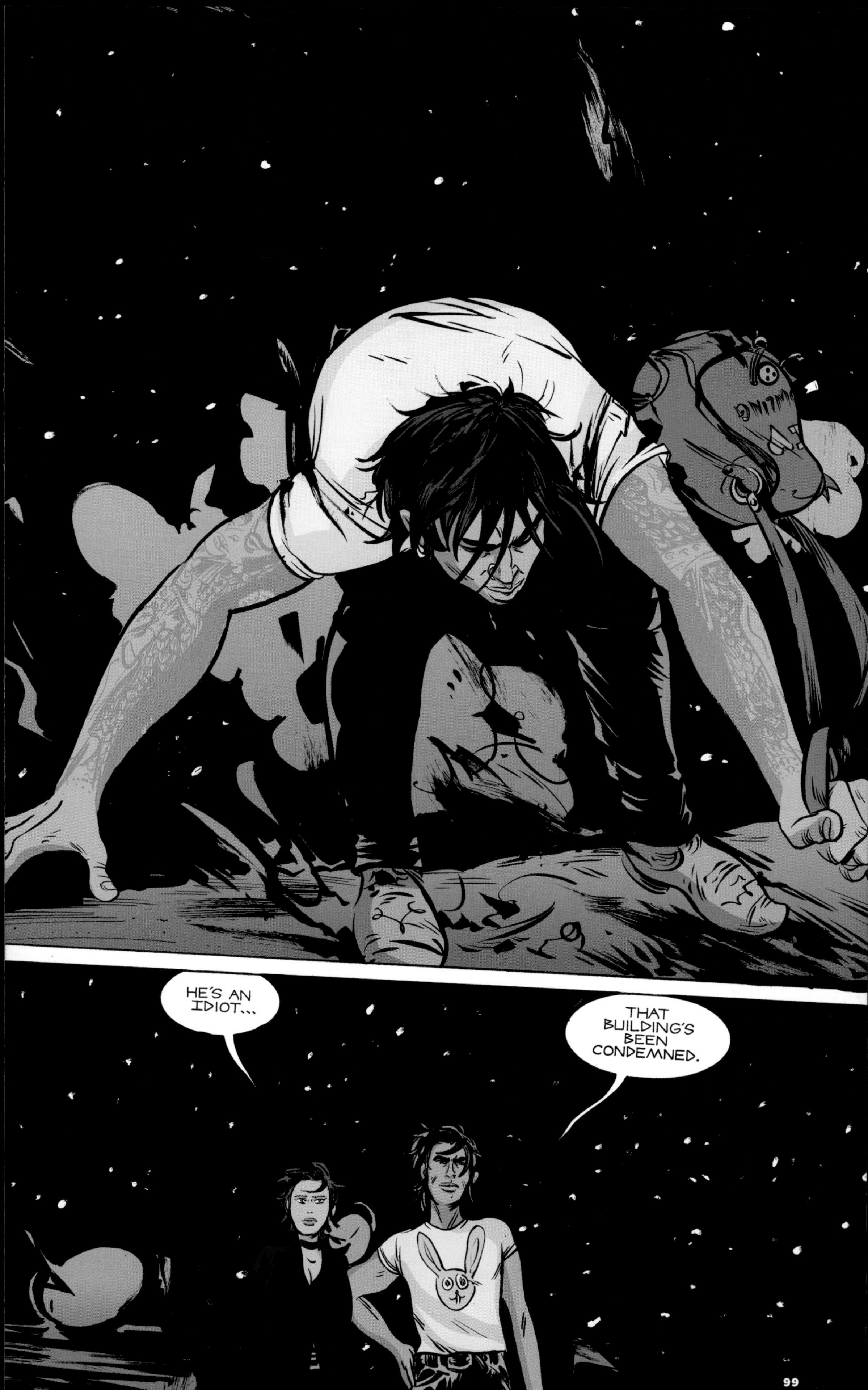
HE'S AN IDIOT...
THAT BUILDING'S BEEN CONDEMNED.

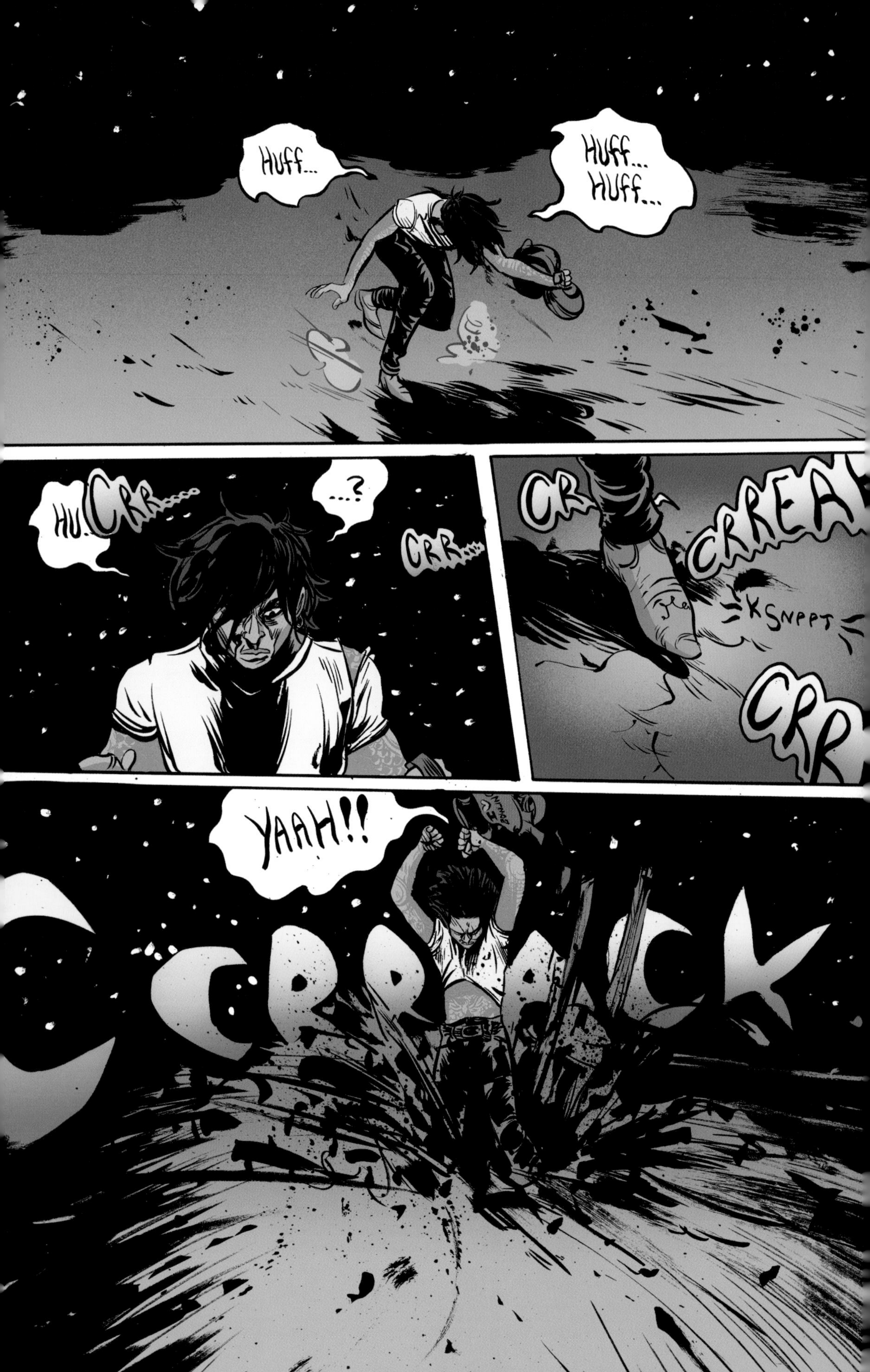
Huff...
Huff... Huff...
Hu..CRR...
...?
CRR...
CR
CRREA
KSNPPT
CRR
YAAH!!
CRRACK

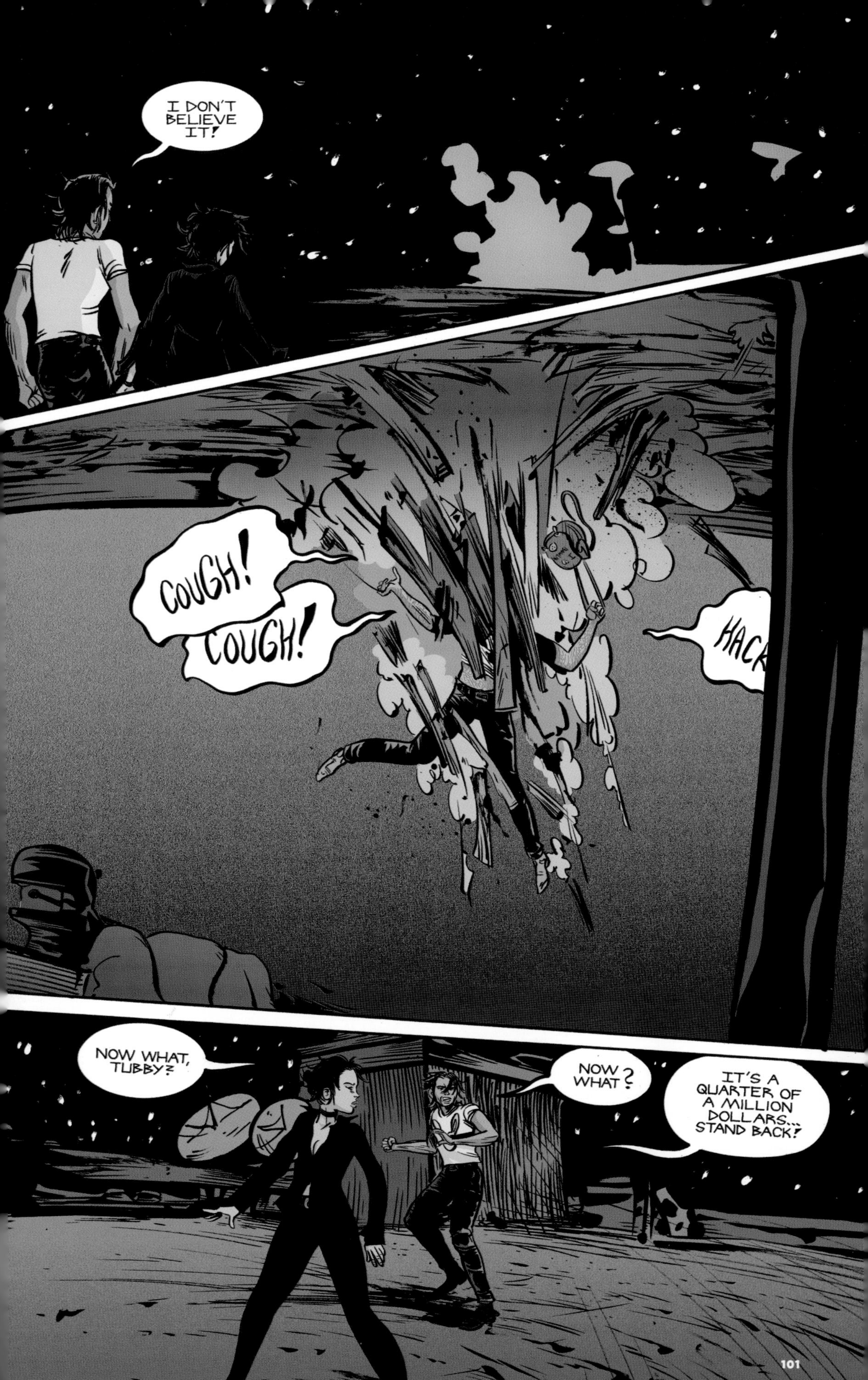
I DON'T BELIEVE IT!
COUGH!
COUGH!
NOW WHAT, TUBBY?
NOW WHAT?
IT'S A QUARTER OF A MILLION DOLLARS... STAND BACK!

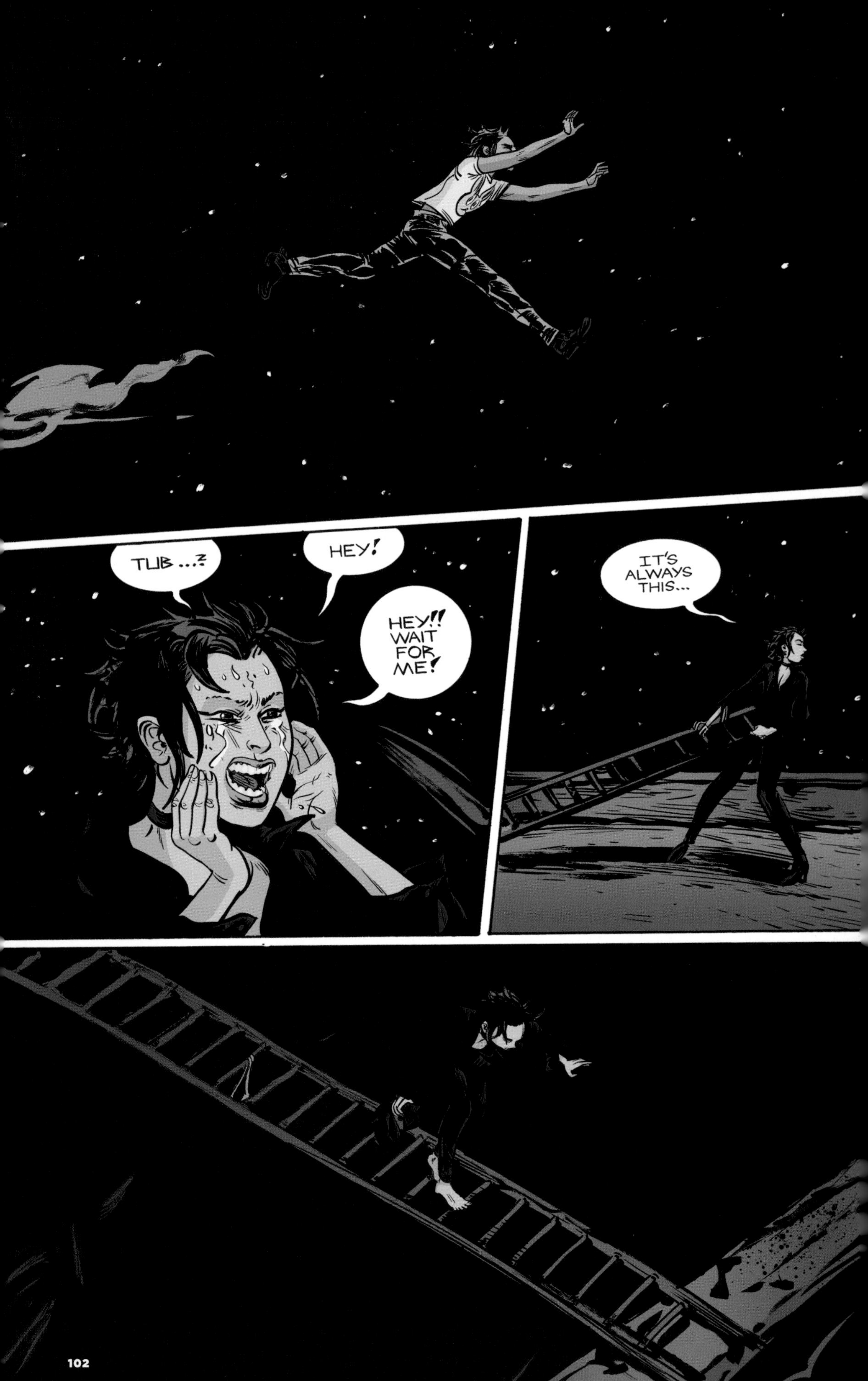
TUB...?
HEY!
HEY!! WAIT FOR ME!
IT'S ALWAYS THIS...

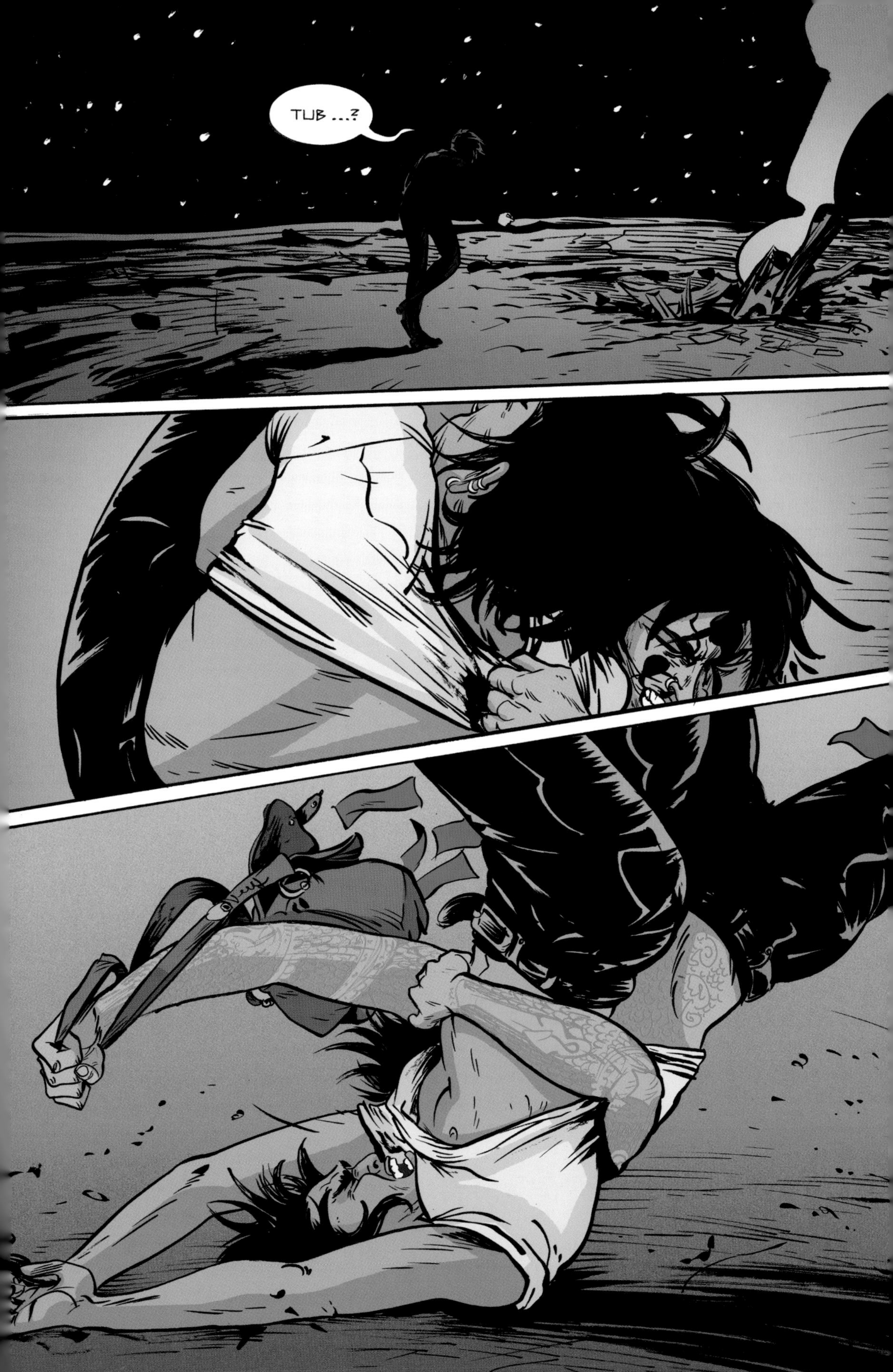
TUB ...?

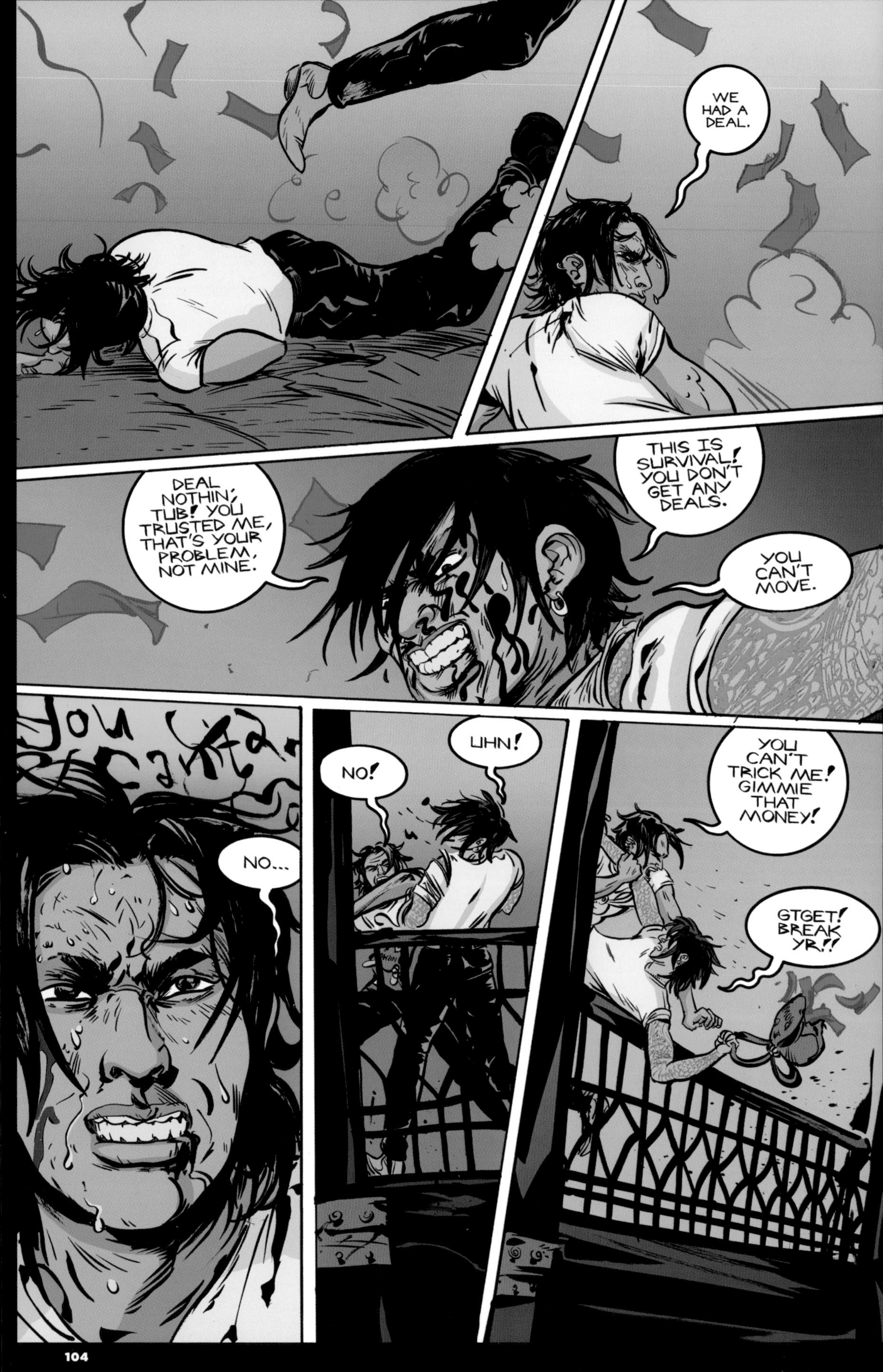

WE HAD A DEAL.
DEAL NOTHIN', TUB! YOU TRUSTED ME, THAT'S YOUR PROBLEM, NOT MINE.
THIS IS SURVIVAL! YOU DON'T GET ANY DEALS.
YOU CAN'T MOVE.
NO...
NO!
UHN!
YOU CAN'T TRICK ME! GIMMIE THAT MONEY!
GTGET! BREAK YR!!

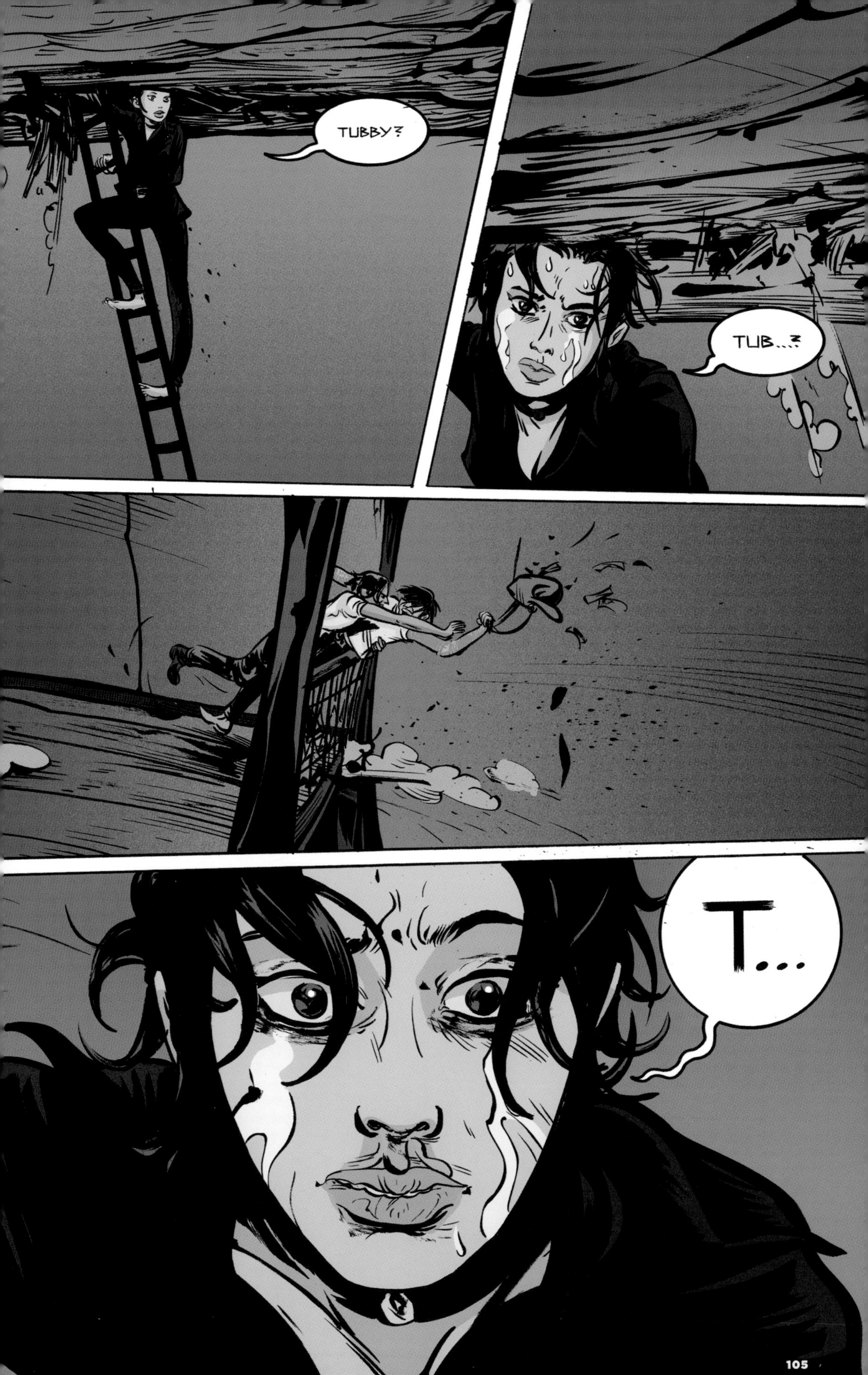
TUBBY?
TUB...?
T...

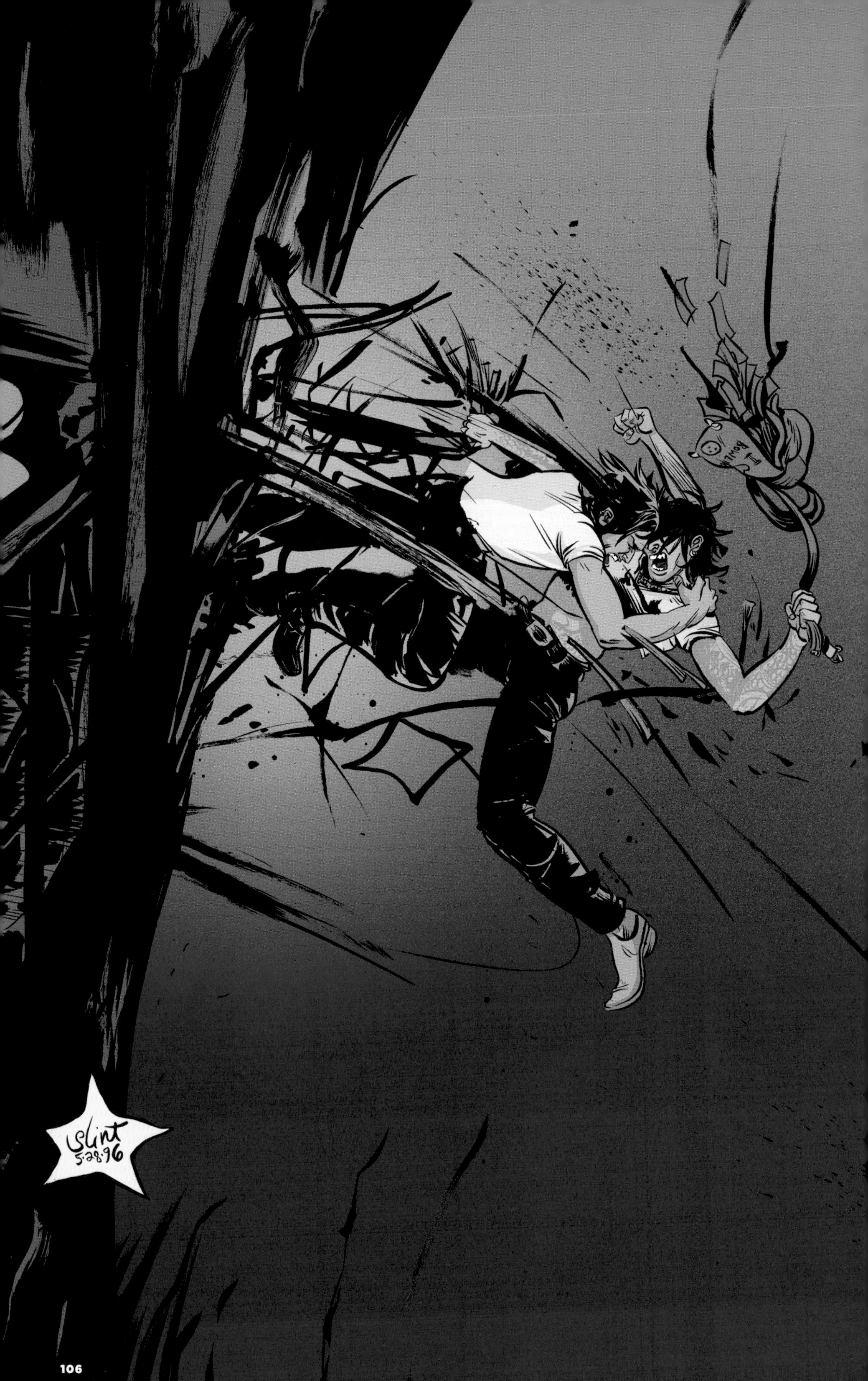
Clint
5·28·96

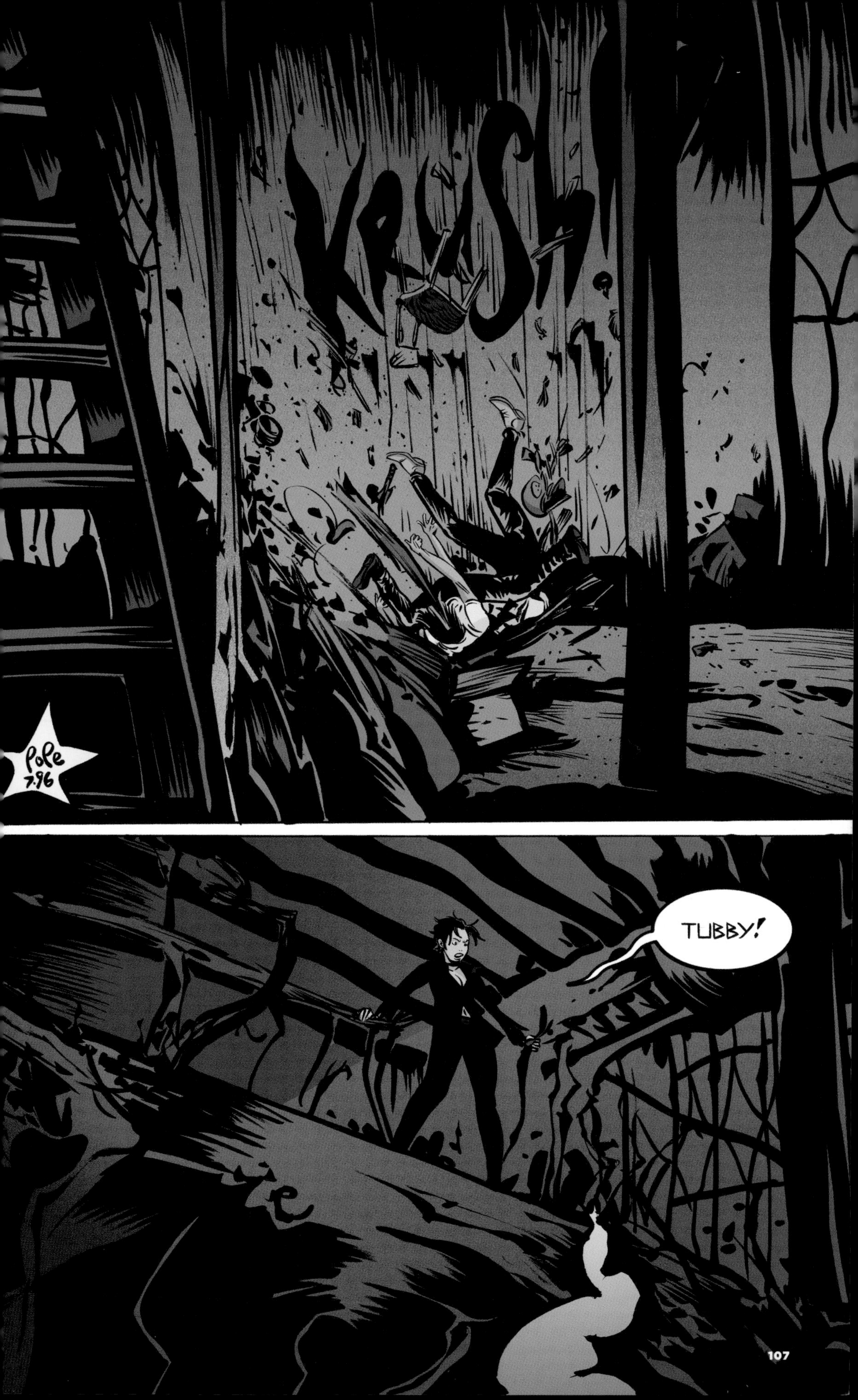
KRUSH
TUBBY!

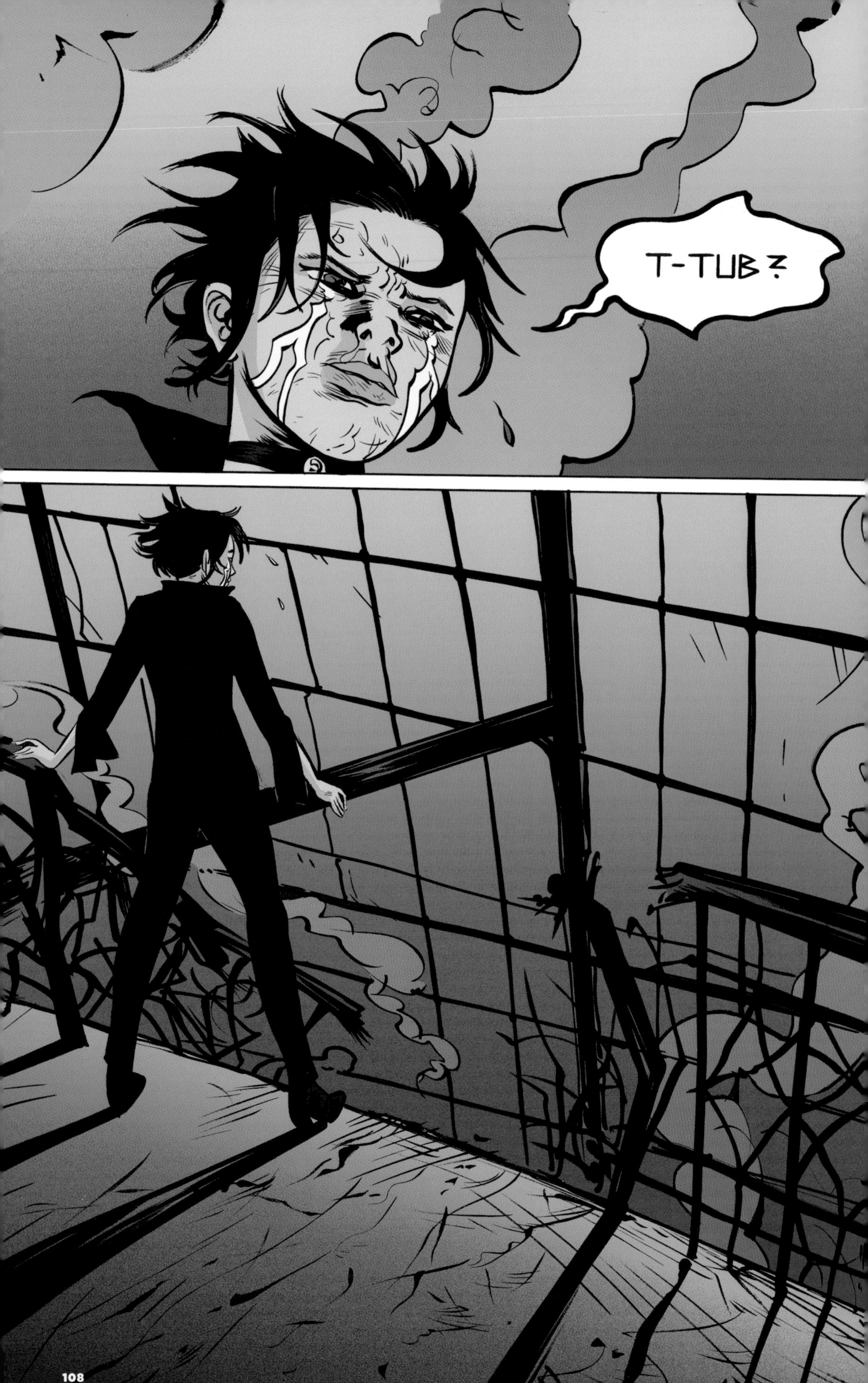
T-TUB?

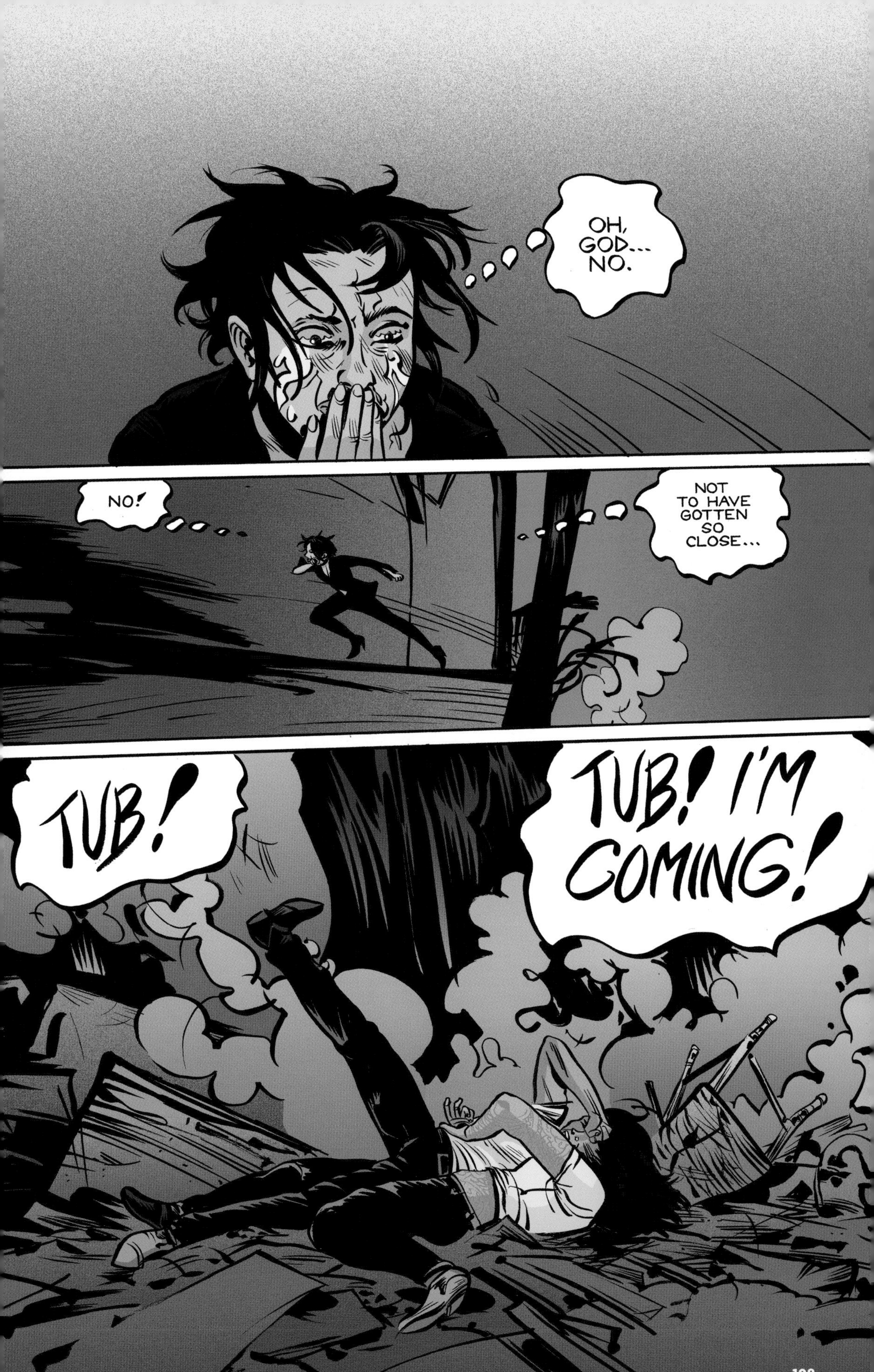
OH, GOD... NO.
NO!
NOT TO HAVE GOTTEN SO CLOSE...
TUB!
TUB! I'M COMING!

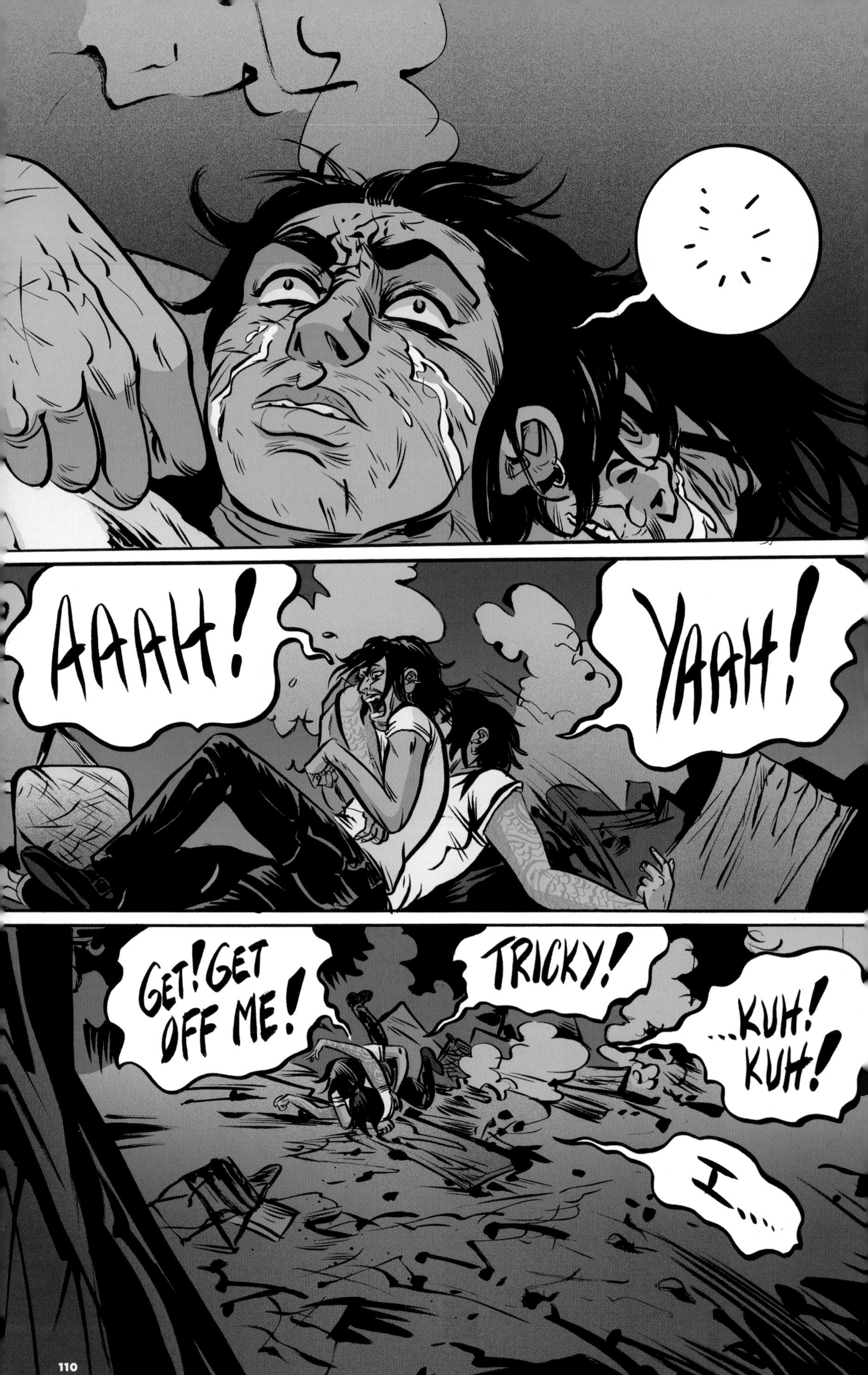
AAAH!
YAAH!
GET! GET OFF ME!
TRICKY!
...KUH! KUH!
I...

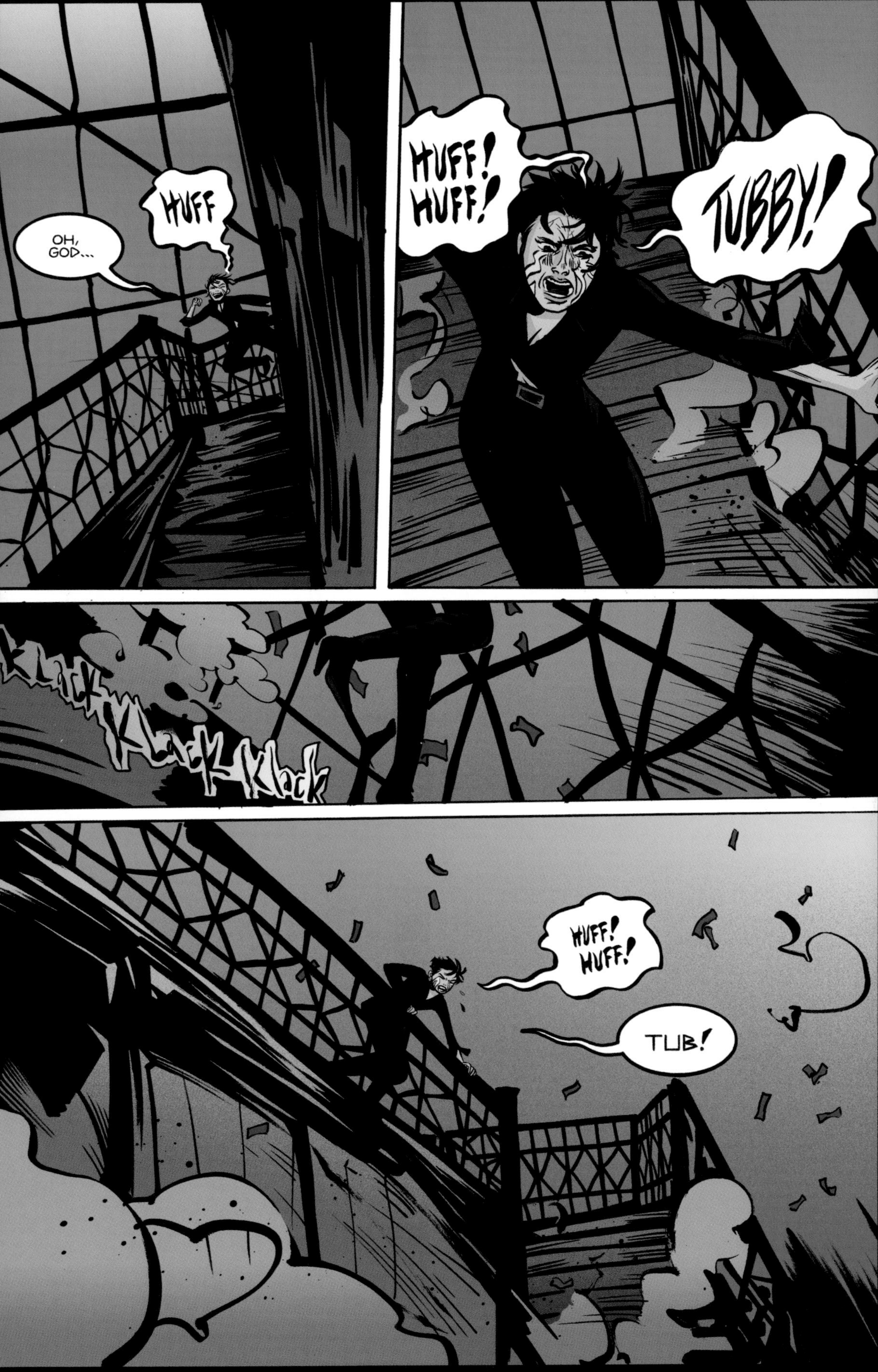
OH, GOD...
HUFF
HUFF! HUFF!
TUBBY!
KLACK KLACK KLACK
HUFF! HUFF!
TUB!

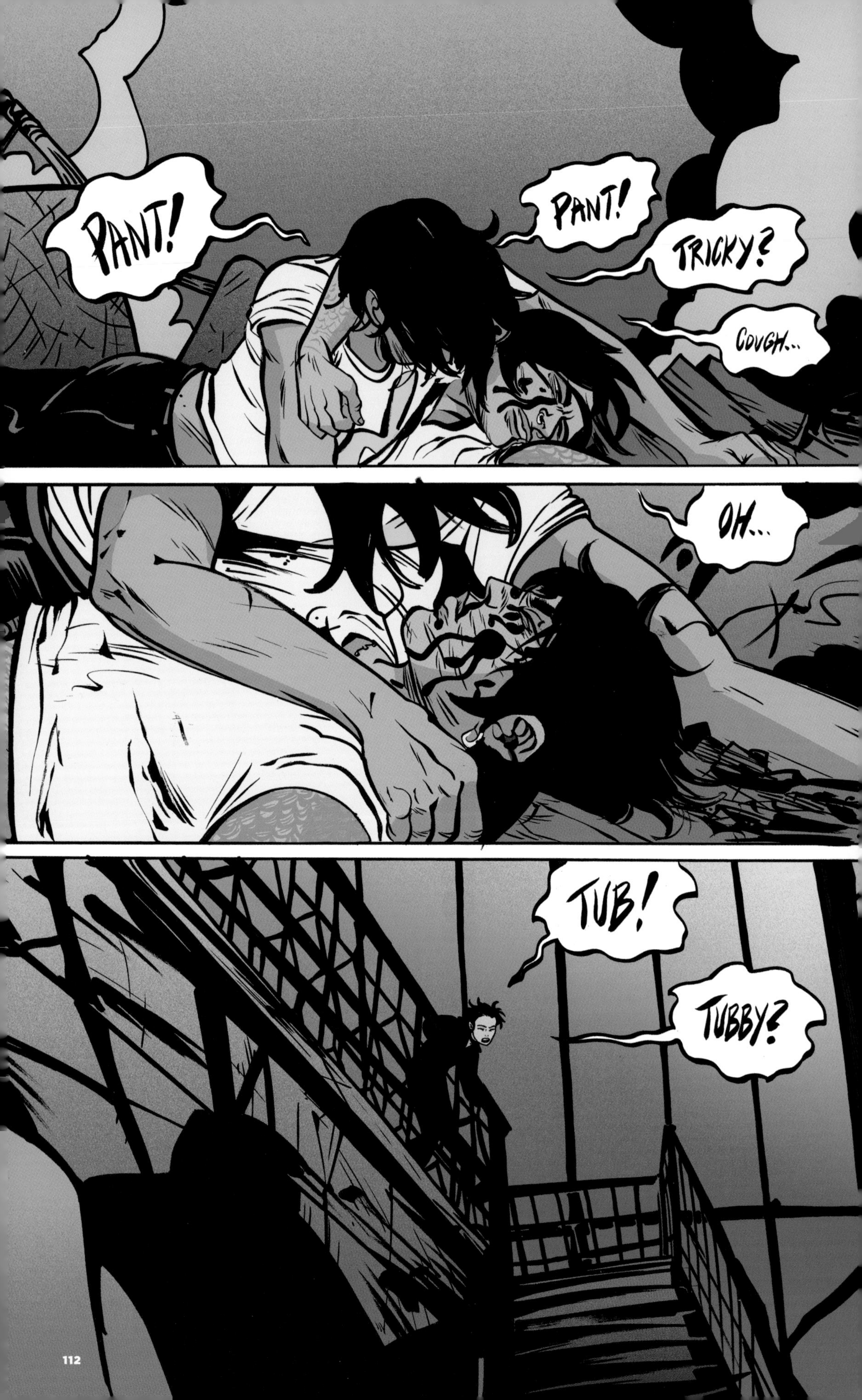
PANT!
PANT!
TRICKY?
COUGH...
OH...
TUB!
TUBBY?

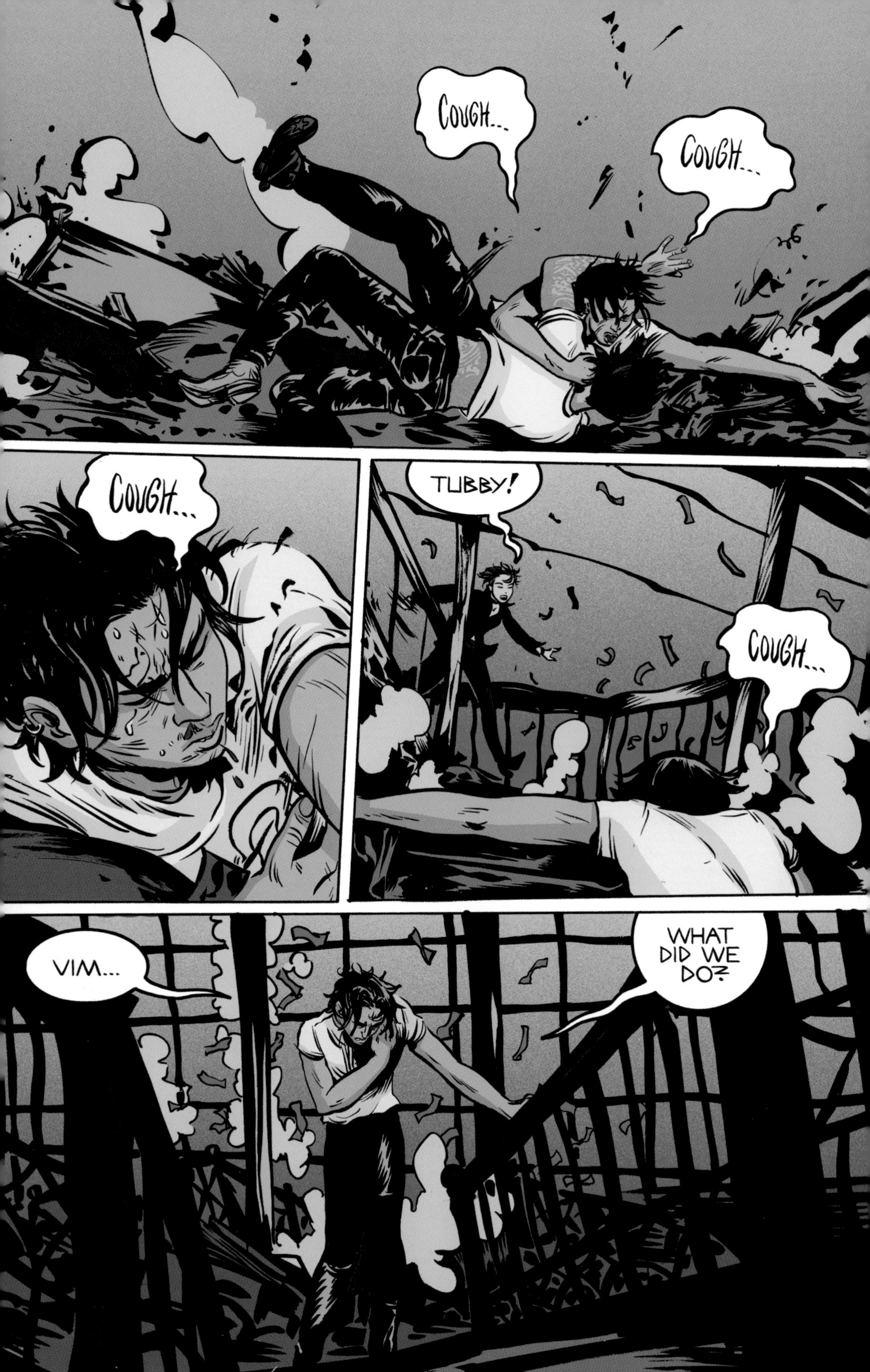
COUGH...
COUGH...
COUGH...
TUBBY!
COUGH...
VIM...
WHAT DID WE DO?

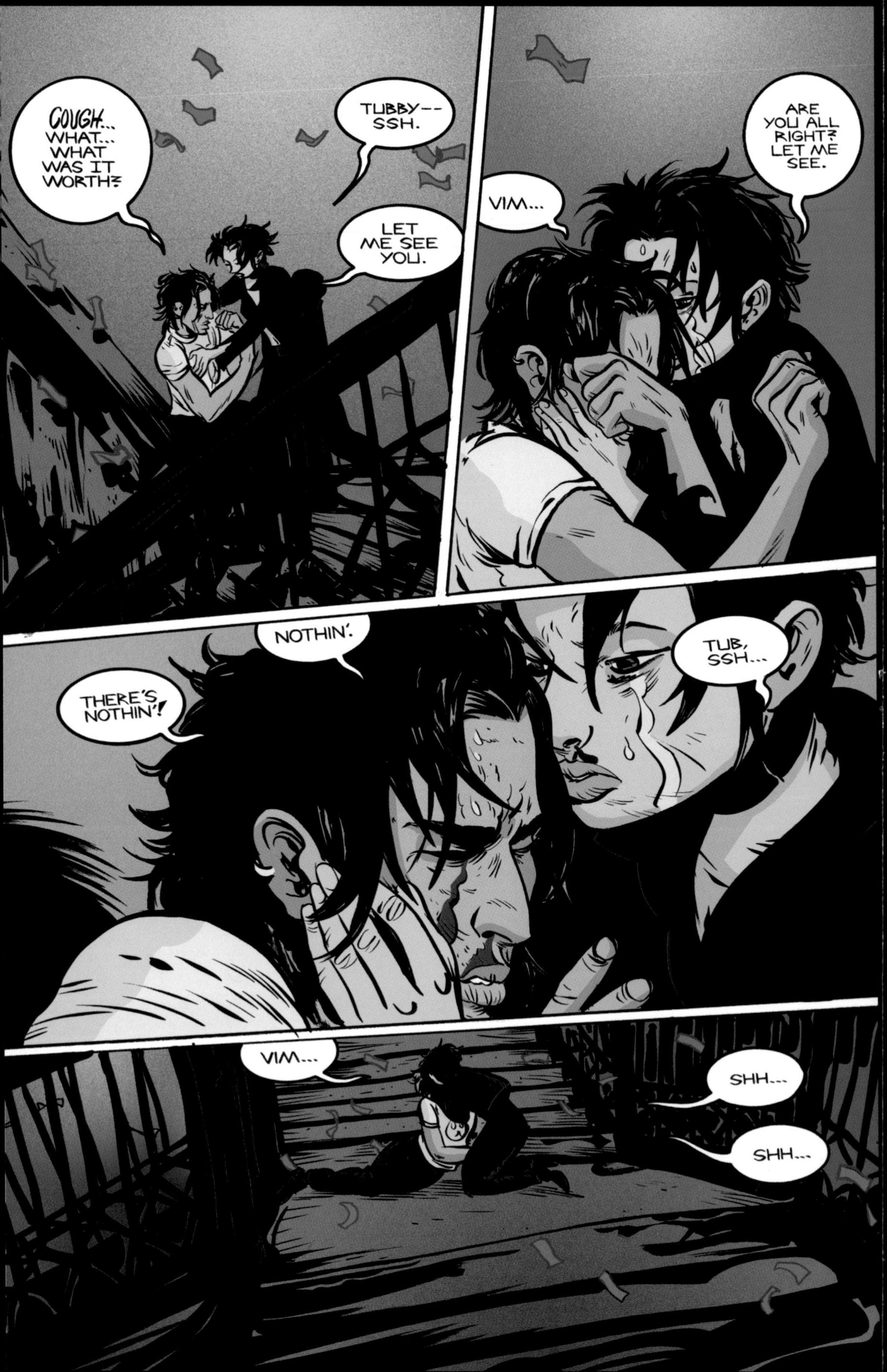
COUGH... WHAT... WHAT WAS IT WORTH?
TUBBY-- SSH.
LET ME SEE YOU.
VIM...
ARE YOU ALL RIGHT? LET ME SEE.
NOTHIN'.
THERE'S NOTHIN'!
TUB, SSH...
VIM...
SHH...
SHH...

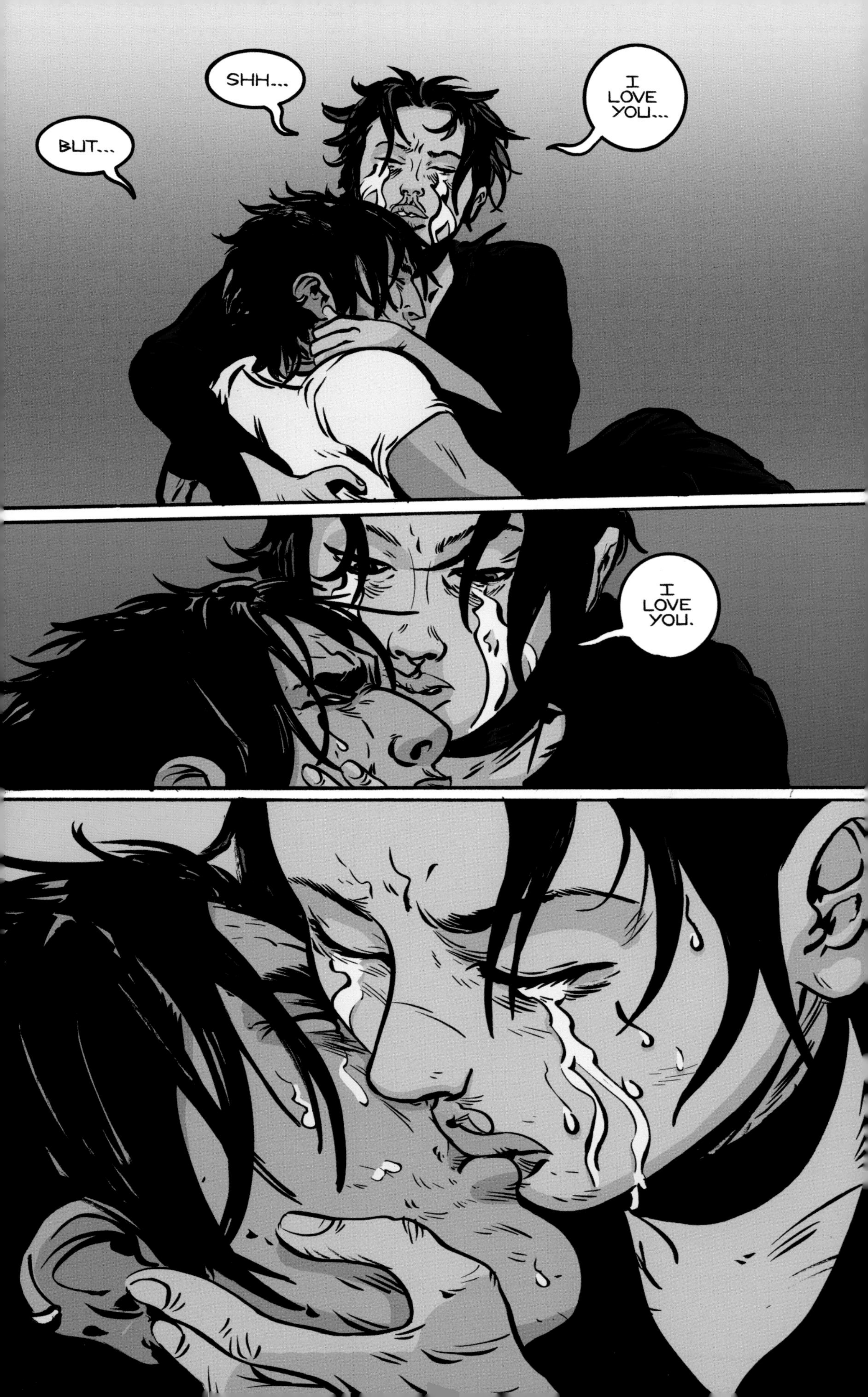
BUT...
SHH...
I LOVE YOU...
I LOVE YOU.

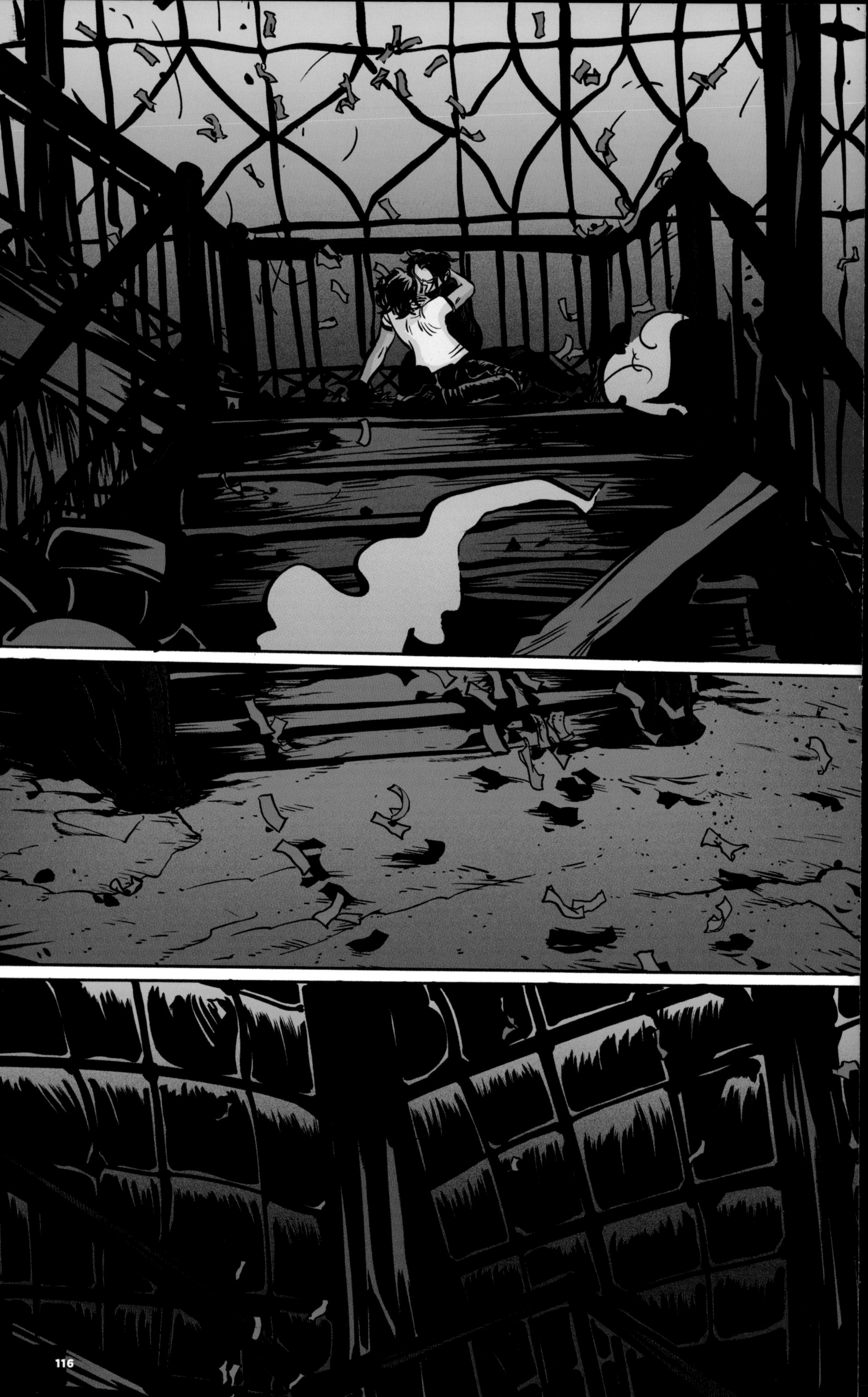

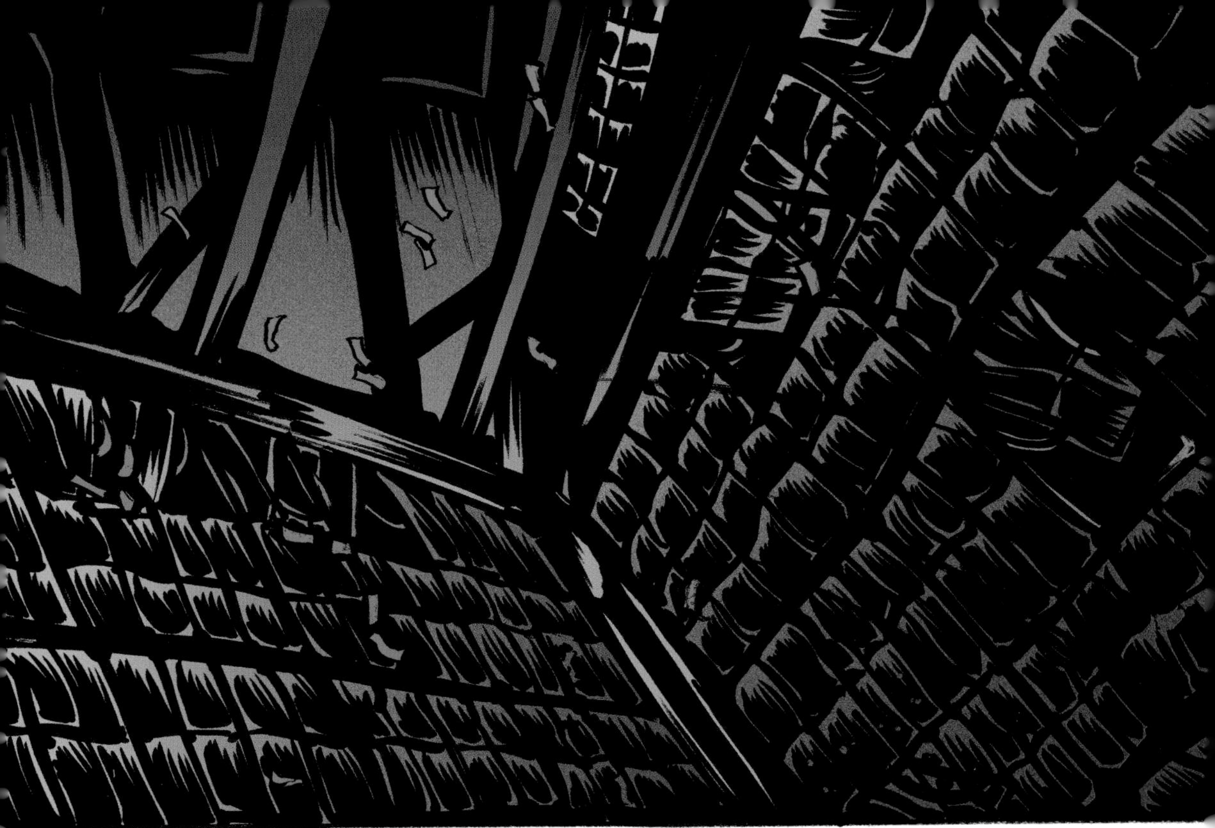

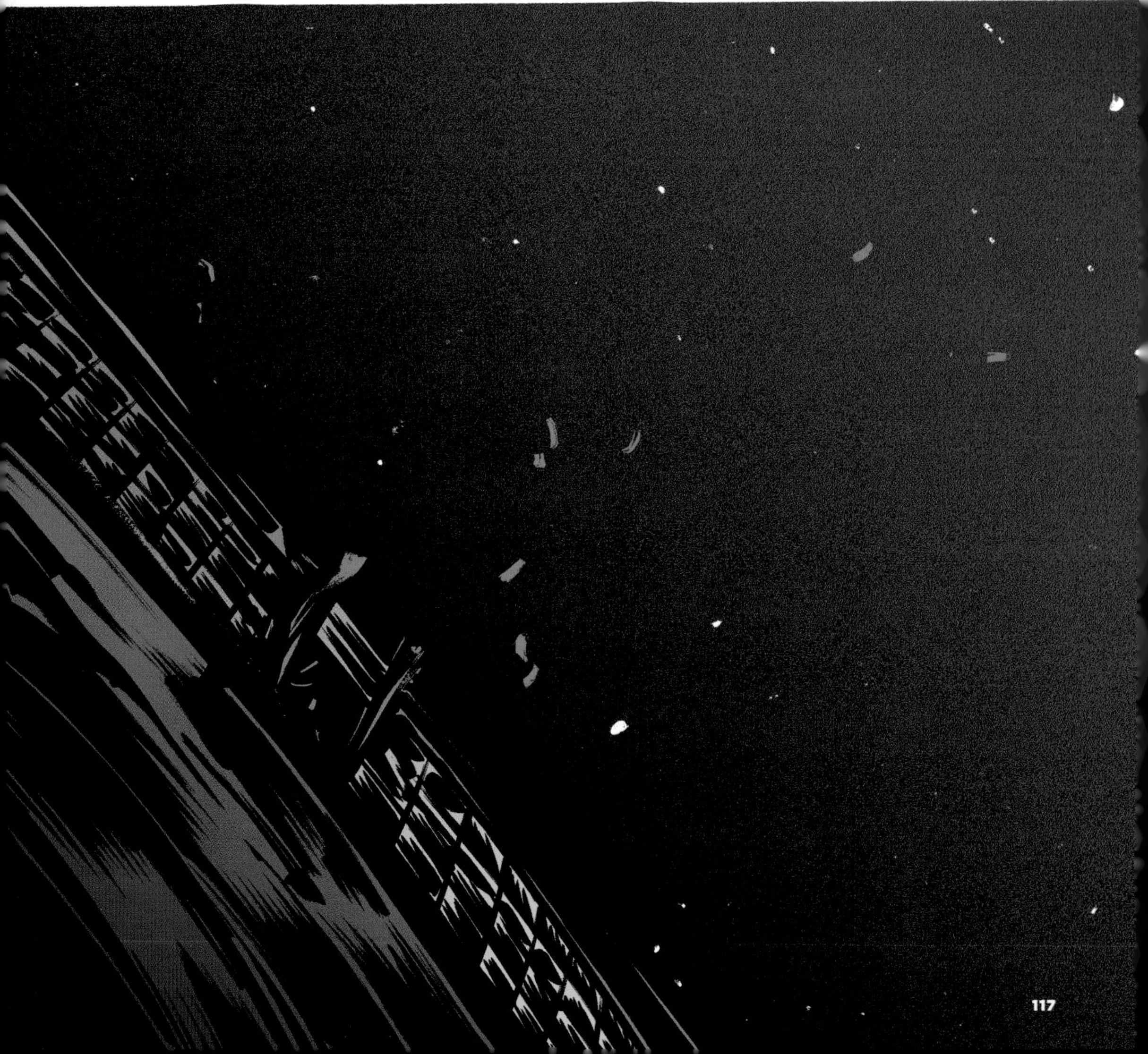

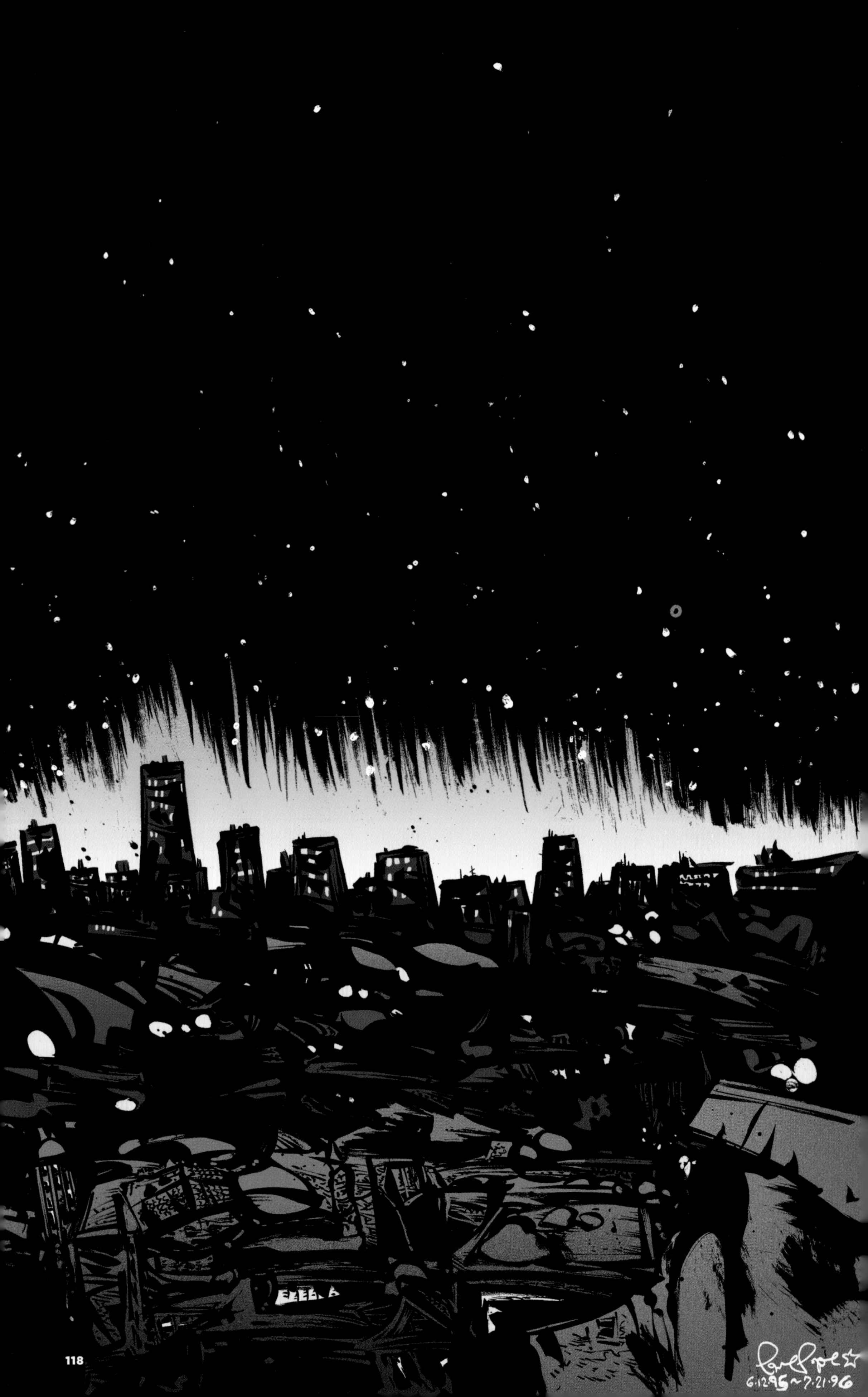
PaulPope☆
6·12·95~7·21·96

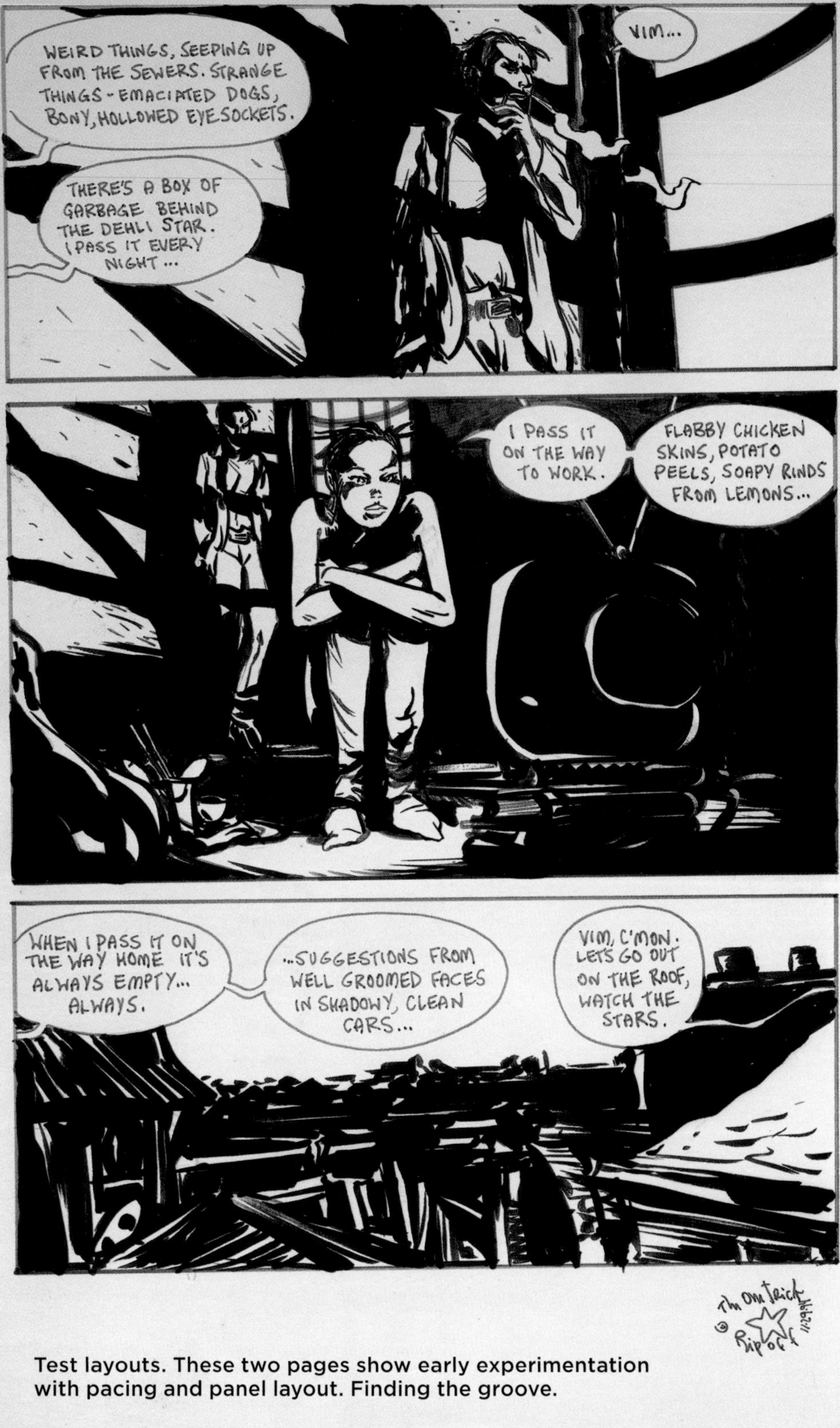
WEIRD THINGS, SEEPING UP FROM THE SEWERS. STRANGE THINGS - EMACIATED DOGS, BONY, HOLLOWED EYE SOCKETS.
THERE'S A BOX OF GARBAGE BEHIND THE DEHLI STAR. I PASS IT EVERY NIGHT...
VIM...
I PASS IT ON THE WAY TO WORK.
FLABBY CHICKEN SKINS, POTATO PEELS, SOAPY RINDS FROM LEMONS...
WHEN I PASS IT ON THE WAY HOME IT'S ALWAYS EMPTY... ALWAYS.
...SUGGESTIONS FROM WELL GROOMED FACES IN SHADOWY, CLEAN CARS...
VIM, C'MON. LET'S GO OUT ON THE ROOF, WATCH THE STARS.

Test layouts. These two pages show early experimentation with pacing and panel layout. Finding the groove.

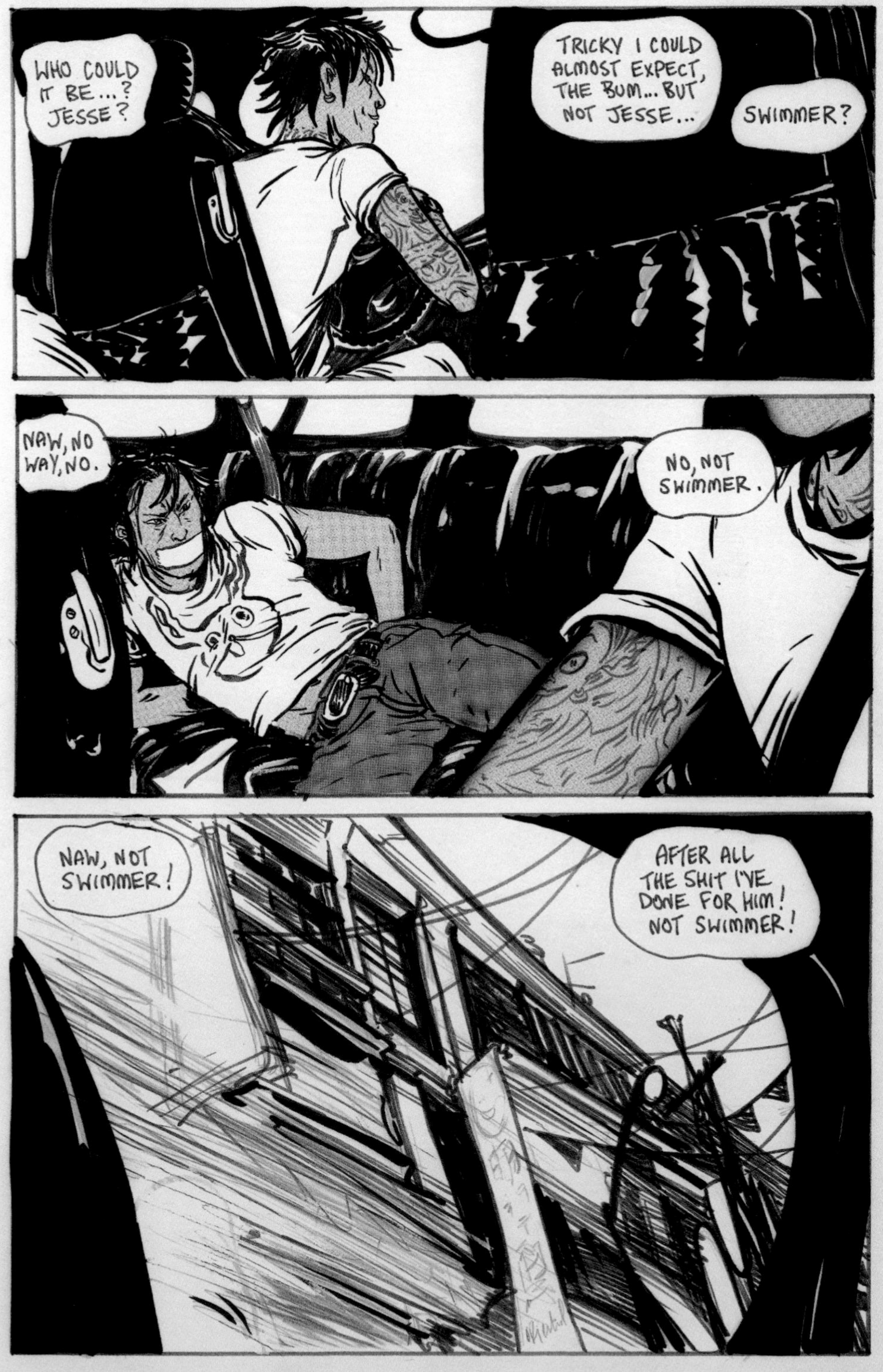
WHO COULD IT BE...? JESSE?
TRICKY I COULD ALMOST EXPECT, THE BUM... BUT NOT JESSE...
SWIMMER?
NAW, NO WAY, NO.
NO, NOT SWIMMER.
NAW, NOT SWIMMER!
AFTER ALL THE SHIT I'VE DONE FOR HIM! NOT SWIMMER!

The One Trick Rip Off .. Tubby realizes "Swimmer" Doublecrossed him ... ©P.P. 12.1.94

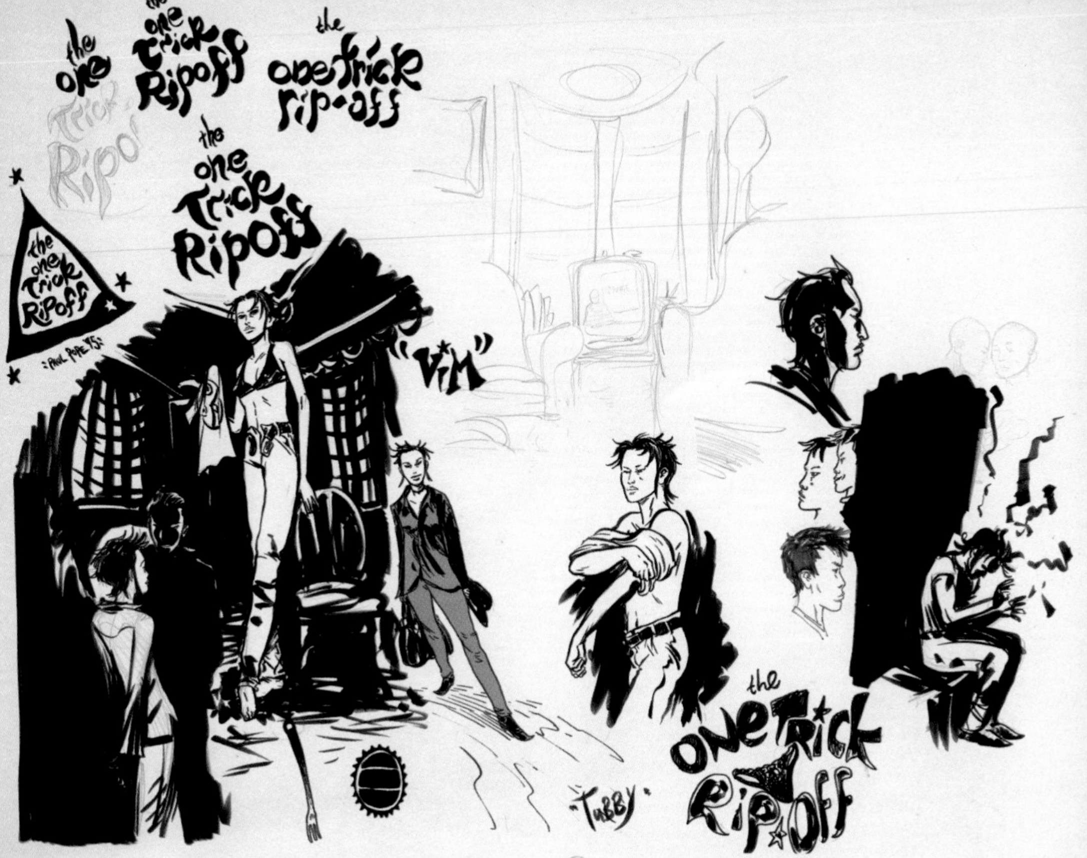

the one Trick Ripoff
the one Trick Ripoff
the onetrick rip-offs
the one Trick Ripoff
the one Trick Ripoff
PAUL POPE '95
"VIM"
"Tubby"
the ONE TRICK RIP OFF

Character studies combined with experiments with typography.

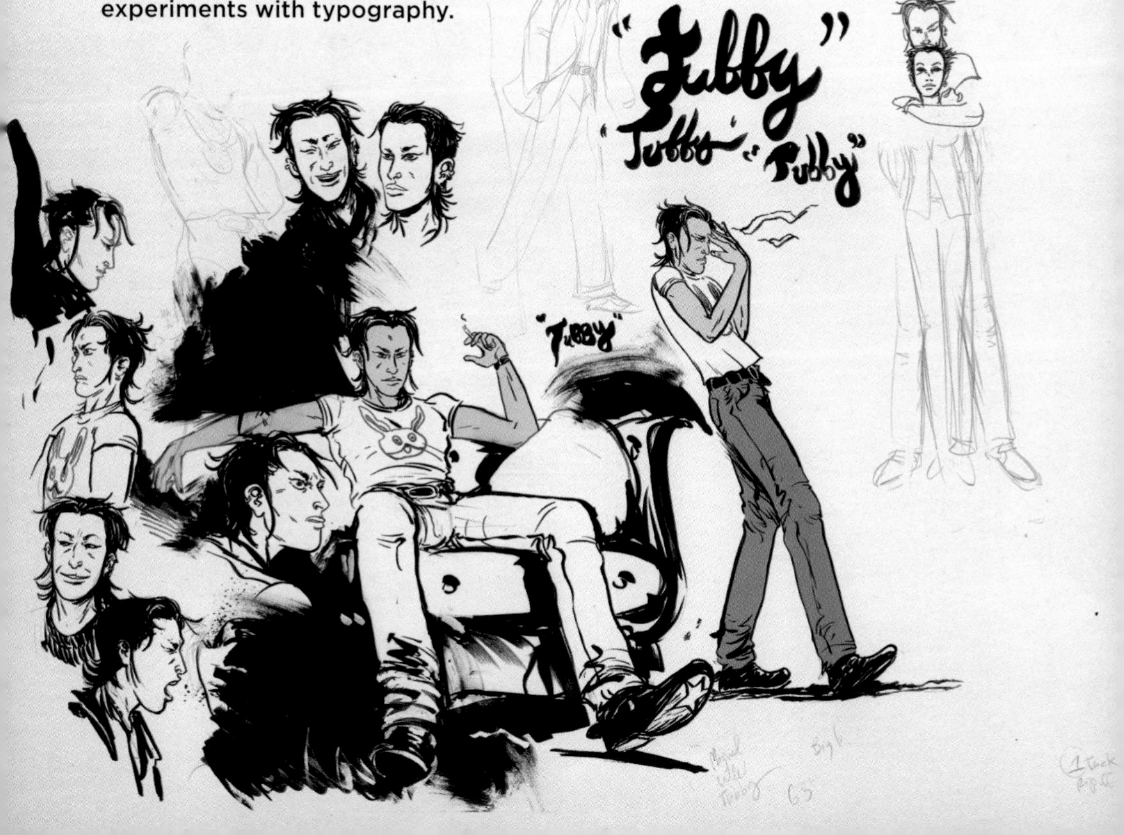

"Tubby"
"Tubby" "Tubby"
"TUBBY"

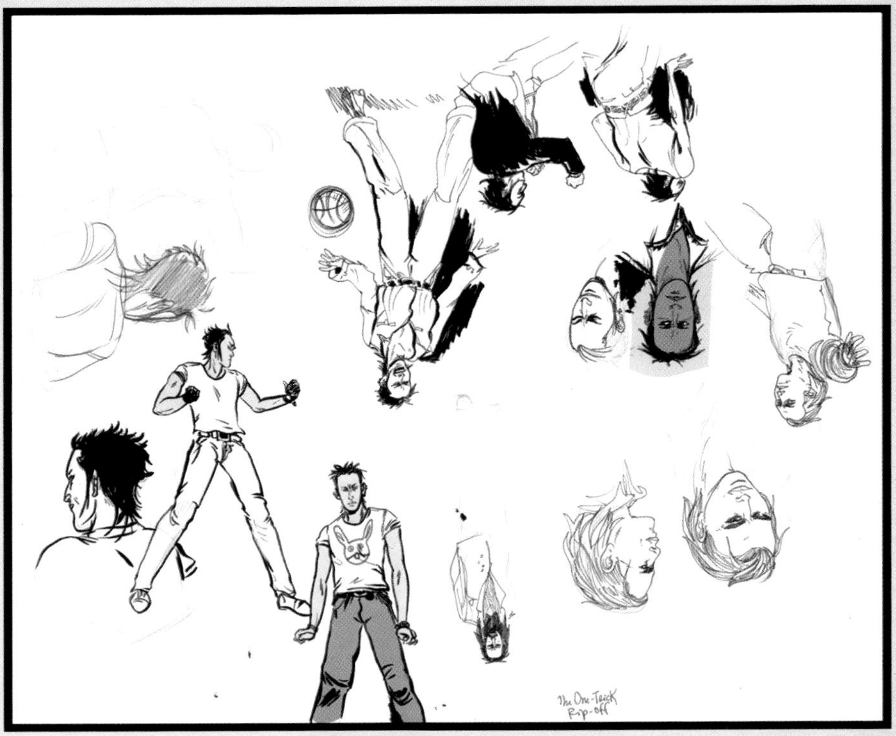
The One-Trick
Rip-off

Character sketch ramp-up.

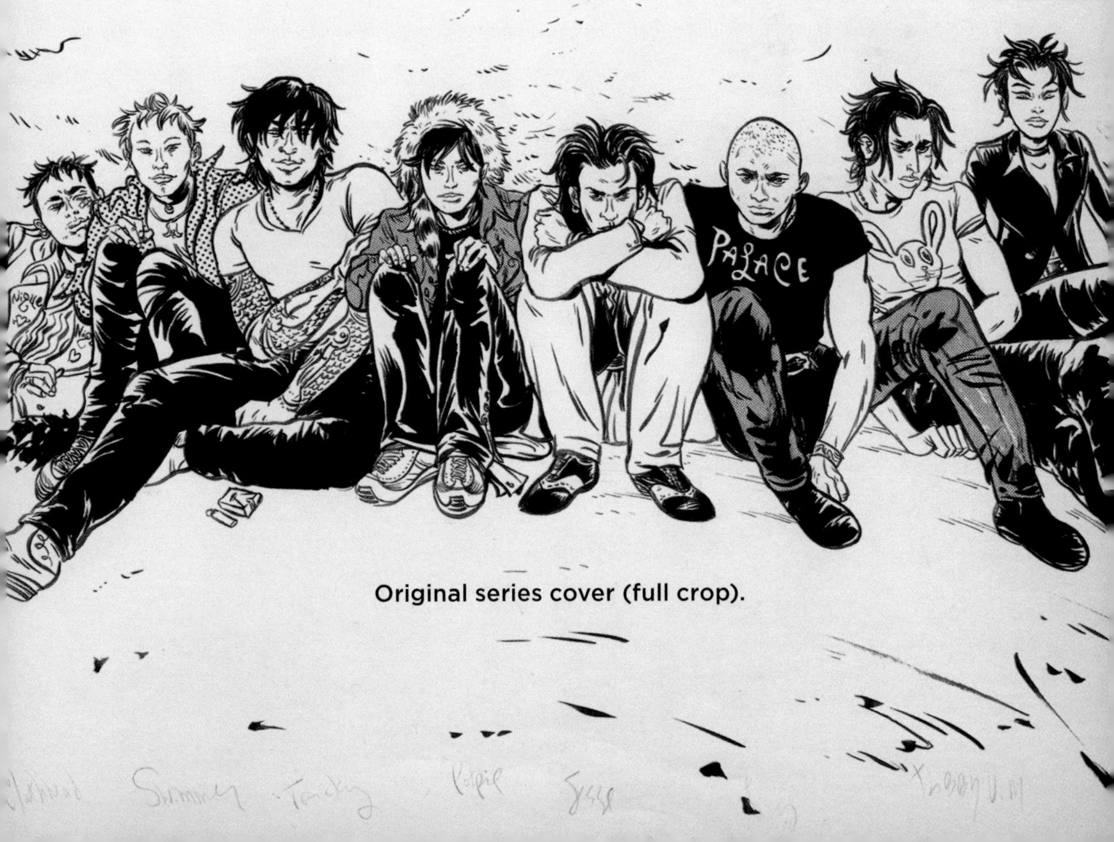

Original series cover (full crop).

Tubby 1.22.97★
PaulPope

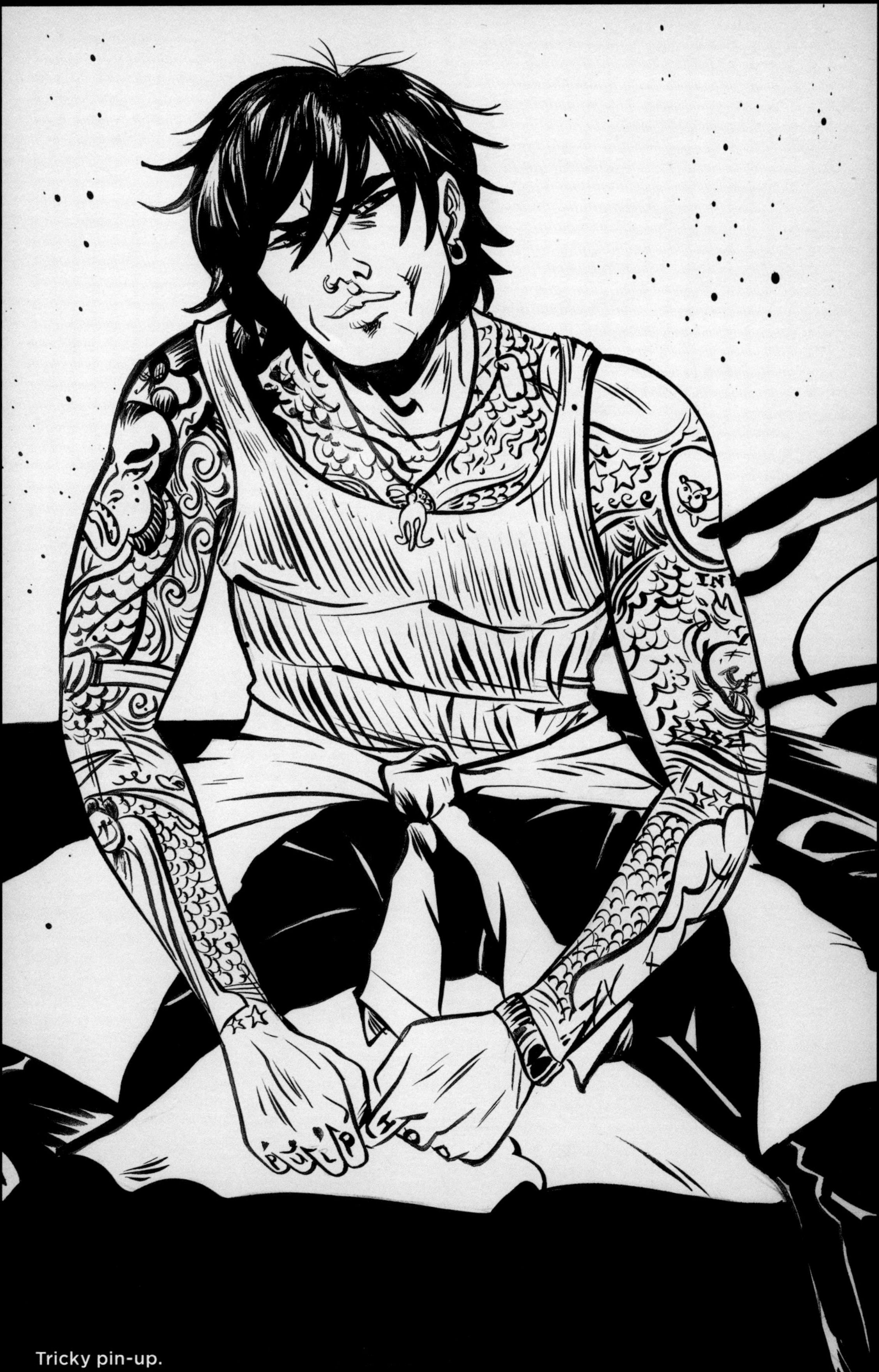

Tricky pin-up.

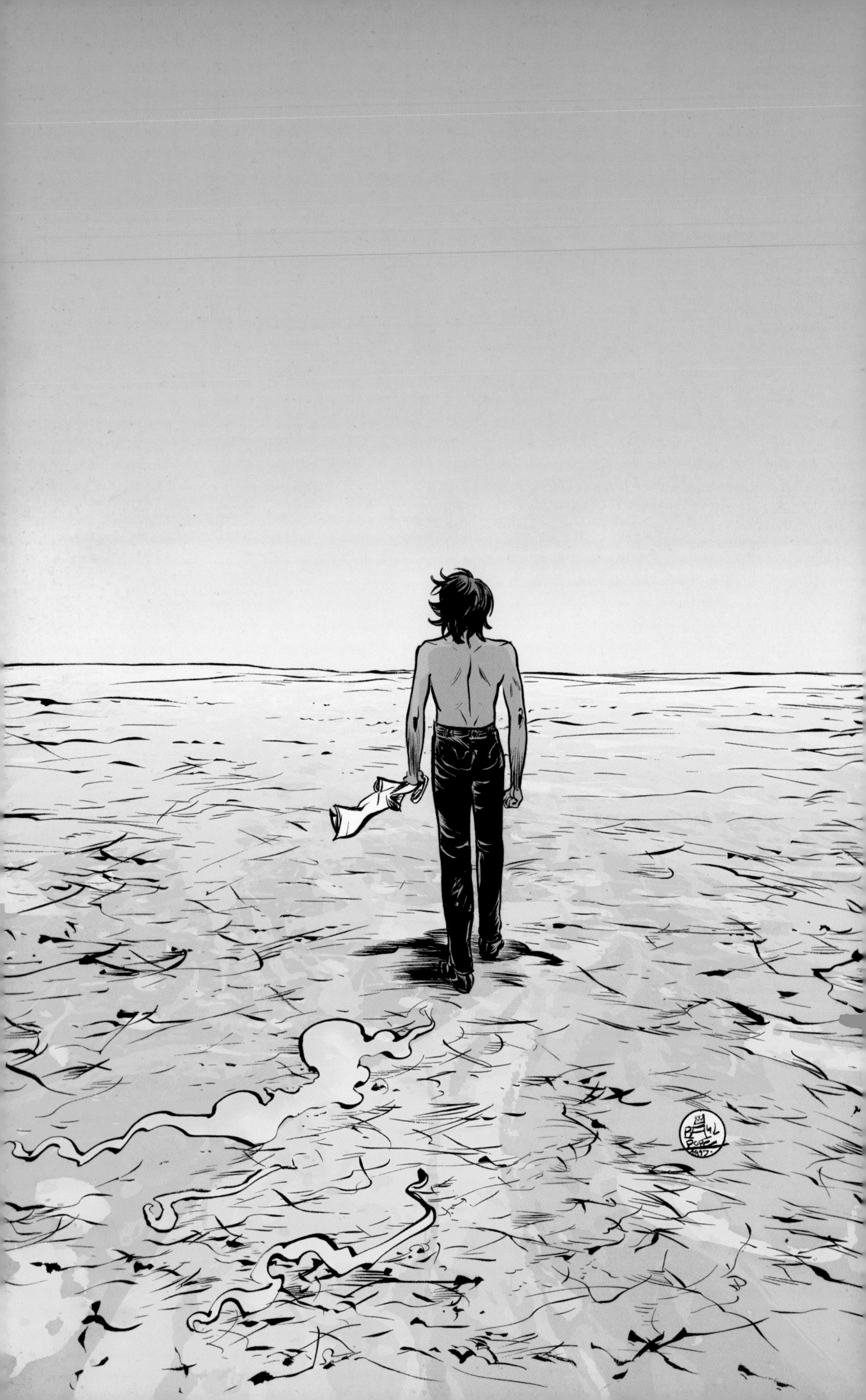

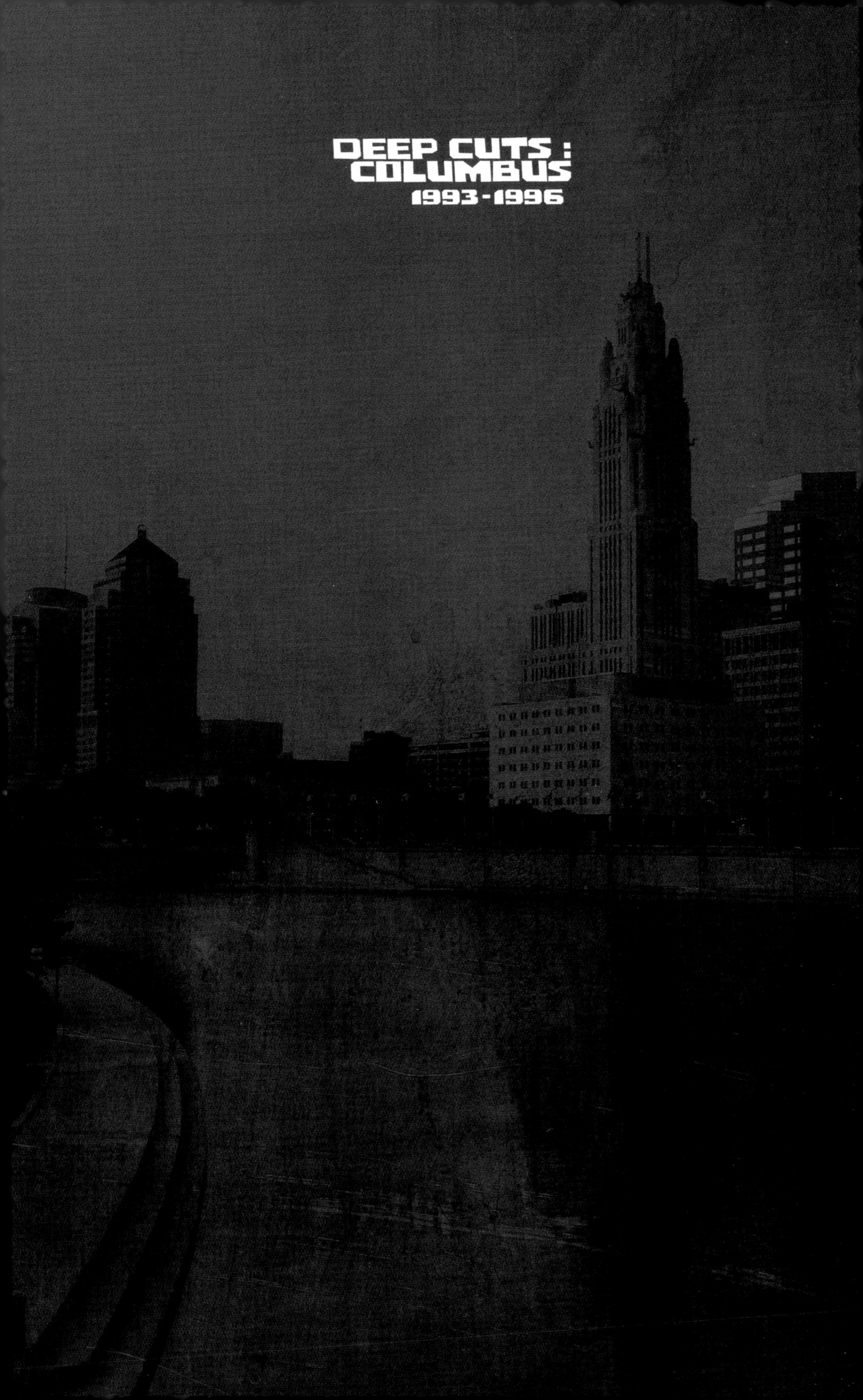
DEEP CUTS :
COLUMBUS
1993-1996

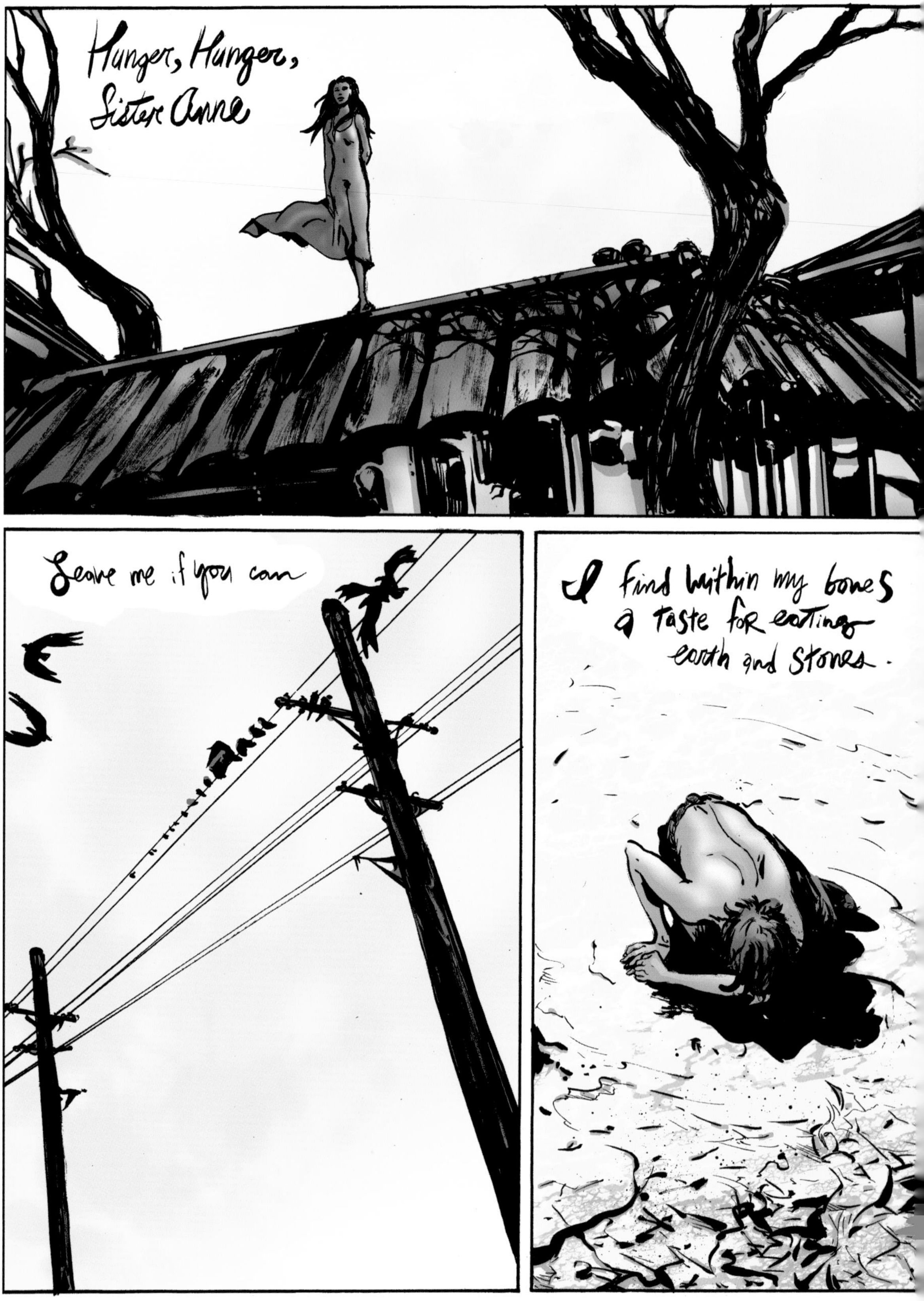
Hunger, Hunger,
Sister Anne
Leave me if you can
I find within my bones
a taste for eating
earth and stones.

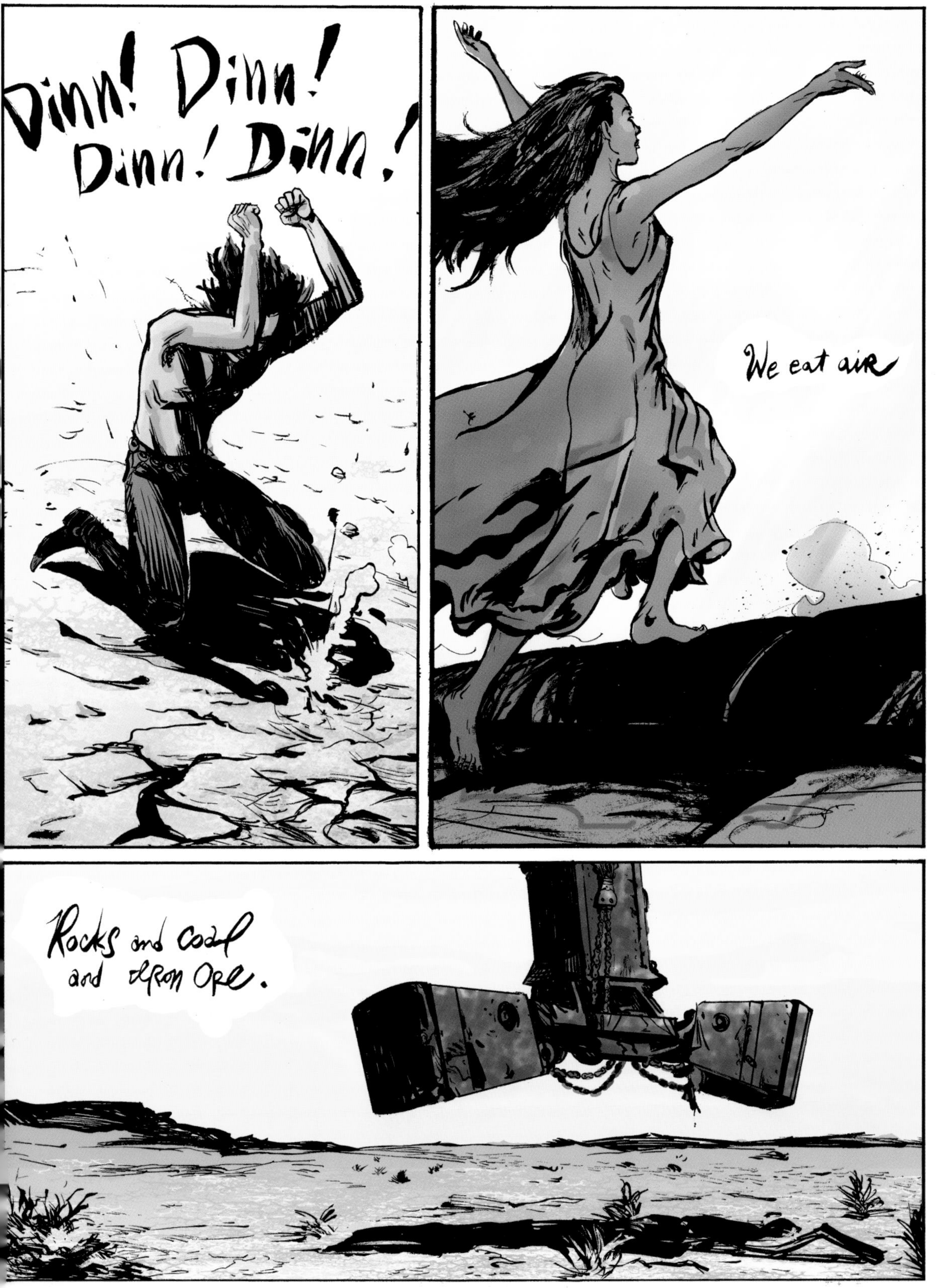
Dinn! Dinn!
Dinn! Dinn!
We eat air
Rocks and coal
and iron ore.

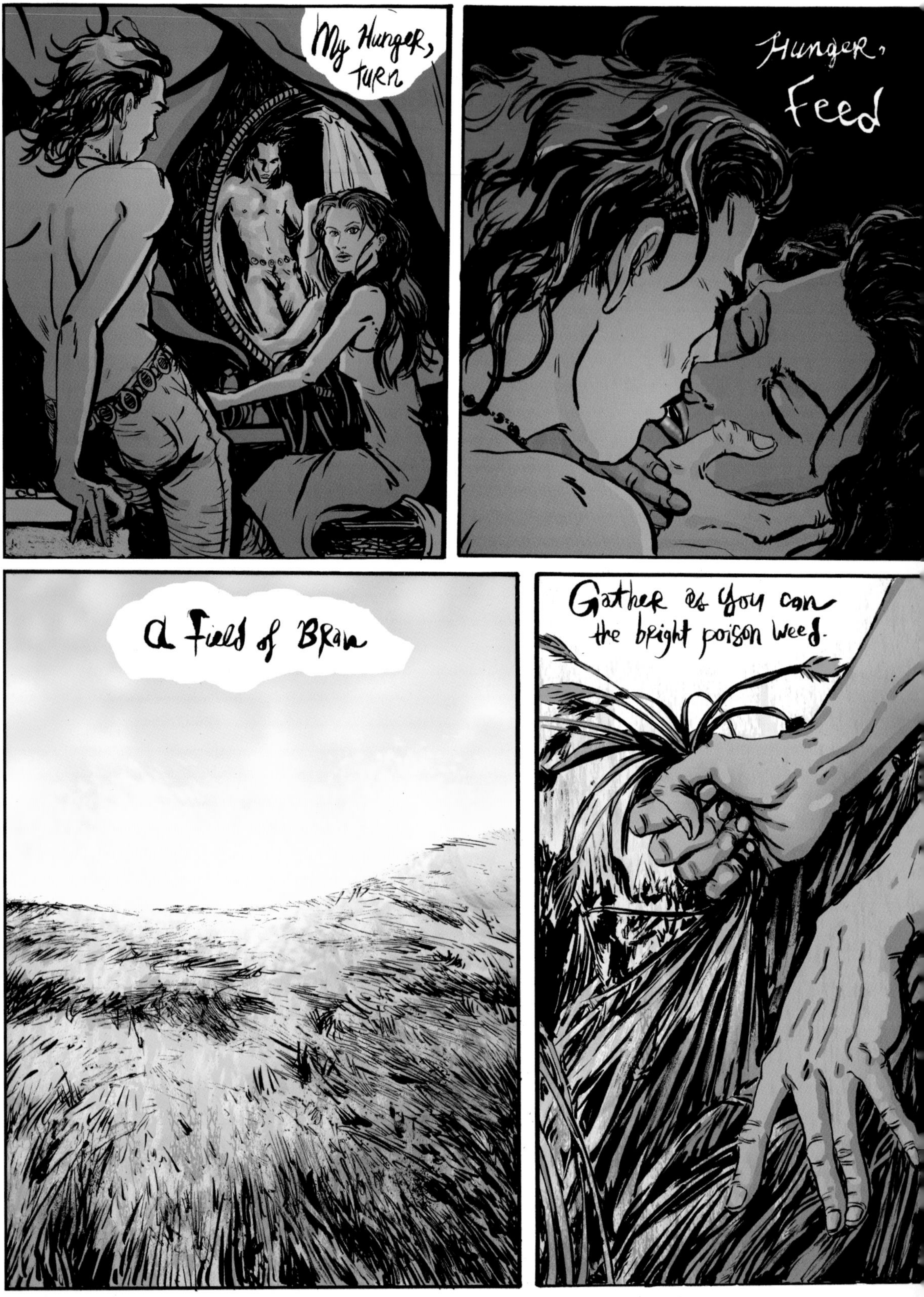
My Hunger, turn
Hunger, Feed
a Field of Bran
Gather as you can the bright poison weed.

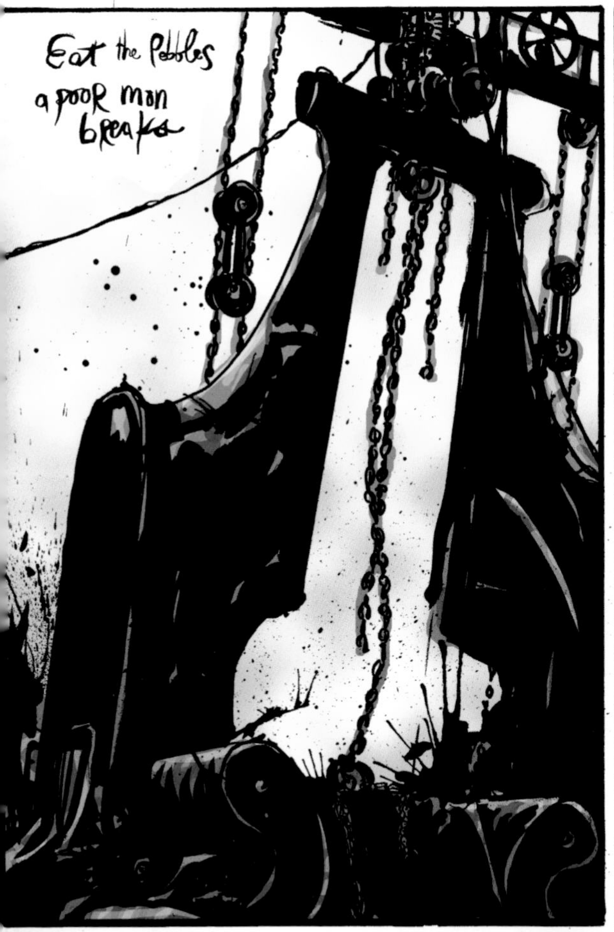
Eat the Pebbles
a poor man
breaks
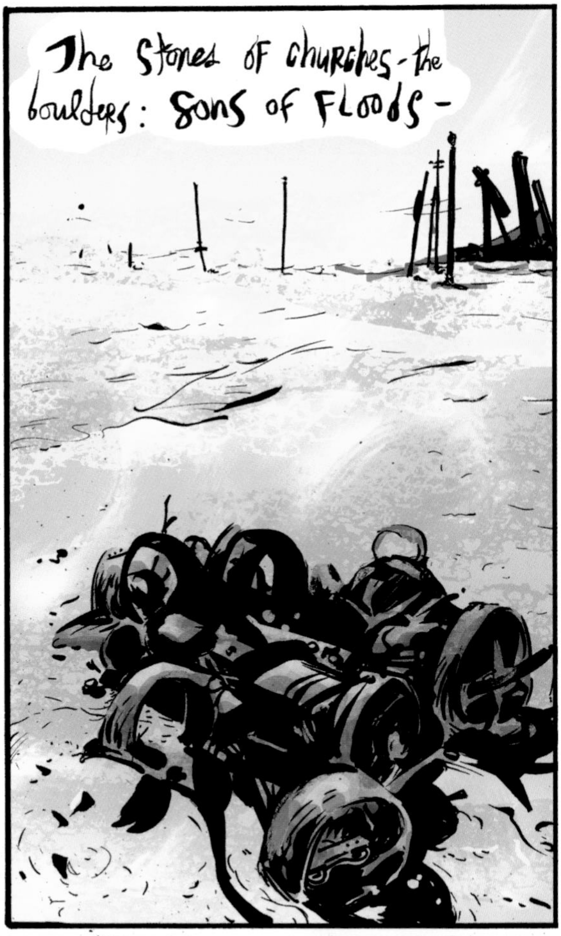
The stones of churches - the
boulders: sons of floods -
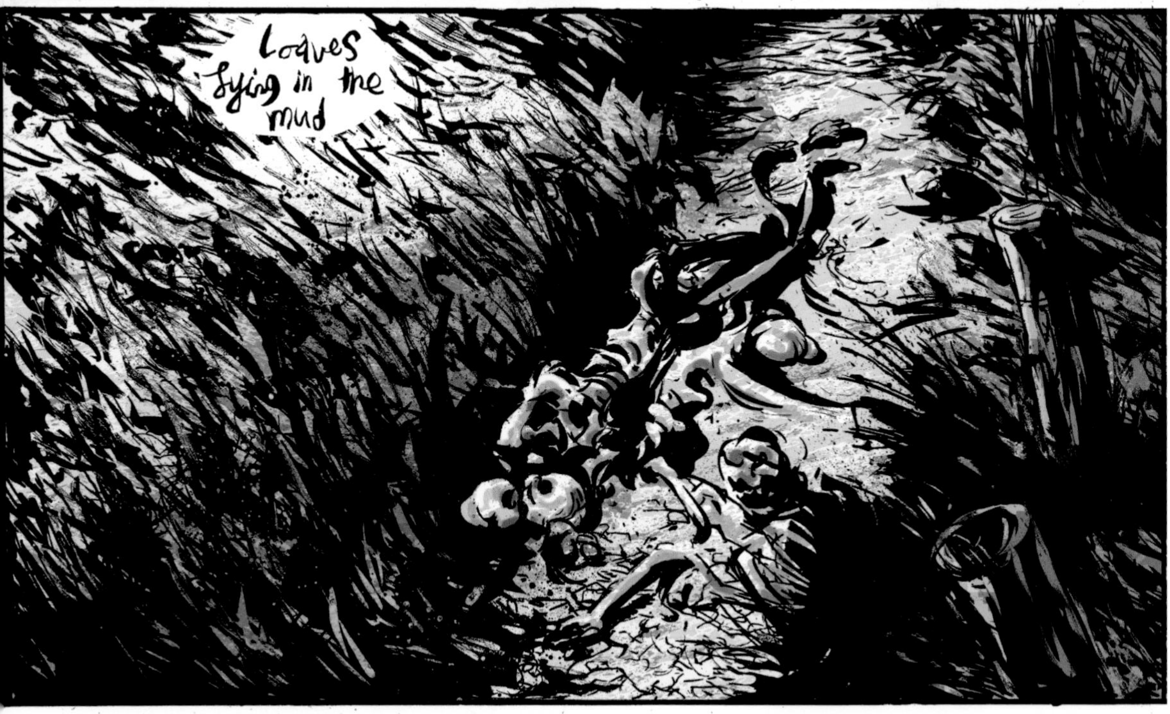
Loaves
lying in the
mud

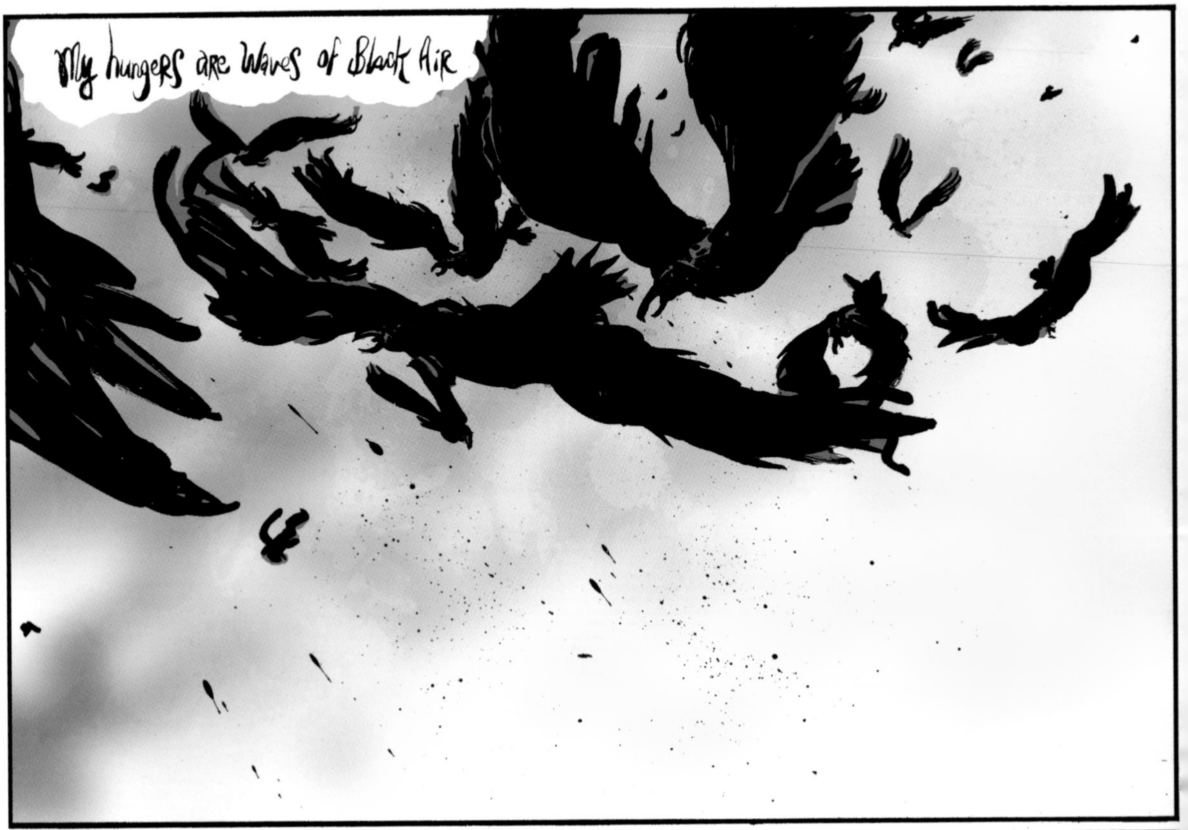
My hungers are Waves of Black Air

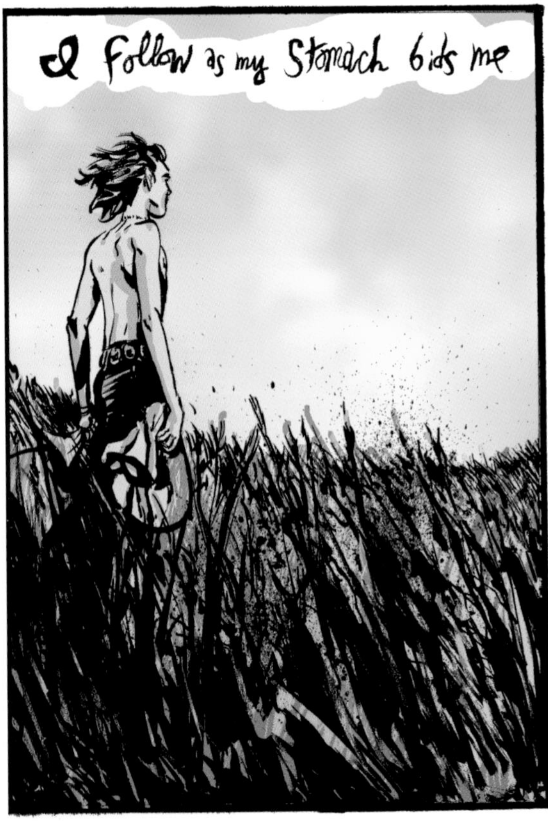
I Follow as my Stomach bids me

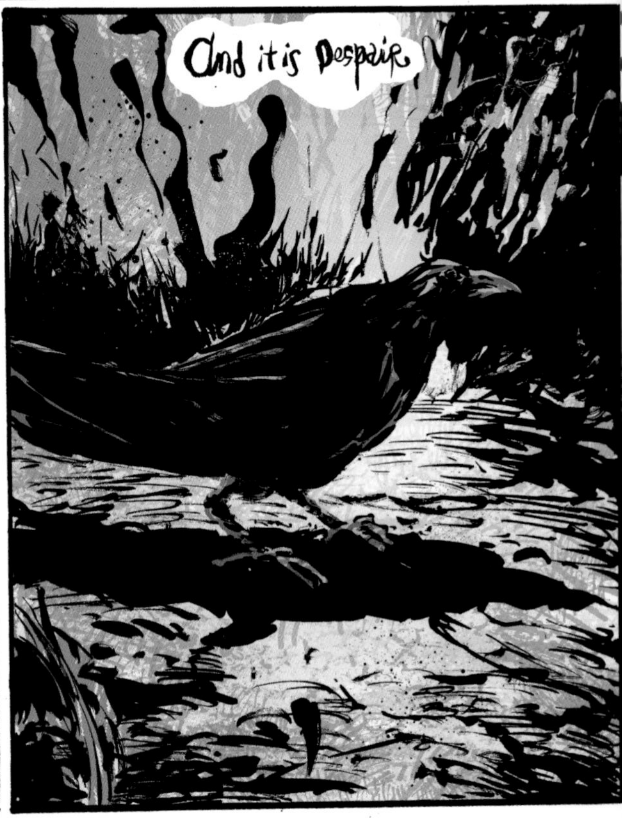
And it is Despair

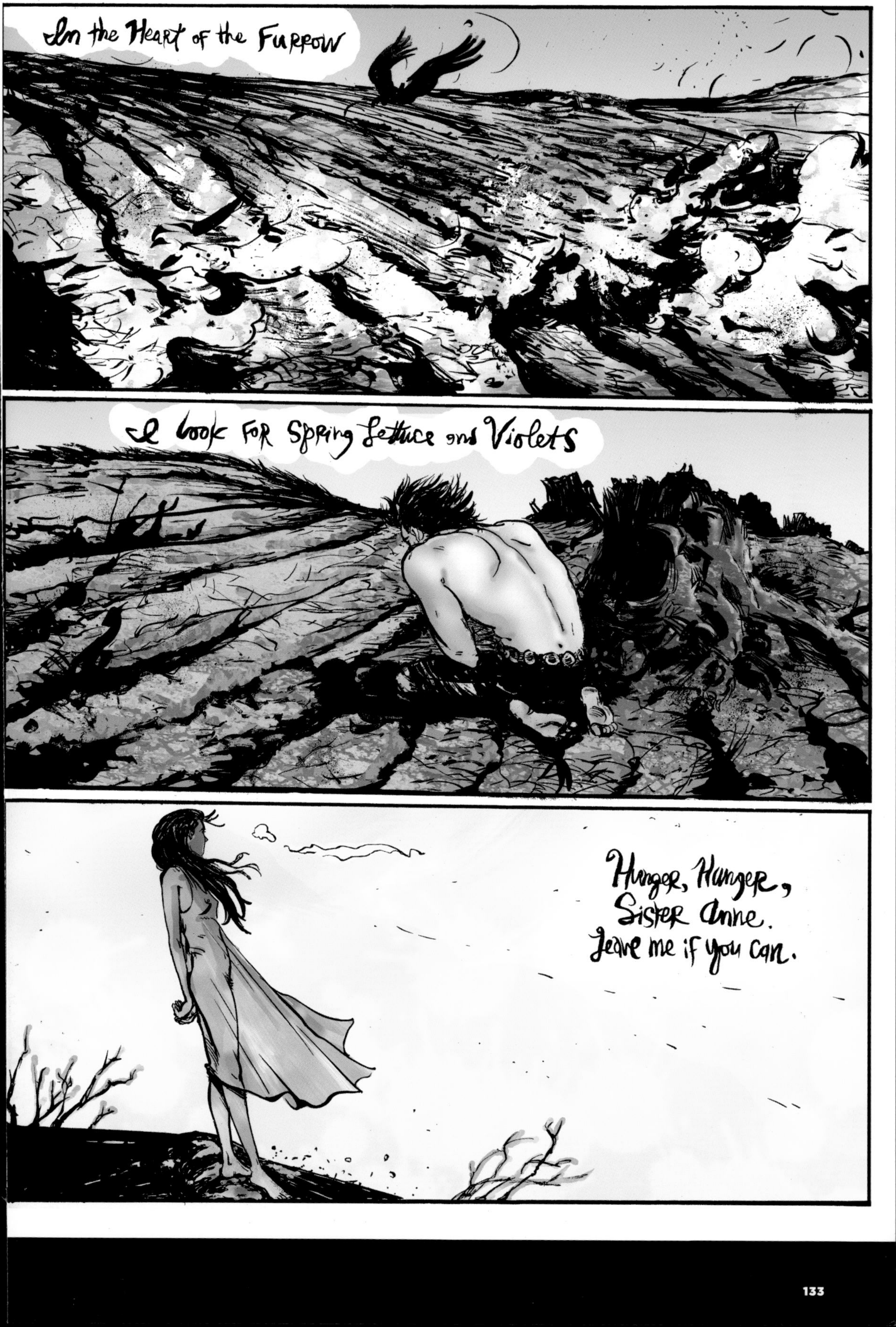
In the Heart of the Furrow
I look for Spring Lettuce and Violets
Hunger, Hunger, Sister Anne. Leave me if you can.

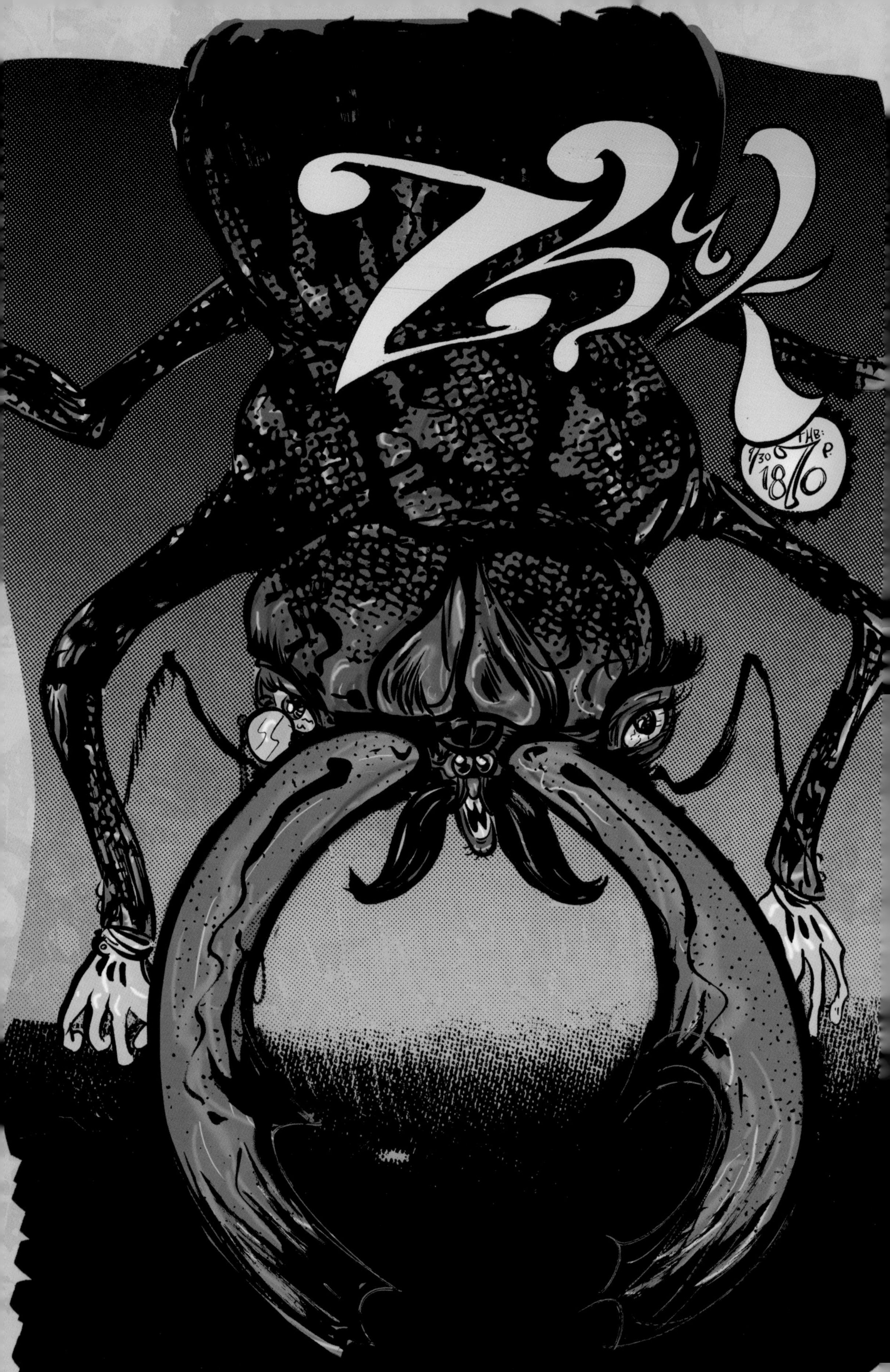
Zhuk

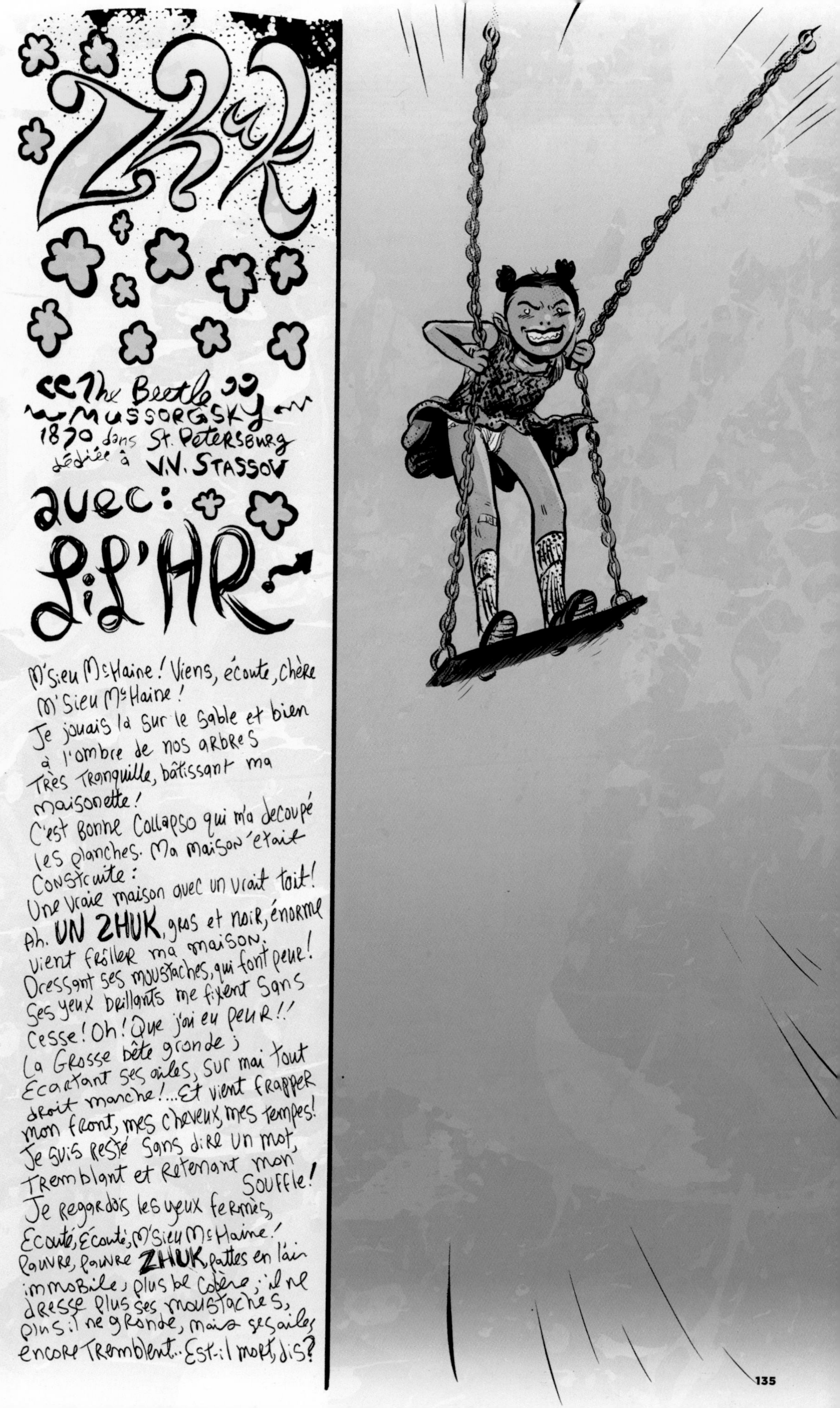
ZHUK
"The Beetle"
MUSSORGSKY
1870 dans St. Petersburg
dédiée à V.V. STASSOV
avec:
Lil'HR
M'sieu McHaine! Viens, écoute, chère
M'sieu McHaine!
Je jouais là sur le sable et bien
à l'ombre de nos arbres
Très tranquille, bâtissant ma
maisonette!
C'est Bonne Collapso qui m'a decoupé
les planches. Ma maison était
constcuite:
Une vraie maison avec un vrait toit!
Ah. UN ZHUK, gros et noir, énorme
vient fröller ma maison.
Dressant ses moustaches, qui font peur!
Ses yeux brillants me fixent sans
cesse! Oh! Que j'ai eu peur!!
La grosse bête gronde;
Écartant ses ailes, sur moi tout
droit marche!... Et vient frapper
mon front, mes cheveux, mes tempes!
Je suis resté sans dire un mot,
Tremblant et retenant mon
souffle!
Je regardais les yeux fermés,
Écouté, Écouté, M'sieu McHaine!
Pauvre, pauvre ZHUK, pattes en l'air
immobile, plus de colère; il ne
dresse plus ses moustaches,
plus il ne gronde, mais ses ailes
encore tremblent... Est-il mort, dis?

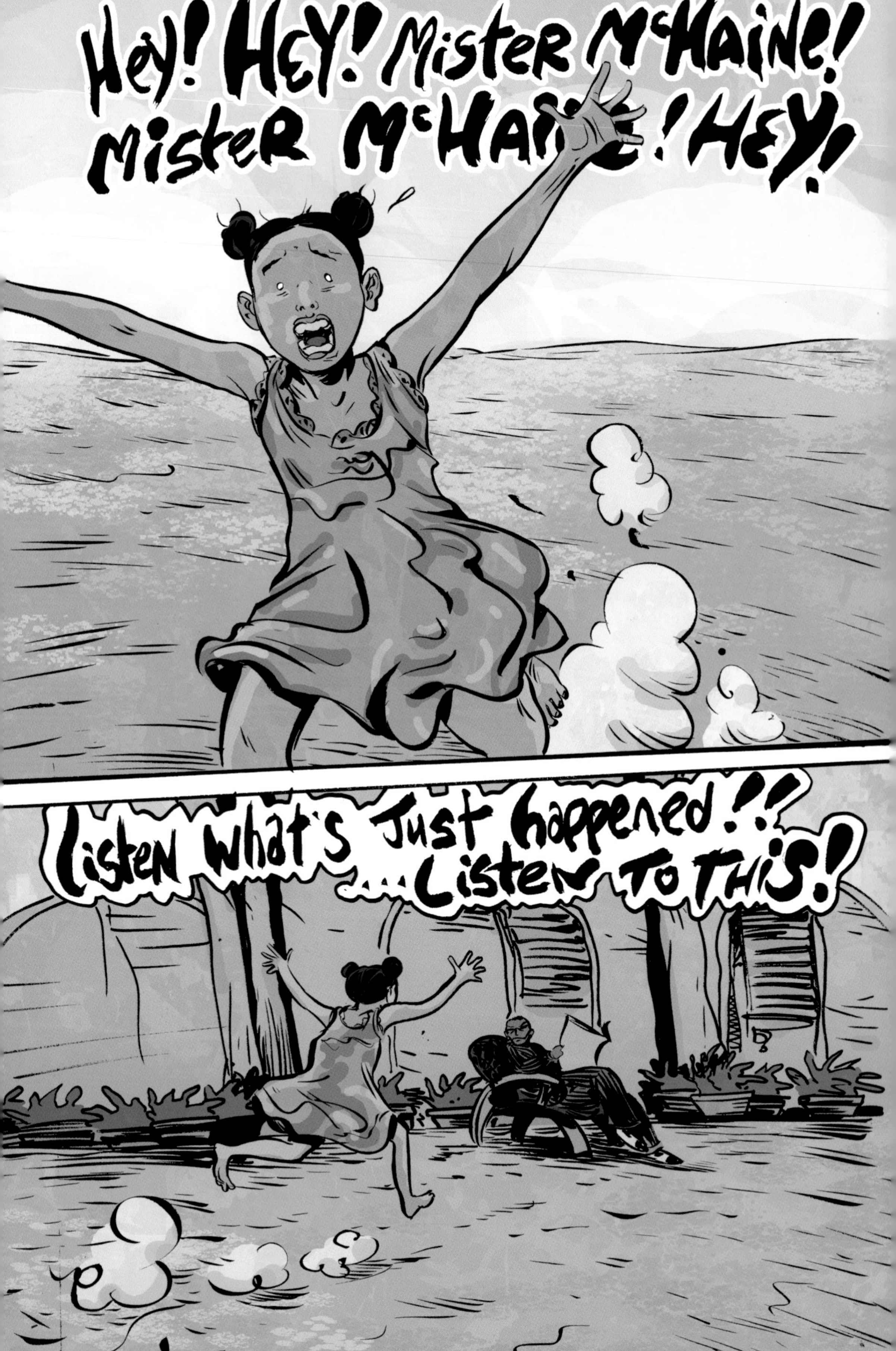
HEY! HEY! MISTER McHAINE! MISTER McHAINE! HEY!
LISTEN WHAT'S JUST HAPPENED!! ...LISTEN TO THIS!

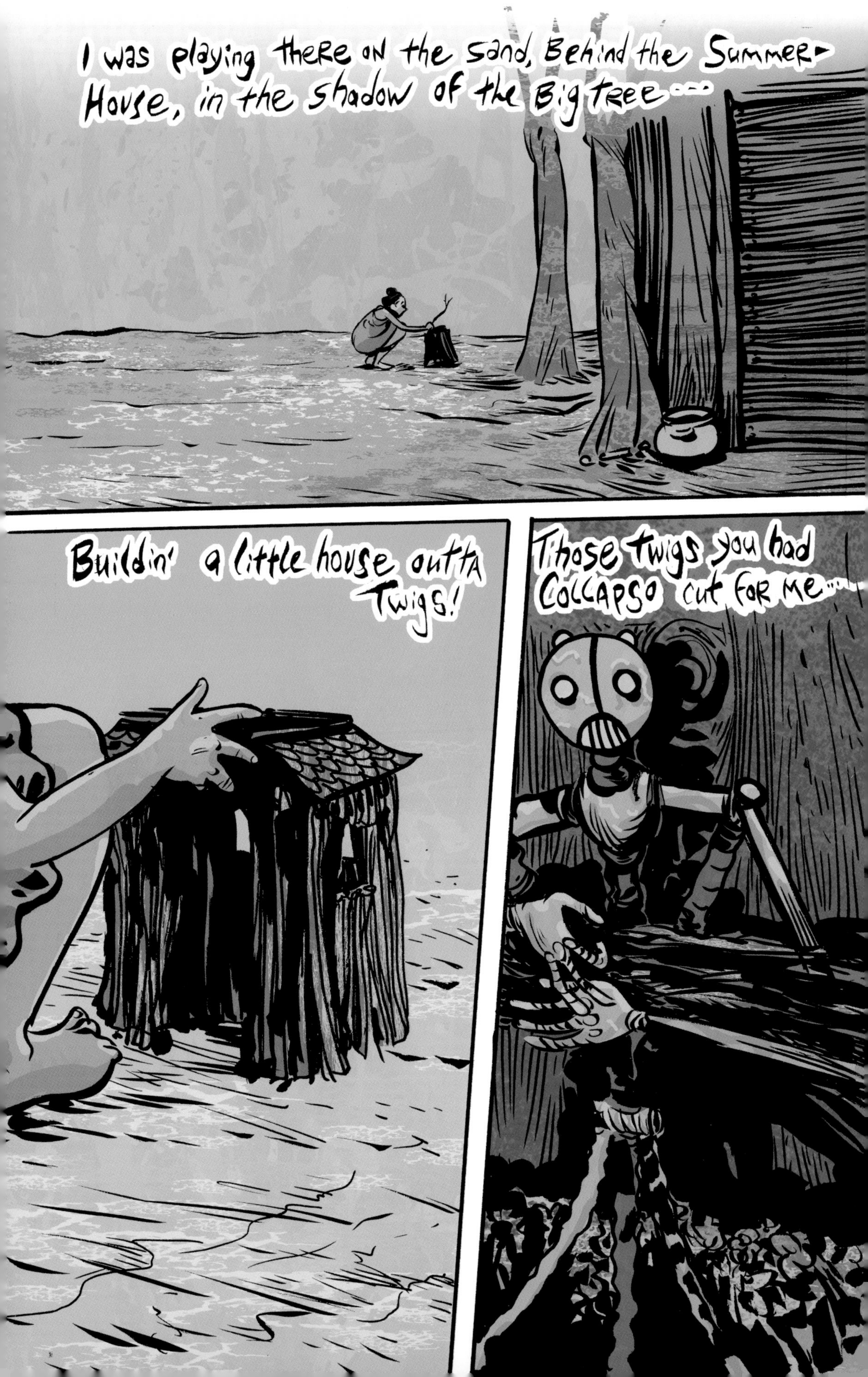
I was playing there on the sand, Behind the Summer-House, in the shadow of the Big tree...
Buildin' a little house outta Twigs!
Those twigs you had Collapso cut for me...

I had already finished buildin' it, the little house! And what a proper little house it was, with a proper little roof an' everything!
When all of the sudden:

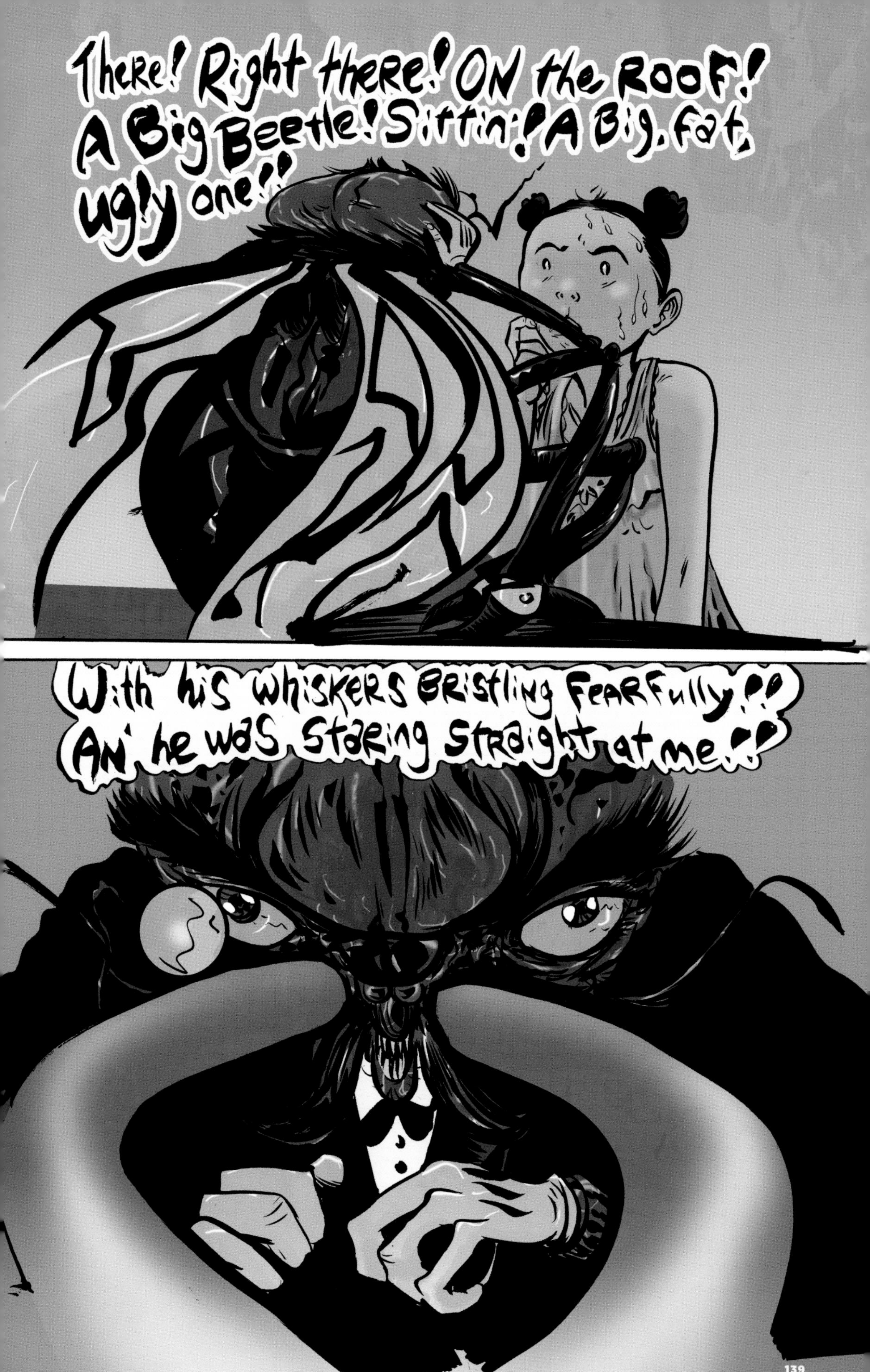
There! Right there! ON the ROOF! A Big Beetle! Sittin'! A Big, fat, ugly one!!
With his whiskers Bristling fearfully!!
An' he was staring straight at me!!

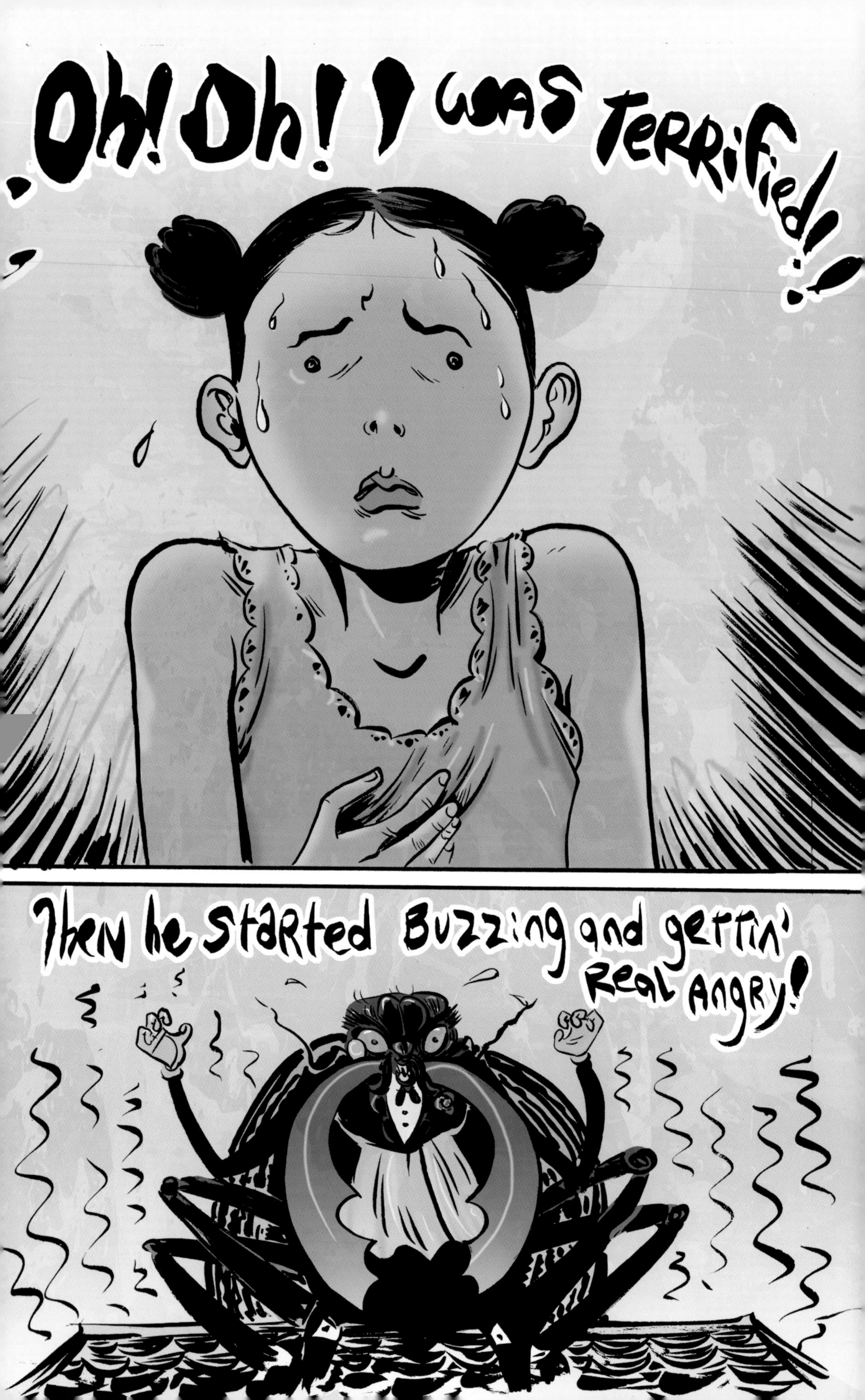
Oh! Oh! I was terrified!!
Then he started buzzing and gettin' real angry!

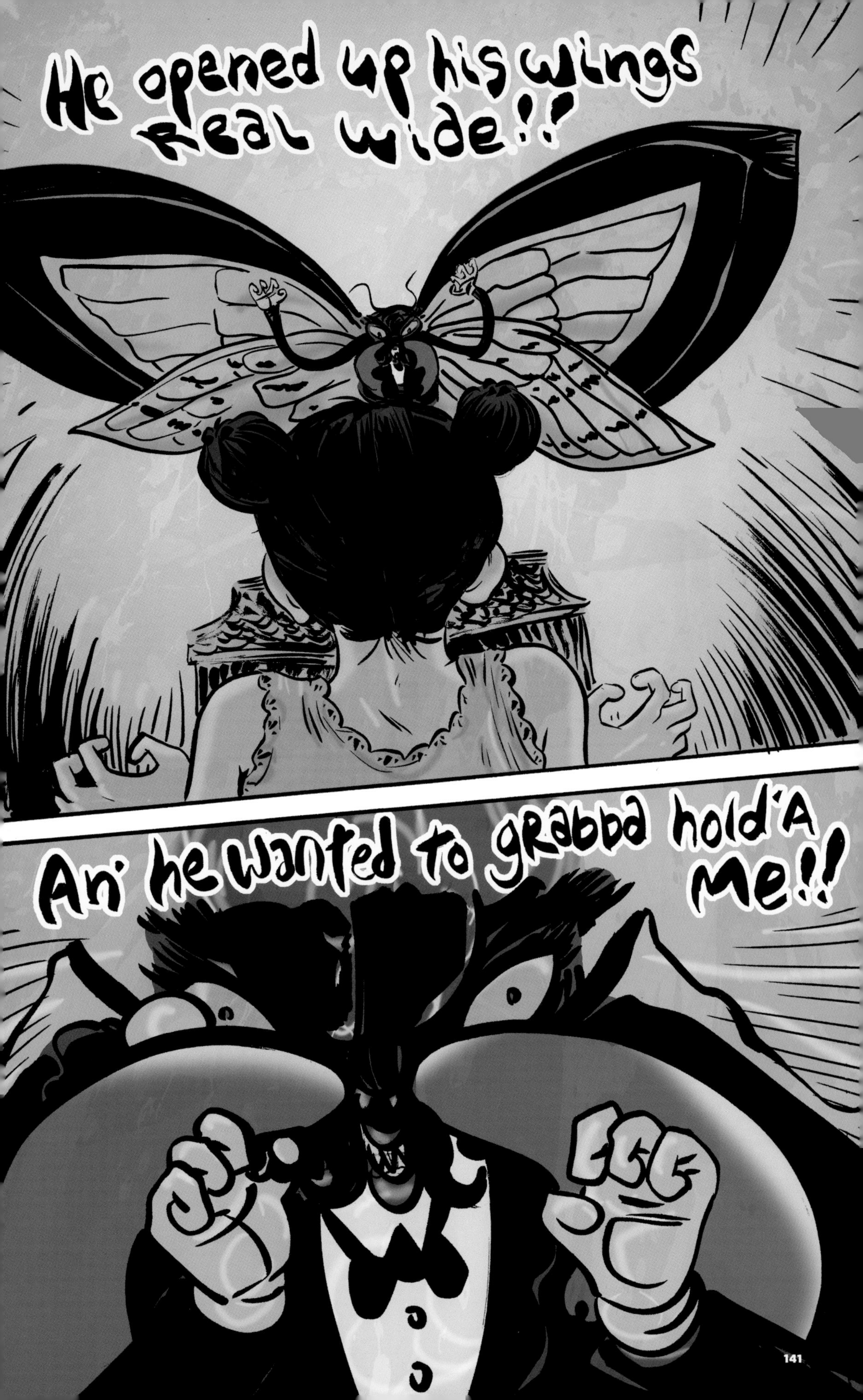
He opened up his wings real wide!!
An' he wanted to grabba hold'a me!!

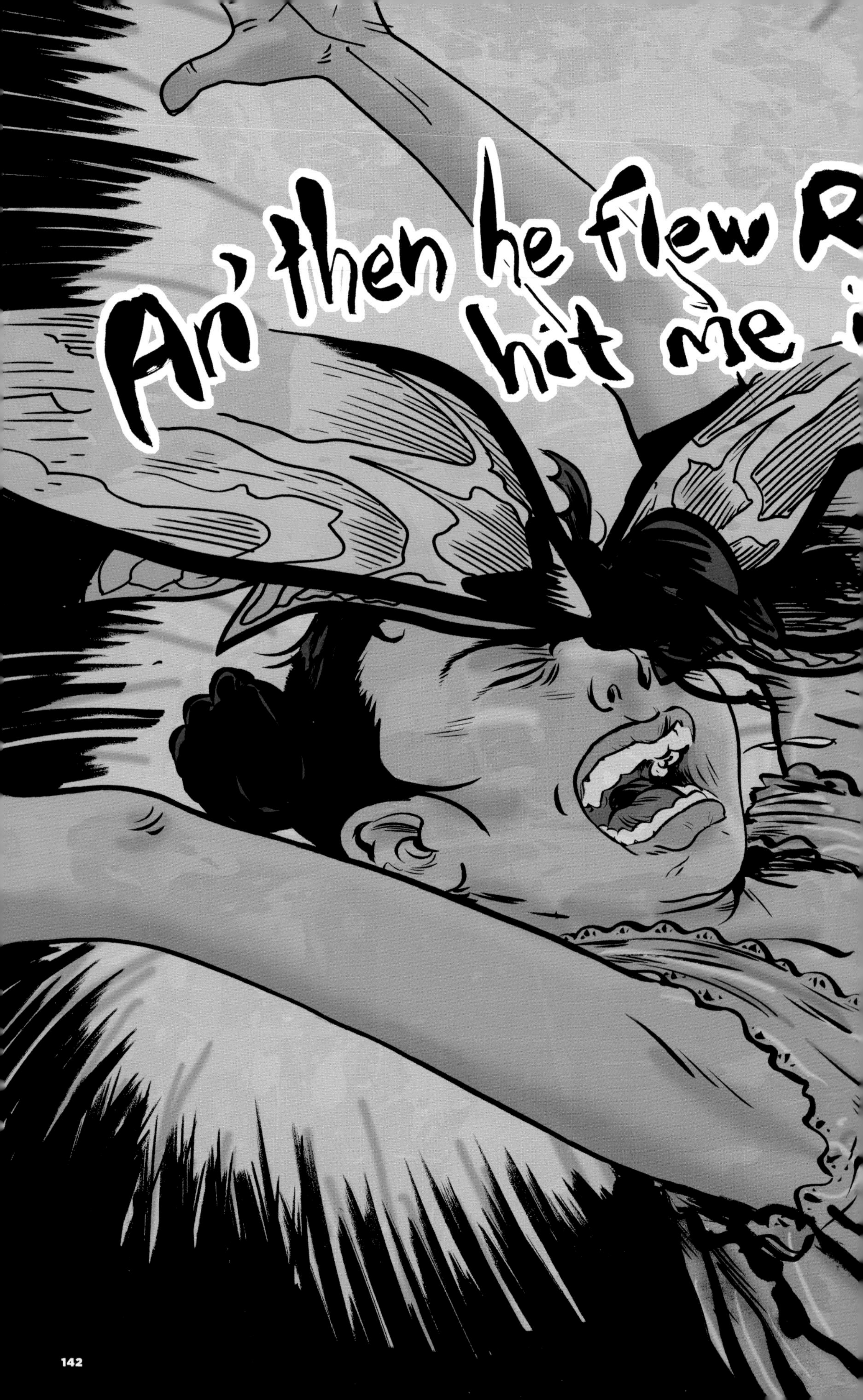
An' then he flew
hit me

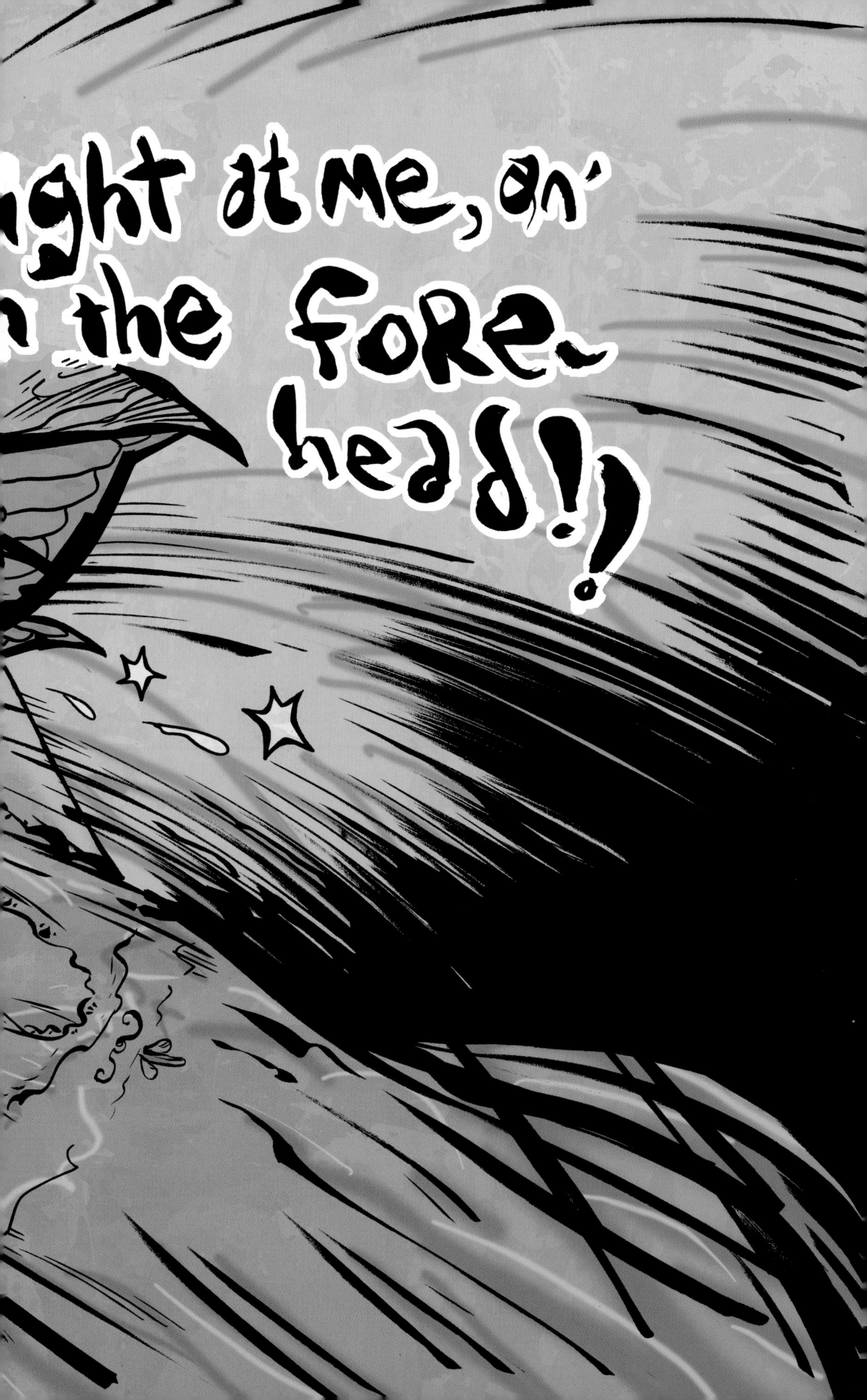
ght at me, an'
n the fore-
head!!

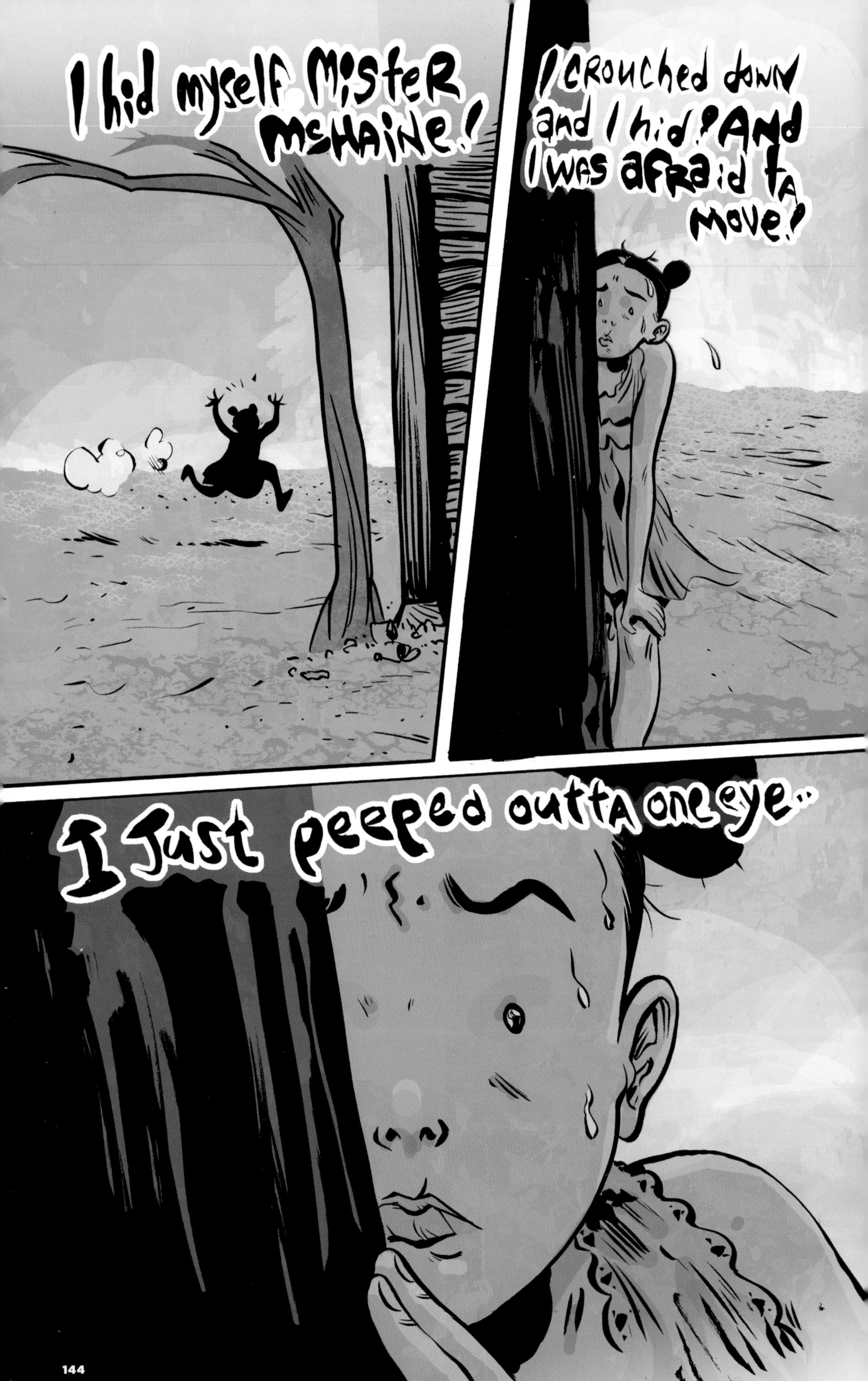
I hid myself Mister McShaine!
I crouched down and I hid! And I was afraid ta move!
I just peeped outta one eye..

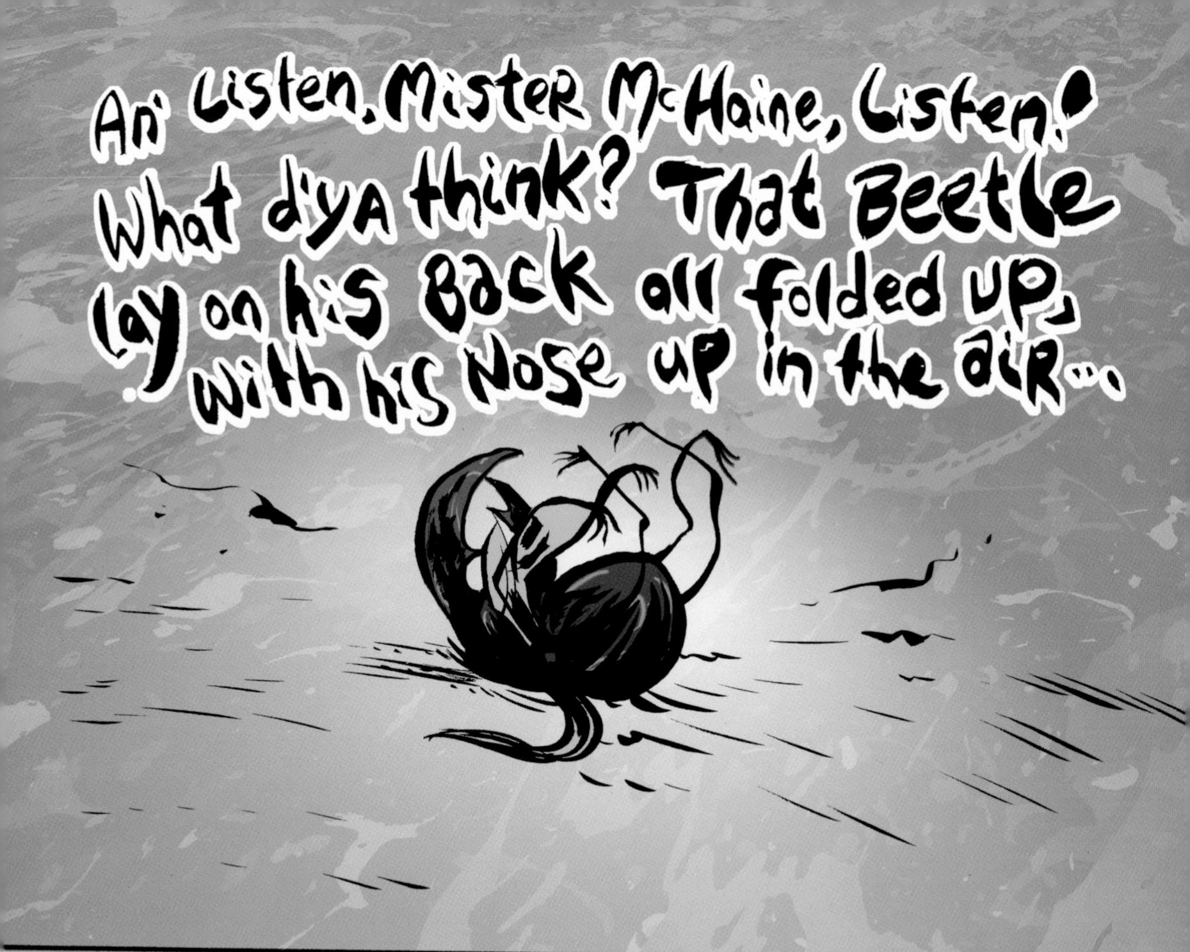
An' Listen, Mister McHaine, Listen!
What d'ya think? That Beetle lay on his Back all folded up, with his Nose up in the air...

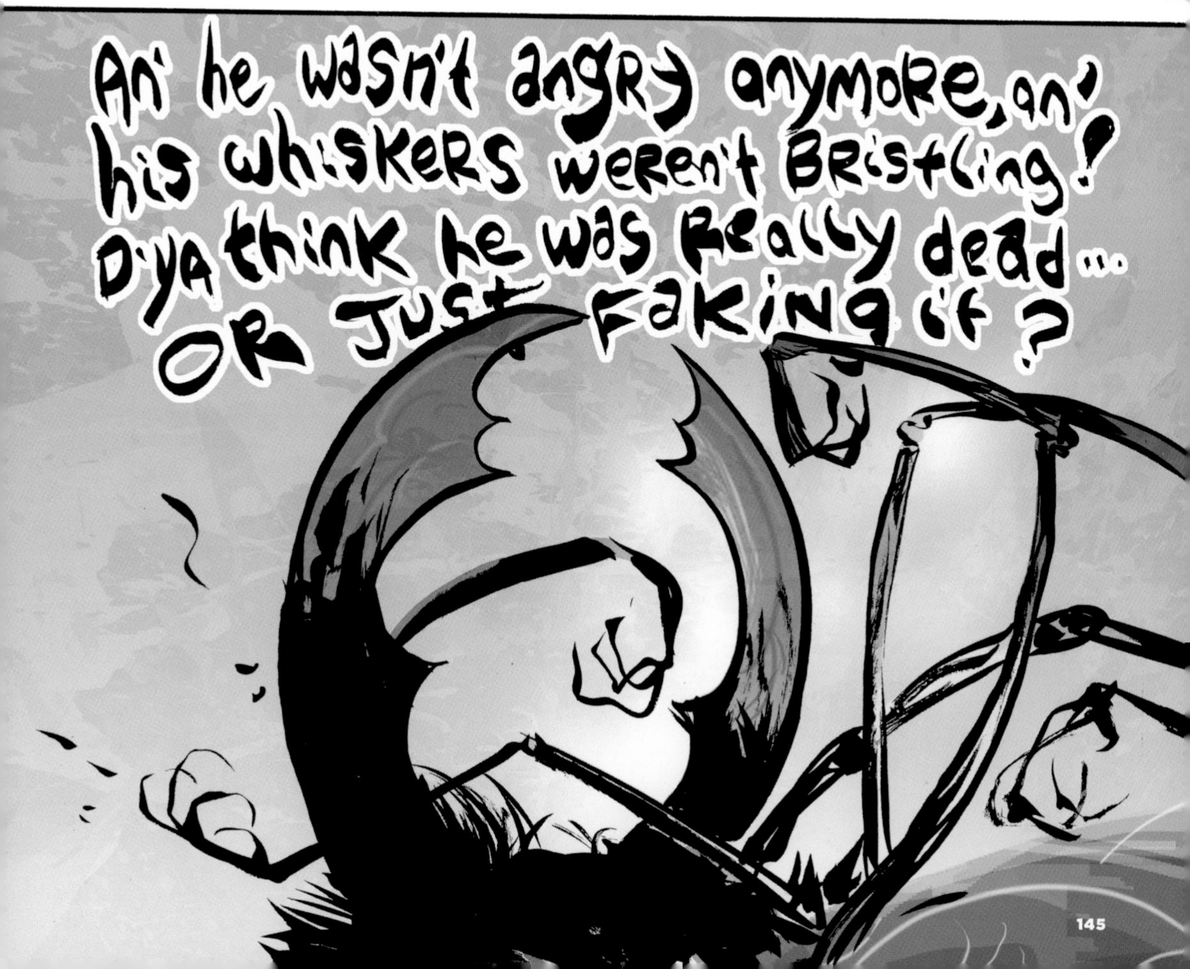
An' he wasn't angry anymore, an' his whiskers weren't Bristling!
D'ya think he was really dead... OR Just faking it?

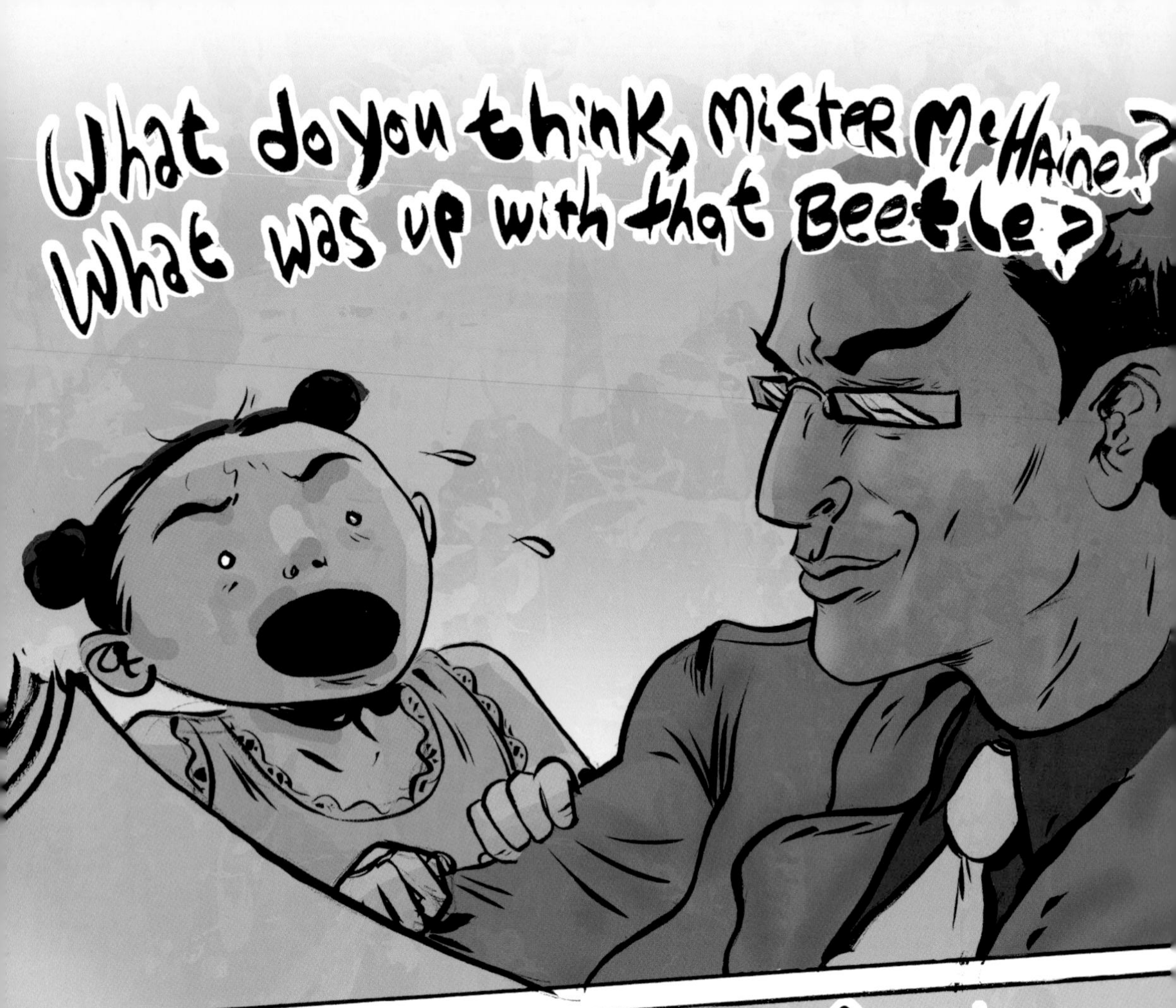
What do you think, Mister McHaine? What was up with that Beetle?

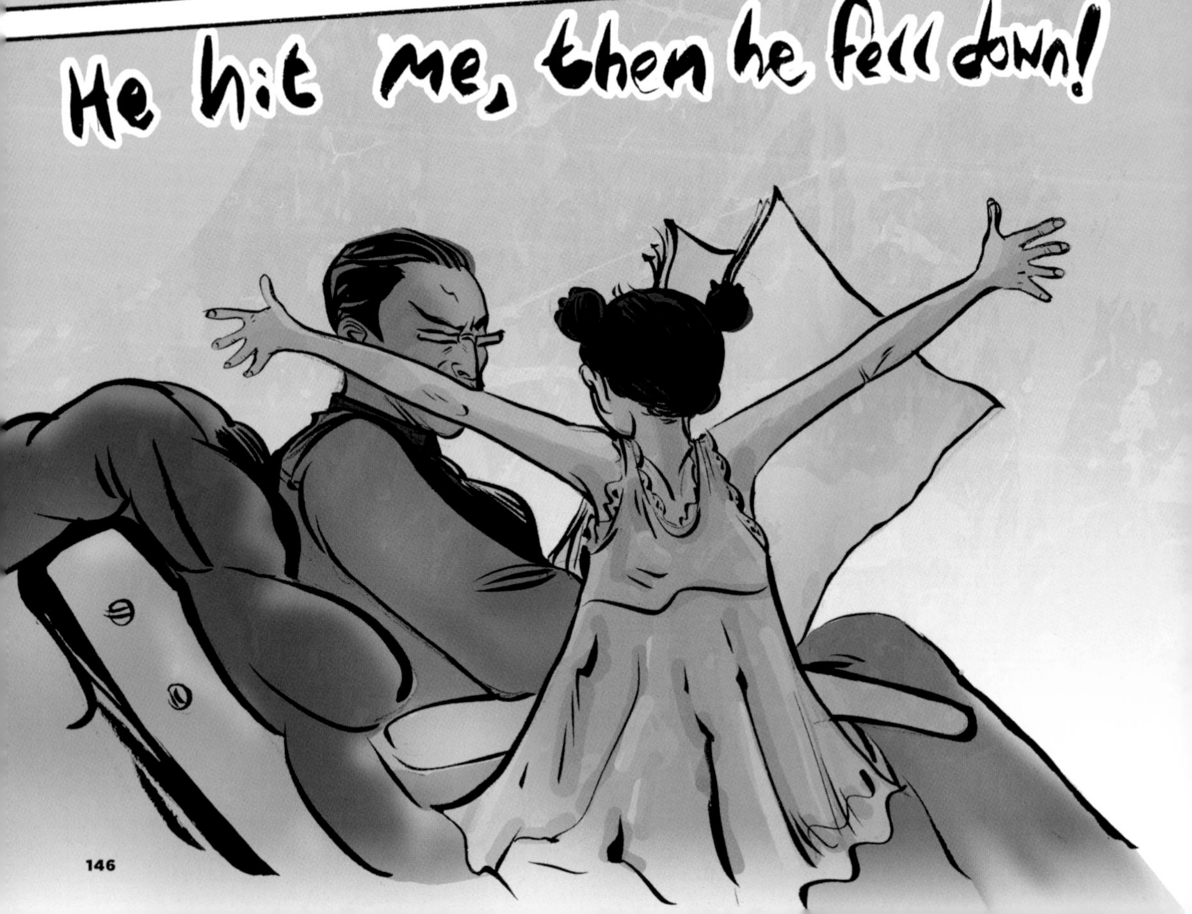
He hit me, then he fell down!

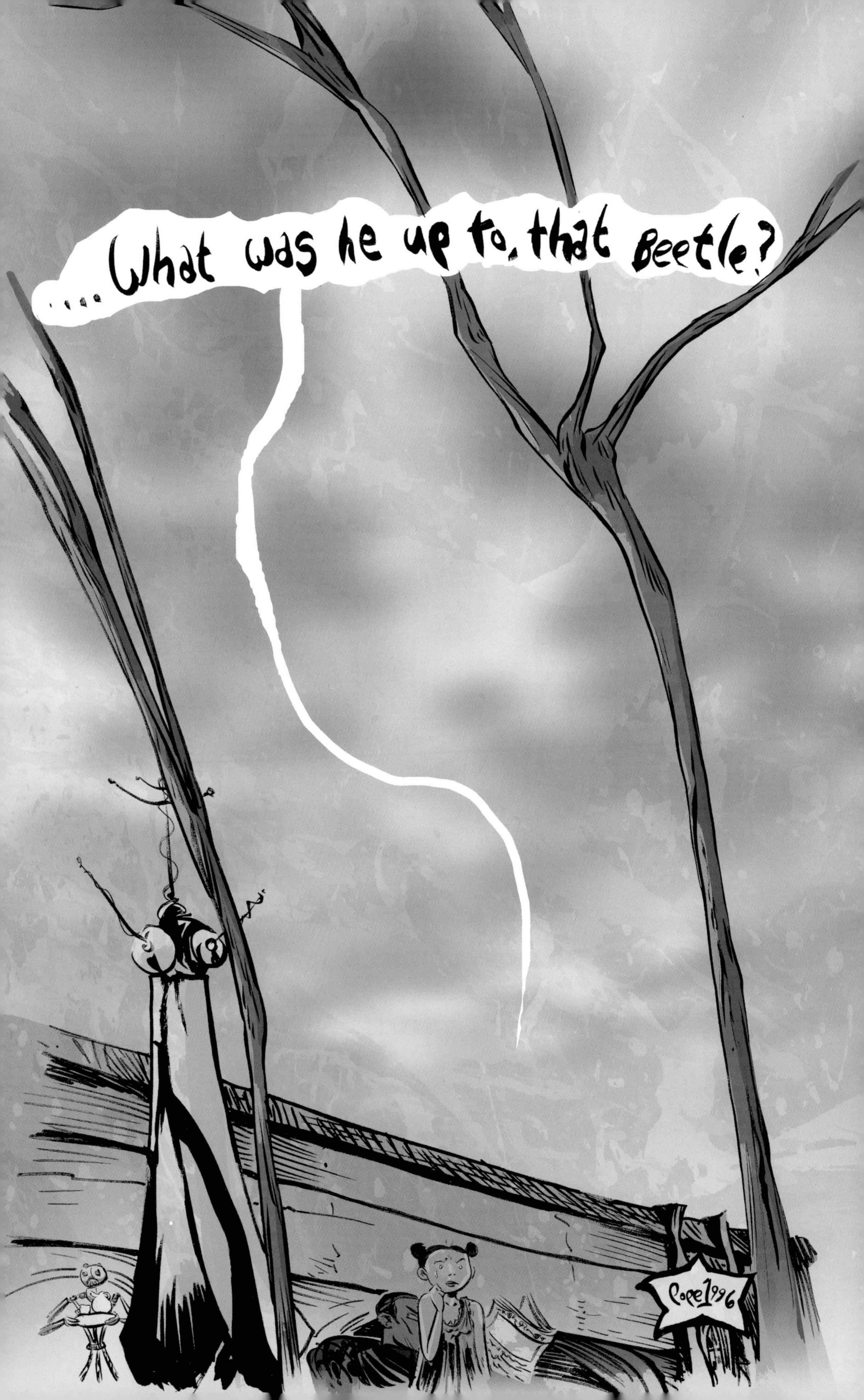
....What was he up to, that Beetle?
Pope 1996

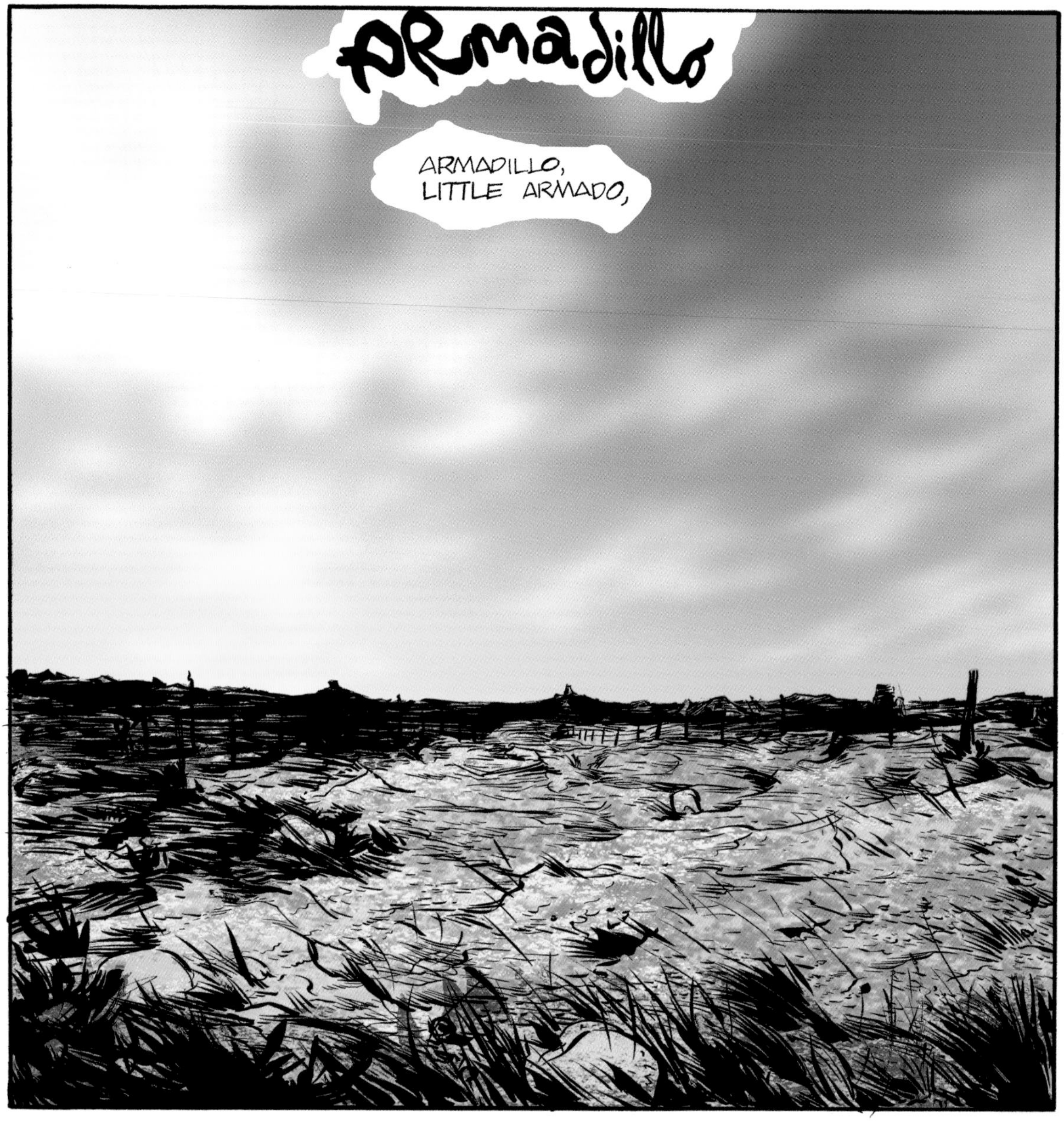
ARMADILLO
ARMADILLO, LITTLE ARMADO,

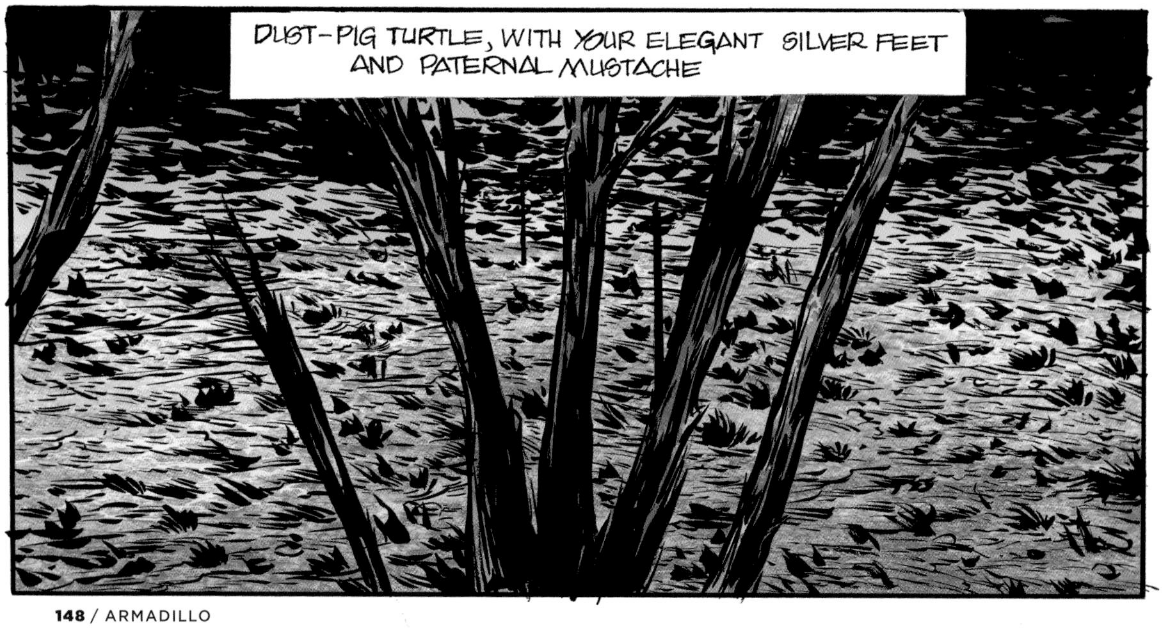
DUST-PIG TURTLE, WITH YOUR ELEGANT SILVER FEET AND PATERNAL MUSTACHE

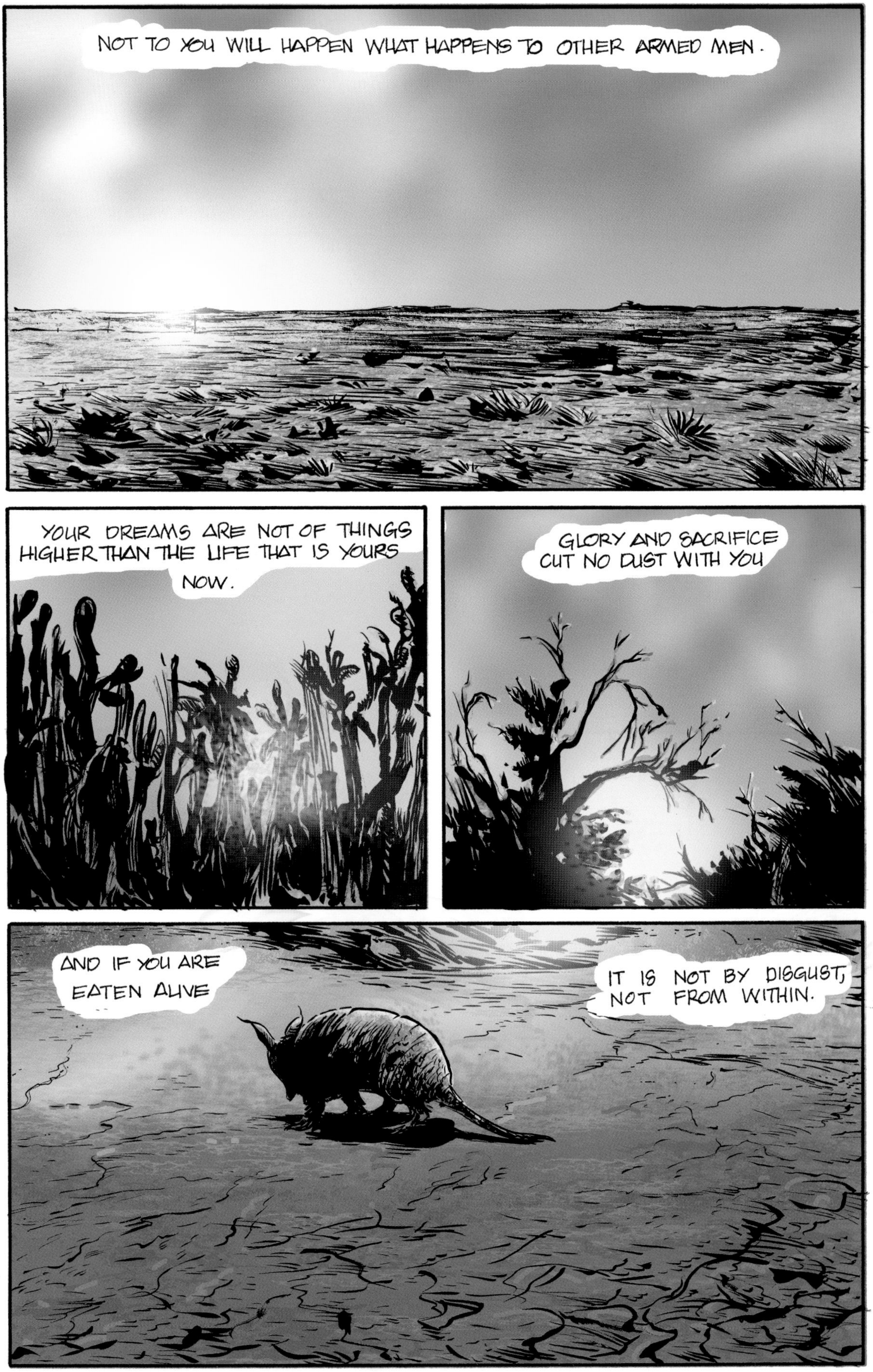
NOT TO YOU WILL HAPPEN WHAT HAPPENS TO OTHER ARMED MEN.
YOUR DREAMS ARE NOT OF THINGS HIGHER THAN THE LIFE THAT IS YOURS NOW.
GLORY AND SACRIFICE CUT NO DUST WITH YOU
AND IF YOU ARE EATEN ALIVE
IT IS NOT BY DISGUST, NOT FROM WITHIN.

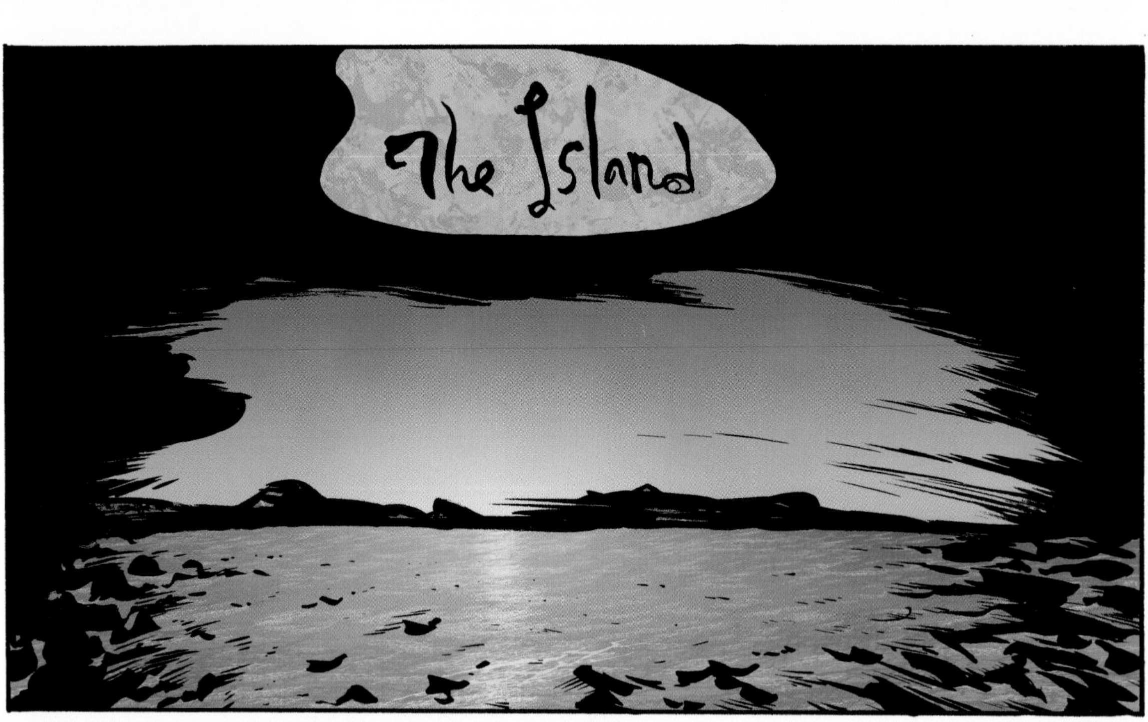
The Island

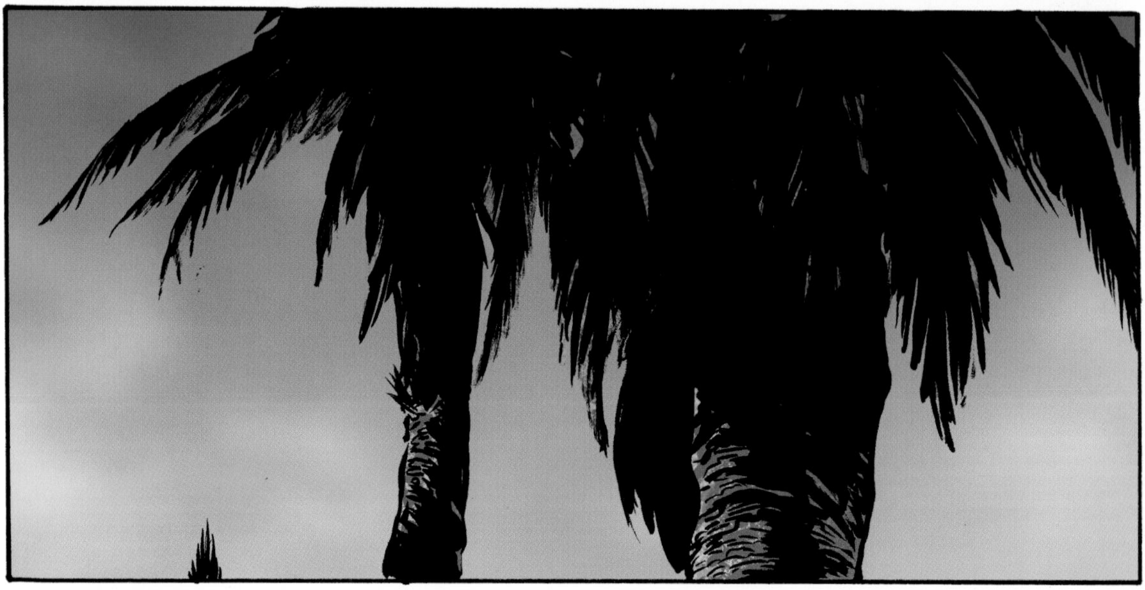

HERE, AFTER THE DAILY RAIN, THE GABI PLANT HOLDS OUT ITS GREAT LEAVES LIKE BAROQUE PLATTERS HEAPED WITH LIGHT, EACH A GREEN SIGH.

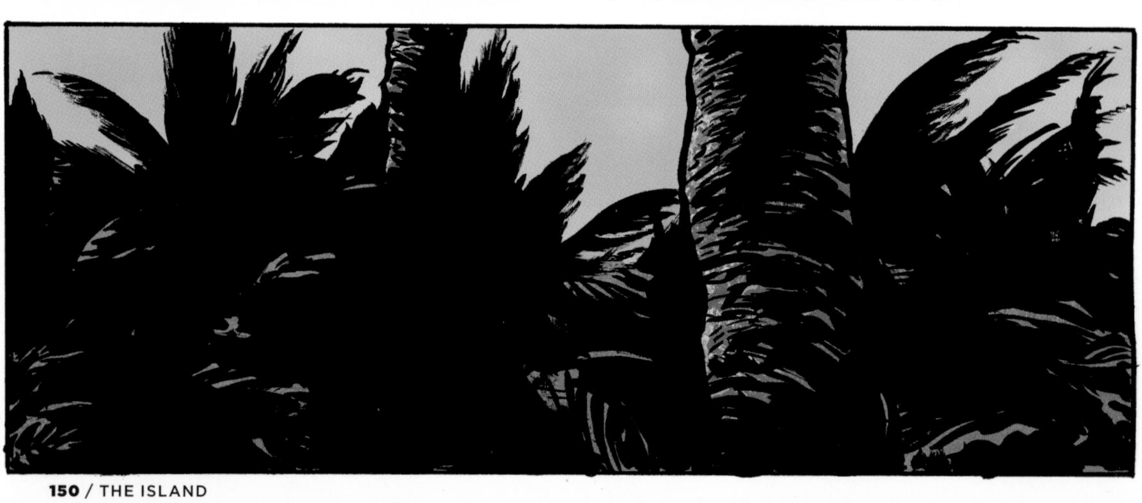

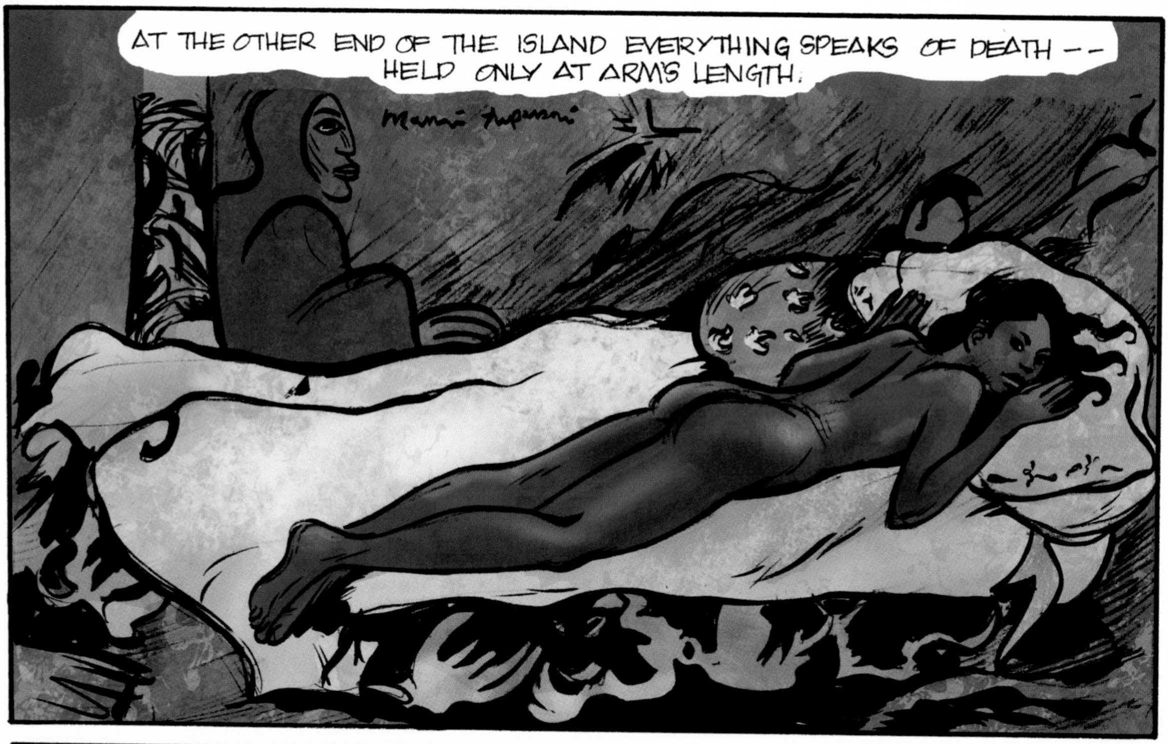
AT THE OTHER END OF THE ISLAND EVERYTHING SPEAKS OF DEATH -- HELD ONLY AT ARM'S LENGTH.

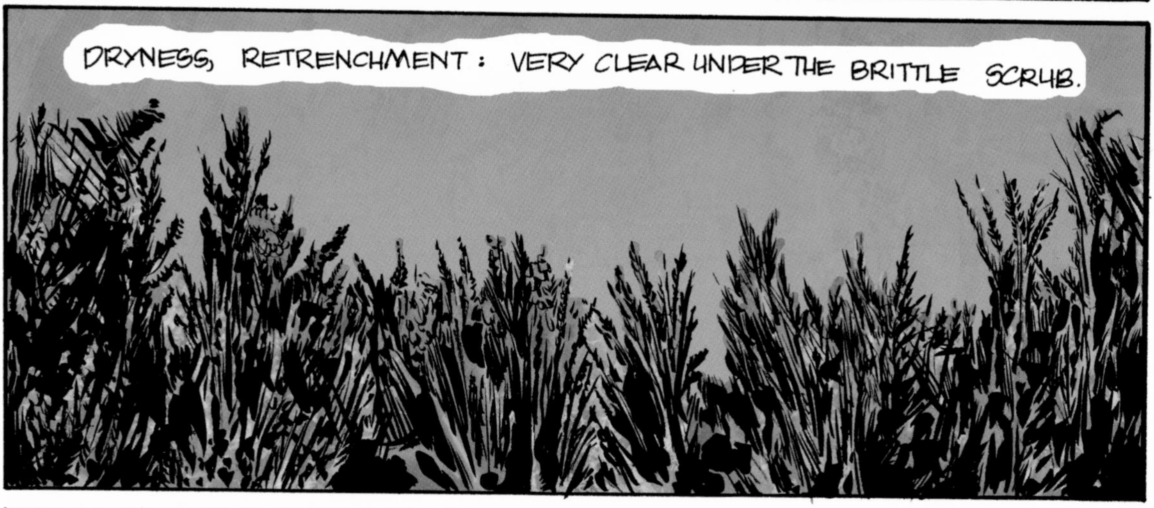
DRYNESS, RETRENCHMENT: VERY CLEAR UNDER THE BRITTLE SCRUB.

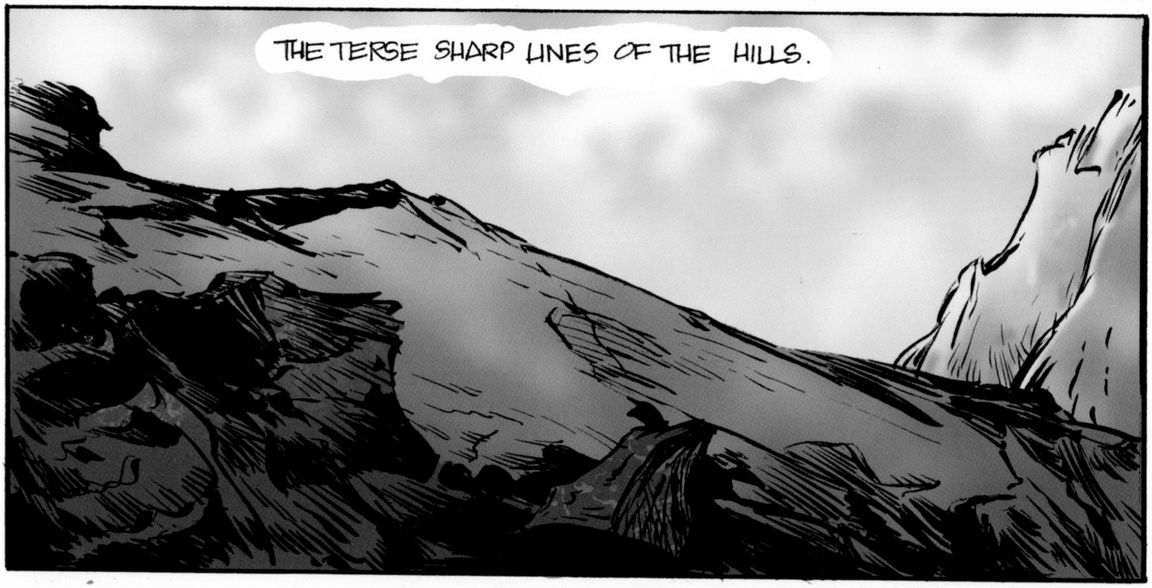
THE TERSE SHARP LINES OF THE HILLS.

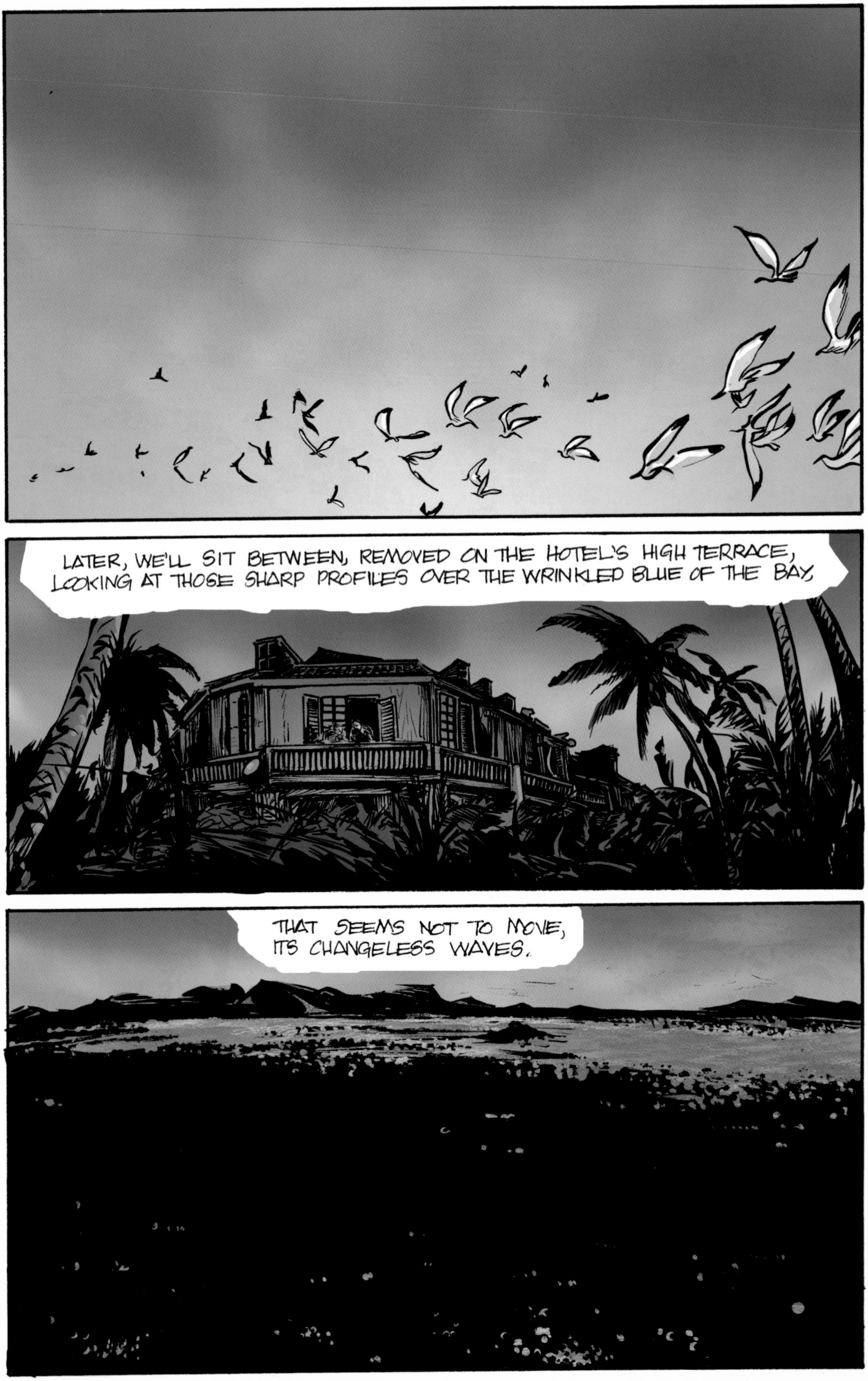
LATER, WE'LL SIT BETWEEN, REMOVED ON THE HOTEL'S HIGH TERRACE, LOOKING AT THOSE SHARP PROFILES OVER THE WRINKLED BLUE OF THE BAY,
THAT SEEMS NOT TO MOVE, ITS CHANGELESS WAVES.

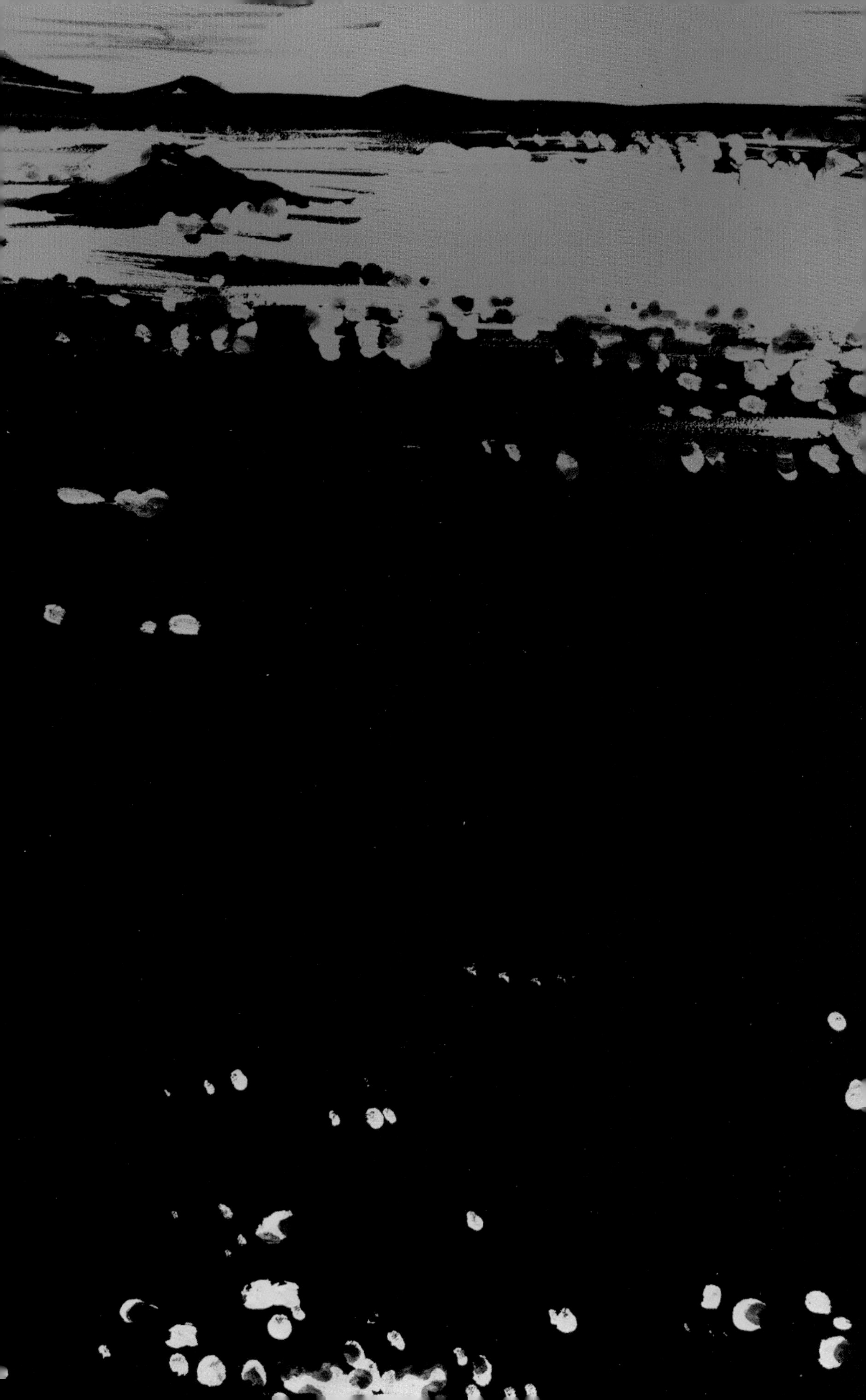

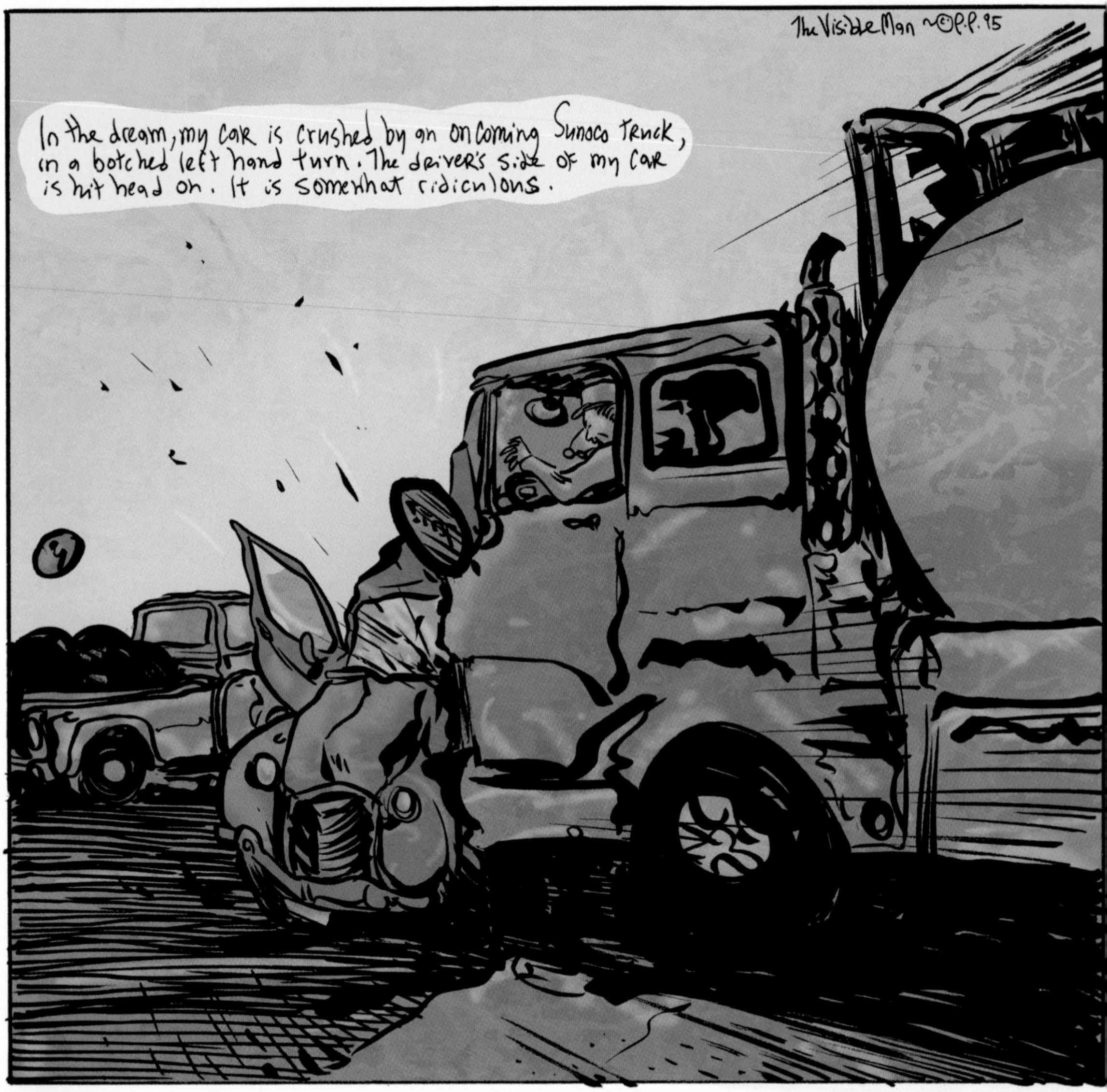
The Visible Man ~©P.P. 95
In the dream, my car is crushed by an oncoming Sunoco truck, in a botched left hand turn. The driver's side of my car is hit head on. It is somewhat ridiculous.

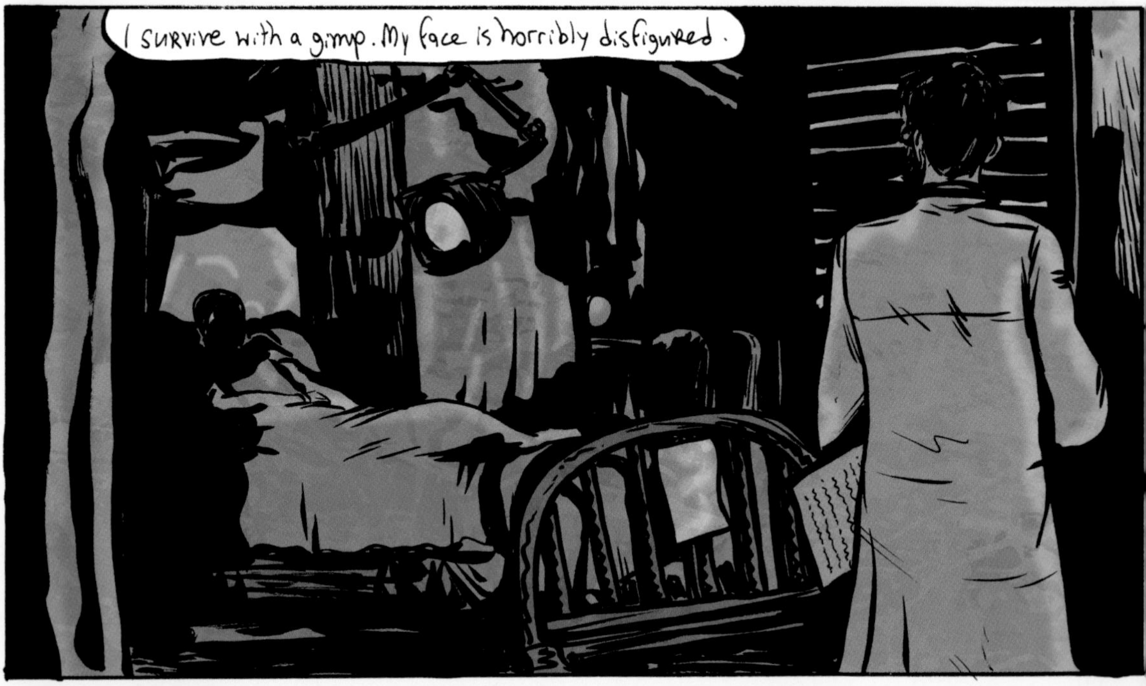
I survive with a gimp. My face is horribly disfigured.

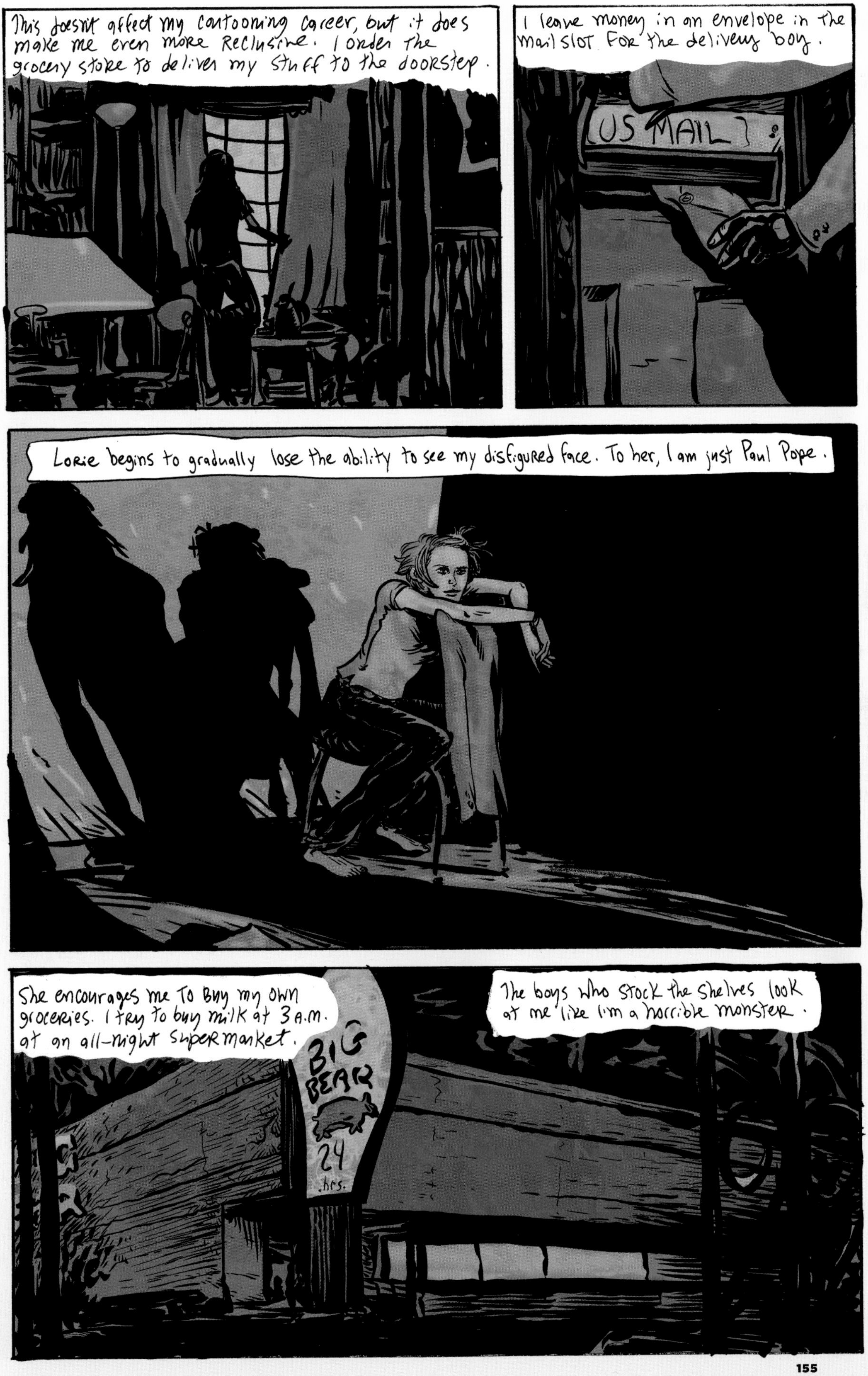
This doesn't affect my cartooning career, but it does
make me even more reclusive. I order the
grocery store to deliver my stuff to the doorstep.
I leave money in an envelope in the
mail slot for the delivery boy.
US MAIL
Lorie begins to gradually lose the ability to see my disfigured face. To her, I am just Paul Pope.
She encourages me to buy my own
groceries. I try to buy milk at 3 A.M.
at an all-night supermarket.
BIG BEAR
24
hrs.
The boys who stock the shelves look
at me like I'm a horrible monster.

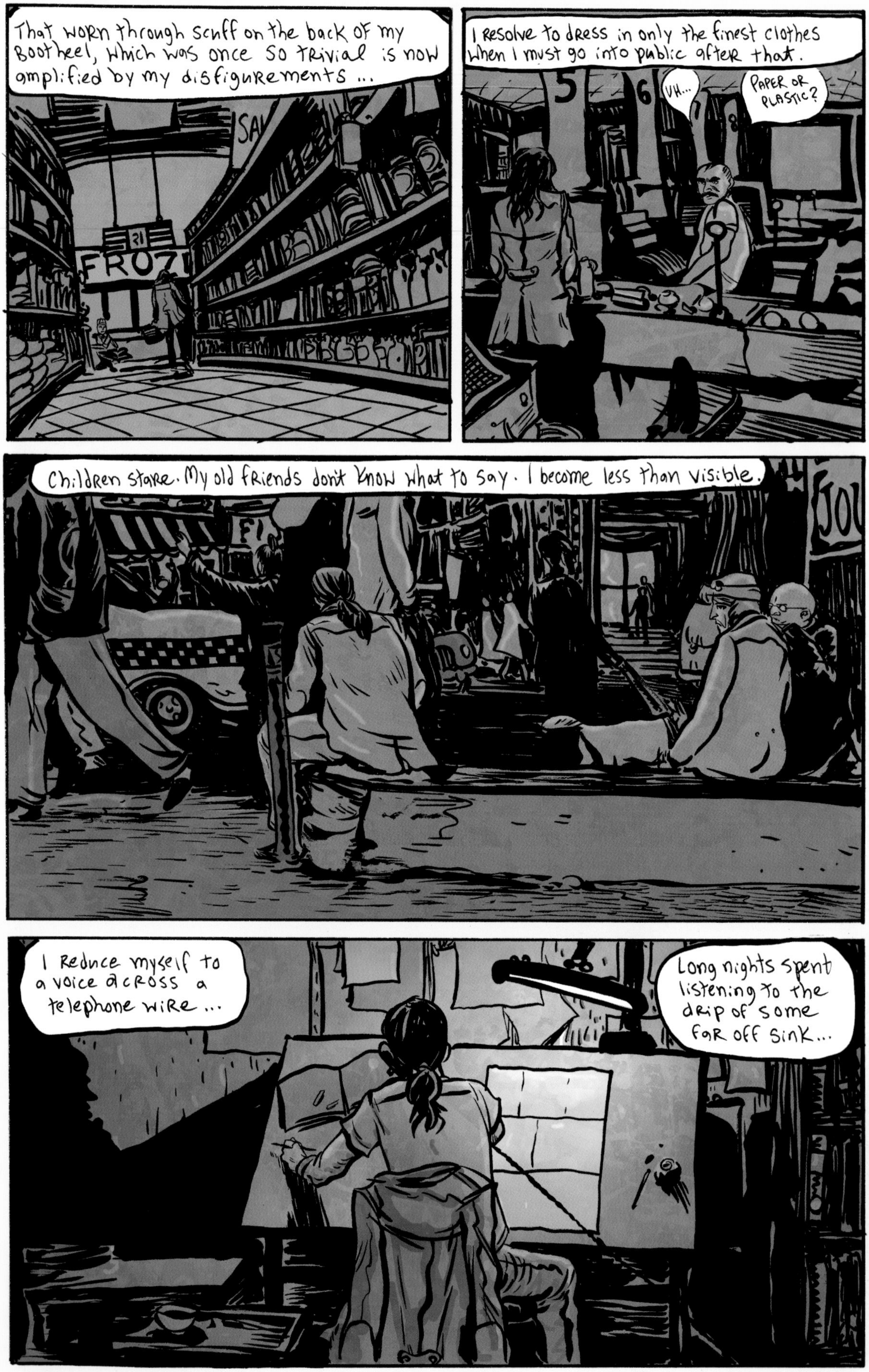
That worn through scuff on the back of my bootheel, which was once so trivial is now amplified by my disfigurements ...
I resolve to dress in only the finest clothes when I must go into public after that.
UH...
PAPER OR PLASTIC?
Children stare. My old friends don't know what to say. I become less than visible.
I reduce myself to a voice across a telephone wire ...
Long nights spent listening to the drip of some far off sink...

Then I go out to the river and I find the smoothest, flattest stone I can find.

I keep it in my pocket for courage and rub it whenever I am afraid.

"I will be strong," I say to myself, "because this is the smoothest, flattest stone I've ever felt."

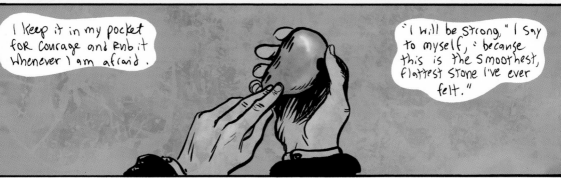

I shave my head and wrap my face with thin, cotton gauze. Lorie helps me.

We experiment with different styles. The final version takes four hours to perfect.

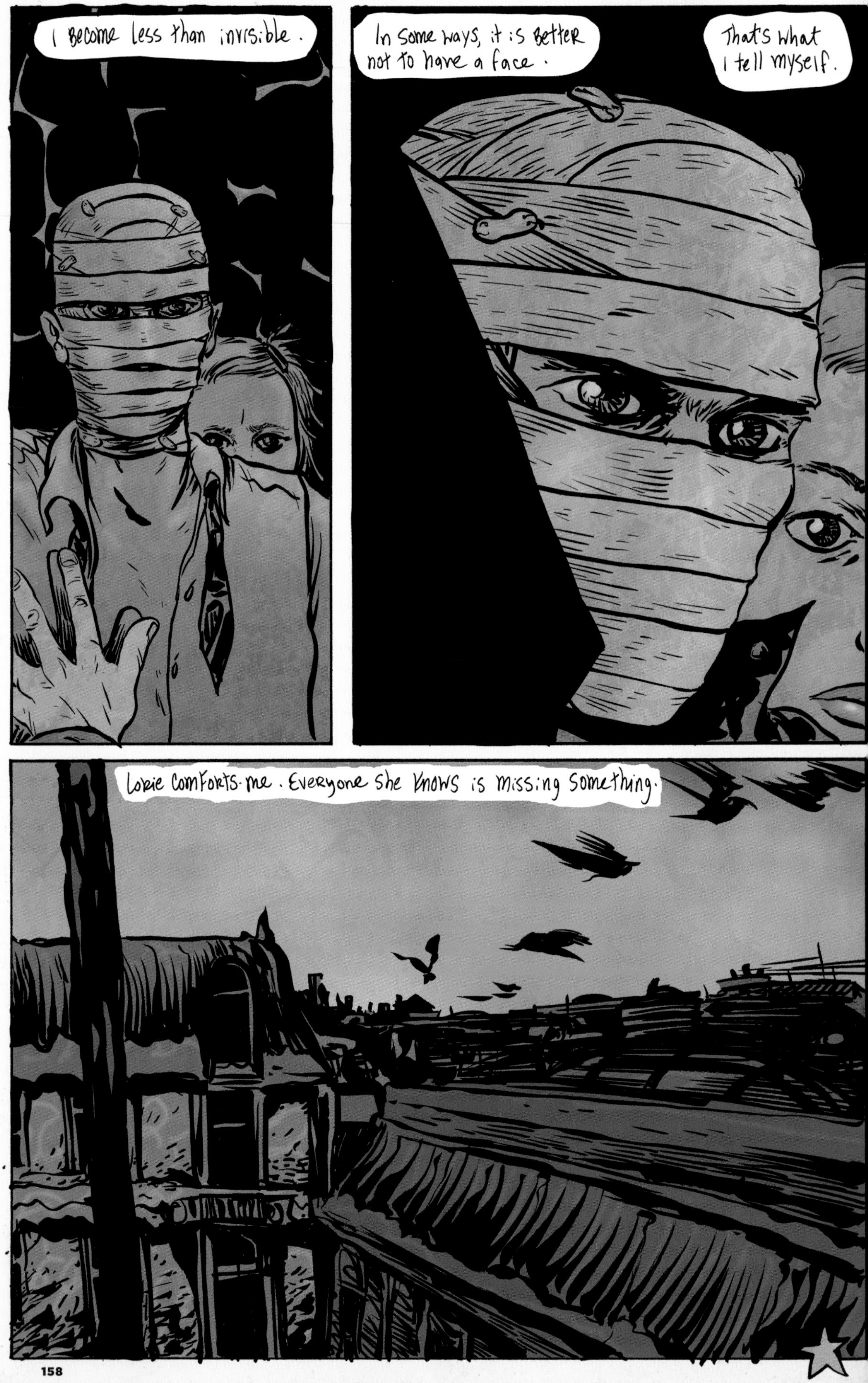
I become less than invisible.
In some ways, it is better not to have a face.
That's what I tell myself.
Lorie comforts me. Everyone she knows is missing something.

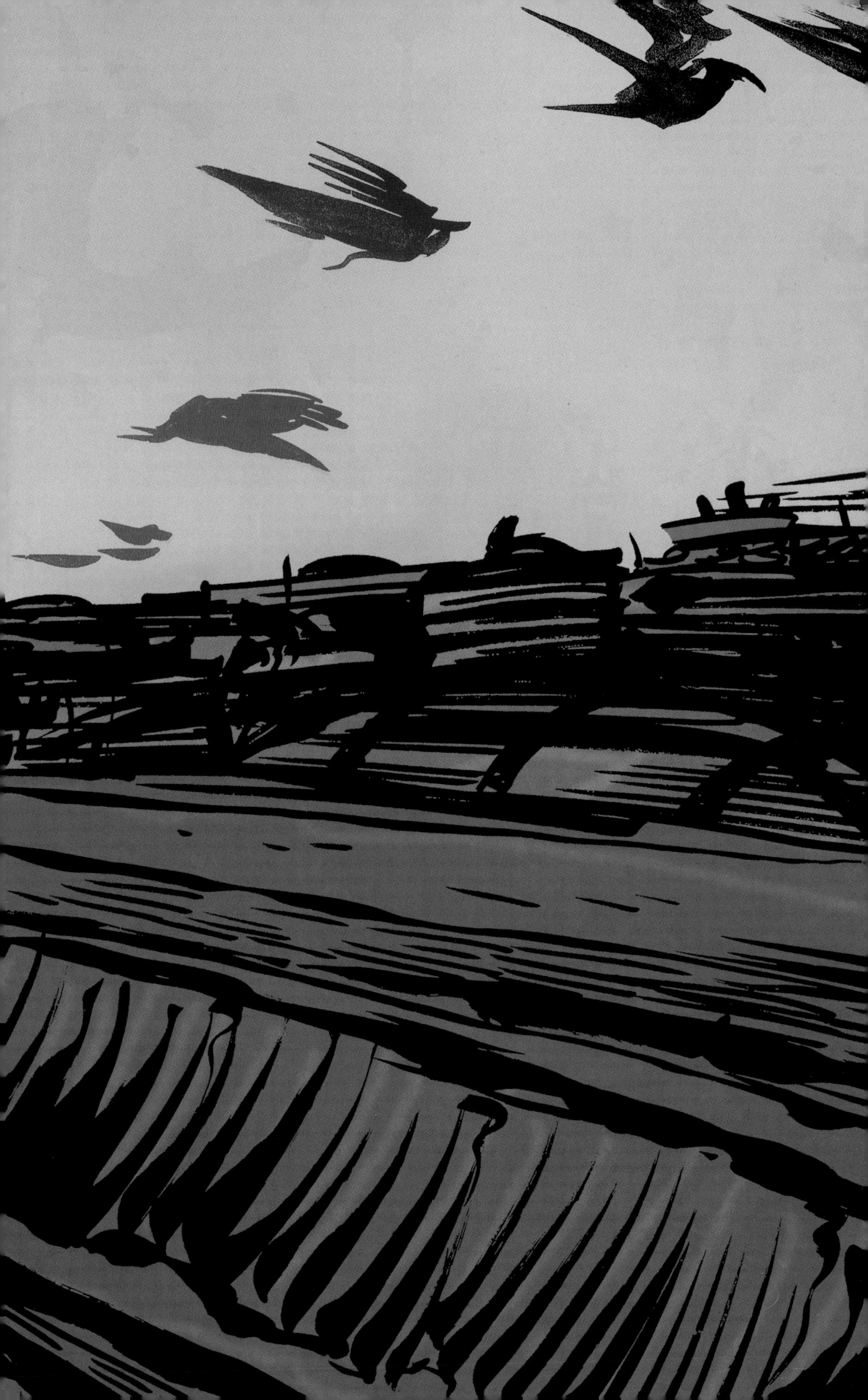

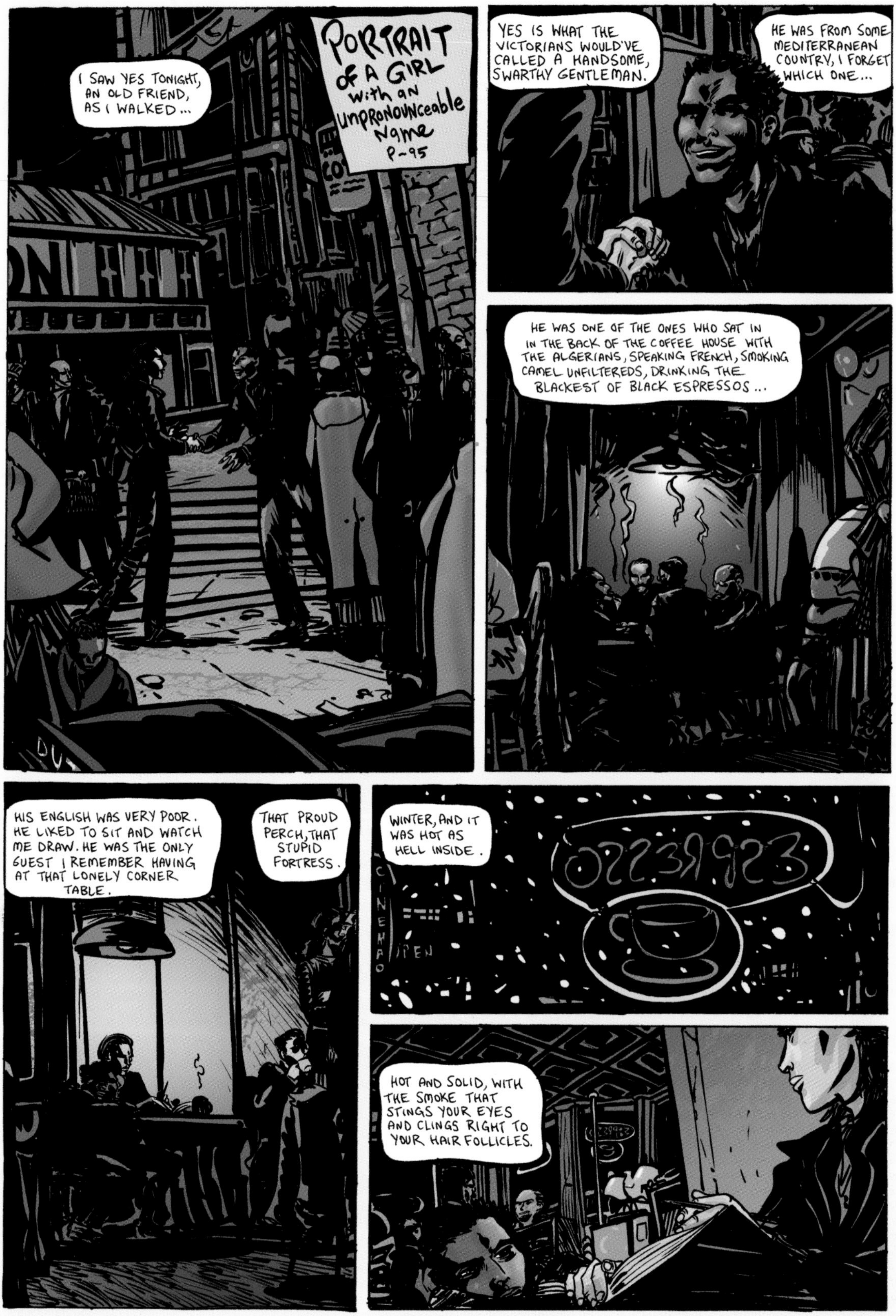
I SAW YES TONIGHT, AN OLD FRIEND, AS I WALKED...
PORTRAIT OF A GIRL with an Unpronounceable Name P~95
YES IS WHAT THE VICTORIANS WOULD'VE CALLED A HANDSOME, SWARTHY GENTLEMAN.
HE WAS FROM SOME MEDITERRANEAN COUNTRY, I FORGET WHICH ONE...
HE WAS ONE OF THE ONES WHO SAT IN IN THE BACK OF THE COFFEE HOUSE WITH THE ALGERIANS, SPEAKING FRENCH, SMOKING CAMEL UNFILTEREDS, DRINKING THE BLACKEST OF BLACK ESPRESSOS...
HIS ENGLISH WAS VERY POOR. HE LIKED TO SIT AND WATCH ME DRAW. HE WAS THE ONLY GUEST I REMEMBER HAVING AT THAT LONELY CORNER TABLE.
THAT PROUD PERCH, THAT STUPID FORTRESS.
WINTER, AND IT WAS HOT AS HELL INSIDE.
HOT AND SOLID, WITH THE SMOKE THAT STINGS YOUR EYES AND CLINGS RIGHT TO YOUR HAIR FOLLICLES.

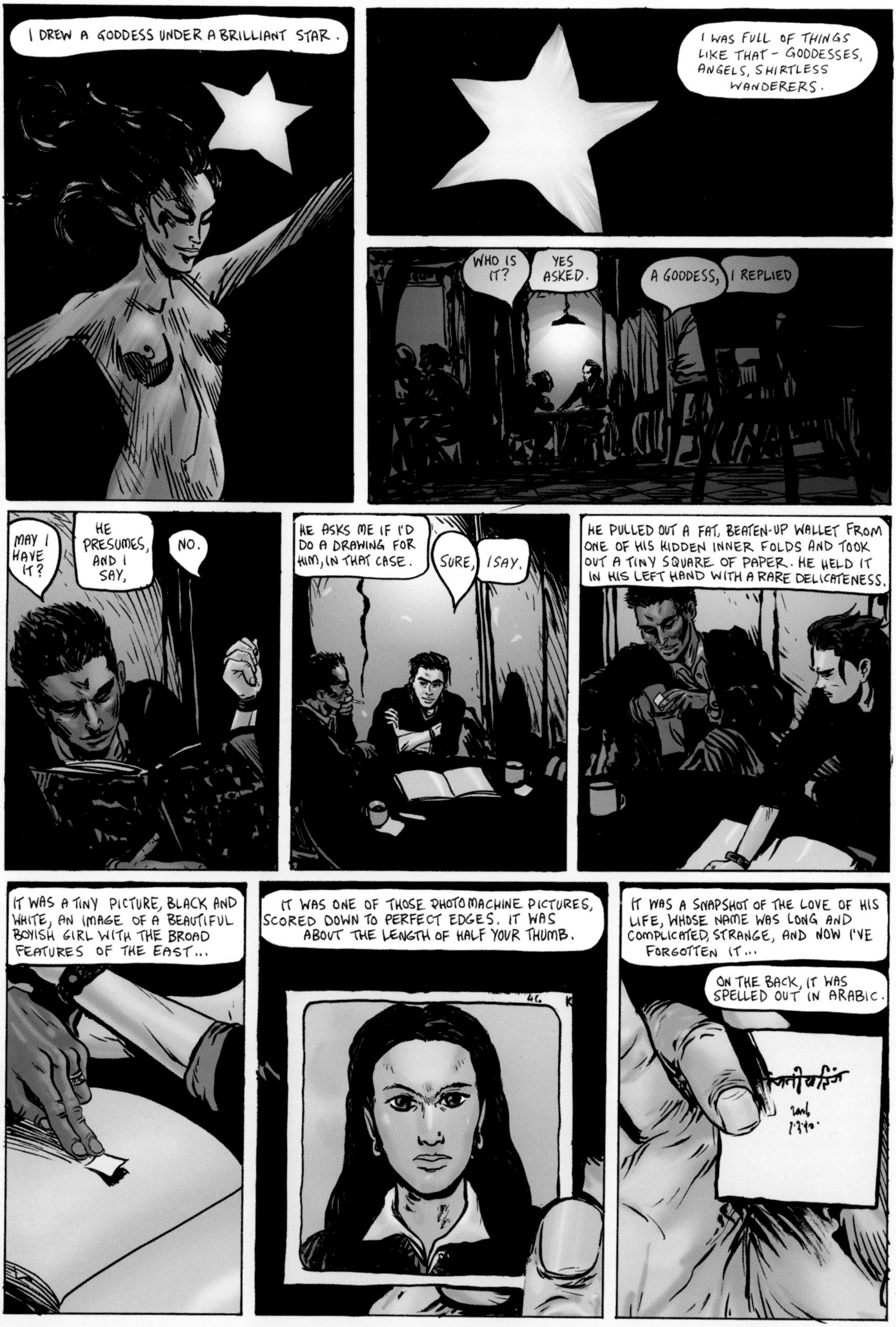
I DREW A GODDESS UNDER A BRILLIANT STAR.
I WAS FULL OF THINGS LIKE THAT - GODDESSES, ANGELS, SHIRTLESS WANDERERS.
WHO IS IT?
YES ASKED.
A GODDESS,
I REPLIED
MAY I HAVE IT?
HE PRESUMES, AND I SAY,
NO.
HE ASKS ME IF I'D DO A DRAWING FOR HIM, IN THAT CASE.
SURE,
I SAY.
HE PULLED OUT A FAT, BEATEN-UP WALLET FROM ONE OF HIS HIDDEN INNER FOLDS AND TOOK OUT A TINY SQUARE OF PAPER. HE HELD IT IN HIS LEFT HAND WITH A RARE DELICATENESS.
IT WAS A TINY PICTURE, BLACK AND WHITE, AN IMAGE OF A BEAUTIFUL BOYISH GIRL WITH THE BROAD FEATURES OF THE EAST...
IT WAS ONE OF THOSE PHOTOMACHINE PICTURES, SCORED DOWN TO PERFECT EDGES. IT WAS ABOUT THE LENGTH OF HALF YOUR THUMB.
IT WAS A SNAPSHOT OF THE LOVE OF HIS LIFE, WHOSE NAME WAS LONG AND COMPLICATED, STRANGE, AND NOW I'VE FORGOTTEN IT...
ON THE BACK, IT WAS SPELLED OUT IN ARABIC.

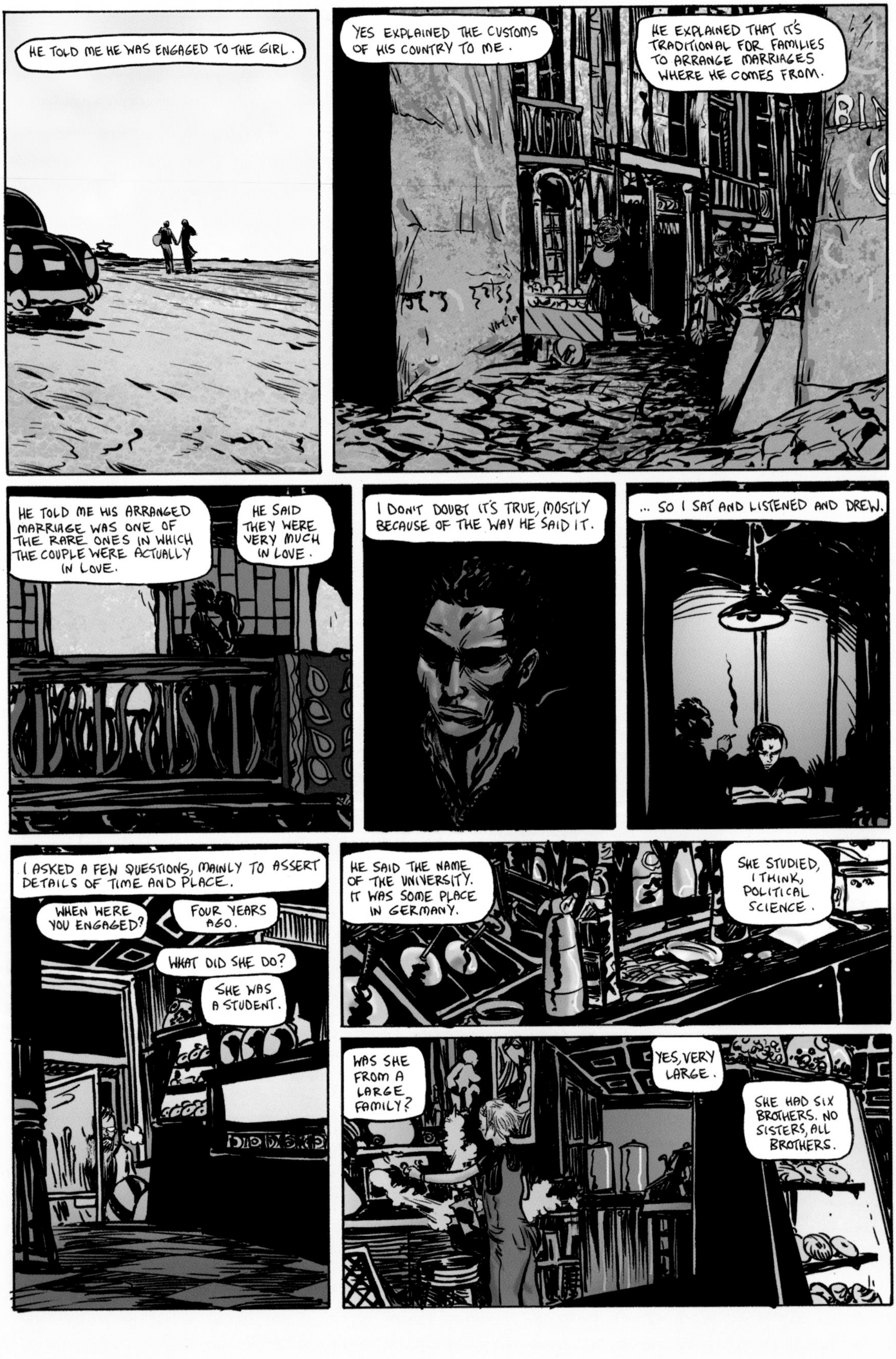
HE TOLD ME HE WAS ENGAGED TO THE GIRL.
YES EXPLAINED THE CUSTOMS OF HIS COUNTRY TO ME.
HE EXPLAINED THAT IT'S TRADITIONAL FOR FAMILIES TO ARRANGE MARRIAGES WHERE HE COMES FROM.
HE TOLD ME HIS ARRANGED MARRIAGE WAS ONE OF THE RARE ONES IN WHICH THE COUPLE WERE ACTUALLY IN LOVE.
HE SAID THEY WERE VERY MUCH IN LOVE.
I DON'T DOUBT IT'S TRUE, MOSTLY BECAUSE OF THE WAY HE SAID IT.
... SO I SAT AND LISTENED AND DREW.
I ASKED A FEW QUESTIONS, MAINLY TO ASSERT DETAILS OF TIME AND PLACE.
WHEN WERE YOU ENGAGED?
FOUR YEARS AGO.
WHAT DID SHE DO?
SHE WAS A STUDENT.
HE SAID THE NAME OF THE UNIVERSITY. IT WAS SOME PLACE IN GERMANY.
SHE STUDIED, I THINK, POLITICAL SCIENCE.
WAS SHE FROM A LARGE FAMILY?
YES, VERY LARGE.
SHE HAD SIX BROTHERS. NO SISTERS, ALL BROTHERS.

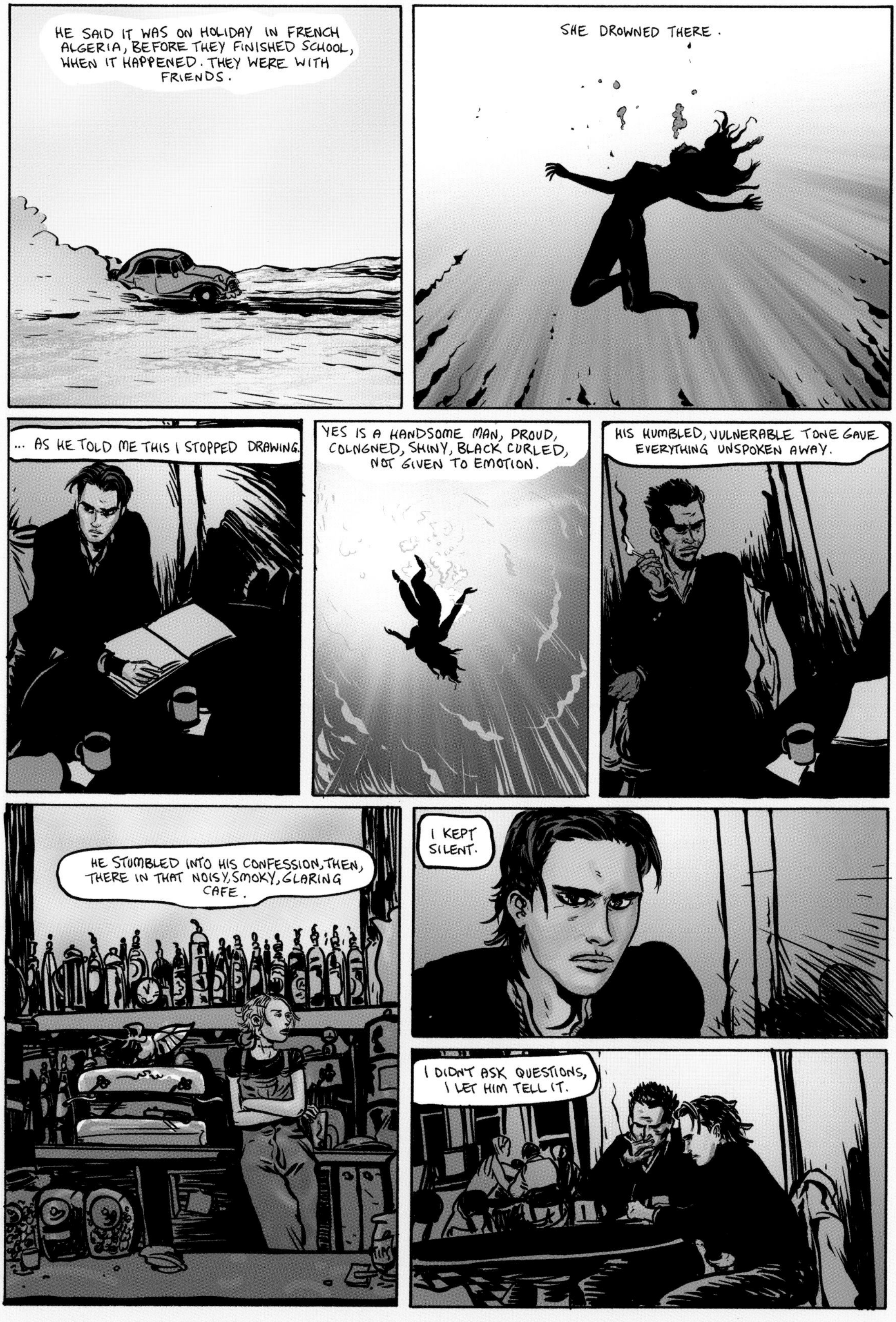
HE SAID IT WAS ON HOLIDAY IN FRENCH ALGERIA, BEFORE THEY FINISHED SCHOOL, WHEN IT HAPPENED. THEY WERE WITH FRIENDS.
SHE DROWNED THERE.
... AS HE TOLD ME THIS I STOPPED DRAWING.
YES IS A HANDSOME MAN, PROUD, COLOGNED, SHINY, BLACK CURLED, NOT GIVEN TO EMOTION.
HIS HUMBLED, VULNERABLE TONE GAVE EVERYTHING UNSPOKEN AWAY.
HE STUMBLED INTO HIS CONFESSION, THEN, THERE IN THAT NOISY, SMOKY, GLARING CAFE.
I KEPT SILENT.
I DIDN'T ASK QUESTIONS, I LET HIM TELL IT.

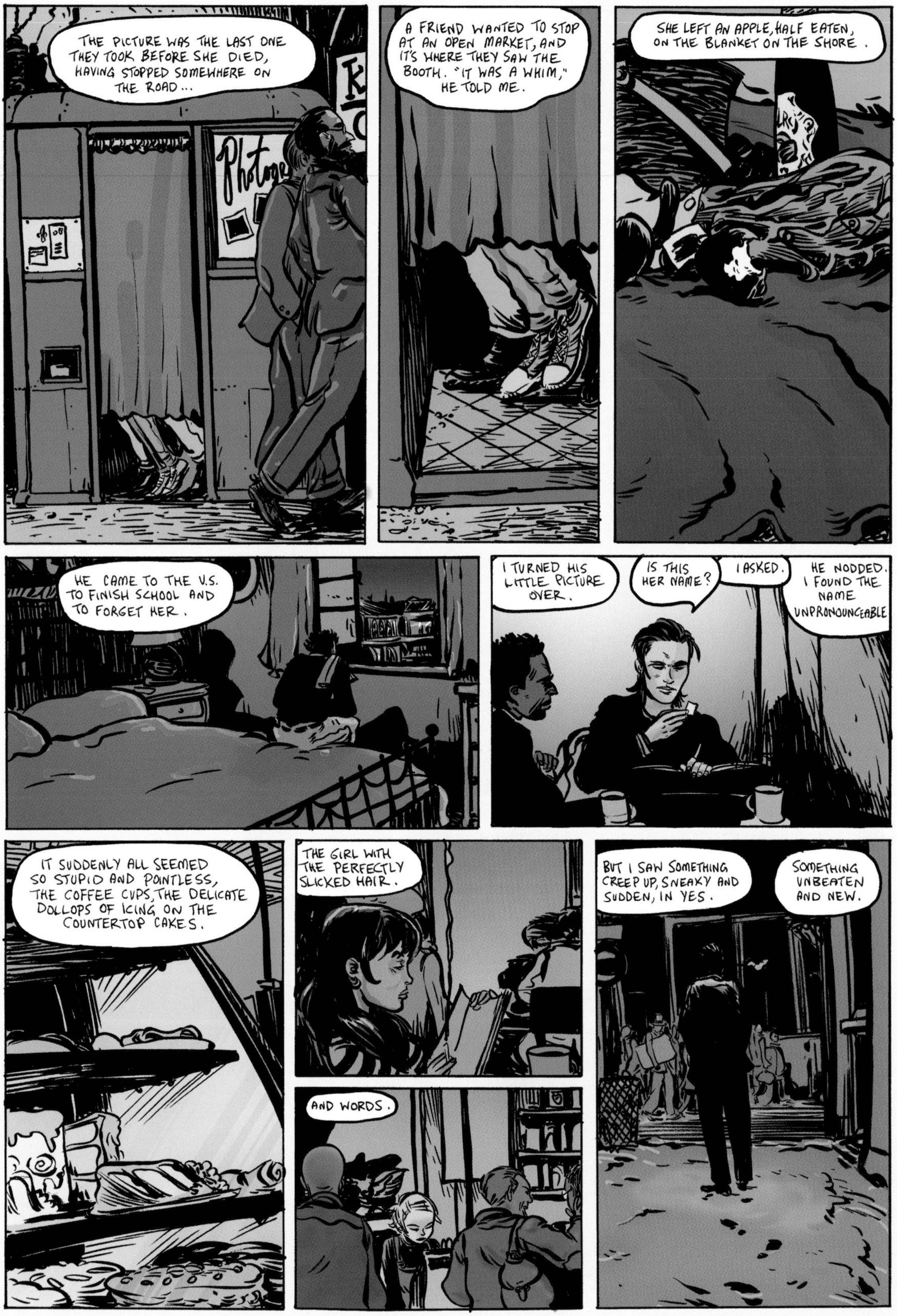
THE PICTURE WAS THE LAST ONE THEY TOOK BEFORE SHE DIED, HAVING STOPPED SOMEWHERE ON THE ROAD...
A FRIEND WANTED TO STOP AT AN OPEN MARKET, AND IT'S WHERE THEY SAW THE BOOTH. "IT WAS A WHIM," HE TOLD ME.
SHE LEFT AN APPLE, HALF EATEN, ON THE BLANKET ON THE SHORE.
HE CAME TO THE U.S. TO FINISH SCHOOL AND TO FORGET HER.
I TURNED HIS LITTLE PICTURE OVER.
IS THIS HER NAME?
I ASKED.
HE NODDED. I FOUND THE NAME UNPRONOUNCEABLE
IT SUDDENLY ALL SEEMED SO STUPID AND POINTLESS, THE COFFEE CUPS, THE DELICATE DOLLOPS OF ICING ON THE COUNTERTOP CAKES.
THE GIRL WITH THE PERFECTLY SLICKED HAIR.
AND WORDS.
BUT I SAW SOMETHING CREEP UP, SNEAKY AND SUDDEN, IN YES.
SOMETHING UNBEATEN AND NEW.

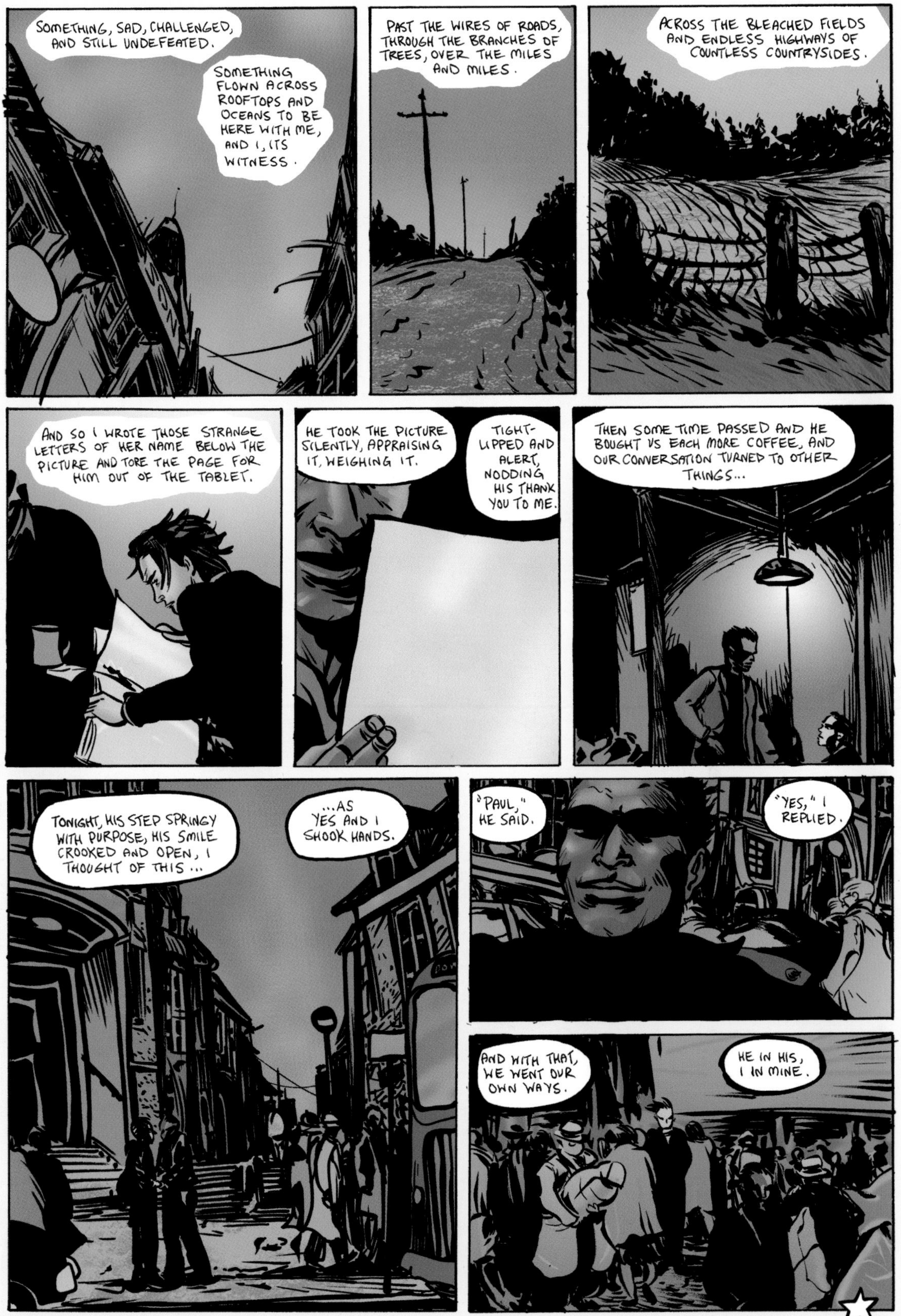
SOMETHING, SAD, CHALLENGED, AND STILL UNDEFEATED.
SOMETHING FLOWN ACROSS ROOFTOPS AND OCEANS TO BE HERE WITH ME, AND I, ITS WITNESS.
PAST THE WIRES OF ROADS, THROUGH THE BRANCHES OF TREES, OVER THE MILES AND MILES.
ACROSS THE BLEACHED FIELDS AND ENDLESS HIGHWAYS OF COUNTLESS COUNTRYSIDES.
AND SO I WROTE THOSE STRANGE LETTERS OF HER NAME BELOW THE PICTURE AND TORE THE PAGE FOR HIM OUT OF THE TABLET.
HE TOOK THE PICTURE SILENTLY, APPRAISING IT, WEIGHING IT.
TIGHT-LIPPED AND ALERT, NODDING HIS THANK YOU TO ME.
THEN SOME TIME PASSED AND HE BOUGHT US EACH MORE COFFEE, AND OUR CONVERSATION TURNED TO OTHER THINGS...
TONIGHT, HIS STEP SPRINGY WITH PURPOSE, HIS SMILE CROOKED AND OPEN, I THOUGHT OF THIS...
...AS YES AND I SHOOK HANDS.
"PAUL," HE SAID.
"YES," I REPLIED.
AND WITH THAT, WE WENT OUR OWN WAYS.
HE IN HIS, I IN MINE.

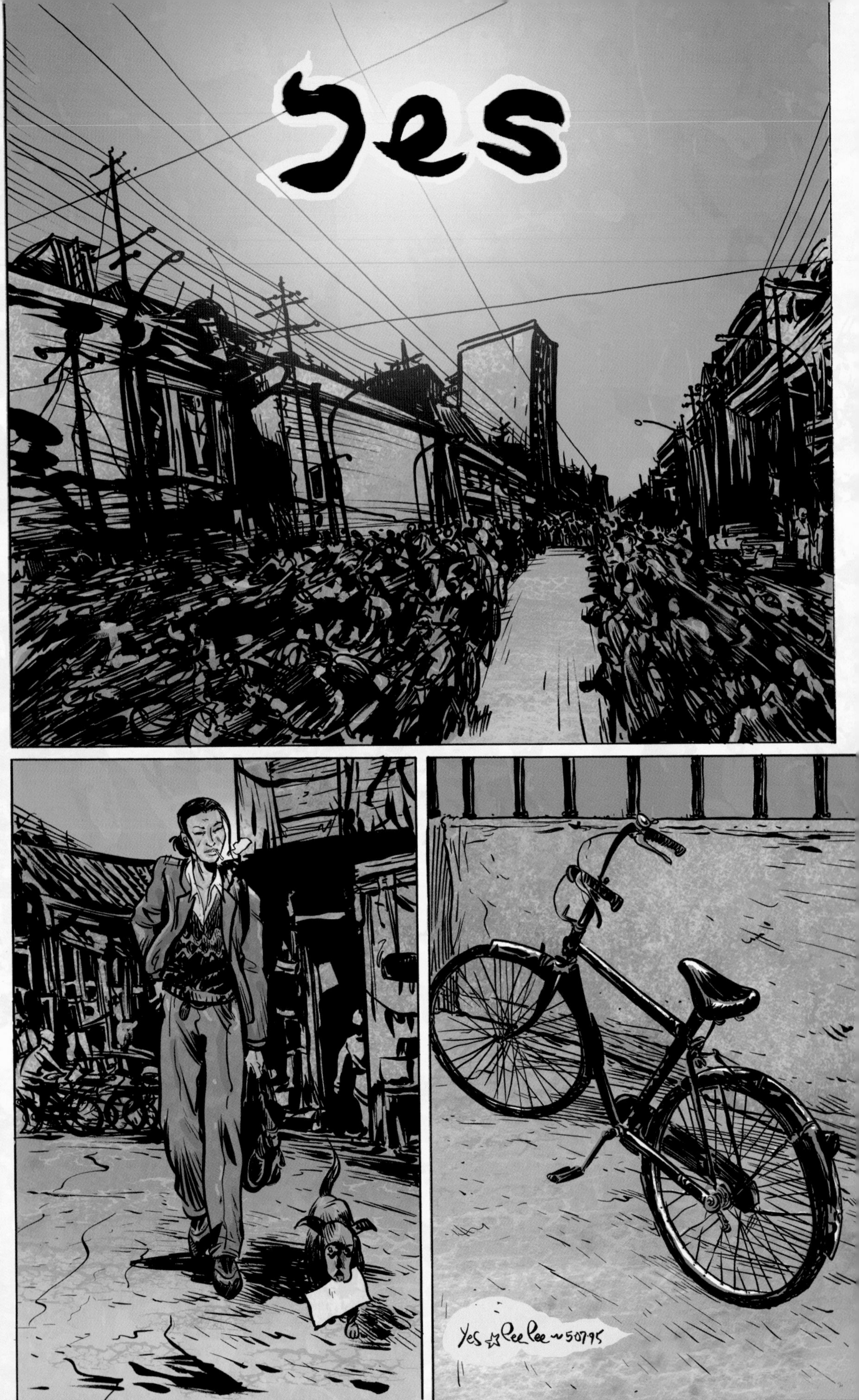
Yes
Yes ☆ Lee Lee ~ 5.07.95

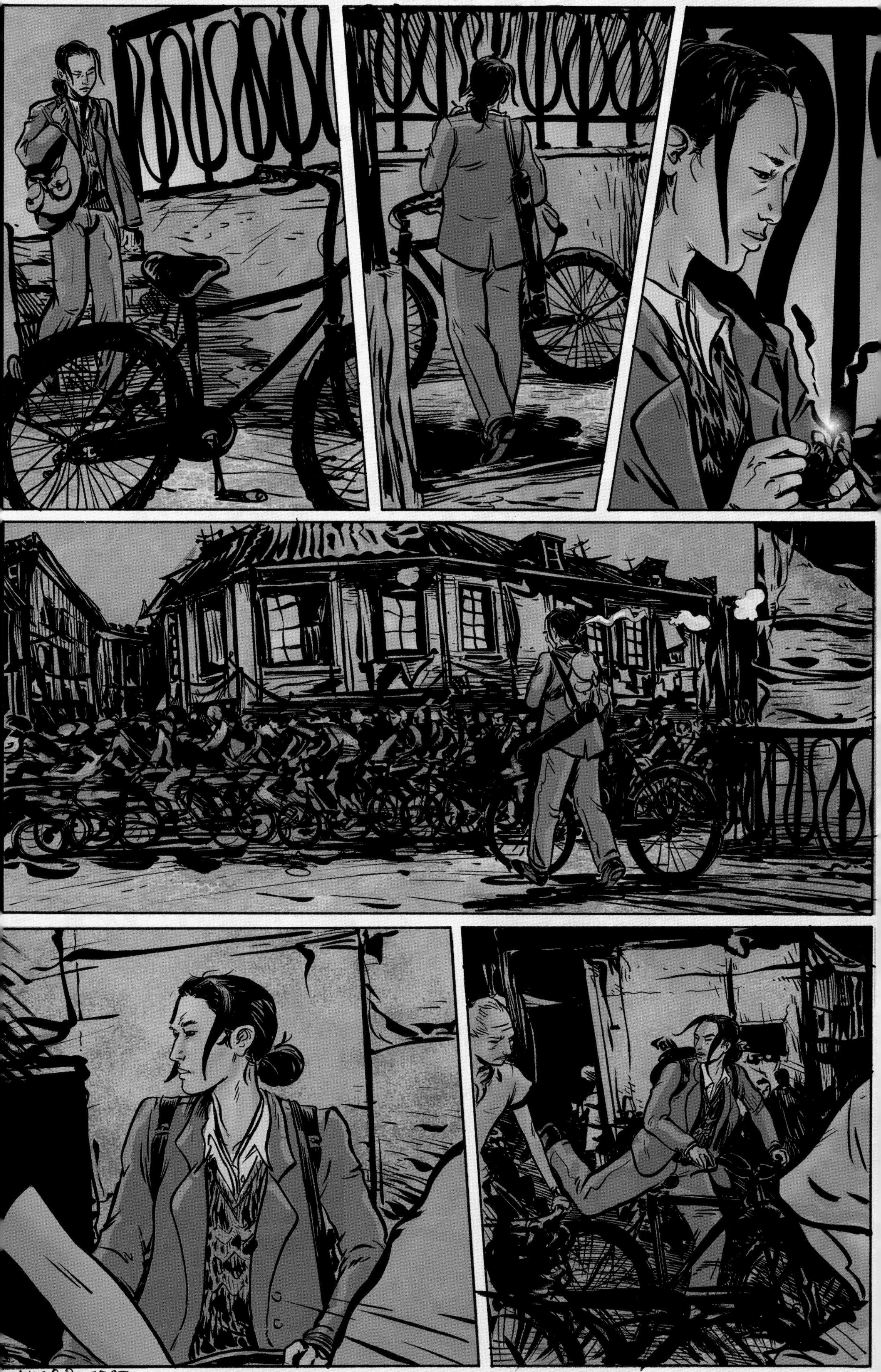
☆yes/ReeRee 5·7·95

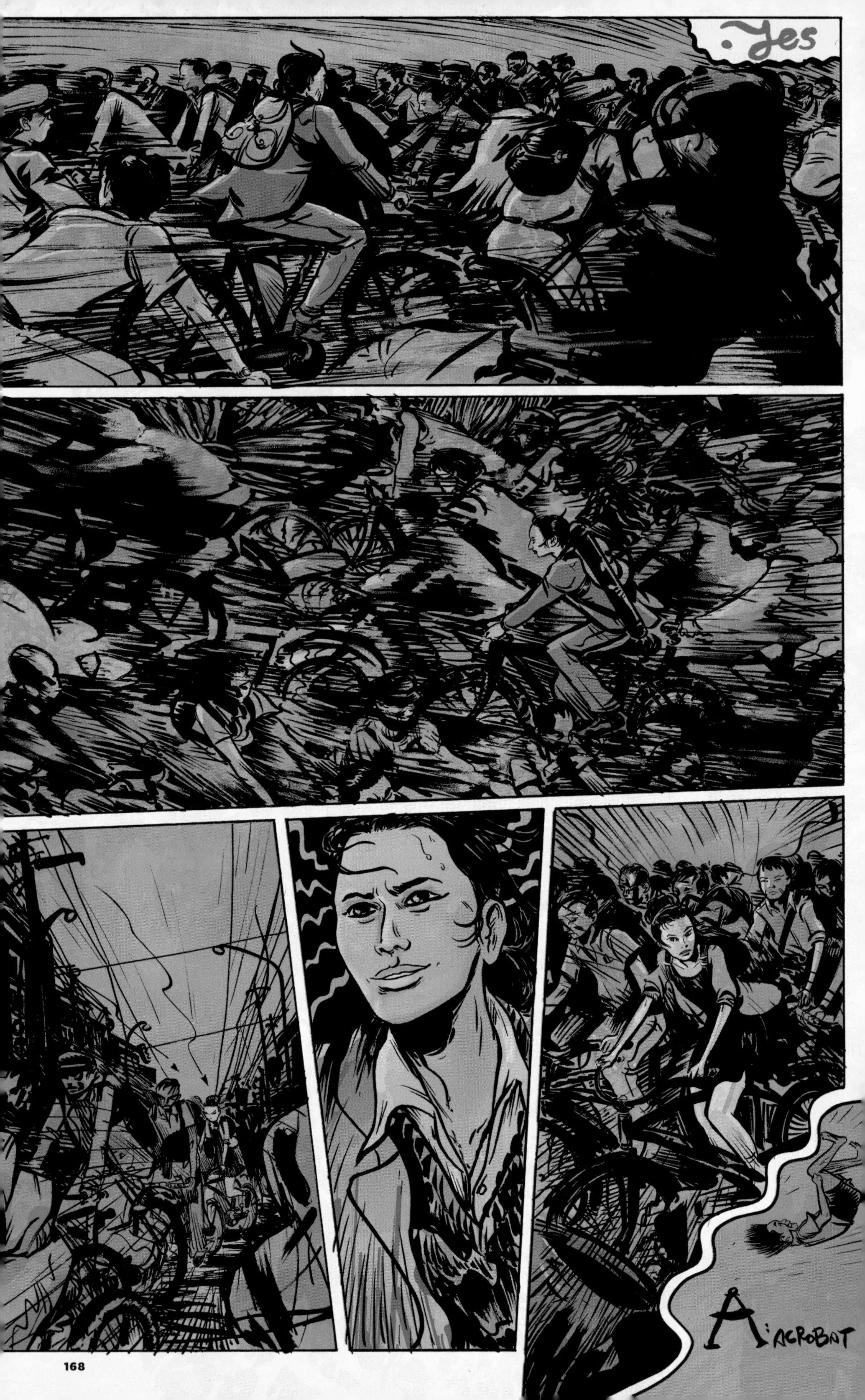
Yes
A: ACROBAT

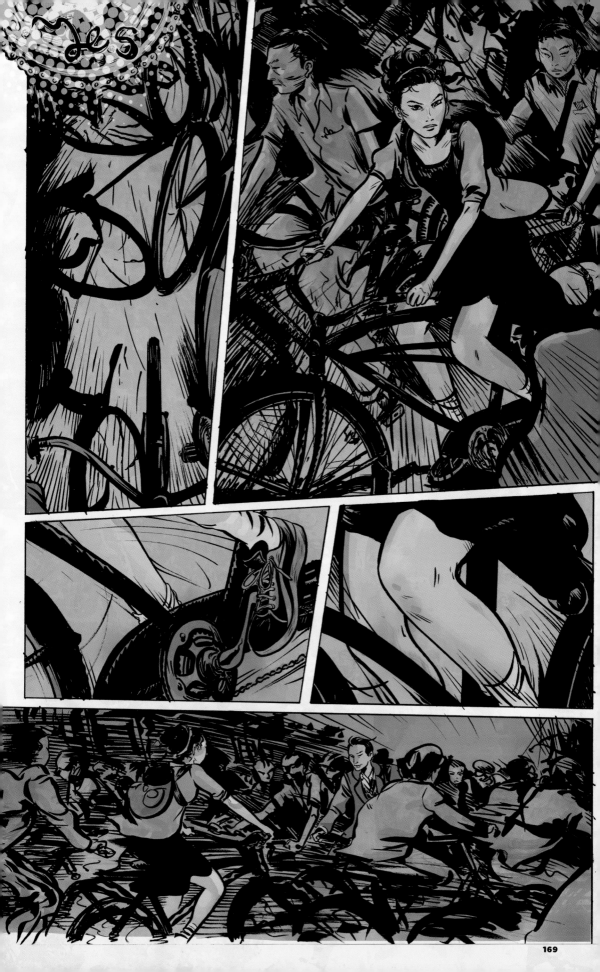

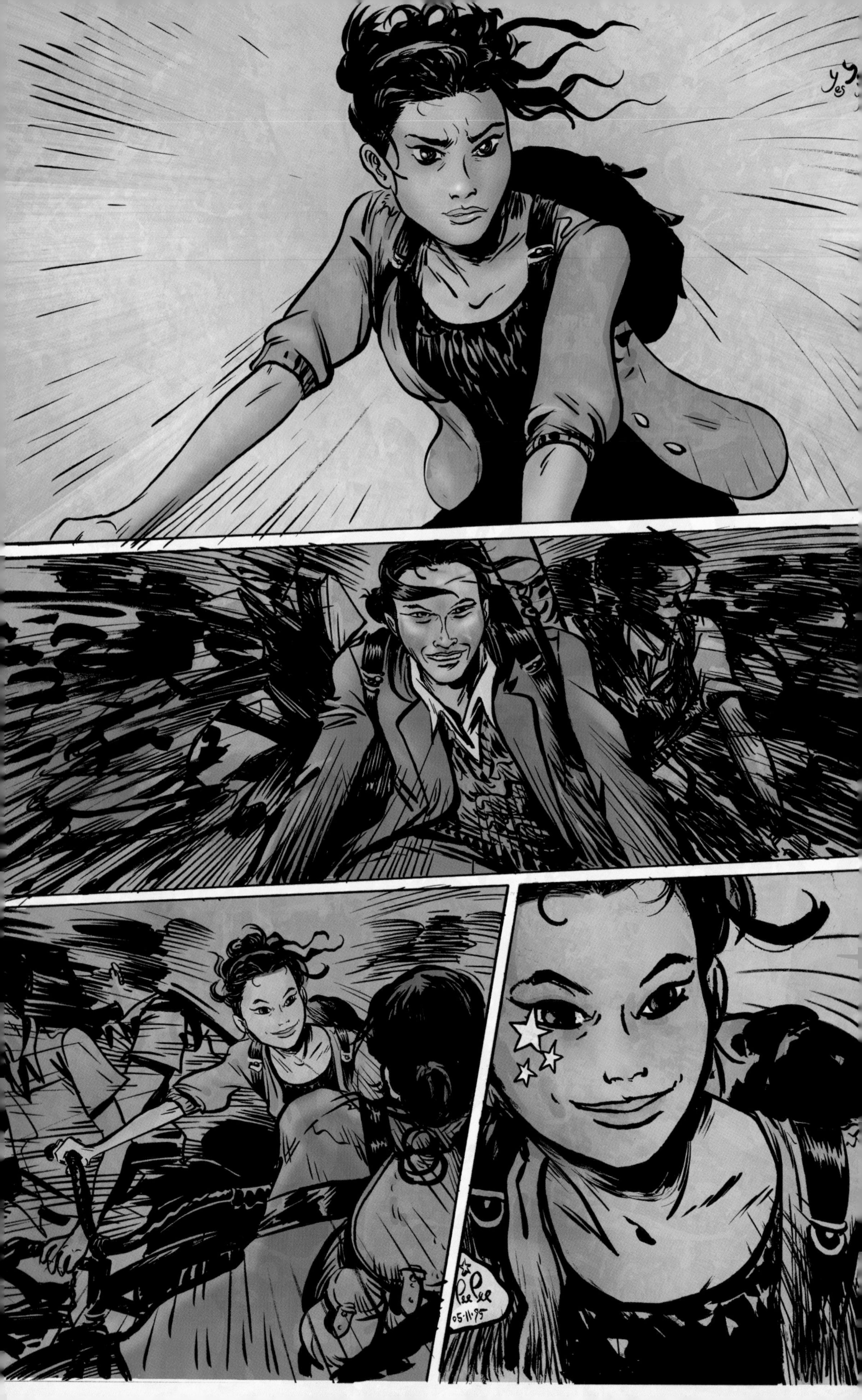
yes
05-11-95

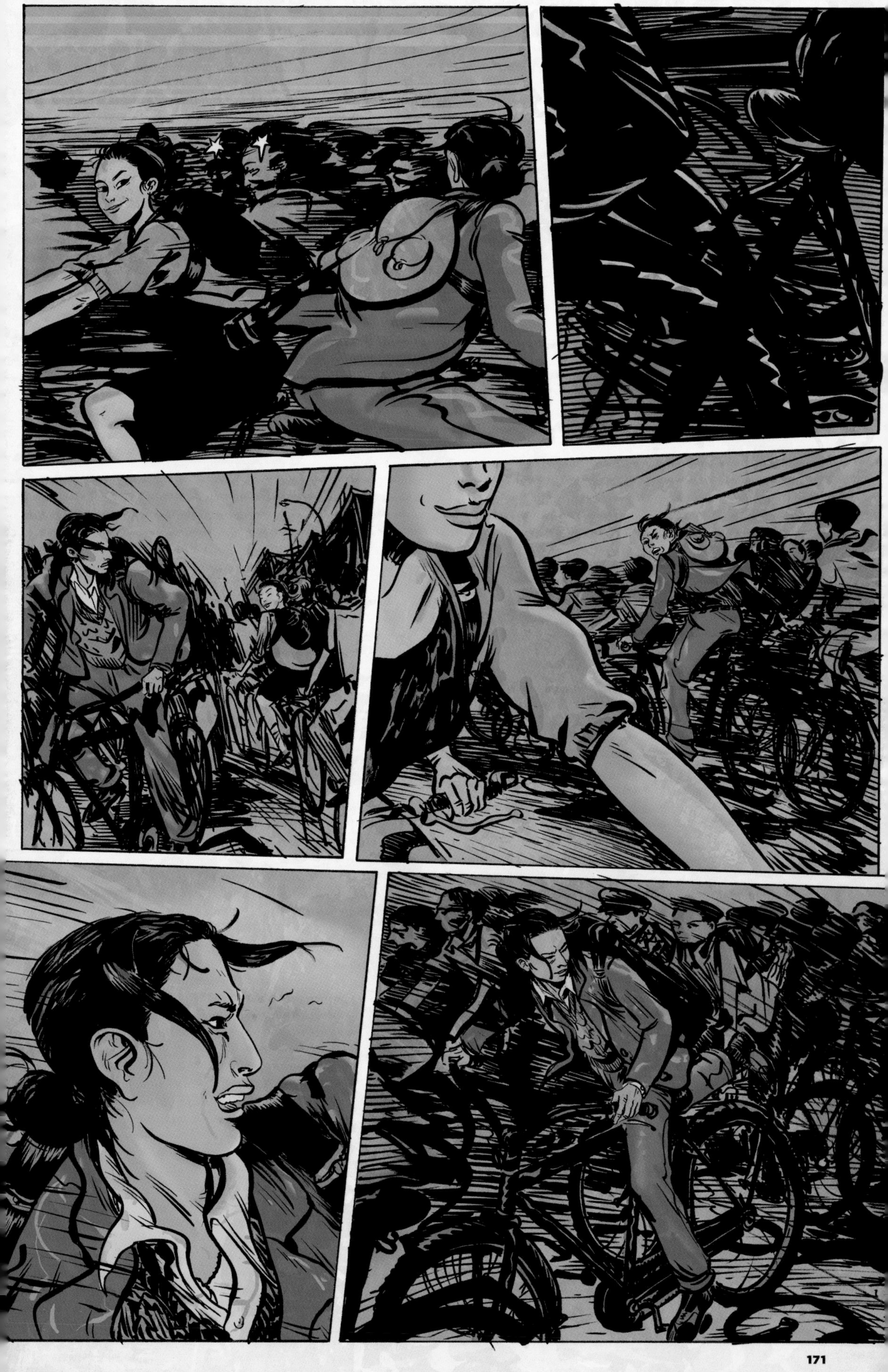

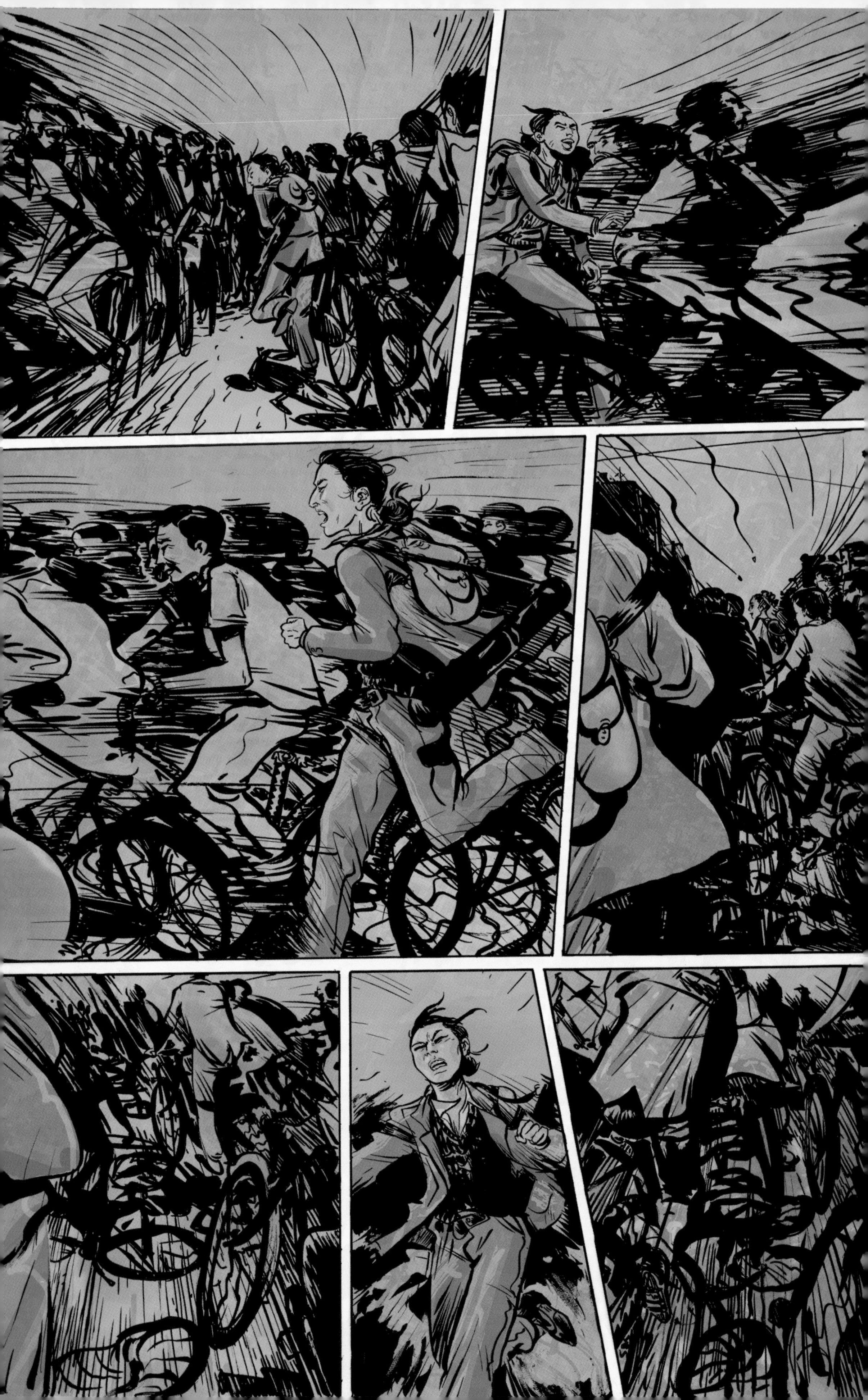

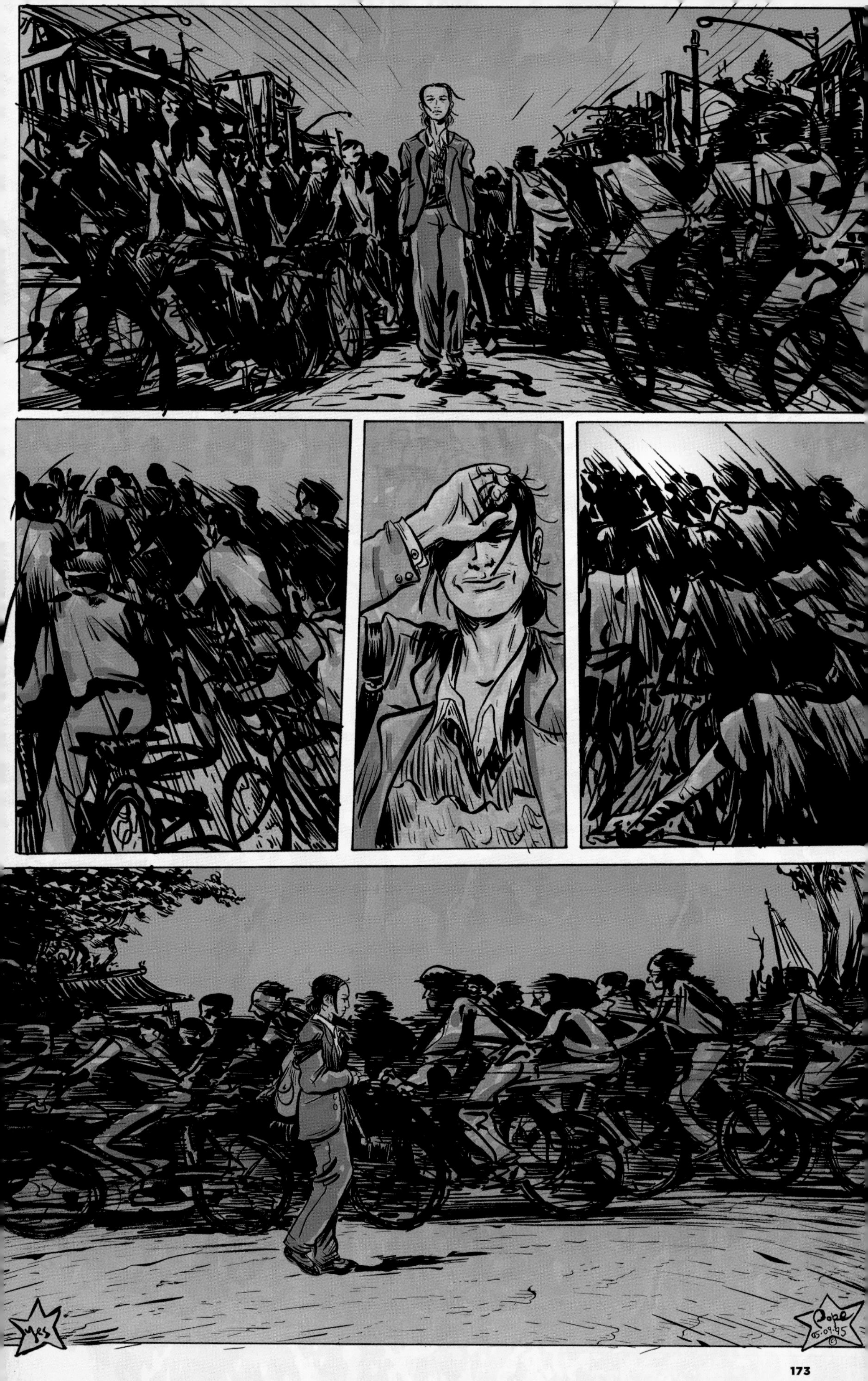
Mes
Pope
05.09.95
©

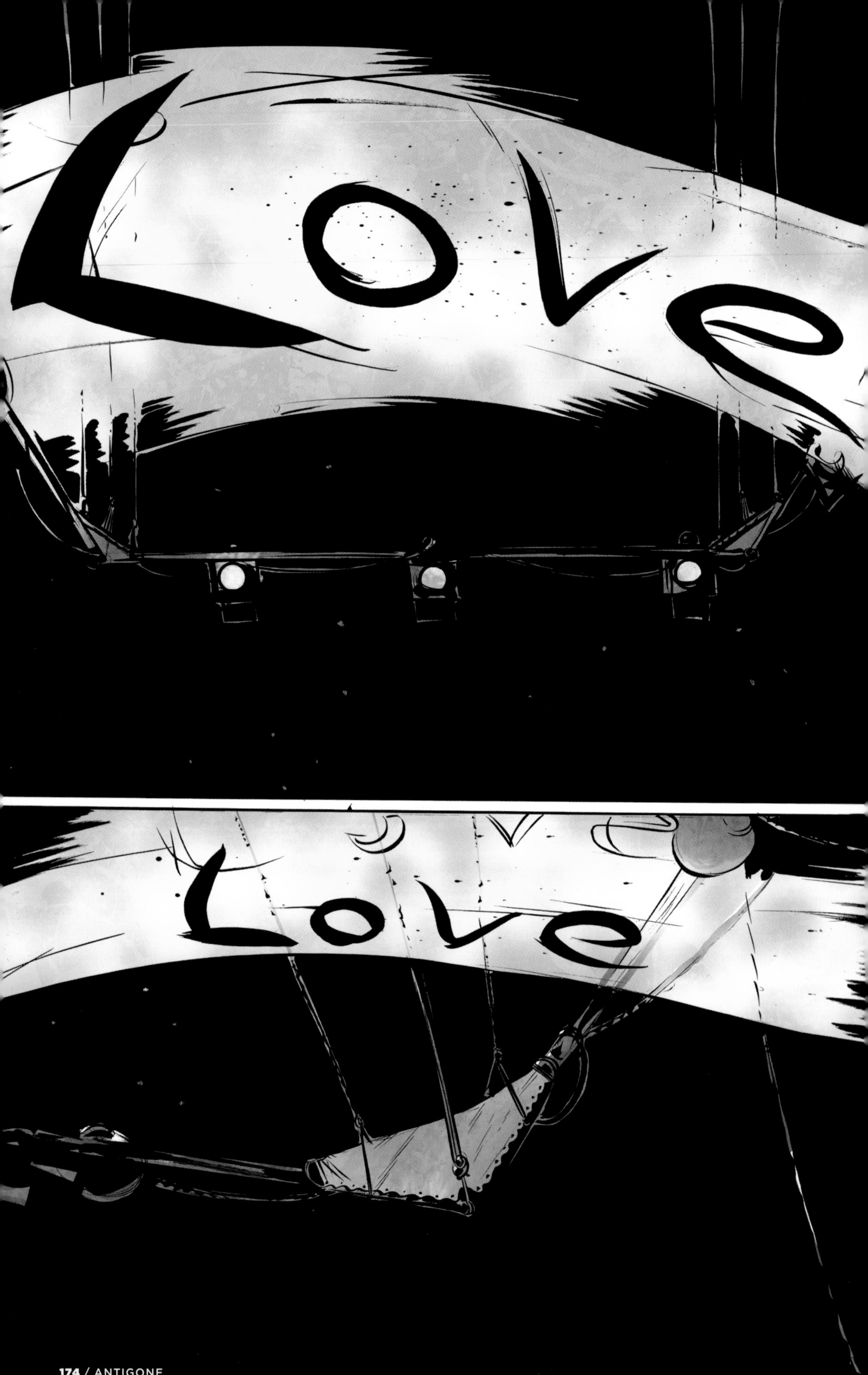
Love
Love

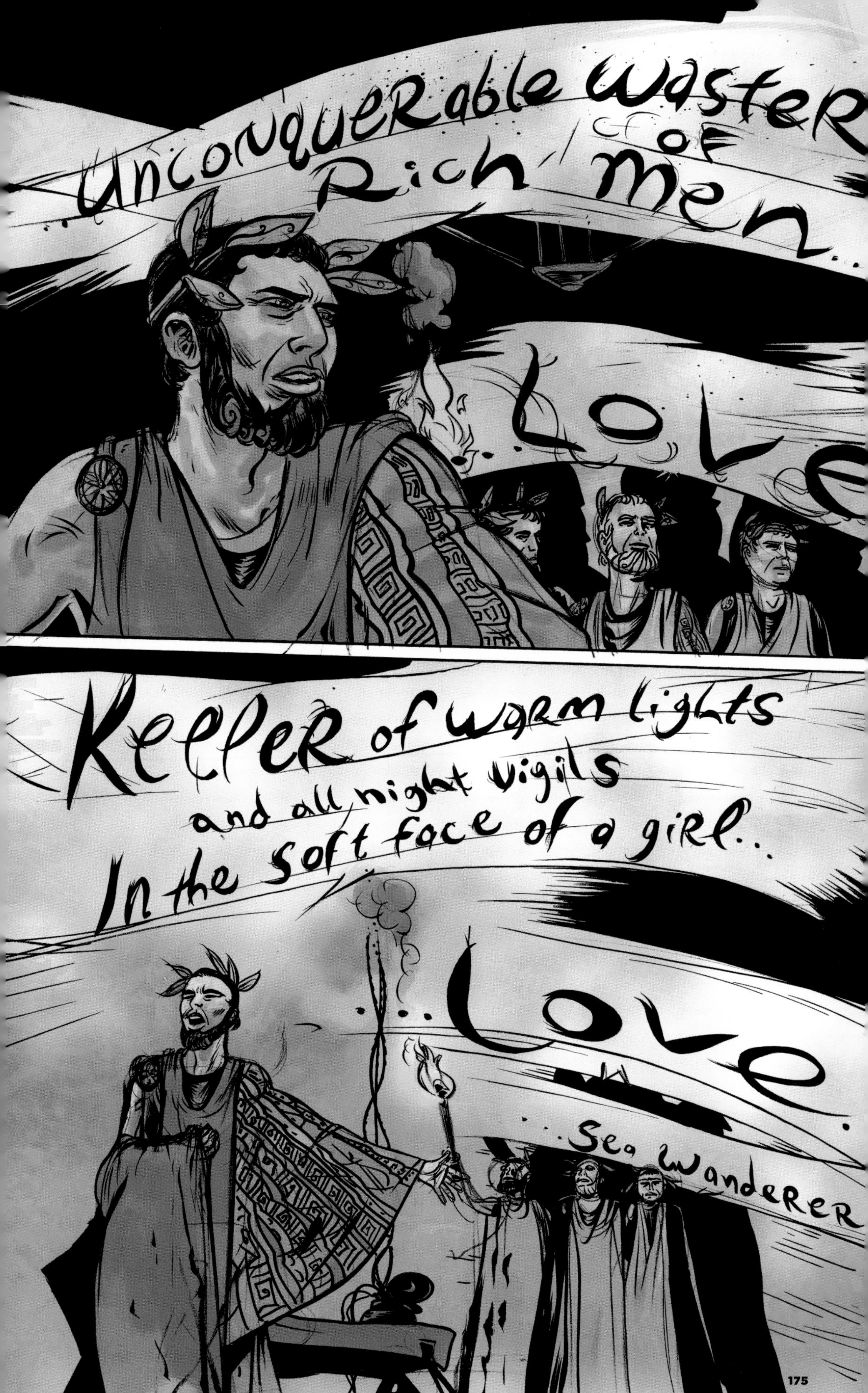

Unconquerable master of rich men...
...Love
Keeper of warm lights and all night vigils
In the soft face of a girl...
...Love.
...Sea wanderer

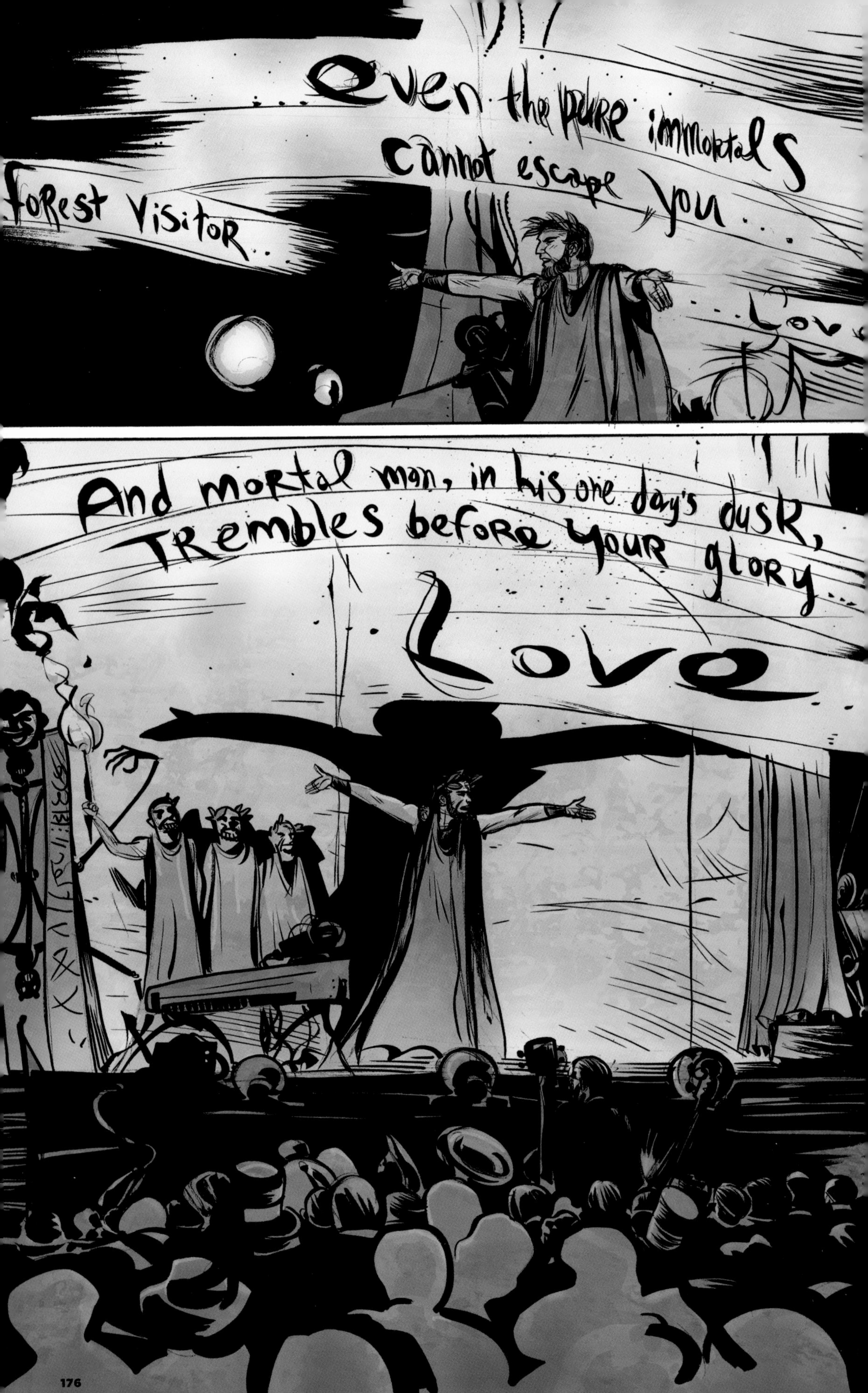

...even the pure immortals cannot escape you...
forest visitor...
...Love
And mortal man, in his one day's dusk, trembles before your glory...
...Love

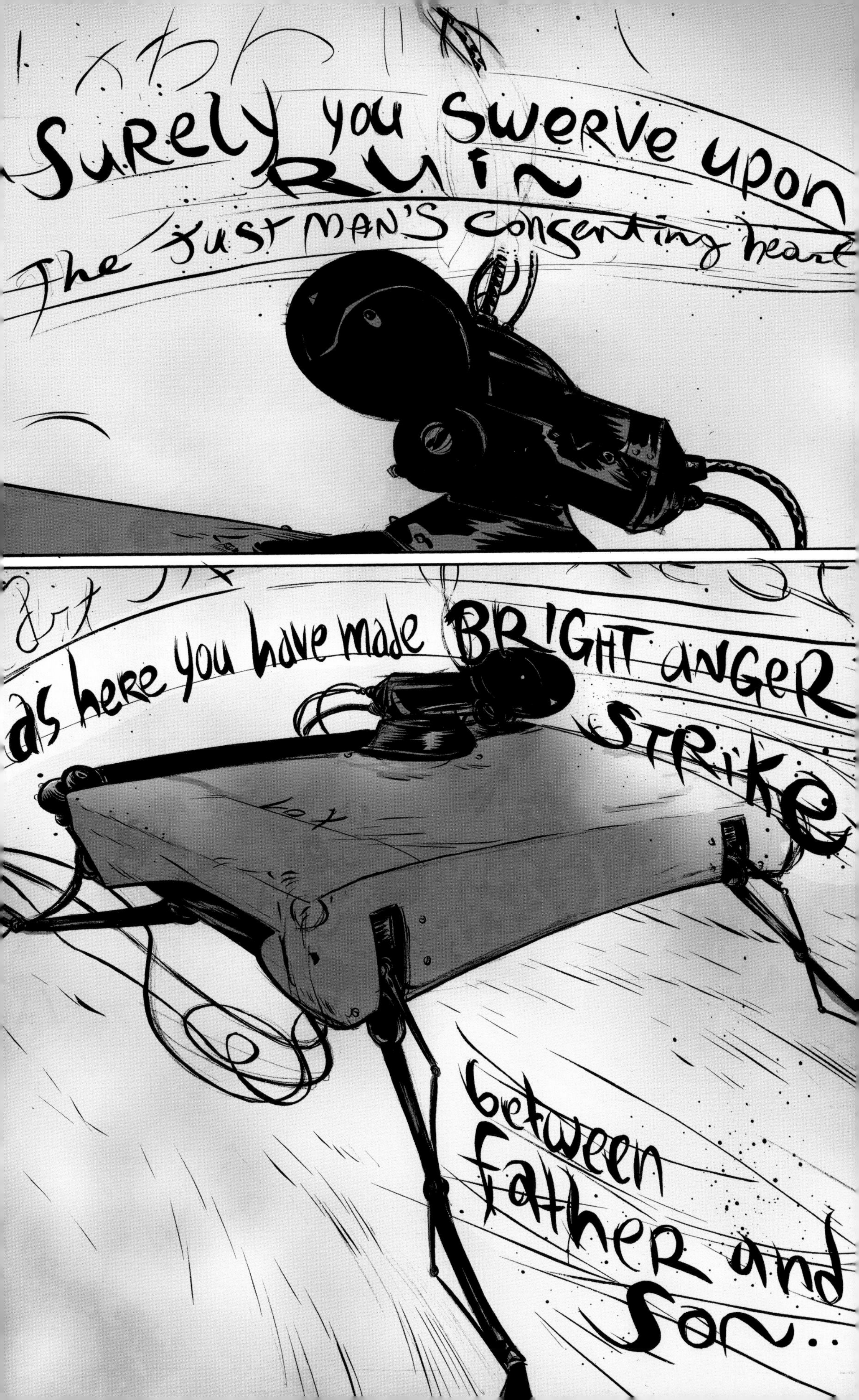
Surely you swerve upon RUIN
The JUST MAN'S consenting heart
But as here you have made BRIGHT anger STRIKE
between father and son...

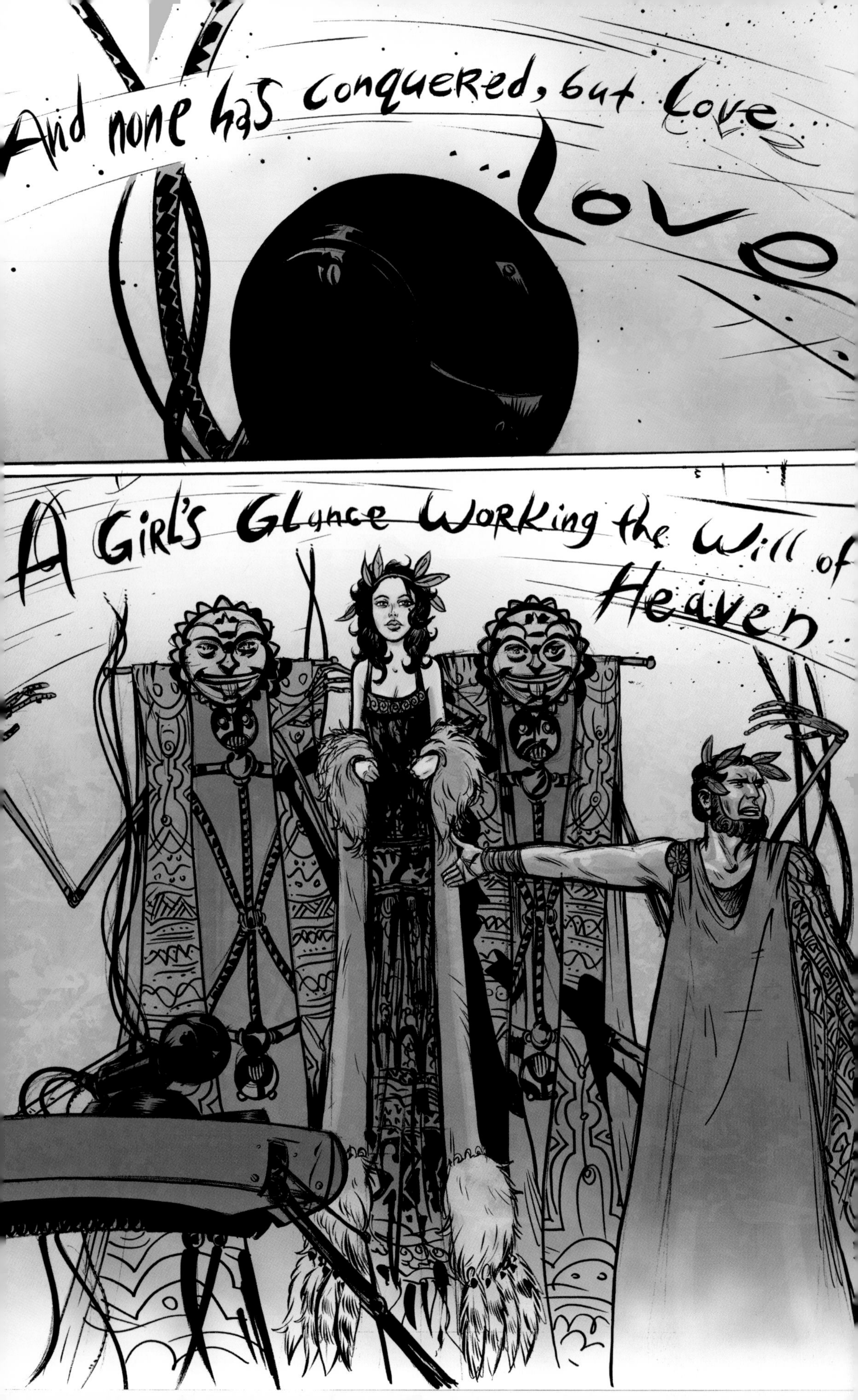
And none has conquered, but Love...
...Love
A Girl's Glance Working the Will of Heaven

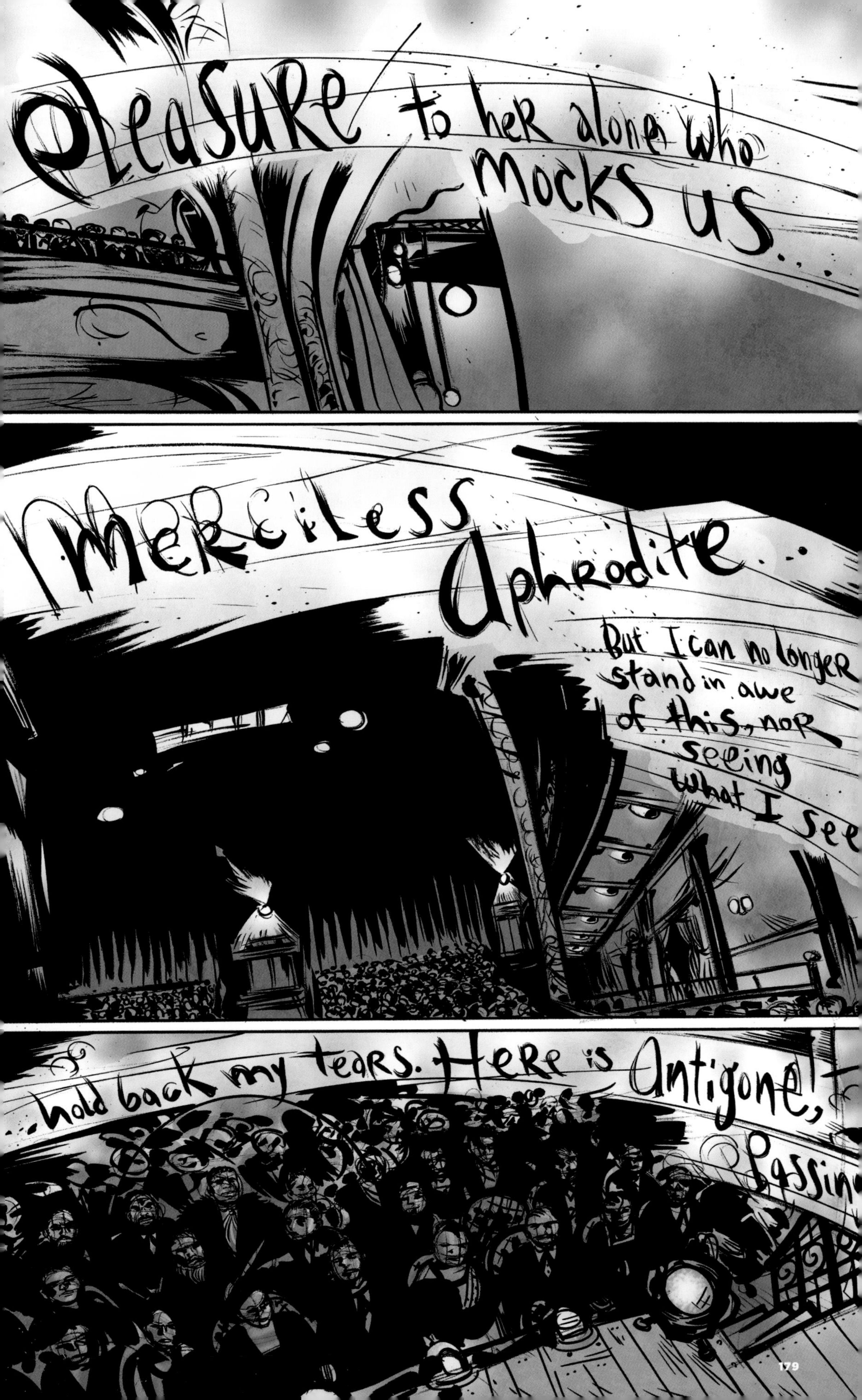
Pleasure to her alone who mocks us...
Merciless Aphrodite
...But I can no longer stand in awe of this, nor seeing what I see
...hold back my tears. Here is Antigone,
Passin

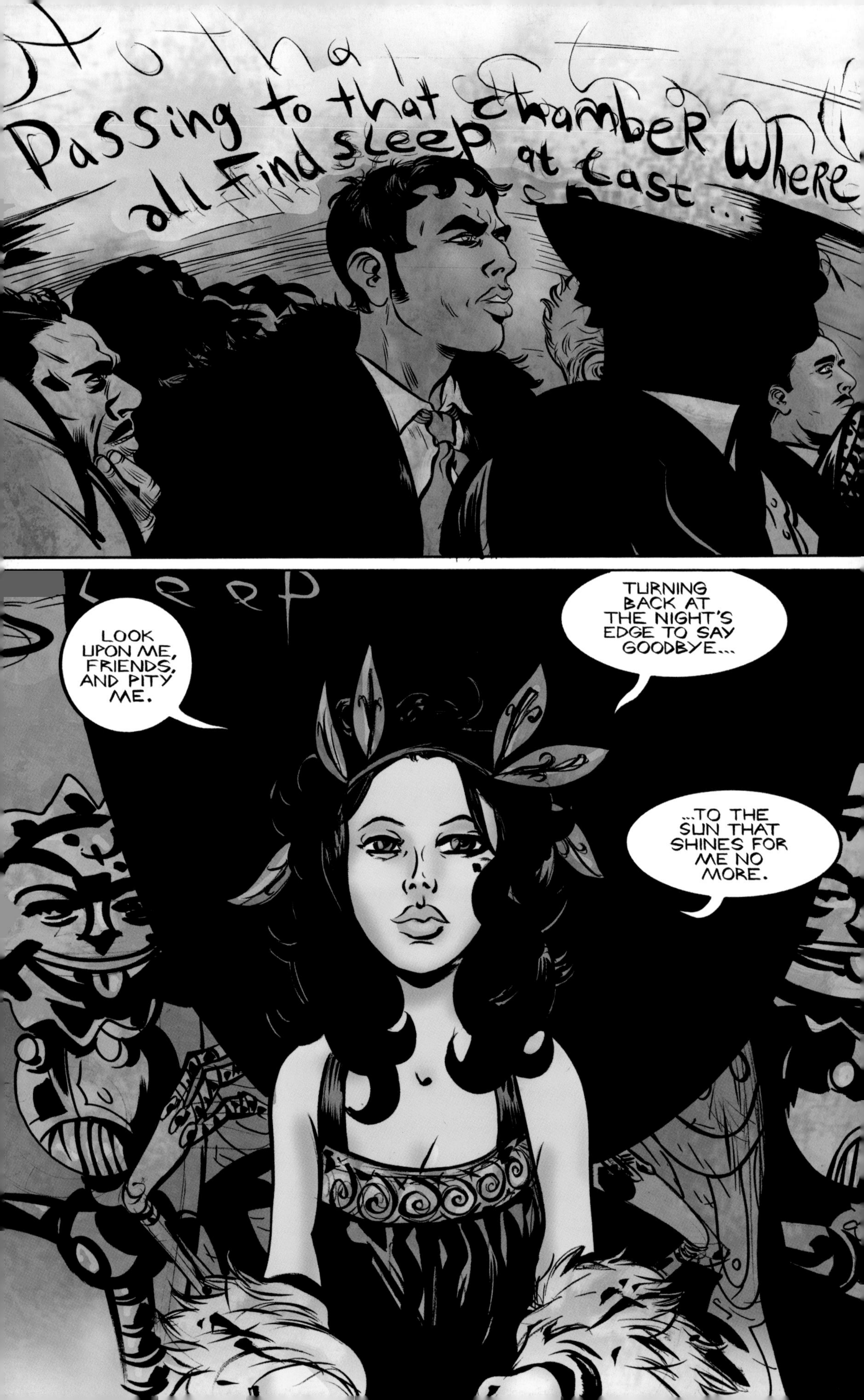
Passing to that chamber where all find sleep at last...
LOOK UPON ME, FRIENDS, AND PITY ME.
TURNING BACK AT THE NIGHT'S EDGE TO SAY GOODBYE...
...TO THE SUN THAT SHINES FOR ME NO MORE.

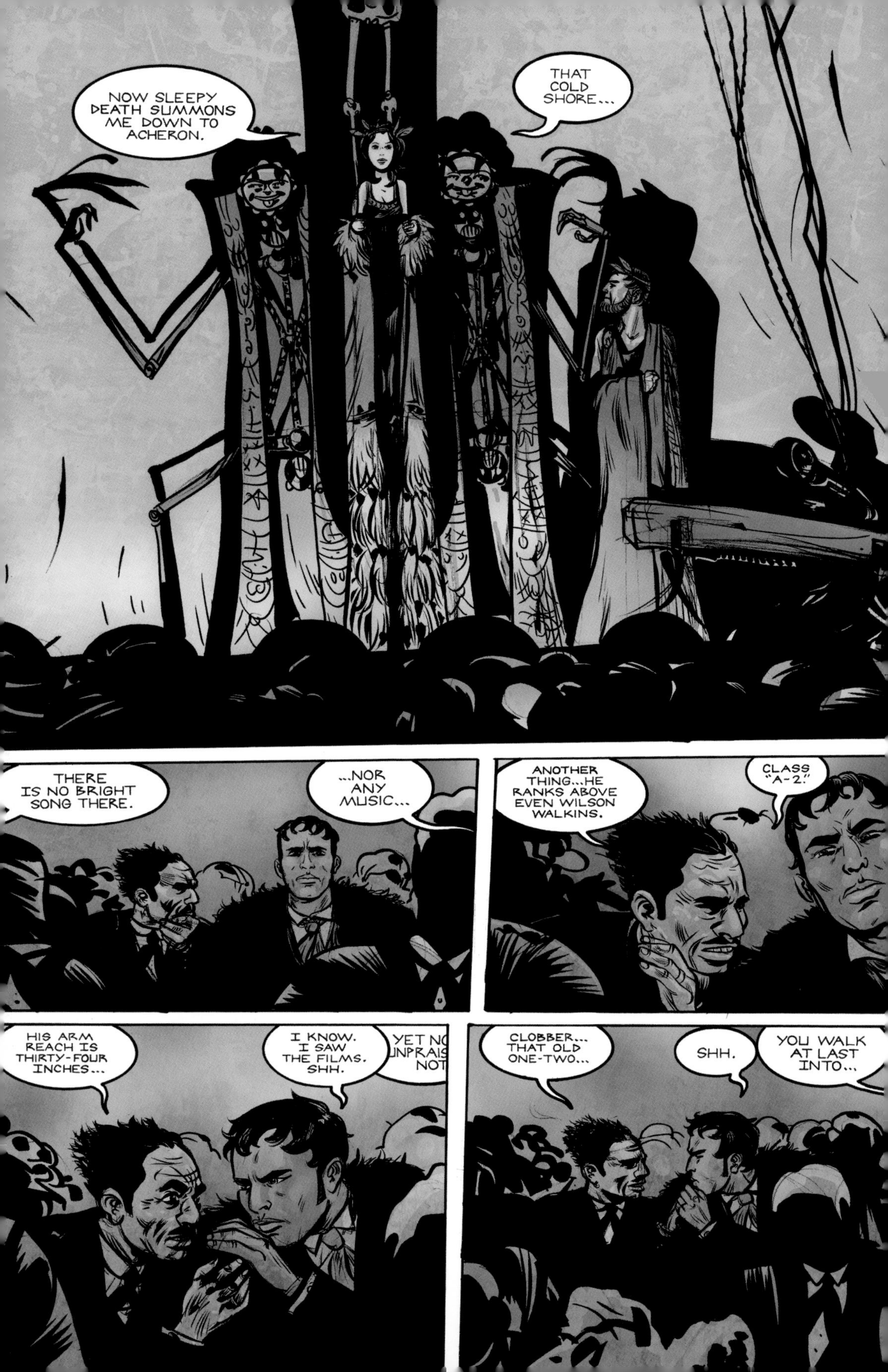
NOW SLEEPY DEATH SUMMONS ME DOWN TO ACHERON.
THAT COLD SHORE...
THERE IS NO BRIGHT SONG THERE.
...NOR ANY MUSIC...
ANOTHER THING...HE RANKS ABOVE EVEN WILSON WALKINS.
CLASS "A-2."
HIS ARM REACH IS THIRTY-FOUR INCHES...
I KNOW. I SAW THE FILMS. SHH.
CLOBBER... THAT OLD ONE-TWO...
SHH.
YOU WALK AT LAST INTO...

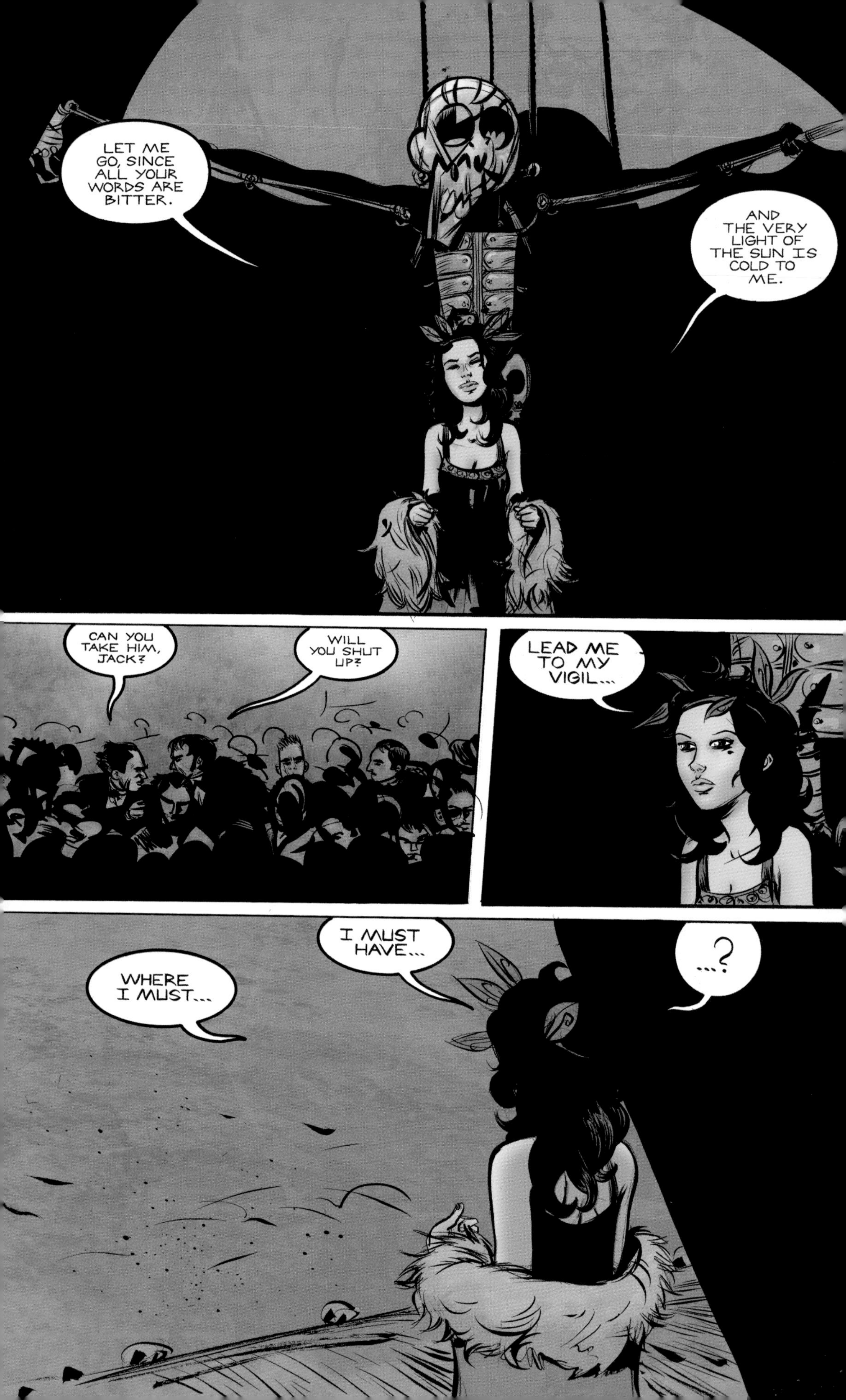
LET ME GO, SINCE ALL YOUR WORDS ARE BITTER.
AND THE VERY LIGHT OF THE SUN IS COLD TO ME.
CAN YOU TAKE HIM, JACK?
WILL YOU SHUT UP?
LEAD ME TO MY VIGIL...
WHERE I MUST...
I MUST HAVE...
...?

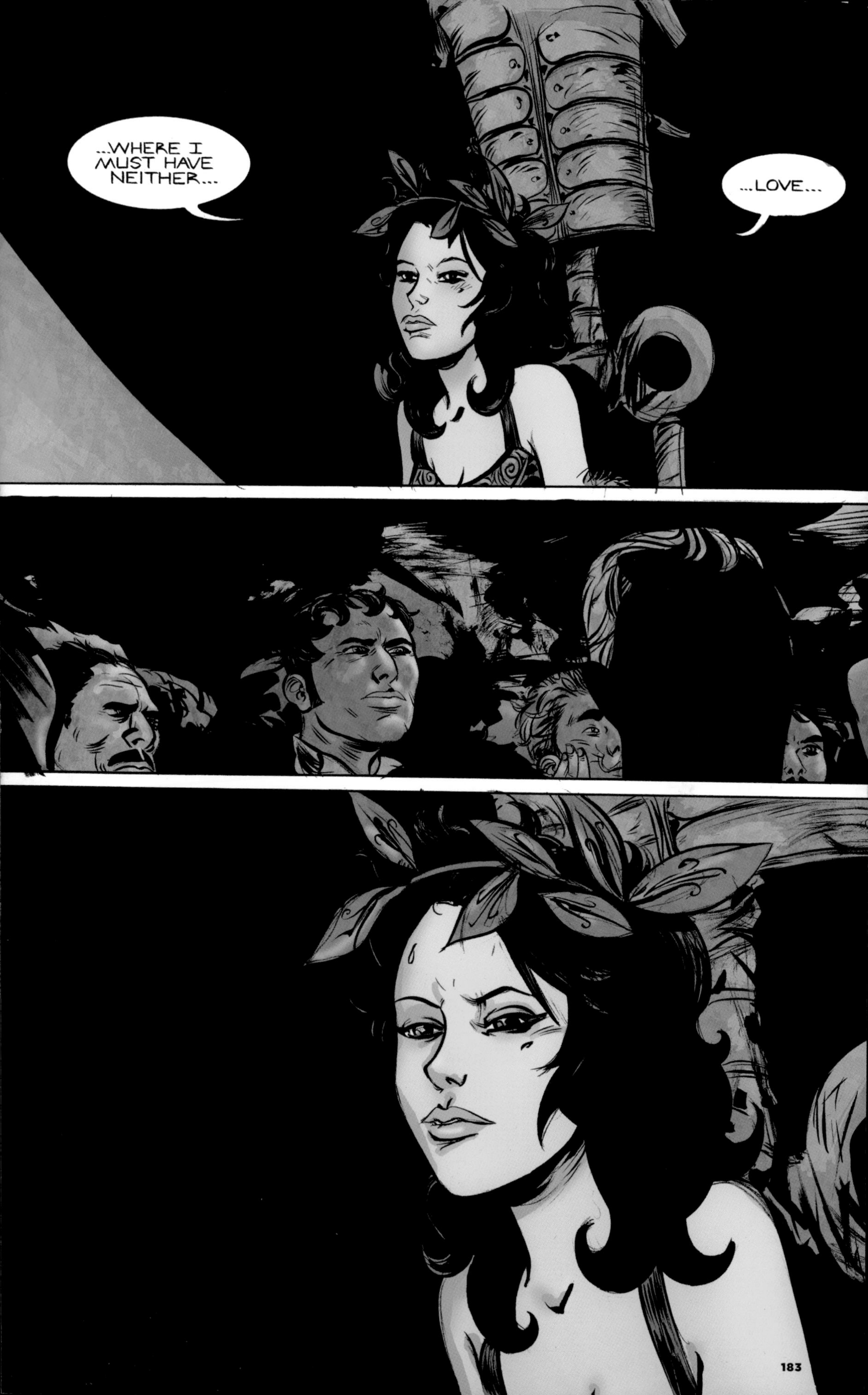
...WHERE I MUST HAVE NEITHER...
...LOVE...

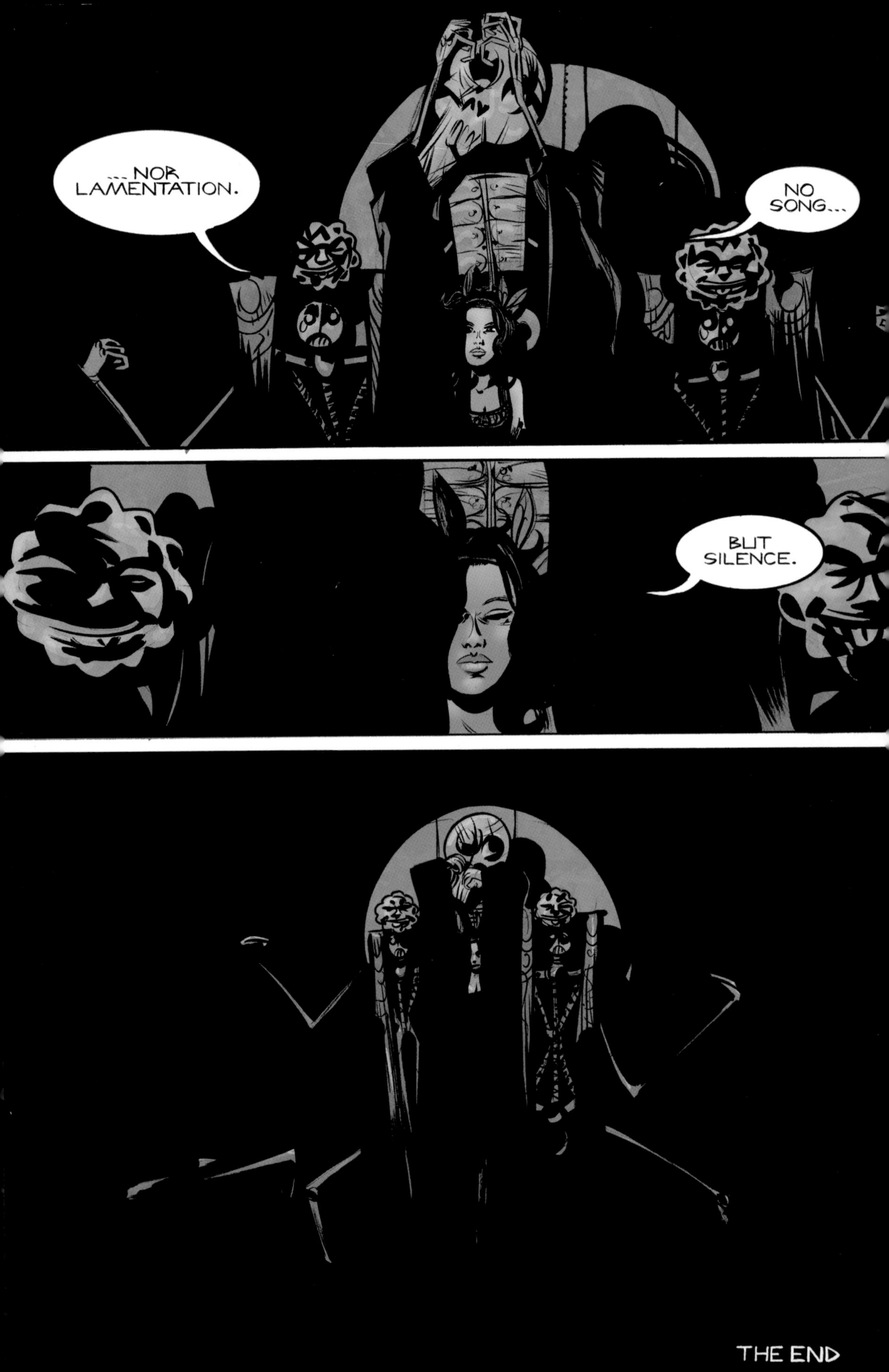
...NOR LAMENTATION.
NO SONG...
BUT SILENCE.
THE END

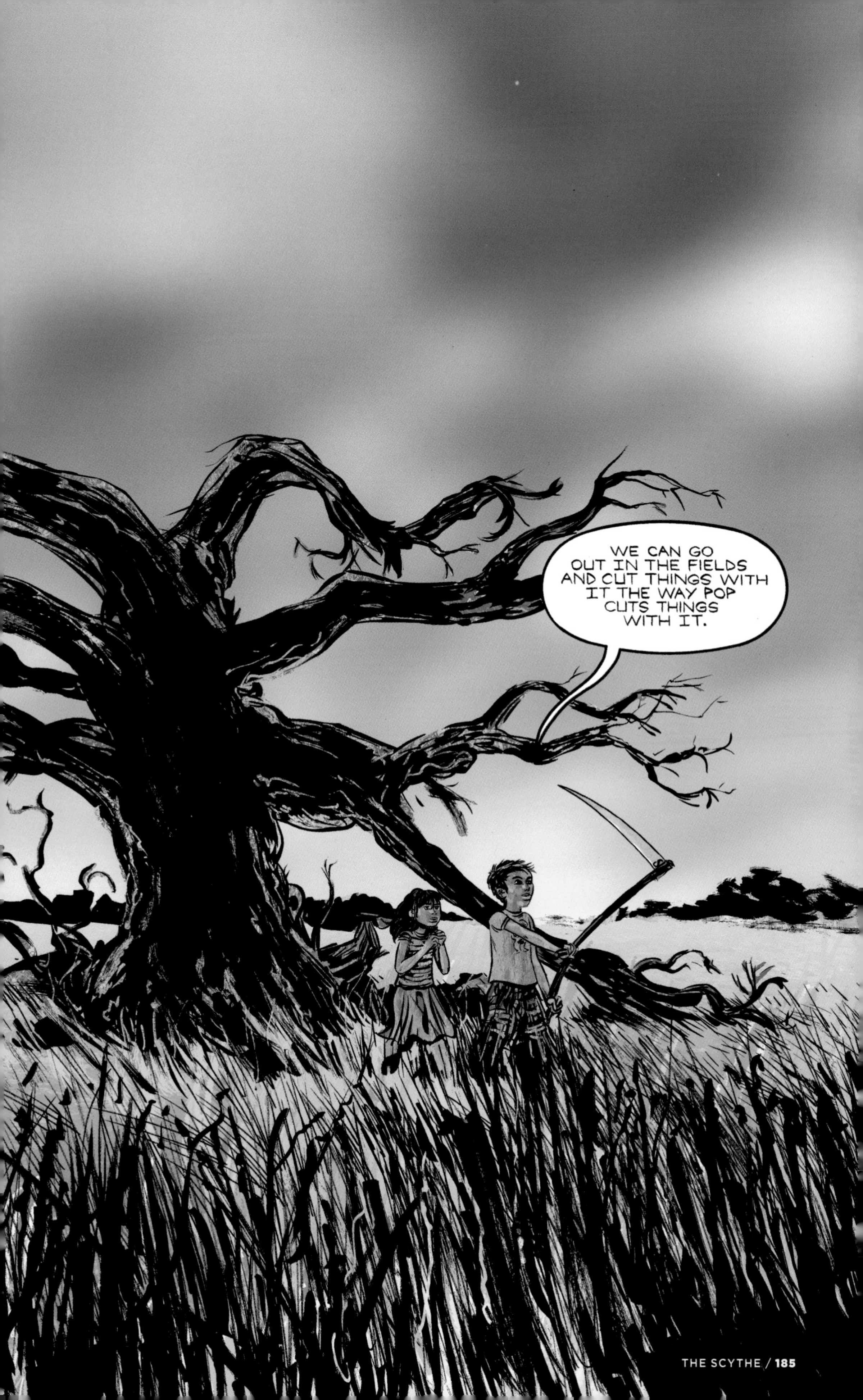
WE CAN GO OUT IN THE FIELDS AND CUT THINGS WITH IT THE WAY POP CUTS THINGS WITH IT.

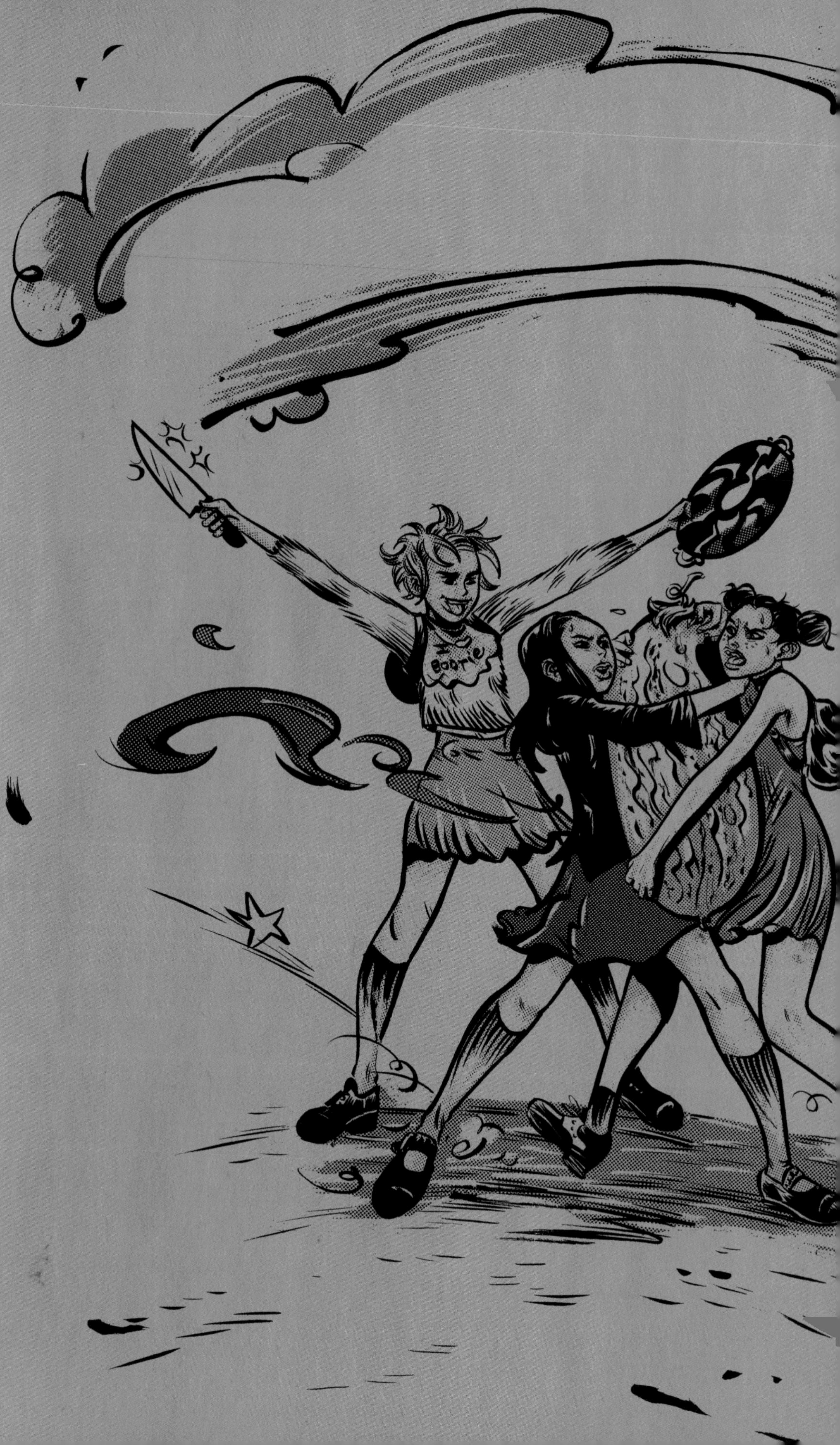
Bootie

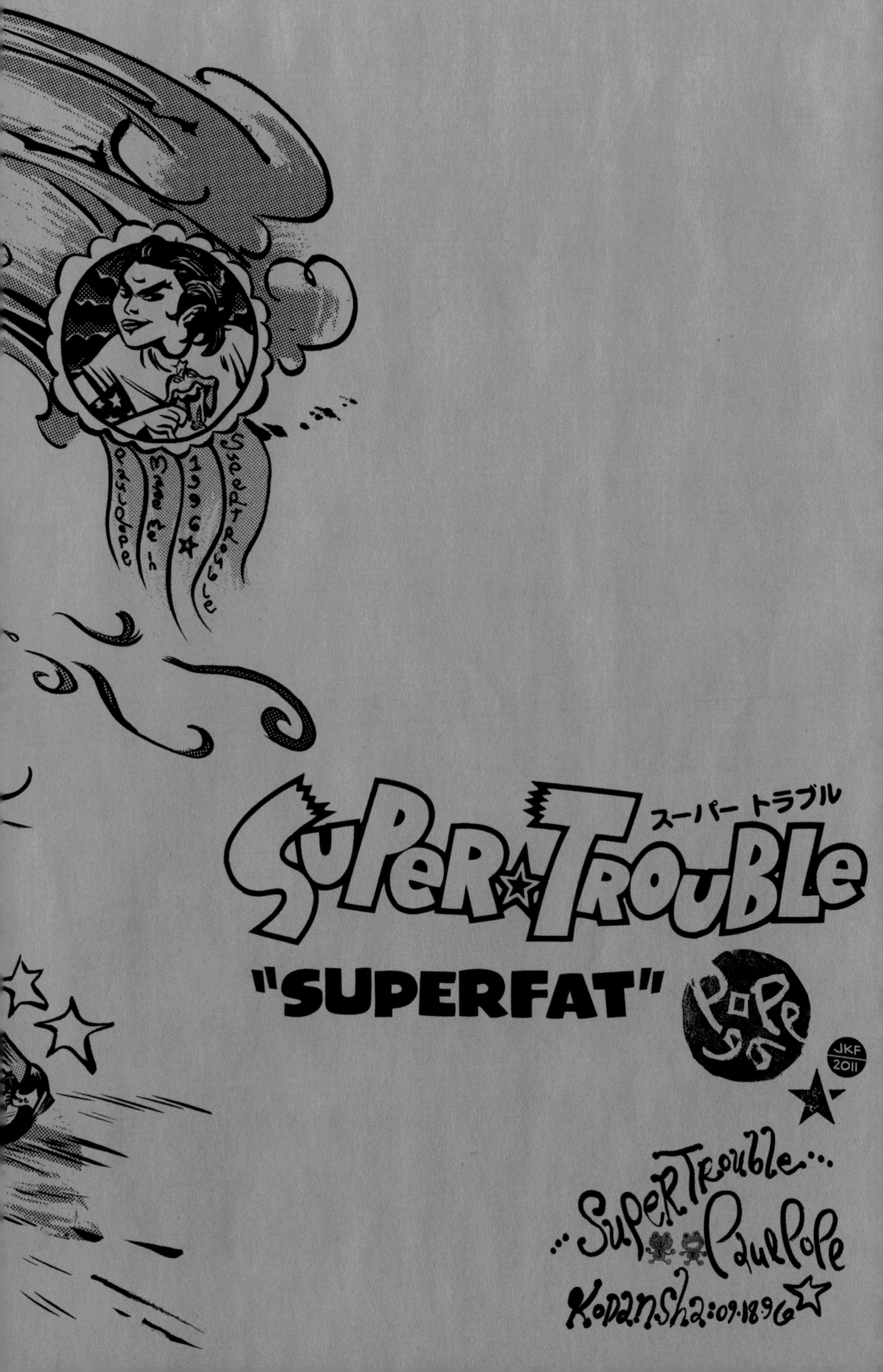

SUPER☆TROUBLE
スーパー トラブル

"SUPERFAT"

Pope

JKF 2011

SuperTrouble...

...Super Paul Pope

Kodansha: 09.18.96☆

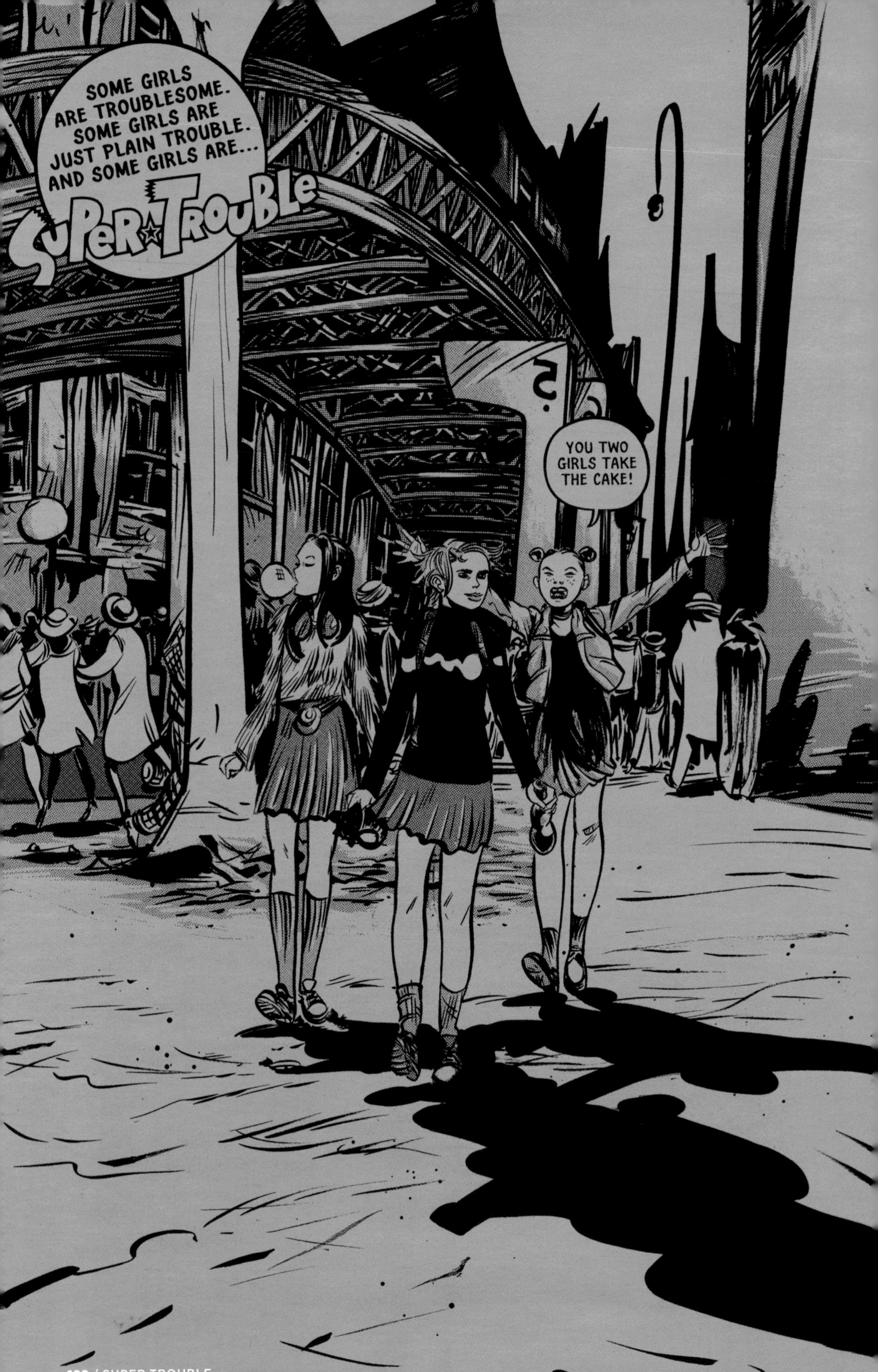
SOME GIRLS ARE TROUBLESOME. SOME GIRLS ARE JUST PLAIN TROUBLE. AND SOME GIRLS ARE...
SUPER☆TROUBLE
YOU TWO GIRLS TAKE THE CAKE!

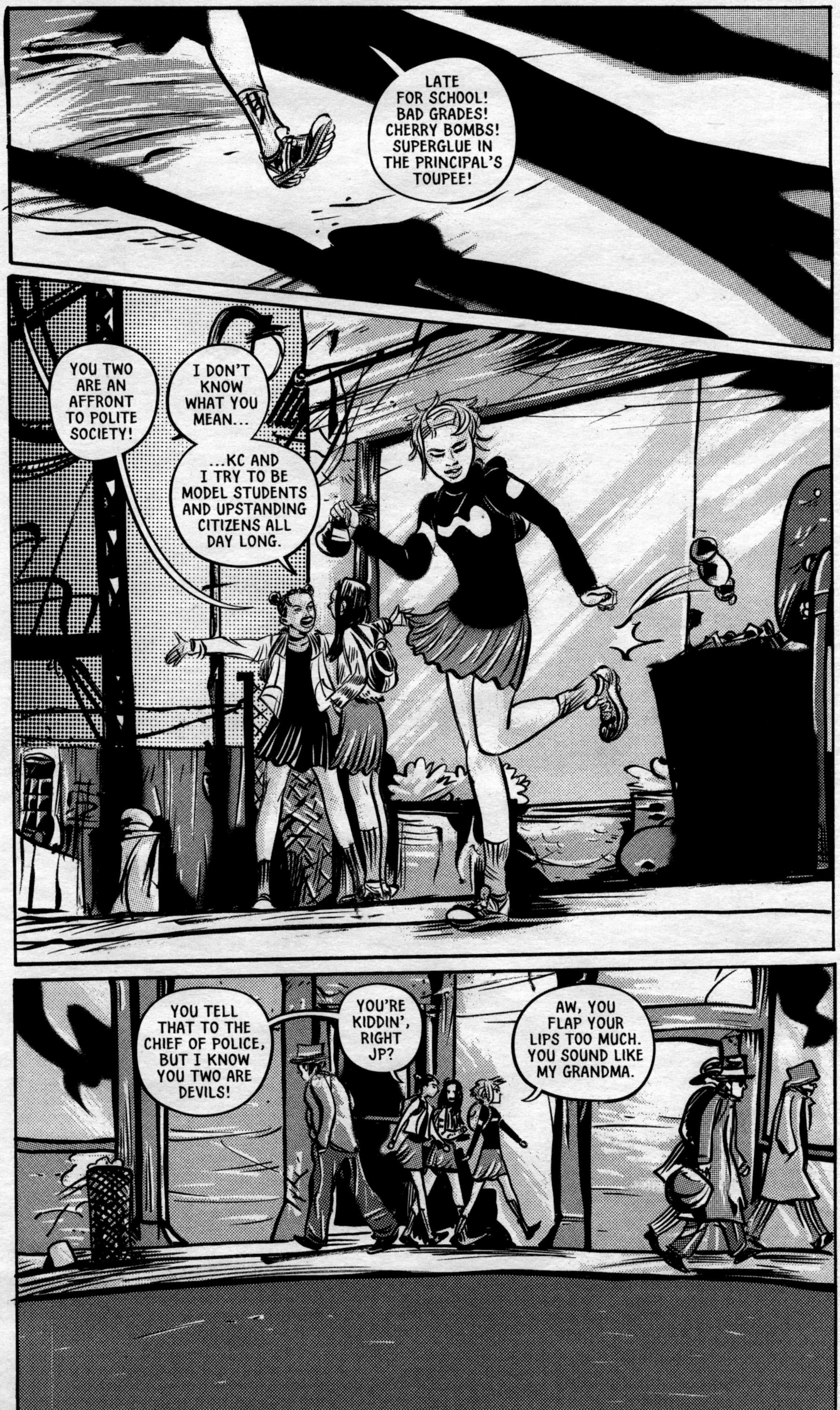
LATE FOR SCHOOL! BAD GRADES! CHERRY BOMBS! SUPERGLUE IN THE PRINCIPAL'S TOUPEE!
YOU TWO ARE AN AFFRONT TO POLITE SOCIETY!
I DON'T KNOW WHAT YOU MEAN...
...KC AND I TRY TO BE MODEL STUDENTS AND UPSTANDING CITIZENS ALL DAY LONG.
YOU TELL THAT TO THE CHIEF OF POLICE, BUT I KNOW YOU TWO ARE DEVILS!
YOU'RE KIDDIN', RIGHT JP?
AW, YOU FLAP YOUR LIPS TOO MUCH. YOU SOUND LIKE MY GRANDMA.

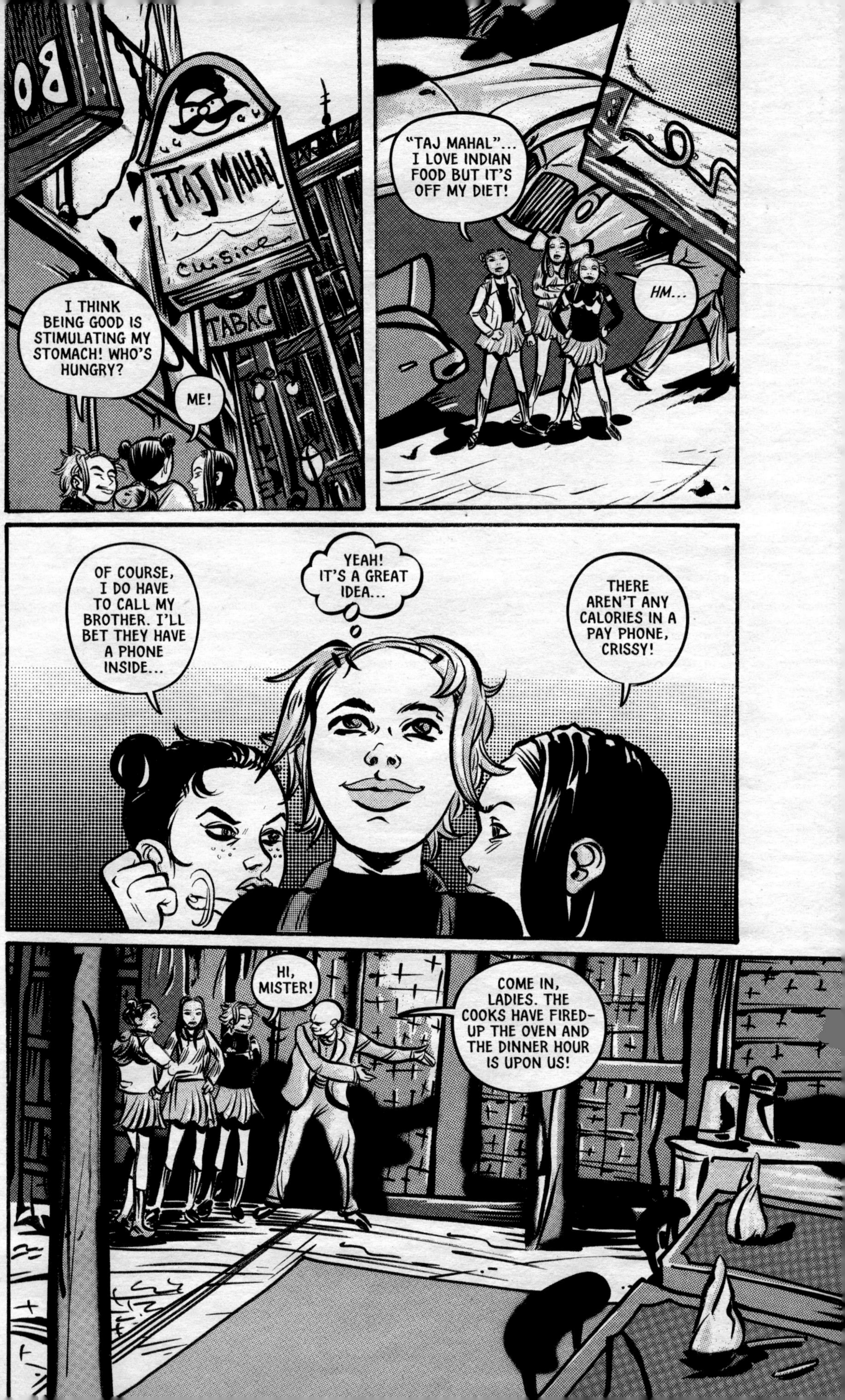
TAJ MAHAL
CUISINE
TABAC
I THINK BEING GOOD IS STIMULATING MY STOMACH! WHO'S HUNGRY?
ME!
"TAJ MAHAL"... I LOVE INDIAN FOOD BUT IT'S OFF MY DIET!
HM...
OF COURSE, I DO HAVE TO CALL MY BROTHER. I'LL BET THEY HAVE A PHONE INSIDE...
YEAH! IT'S A GREAT IDEA...
THERE AREN'T ANY CALORIES IN A PAY PHONE, CRISSY!
HI, MISTER!
COME IN, LADIES. THE COOKS HAVE FIRED-UP THE OVEN AND THE DINNER HOUR IS UPON US!

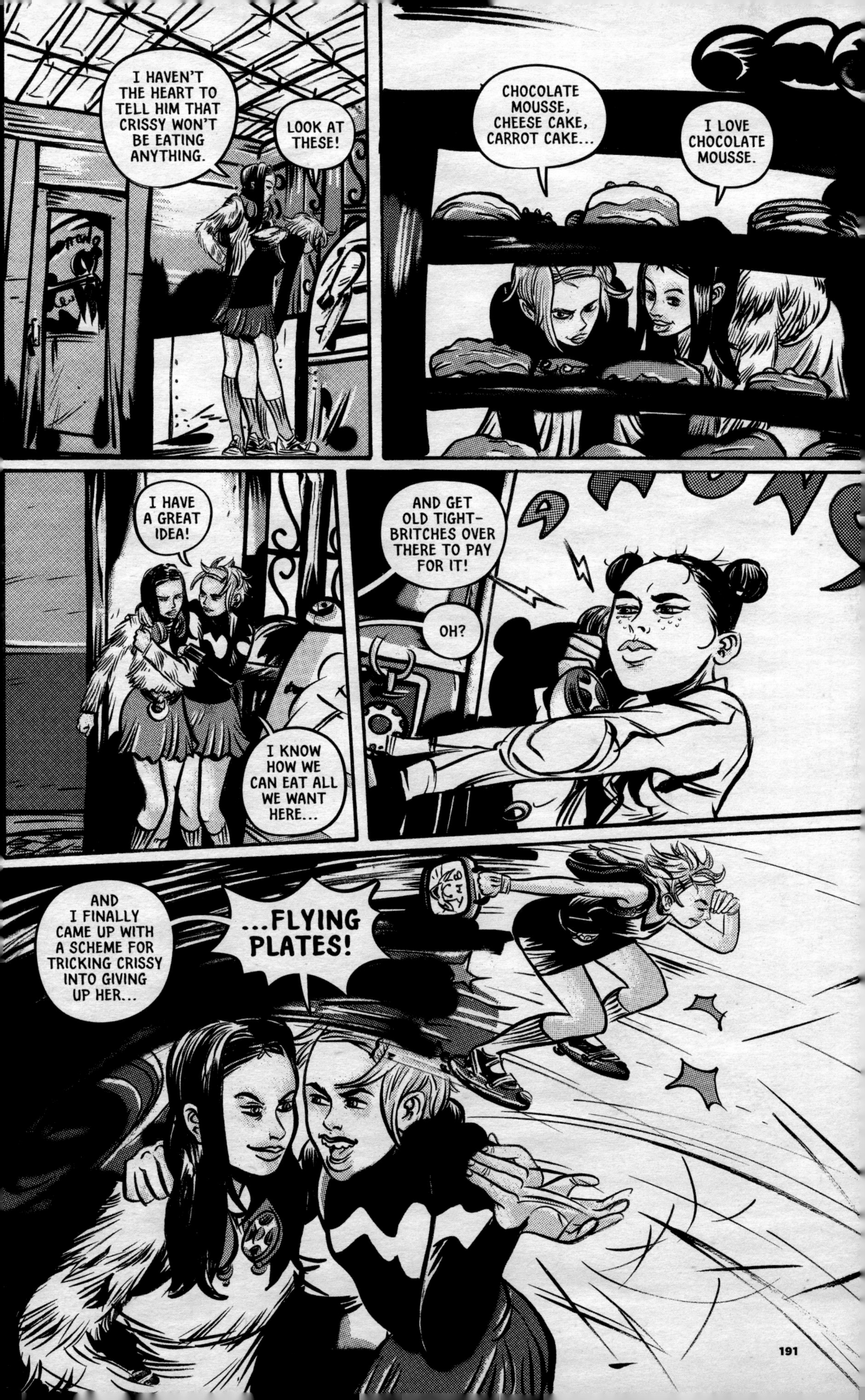
I HAVEN'T THE HEART TO TELL HIM THAT CRISSY WON'T BE EATING ANYTHING.
LOOK AT THESE!
CHOCOLATE MOUSSE, CHEESE CAKE, CARROT CAKE...
I LOVE CHOCOLATE MOUSSE.
I HAVE A GREAT IDEA!
I KNOW HOW WE CAN EAT ALL WE WANT HERE...
AND GET OLD TIGHT-BRITCHES OVER THERE TO PAY FOR IT!
OH?
AND I FINALLY CAME UP WITH A SCHEME FOR TRICKING CRISSY INTO GIVING UP HER...
...FLYING PLATES!

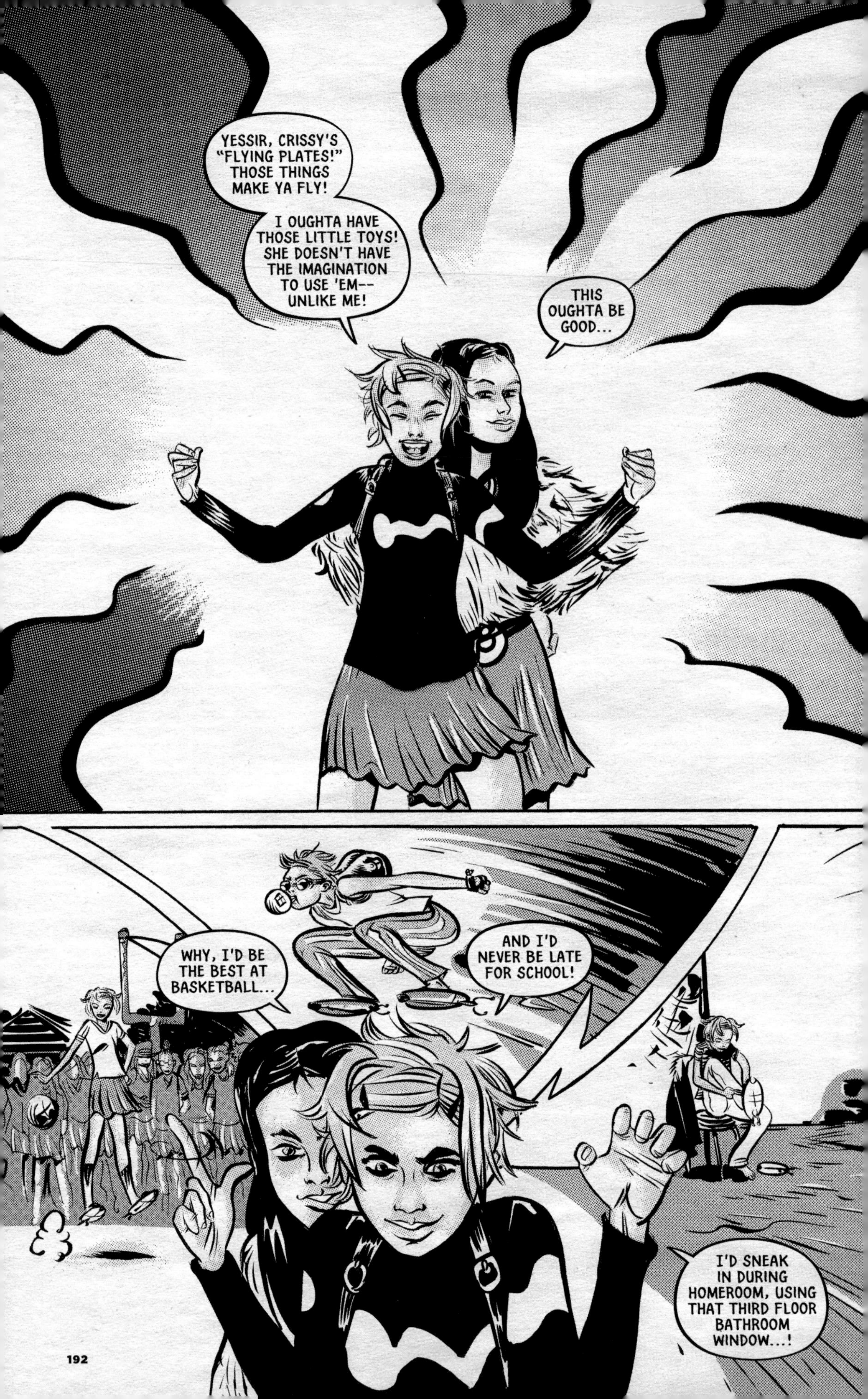
YESSIR, CRISSY'S "FLYING PLATES!" THOSE THINGS MAKE YA FLY!
I OUGHTA HAVE THOSE LITTLE TOYS! SHE DOESN'T HAVE THE IMAGINATION TO USE 'EM-- UNLIKE ME!
THIS OUGHTA BE GOOD...
WHY, I'D BE THE BEST AT BASKETBALL...
AND I'D NEVER BE LATE FOR SCHOOL!
I'D SNEAK IN DURING HOMEROOM, USING THAT THIRD FLOOR BATHROOM WINDOW...!

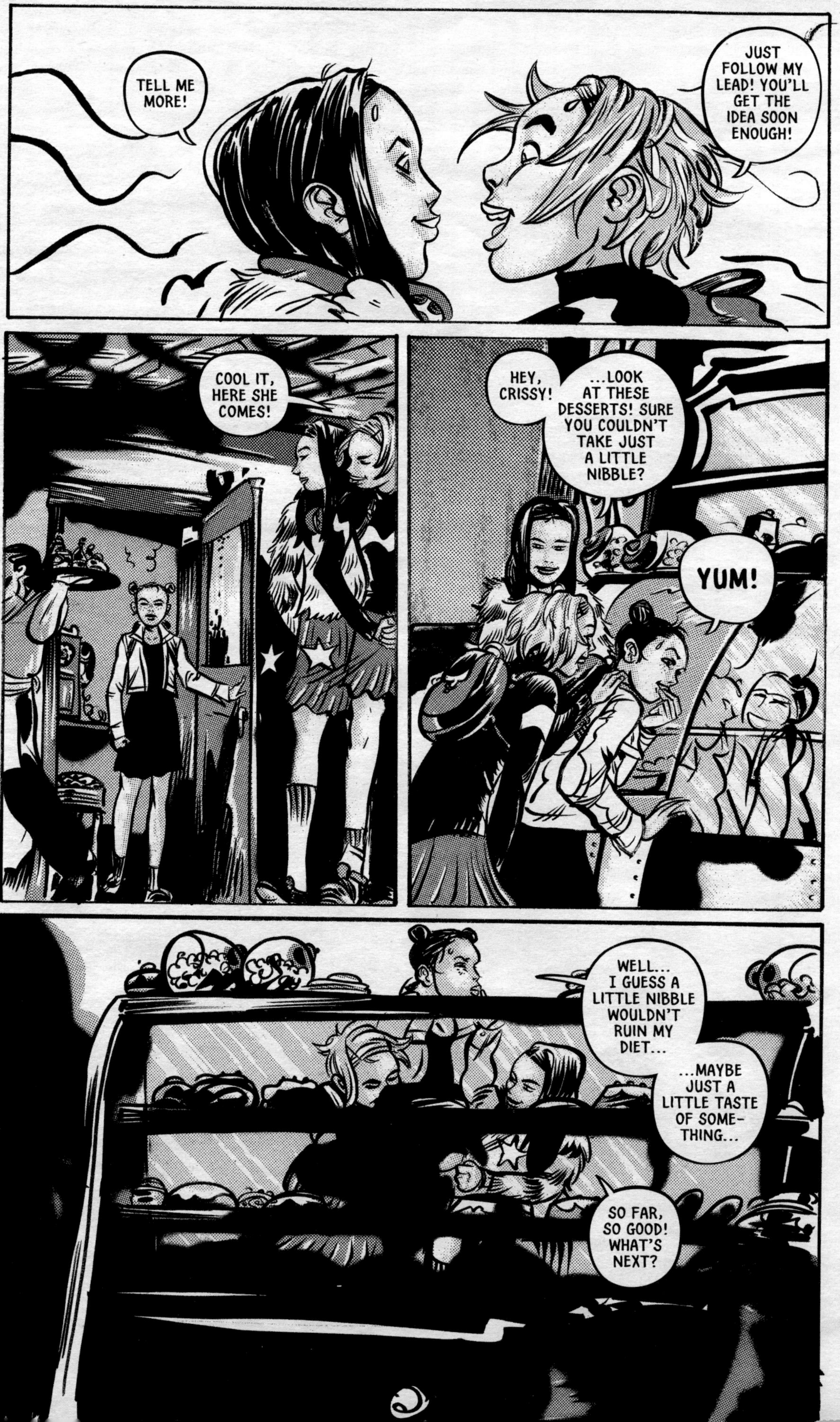
TELL ME MORE!
JUST FOLLOW MY LEAD! YOU'LL GET THE IDEA SOON ENOUGH!
COOL IT, HERE SHE COMES!
HEY, CRISSY!
...LOOK AT THESE DESSERTS! SURE YOU COULDN'T TAKE JUST A LITTLE NIBBLE?
YUM!
WELL... I GUESS A LITTLE NIBBLE WOULDN'T RUIN MY DIET...
...MAYBE JUST A LITTLE TASTE OF SOME-THING...
SO FAR, SO GOOD! WHAT'S NEXT?

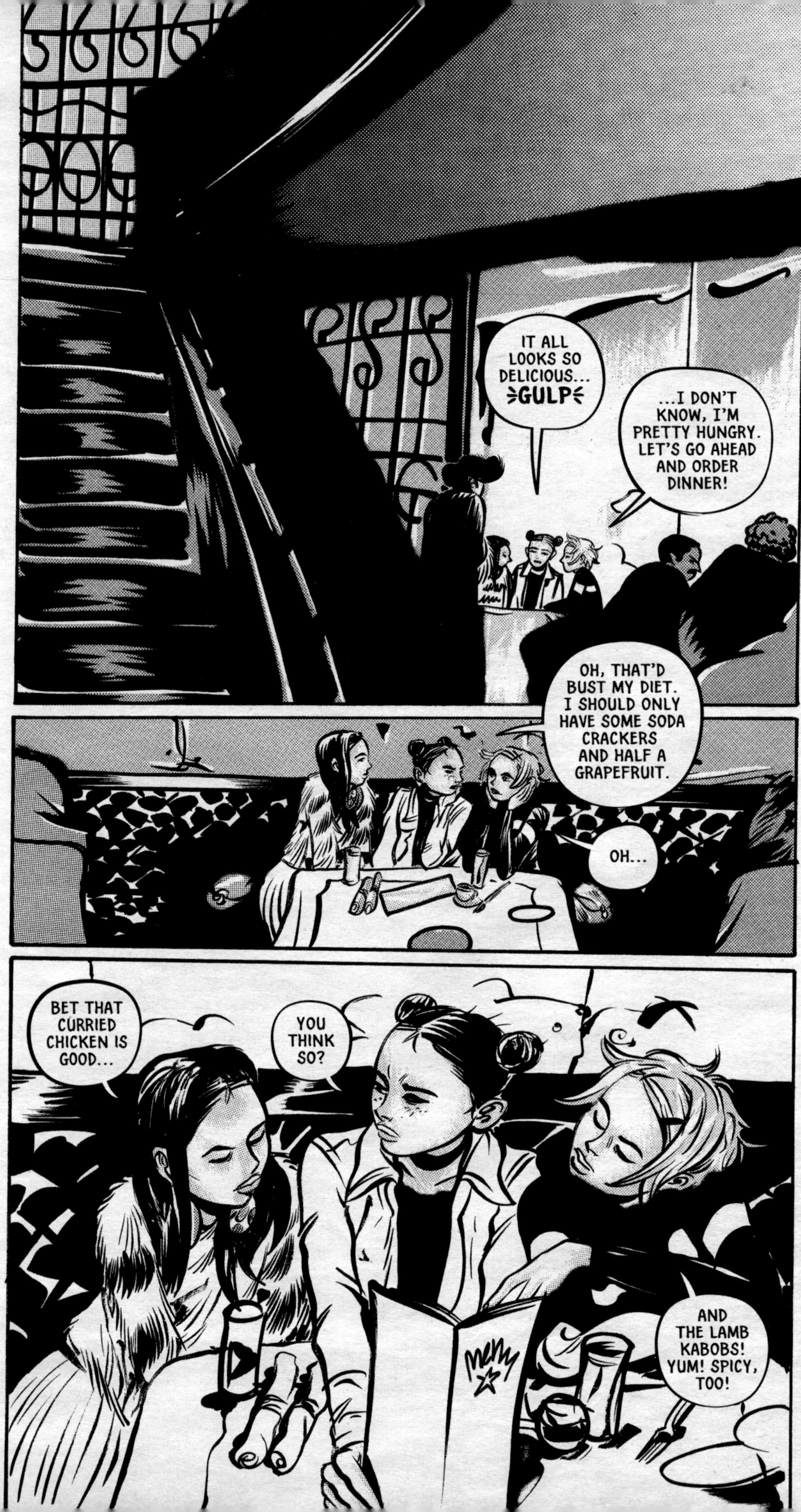
IT ALL LOOKS SO DELICIOUS... GULP
...I DON'T KNOW, I'M PRETTY HUNGRY. LET'S GO AHEAD AND ORDER DINNER!
OH, THAT'D BUST MY DIET. I SHOULD ONLY HAVE SOME SODA CRACKERS AND HALF A GRAPEFRUIT.
OH...
BET THAT CURRIED CHICKEN IS GOOD...
YOU THINK SO?
AND THE LAMB KABOBS! YUM! SPICY, TOO!
MENU

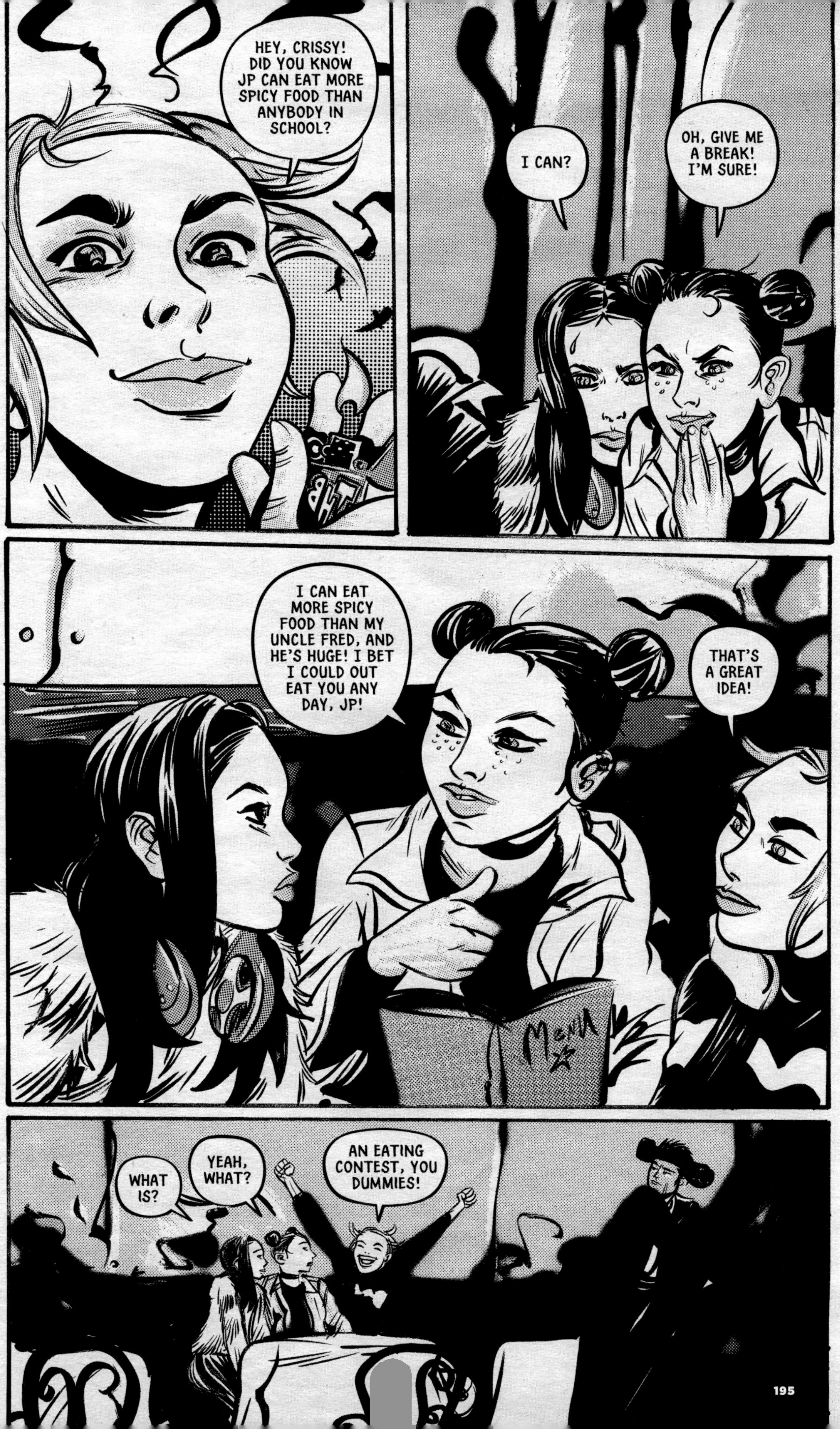
HEY, CRISSY! DID YOU KNOW JP CAN EAT MORE SPICY FOOD THAN ANYBODY IN SCHOOL?
I CAN?
OH, GIVE ME A BREAK! I'M SURE!
I CAN EAT MORE SPICY FOOD THAN MY UNCLE FRED, AND HE'S HUGE! I BET I COULD OUT EAT YOU ANY DAY, JP!
THAT'S A GREAT IDEA!
MENU
WHAT IS?
YEAH, WHAT?
AN EATING CONTEST, YOU DUMMIES!

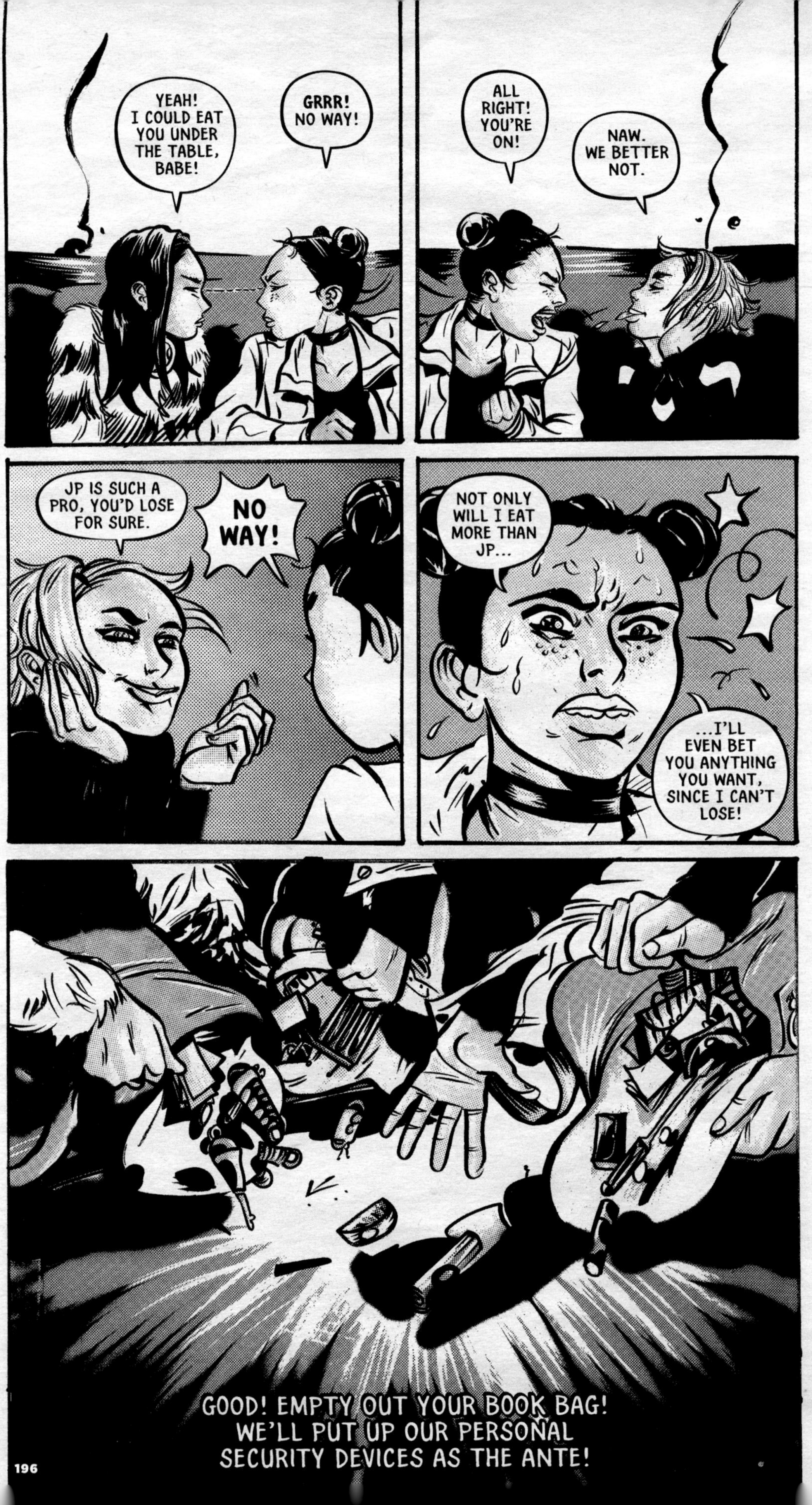
YEAH! I COULD EAT YOU UNDER THE TABLE, BABE!
GRRR! NO WAY!
ALL RIGHT! YOU'RE ON!
NAW. WE BETTER NOT.
JP IS SUCH A PRO, YOU'D LOSE FOR SURE.
NO WAY!
NOT ONLY WILL I EAT MORE THAN JP...
...I'LL EVEN BET YOU ANYTHING YOU WANT, SINCE I CAN'T LOSE!
GOOD! EMPTY OUT YOUR BOOK BAG! WE'LL PUT UP OUR PERSONAL SECURITY DEVICES AS THE ANTE!

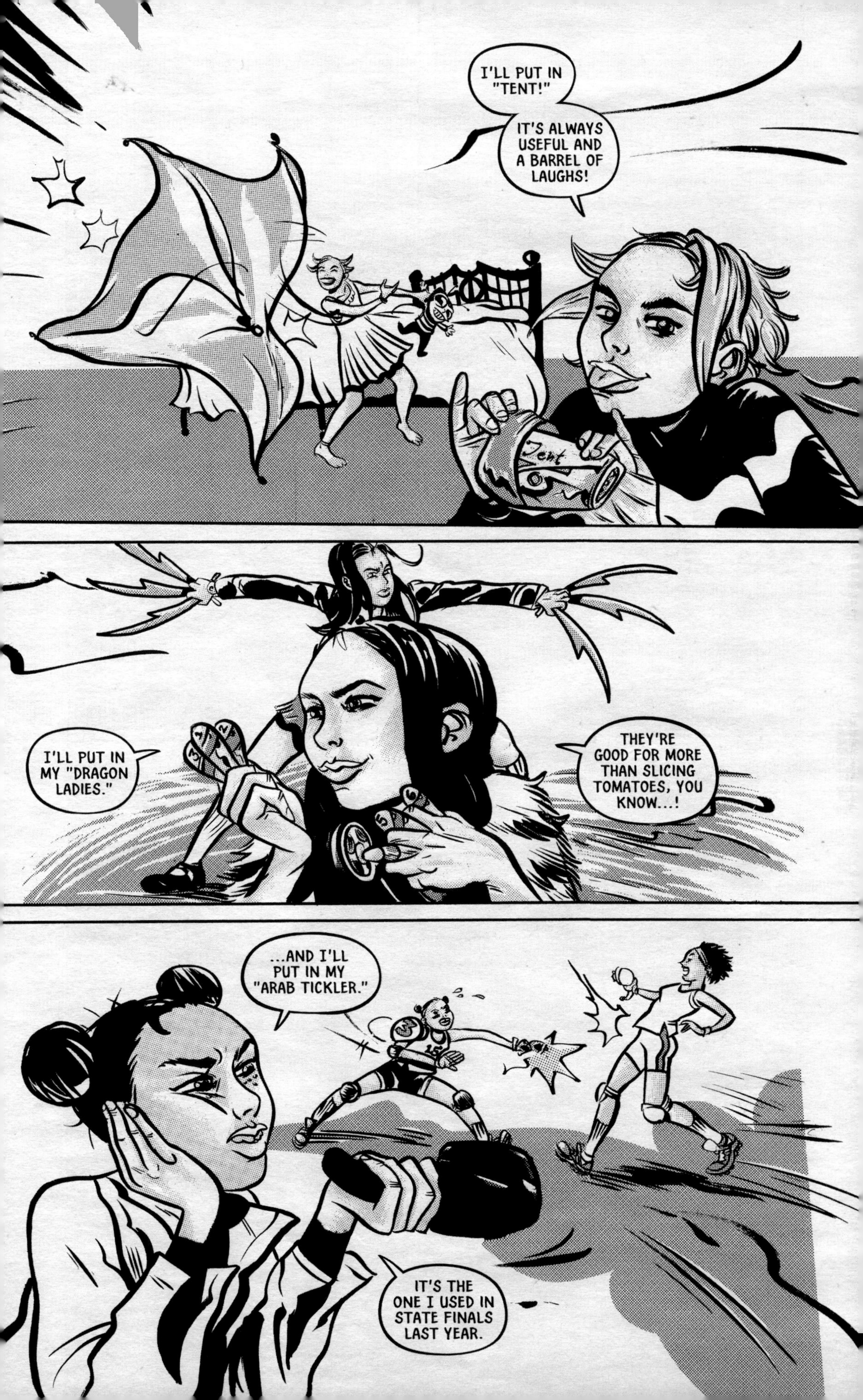
I'LL PUT IN "TENT!"
IT'S ALWAYS USEFUL AND A BARREL OF LAUGHS!
Tent
I'LL PUT IN MY "DRAGON LADIES."
THEY'RE GOOD FOR MORE THAN SLICING TOMATOES, YOU KNOW...!
...AND I'LL PUT IN MY "ARAB TICKLER."
IT'S THE ONE I USED IN STATE FINALS LAST YEAR.

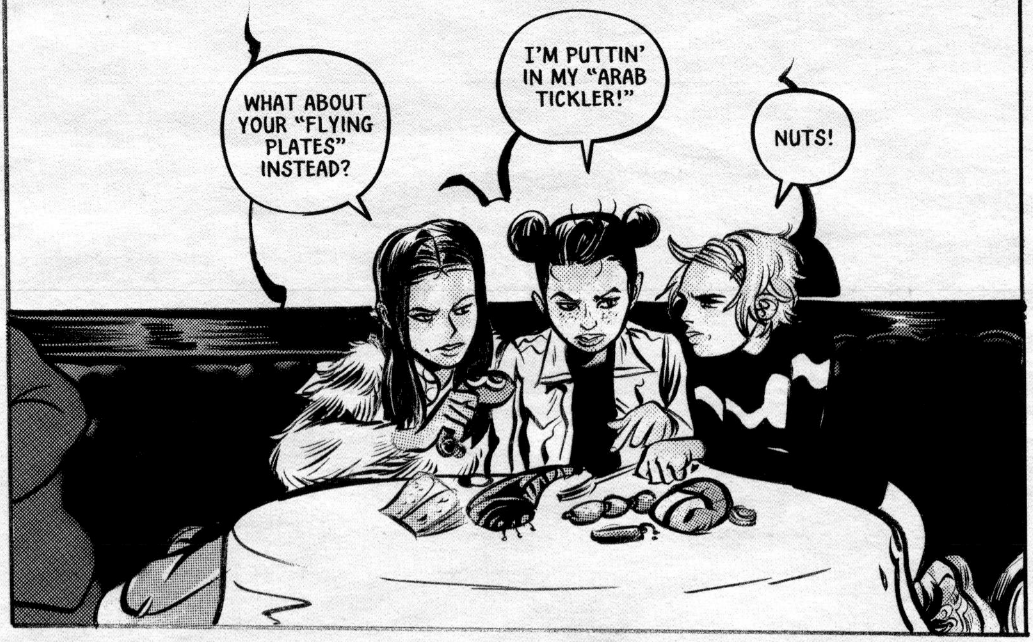
WHAT ABOUT YOUR "FLYING PLATES" INSTEAD?
I'M PUTTIN' IN MY "ARAB TICKLER!"
NUTS!

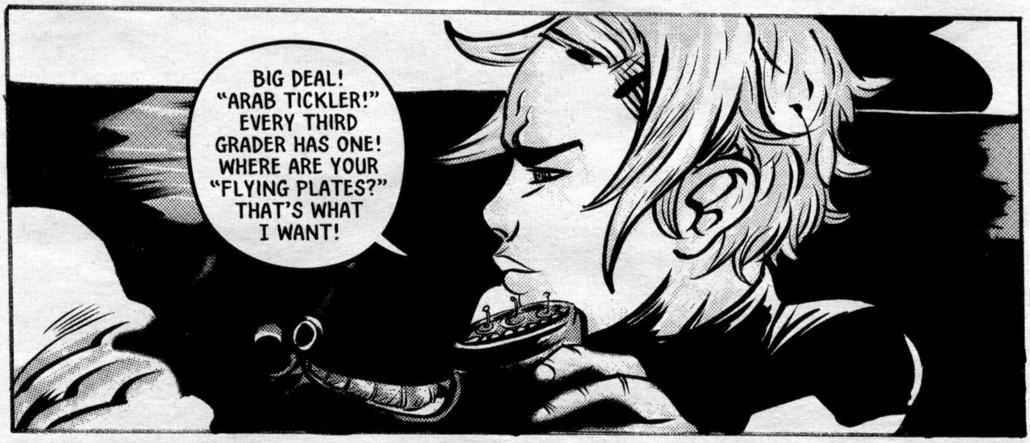
BIG DEAL! "ARAB TICKLER!" EVERY THIRD GRADER HAS ONE! WHERE ARE YOUR "FLYING PLATES?" THAT'S WHAT I WANT!

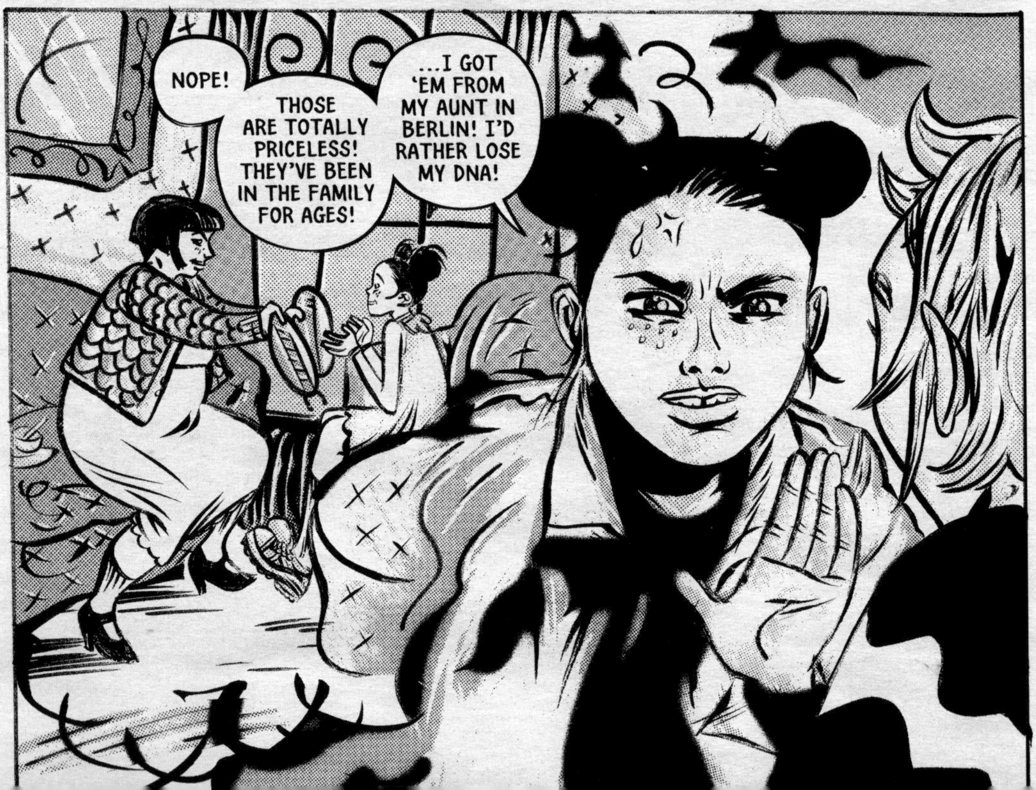
NOPE!
THOSE ARE TOTALLY PRICELESS! THEY'VE BEEN IN THE FAMILY FOR AGES!
...I GOT 'EM FROM MY AUNT IN BERLIN! I'D RATHER LOSE MY DNA!

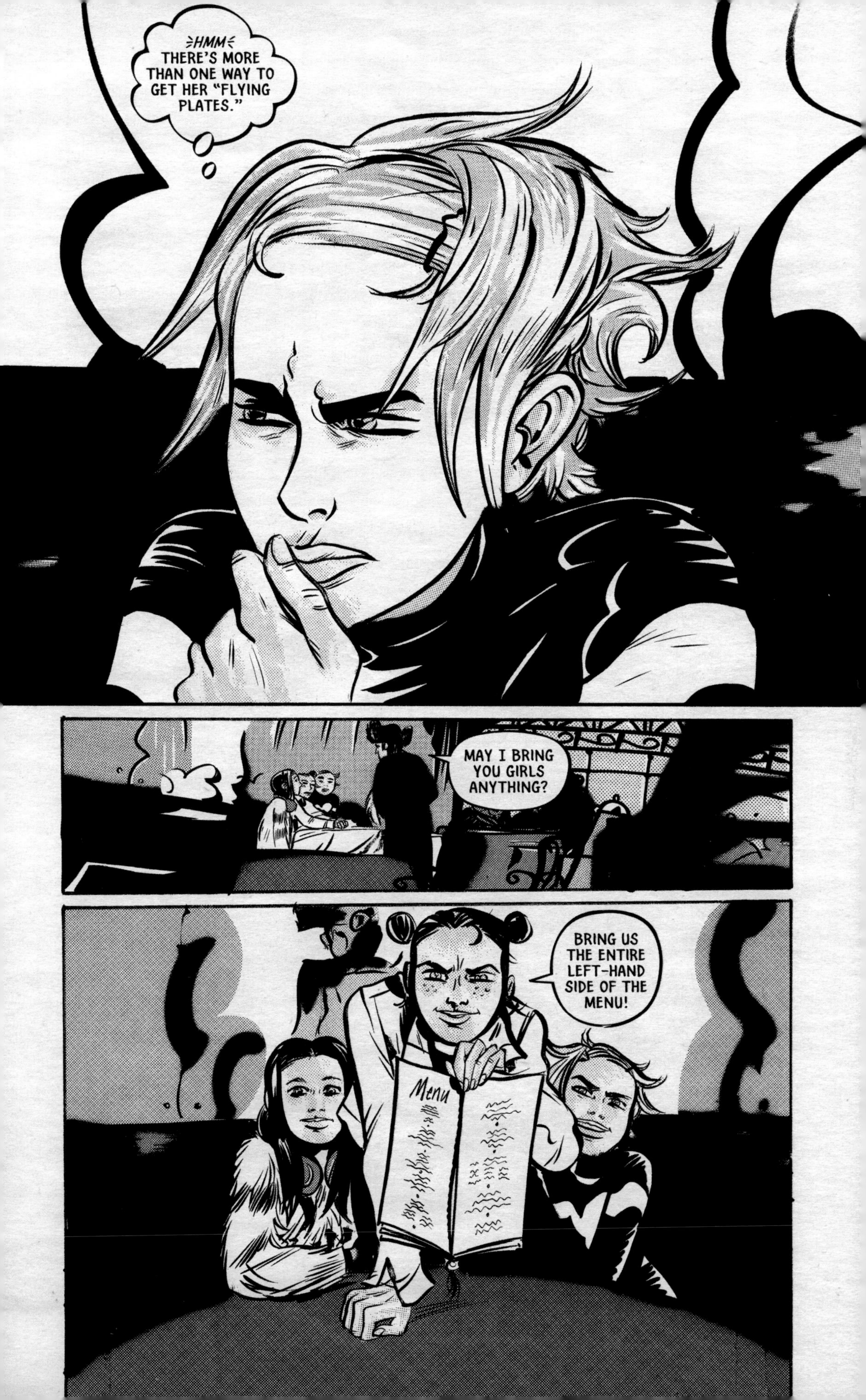
HMM
THERE'S MORE THAN ONE WAY TO GET HER "FLYING PLATES."
MAY I BRING YOU GIRLS ANYTHING?
BRING US THE ENTIRE LEFT-HAND SIDE OF THE MENU!
Menu

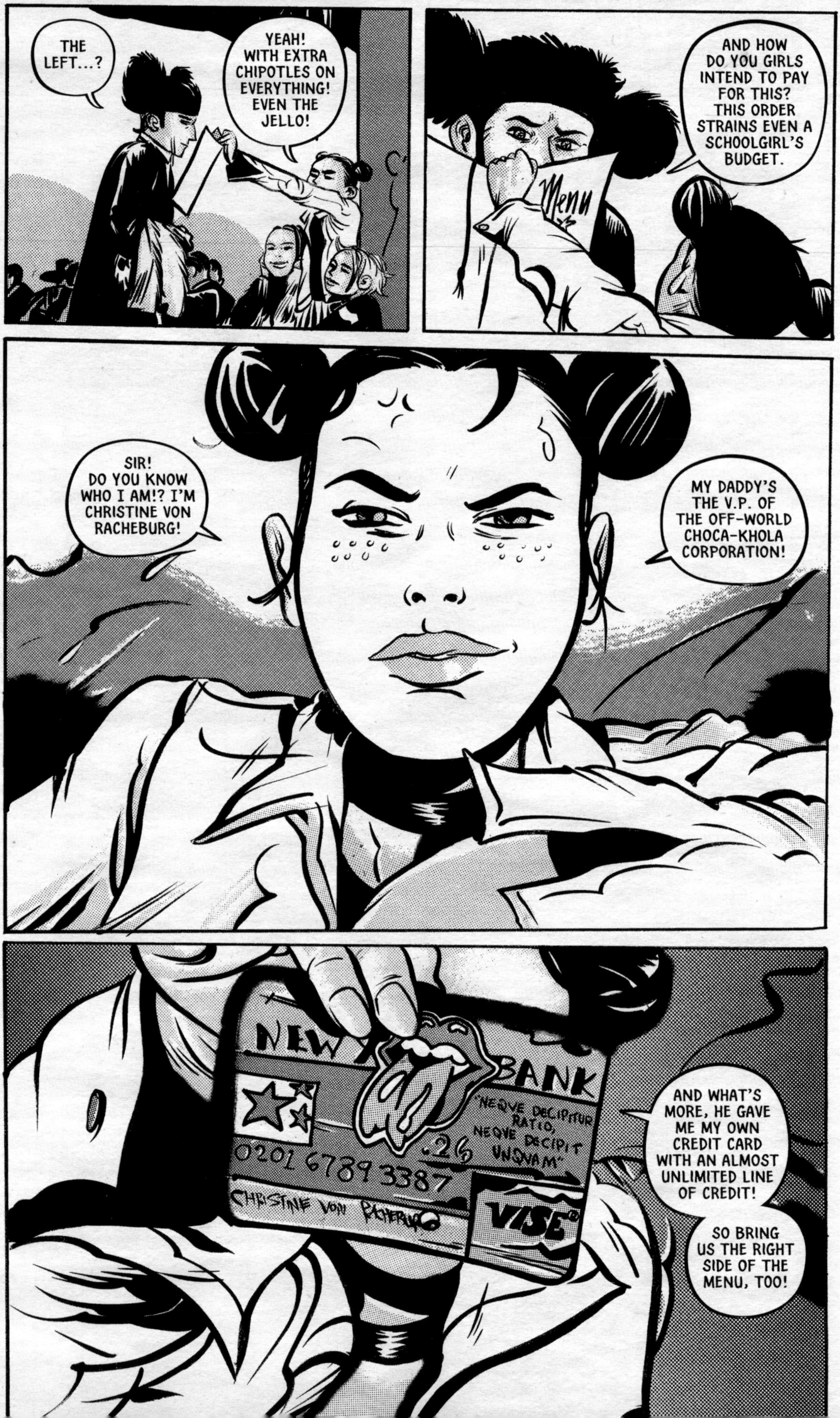
THE LEFT...?
YEAH! WITH EXTRA CHIPOTLES ON EVERYTHING! EVEN THE JELLO!
AND HOW DO YOU GIRLS INTEND TO PAY FOR THIS? THIS ORDER STRAINS EVEN A SCHOOLGIRL'S BUDGET.
Menu
SIR! DO YOU KNOW WHO I AM!? I'M CHRISTINE VON RACHEBURG!
MY DADDY'S THE V.P. OF THE OFF-WORLD CHOCA-KHOLA CORPORATION!
NEW
BANK
"NEQVE DECIPITUR RATIO, NEQVE DECIPIT UNQVAM"
0201 6789 3387
VISE
AND WHAT'S MORE, HE GAVE ME MY OWN CREDIT CARD WITH AN ALMOST UNLIMITED LINE OF CREDIT!
SO BRING US THE RIGHT SIDE OF THE MENU, TOO!

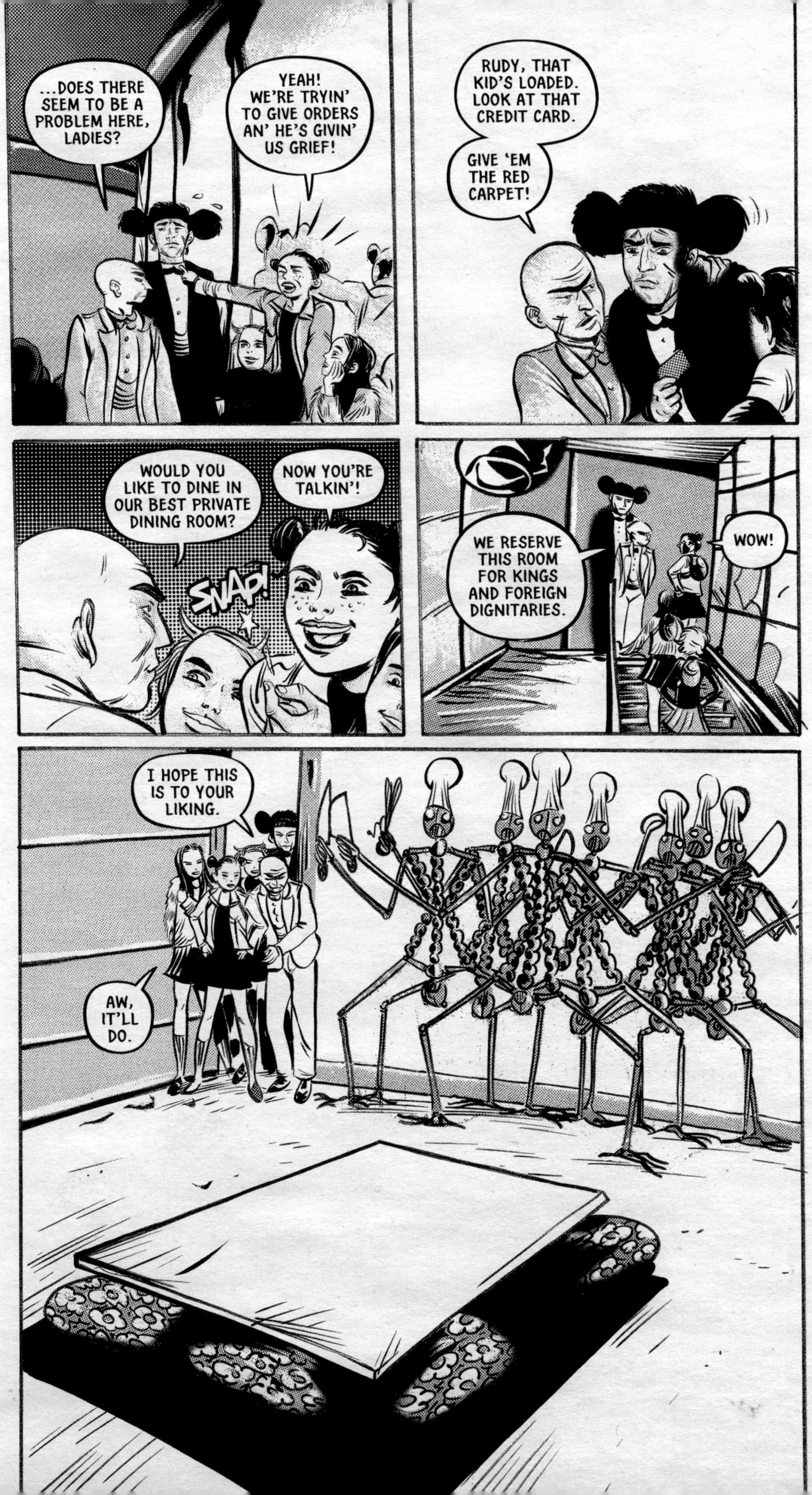
...DOES THERE SEEM TO BE A PROBLEM HERE, LADIES?
YEAH! WE'RE TRYIN' TO GIVE ORDERS AN' HE'S GIVIN' US GRIEF!
RUDY, THAT KID'S LOADED. LOOK AT THAT CREDIT CARD.
GIVE 'EM THE RED CARPET!
WOULD YOU LIKE TO DINE IN OUR BEST PRIVATE DINING ROOM?
NOW YOU'RE TALKIN'!
SNAP!
WE RESERVE THIS ROOM FOR KINGS AND FOREIGN DIGNITARIES.
WOW!
I HOPE THIS IS TO YOUR LIKING.
AW, IT'LL DO.

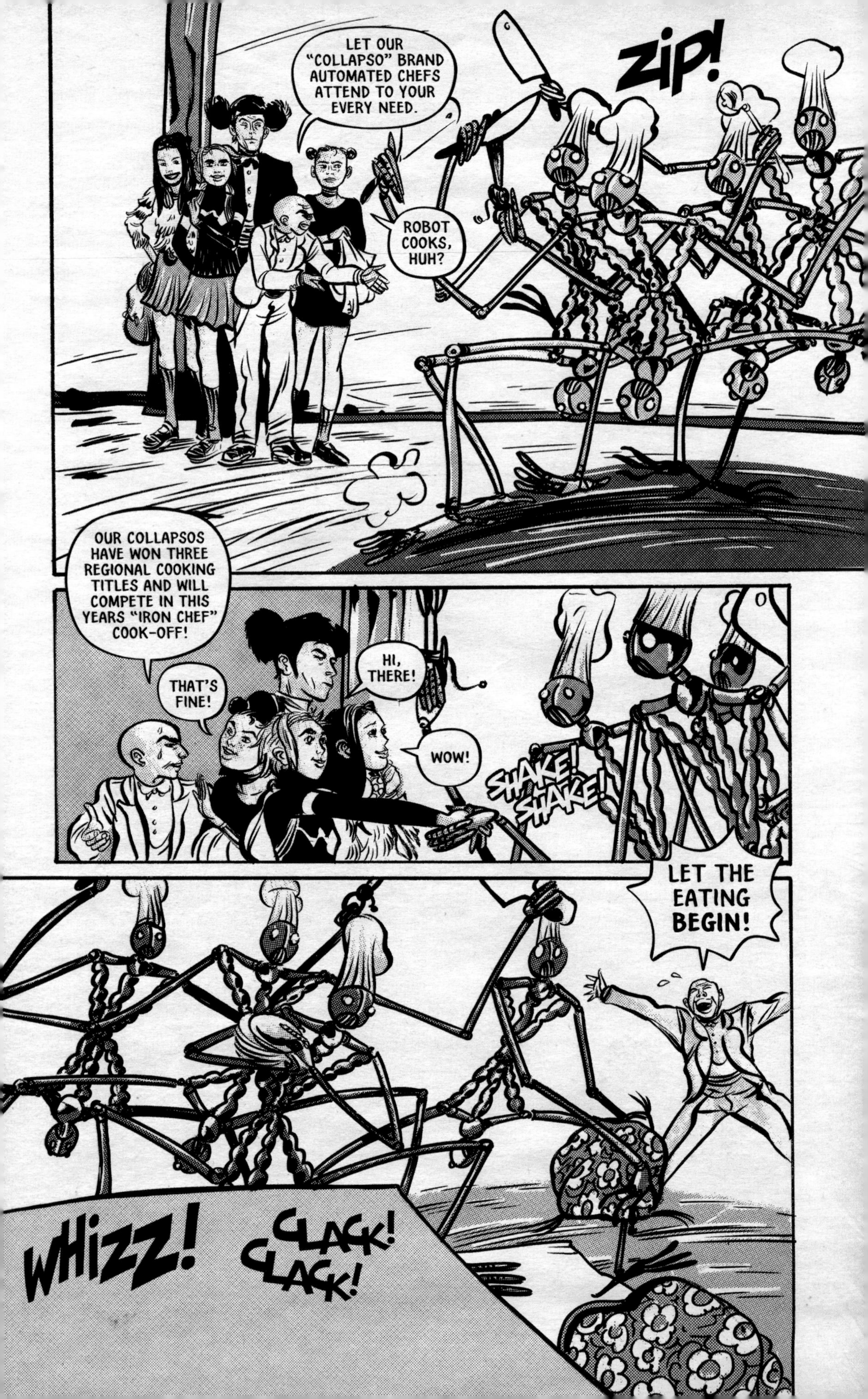
LET OUR "COLLAPSO" BRAND AUTOMATED CHEFS ATTEND TO YOUR EVERY NEED.
ZIP!
ROBOT COOKS, HUH?
OUR COLLAPSOS HAVE WON THREE REGIONAL COOKING TITLES AND WILL COMPETE IN THIS YEARS "IRON CHEF" COOK-OFF!
THAT'S FINE!
HI, THERE!
WOW!
SHAKE! SHAKE!
LET THE EATING BEGIN!
WHIZZ!
CLACK! CLACK!

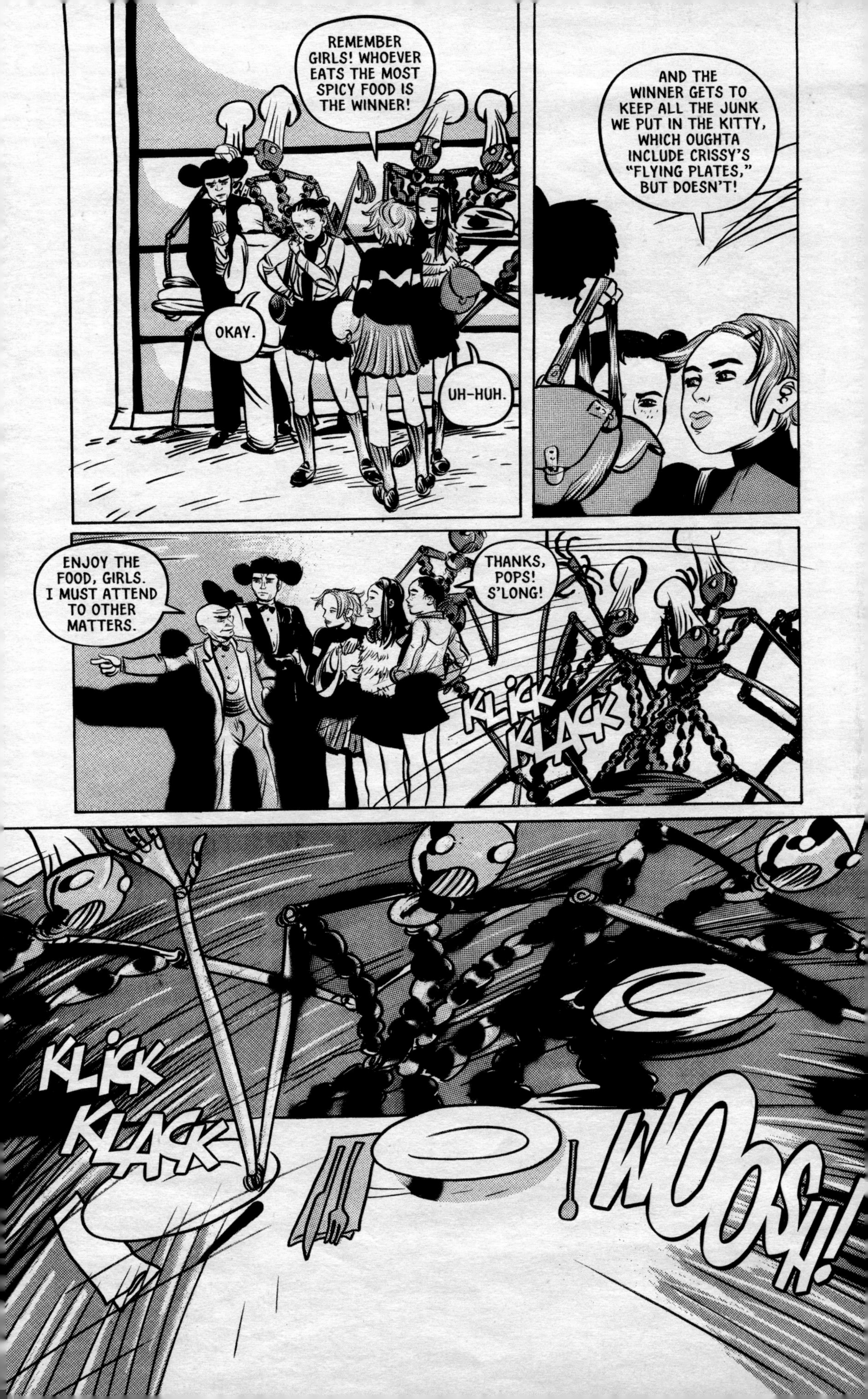
REMEMBER GIRLS! WHOEVER EATS THE MOST SPICY FOOD IS THE WINNER!
OKAY.
UH-HUH.
AND THE WINNER GETS TO KEEP ALL THE JUNK WE PUT IN THE KITTY, WHICH OUGHTA INCLUDE CRISSY'S "FLYING PLATES," BUT DOESN'T!
ENJOY THE FOOD, GIRLS. I MUST ATTEND TO OTHER MATTERS.
THANKS, POPS! S'LONG!
KLICK KLACK
KLICK KLACK
WOOSH!

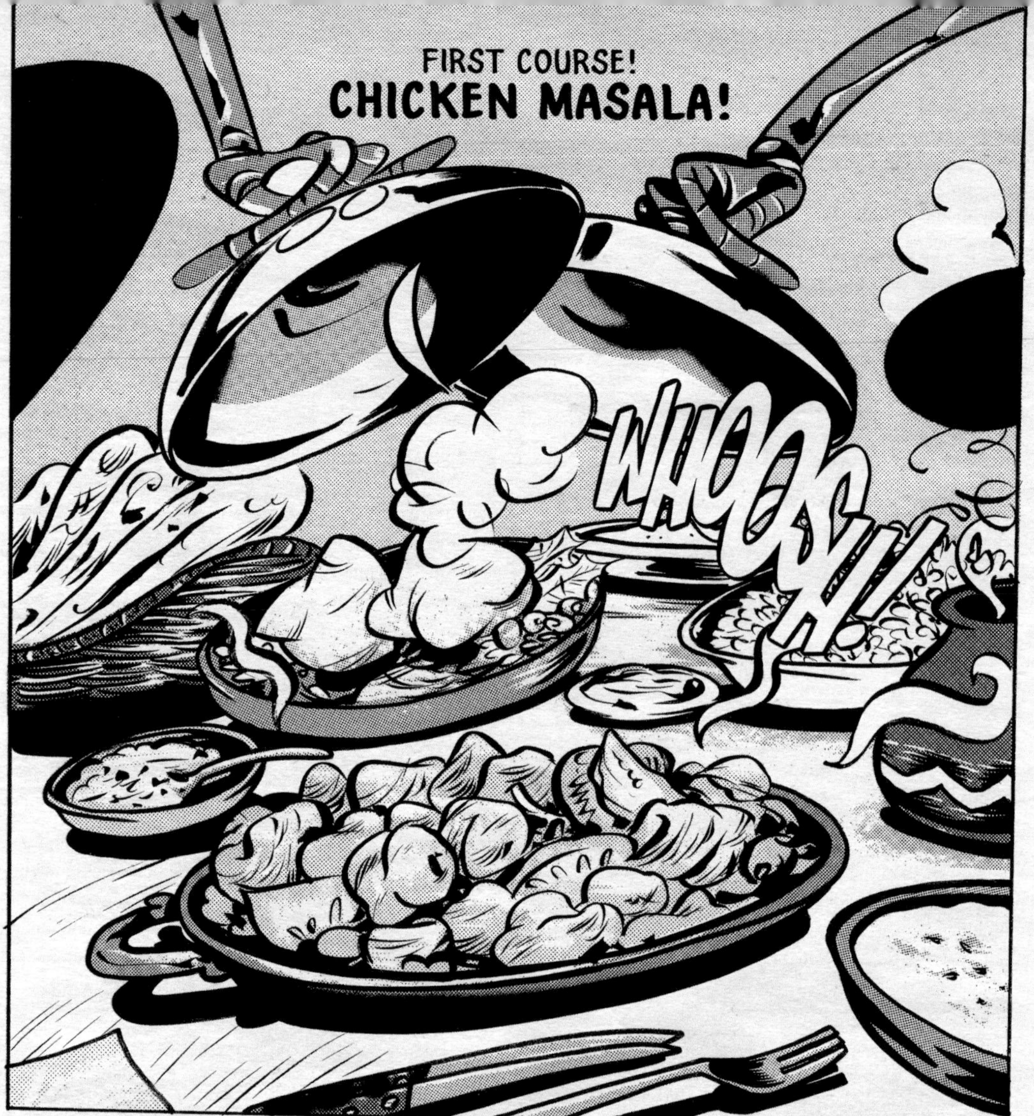
FIRST COURSE!
CHICKEN MASALA!
WHOOSH!

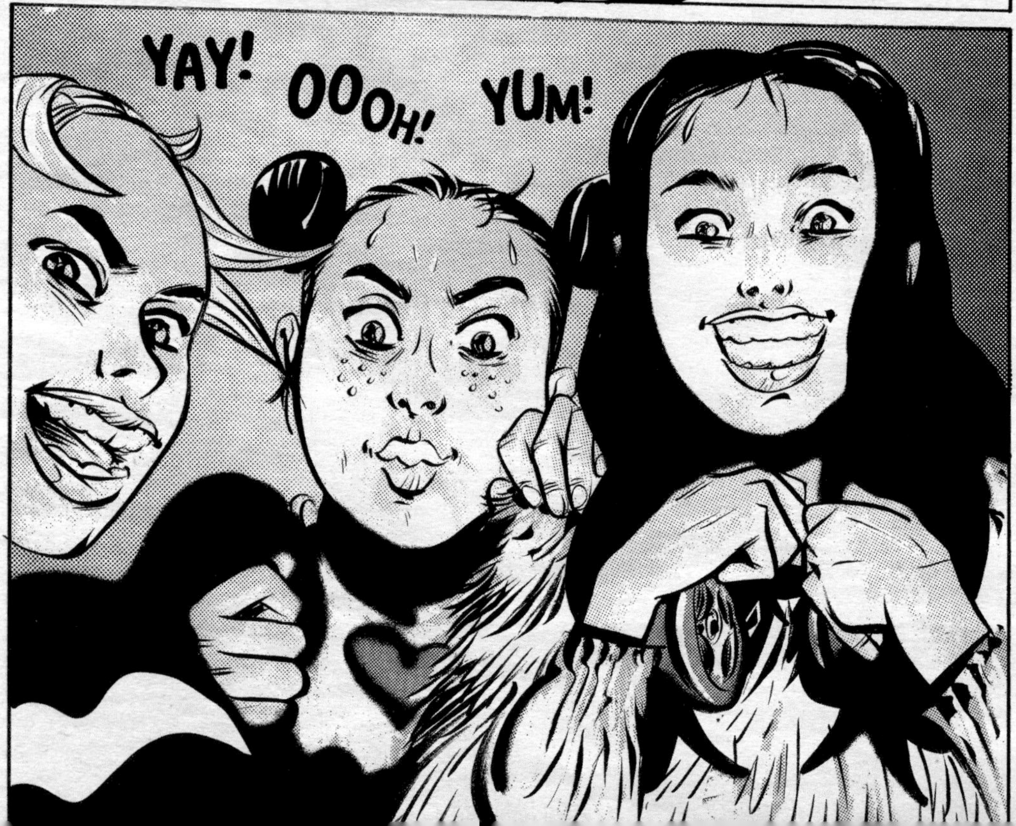
YAY!
OOOH!
YUM!

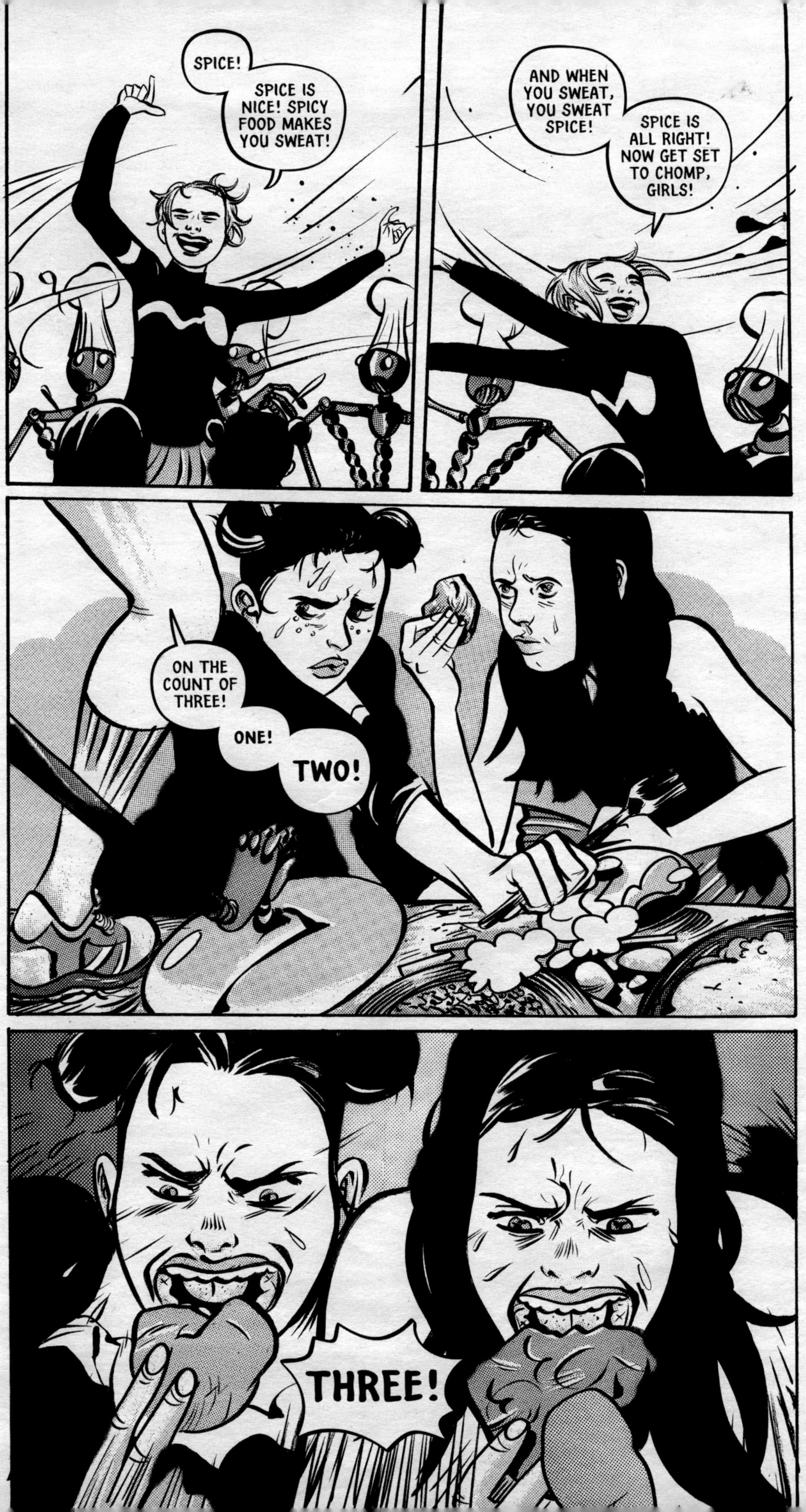
SPICE!
SPICE IS NICE! SPICY FOOD MAKES YOU SWEAT!
AND WHEN YOU SWEAT, YOU SWEAT SPICE!
SPICE IS ALL RIGHT! NOW GET SET TO CHOMP, GIRLS!
ON THE COUNT OF THREE!
ONE!
TWO!
THREE!

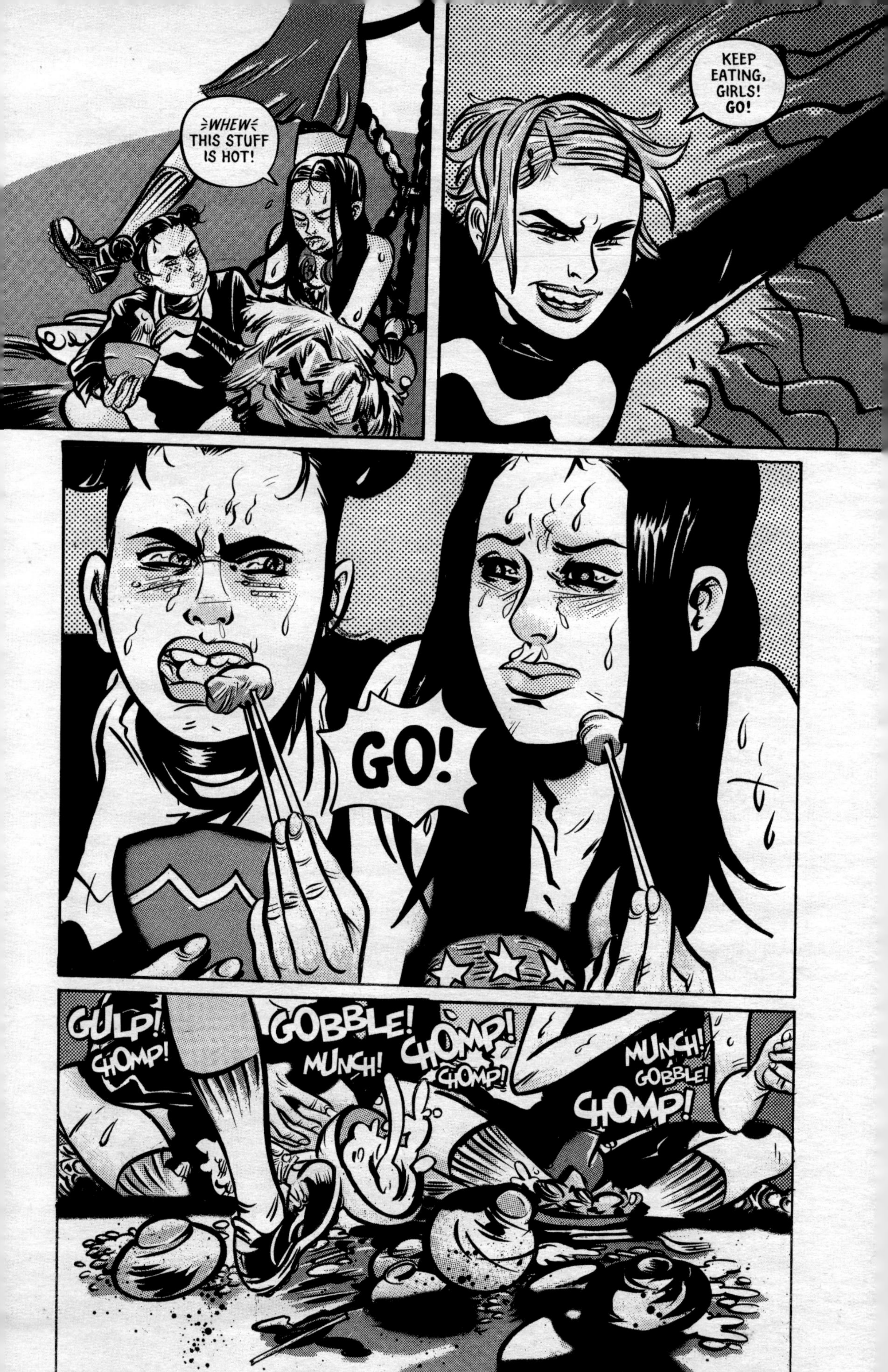
WHEW
THIS STUFF IS HOT!
KEEP EATING, GIRLS! GO!
GO!
GULP!
CHOMP!
GOBBLE!
MUNCH!
CHOMP!
CHOMP!
MUNCH!
GOBBLE!
CHOMP!

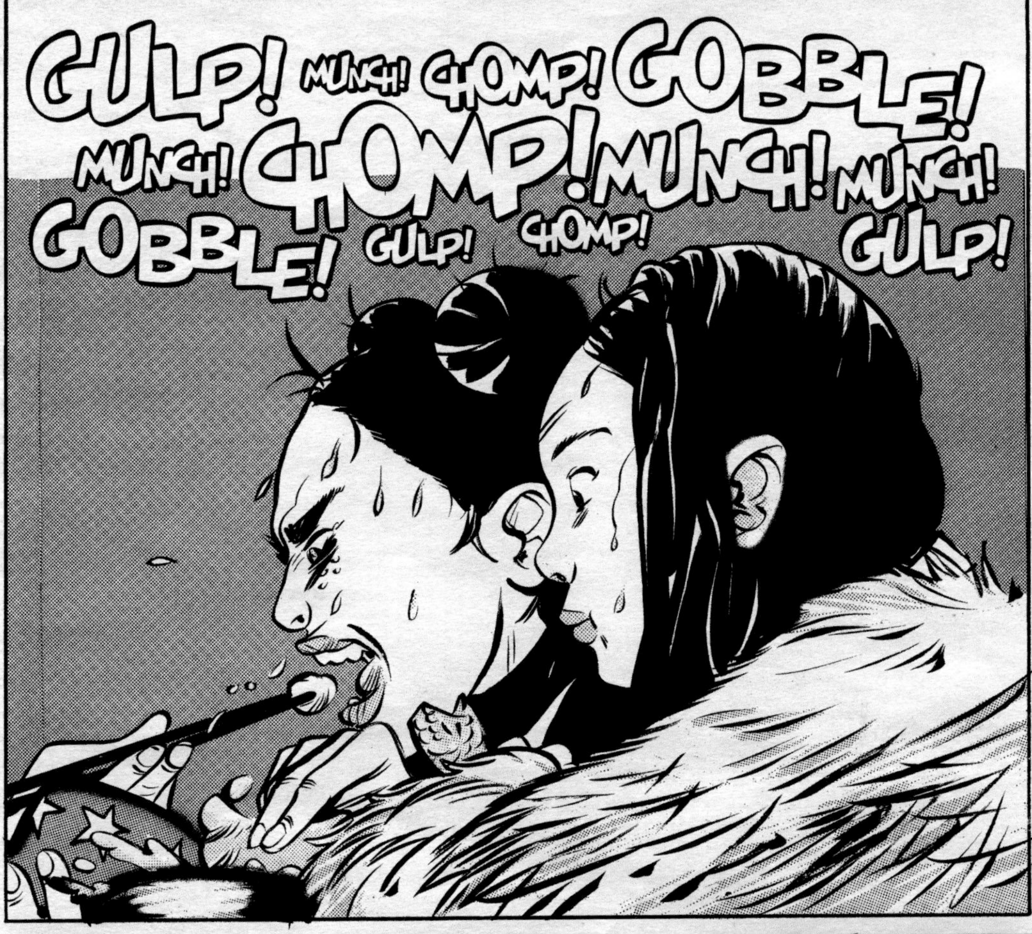
GULP! MUNCH! CHOMP! GOBBLE!
MUNCH! CHOMP! MUNCH! MUNCH!
GOBBLE! GULP! CHOMP! GULP!

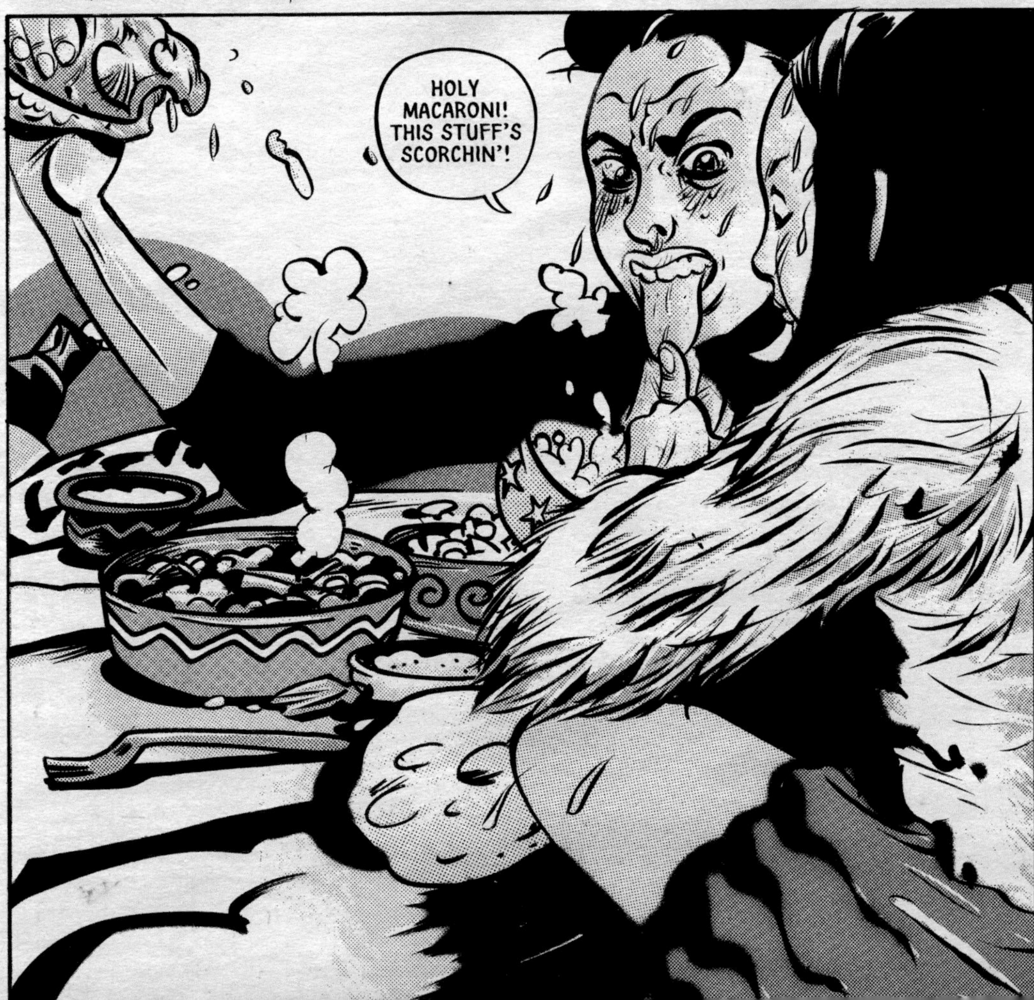
HOLY MACARONI! THIS STUFF'S SCORCHIN'!

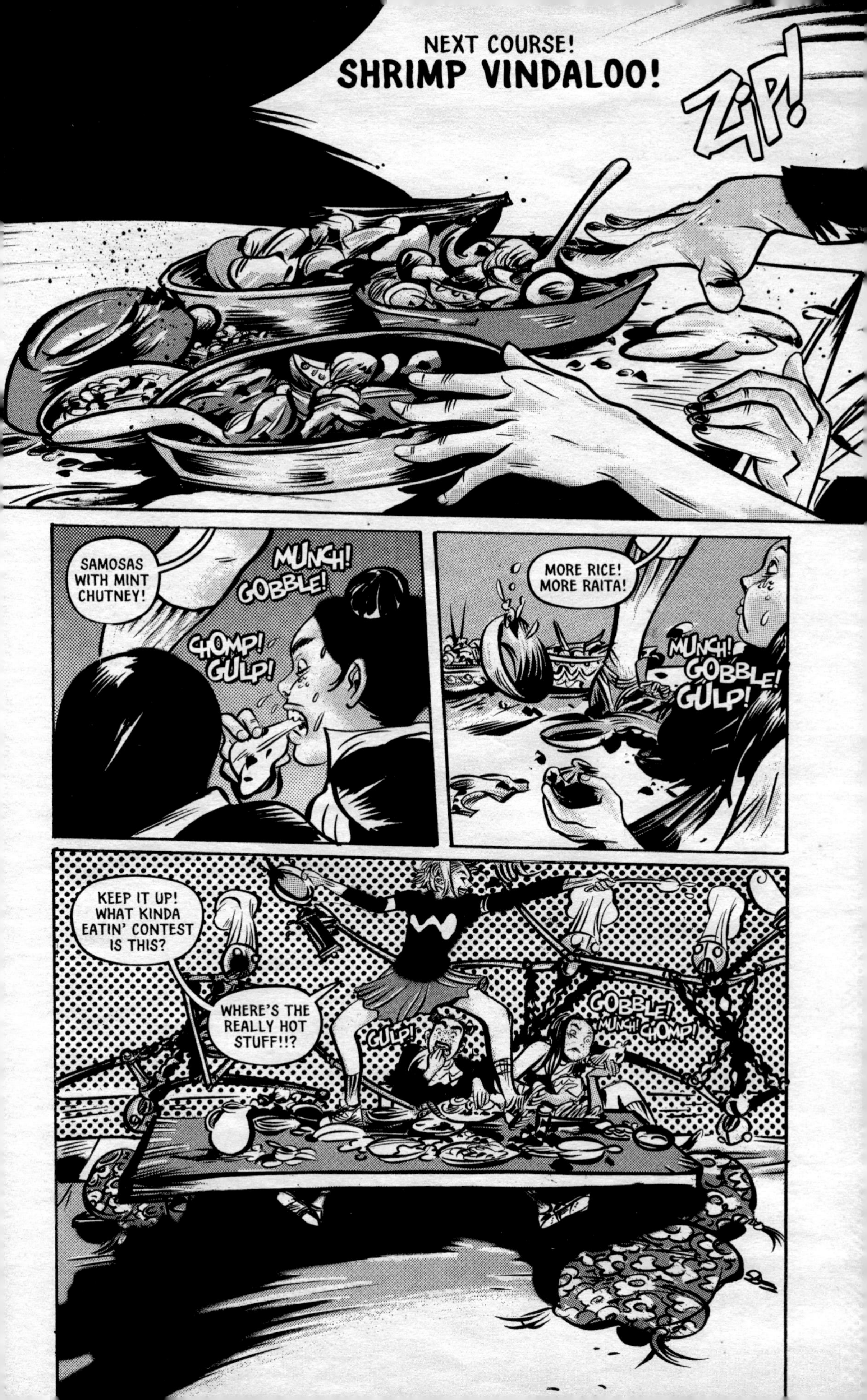
NEXT COURSE!
SHRIMP VINDALOO!
ZIP!
SAMOSAS WITH MINT CHUTNEY!
MUNCH! GOBBLE!
CHOMP! GULP!
MORE RICE! MORE RAITA!
MUNCH! GOBBLE! GULP!
KEEP IT UP! WHAT KINDA EATIN' CONTEST IS THIS?
WHERE'S THE REALLY HOT STUFF!!?
GULP!
GOBBLE! MUNCH! CHOMP!

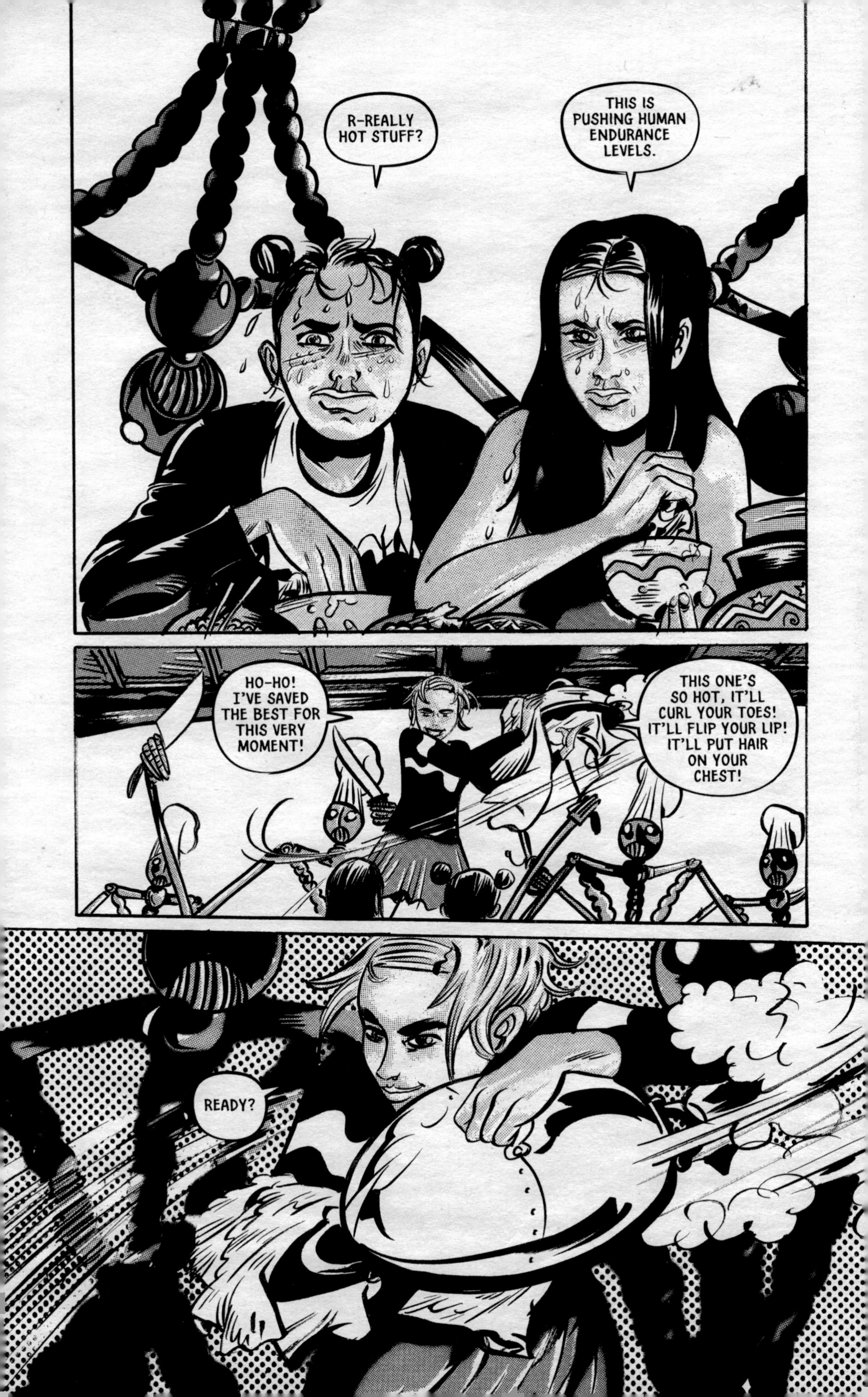
R-REALLY HOT STUFF?
THIS IS PUSHING HUMAN ENDURANCE LEVELS.
HO-HO! I'VE SAVED THE BEST FOR THIS VERY MOMENT!
THIS ONE'S SO HOT, IT'LL CURL YOUR TOES! IT'LL FLIP YOUR LIP! IT'LL PUT HAIR ON YOUR CHEST!
READY?

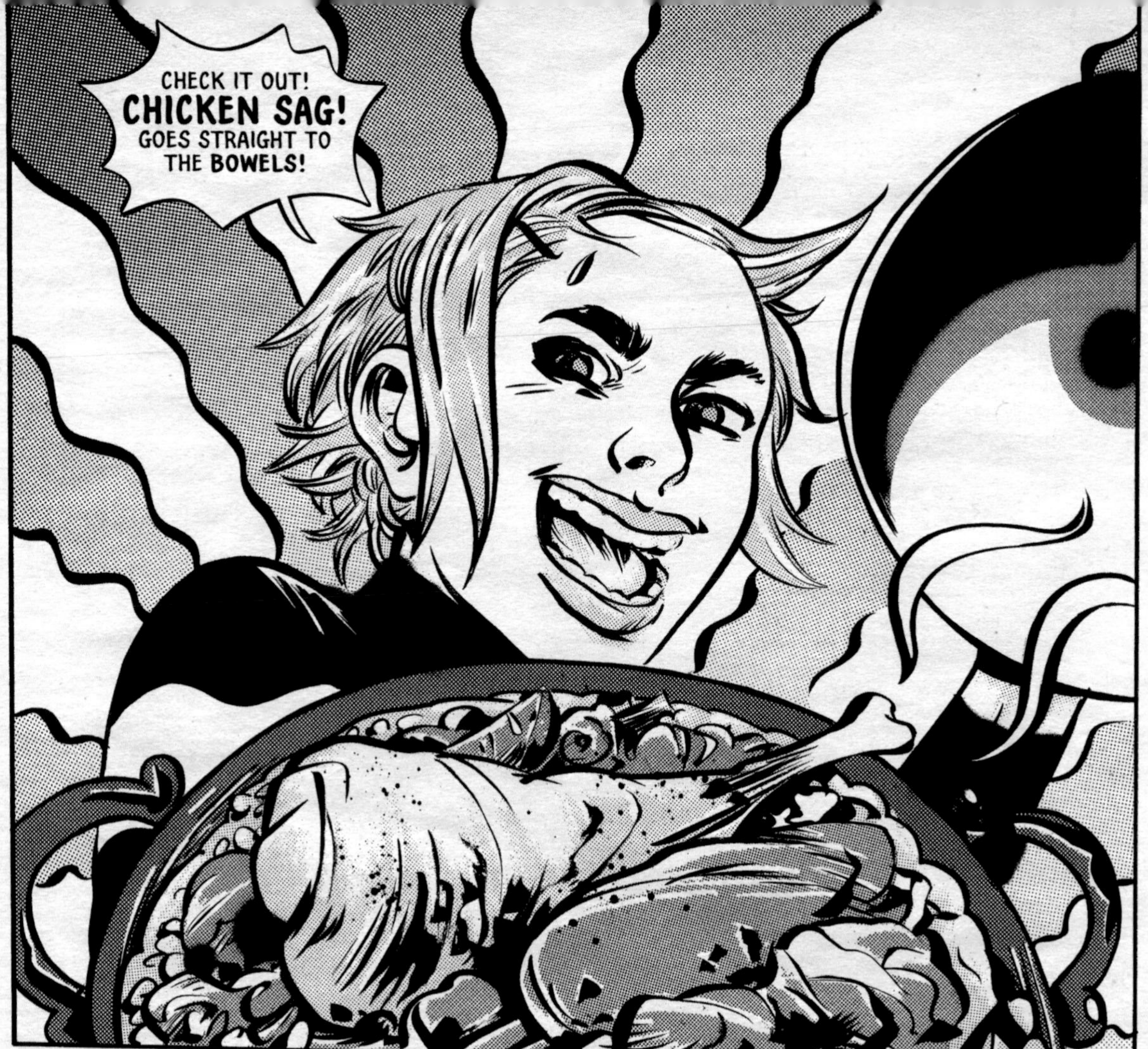
CHECK IT OUT! CHICKEN SAG! GOES STRAIGHT TO THE BOWELS!

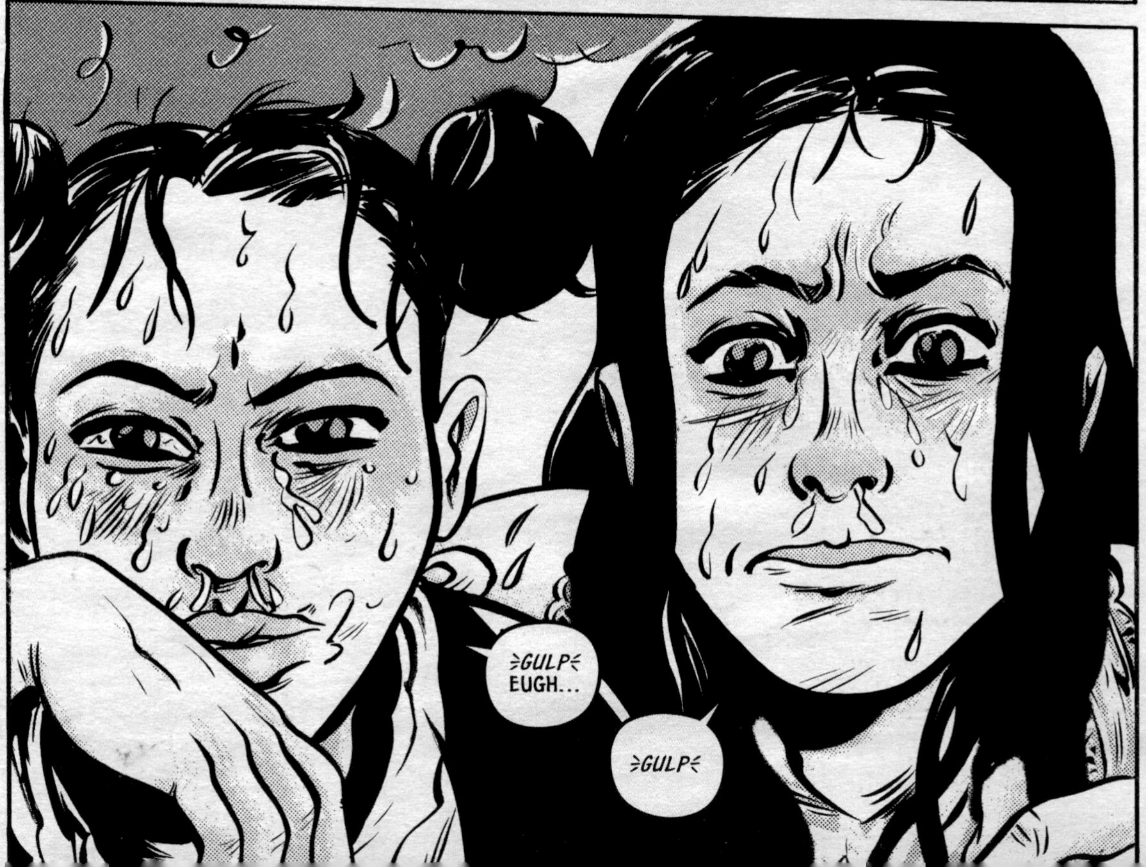
≥GULP≤ EUGH...
≥GULP≤

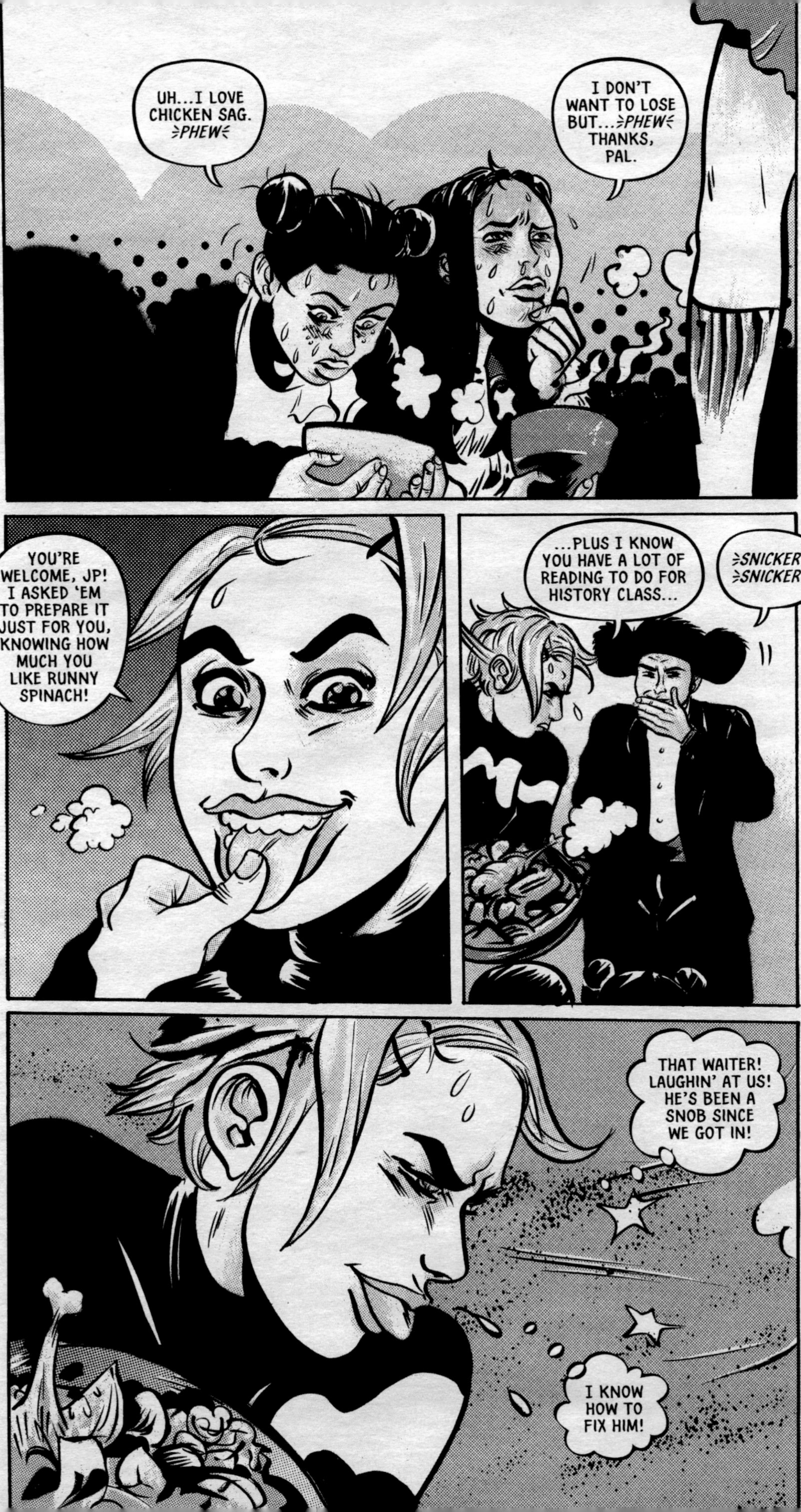
UH...I LOVE CHICKEN SAG. ⪢PHEW⪡
I DON'T WANT TO LOSE BUT...⪢PHEW⪡ THANKS, PAL.
YOU'RE WELCOME, JP! I ASKED 'EM TO PREPARE IT JUST FOR YOU, KNOWING HOW MUCH YOU LIKE RUNNY SPINACH!
...PLUS I KNOW YOU HAVE A LOT OF READING TO DO FOR HISTORY CLASS...
⪢SNICKER⪡ ⪢SNICKER⪡
THAT WAITER! LAUGHIN' AT US! HE'S BEEN A SNOB SINCE WE GOT IN!
I KNOW HOW TO FIX HIM!

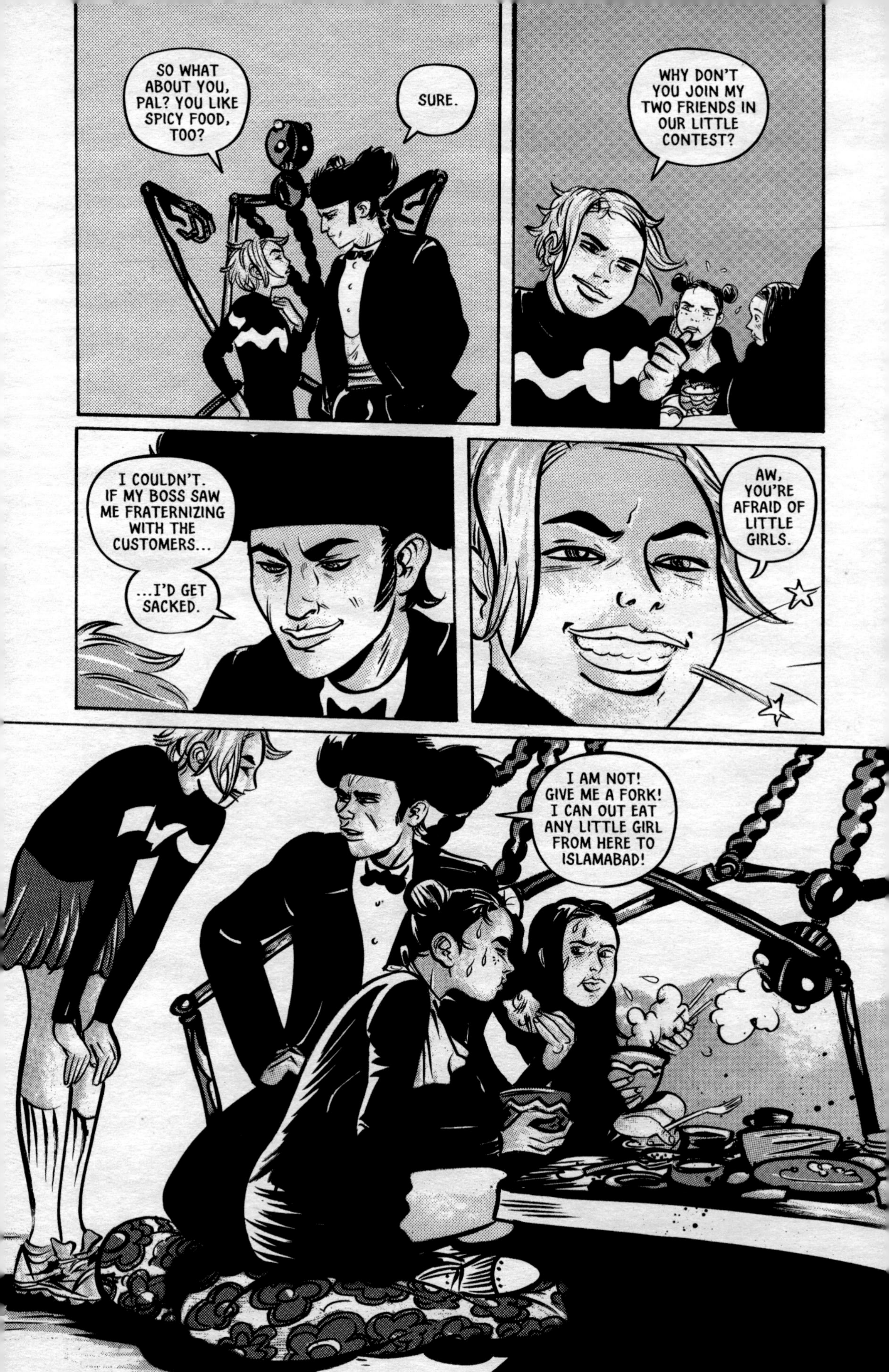
SO WHAT ABOUT YOU, PAL? YOU LIKE SPICY FOOD, TOO?
SURE.
WHY DON'T YOU JOIN MY TWO FRIENDS IN OUR LITTLE CONTEST?
I COULDN'T. IF MY BOSS SAW ME FRATERNIZING WITH THE CUSTOMERS...
...I'D GET SACKED.
AW, YOU'RE AFRAID OF LITTLE GIRLS.
I AM NOT! GIVE ME A FORK! I CAN OUT EAT ANY LITTLE GIRL FROM HERE TO ISLAMABAD!

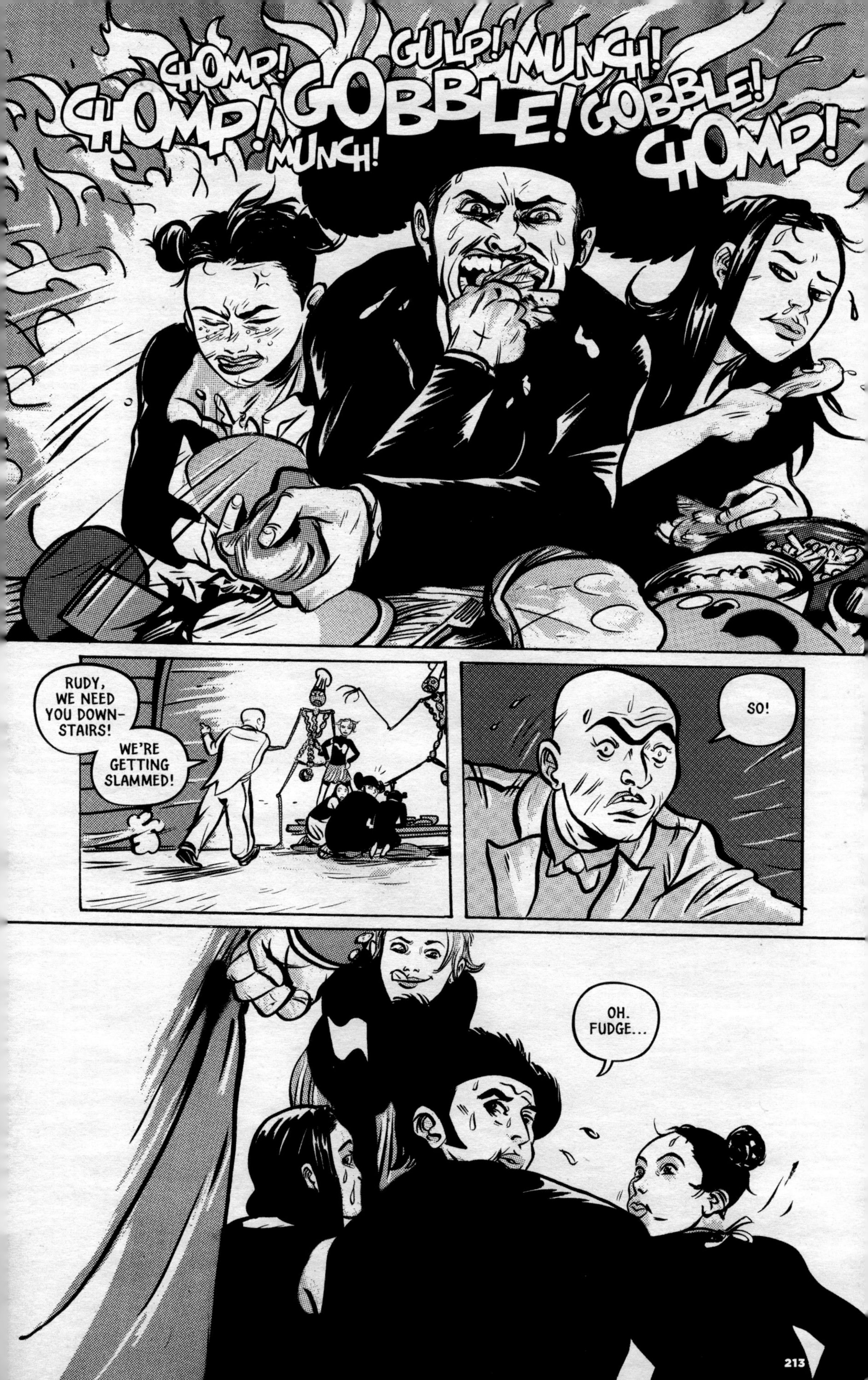
CHOMP!
CHOMP!
GULP!
MUNCH!
GOBBLE!
MUNCH!
GOBBLE!
CHOMP!
RUDY, WE NEED YOU DOWN-STAIRS!
WE'RE GETTING SLAMMED!
SO!
OH. FUDGE...

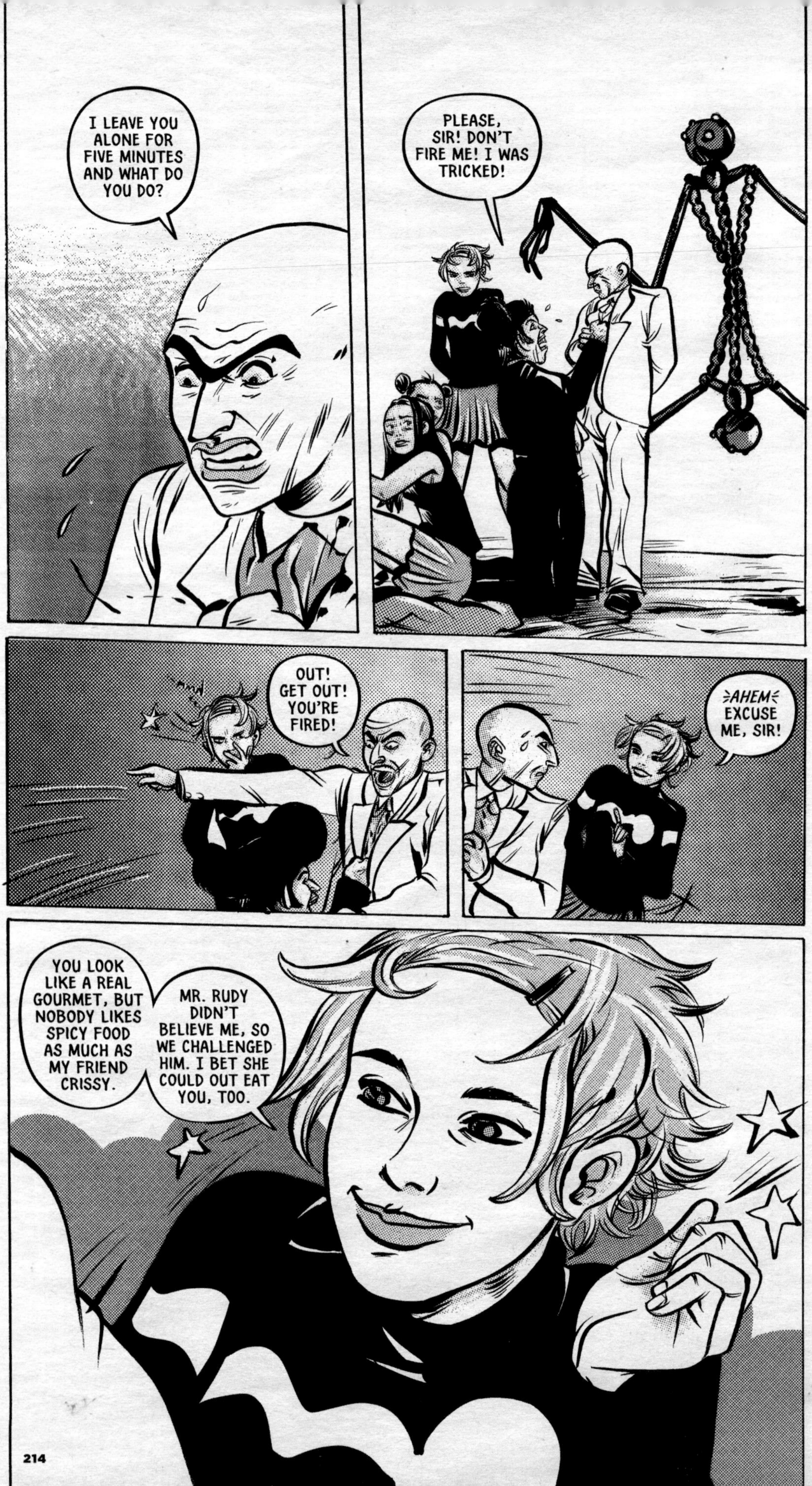
I LEAVE YOU ALONE FOR FIVE MINUTES AND WHAT DO YOU DO?
PLEASE, SIR! DON'T FIRE ME! I WAS TRICKED!
OUT! GET OUT! YOU'RE FIRED!
AHEM EXCUSE ME, SIR!
YOU LOOK LIKE A REAL GOURMET, BUT NOBODY LIKES SPICY FOOD AS MUCH AS MY FRIEND CRISSY.
MR. RUDY DIDN'T BELIEVE ME, SO WE CHALLENGED HIM. I BET SHE COULD OUT EAT YOU, TOO.

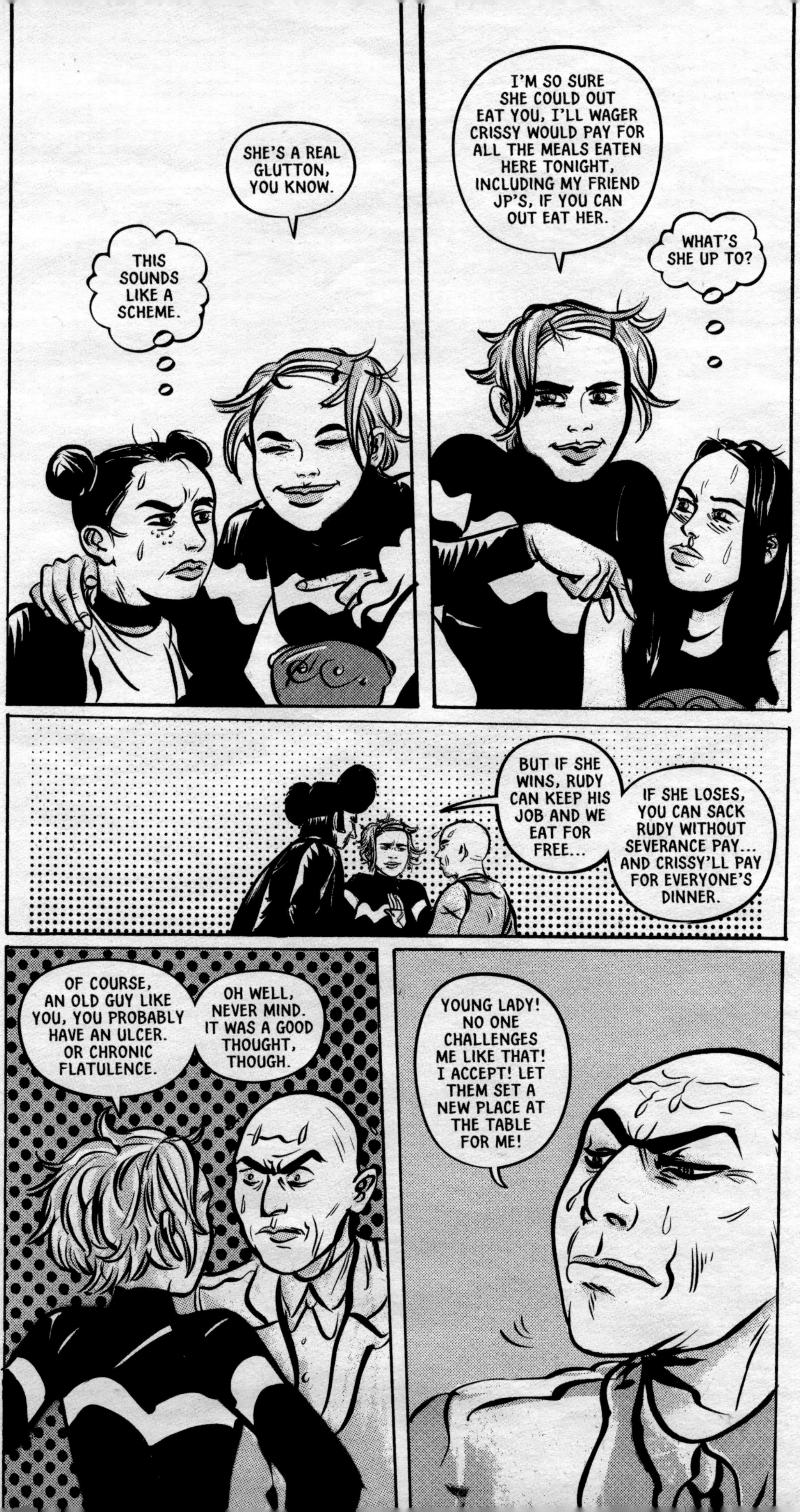
SHE'S A REAL GLUTTON, YOU KNOW.
THIS SOUNDS LIKE A SCHEME.
I'M SO SURE SHE COULD OUT EAT YOU, I'LL WAGER CRISSY WOULD PAY FOR ALL THE MEALS EATEN HERE TONIGHT, INCLUDING MY FRIEND JP'S, IF YOU CAN OUT EAT HER.
WHAT'S SHE UP TO?
BUT IF SHE WINS, RUDY CAN KEEP HIS JOB AND WE EAT FOR FREE...
IF SHE LOSES, YOU CAN SACK RUDY WITHOUT SEVERANCE PAY... AND CRISSY'LL PAY FOR EVERYONE'S DINNER.
OF COURSE, AN OLD GUY LIKE YOU, YOU PROBABLY HAVE AN ULCER. OR CHRONIC FLATULENCE.
OH WELL, NEVER MIND. IT WAS A GOOD THOUGHT, THOUGH.
YOUNG LADY! NO ONE CHALLENGES ME LIKE THAT! I ACCEPT! LET THEM SET A NEW PLACE AT THE TABLE FOR ME!

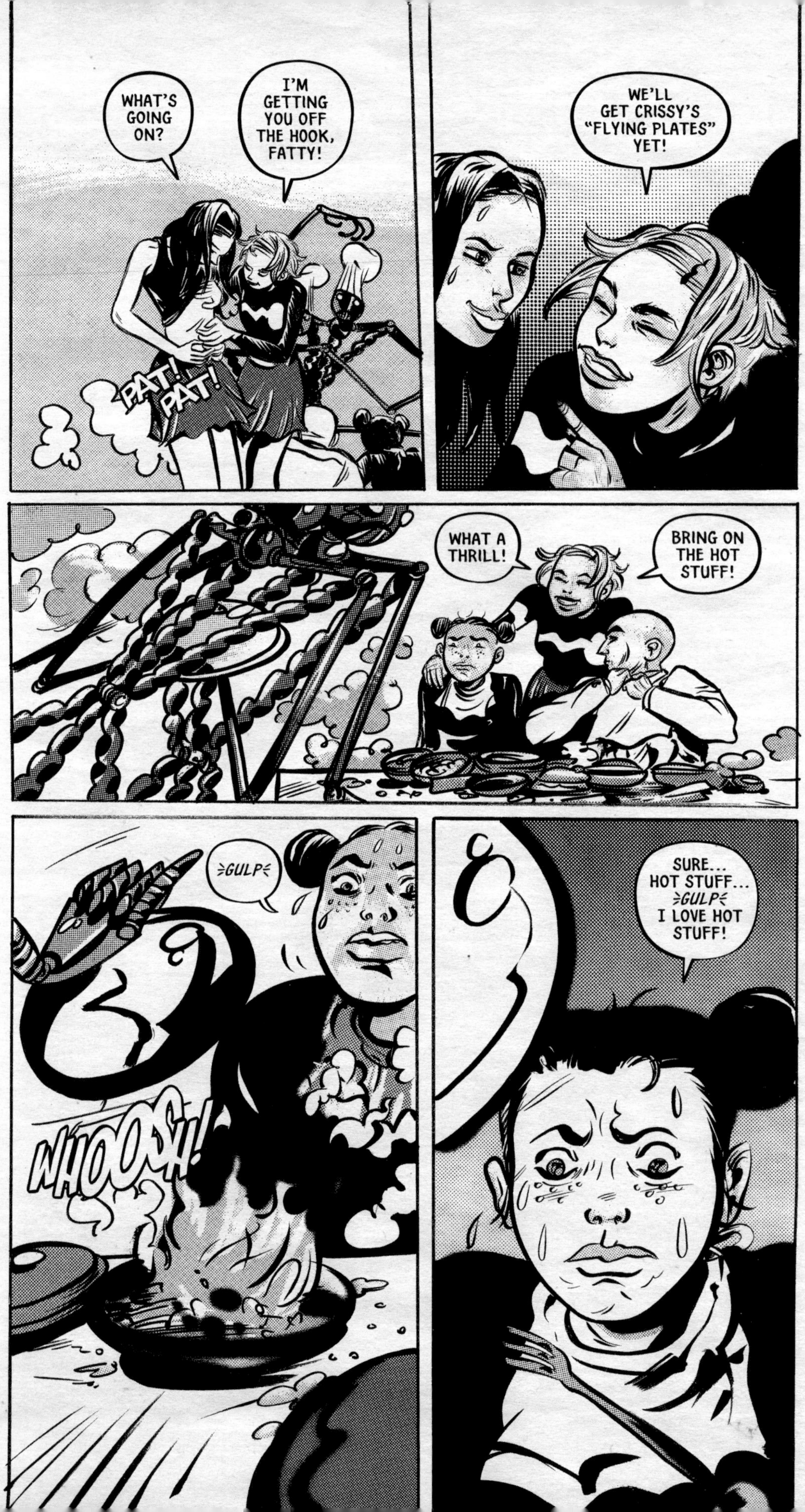
WHAT'S GOING ON?
I'M GETTING YOU OFF THE HOOK, FATTY!
PAT! PAT!
WE'LL GET CRISSY'S "FLYING PLATES" YET!
WHAT A THRILL!
BRING ON THE HOT STUFF!
GULP
WHOOSH!
SURE... HOT STUFF... GULP I LOVE HOT STUFF!

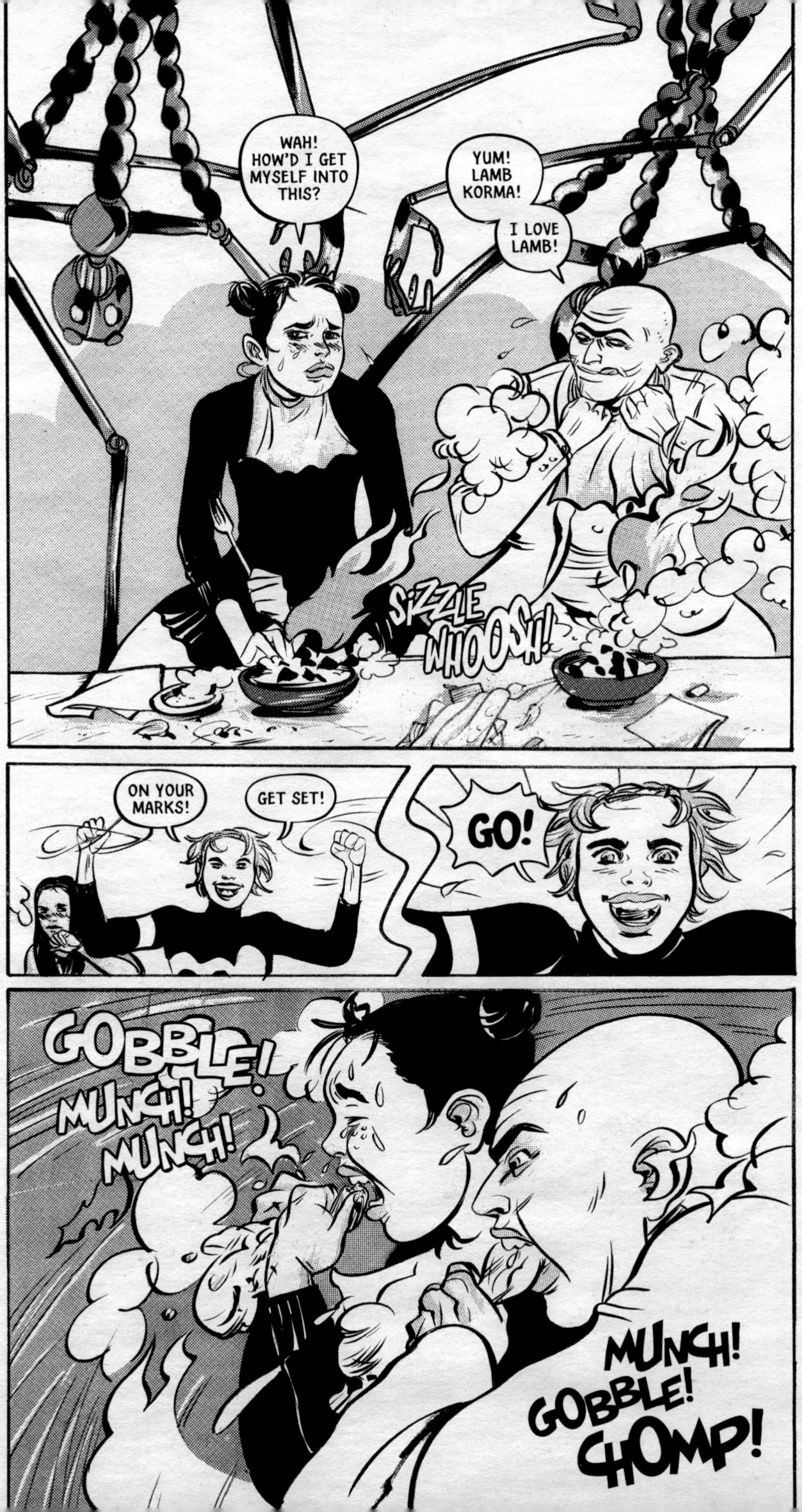
WAH! HOW'D I GET MYSELF INTO THIS?
YUM! LAMB KORMA!
I LOVE LAMB!
SIZZLE
WHOOSH!
ON YOUR MARKS!
GET SET!
GO!
GOBBLE!
MUNCH! MUNCH!
MUNCH!
GOBBLE!
CHOMP!

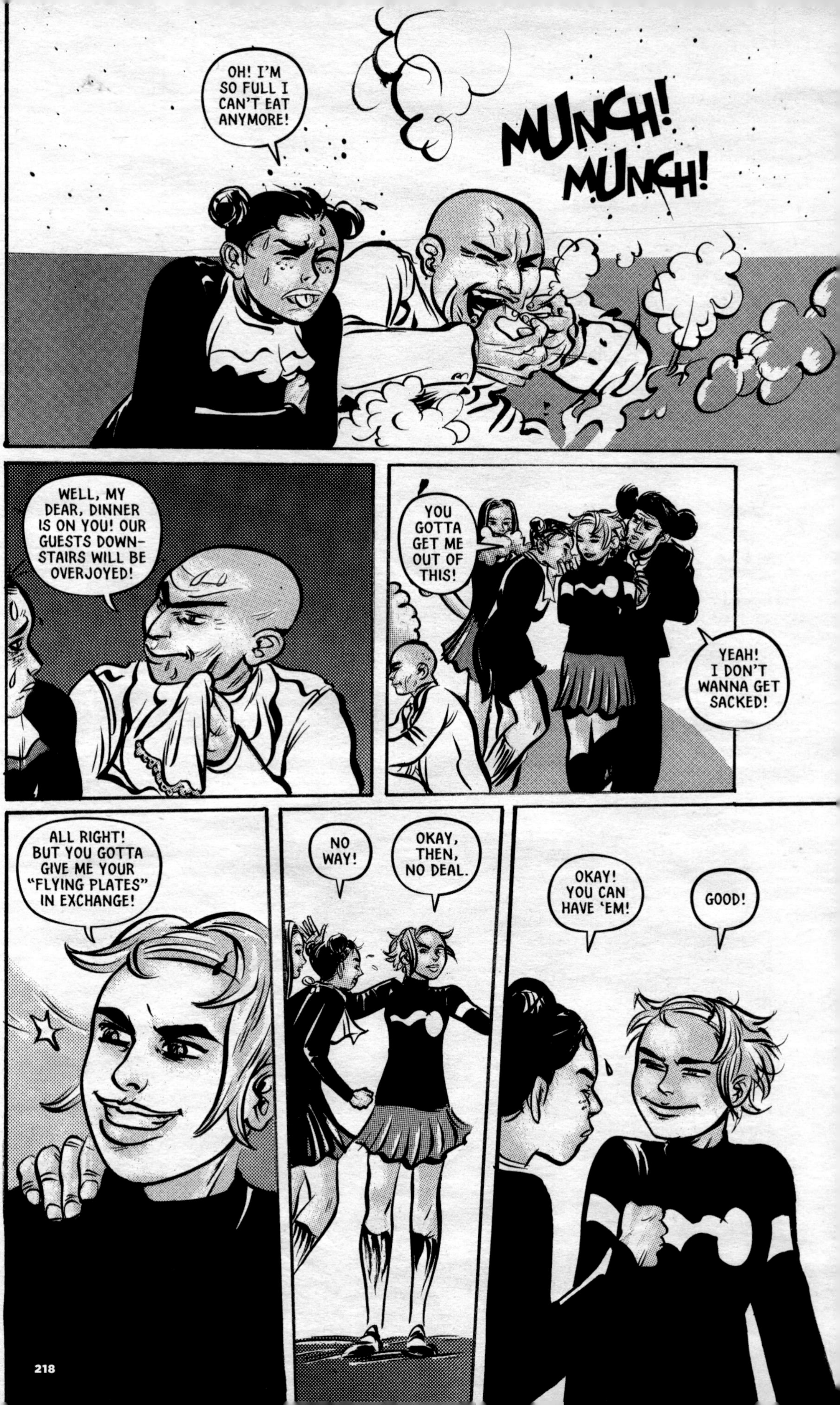
OH! I'M SO FULL I CAN'T EAT ANYMORE!
MUNCH! MUNCH!
WELL, MY DEAR, DINNER IS ON YOU! OUR GUESTS DOWN-STAIRS WILL BE OVERJOYED!
YOU GOTTA GET ME OUT OF THIS!
YEAH! I DON'T WANNA GET SACKED!
ALL RIGHT! BUT YOU GOTTA GIVE ME YOUR "FLYING PLATES" IN EXCHANGE!
NO WAY!
OKAY, THEN, NO DEAL.
OKAY! YOU CAN HAVE 'EM!
GOOD!

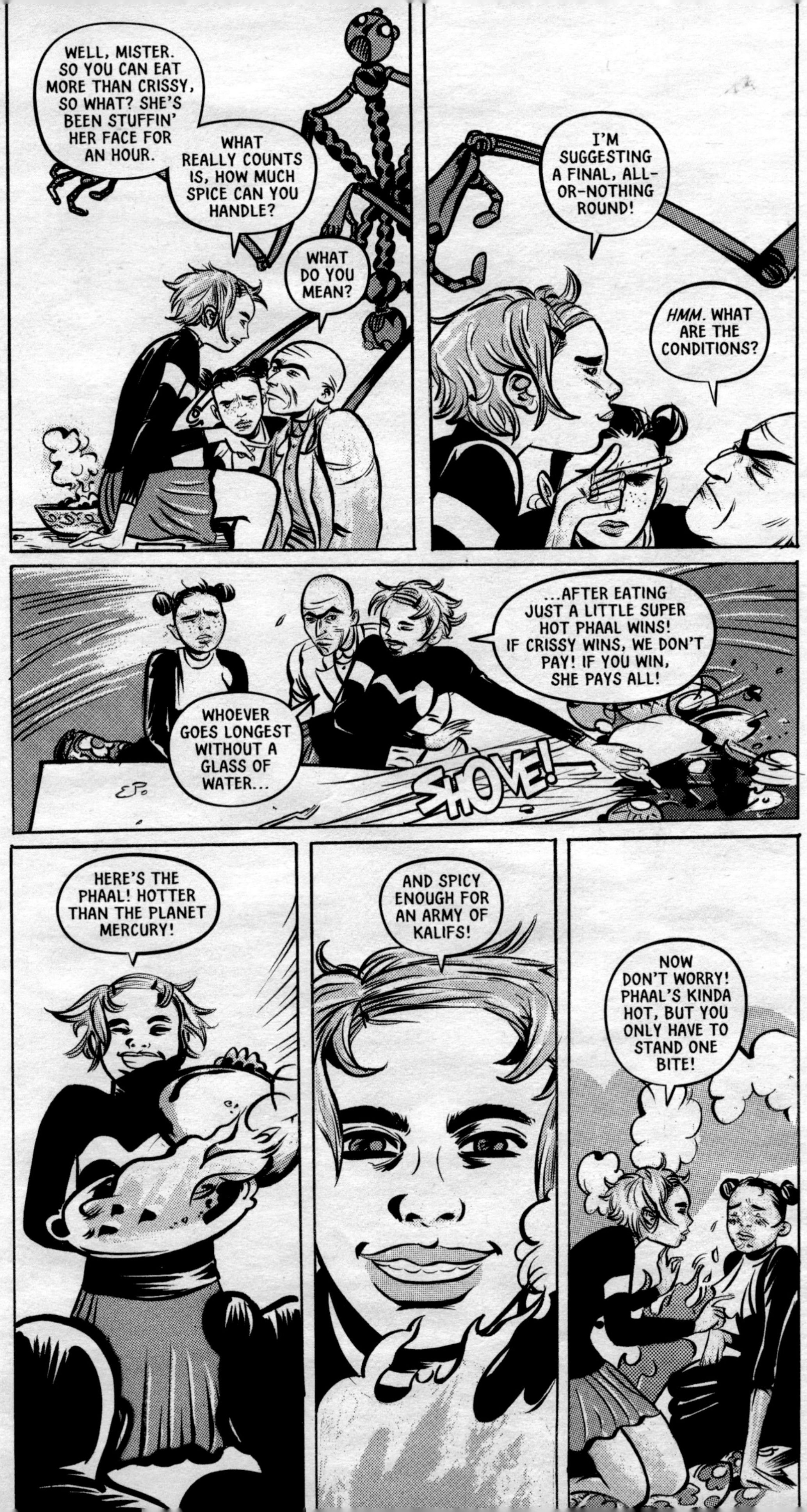
WELL, MISTER. SO YOU CAN EAT MORE THAN CRISSY, SO WHAT? SHE'S BEEN STUFFIN' HER FACE FOR AN HOUR.
WHAT REALLY COUNTS IS, HOW MUCH SPICE CAN YOU HANDLE?
WHAT DO YOU MEAN?
I'M SUGGESTING A FINAL, ALL-OR-NOTHING ROUND!
HMM. WHAT ARE THE CONDITIONS?
WHOEVER GOES LONGEST WITHOUT A GLASS OF WATER...
...AFTER EATING JUST A LITTLE SUPER HOT PHAAL WINS! IF CRISSY WINS, WE DON'T PAY! IF YOU WIN, SHE PAYS ALL!
SHOVE!
HERE'S THE PHAAL! HOTTER THAN THE PLANET MERCURY!
AND SPICY ENOUGH FOR AN ARMY OF KALIFS!
NOW DON'T WORRY! PHAAL'S KINDA HOT, BUT YOU ONLY HAVE TO STAND ONE BITE!

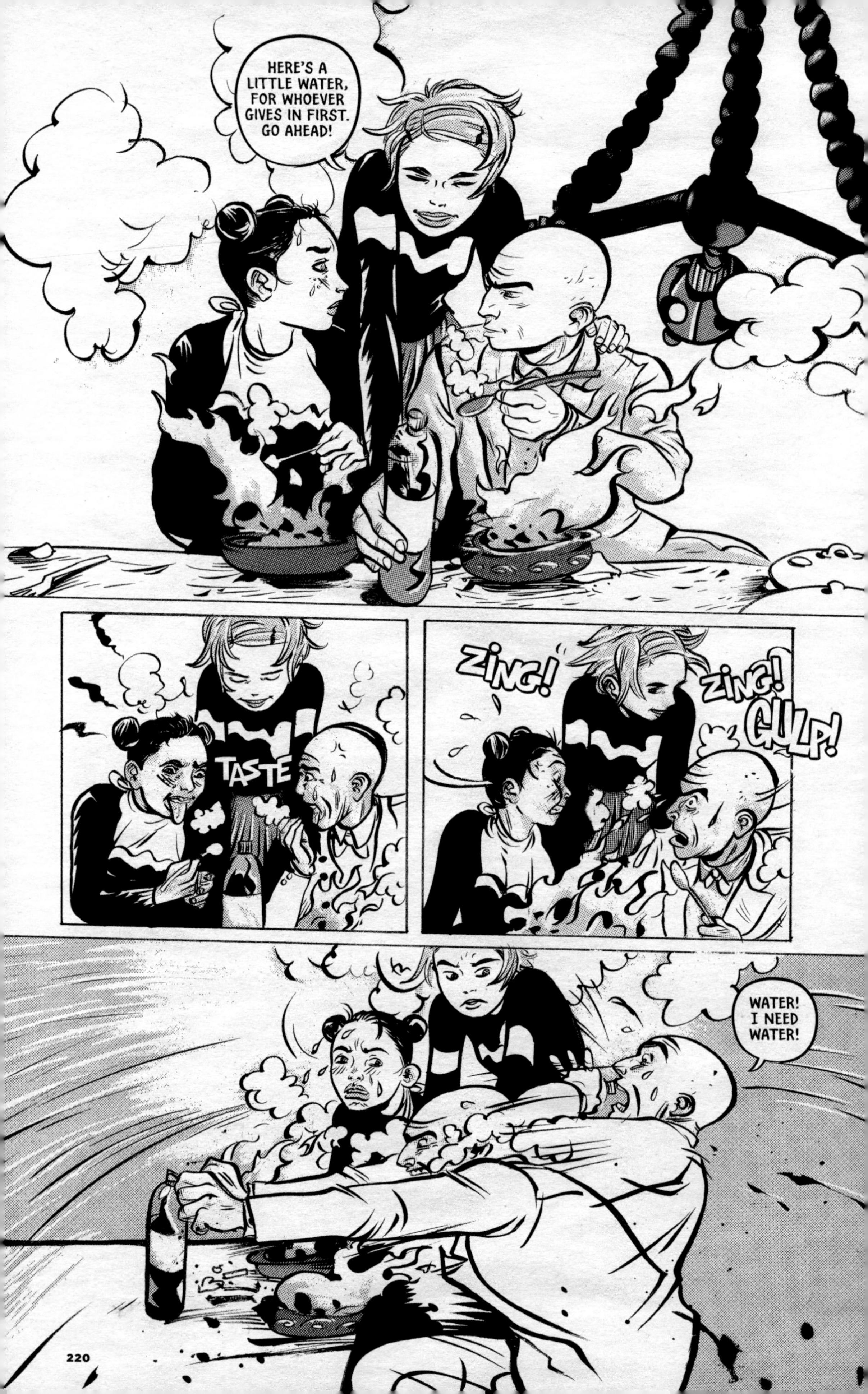
HERE'S A LITTLE WATER, FOR WHOEVER GIVES IN FIRST. GO AHEAD!
TASTE
ZING!
ZING!
GULP!
WATER! I NEED WATER!

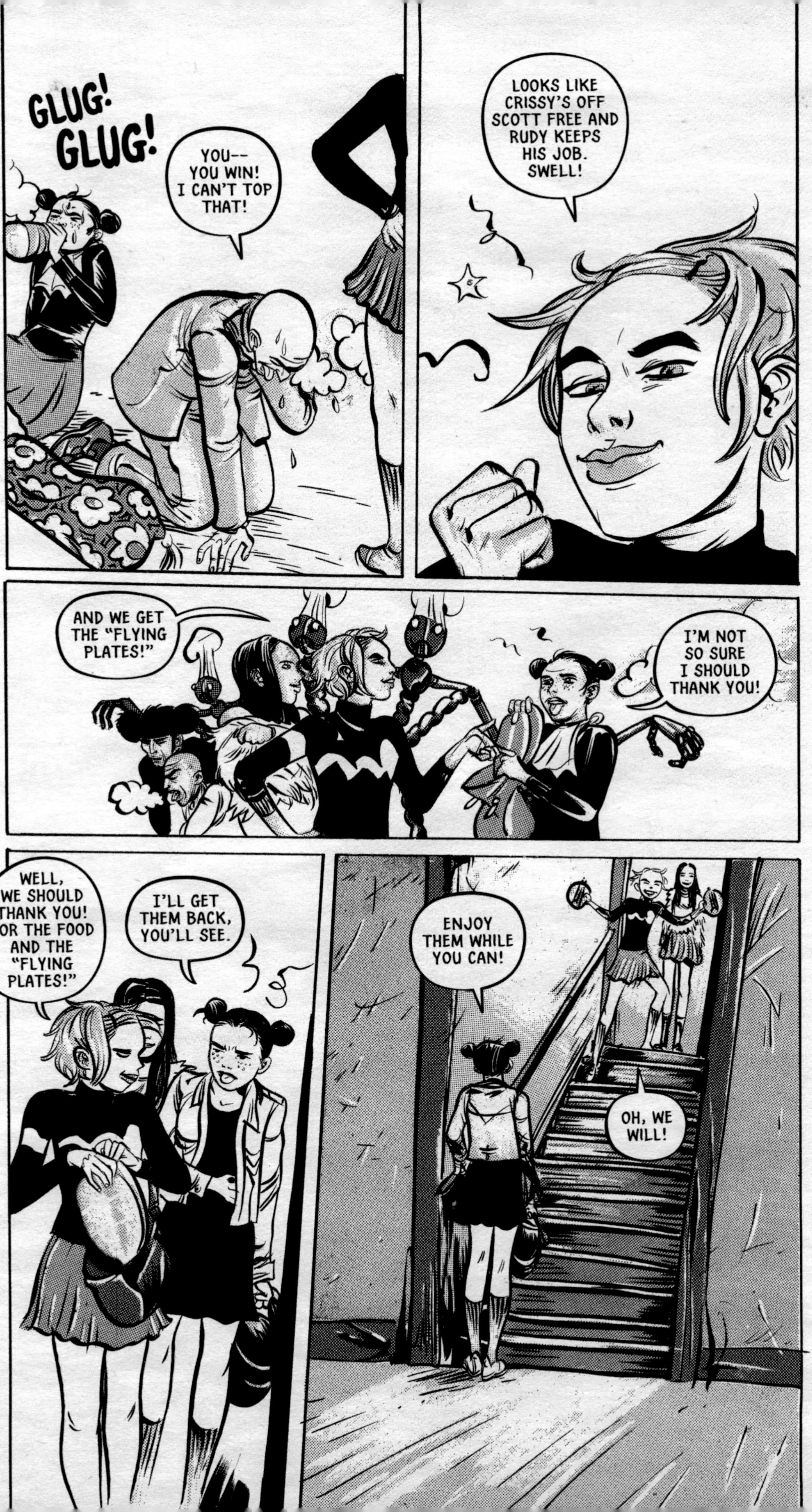
GLUG! GLUG!
YOU-- YOU WIN! I CAN'T TOP THAT!
LOOKS LIKE CRISSY'S OFF SCOTT FREE AND RUDY KEEPS HIS JOB. SWELL!
AND WE GET THE "FLYING PLATES!"
I'M NOT SO SURE I SHOULD THANK YOU!
WELL, WE SHOULD THANK YOU! FOR THE FOOD AND THE "FLYING PLATES!"
I'LL GET THEM BACK, YOU'LL SEE.
ENJOY THEM WHILE YOU CAN!
OH, WE WILL!

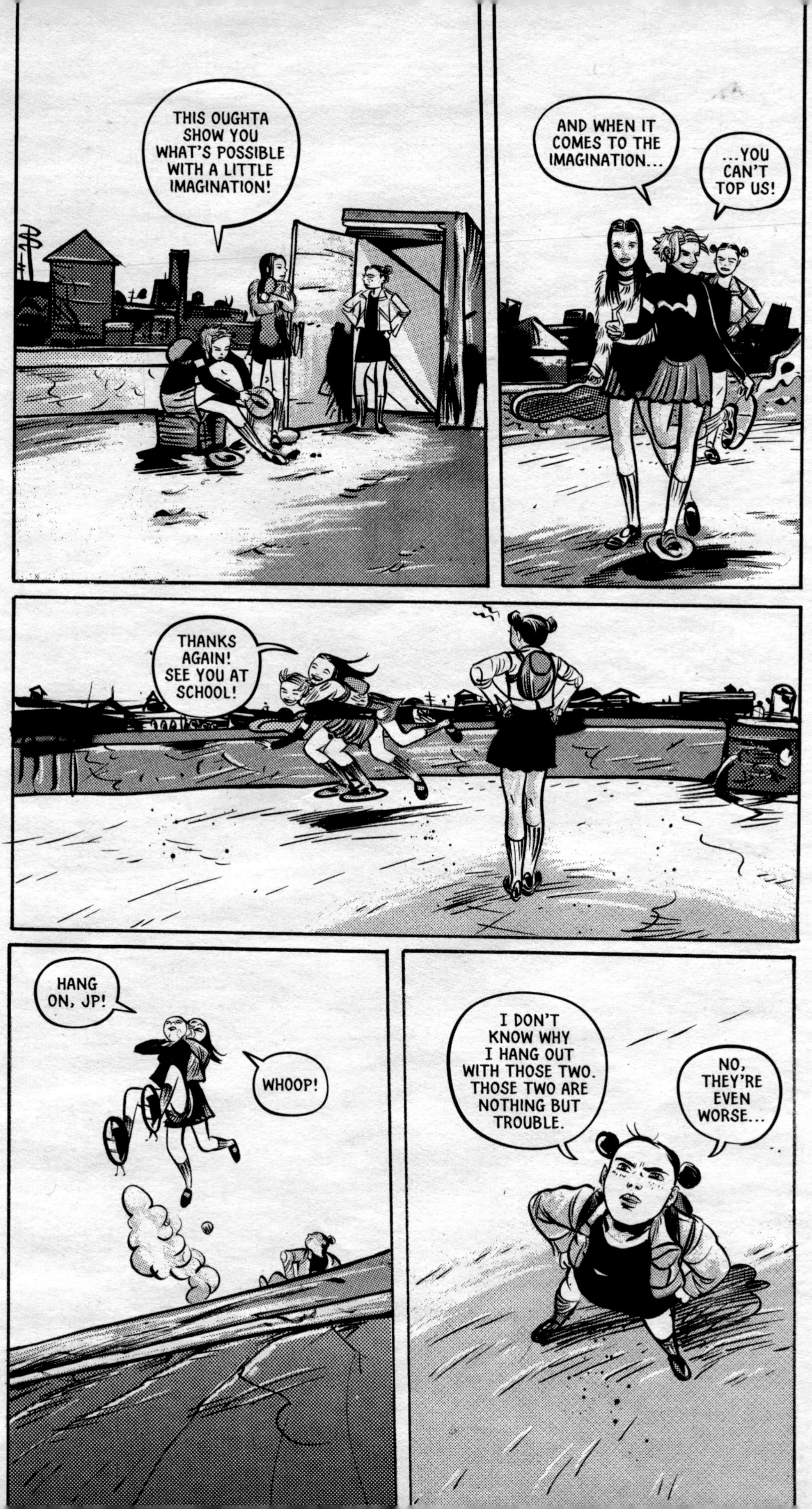
THIS OUGHTA SHOW YOU WHAT'S POSSIBLE WITH A LITTLE IMAGINATION!
AND WHEN IT COMES TO THE IMAGINATION...
...YOU CAN'T TOP US!
THANKS AGAIN! SEE YOU AT SCHOOL!
HANG ON, JP!
WHOOP!
I DON'T KNOW WHY I HANG OUT WITH THOSE TWO. THOSE TWO ARE NOTHING BUT TROUBLE.
NO, THEY'RE EVEN WORSE...

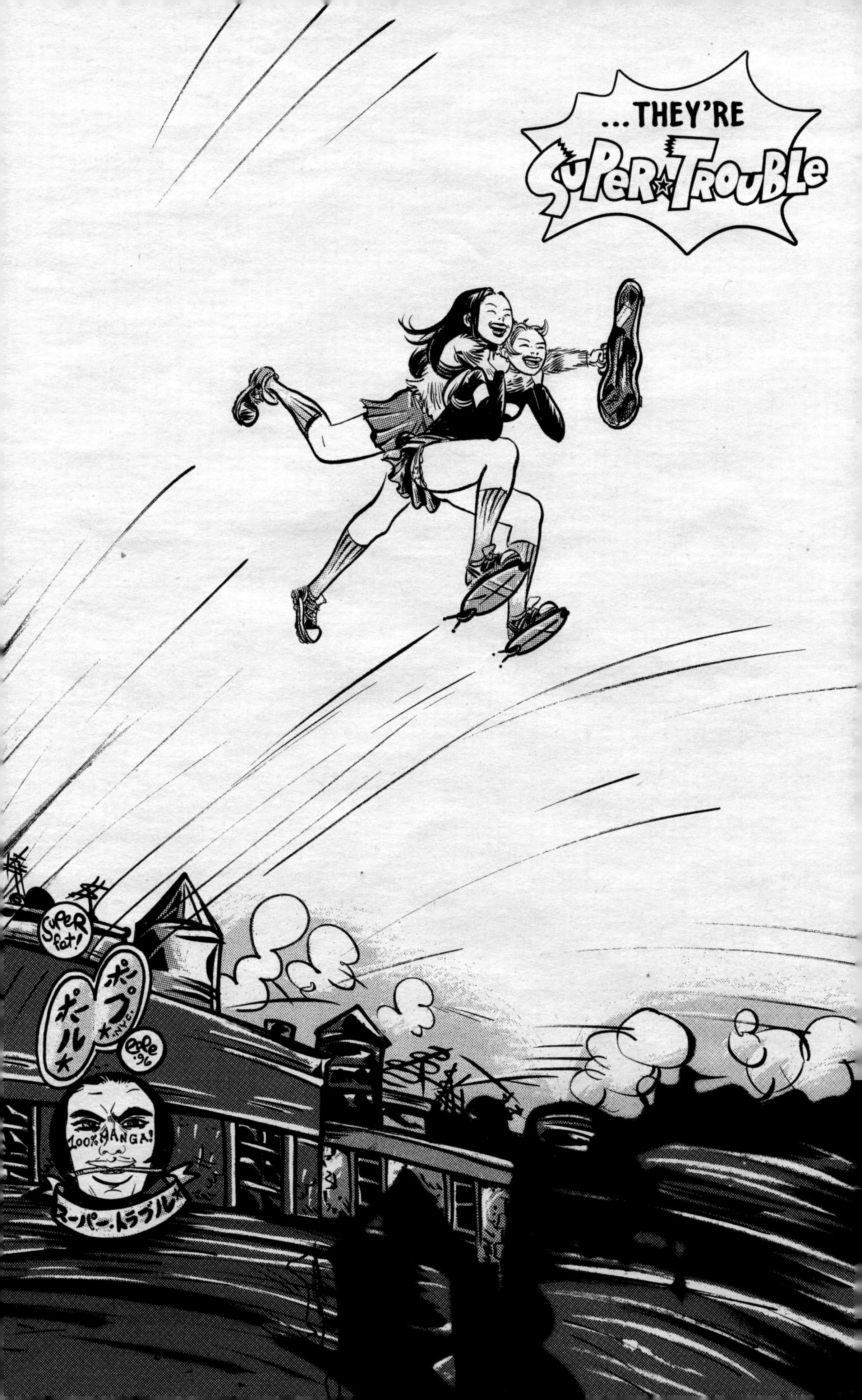
...THEY'RE
SUPER☆TROUBLE
SUPER fat!
ポップ★NYC
ポール★
100% MANGA!
スーパー・トラブル★

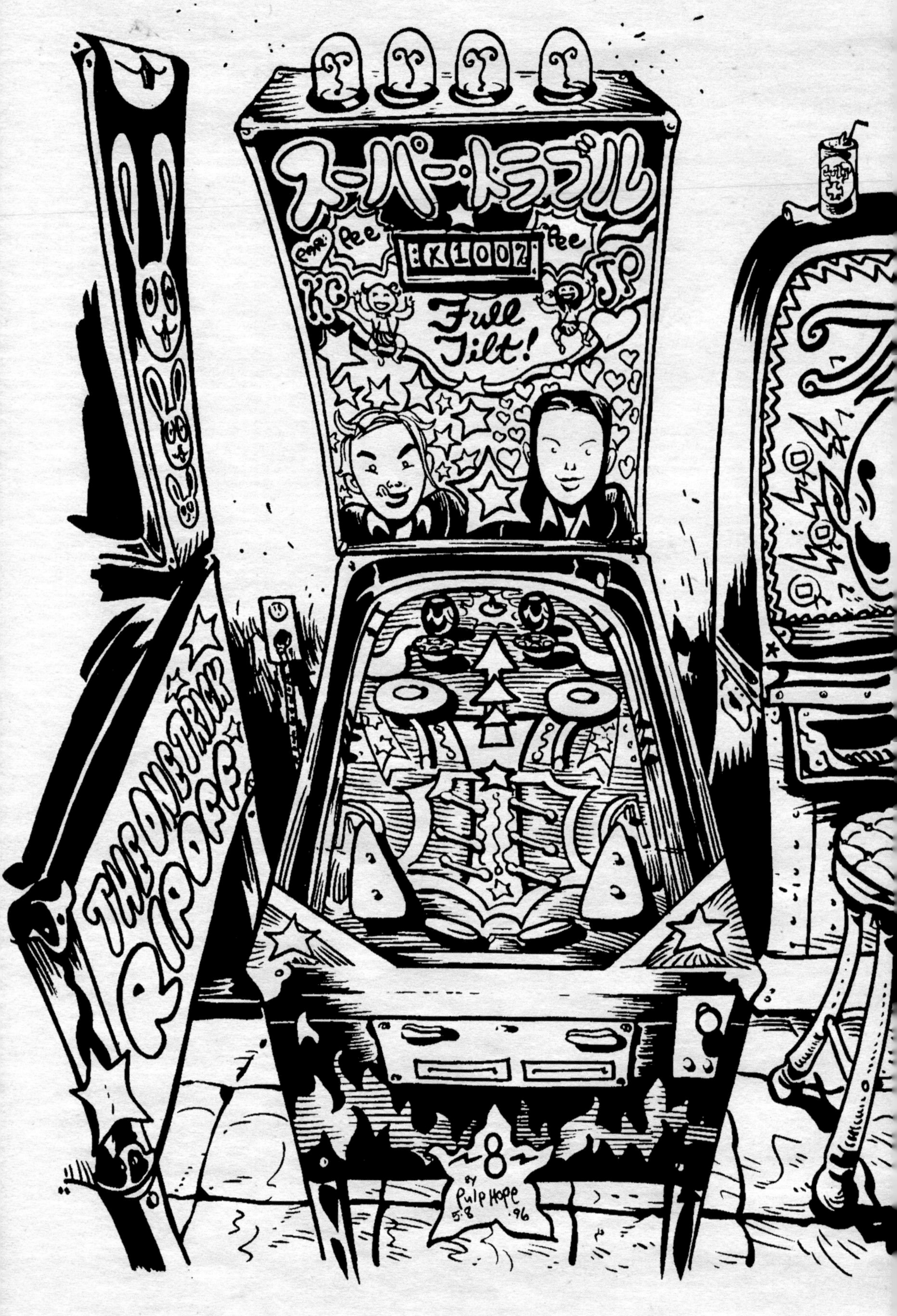

スーパー・トラブル
Pee
Pee
KC
JP
Full Tilt!
THE ONE TRICK RIPOFF
8
BY
Pulp Hope
5.8.96

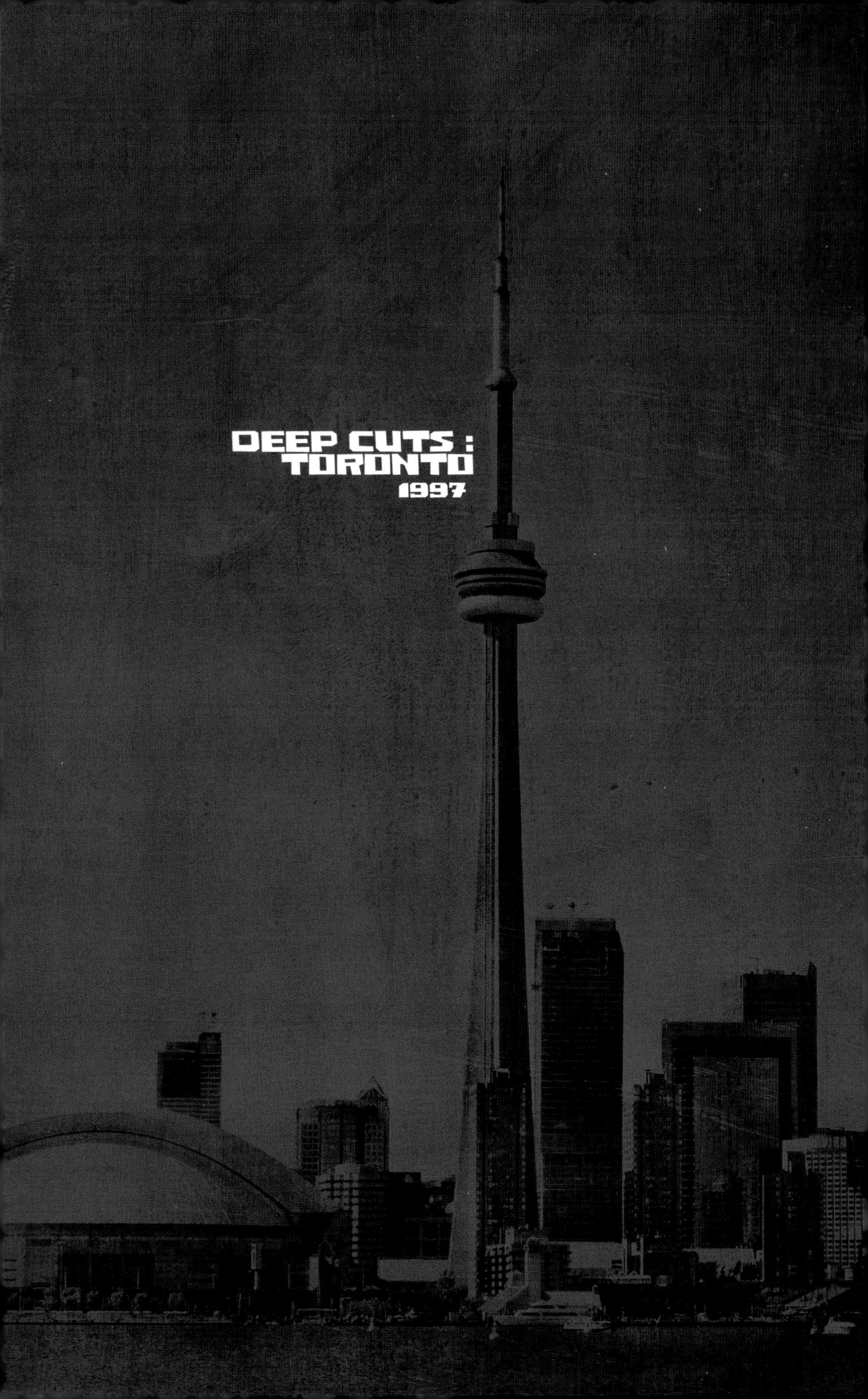
DEEP CUTS :
TORONTO
1997

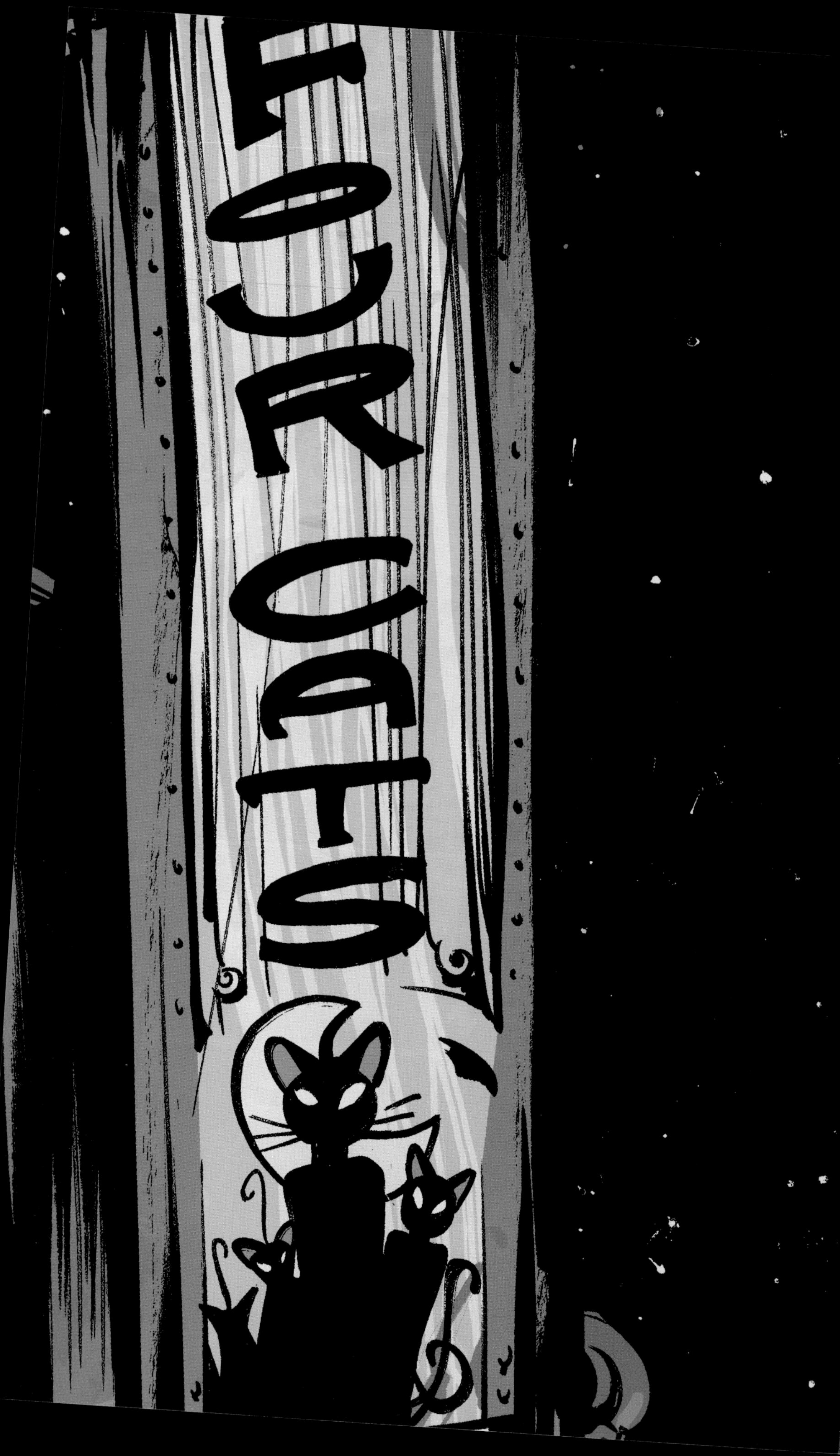
OUR CATS

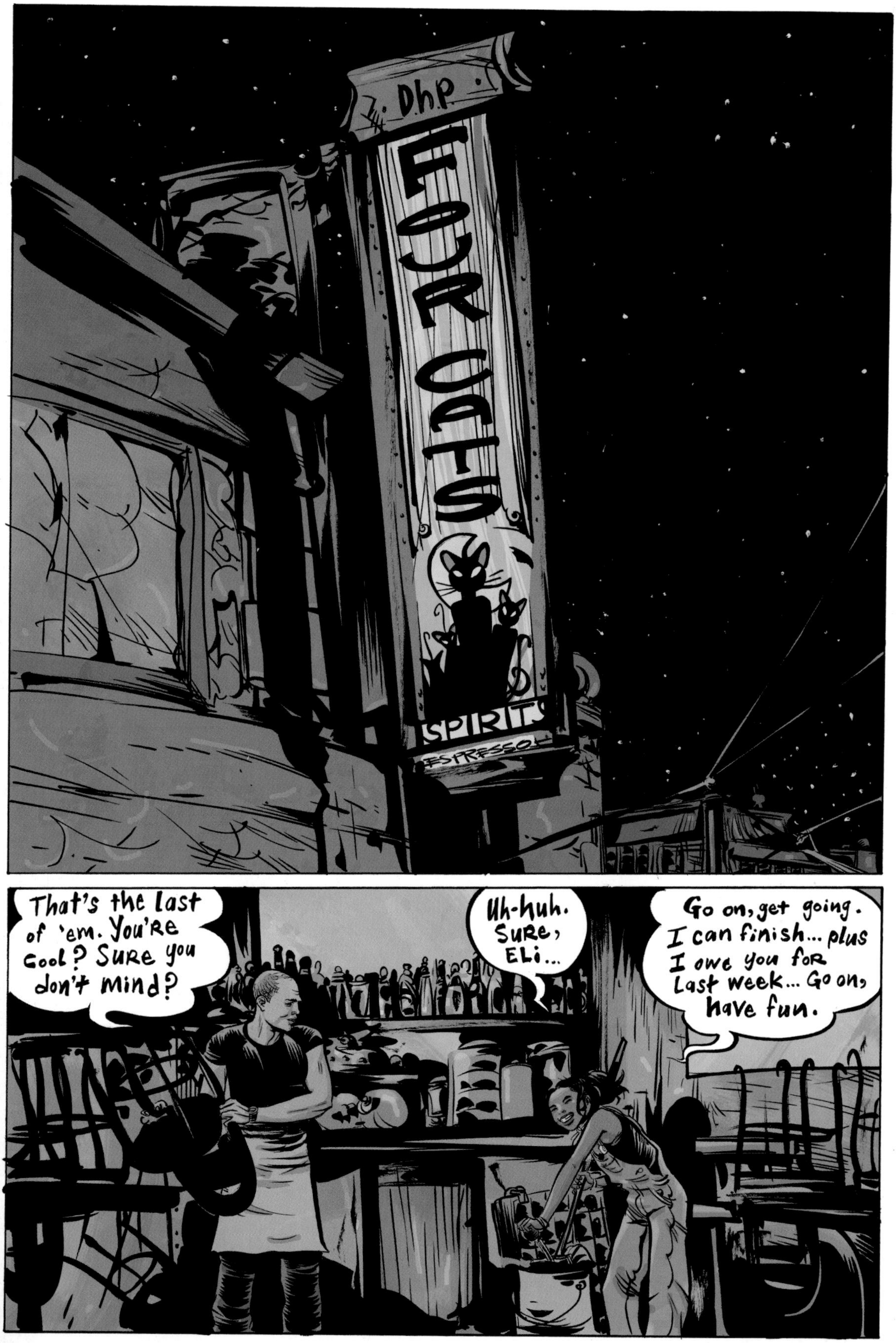
Dhp
FOUR CATS
SPIRITS
ESPRESSO
That's the last of 'em. You're cool? Sure you don't mind?
Uh-huh. Sure, Eli...
Go on, get going. I can finish... plus I owe you for last week... Go on, have fun.

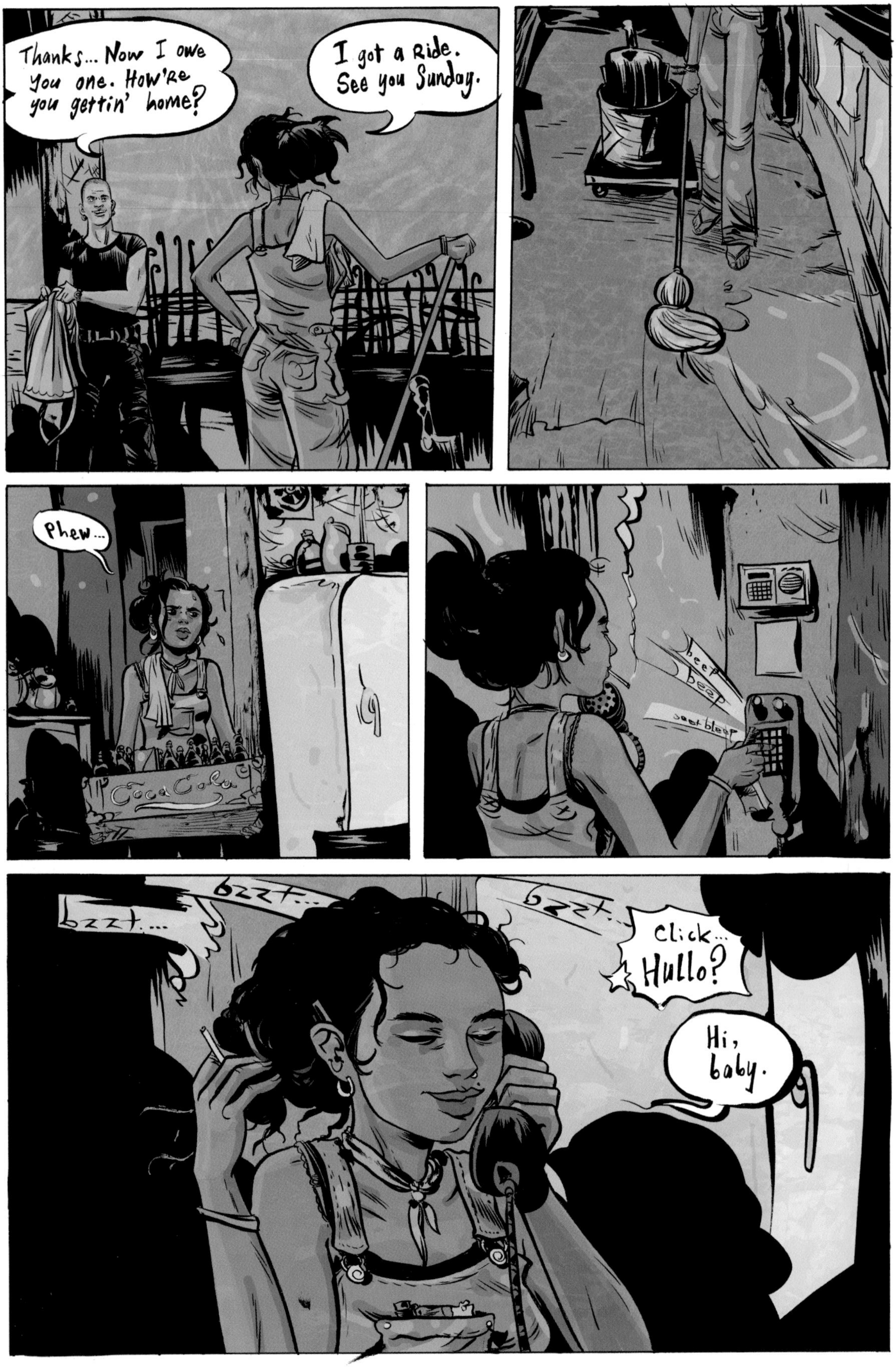
Thanks... Now I owe you one. How're you gettin' home?
I got a Ride. See you Sunday.
Phew...
beep
beep
beep bleep
bzzt...
bzzt...
bzzt...
Click... Hullo?
Hi, baby.

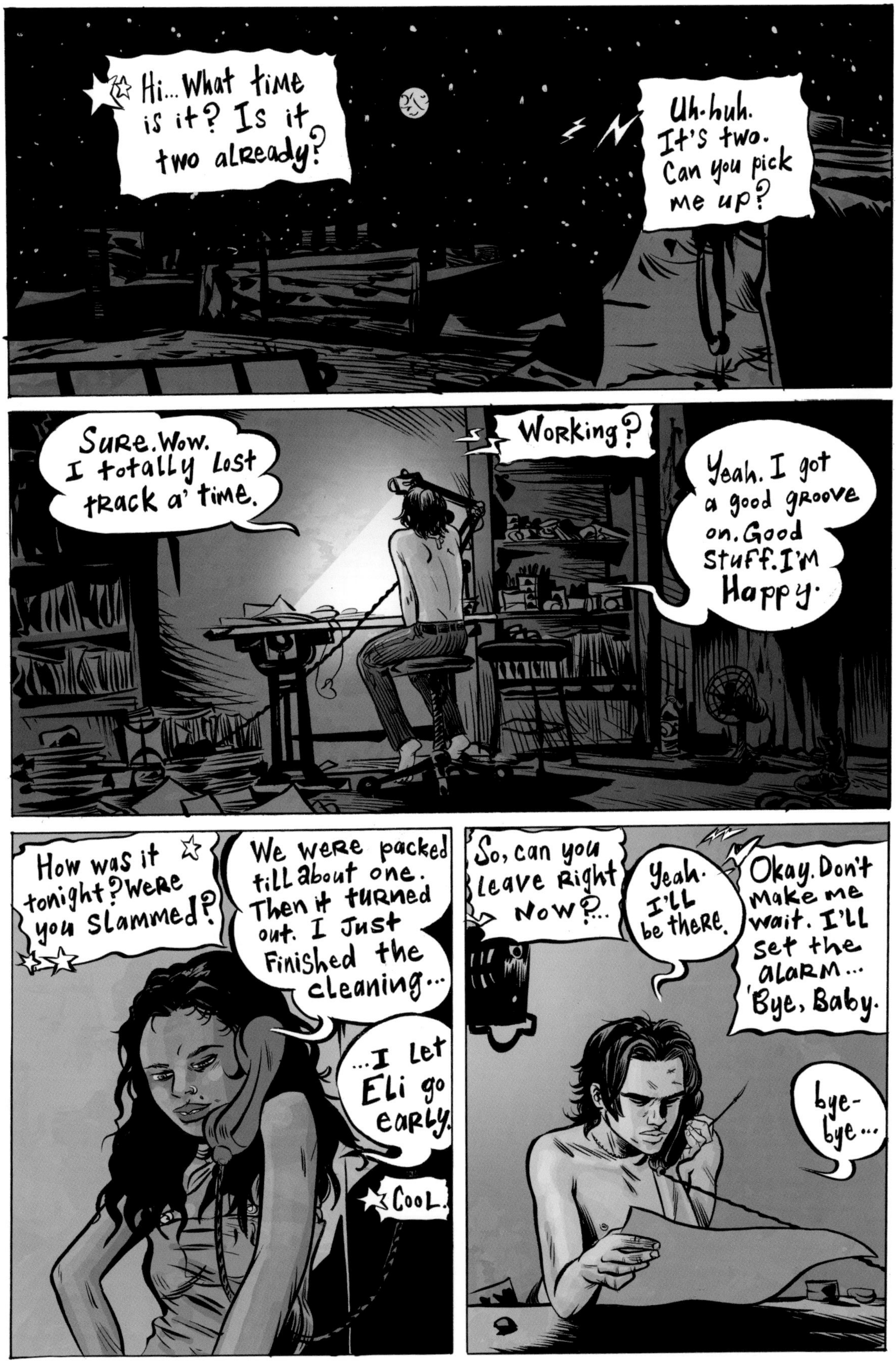
Hi... What time is it? Is it two already?
Uh-huh. It's two. Can you pick me up?
Sure. Wow. I totally lost track a' time.
Working?
Yeah. I got a good groove on. Good stuff. I'm happy.
How was it tonight? Were you slammed?
We were packed till about one. Then it turned out. I just finished the cleaning...
...I let Eli go early.
Cool.
So, can you leave right now?...
Yeah. I'll be there.
Okay. Don't make me wait. I'll set the alarm... 'Bye, Baby.
bye-bye...

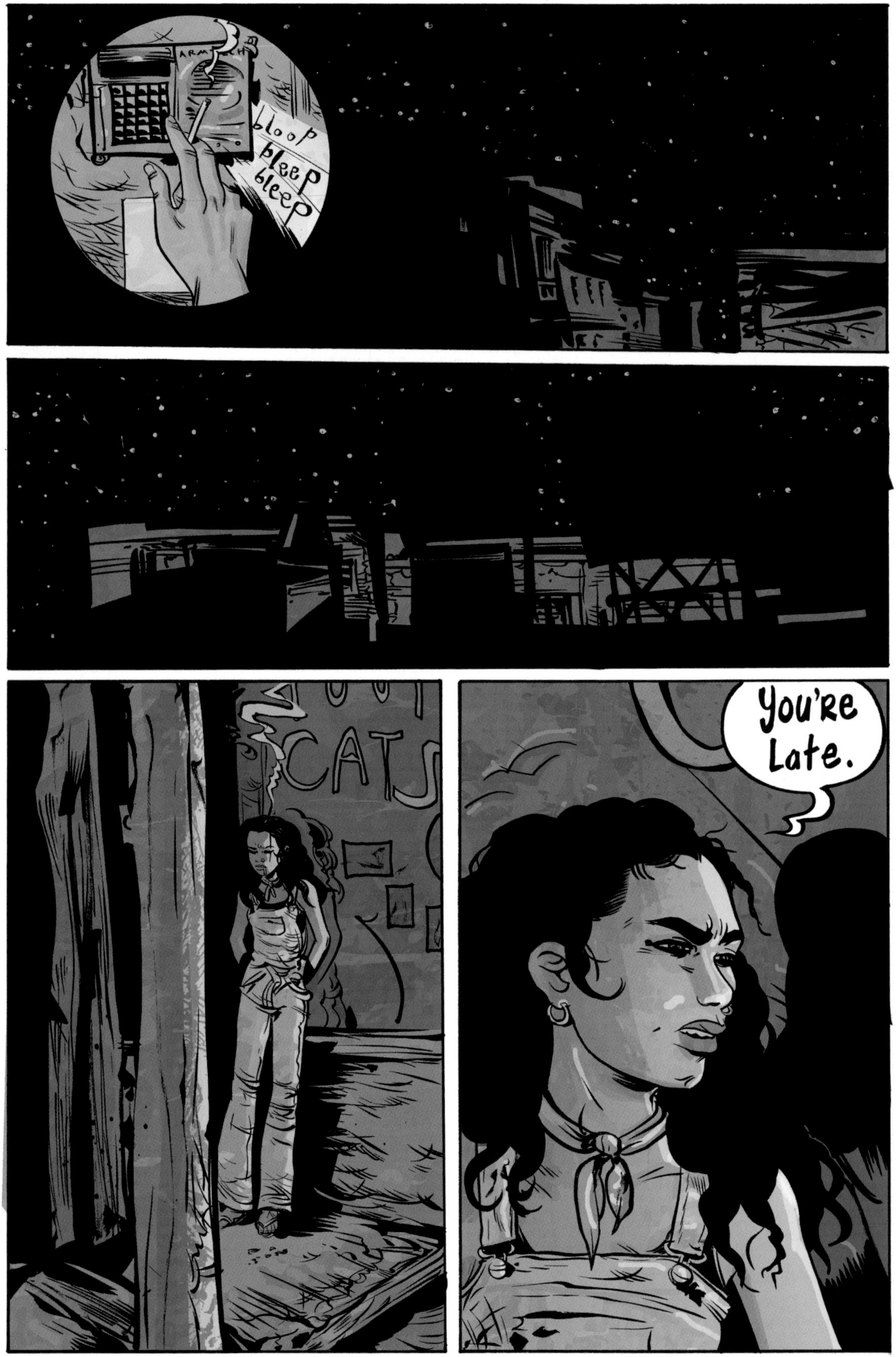
bloop
bleep
bleep
CATS
You're Late.

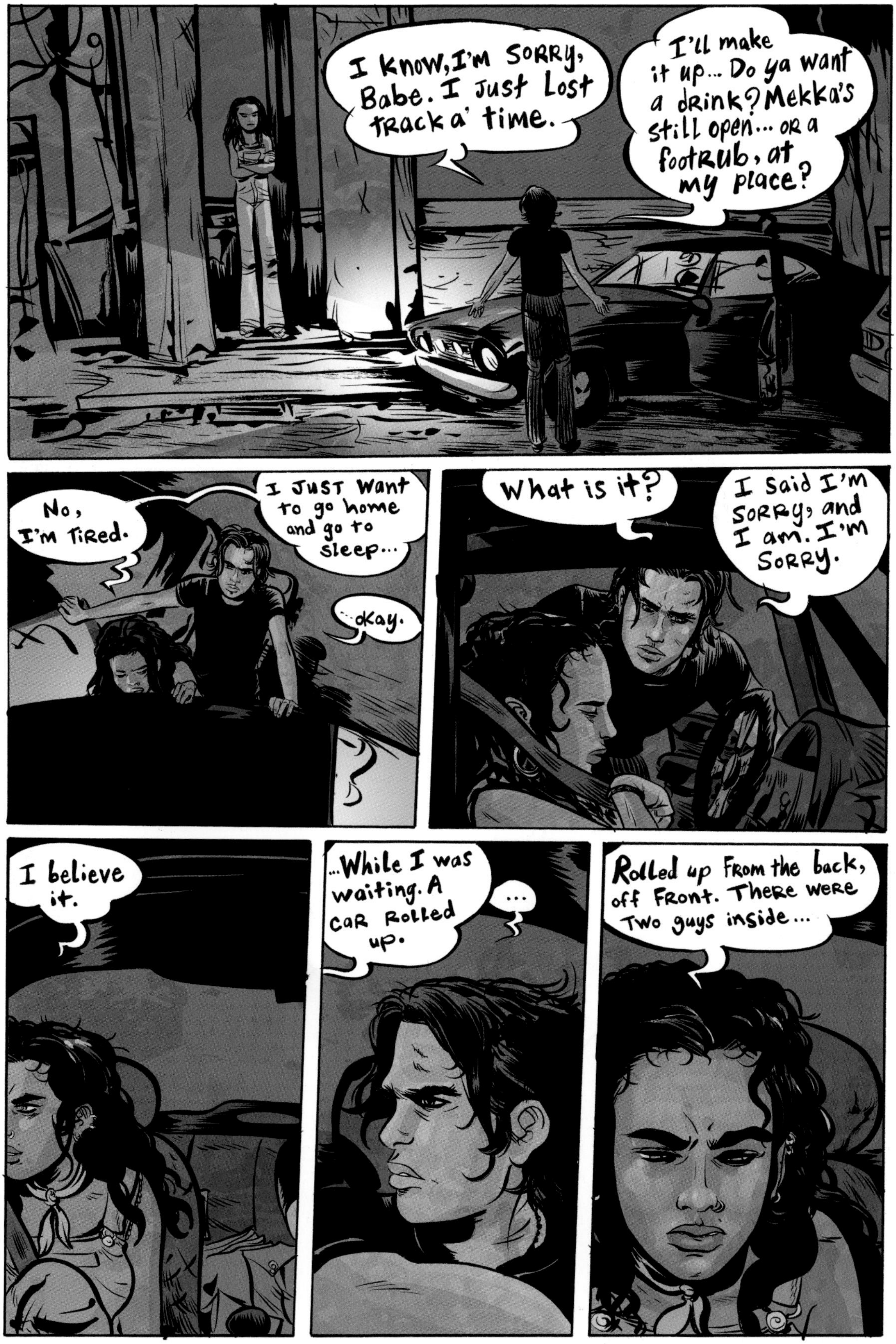
I know, I'm sorry, Babe. I just lost track a' time.
I'll make it up... Do ya want a drink? Mekka's still open... or a footrub, at my place?
No, I'm tired.
I just want to go home and go to sleep...
...okay.
What is it?
I said I'm sorry, and I am. I'm sorry.
I believe it.
...While I was waiting. A car rolled up.
...
Rolled up from the back, off front. There were two guys inside...

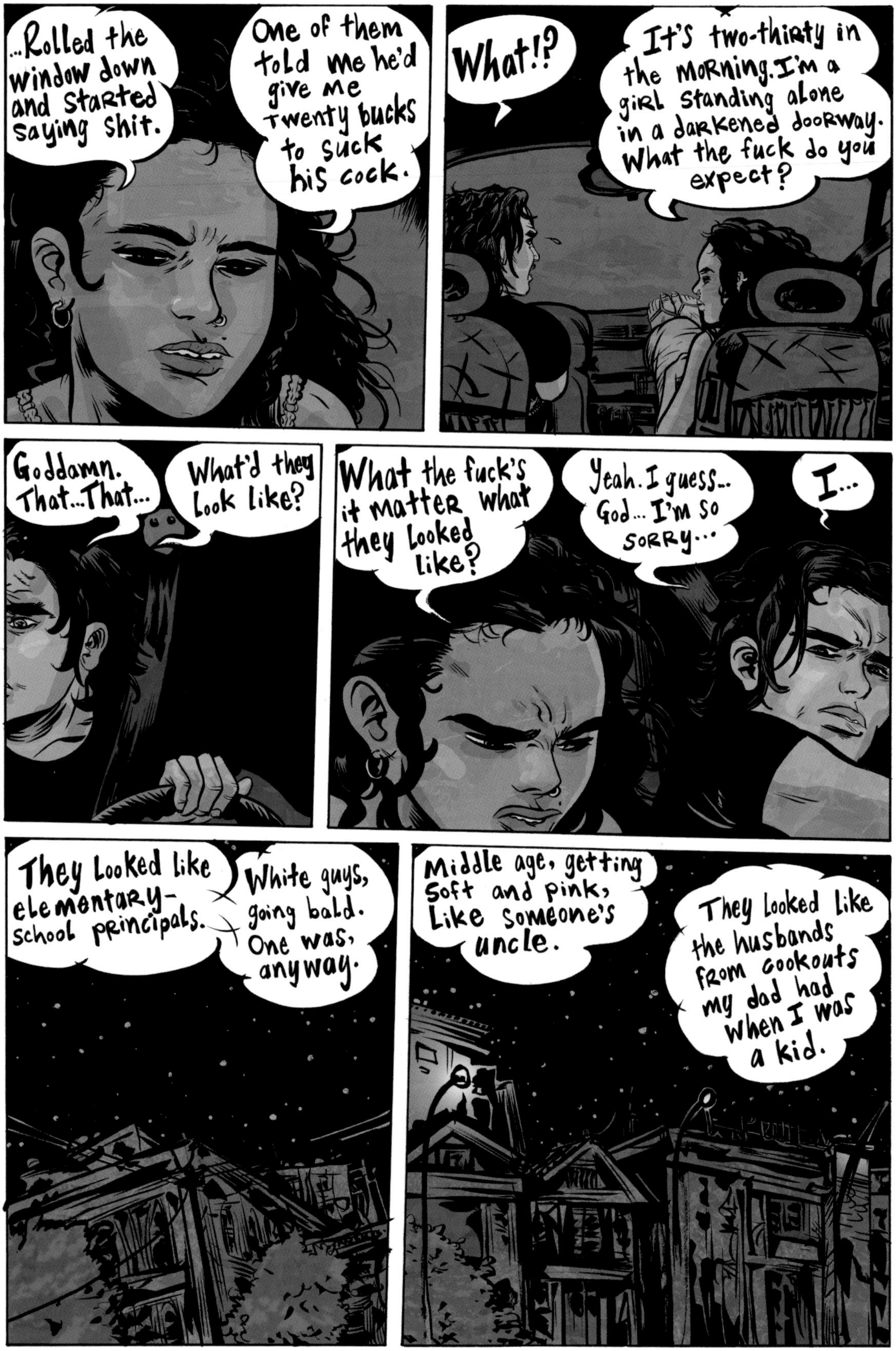
...Rolled the window down and started saying shit.
One of them told me he'd give me twenty bucks to suck his cock.
What!?
It's two-thirty in the morning. I'm a girl standing alone in a darkened doorway. What the fuck do you expect?
Goddamn. That...That...
What'd they look like?
What the fuck's it matter what they looked like?
Yeah. I guess.. God... I'm so sorry...
I...
They looked like elementary-school principals.
White guys, going bald. One was, anyway.
Middle age, getting soft and pink, like someone's uncle.
They looked like the husbands from cookouts my dad had when I was a kid.

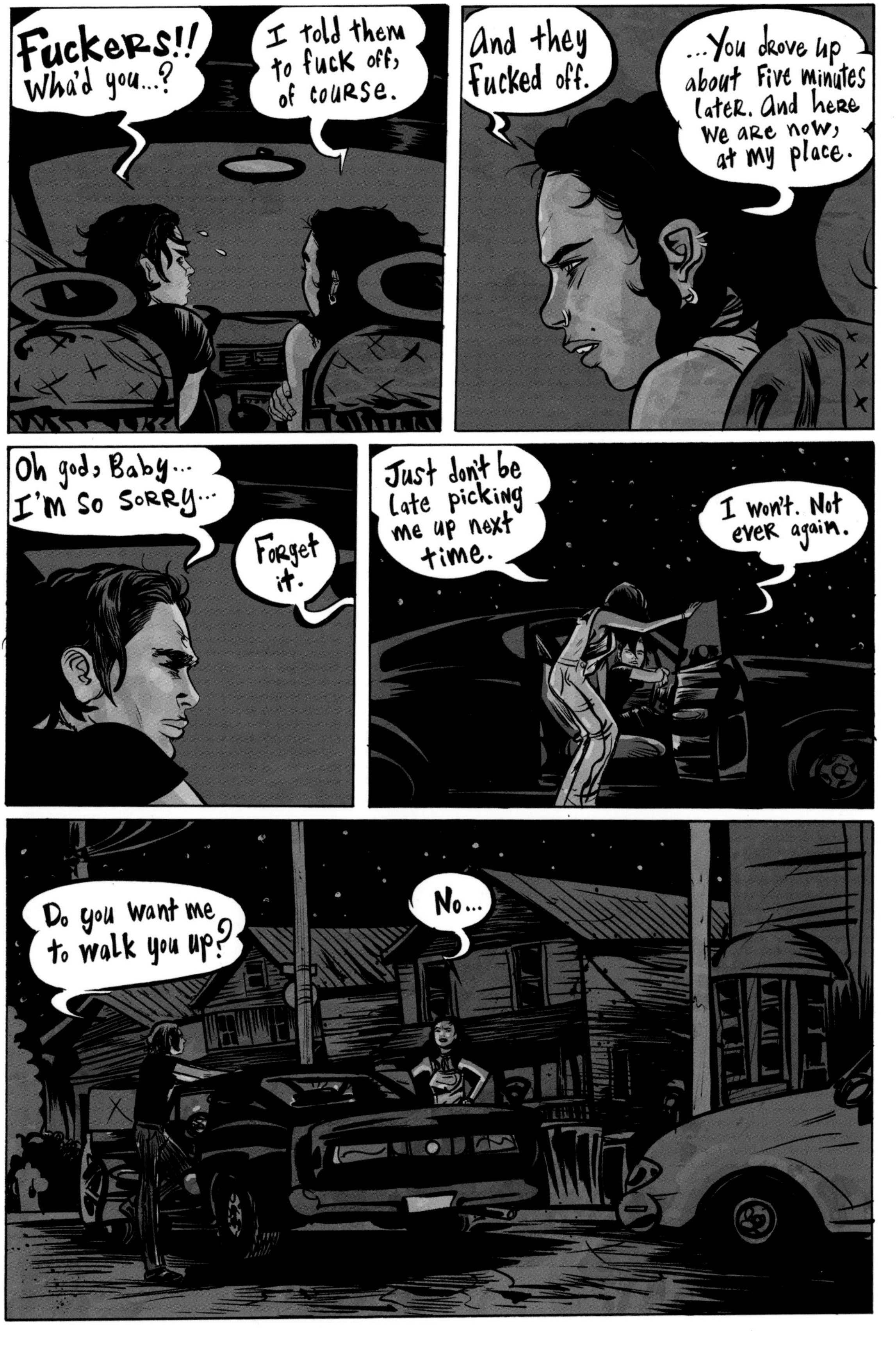
FUCKERS!! Wha'd you...?
I told them to fuck off, of course.
And they fucked off.
...You drove up about five minutes later. And here we are now, at my place.
Oh god, Baby... I'm so sorry...
Forget it.
Just don't be late picking me up next time.
I won't. Not ever again.
Do you want me to walk you up?
No...

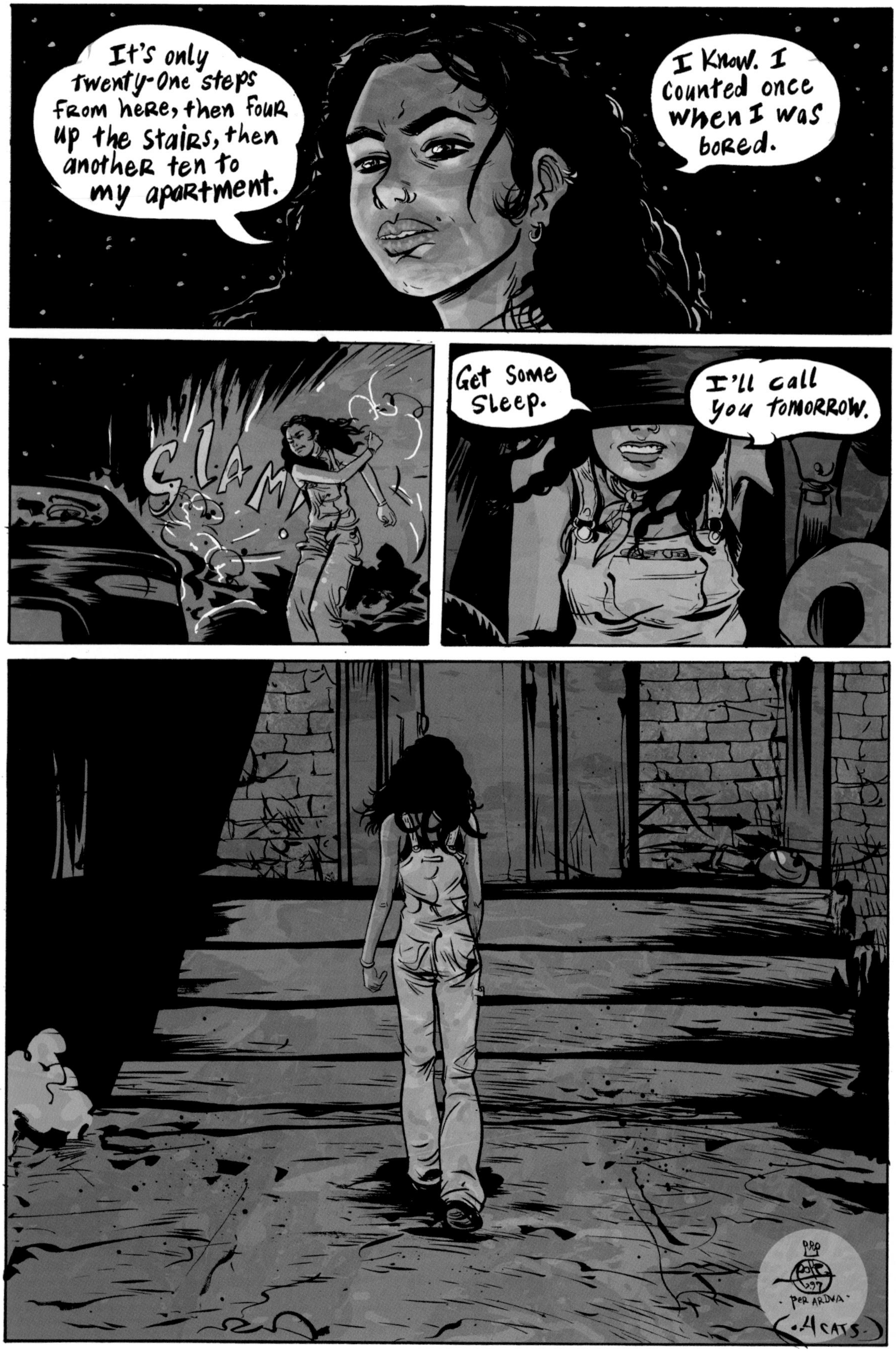
It's only twenty-one steps from here, then four up the stairs, then another ten to my apartment.
I know. I counted once when I was bored.
SLAM
Get some sleep.
I'll call you tomorrow.
PER ARDUA
41 CATS

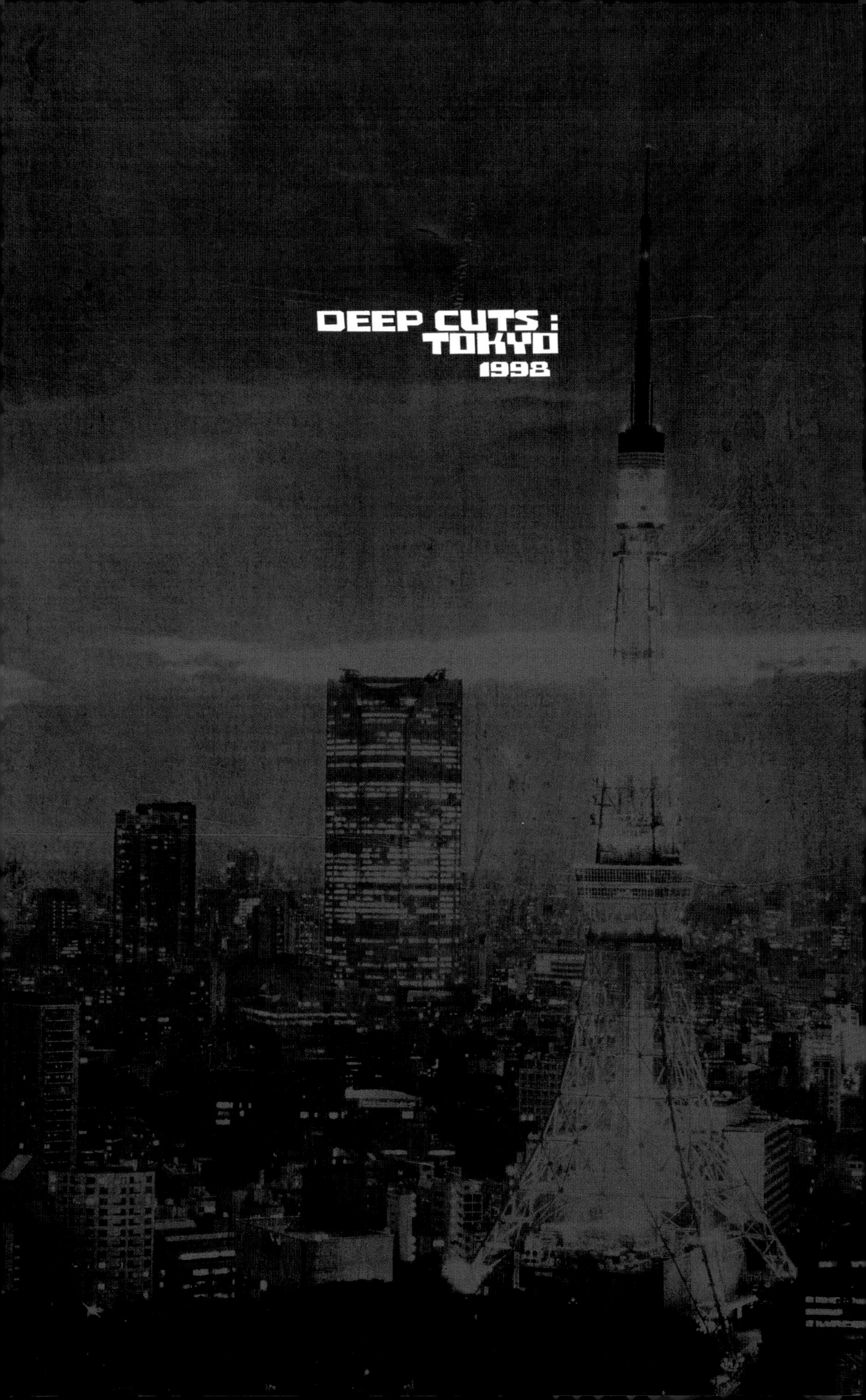
DEEP CUTS :
TOKYO
1998

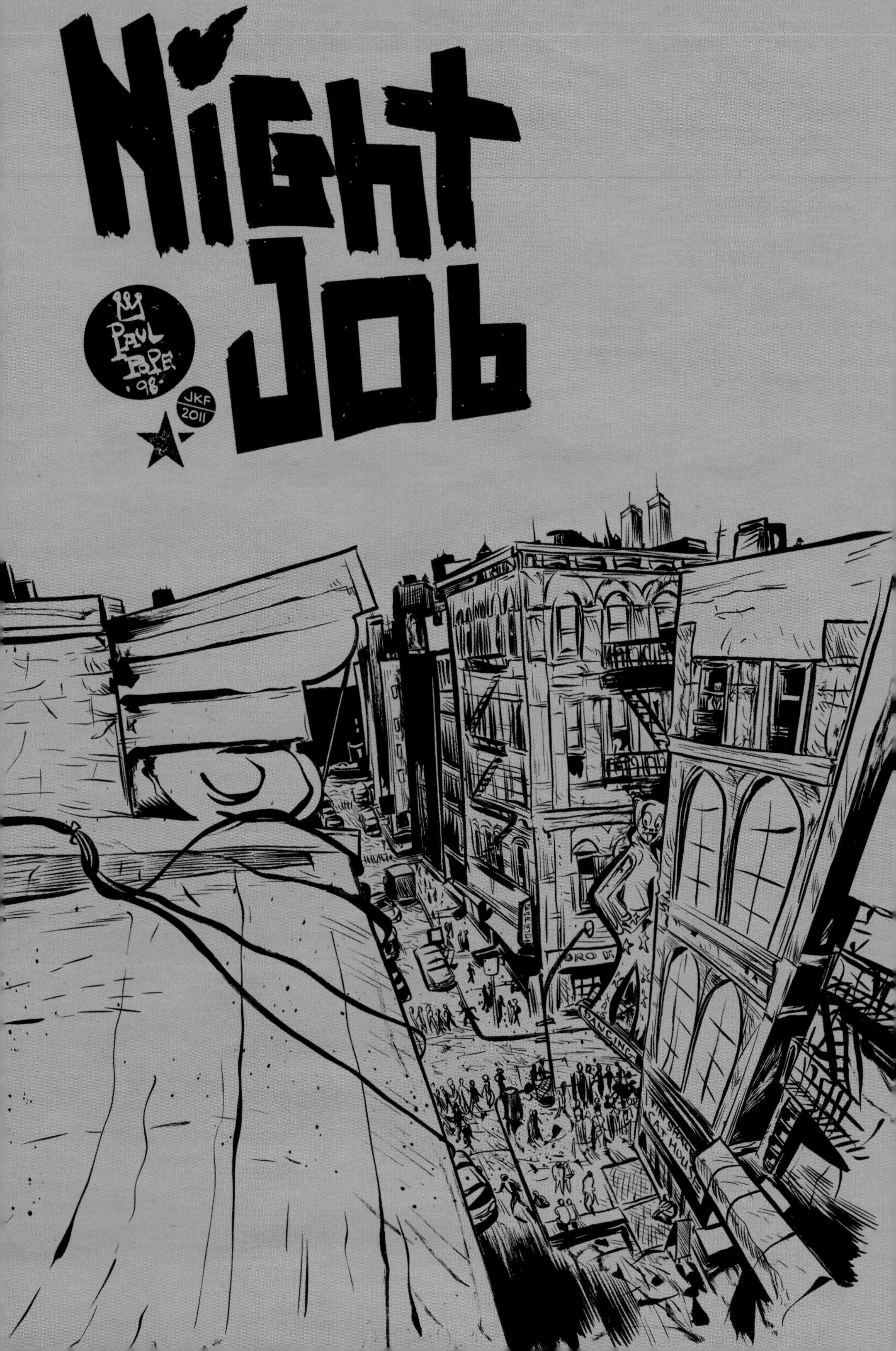
Night Job
Paul Pope 98
JKF 2011
DANCING
CAT HOUSE

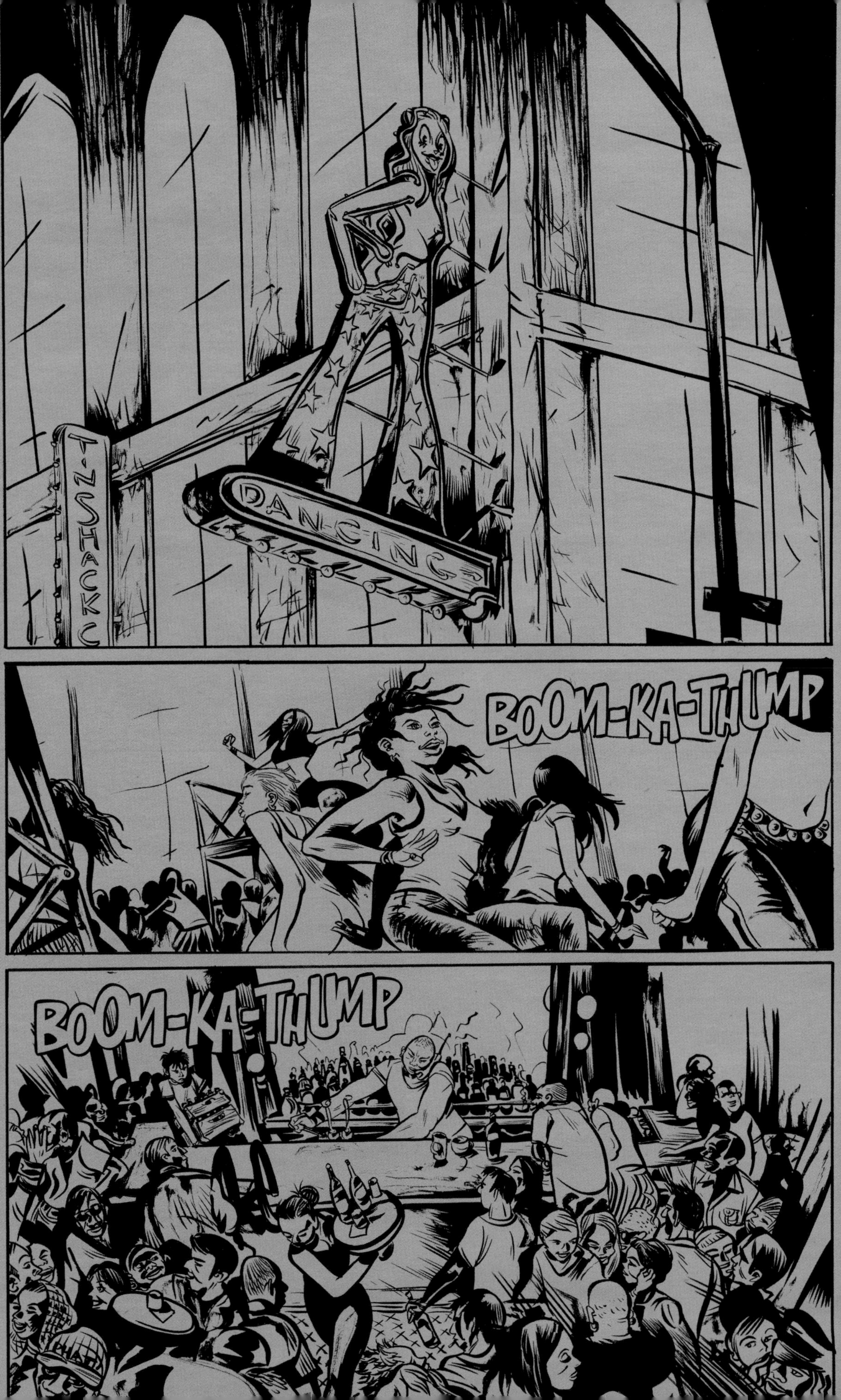
DANCING
BOOM-KA-THUMP
BOOM-KA-THUMP

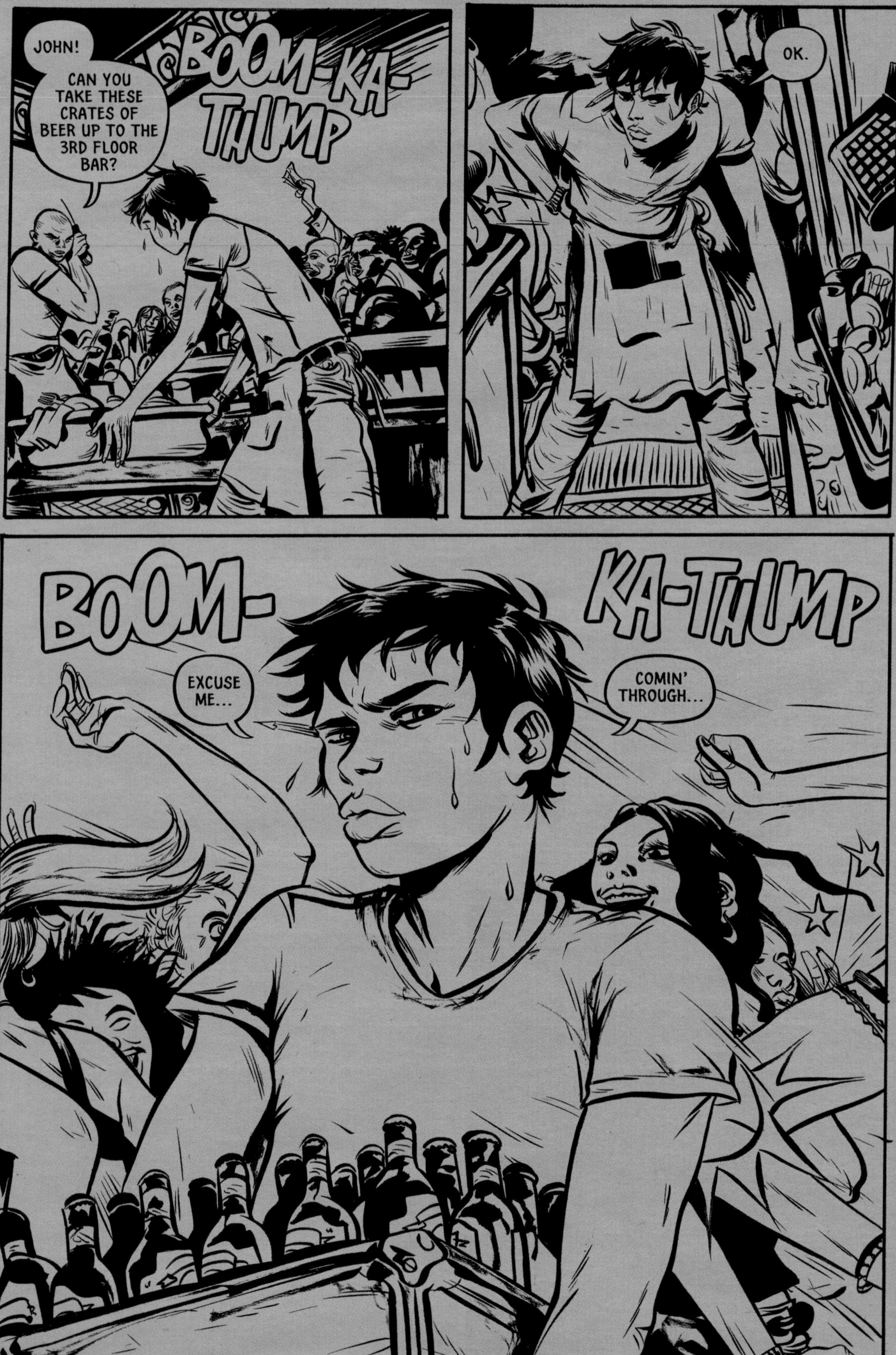
JOHN!
CAN YOU TAKE THESE CRATES OF BEER UP TO THE 3RD FLOOR BAR?
BOOM-KA-THUMP
OK.
BOOM-
KA-THUMP
EXCUSE ME...
COMIN' THROUGH...

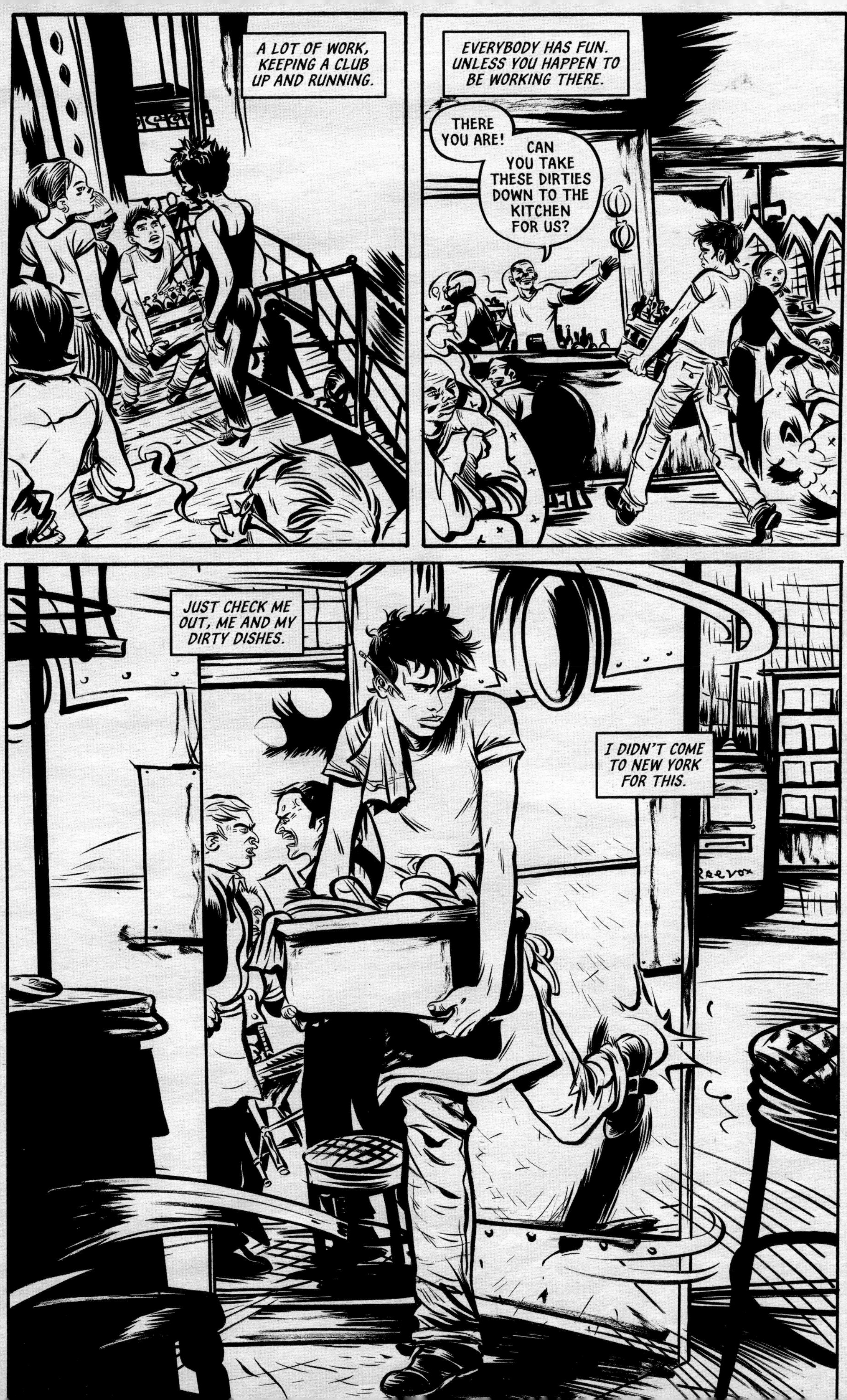
A LOT OF WORK, KEEPING A CLUB UP AND RUNNING.
EVERYBODY HAS FUN. UNLESS YOU HAPPEN TO BE WORKING THERE.
THERE YOU ARE!
CAN YOU TAKE THESE DIRTIES DOWN TO THE KITCHEN FOR US?
JUST CHECK ME OUT, ME AND MY DIRTY DISHES.
I DIDN'T COME TO NEW YORK FOR THIS.

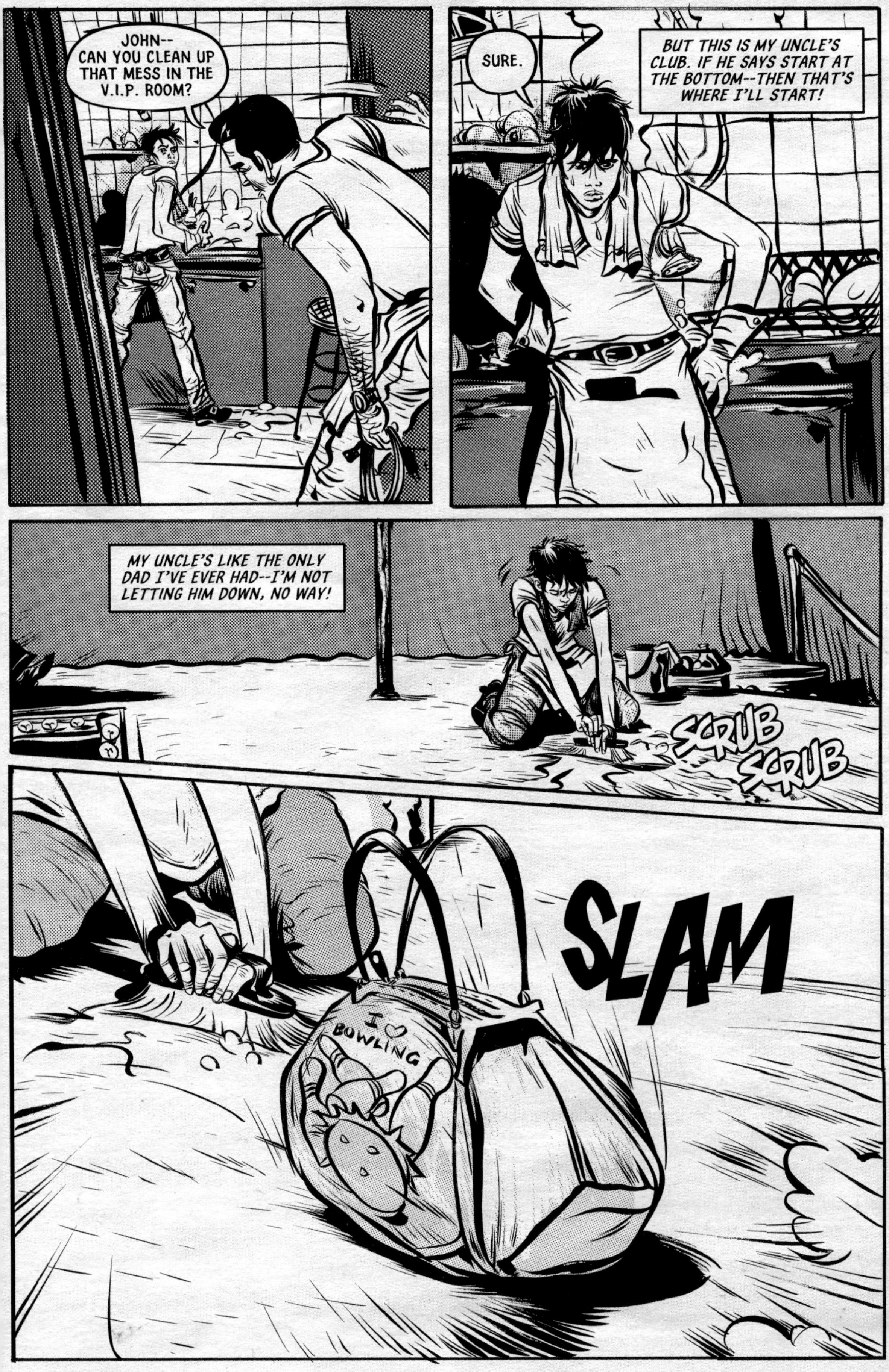
JOHN-- CAN YOU CLEAN UP THAT MESS IN THE V.I.P. ROOM?
SURE.
BUT THIS IS MY UNCLE'S CLUB. IF HE SAYS START AT THE BOTTOM--THEN THAT'S WHERE I'LL START!
MY UNCLE'S LIKE THE ONLY DAD I'VE EVER HAD--I'M NOT LETTING HIM DOWN, NO WAY!
SCRUB SCRUB
I ♡ BOWLING
SLAM

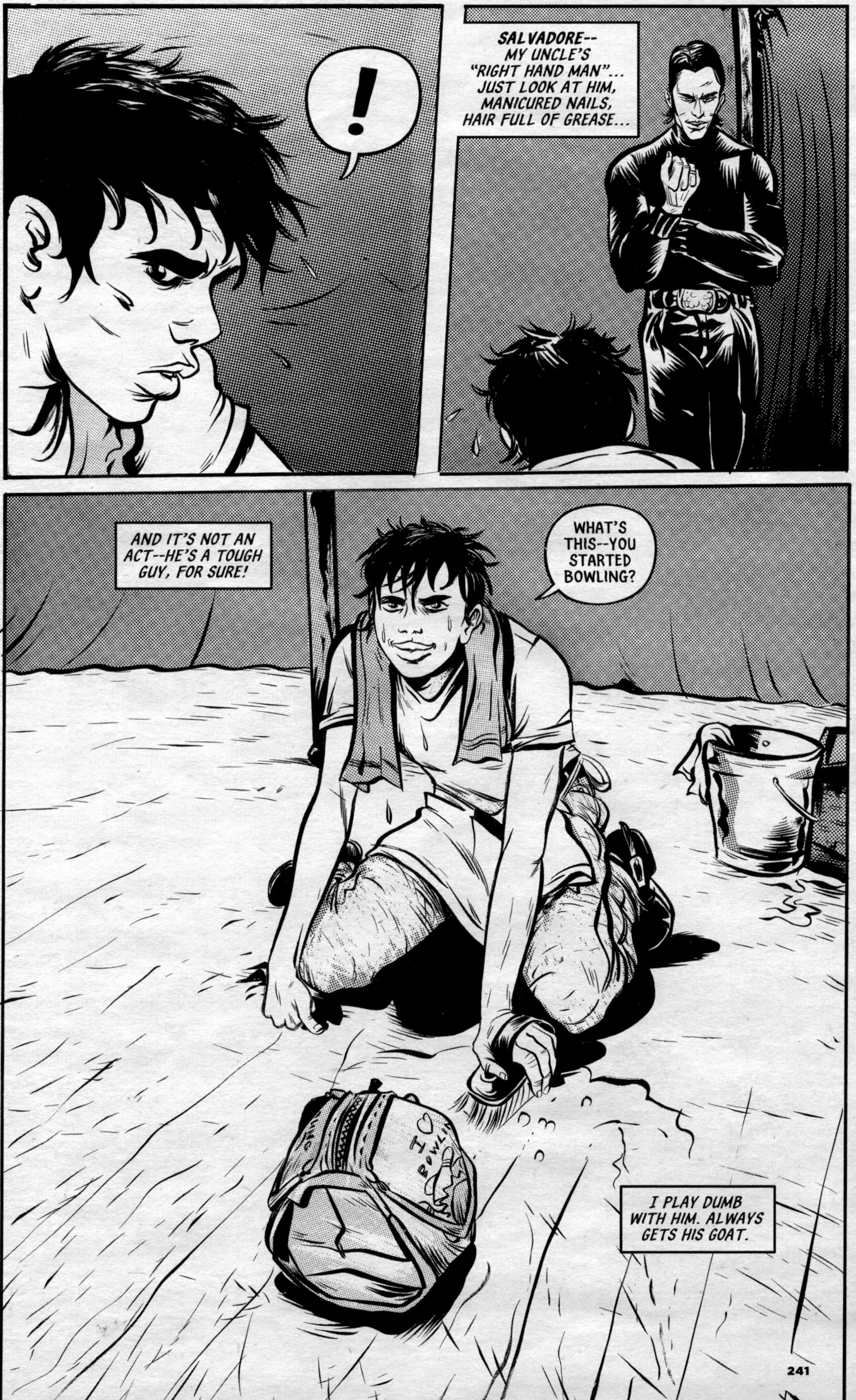
!
SALVADORE-- MY UNCLE'S "RIGHT HAND MAN"... JUST LOOK AT HIM, MANICURED NAILS, HAIR FULL OF GREASE...
AND IT'S NOT AN ACT--HE'S A TOUGH GUY, FOR SURE!
WHAT'S THIS--YOU STARTED BOWLING?
I PLAY DUMB WITH HIM. ALWAYS GETS HIS GOAT.

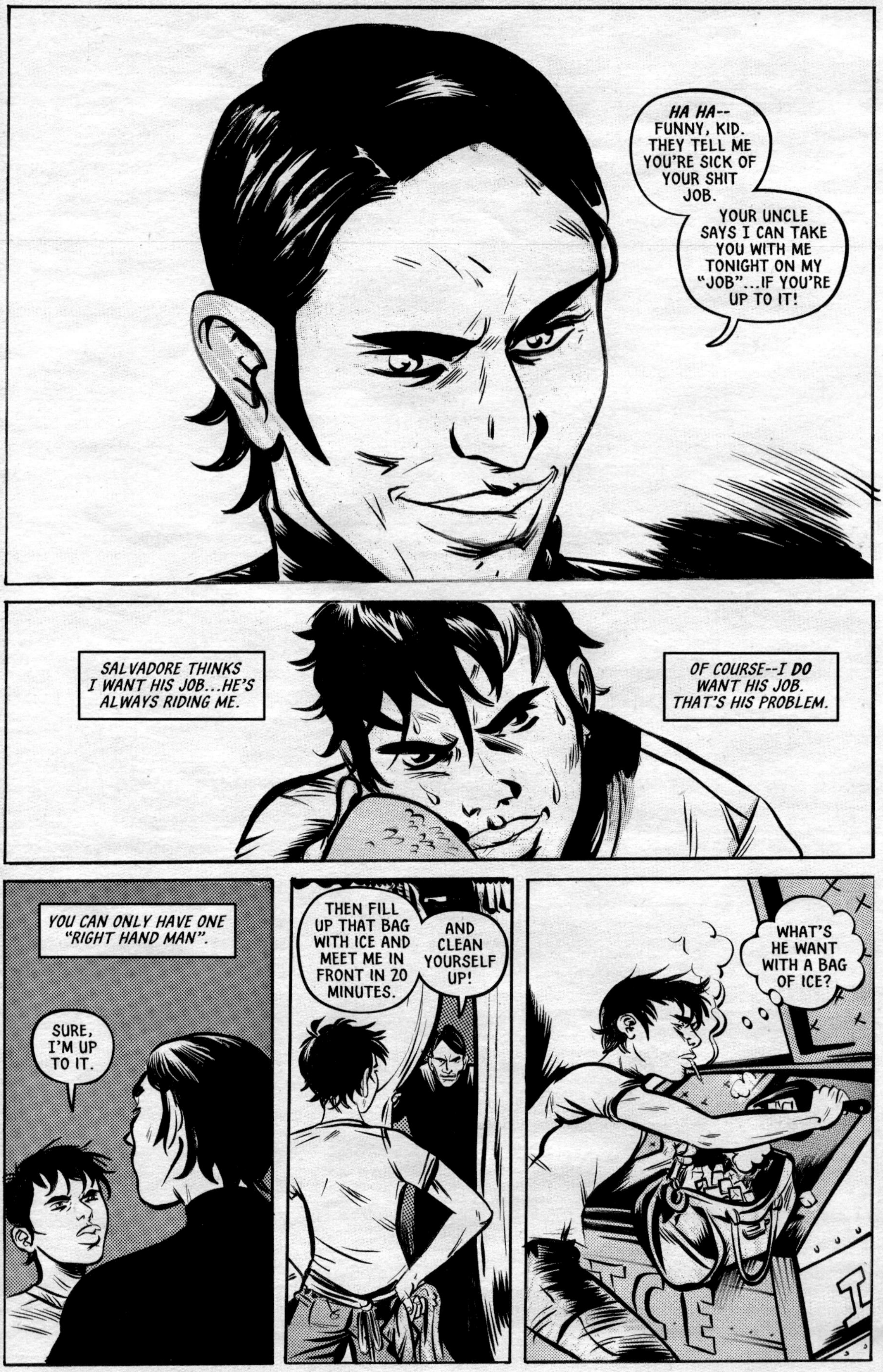
HA HA--
FUNNY, KID. THEY TELL ME YOU'RE SICK OF YOUR SHIT JOB.
YOUR UNCLE SAYS I CAN TAKE YOU WITH ME TONIGHT ON MY "JOB"...IF YOU'RE UP TO IT!
SALVADORE THINKS I WANT HIS JOB...HE'S ALWAYS RIDING ME.
OF COURSE--I DO WANT HIS JOB. THAT'S HIS PROBLEM.
YOU CAN ONLY HAVE ONE "RIGHT HAND MAN".
SURE, I'M UP TO IT.
THEN FILL UP THAT BAG WITH ICE AND MEET ME IN FRONT IN 20 MINUTES.
AND CLEAN YOURSELF UP!
WHAT'S HE WANT WITH A BAG OF ICE?
ICE

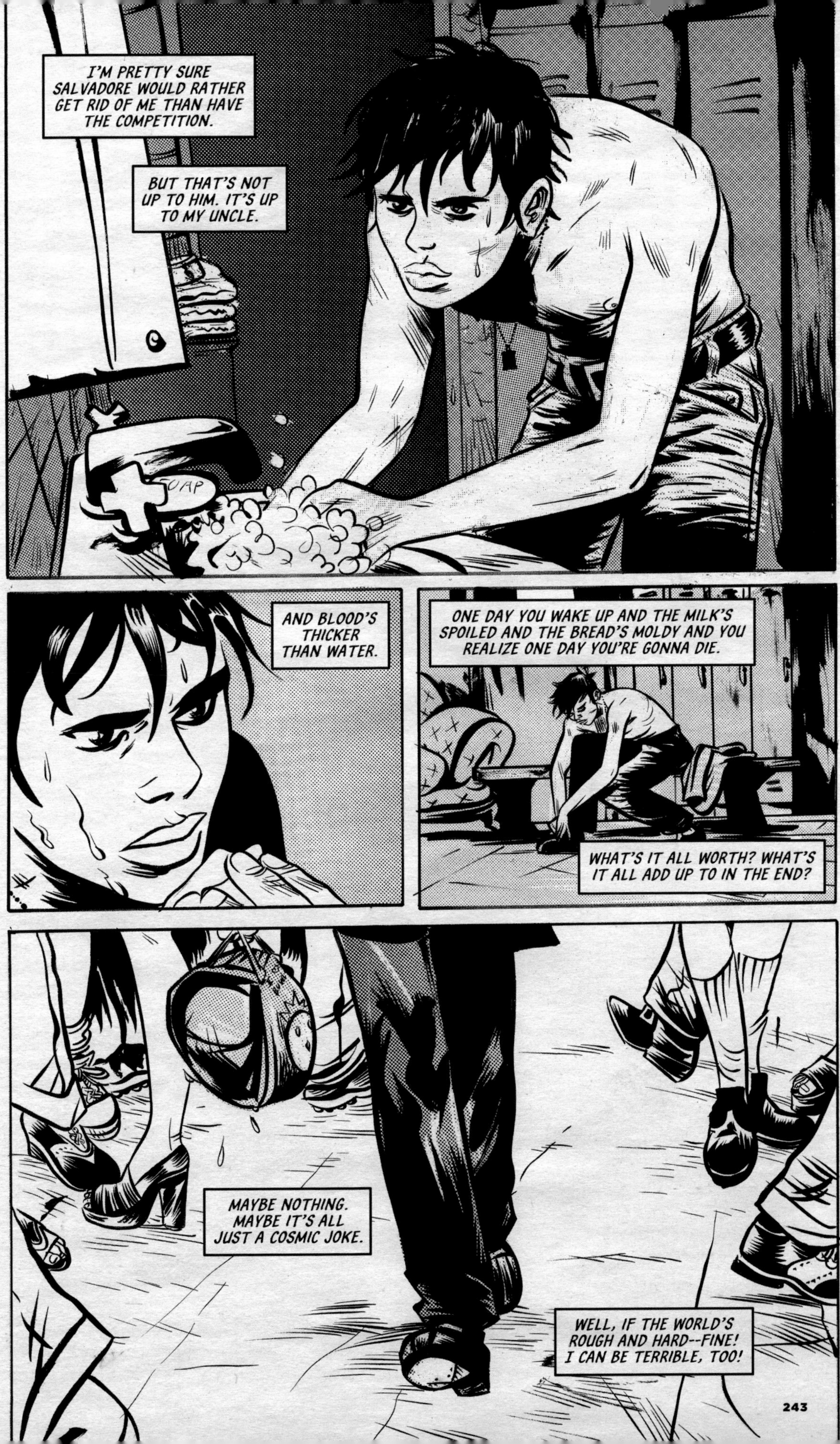
I'M PRETTY SURE SALVADORE WOULD RATHER GET RID OF ME THAN HAVE THE COMPETITION.
BUT THAT'S NOT UP TO HIM. IT'S UP TO MY UNCLE.
SOAP
AND BLOOD'S THICKER THAN WATER.
ONE DAY YOU WAKE UP AND THE MILK'S SPOILED AND THE BREAD'S MOLDY AND YOU REALIZE ONE DAY YOU'RE GONNA DIE.
WHAT'S IT ALL WORTH? WHAT'S IT ALL ADD UP TO IN THE END?
MAYBE NOTHING. MAYBE IT'S ALL JUST A COSMIC JOKE.
WELL, IF THE WORLD'S ROUGH AND HARD--FINE! I CAN BE TERRIBLE, TOO!

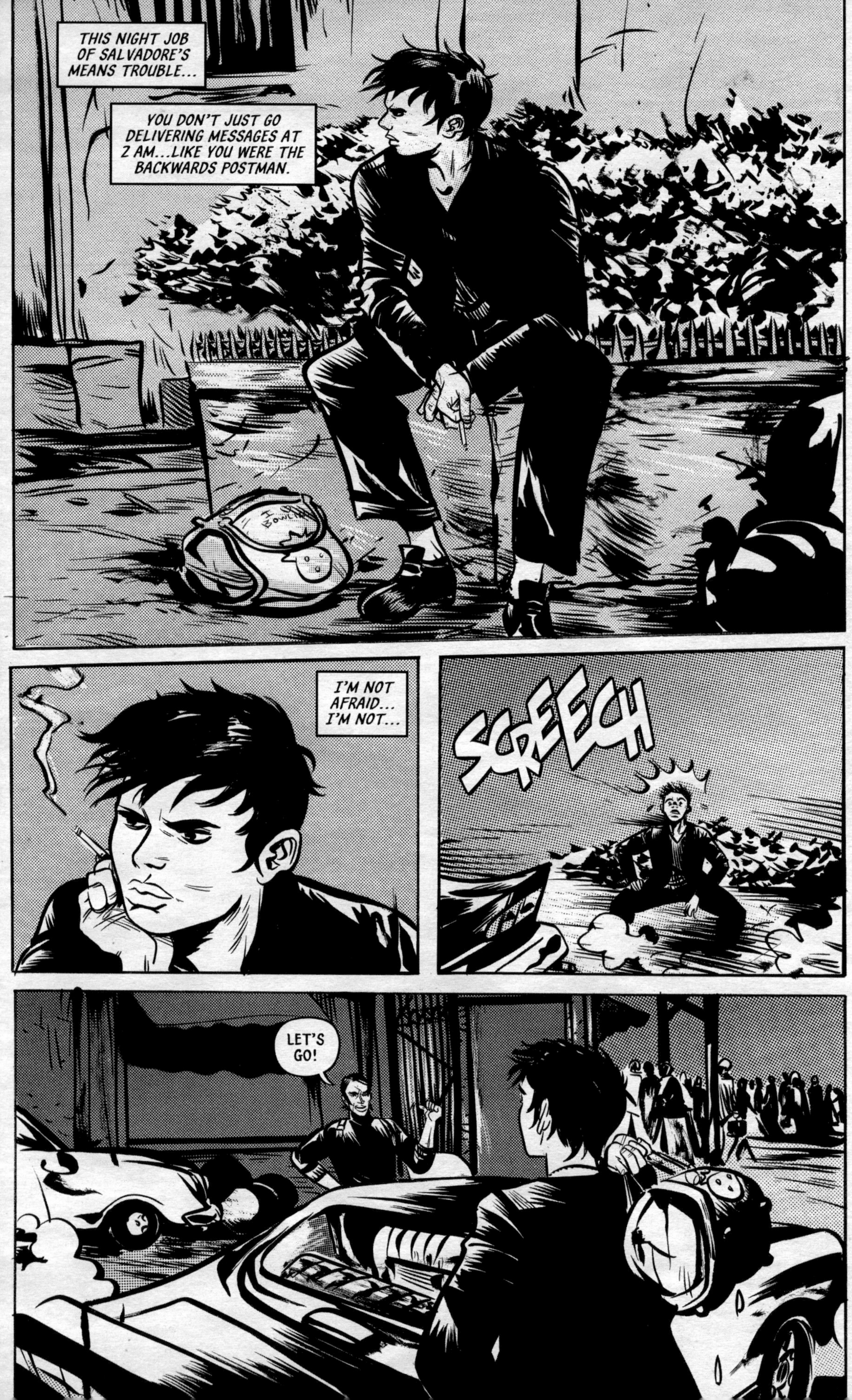

THIS NIGHT JOB OF SALVADORE'S MEANS TROUBLE...
YOU DON'T JUST GO DELIVERING MESSAGES AT 2 AM...LIKE YOU WERE THE BACKWARDS POSTMAN.
I'M NOT AFRAID... I'M NOT...
SCREECH
LET'S GO!

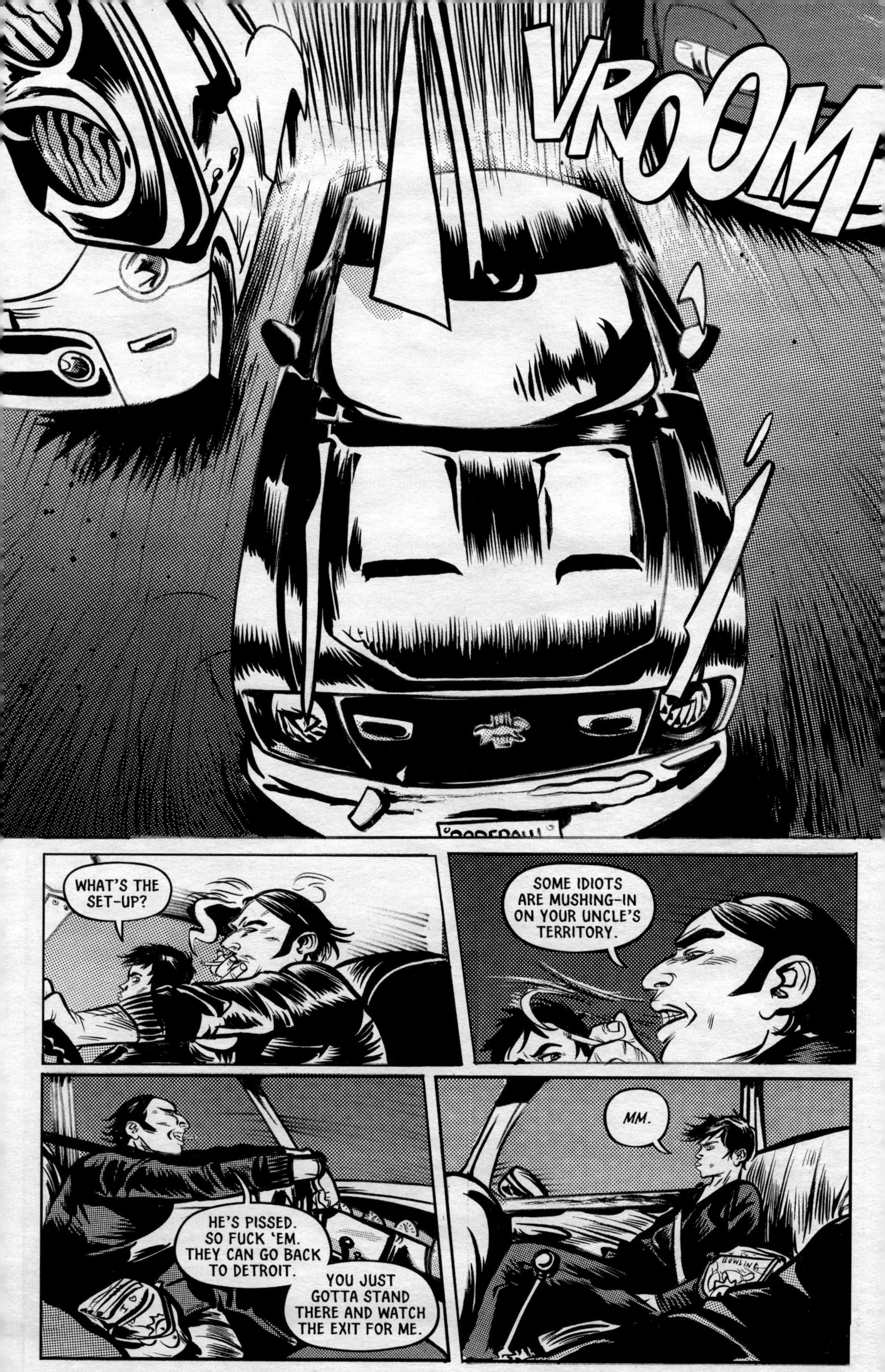
VROOM
WHAT'S THE SET-UP?
SOME IDIOTS ARE MUSHING-IN ON YOUR UNCLE'S TERRITORY.
HE'S PISSED. SO FUCK 'EM. THEY CAN GO BACK TO DETROIT.
YOU JUST GOTTA STAND THERE AND WATCH THE EXIT FOR ME.
MM.
BOWLING

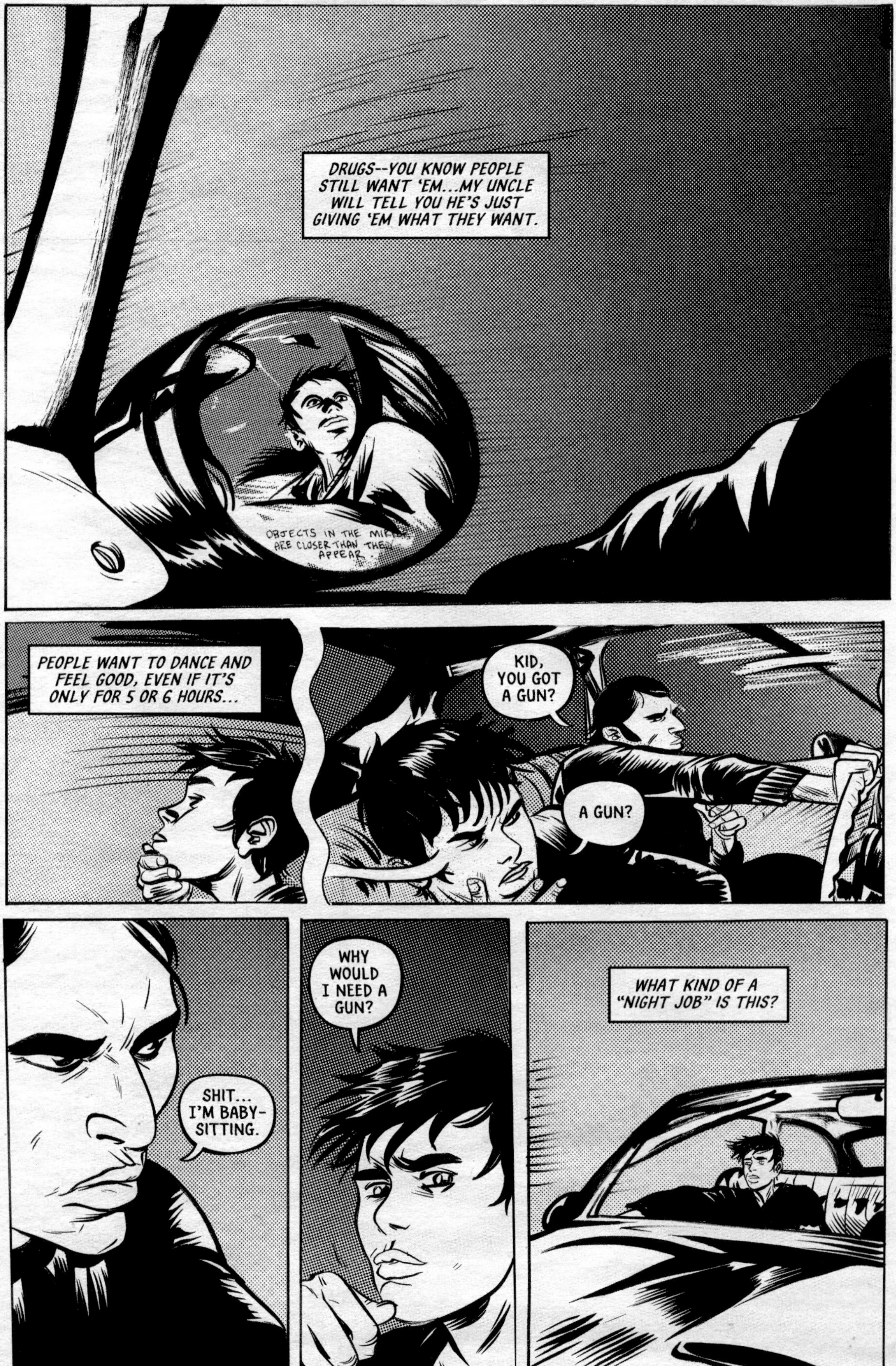
DRUGS--YOU KNOW PEOPLE STILL WANT 'EM...MY UNCLE WILL TELL YOU HE'S JUST GIVING 'EM WHAT THEY WANT.
OBJECTS IN THE
ARE CLOSER THAN
APPEAR
PEOPLE WANT TO DANCE AND FEEL GOOD, EVEN IF IT'S ONLY FOR 5 OR 6 HOURS...
KID, YOU GOT A GUN?
A GUN?
SHIT... I'M BABY-SITTING.
WHY WOULD I NEED A GUN?
WHAT KIND OF A "NIGHT JOB" IS THIS?

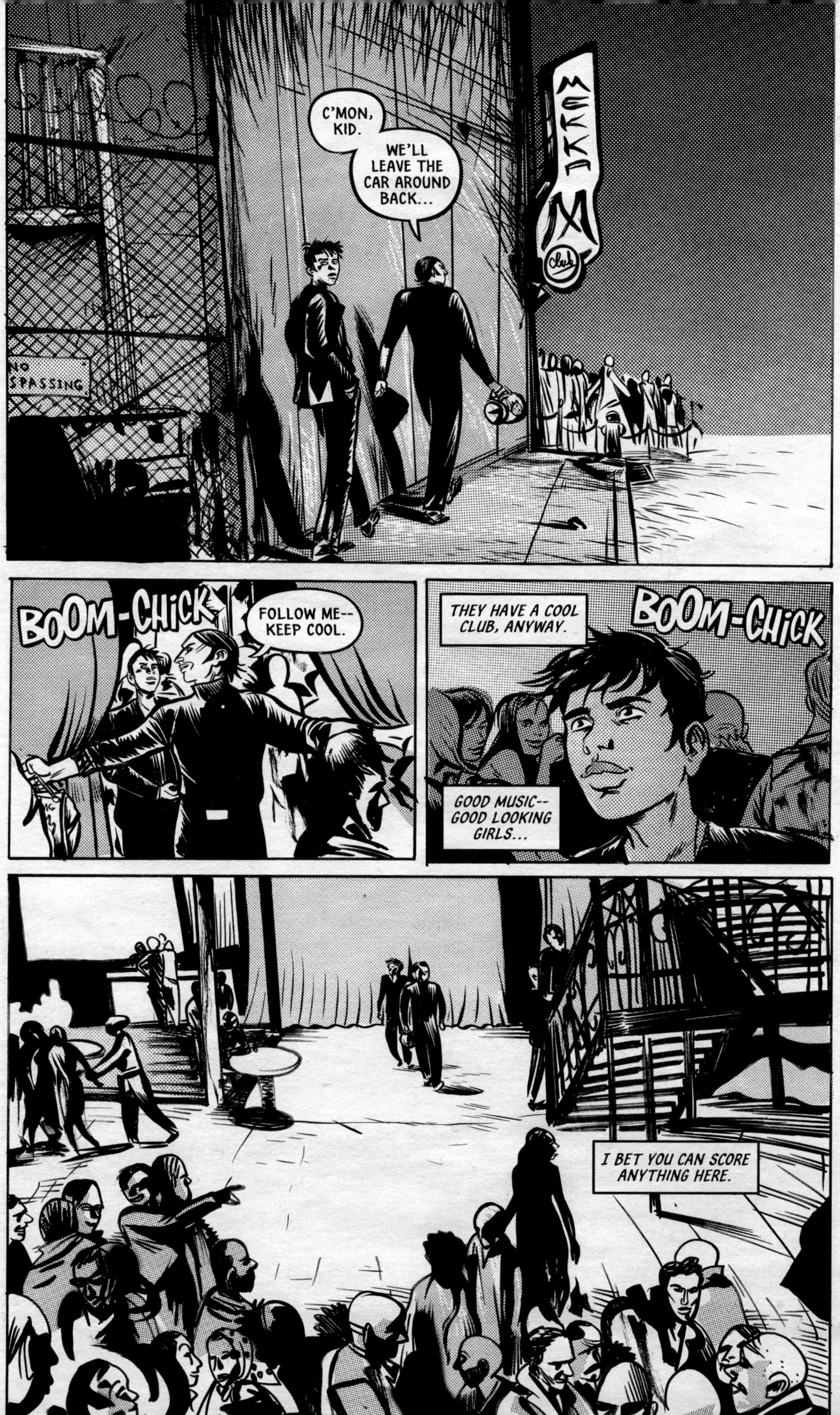
C'MON, KID.
WE'LL LEAVE THE CAR AROUND BACK...
BOOM-CHICK
FOLLOW ME-- KEEP COOL.
THEY HAVE A COOL CLUB, ANYWAY.
BOOM-CHICK
GOOD MUSIC-- GOOD LOOKING GIRLS...
I BET YOU CAN SCORE ANYTHING HERE.

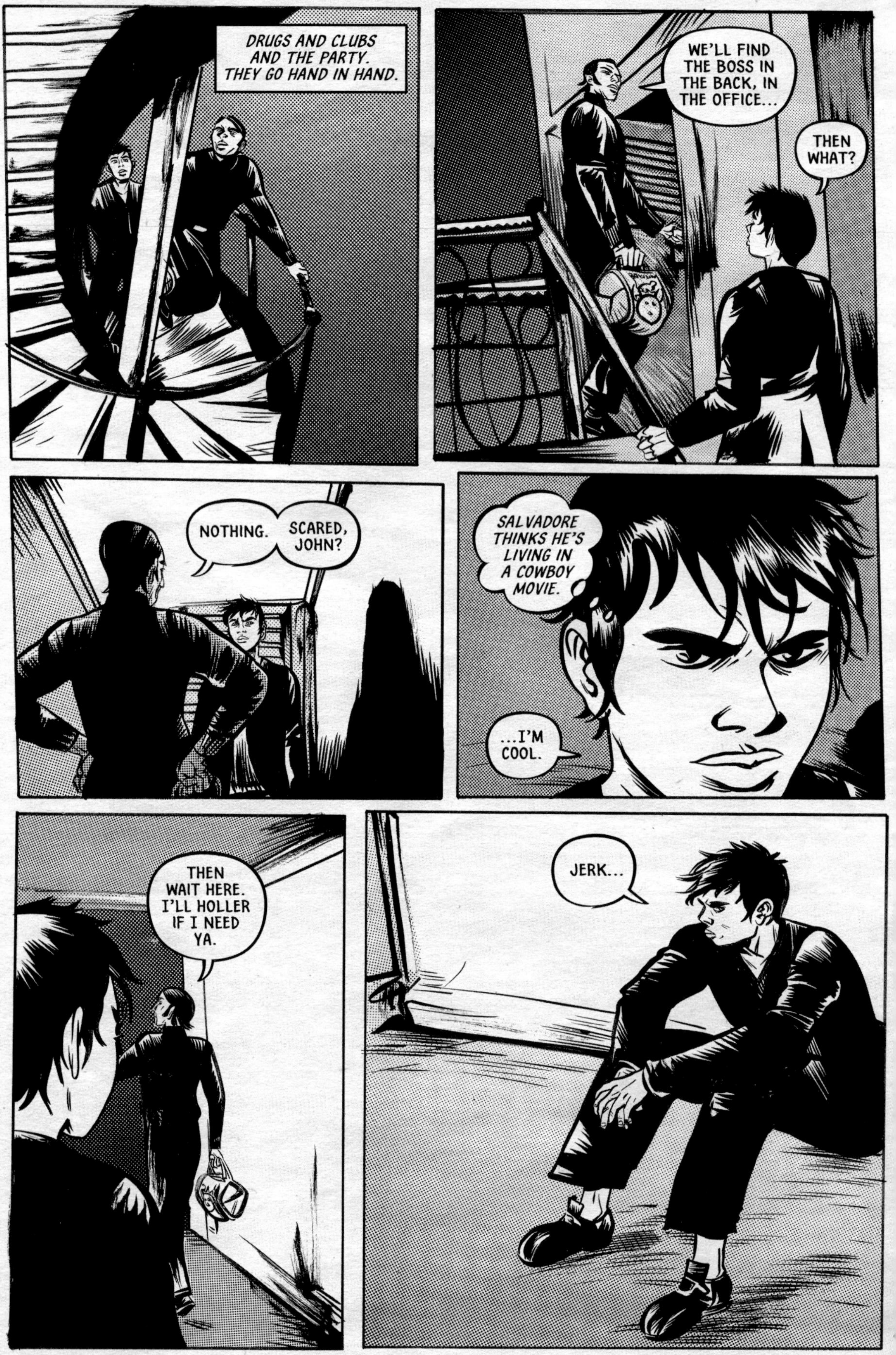
DRUGS AND CLUBS AND THE PARTY. THEY GO HAND IN HAND.
WE'LL FIND THE BOSS IN THE BACK, IN THE OFFICE...
THEN WHAT?
NOTHING.
SCARED, JOHN?
SALVADORE THINKS HE'S LIVING IN A COWBOY MOVIE.
...I'M COOL.
THEN WAIT HERE. I'LL HOLLER IF I NEED YA.
JERK...

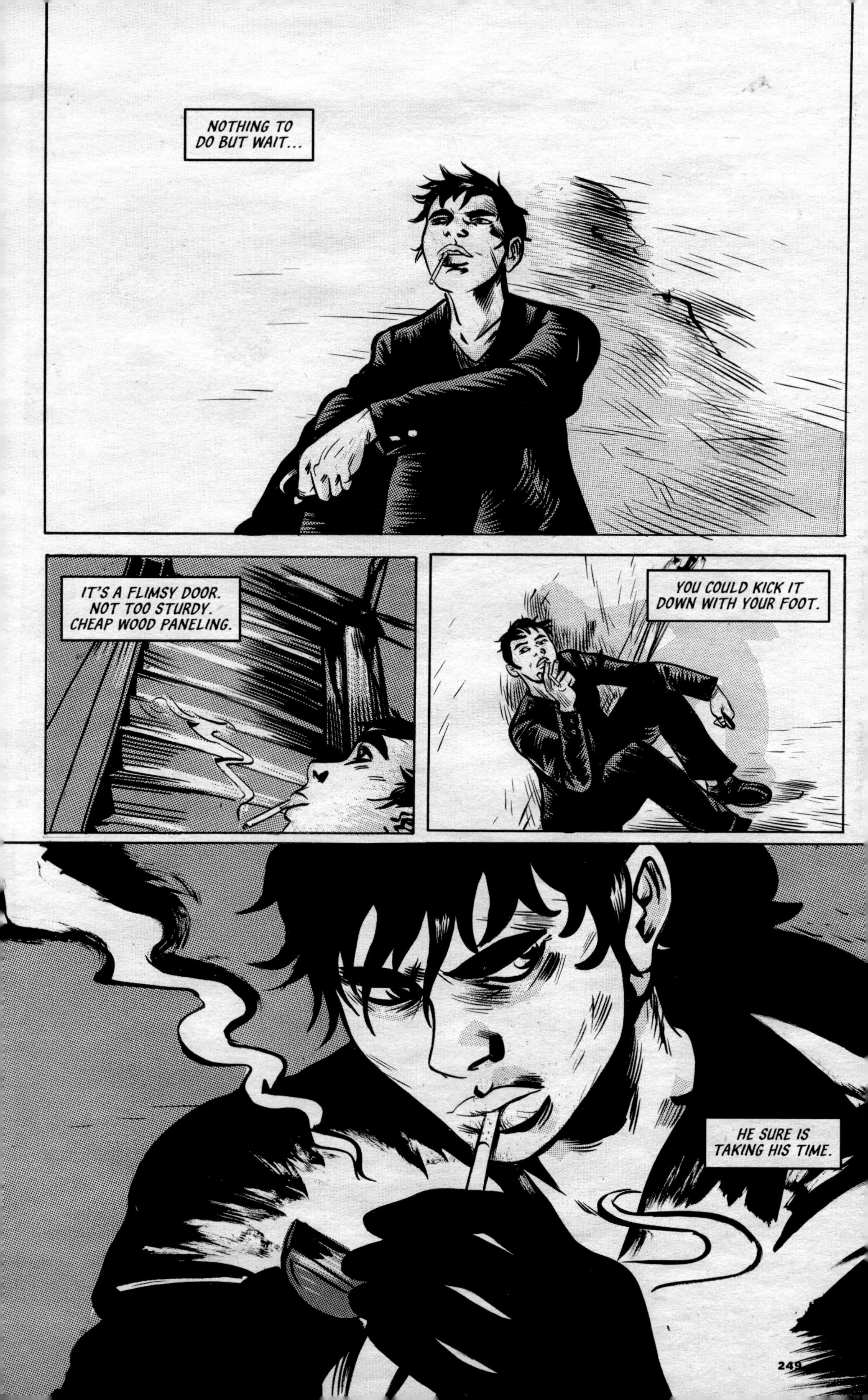

NOTHING TO DO BUT WAIT...
IT'S A FLIMSY DOOR. NOT TOO STURDY. CHEAP WOOD PANELING.
YOU COULD KICK IT DOWN WITH YOUR FOOT.
HE SURE IS TAKING HIS TIME.

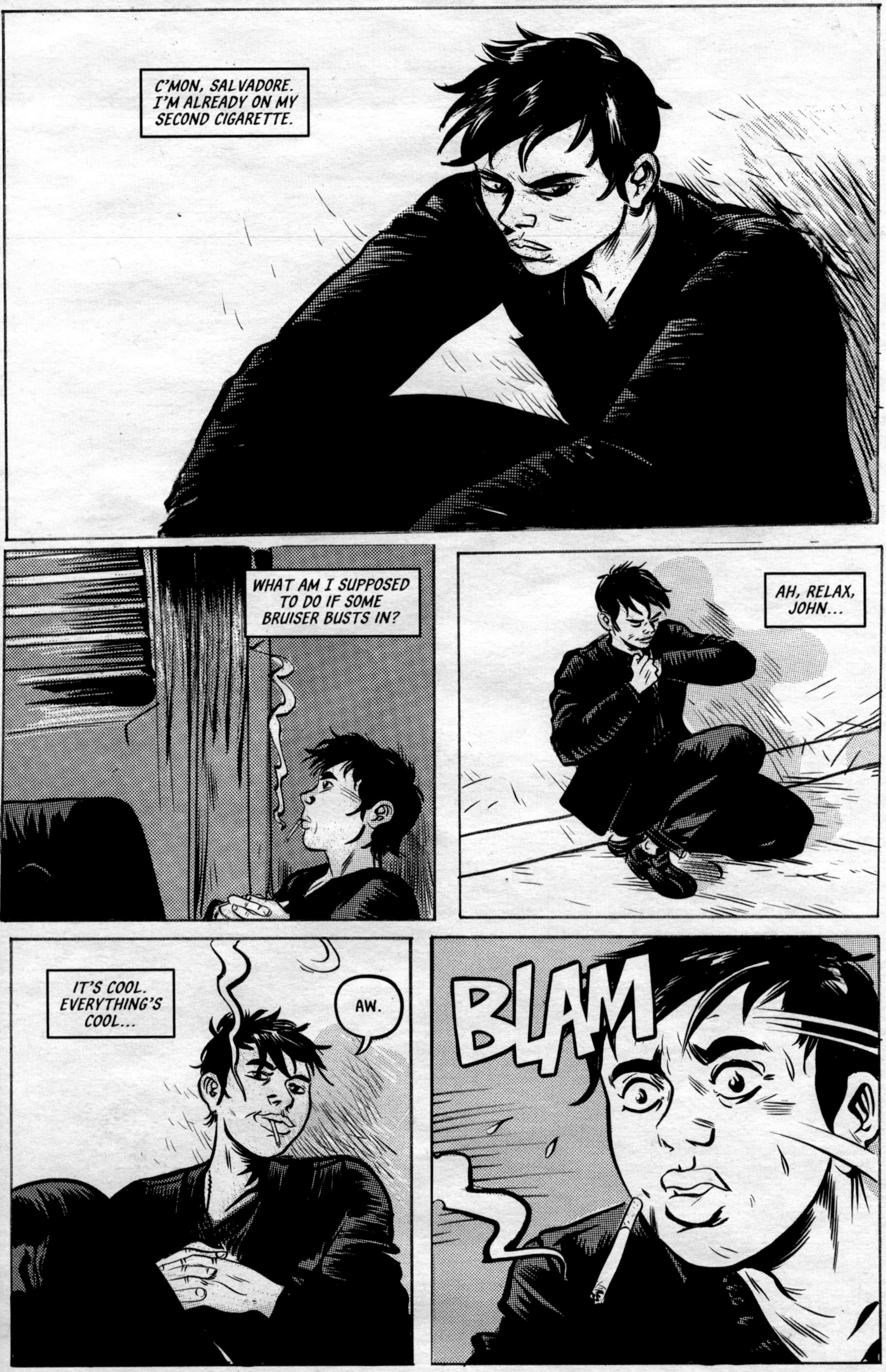
C'MON, SALVADORE. I'M ALREADY ON MY SECOND CIGARETTE.
WHAT AM I SUPPOSED TO DO IF SOME BRUISER BUSTS IN?
AH, RELAX, JOHN...
IT'S COOL. EVERYTHING'S COOL...
AW.
BLAM

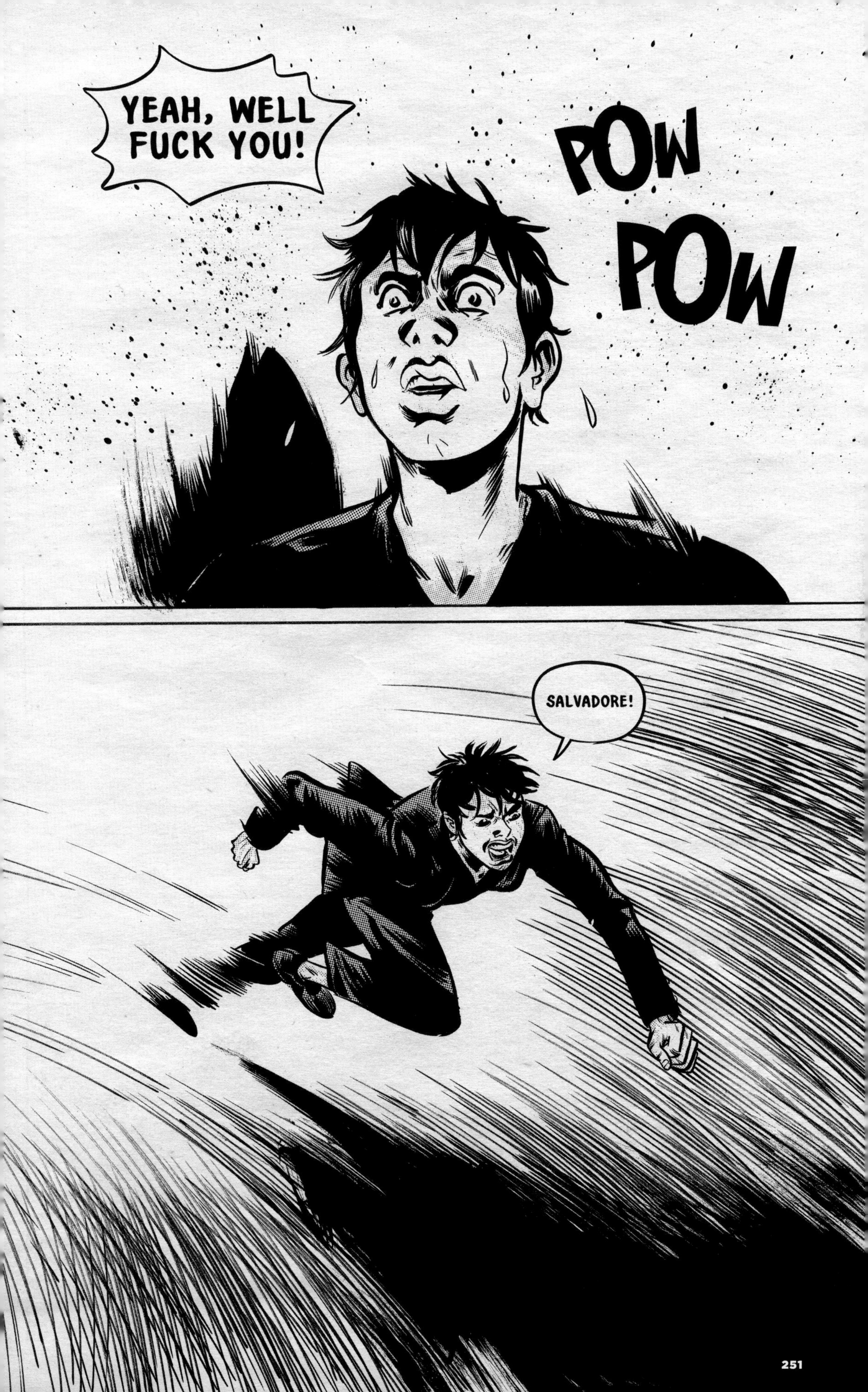
YEAH, WELL FUCK YOU!
POW
POW
SALVADORE!

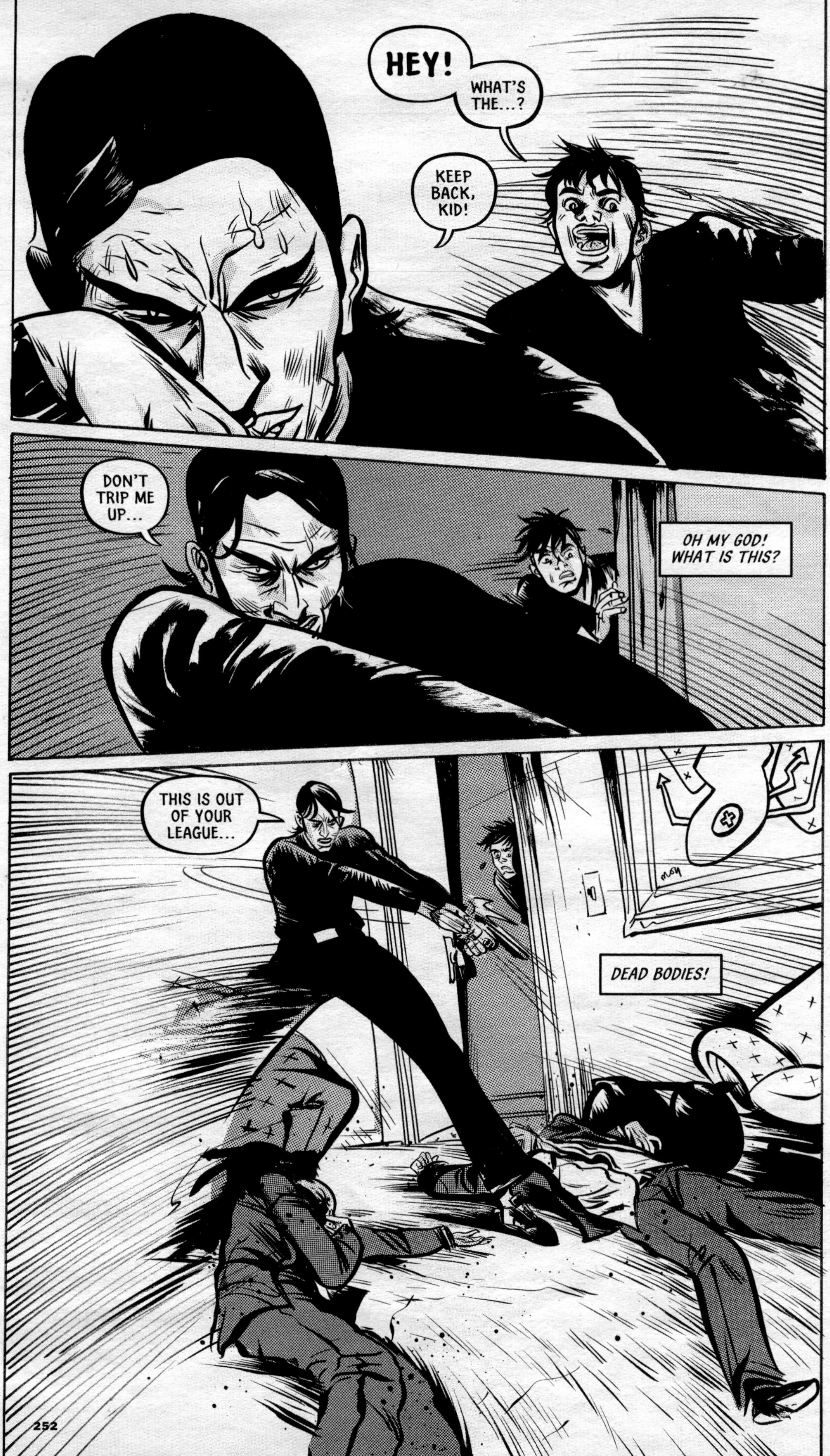
HEY!
WHAT'S THE...?
KEEP BACK, KID!
DON'T TRIP ME UP...
OH MY GOD! WHAT IS THIS?
THIS IS OUT OF YOUR LEAGUE...
DEAD BODIES!

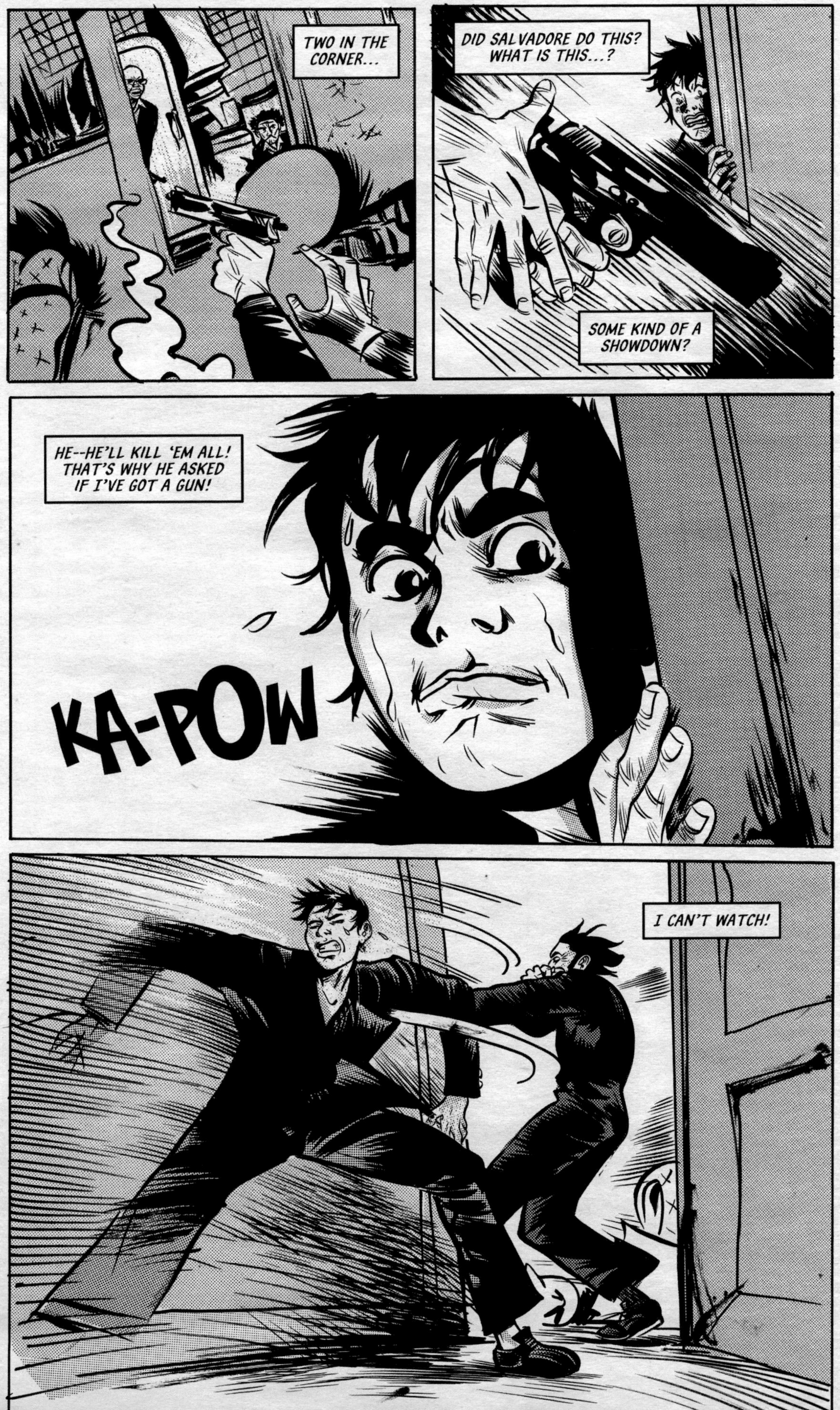
TWO IN THE CORNER...
DID SALVADORE DO THIS? WHAT IS THIS...?
SOME KIND OF A SHOWDOWN?
HE--HE'LL KILL 'EM ALL! THAT'S WHY HE ASKED IF I'VE GOT A GUN!
KA-POW
I CAN'T WATCH!

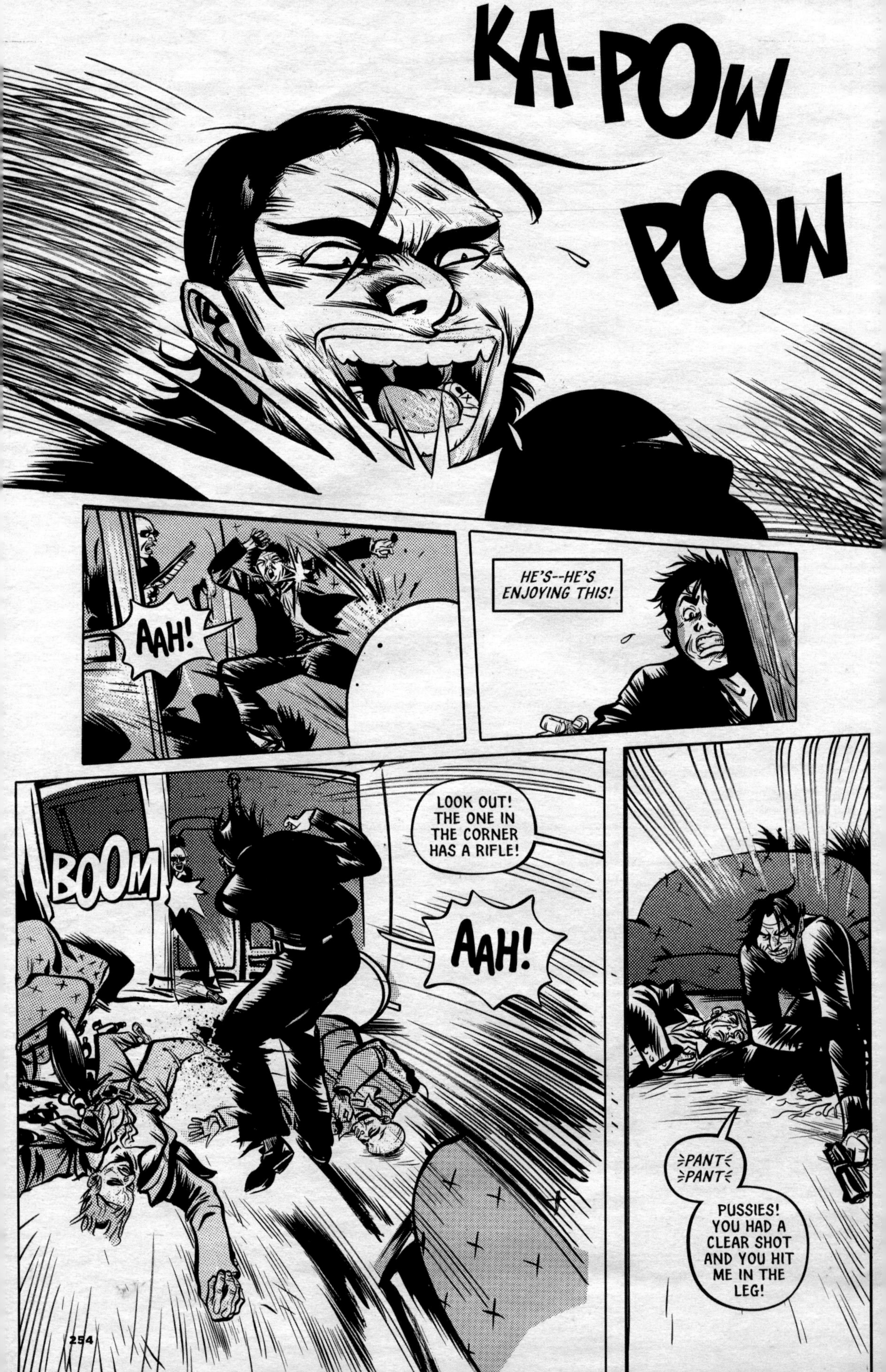
KA-POW
POW
AAH!
HE'S--HE'S ENJOYING THIS!
BOOM
LOOK OUT! THE ONE IN THE CORNER HAS A RIFLE!
AAH!
PANT PANT
PUSSIES! YOU HAD A CLEAR SHOT AND YOU HIT ME IN THE LEG!

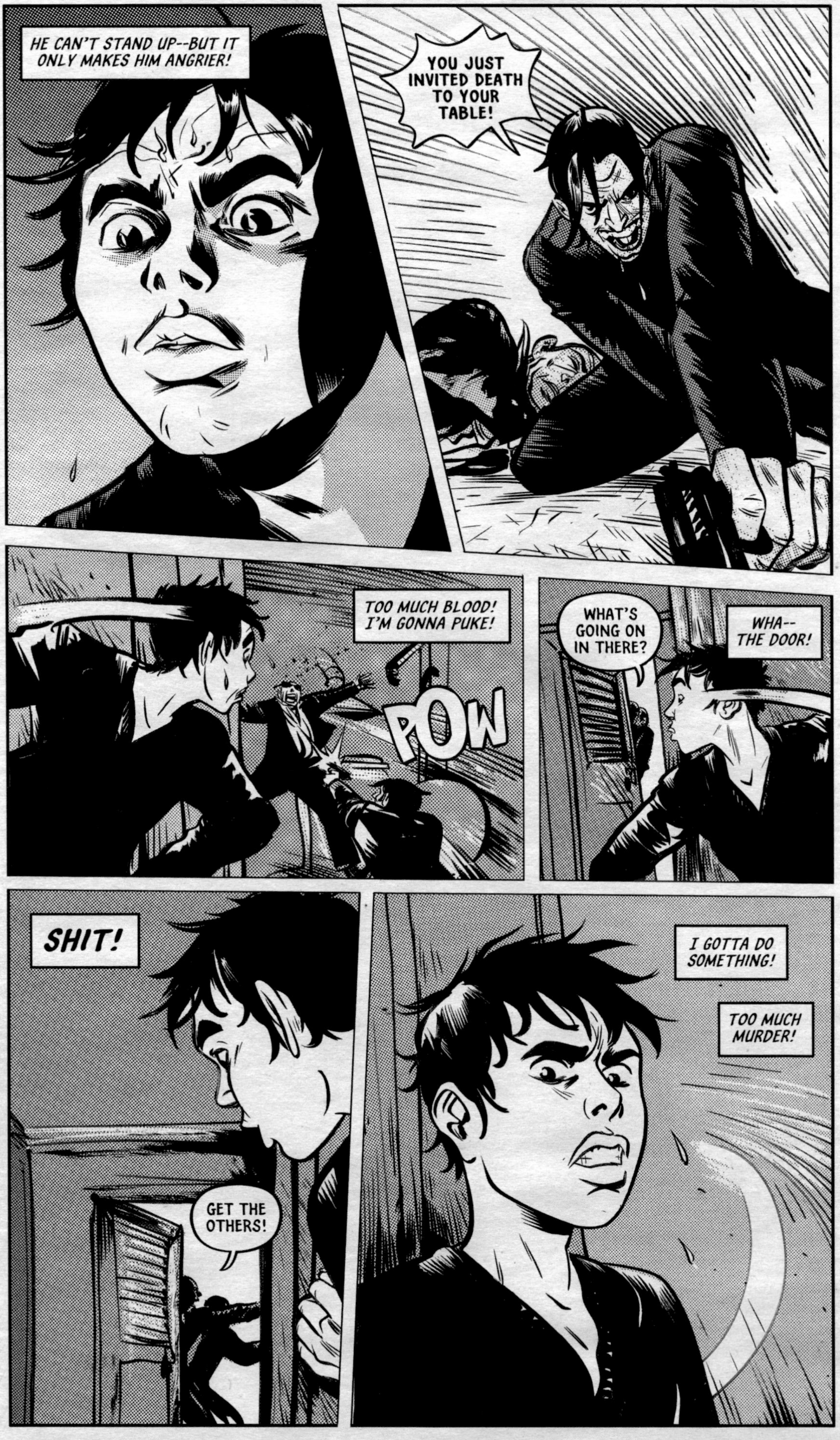
HE CAN'T STAND UP--BUT IT ONLY MAKES HIM ANGRIER!
YOU JUST INVITED DEATH TO YOUR TABLE!
TOO MUCH BLOOD! I'M GONNA PUKE!
POW
WHAT'S GOING ON IN THERE?
WHA-- THE DOOR!
SHIT!
GET THE OTHERS!
I GOTTA DO SOMETHING!
TOO MUCH MURDER!

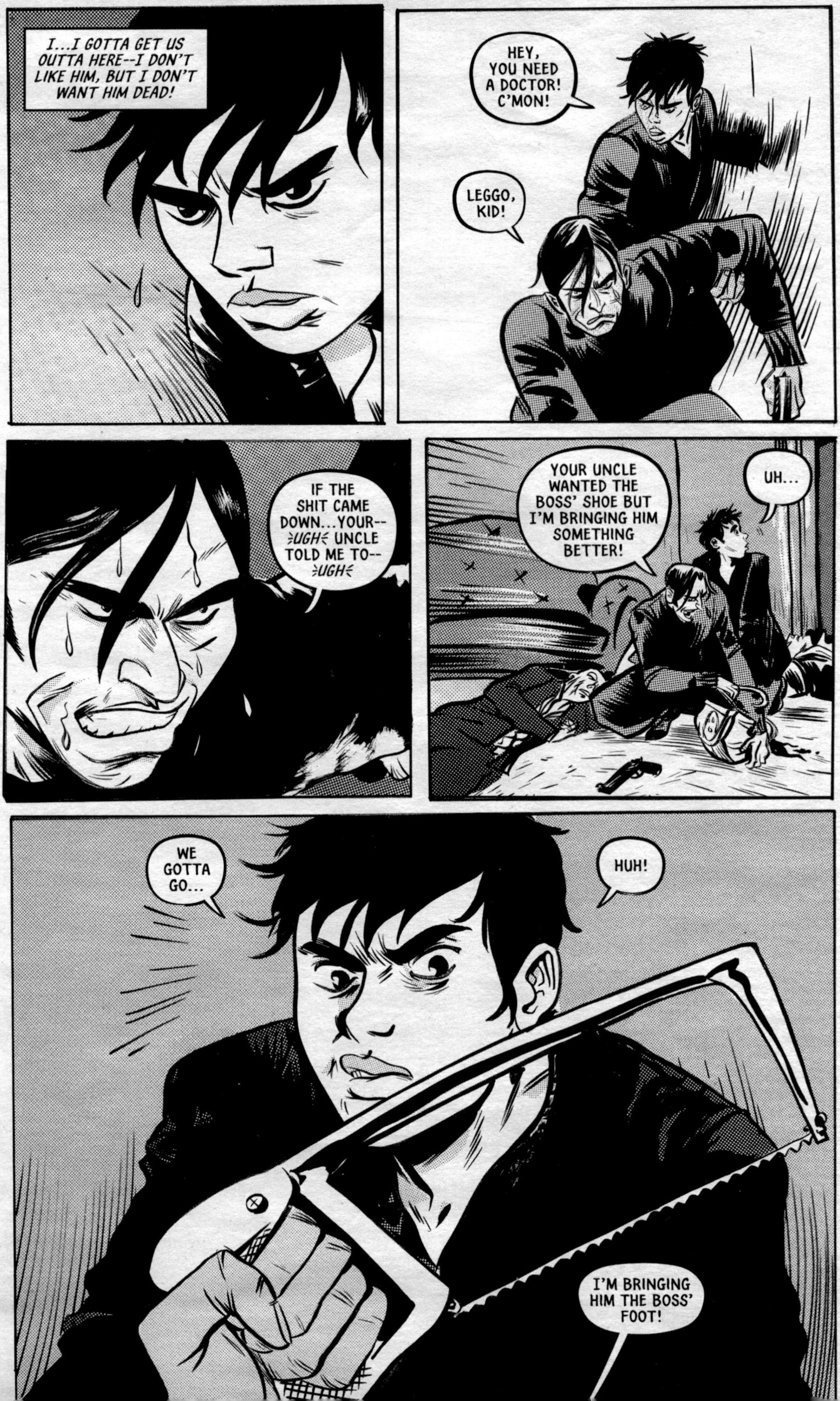
I...I GOTTA GET US OUTTA HERE--I DON'T LIKE HIM, BUT I DON'T WANT HIM DEAD!
HEY, YOU NEED A DOCTOR! C'MON!
LEGGO, KID!
IF THE SHIT CAME DOWN...YOUR-- UGH UNCLE TOLD ME TO-- UGH
YOUR UNCLE WANTED THE BOSS' SHOE BUT I'M BRINGING HIM SOMETHING BETTER!
UH...
WE GOTTA GO...
HUH!
I'M BRINGING HIM THE BOSS' FOOT!

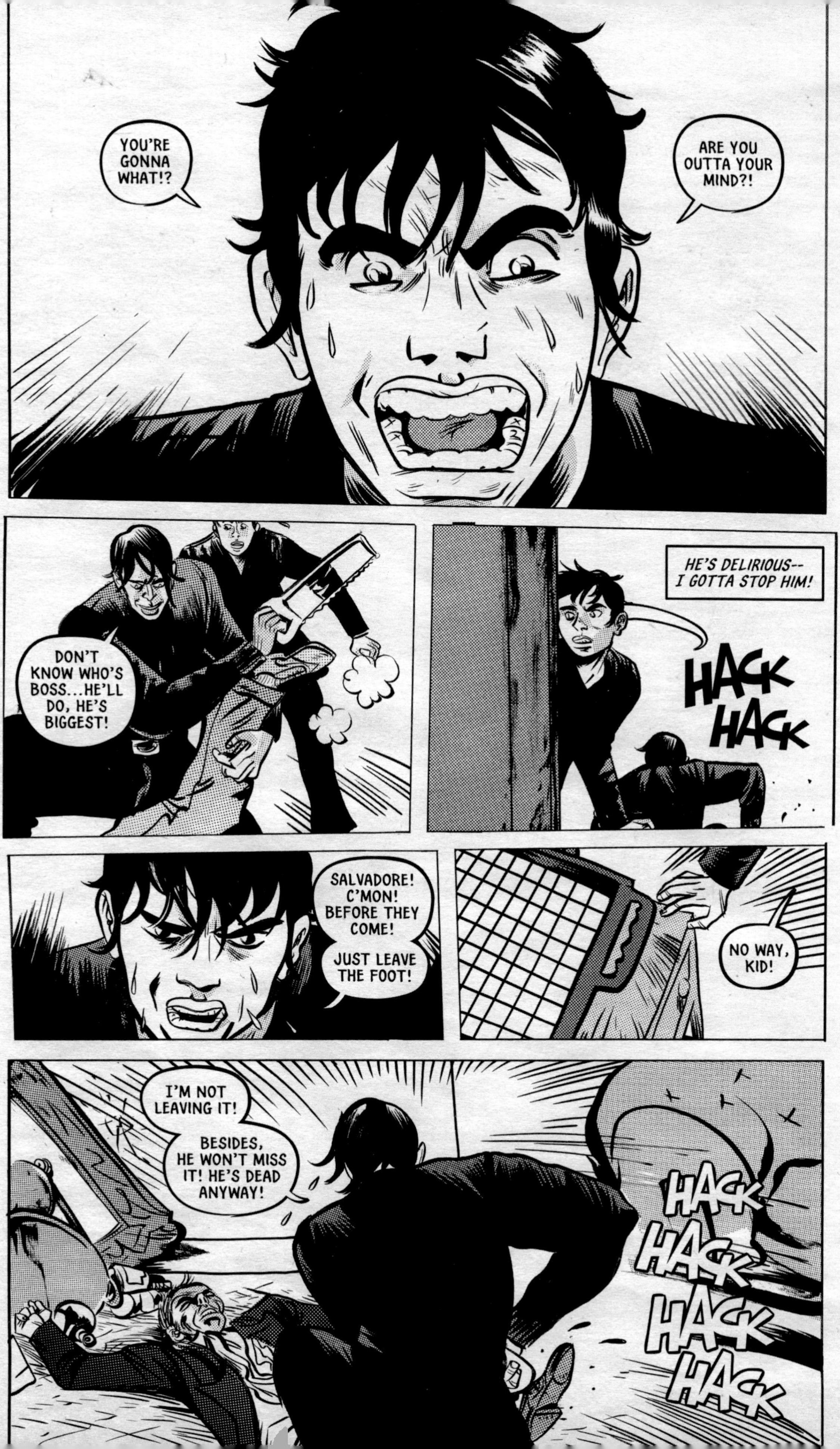
YOU'RE GONNA WHAT!?
ARE YOU OUTTA YOUR MIND?!
DON'T KNOW WHO'S BOSS...HE'LL DO, HE'S BIGGEST!
HE'S DELIRIOUS-- I GOTTA STOP HIM!
HACK HACK
SALVADORE! C'MON! BEFORE THEY COME!
JUST LEAVE THE FOOT!
NO WAY, KID!
I'M NOT LEAVING IT!
BESIDES, HE WON'T MISS IT! HE'S DEAD ANYWAY!
HACK HACK HACK HACK

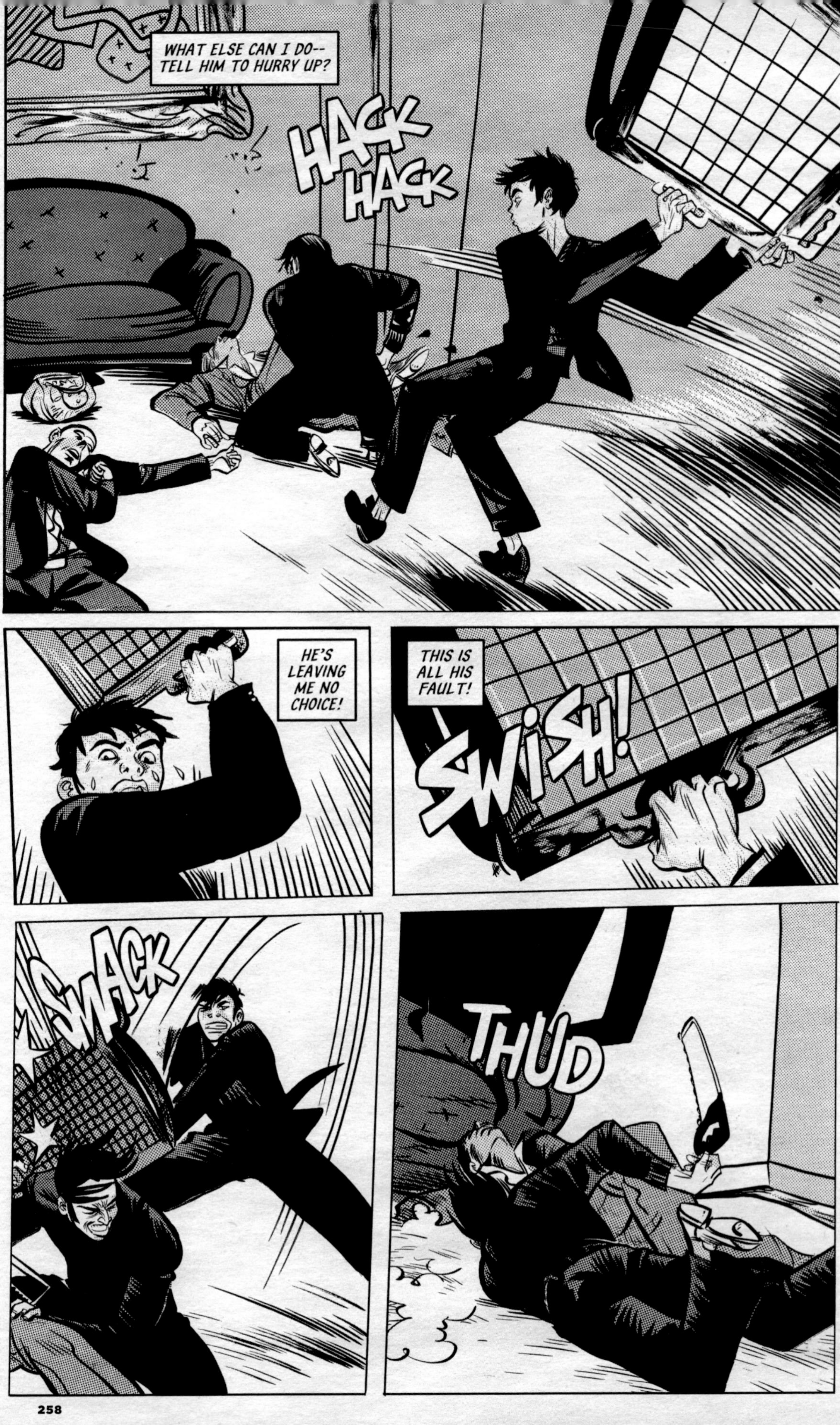
WHAT ELSE CAN I DO--
TELL HIM TO HURRY UP?
HACK
HACK
HE'S LEAVING ME NO CHOICE!
THIS IS ALL HIS FAULT!
SWISH!
SMACK
THUD

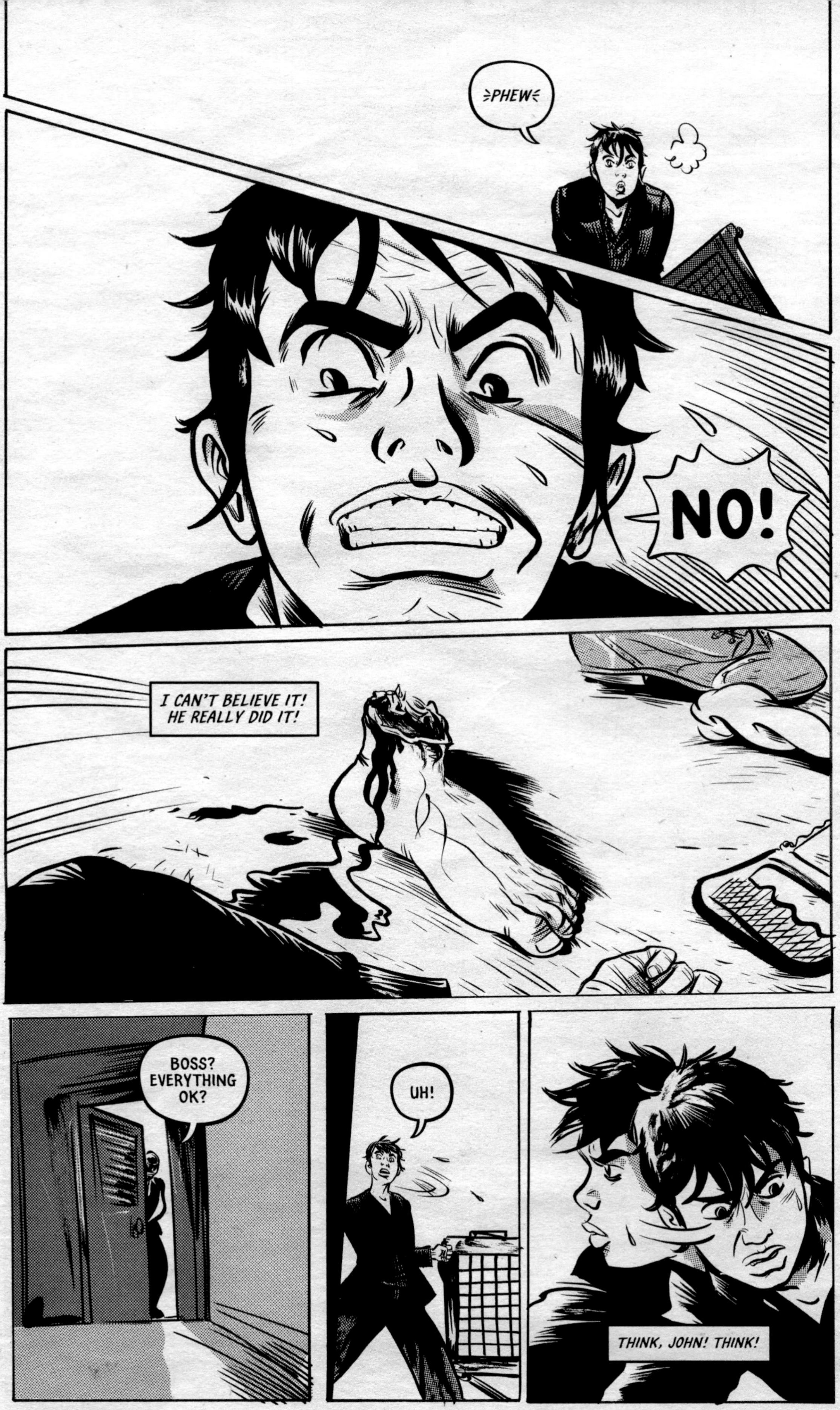
PHEW
NO!
I CAN'T BELIEVE IT! HE REALLY DID IT!
BOSS? EVERYTHING OK?
UH!
THINK, JOHN! THINK!

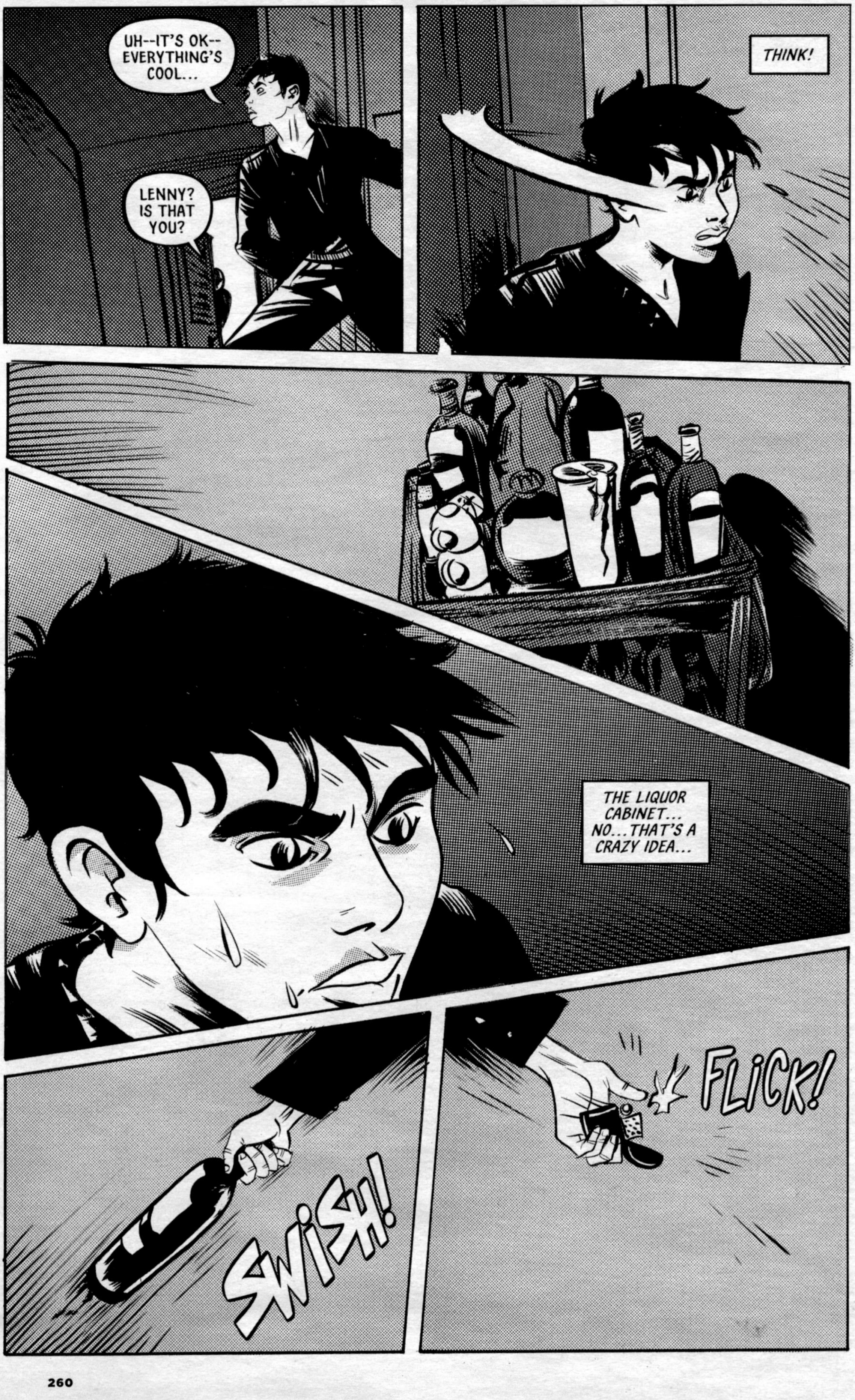
UH--IT'S OK--
EVERYTHING'S
COOL...
LENNY?
IS THAT
YOU?
THINK!
THE LIQUOR
CABINET...
NO...THAT'S A
CRAZY IDEA...
SWISH!
FLICK!

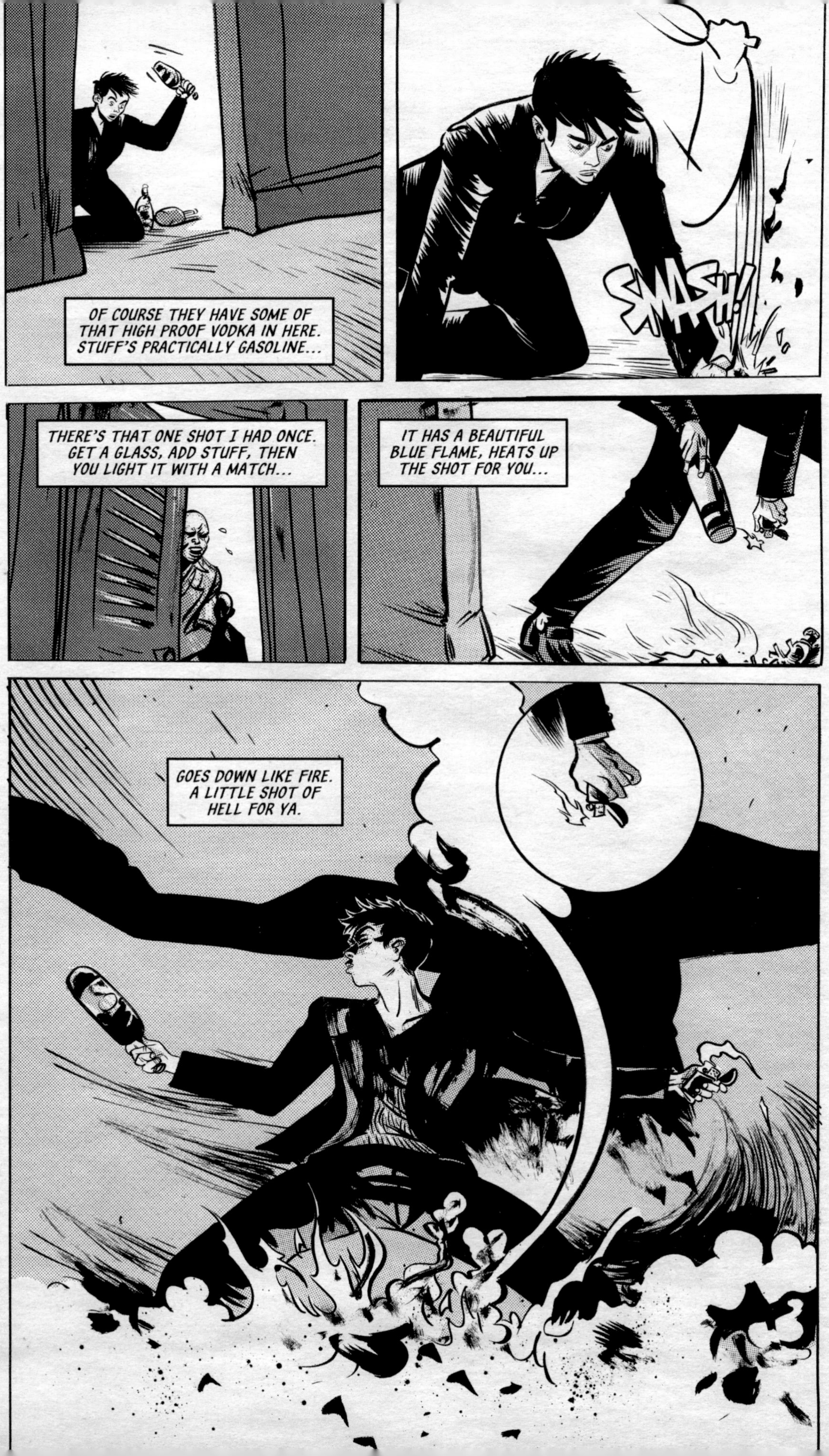

OF COURSE THEY HAVE SOME OF THAT HIGH PROOF VODKA IN HERE. STUFF'S PRACTICALLY GASOLINE...
SMASH!
THERE'S THAT ONE SHOT I HAD ONCE. GET A GLASS, ADD STUFF, THEN YOU LIGHT IT WITH A MATCH...
IT HAS A BEAUTIFUL BLUE FLAME, HEATS UP THE SHOT FOR YOU...
GOES DOWN LIKE FIRE. A LITTLE SHOT OF HELL FOR YA.

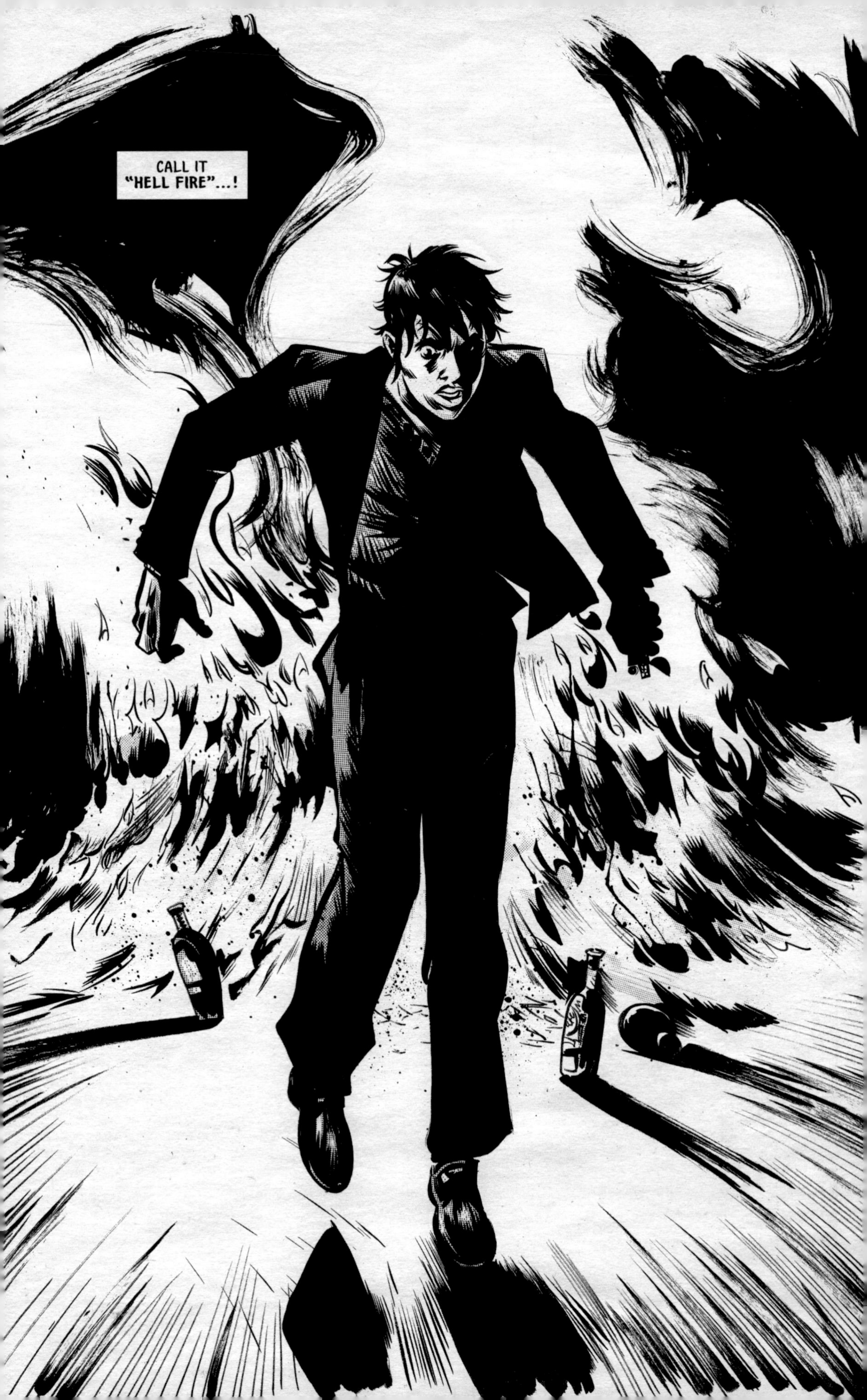
CALL IT "HELL FIRE"...!

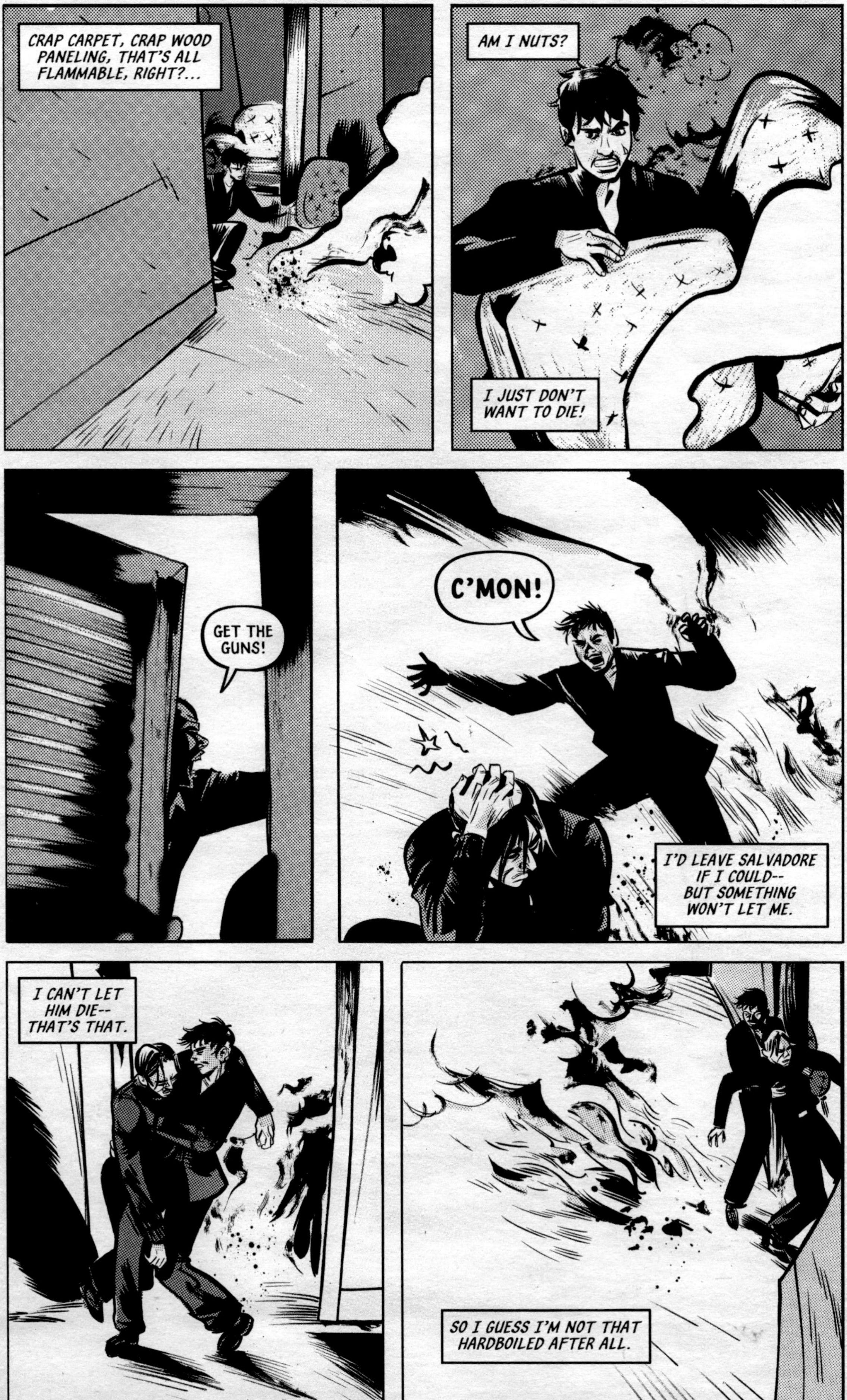
CRAP CARPET, CRAP WOOD PANELING, THAT'S ALL FLAMMABLE, RIGHT?...
AM I NUTS?
I JUST DON'T WANT TO DIE!
GET THE GUNS!
C'MON!
I'D LEAVE SALVADORE IF I COULD-- BUT SOMETHING WON'T LET ME.
I CAN'T LET HIM DIE-- THAT'S THAT.
SO I GUESS I'M NOT THAT HARDBOILED AFTER ALL.

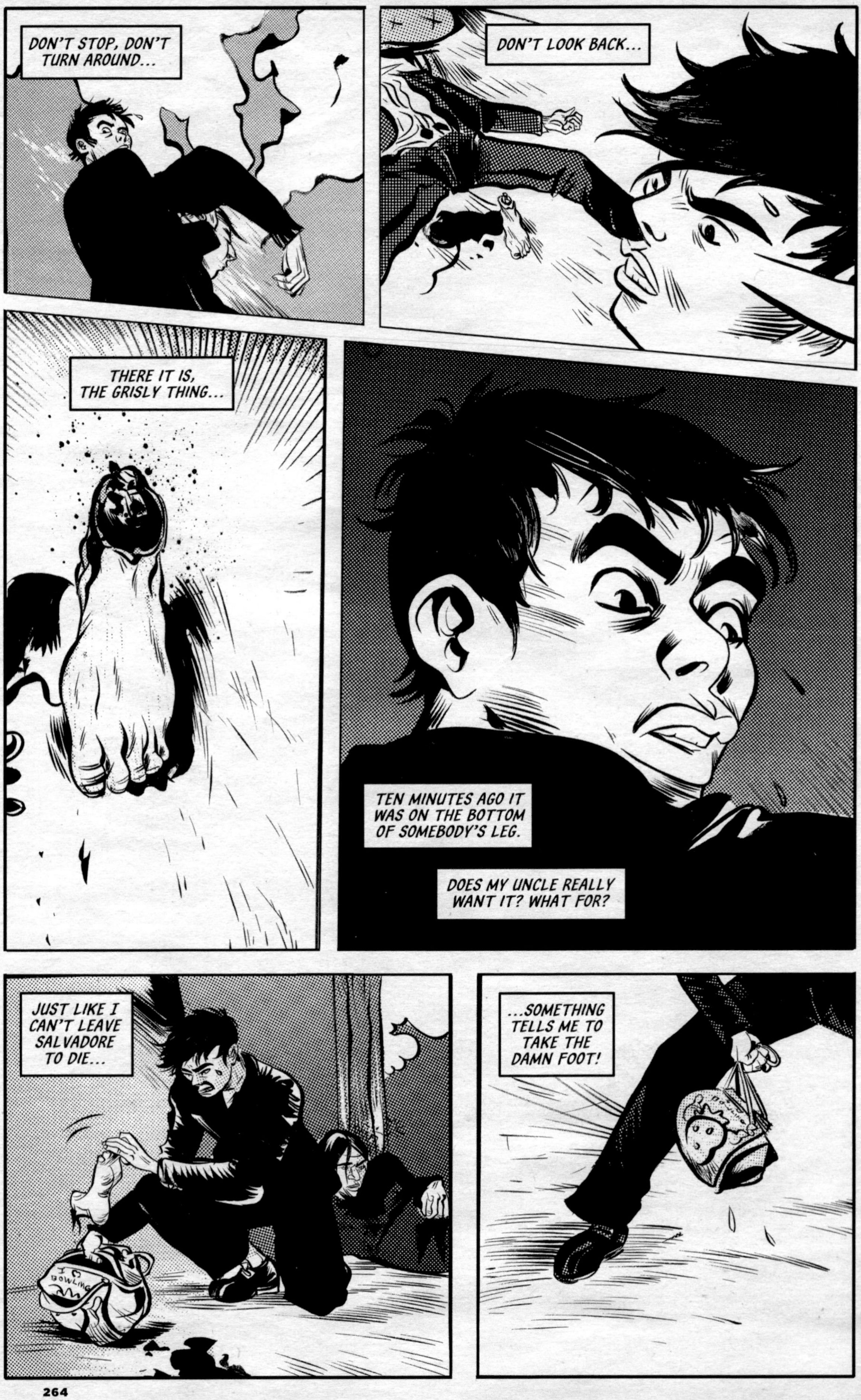
DON'T STOP, DON'T TURN AROUND...
DON'T LOOK BACK...
THERE IT IS, THE GRISLY THING...
TEN MINUTES AGO IT WAS ON THE BOTTOM OF SOMEBODY'S LEG.
DOES MY UNCLE REALLY WANT IT? WHAT FOR?
JUST LIKE I CAN'T LEAVE SALVADORE TO DIE...
...SOMETHING TELLS ME TO TAKE THE DAMN FOOT!

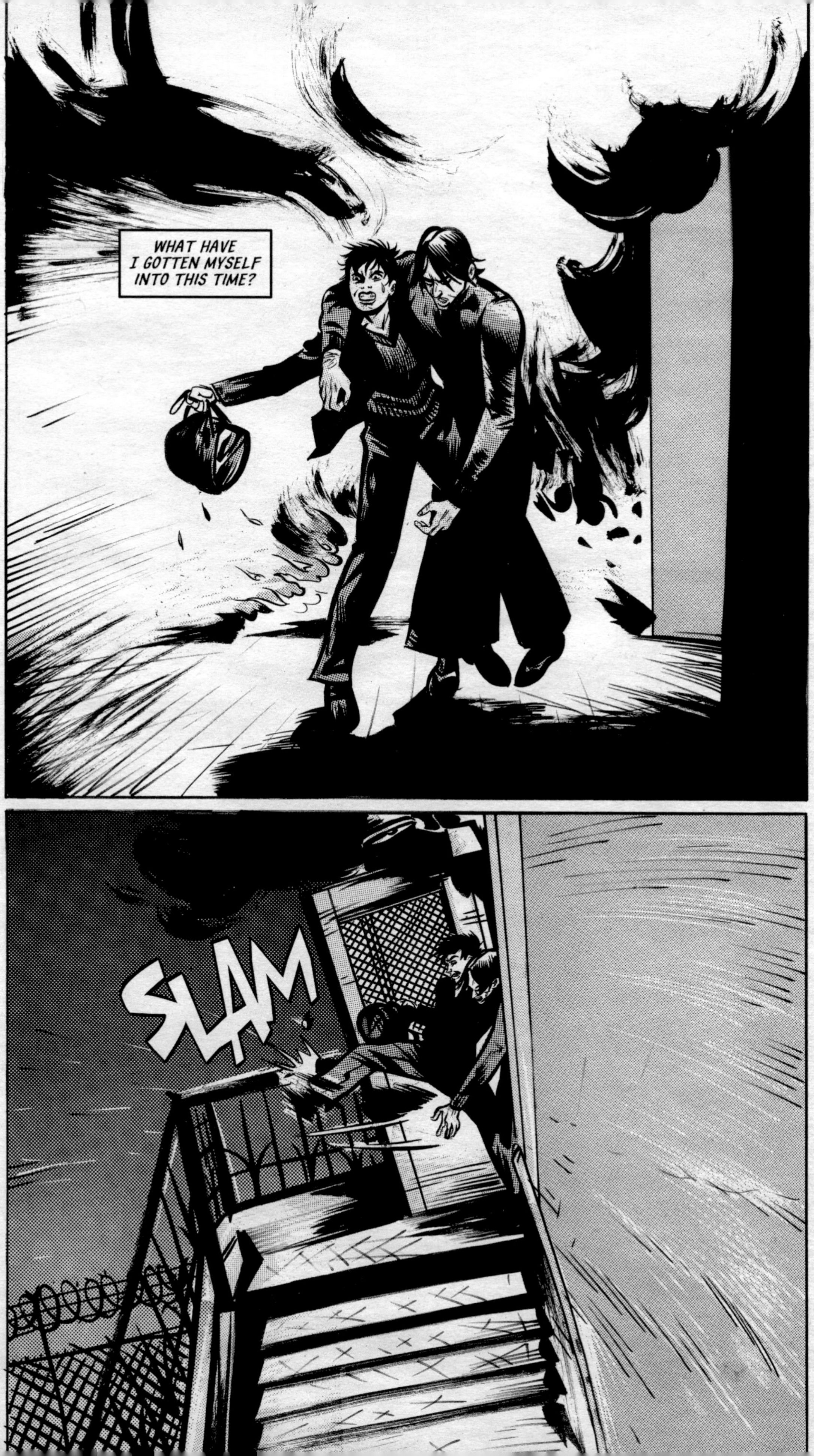
WHAT HAVE I GOTTEN MYSELF INTO THIS TIME?
SLAM

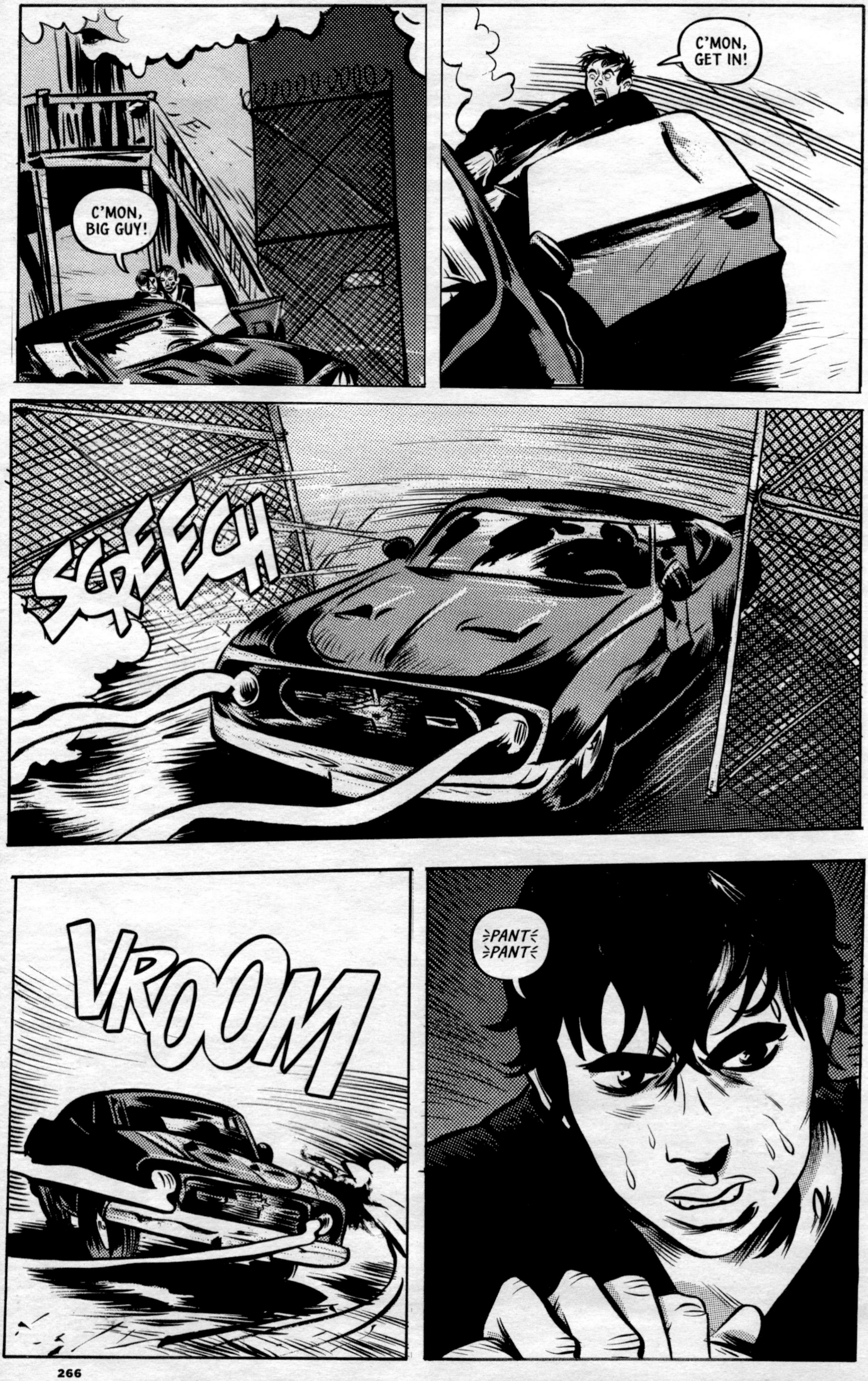
C'MON, BIG GUY!
C'MON, GET IN!
SCREECH
VROOM
PANT PANT

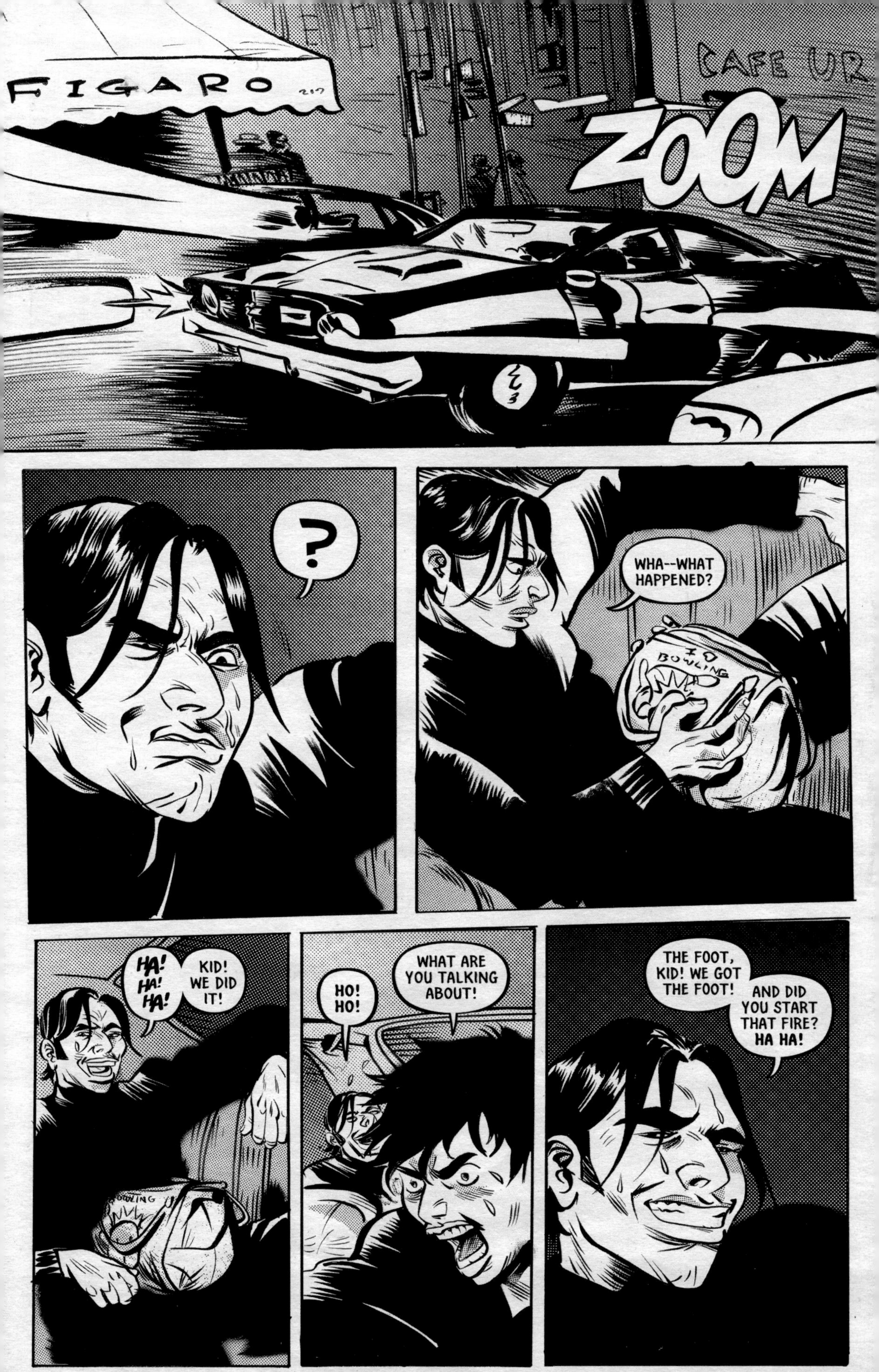
FIGARO
CAFE UR
ZOOM
?
WHA--WHAT HAPPENED?
BOWLING
HA! HA! HA!
KID! WE DID IT!
HO! HO!
WHAT ARE YOU TALKING ABOUT!
THE FOOT, KID! WE GOT THE FOOT!
AND DID YOU START THAT FIRE? HA HA!

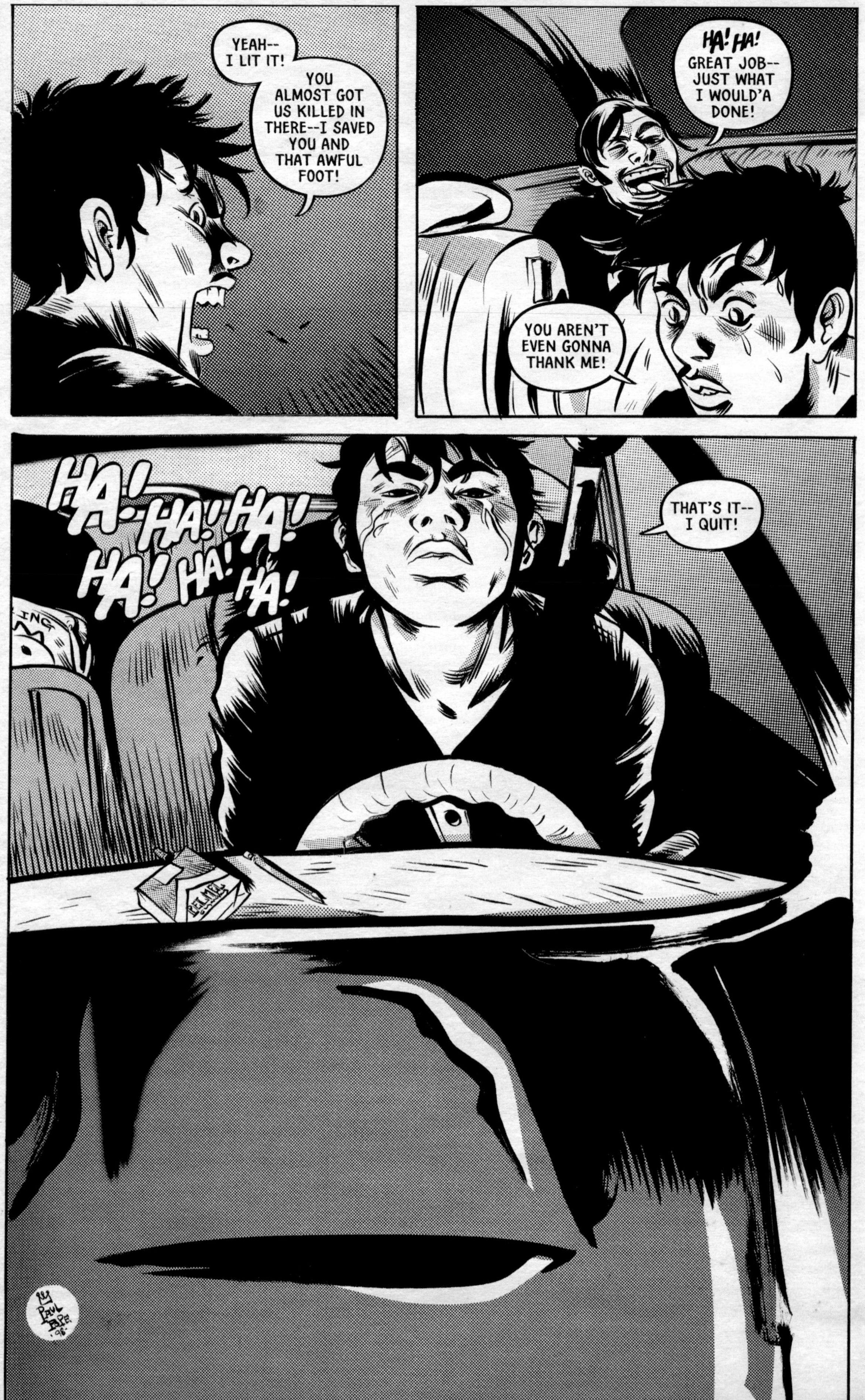
YEAH--
I LIT IT!
YOU ALMOST GOT US KILLED IN THERE--I SAVED YOU AND THAT AWFUL FOOT!
HA! HA!
GREAT JOB--
JUST WHAT I WOULD'A DONE!
YOU AREN'T EVEN GONNA THANK ME!
HA! HA! HA! HA! HA! HA!
THAT'S IT--
I QUIT!

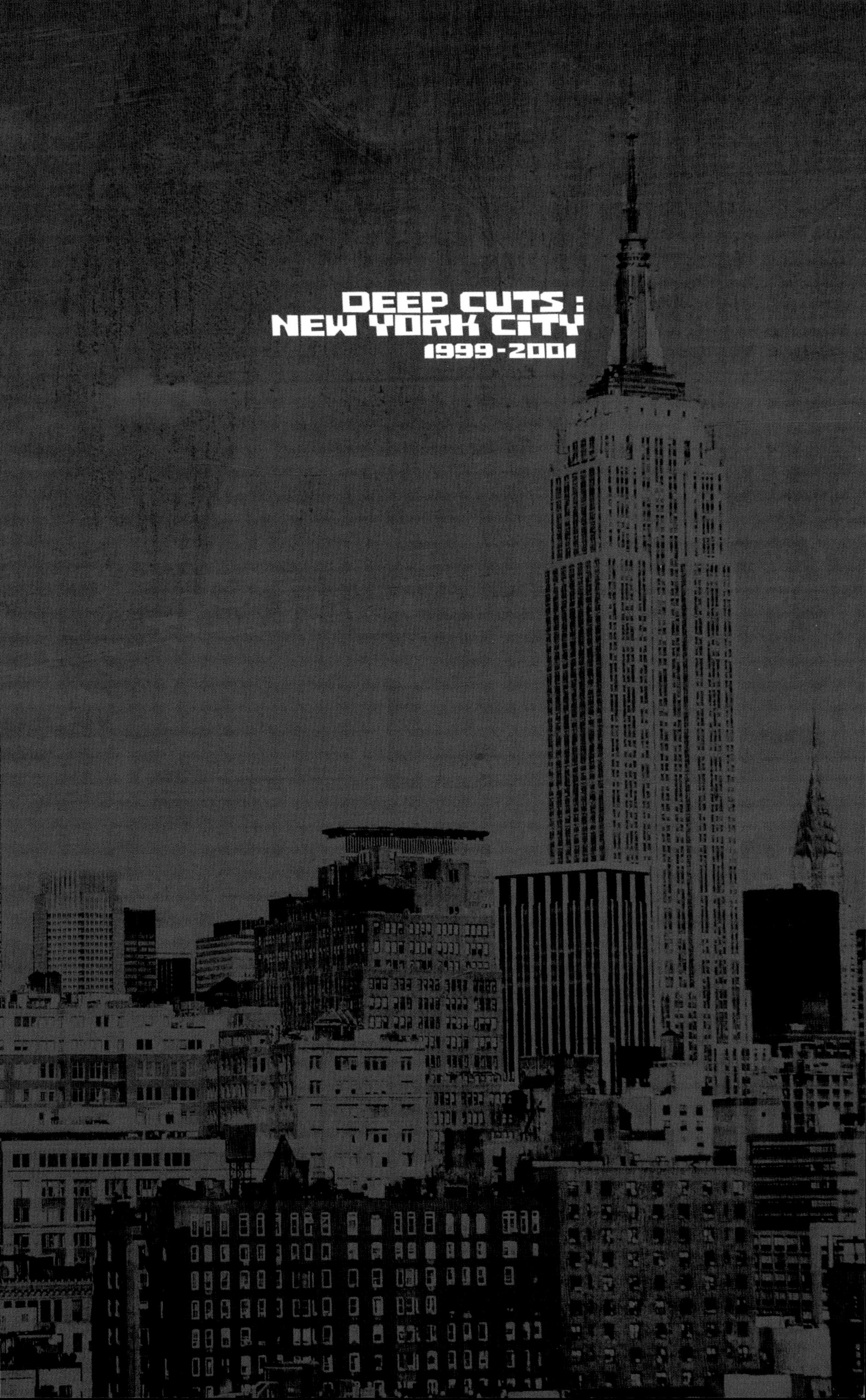
DEEP CUTS :
NEW YORK CITY
1999-2001

せちなりせ せらせい そらもにさ (1999)

THE SCARF

Pope 1999

JKF 2012

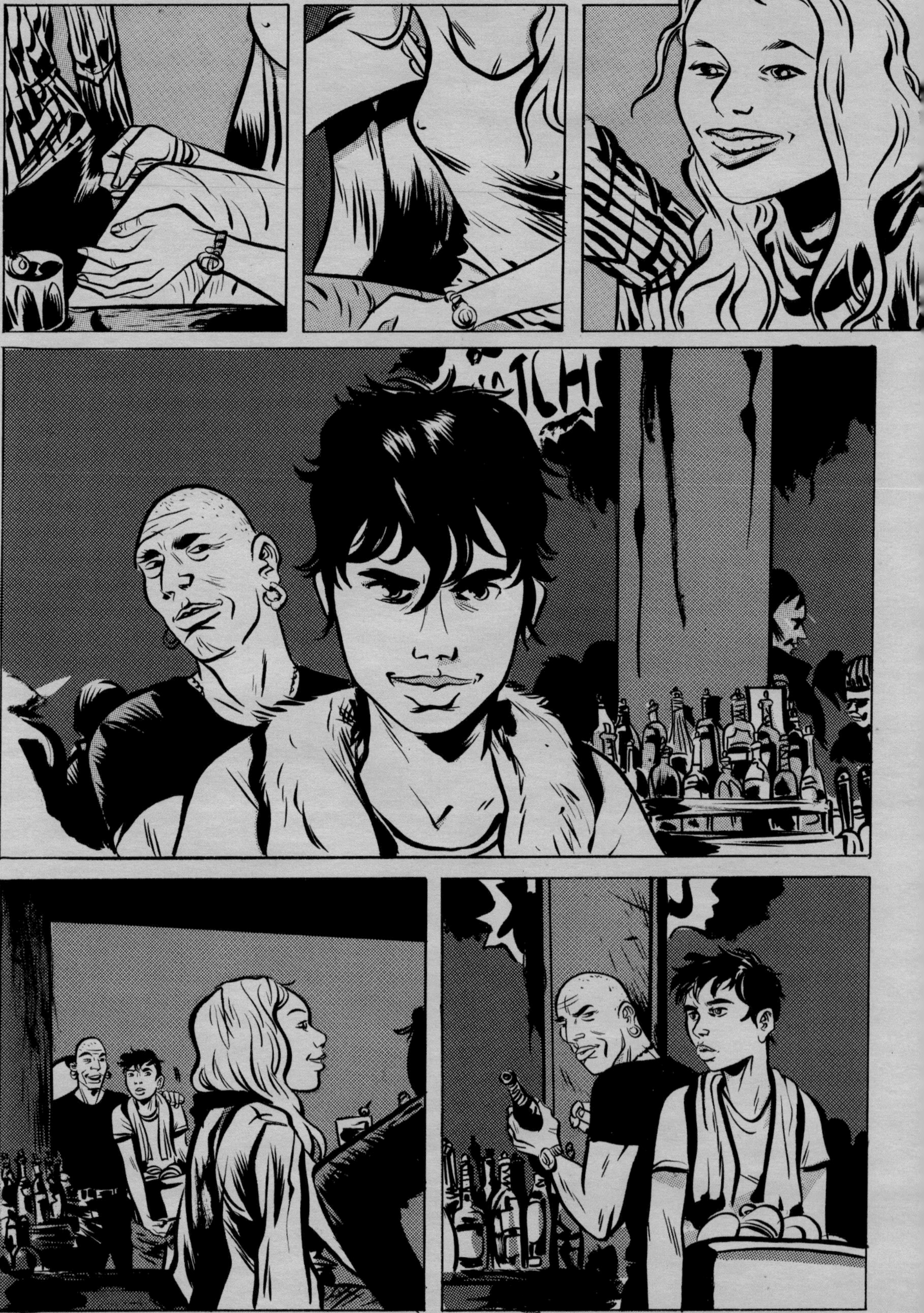

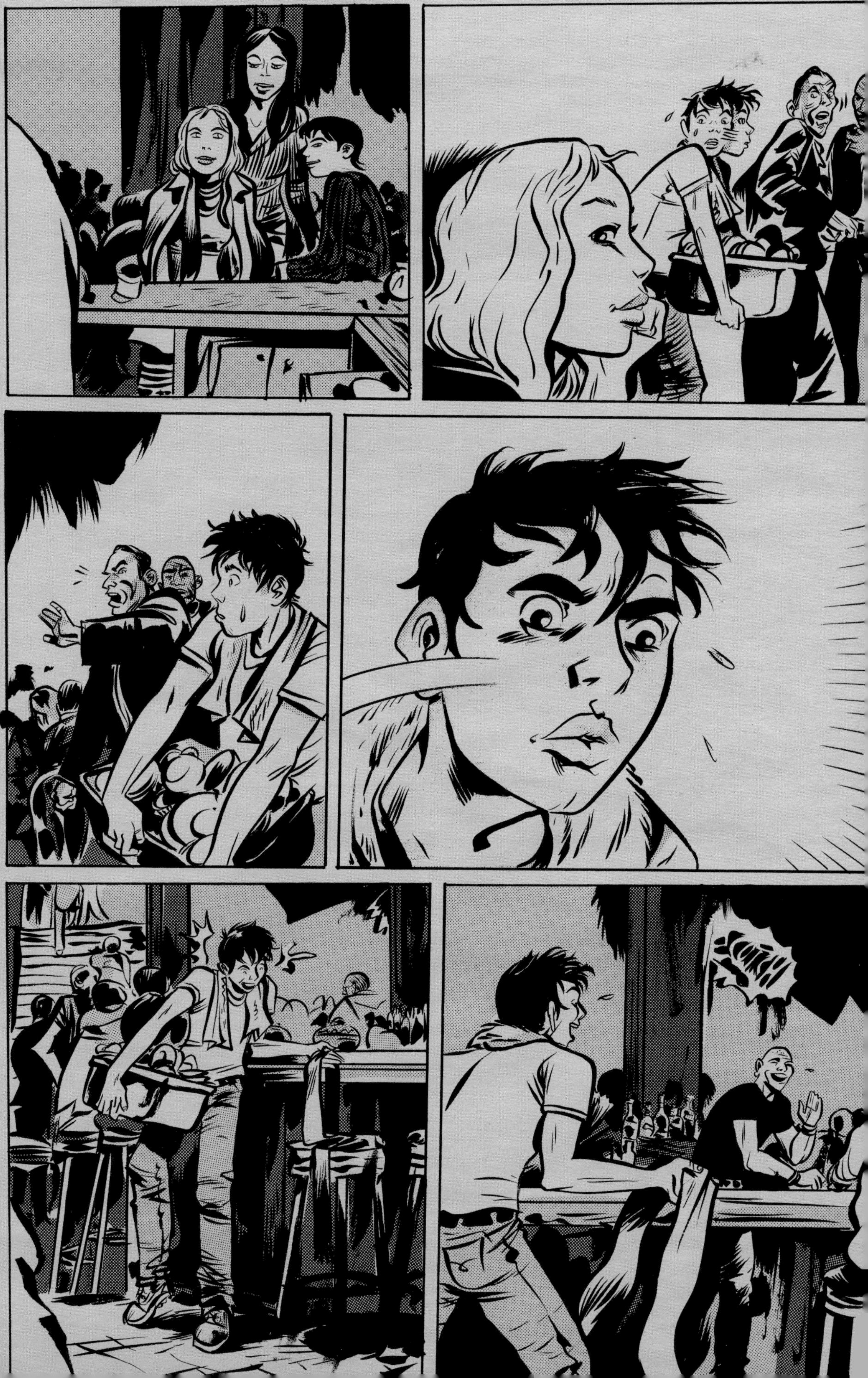

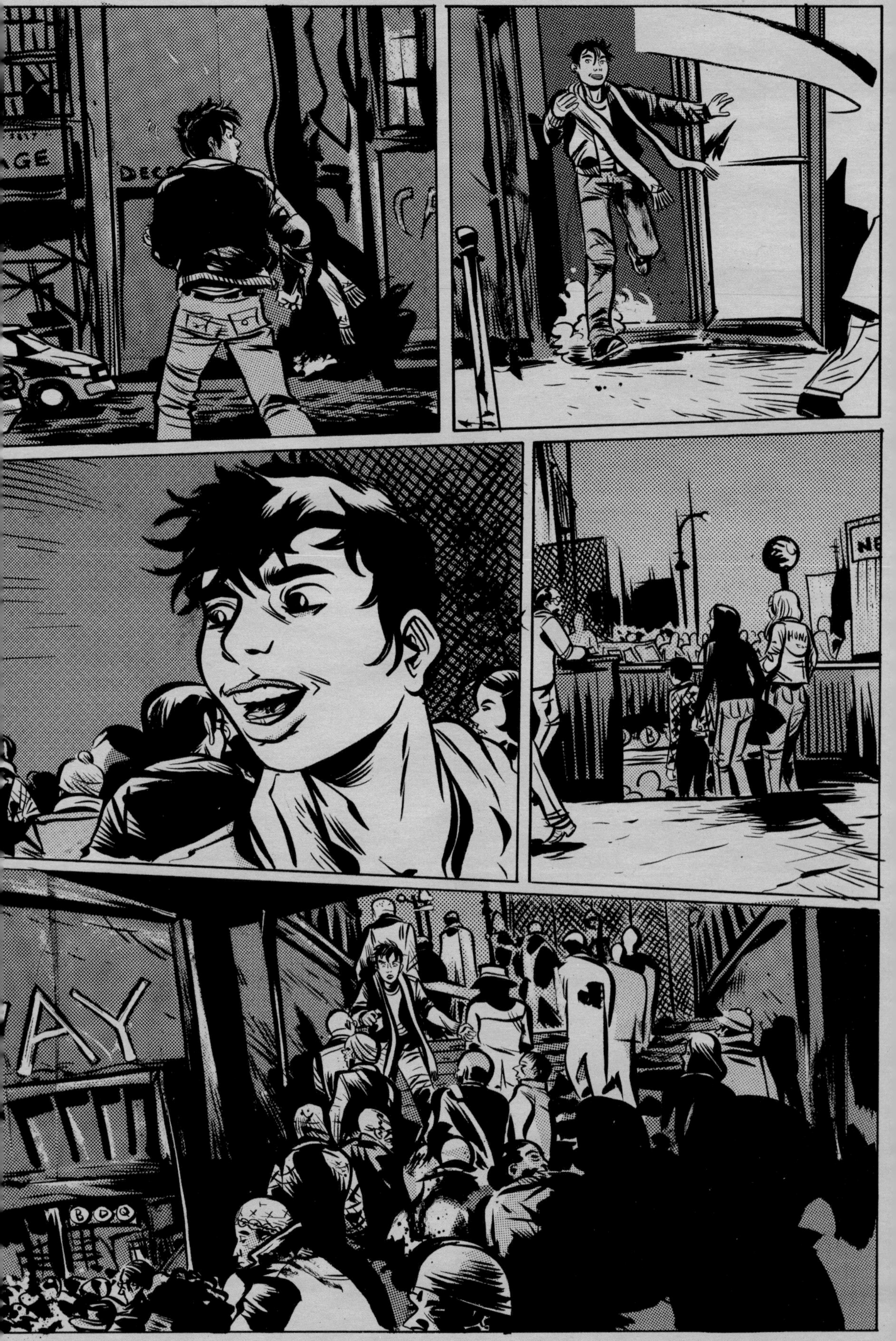

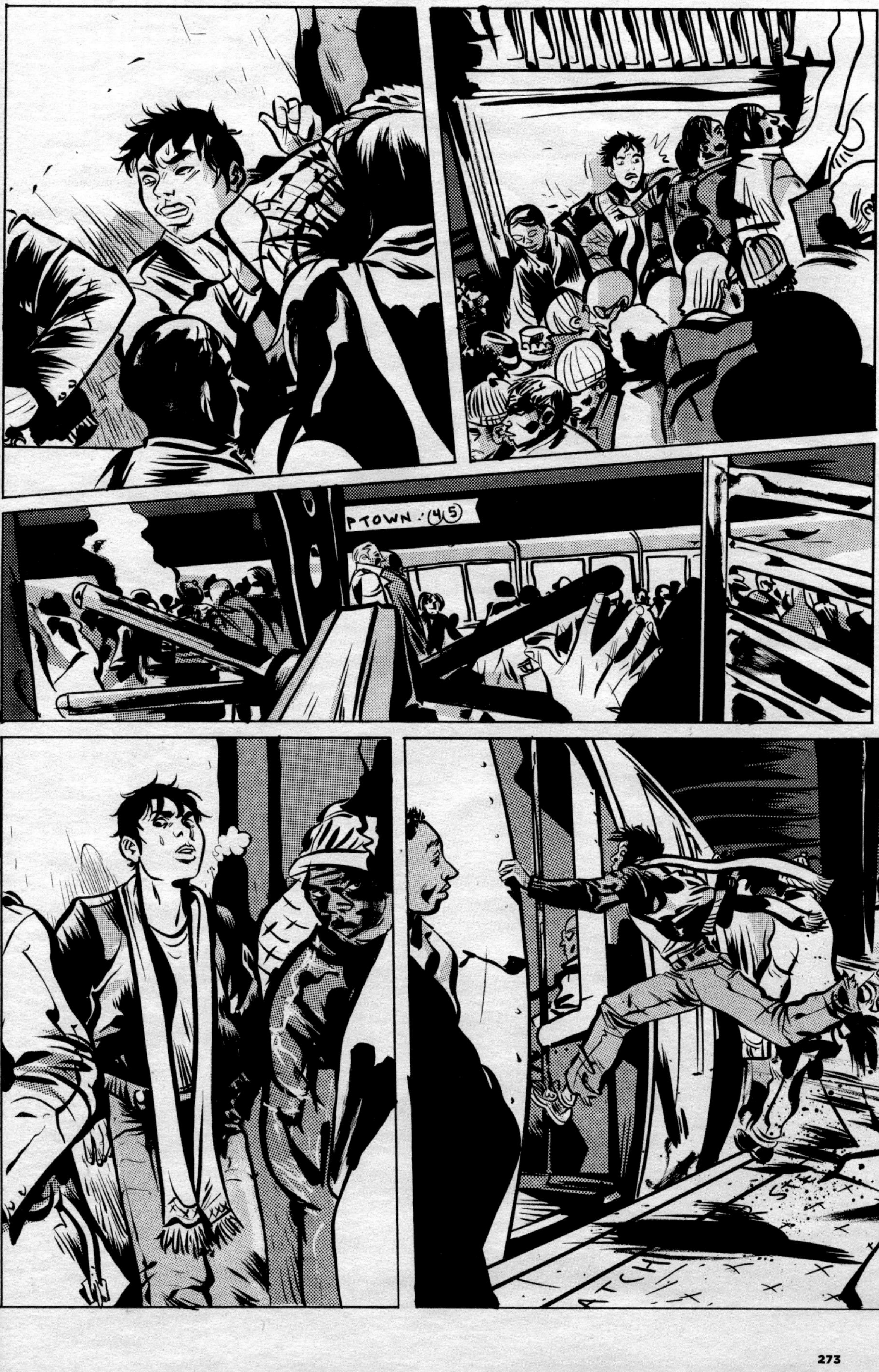
PTOWN (4)(5)

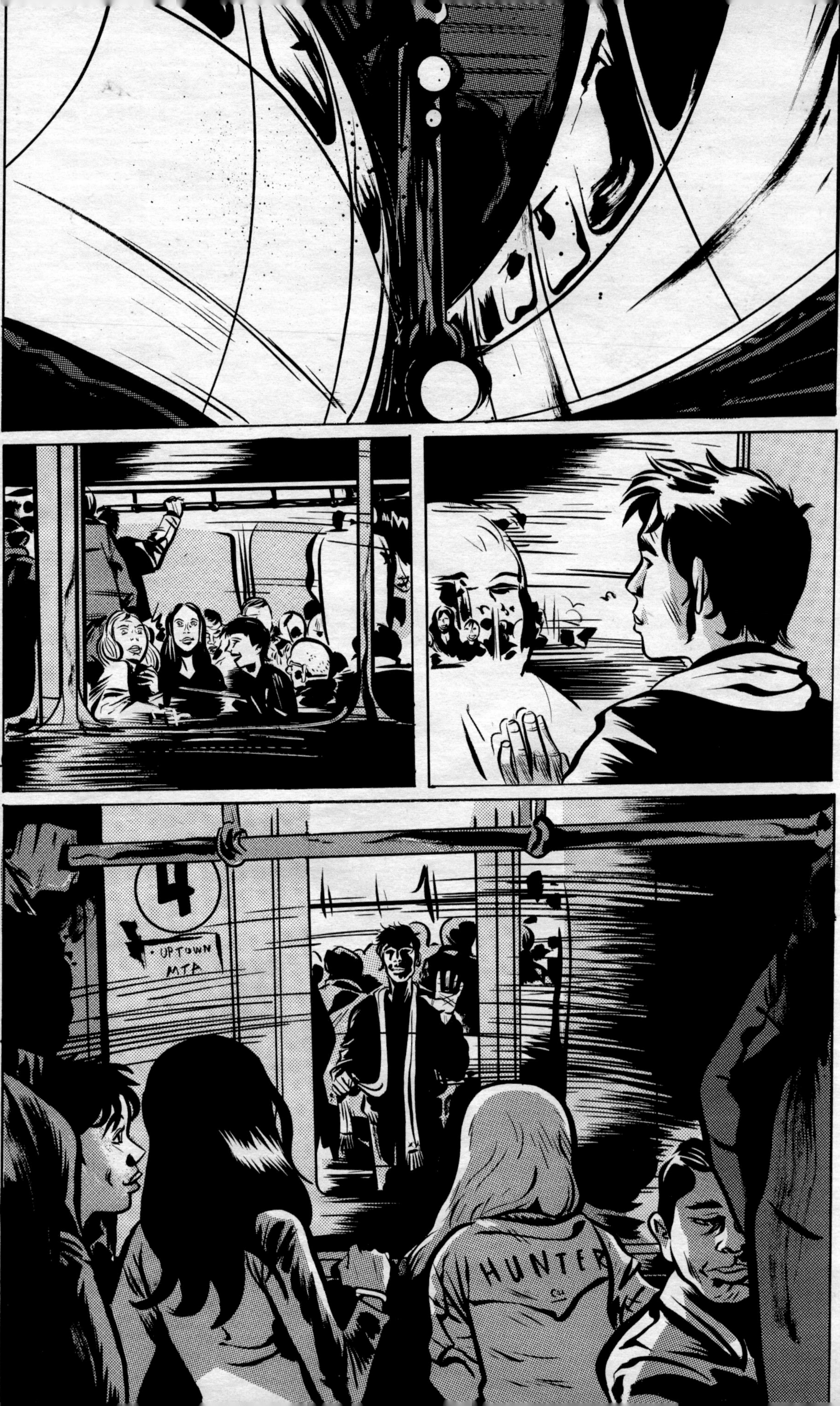
4
UPTOWN
MTA
HUNTER

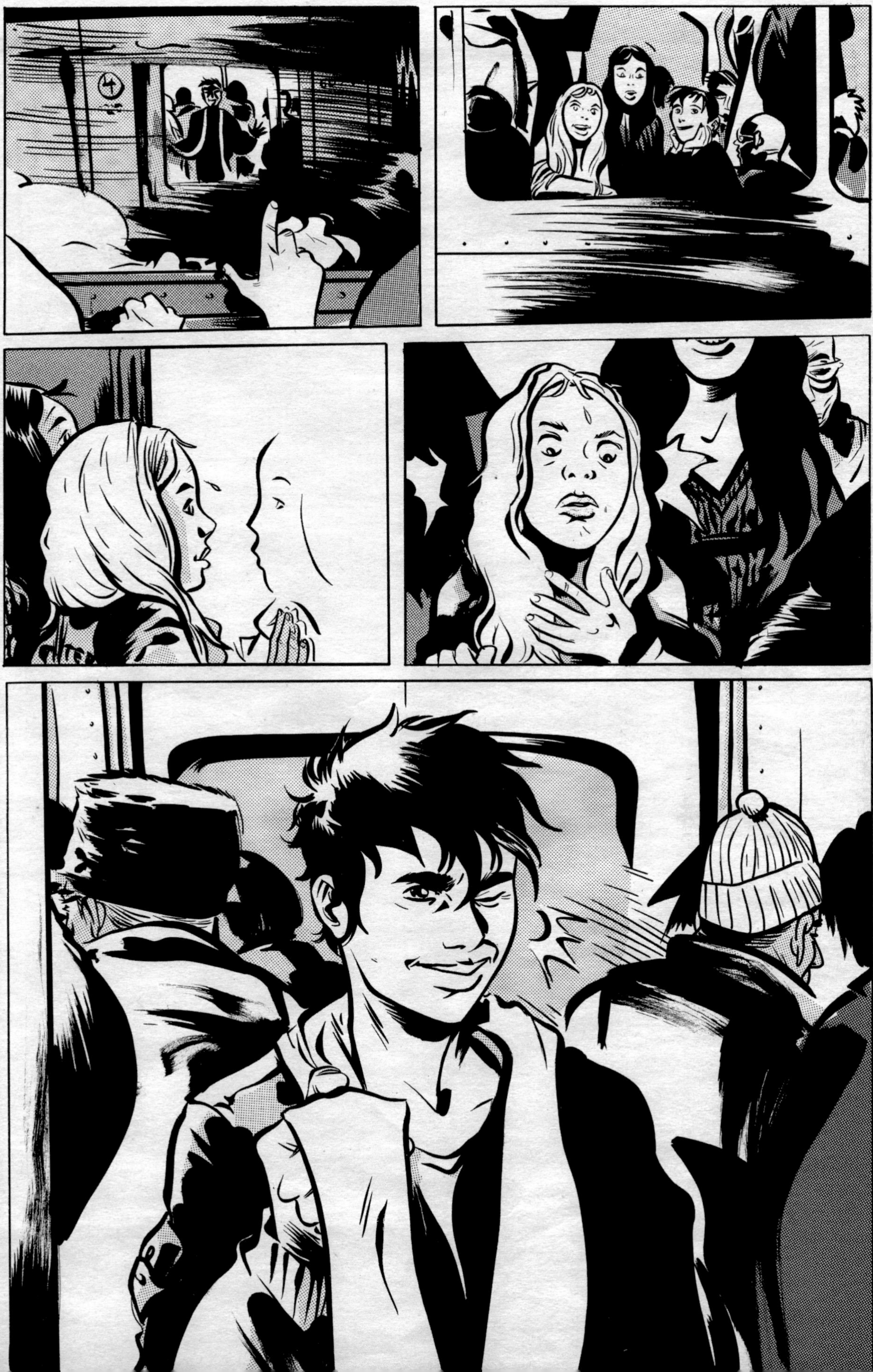

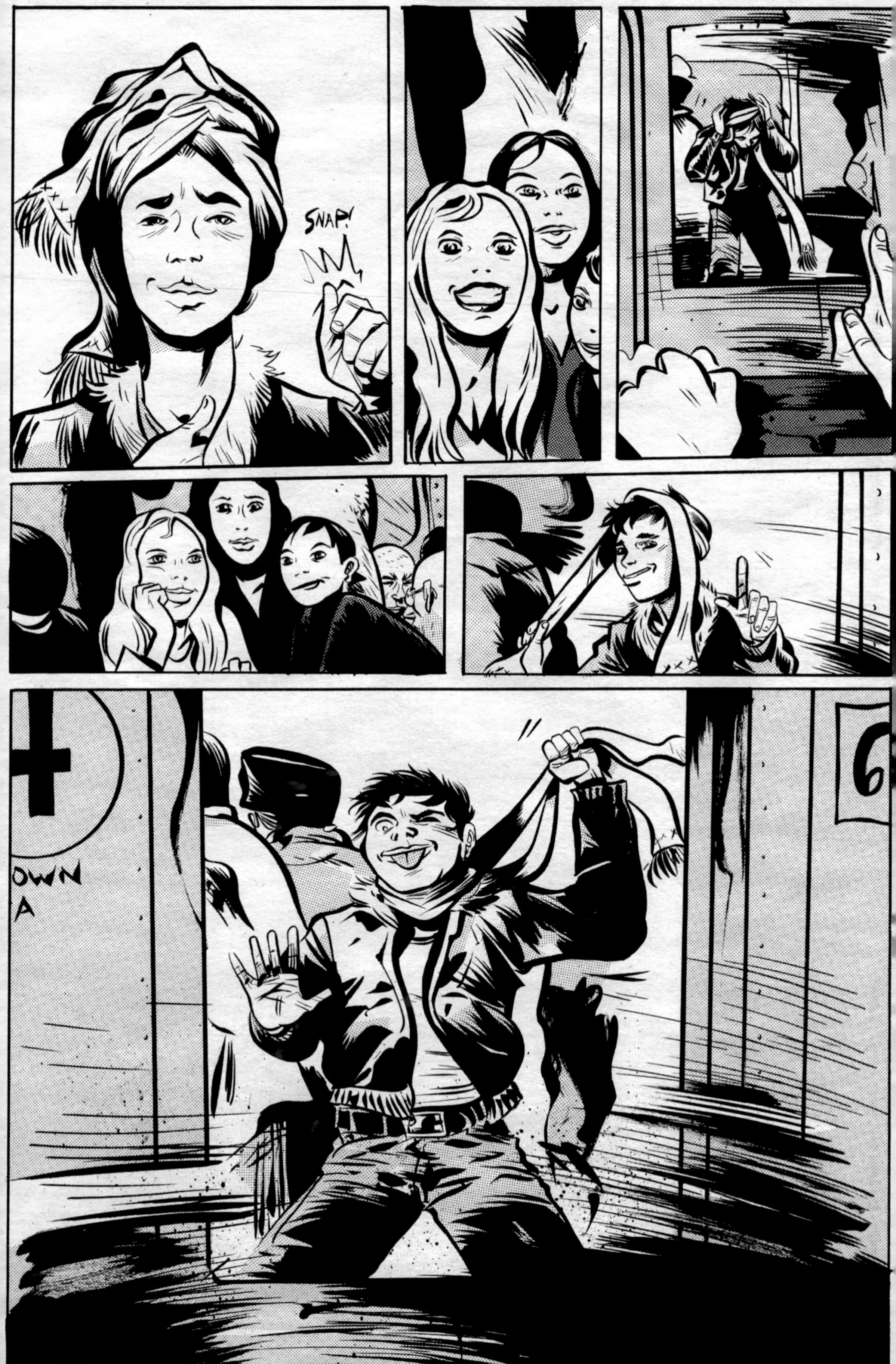
SNAP!

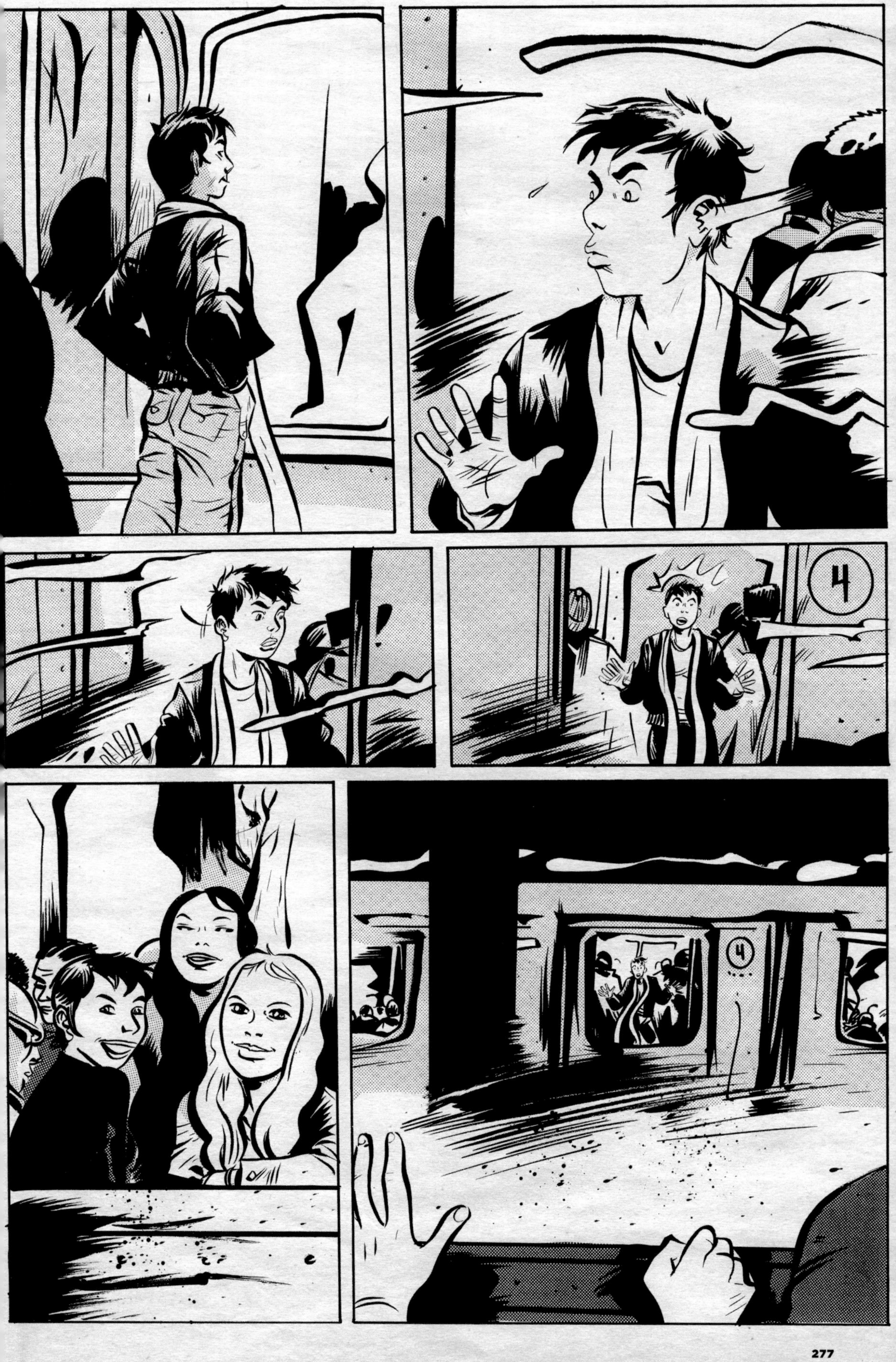

4
4

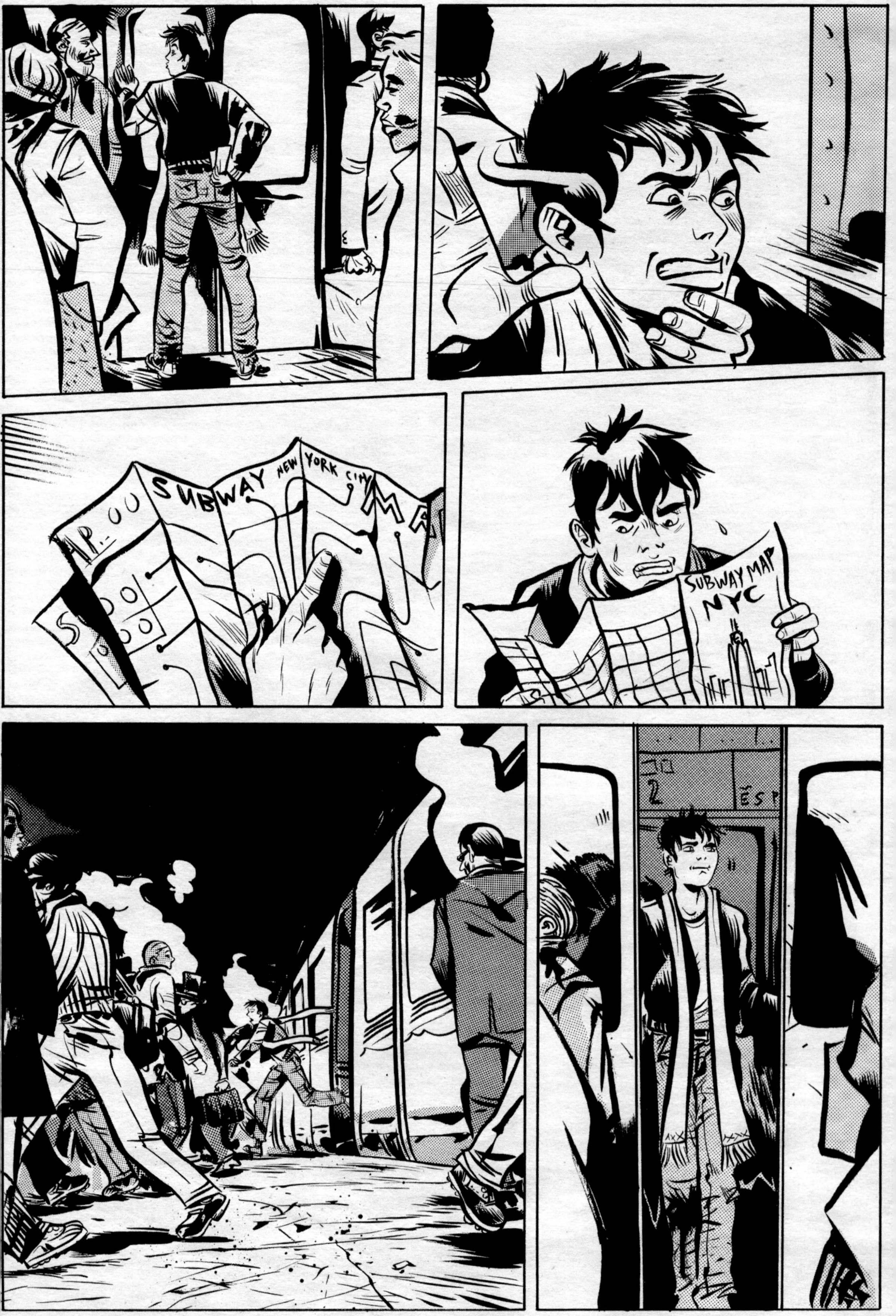
SUBWAY NEW YORK CITY
SUBWAY MAP
NYC

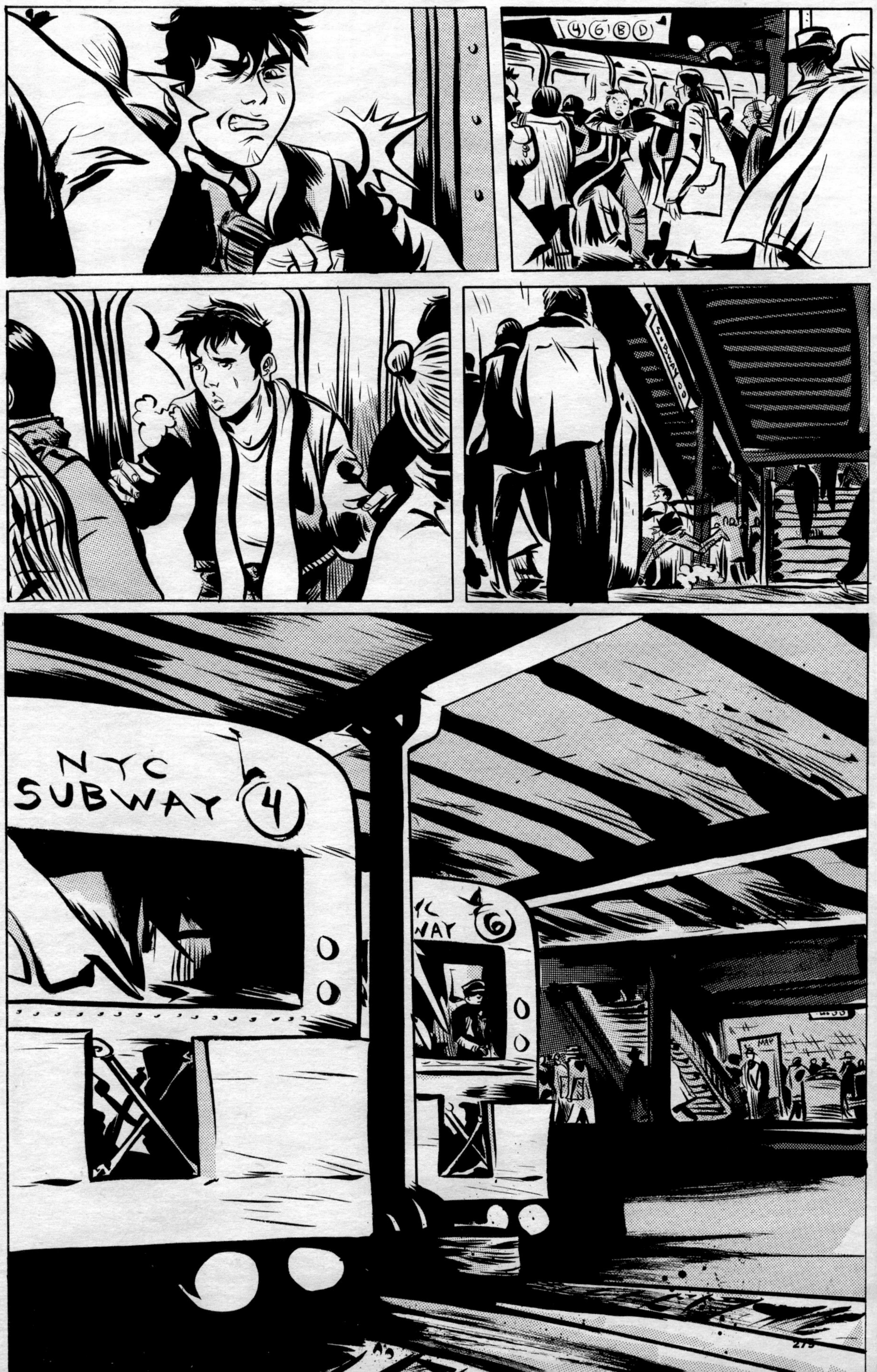
4 6 B D
SUBWAY
NYC
SUBWAY 4
6
MAP

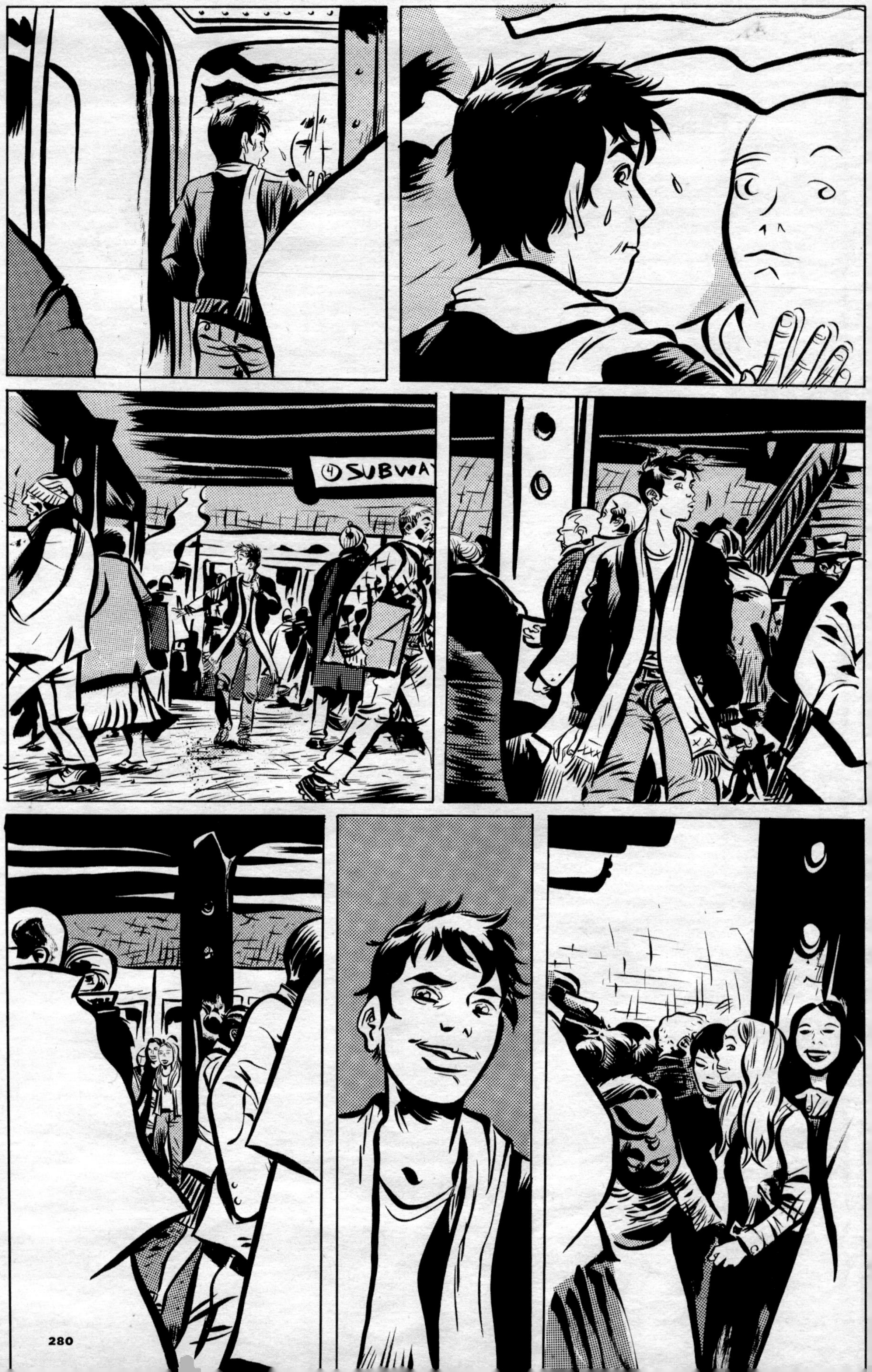

④ SUBWA

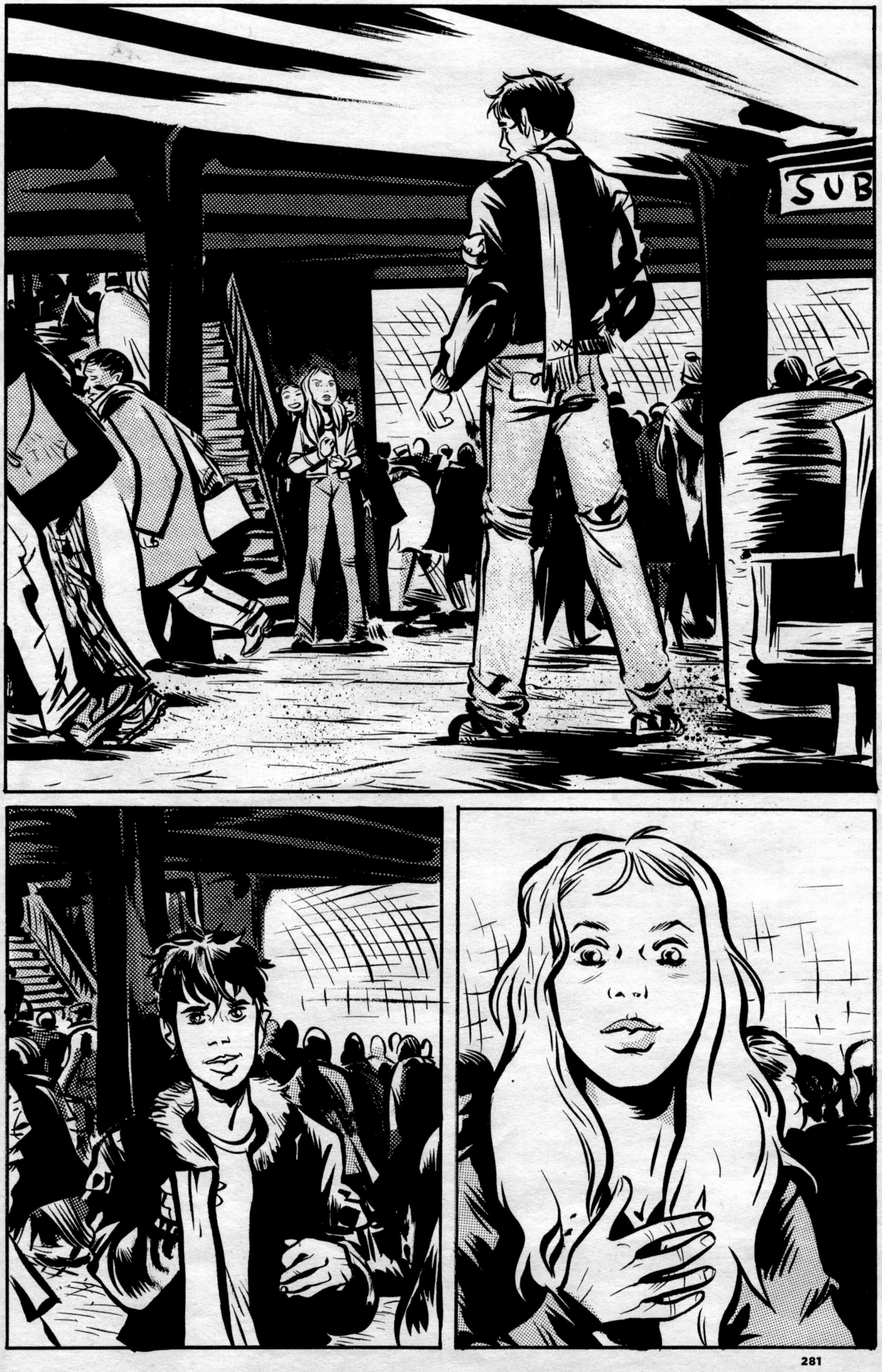
SUB

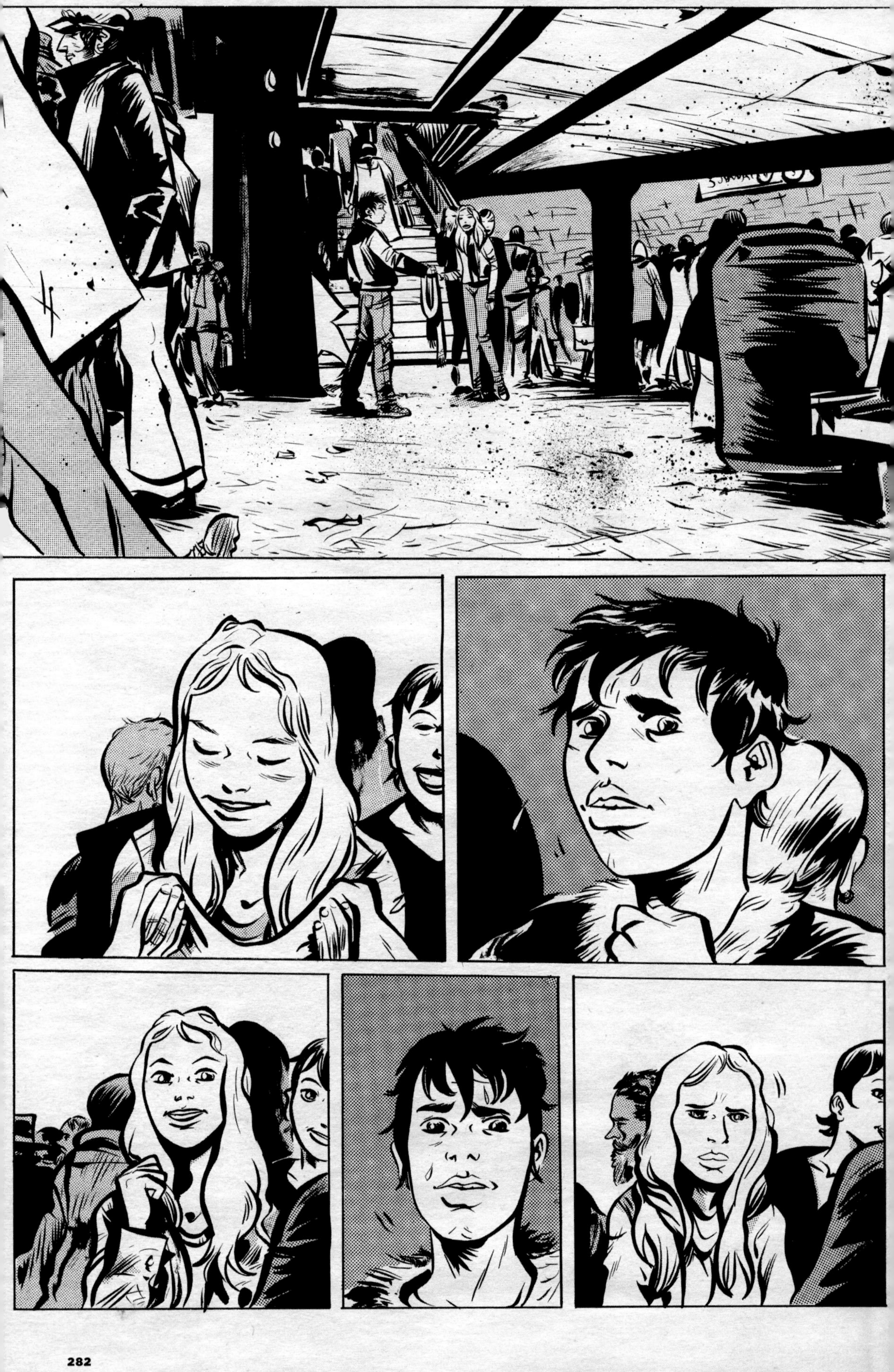

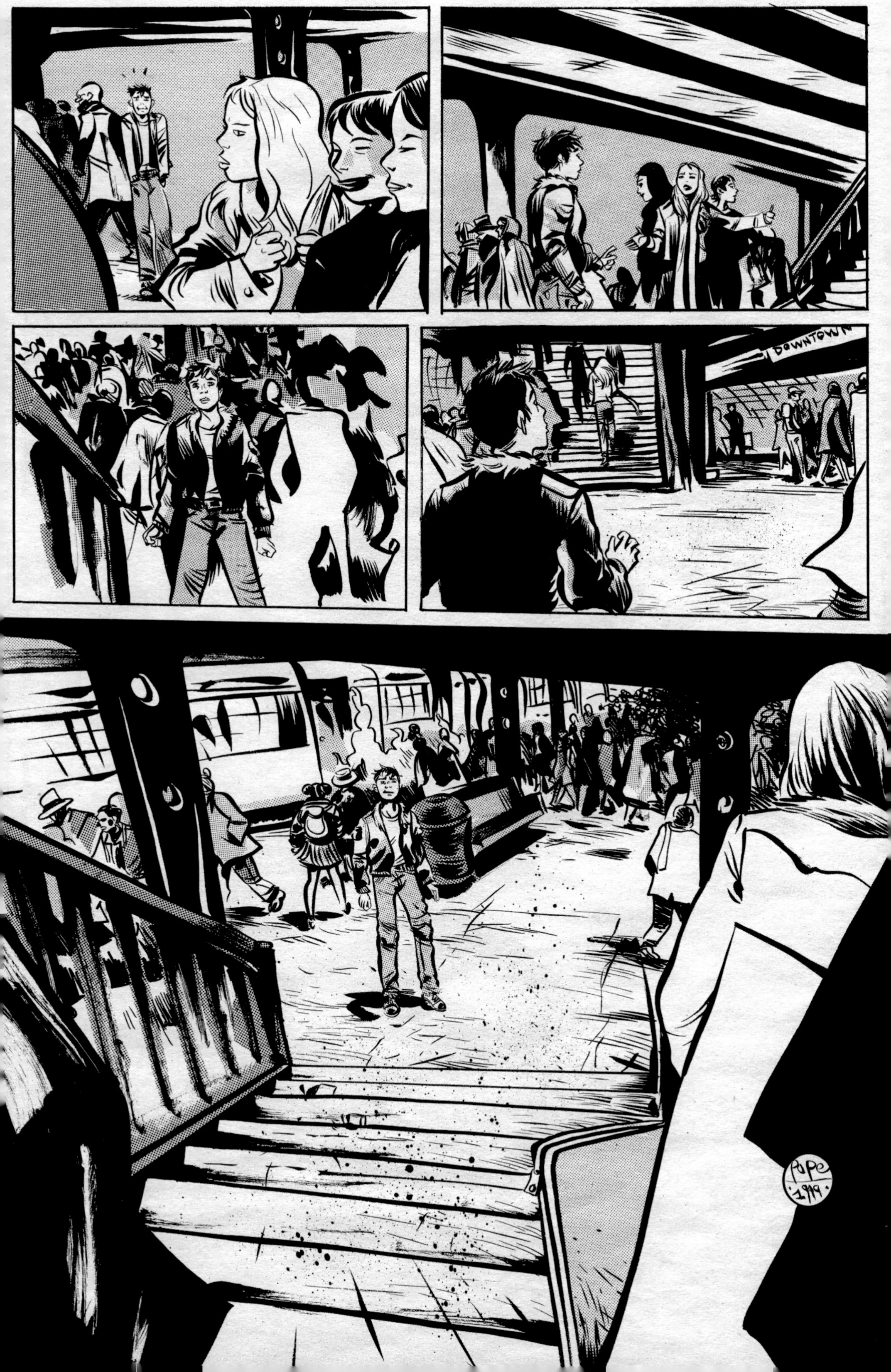
DOWNTOWN
Pope
1999

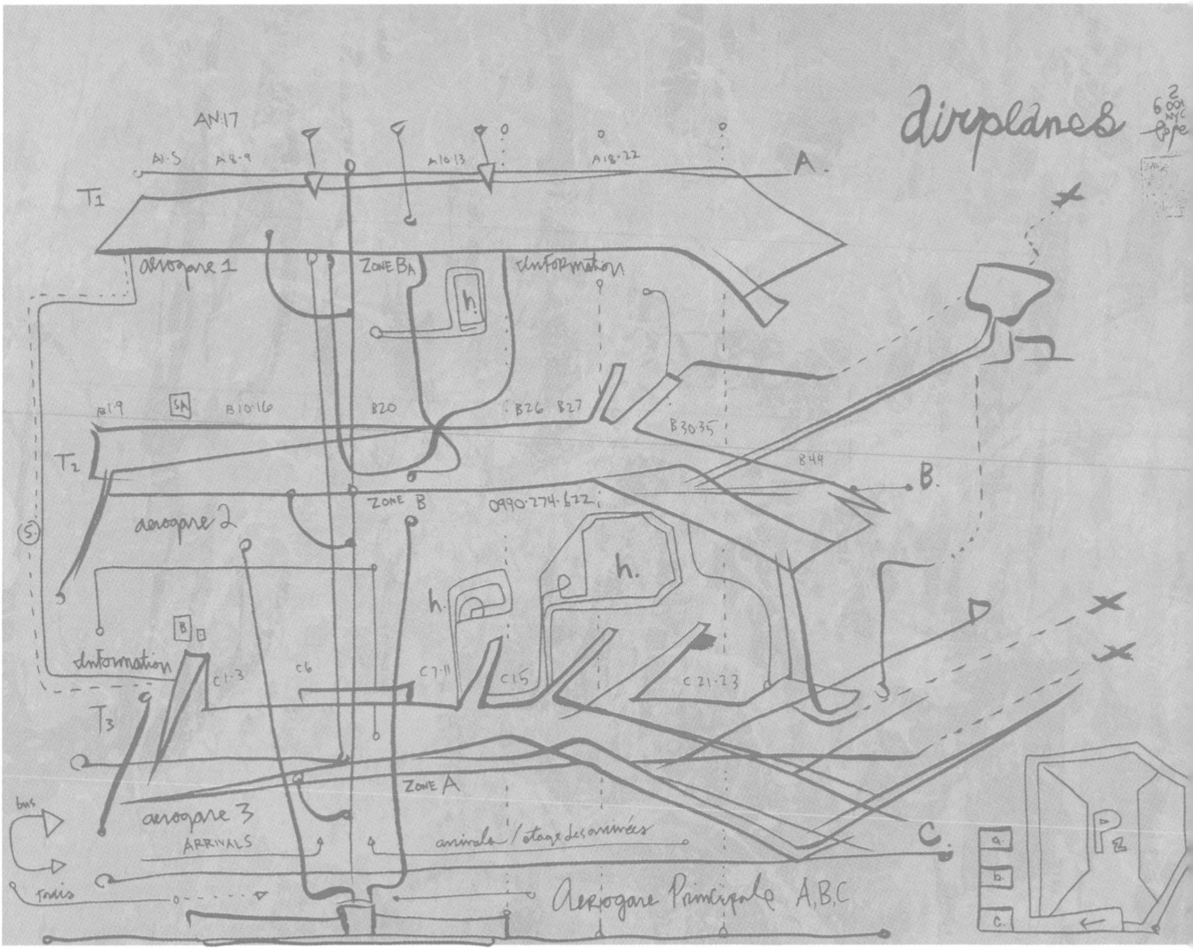
airplanes
AN.17
A1-5
A8-9
A10-13
A18-22
A.
T1
aerogare 1
ZONE BA
information
h.
B19
SA
B10-16
B20
B26 B27
B30-35
B44
B.
T2
ZONE B
0990-274-622
aerogare 2
h.
h.
information
C1-3
C6
C7-11
C15
C21-23
T3
ZONE A
aerogare 3
ARRIVALS
arrivals / etage des arrivées
C.
bus
train
Aerogare Principale A,B,C
a.
b.
c.
P2

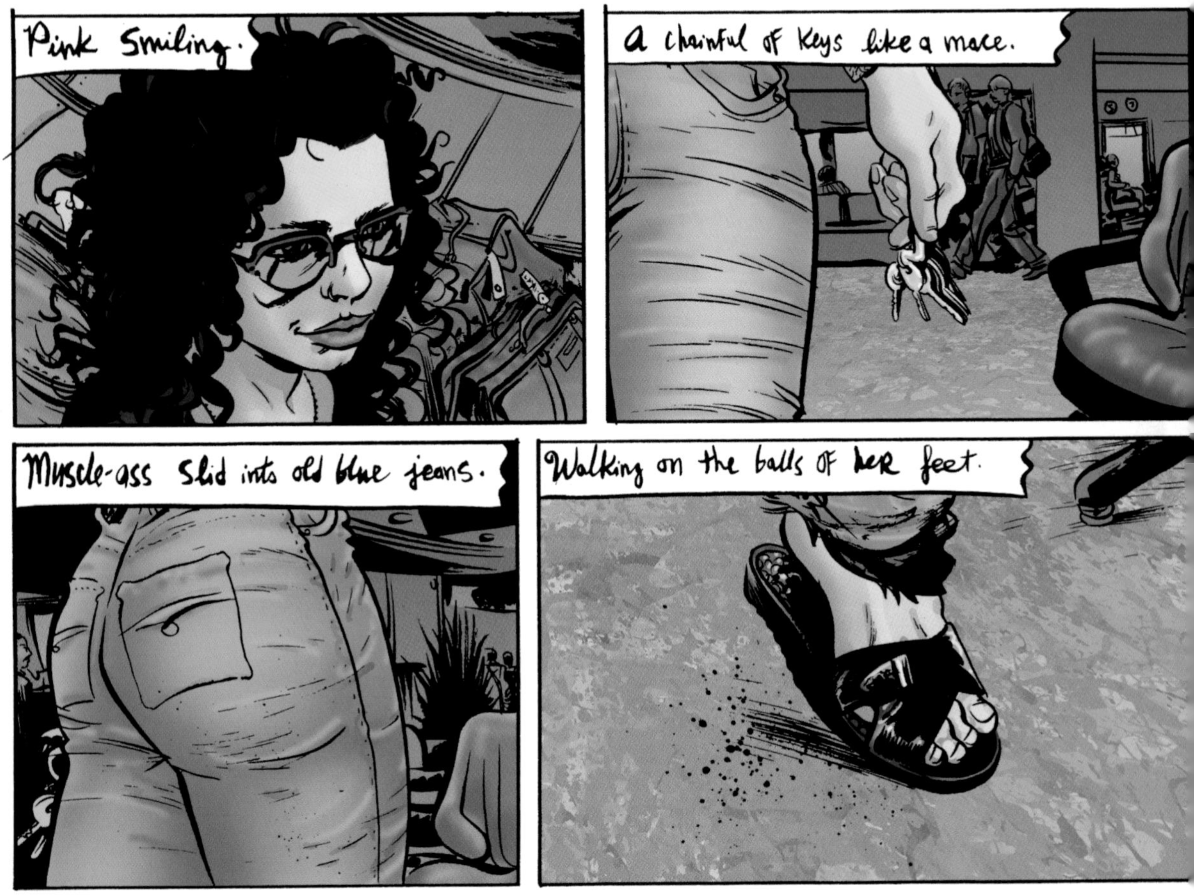
Pink Smiling.
a chainful of keys like a mace.
Muscle-ass slid into old blue jeans.
Walking on the balls of her feet.

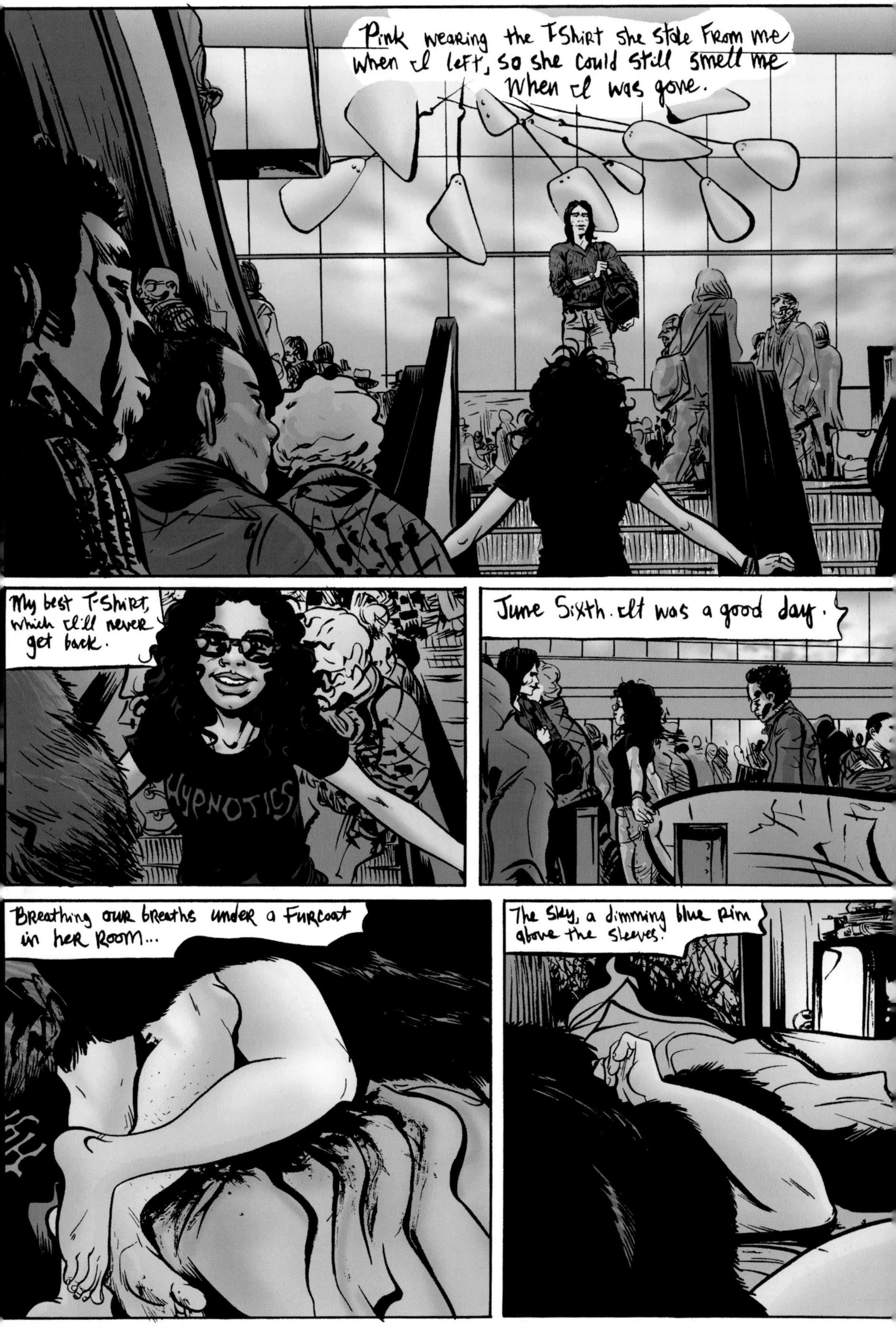
Pink wearing the T-Shirt she stole From me when I left, so she could still smell me when I was gone.
My best T-Shirt, which I'll never get back.
HYPNOTICS
June Sixth. It was a good day.
Breathing our breaths under a Furcoat in her Room...
The Sky, a dimming blue Rim above the Sleeves.

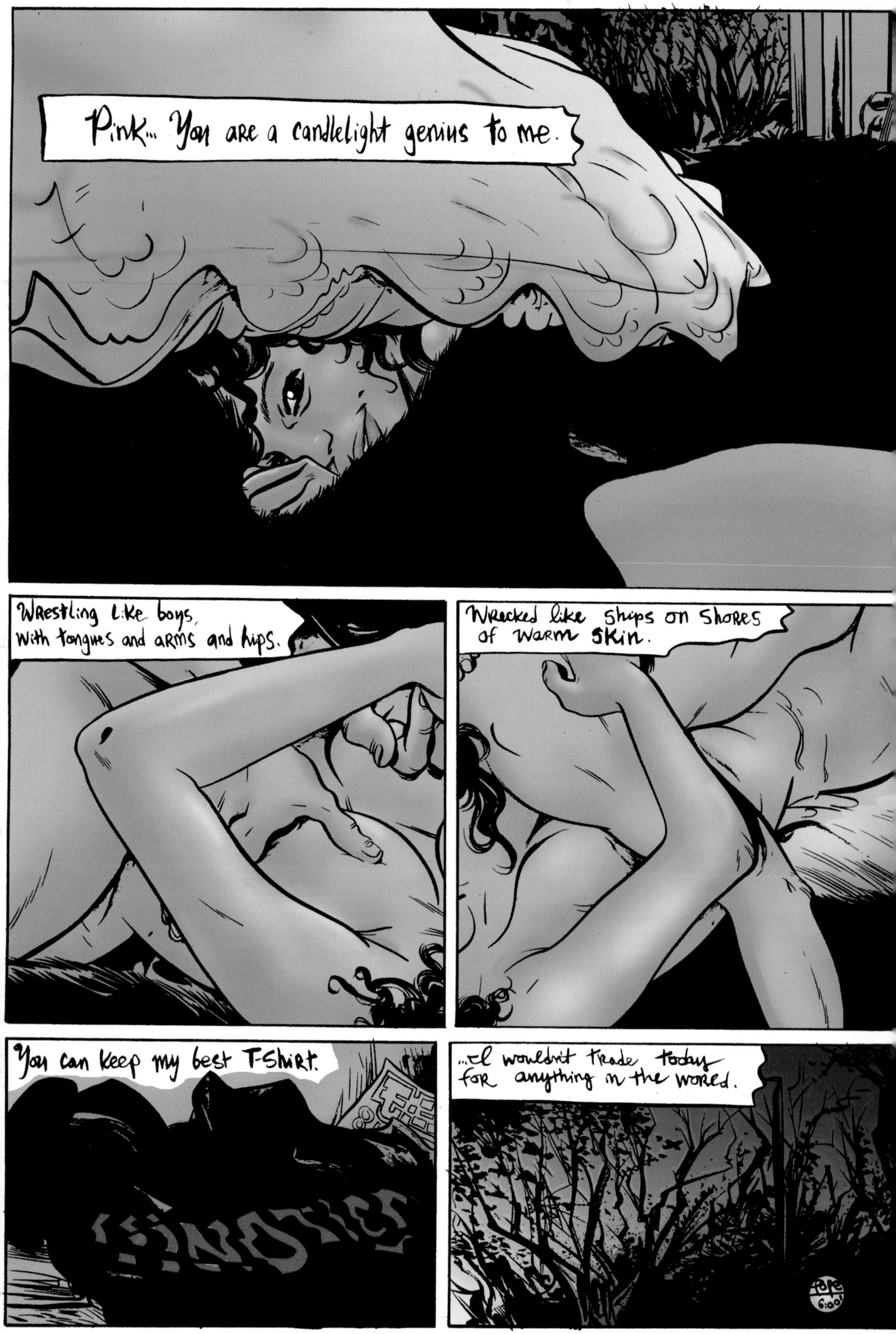
Pink... You are a candlelight genius to me.
Wrestling like boys, with tongues and arms and hips.
Wrecked like ships on shores of warm skin.
You can keep my best T-Shirt.
...I wouldn't trade today for anything in the world.

BIOS

PAUL POPE
(author/illustrator)

PAUL POPE is an American cartoonist living and working in New York City. He has been working primarily in comics since the early '90s, but has also done a number of projects with Italian fashion label Diesel Industries and, in the US, with DKNY. His iconic *Batman: Year 100*, a science fiction take on the classic Batman origin tale, has won numerous awards and seen print in many languages. In 2010, he was recognized as a Master Artist by the American Council of the Arts. His 2010 short science fiction comic strip *Strange Adventures* (DC Comics) — an homage to the Flash Gordon serials of the '30s — won the coveted National Cartoonist Society's Reuben Award for Best Comic Book of the year. He is currently working on *Battling Boy*, a book length epic featuring a young superhero, for First Second/MacMillian.

JAMIE GRANT
(colorist)

JAMIE GRANT is a digital colorist whose work includes *We3*, *All-Star Superman*, *Hellblazer* and *Supergirl*.

DOMINIC REGAN
(colorist)

DOMINIC REGAN lives in the Southside of Glasgow and makes lots of coffee. He also colors comic books for cold, hard cash. In his spare time he likes to sleep.

JARED K. FLETCHER
(colorist/letterer)

JARED K. FLETCHER is the cartoonist behind the *Stranger Fictions* webcomic, a designer, and the occasional letterer of comics like this book, *Batman Year 100*, *DMZ*, *The New Frontier*, and *Ex Machina*. He is also responsible for that recent overhaul of the entire line of X-Men logos for Marvel Comics. And along the way he's picked up Eisner, Harvey, and Eagle Award nominations. Jared lives and works in Brooklyn, NY. For more, visit jaredkfletcher.com.

JIM PASCOE
(book designer)

JIM PASCOE has been designing books and packaging for 15 years. A multiple-award-winning creative director, he produced and designed the interactive TV game JETIX Cards Live, which won an Emmy Award in 2004, and he's responsible for the packaging design of over 100 DVDs, such as *Mad Men*, *Watchmen: Tales of the Black Freighter*, the 2010 *Kubrick Collection* and *Coraline*, which won Best in Show at *The Hollywood Reporter*'s Key Art Awards. He is also the author of several books, including the graphic novel *Undertown* and the pulp novel *By the Balls*. Follow on twitter.com/jimpascoe.

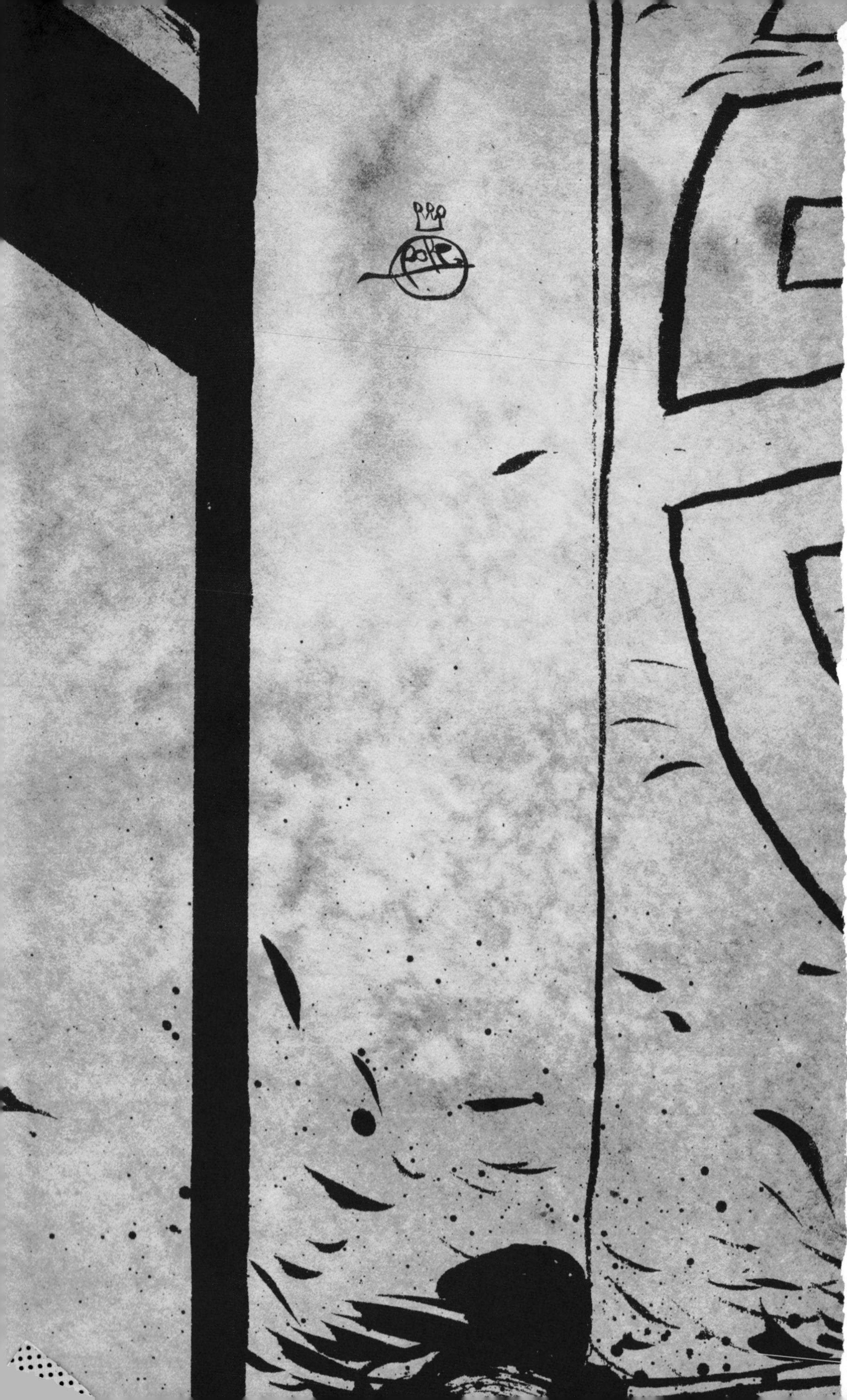

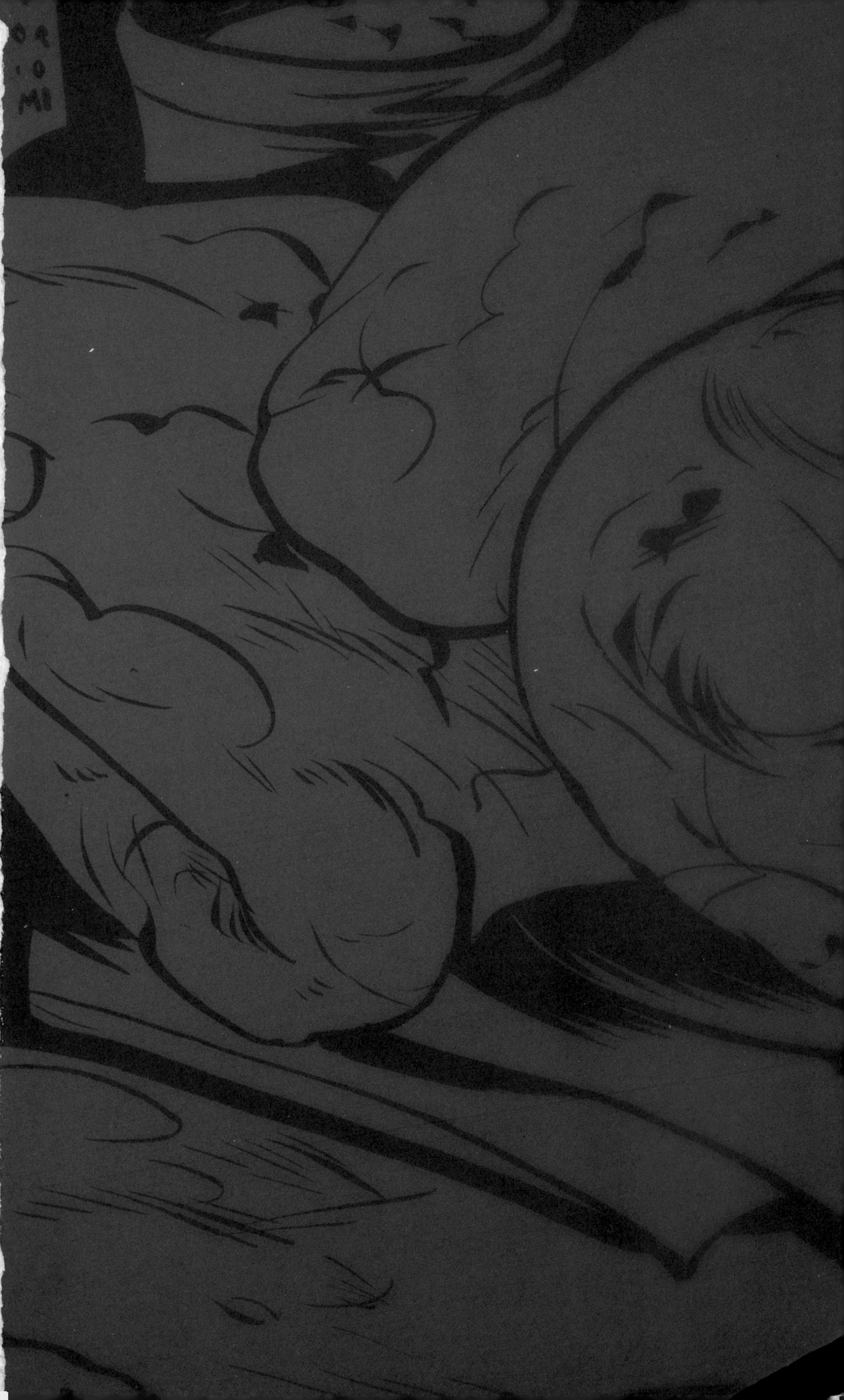

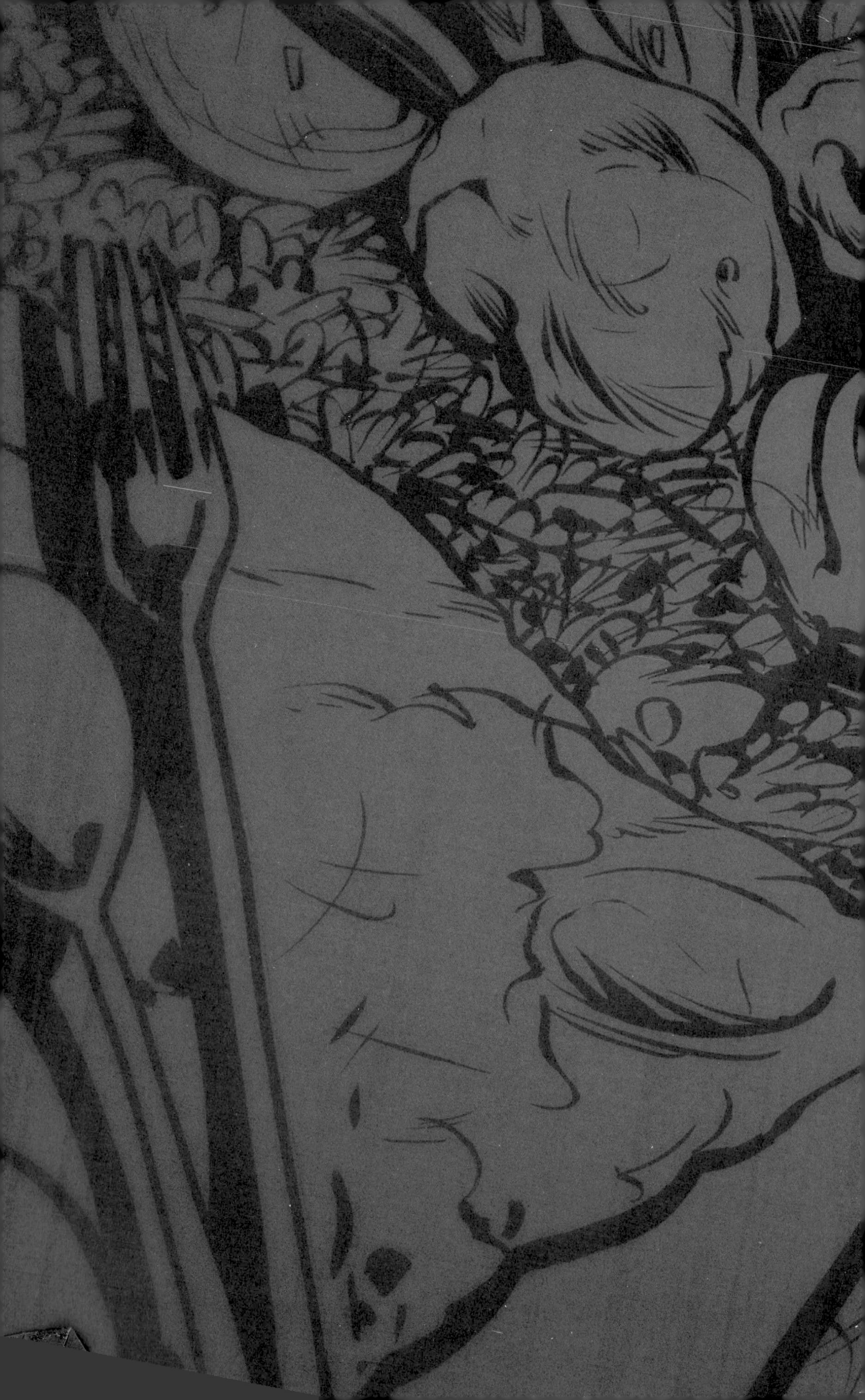